兰研外语

TOPWAY

淘金高阶 *4* 级考试

巅峰训练

主　　编　潘晓燕
副主编　叶常青　潘
编　　者　潘晓燕　叶
　　　　　袁　惠　诺

MP3 版

中山大学出版社
汕头大学出版社

图书在版编目(CIP)数据

淘金高阶4级考试巅峰训练:MP3版/潘晓燕主编. —汕头:汕头大学出版社,2008.6
ISBN 978-7-81120-333-2

I. 淘　　II. 潘…　III. 英语—高等学校—水平考试—习题　IV. H319.6

中国版本图书馆 CIP 数据核字(2008)第 071586 号

淘金高阶4级考试巅峰训练:MP3版

策　　划:华研外语
主　　编:潘晓燕
责任编辑:胡开祥　胡　敏
出版发行:汕头大学出版社
　　　　　(广东省汕头市汕头大学内　邮编:515063)
电　　话:0754-82903126
经　　销:广东省新华书店
印　　刷:湛江南华印务有限公司
字　　数:1010千字
版　　次:2008年9月第1版
　　　　　2009年1月第2次印刷
开　　本:787×1092毫米　16开本
印　　张:26
ISBN 978-7-81120-333-2
ISBN 978-7-88490-235-4(光盘随书附送)
定　　价:26.80元

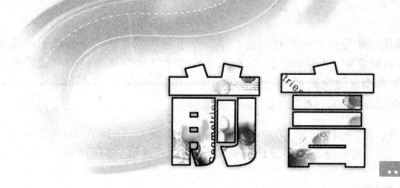

《淘金高阶 4 级考试巅峰训练》是专供 CET-4 考生考前冲刺使用的"一本通"型参考书。

特色 破译 710 分新题型命题规律

一、命题规律破译

本书的作者团队是上海交通大学的精英教师。他们具有多年的教学、应试辅导和阅卷的经验,对 4 级考试的改革方向和命题精神了如指掌。

本书一共有八个部分——快速阅读、听力理解、篇章词汇、篇章阅读、中译英、完型填空、短文写作和考前冲刺。作者在深入研究了每种题型的命题手段、考查角度、考点范围与难点设置之后,归纳出科学、严密的命题规律。这些理论全面剖析出题者的考查目的、出题心理和陷阱设计方法,考生读后往往会恍然大悟。这对在试题迷宫中晕头转向、苦苦摸索的考生来说,无异于"一语道醒梦中人"。

二、答题技巧总结

针对出题者的各种命题手段和规律,本书以图表框的形式为考生总结应对技巧、指明解题捷径。与其他同类图书说得天花乱坠、华而不实的所谓"技巧"不同,本书的图表框只是寥寥数语,却又字字珠玑。这些图表框有的言简意赅地说明某个命题规律的解题方法,有的罗列解题关键词汇,还有的传授在考试中屡屡应验的"应急一招"——不仅巧妙,而且实用。

三、典型题目设计

为了帮助考生进行有效的复习备考,本书根据 4 级考试的命题规律设计了大量有针对性的训练题。这些训练题与真题相比,不仅难度吻合、考查形式类似,而且考法一致。考生运用学到的解题技巧进行训练,能够培养敏锐的"题感",迅速提高应试水平。

编排 分阶突破的复习冲刺

一、480 分达标考点突破

本书每部分的第一章集中阐述该部分题型的考试要点。以历年试题和考纲分析为基础总结出来的考试要点,能让考生对考试最常考、最主要的"基本面"有一个清晰的了解。同时,配置的"专项扫雷训练"能够帮助考生巩固基础知识,积累考试经验。

二、550 分优良应试技巧

在掌握了考试要点的前提下,考生往往只要善于运用一些技巧就可以大幅度地提高考试成绩。有的学生在考试中经常成为"黑马",就是善于运用技巧的结果。本书每部分的第二章点破了应试高手常用"手筋"的内容:急中生智巧猜答案、灵机一动猜答案等,帮助考生达到事半功倍的应试效果。另外,本章还设置了相应的"历年典型真题突破训练",供考生活学活用。

三、610分高分突击训练

每部分的第三章贯彻本书宗旨:突击训练。在考试前适量做一些题目、保持活跃的应试思维,历来被认为是行之有效的热身。本书这部分是精心设计的模拟题,集强化训练、查漏补缺等多种功能于一体。

解析 一针见血,远胜废话连篇

一、全文翻译

为了帮助考生进一步深入地理解和学习,本书对所有的阅读文章都给出了准确、流畅的译文,让考生更加顺利地学习提高。

二、划线点评

本书在听力原文和阅读理解的译文里,给解题的关键句加上了下划线,并标明其对应的题号,帮助考生迅速剔除无关信息,沙里淘金,萃取答题精华。

三、化繁为简

题目的解析并不是越长越好。要做到几长开不难,难的是要"到位"。一人堆儿大系要的东四住住会湮没重点,读完了还是令人迷惑不已。本书的解析力求短小精悍、一针见血,把重点放在"到位"二字上。

四、化英为中

在使用英语应试图书时,很多考生都有这种感觉:解析常常大量引用英语原文,解释是中英文夹杂的长篇大论,考生读起来苦不堪言。本书摒弃了这一得不偿失的解析方法,杜绝大量引用英语原文的做法,而是用精练的中文进行解析,只保留原文中的英文关键词/词组。考生读起来感觉思路清晰,能够更加透彻地理解题目。

五、画龙点睛

考生进行强化训练,目的不只是学会解答这些题目,还要学会解这类题的方法。本书概括总结每一类题的性质、解答方案,或者剖析这类题的命题陷阱。让考生能够触类旁通,在学会解答一道题的同时,也学会解答一类题。

冲刺 710分巅峰训练

本书通过再现各项命题规律,设置了4套巅峰训练题,让考生进行模拟考试,考查自己对解题技巧的掌握情况。一方面,考生在学完理论之后,可以借助完整的试题训练来检验学习成果,看看是否已经融会贯通;另一方面,他们还可以通过实战演练积累应试经验,让自己的临考状态达到巅峰。

编 者

Contents
目录
....710 分新题型巅峰训练..............

第三篇　篇章词汇理解

第四篇　篇章阅读理解

第五篇　中译英

第六篇　完型填空

第七篇　短文写作

第八篇　710分考前冲刺

附录　备考题型

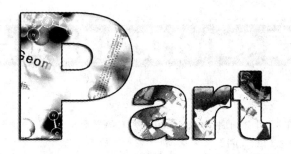

第一篇

快速阅读理解

第一章 稳拿480分快速阅读考点突破

大学英语四级中的快速阅读要求考生在15分钟内阅读一篇1000词左右的文章并完成相应的测试题目。测试题目包括三种题型共10道题：7道是非判断题（包括Y"正"、N"误"和NG"未提及"）或选择题，及3道句子填空题。

快速阅读旨在考查考生对特定或关键信息的快速提取能力以及对阅读材料内容进行快速把握的能力。因为较为强调速度，故对理解的深度要求并不很高，一般更注重字面意思的理解。快速阅读包含两种阅读方法或考查方式：略读和寻读。略读是对文章或段落整体结构、主题句的全局性把握；寻读则主要是对具体细节、事实等局部性的寻找和定位。

快速阅读解题步骤

(1)通读文章开头、结尾及各个小标题，从而弄清文章的结构和大意。

(2)正确理解题目所表述的内容，找出其关键词语，确定题眼。特别注意人物、时间、地点和数字等信息。

(3)将题眼内容与文章各部分小标题的内容对比，大概定位该题是在哪个部分被提及。

(4)阅读相关部分内容，准确定位有关信息。

第一节 命题手段和定位技巧

快速阅读的题型虽然有三种：是非判断题、选择题和句子填空题。但是这三种题型的命题手段基本相同，因此定位信息源的技巧也一致。无论遇到哪种题型，考生所要做的就是根据题意进行准确的定位，然后结合题型特点作答。

1. 主旨题

四级快速阅读的文章通常先简要地介绍文章的总体内容、写作目的或引出文章主题，然后再具体介绍细节（通常用小标题把各部分进行概括和隔离开来）。因此，考生只需阅读文章开头的段落及各个小标题，就可以判断考题是否只是概括了部分内容还是过于宽泛。这种题不会有 NG 的情况出现。

主旨题的主要命题方式如下：

> The passage is mainly about...
>
> The passage mainly discusses...
>
> The passage tends/aims to tell the readers about...
>
> The passage compares...
>
> The passage mainly shows/indicates/introduces that...
>
> The passage agrees that...

下面以四级样题中的快速阅读文章为例。

【例1】标题:**Landfills**

　...

　小标题:How Much Trash Is Generated?

　...

　How Is Trash Disposed Of?

　...

　What Is a Landfill?

　...

　Proposing the Landfill

　...

　Building the Landfill

　...

　What Happens to Trash in a Landfill?

　...

　How Is a Landfill Operated?

　...

【题目】The passage gives a general description of the structure and use of a landfill.

【解析】原文一共有7个小标题,其中第3至第7个小标题都与landfill有关,综合这五个小标题的内容可以知道,这五部分应该介绍了landfill的构成与用途,这正是题目所表达的内容,因此可断定本题答案为Y。

2. 细节题

快速阅读的命题点比较有规律性。一般来说,快速阅读的命题点包括:数字(含时间)、地点、人物、因果关系、时间顺序、目的、比较关系(含对比和类比)、方式、条件等。

命题规律1:与数字有关的细节

> 数字在文章中通常以阿拉伯数字的形式书写,比较容易定位,因此考题中含有的数字往往可以成为最有利的定位工具。

【例2】The interstate highway system was finally launched in 1956 and has been hailed as one of the greatest public works projects of the century. To build its 44,000-mile web of highways, bridges, and tunnels, hundreds of unique engineering designs and solutions had to be worked out. Consider the many geographic features of the country: mountains, steep grades, wetlands, rivers, deserts, and plains. ...

【题目】It was in the 1950s that the American government finally took action to build a national highway system.

[2006.6/T3]

【解析】解题时,应先以题目中的数字"1950s"为题眼在原文定位信息源于上文首句,然后,对比题目和原文可以知道,虽然它们的主语和宾语位置相反,但是表达的内容一致,所以答案为Y。

命题规律2:与地点或人物有关的细节

> 地点和人物作为对某一事件的具体描述中不可或缺的部分,特别是一些专有名词(人名或地名),通常以大写字母开头,在文章中显得比较突出,容易寻找,可成为题眼帮助定位信息源。

【例3】By the end of the century there was an immense network of paved roads, residential streets, expressways, and freeways built to support millions of vehicles. The highway system was officially renamed for Eisenhower to honor his vision and leadership. The year construction began he said: "Together, the united forces of our communication and transportation systems are dynamic elements in the very name we bear—United States. Without them, we would be a mere alliance of many separate parts."

【题目】The interstate system was renamed after Eisenhower in recognition of _____.

[2006.6/T10]

【解析】以Eisenhower这个专有名词为本题题眼,将信息源定位于上述段落第2句,可以看出题目中的in recognition

of 和原文的 to honor 表达的都是目的,而且它们的意思相同,因此空白处应该是 honor 的宾语 his vision and leadership。

命题规律 3:与因果关系有关的细节

含有因果关系的题目在快速阅读中较为常见,考题中往往含有 because, reason, due to, for, as, since, as a result of, so that 等表示因果关系的词语。解题时,题眼可在"因"或"果"中寻找,并可结合其他定位技巧,定位信息源之后要得到答案就不难了。

[例4]... In the wake of September 11, changes in the visa process caused a dramatic decline in the number of foreign students seeking admission to U.S. universities, and a corresponding surge in enrollments in Australia, Singapore and the U.K. ...

[题目]The dramatic decline in the enrollment of foreign students in the U.S. after September 11 was caused by _____. [2007.12/T8]

[解析]空白处前的 caused 表明本题考查因果关系中的"因",在 caused 前的"果"中,应结合命题规律 1 将"September 11"作为题眼,定位上文后,就可发现原文中也有 caused 一词,区别只在于原文和题目中 caused 的主语和宾语的位置相反,由此可见,原文 caused 前的主语 changes in the visa process 为本题答案。

命题规律 4:与时间顺序有关的细节

这种考题往往含有 after, before, when, while, meanwhile, at the same time, prior to, then, later 等表示时间关系的词语,题目包含两个动作或时间,解题时考生可根据这两个动作或时间进行定位并做出判断。

[例5]Career experts say that one of the ways job seekers can stay safe while using the Internet to search out jobs is to conceal their identities. Replace your name on your resume with a generic (泛指的) identifier, such as "Intranet Developer Candidate," or "Experienced Marketing Representative."

[题目]Applicants are advised to use generic names for themselves and their current employers when seeking employment online. [2007.6/T7]

[解析]题目中 when 前的 generic names 和 when 后的 online 都可成为题眼,据此定位于上述段落。原文建议在网上求职不要用真名,而用 generic 的名字,由此看来,题目正是对原文的高度概括,所以答案为 Y。

命题规律 5:与目的、方式、条件有关的细节

此类命题要求考生查找某个事件或动作的目的,或要求考生查找达到某个目的的方式条件,往往含有 to, for, in order to, so as to, in order that, so that, for the purpose of 等表示目的关系的词眼,或引出方式条件的词语,如 with, through, by means of, if, though 等。在解这种考题时,题眼可在条件或目的中寻找,并结合其他命题规律的定位技巧定位信息源之后,再对条件与目的的关系进行判断。

[例6]The first step in solving this meaning shortage is to figure out what you really care about, and then do something about it. A case in point is Ivy, 57, a pioneer in investment banking. "I mistakenly believed that all the money I made would mean something," she says. "But I feel lost, like a 22-year-old wondering what to do with her life." Ivy's solution? She started a program that shows Wall Streeters how to donate time and money to poor children. In the process, Ivy filled her life with meaning.

[题目]Ivy filled her life with meaning by launching a program to help poor children. [2006.12/T6]

[解析]题目中的 by 表明本题要求查找 by 连接的方式——目的关系是否成立。我们可以 Ivy 这个人名为题眼先将信息源定位于上文,然后再以 poor children 等词将信息源精确定位于上文倒数第 2 句,对比原文和题目可以发现题目是对上文最后两句内容的概括,因此本题答案为 Y。

命题规律 6:与比较关系有关的细节

快速阅读中,两个或多个事物之间的比较和最高级也经常成为考点。这种考题一般有形容词或副词的比较级或最高级等较为明显的特征,或者一些信号词如 contrary to, by contrast, unlike, like 等。在此种考题里,除了可将形容词、副词及其比较级、最高级当做题眼外,两个比较的对象也可成为题眼,定位信息源后,就可确定对比关系是否正确。

【例7】Today, the interstate system links every major city in the U.S., and the U.S. with Canada and Mexico. Built with safety in mind, the highways have wide lanes and shoulders, dividing medians or barriers, long entry and exit lanes, curves engineered for safe turns, and limited access. The death rate on highways is half that of all other U.S. roads (0.86 deaths per 100 million passenger miles compared to 1.99 deaths per 100 million on all other roads).

【题目】In spite of safety considerations, the death rate on interstate highways is still higher than that of other American roads.

[2006.6/T5]

【解析】这是一个很典型的考查比较关系的命题。比较的两个对象 interstate highways 和 other American roads 可成为本题题眼帮助定位信息源于上述段落末句。对比题目和原文可知,题目中的 higher than 和 half that of 显然是不相同的,所以答案为 N。

Passage One

Time Pattern in America

Susan Anthony has an eight-to-five job with two 15-minute coffee breaks, a one-hour lunch break, scheduled appointments and weekly deadlines. Every time she enters and leaves her office building she "punches" the clock. Although she is not aware of it, her workday is strongly influenced by her culture's attitudes toward time.

When travelers lack an awareness of how time is regulated in a foreign country, they can expect to feel somewhat *disoriented* (分不清方向或目标的). Since most people take time for granted, the effects of values, customs and social etiquette on the use of time are seldom examined. A culture that values achievement and progress will discourage people from "wasting" time. Highly efficient business people from these cultures may feel frustrated in a country where work proceeds at a slow pace. In religious societies, customs specify times of the day, week, or year for prayer and religious celebrations. If an individual tries to make an appointment during a sacred holiday, he or she could unknowingly offend a religious person. Social etiquette determines appropriate times for visits, meetings, and even phone calls. Arriving two hours late for an appointment may be acceptable in one culture, whereas in another, keeping someone waiting fifteen minutes may be considered rude.

Promptness

Promptness is important in American business, academic and social settings. The importance of punctuality is taught to young children in school. *Tardy* (迟到的) slips and the use of bells signal to the child that punctuality and time itself are to be respected. An amusing report of schoolchild's experience with time appeared in a recent newspaper article.

As a child, my mother used to tell me how crucial it was to be at school when the first bell rang. Preparation for my "on-time" appearance began the night before. I was directed to go to bed early so I could wake up at 7 a.m. with enough time to get ready. Although I usually managed to watch my share of TV cartoons, I knew that in one hour I had to get dressed, eat breakfast, brush my teeth, comb my hair and be on my way to school or I would be violating an important rule of Mom's, the school's, or the world's. It was hard to tell which.

People who keep appointments are considered dependable. If people are late to job interviews, appointments or classes, they are often viewed as unreliable and irresponsible. In the business world, "time is money" and companies may fine their executives for tardiness to business meetings. Of course, it was not always possible to be punctual. Social and business etiquette also provides rules for late arrivals. Calling on the telephone if one is going to be more than a few minutes late for scheduled appointments is considered polite and is often expected. Keeping a date or a friend waiting beyond ten to twenty minutes is considered rude. On the other hand, arriving thirty minutes late

to some parties is acceptable.

Respecting deadlines is also important in academic and professional circles. It is expected that deadlines for class assignments or business reports will be met. Students who hand in assignments late may be surprised to find that the professor will lower their grades or even refuse to grade their work. Whether it is a question of arriving on time or of meeting a deadline, people are culturally conditioned to regulate time.

Division of Time

Time is *tangible* (可以感知的); one can "gain time", "spend time", "waste time", "save time", or even "kill time"! Common questions in American English reveal this concrete quality as though time were a possession. "Do you have time?" "Can you make some time for this?" "How much free time do you have?" The treatment of time as a possession influences the way time is carefully divided.

Generally, Americans are taught to do one thing at a time and may be uncomfortable when an activity is interrupted. In business the careful scheduling of time and the separation of activities are common practices. Appointment calendars are printed with 15-, 30-, and 60-minute time slots. A 2:30–3:00 interview may end in time for a brief break before a 3:15–4:00 meeting. The idea that "there is a time and place for everything" extends to American social life. Visitors who "drop by" without prior notice may interrupt their host's personal time. Thus, calling friends on the telephone before visiting them is generally preferred to visitors "dropping by". To accommodate other people's schedules, Americans make business plans and social engagements several days or weeks in advance.

Future Time

Cultures tend to favor either a past, present, or future orientation with regard to time. A future orientation, *encompassing* (包括) a preference for change, is characteristic of American culture. The society encourages people to look to the future rather than to the past. Technological, social and artistic trends change rapidly and affect people's lifestyles and the relationships.

Given this *inclination* (倾向) toward change, it is not surprising that tradition plays a limited role in the American culture. Those who try to uphold traditional patterns of living or thought may be seen as rigid or "old-fashioned". In a society where change is so rapid, it is not uncommon for every generation to experience a "generation gap". Sometimes parents struggle to understand the values of their children. Even religious institutions have had to adapt to contemporary needs of their followers. Folk singers in church services, women religious leaders, slang versions of the Bible, all reflect attempts made by traditional institutions to "keep up with the times".

High rates of changes, particularly in urban areas, have contributed to a focus on the future rather than the past or present. Some Americans believe that the benefits of the future orientation are achievement and progress and stomach *ulcers* (溃疡) are the results of such a lifestyle.

As individuals in a culture, we all have an intuitive understanding about how time is regulated. Usually we do not think about the concept of time until we interact with others who have a different time orientation. Although individuals from any two cultures may view time similarly, we often sense that in another culture, life seems to proceed either at a slower or faster pace. Knowing how time is regulated, divided and perceived can provide valuable insights into individuals and their cultures.

1. Highly efficient business people are always from cultures that value achievement and progress.
2. Arriving two hours late for an appointment is considered rude in every culture.
3. If a student hands in his assignments late, the professor may refuse to grade his work.
4. The idea that "there is a time and place for everything" is not only restrained in the business circle.
5. The American culture favors future orientation with regard to time.
6. There are as many women leaders as men leaders now in the religious institutions.
7. It is quite impossible for people from different cultures to have similar time orientation.
8. People who do not keep appointment are often considered _____ or _____.
9. The careful division of time is greatly influenced by _____.
10. Tradition plays a limited role in the American culture considering _____.

Passage Two
The International Monetary Fund

In 1944, officials from forty-four nations gathered together for a historic meeting at Bretton Woods in the United States. They wanted to make provisions for the economic problems they expected to follow the end of the World War II. These efforts resulted in the formation of the International Monetary Fund, which was officially established on December 27, 1945, with 30 members. Membership in the IMF is open to every *sovereign* (主权) state that is willing and able to fulfill its obligation. The Fund has grown rapidly, and has 183 countries by the end of 2000. China resumed her membership of IMF in April 1980.

Objective of the IMF

The IMF is established to promote international monetary cooperation and exchange stability, to avoid competitive exchange *depreciation* (贬值) and to provide temporary financial assistance to countries to help ease balance of payments *deficits* (赤字).

Under the Bretton Woods System, all members joining the Fund had to define the exchange rate of their currencies in terms of gold, while one ounce of gold was equal to exactly 35 US dollars.

Since the abandonment of the Bretton Wood System, the Fund has agreed to allow each member to choose its own method of determining an exchange rate for its currency. The only requirements are that the member country no longer bases the value of its currency on gold and informs other members about how it is determining the currency's value.

At any time, the Fund keeps on *supervising* (监督) exchange rate of the member states by asking for necessary data from the members and by collecting materials required to discuss and evaluate the prevailing exchange rate policies globally.

Finance Resources of the Fund

In order to attain these objectives, however, very large financial reserves are needed. There are three financial resources for the Fund, namely, the *quota* (配额) subscriptions, the borrowing money and the trust fund.

The quota is the heart of the International Monetary Fund. The size of the quota is set by the Fund authorities. It is based on the economic importance of a country by such indicators as population, international trade, and GNP. The quota of P. R. China on January 28, 2001, for example, is 4,687.2 million of *SDRs* (特别提款权). The member states need to pay subscription to the IMF, also called membership fee, which is the contribution that the member states must make to the IMF's funds, just like the share capital paid by a stockholder to join in a stock company. It is expressed in SDRs and equal in value to the member's quota. 75% of the subscription is payable in the member state's own currency and 25% is payable in SDRs or in one of the *designated* (指定) reserve currencies. Voting power and qualification to draw on the Fund are linked to the size of the quota. Quota is important because it determines the maximum amount that the member can draw out in times of difficulty. Quotas are reviewed every five years and adjusted accordingly.

Beginning with 1956, IMF activities increased sharply, mainly because of large drawings by the United Kingdom to cope with various crises of the British monetary system. Since then steps have been taken to strengthen the Fund's resources. Besides four general quota increases, the Fund has also sold gold to its principal members to increase its holdings of their currencies. In 1962, the Fund entered into "general arrangement to borrow". In these, the leading nations agreed to lend it up to the equivalent of $6 billion. By borrowing money from member governments or their monetary authorities, the Fund assists special programs that benefit its members.

In 1976, IMF decided to sell one-sixth of its gold at the market rate during four years and use the profit obtained as Trust Fund. The purpose was to provide prime loans to the low-income countries.

Loan and Repayments

As an international regulatory and financing institution, the Fund is entitled to exercise supervision over the policies of its member countries' own currency with gold, or a currency acceptable to the Fund or SDRs.

1. Normal credit

This is the most basic kind of loan provided by the IMF to solve the temporary difficulty with the member's balance of payments. The maximum amount of such a credit is 125% of the member's quota subscriptions and the term is three to five years.

The Fund uses its financial resources to assist its members to resolve their balance-of-payments problems in a manner that is consistent with a stable international or national prosperity. The Fund conducts operations only with the ministry of finance, central bank, and similar financial institutions of its members. Whenever it makes a loan it provides foreign currencies or SDRs from its holdings to the borrower, and the borrower pays the Fund the equivalent amount in its own currency. A loan, called a drawing, thus consists of a member's purchase of foreign currencies or SDRs with its own currency.

2. Special facilities

To help the member countries solve some special problems, the Fund provides them some special facilities, such as the Oil Facility, the Trust Fund Facility, and the Structural Adjustment Facility. Each of the special facilities is targeted at a specific monetary problem.

3. Repayments

Members undertake repayments to the Fund within a maximum of three to five years, which in certain cases can be extended up to ten years. Earlier repurchases are often made either voluntarily or according to a requirement that a member makes a repurchase if its gold and foreign exchange reserves increase sufficiently.

Special Drawing Rights (SDRs)

The SDRs are special rights to borrow or draw from the IMF extended by the IMF to its member countries as an addition to the general drawing rights they already hold. SDRs do not represent actual money, but simply a form of credit. SDRs may be exchanged between member countries or between those countries and IMF.

SDRs are distributed among member countries in proportion to their subscription to the IMF. At first the value of the SDRs was expressed in terms of gold. Since 1974, the SDR's value has been based on a basket of currencies whose allocation is reviewed every five years.

1. What is true about the first members of the IMF?
   A) China was among the first members.　　　B) They had a meeting at Bretton Woods.
   C) The first members included 30 nations.　　D) Some of them withdrew from the IMF.

2. The Bretton Woods System required that the IMF members define the exchange rate of their currencies by means of _____.
   A) American dollar　　B) Euro　　C) gold　　D) pound

3. After the Bretton Woods System was abandoned, the exchange rate of the member countries is monitored by _____.
   A) the United Nations　　　　　　　　　　B) the IMF itself
   C) the countries themselves　　　　　　　D) an unknown organization under the IMF

4. Which of the following is regarded as the membership fee of the IMF members?
   A) The subscription.　　B) The borrowing money.　　C) The trust fund.　　D) The quota.

5. The membership fee of the IMF members can be paid in SDRs up to _____.
   A) a half　　B) one third　　C) a quarter　　D) three quarters

6. The IMF entered the "general arrangement to borrow" in _____.
   A) 1956　　B) 1962　　C) 1976　　D) 1980

7. The Trust Fund was established to help _____.
   A) the developing members　　　　　　　B) the low-income members
   C) stabilize the market rate of gold　　　D) cope with the IMF special plans

8. A normal credit is provided by the IMF to help the members that have problems with their _____.

9. When the IMF makes a loan to a member, the borrower must exchange its own currency for equivalent amount of _____.

10. Each member's SDRs are determined in accordance with _____.

Passage Three
How Should You Build up Your Vocabulary

Exactly what do you do during a normal day? How do you spend your time? Paul T. Rankin very much wanted an answer to that question. To get it, he asked sixty-eight individuals to keep an accurate, detailed record of what they did every minute of their waking hours. When he *consolidated* (巩固) his findings, he discovered that the average individual spent 70 percent of his waking time doing one thing only—communication. That meant either reading, writing, speaking or listening.

Put that evidence alongside of the research findings uncovered by the Human Engineering Laboratories. In exploring *aptitudes* (智能) and careers involving, among other things, data from 30,000 vocabulary tests given yearly, they discovered that big incomes and big vocabularies go together. Vocabulary, more than any other factor yet known, predicts financial success.

And it all fits. Each word you add to your vocabulary makes you a better reader, writer, speaker and listener. Furthermore, linguistic scientists are quick to point out that we actually think with words. If that is so, new words make us better thinkers as well as communicators. No wonder more words are likely to mean more money. What better reason for beginning right now to extend your vocabulary?

Take reading. What exactly do you read? Common sense says you read words. Research confirms that fact. "Vocabulary in context" contributes 39 percent to comprehension. That's more than any other factor isolated and studied—even more than intelligence. And "word discrimination" contributes more to speed of reading than any other factor—28 percent. In short, your efforts to improve vocabulary will pay off in both comprehension and speed.

Suppose, as you're reading along, you lumtebs across a strange word. Did you find yourself stopping for a closer look at lumtebs? Pardon the spelling slip. That's actually the word *stumble* (偶然发现). The letter just got mixed around. Obviously you now know that strange words do slow you down—or even stop you completely. Furthermore, strange words *hinder* (妨碍) comprehension. Which is easier to understand, "Eschew garrulity" or "Avoiding talking too much"?

What you need is a vital, dynamic approach to vocabulary building. *Hybrid* (混合种) corn combines the best qualities of several varieties to ensure maximum productivity. A hybrid approach to vocabulary should, in the same way, ensure maximum results. That's why you should use the CPD formula.

Through Context

When students in a college class were asked what should be done when they came across an unknown word in their reading, 84 percent said, "Look it up in the dictionary." If you do, however, you short-circuit the very mental processes needed to make your efforts most productive.

But there's another reason. Suppose someone asks you what the word fast means. You answer, "speedy or swift". But does it mean that in such contexts as "fast color", "fast woman", or "fast friend"? And if a horse is fast, is it securely tied or *galloping* (飞驰) at top speed? It could be either. It all depends. On the dictionary? No, on context—on how the word is actually used. After all, there are over twenty different meanings for fast in the dictionary. But the dictionary doesn't tell you which meaning is intended. That's why it makes such good sense to begin with context.

Through Word Parts

Now for the next step. Often unfamiliar words contain one or more parts, which, if recognized, provide definite help with meaning. Suppose you read that someone "had a predilection for reading mysteries". The context certainly isn't too helpful. But do you see a prefix, suffix or root that you know? Well, there's the familiar prefix pre-, meaning "before". Look back at the context and try inserting "before". Reading mysteries apparently comes "before" other kinds of reading. Yes, a pre-dilection—or preference—is something put "before" something else.

Or take the word monolithic. Try to isolate the parts. There is the prefix mono-, meaning "one", and the root lith, meaning "stone". Finally, there's the suffix -ic, meaning "consisting of". Those three parts add up to this defi-

nition: "consisting of one stone".

To speed up your use of word parts, you will be introduced to the fourteen most important words in the English language. The prefix and root elements in those few words are found in over 14,000 words of desk dictionary size. With those amazingly useful shortcuts, you can build vocabulary, not a snail's pace, one word at a time, but in giant strides, up to a thousand words at a time.

Your second step, then, is to look for familiar word parts. If they do not give you exact meanings, they should at least bring you much closer.

Through the Dictionary

Now you can see why you should consult the dictionary last, not first. You've looked carefully at the context. You've looked for familiar word parts. Now you play Sherlock Holmes—an exciting role. You hypothesize. In light of context or word parts, you try to solve a mystery. What exactly does that strange word mean? Only after you go through the mental gymnastics to come up with a tentative definition should you open the dictionary to see if you're right.

After all, those first two steps or approaches spark a stronger than usual interest in that dictionary definition. You're now personally involved. Did you figure out the word meaning? Your heightened interest will lead to a better memory of both word and meaning. It also encourages your development of the habits needed to accelerate your progress. And when you see in black and white the definition you had expected, what a feeling of accomplishment is yours. In that way, the CPD Formula provides the exact dynamic interplay of approaches for maximum effectiveness.

Well, there it is, your new formula—Context, Parts, Dictionary. Use it! The exercises that follow will give you specific, step-by-step help in sharpening your awareness of contextual clues, learning the most useful word parts, and using the dictionary with increased accuracy and ease. The results will be like the money in the bank.

1. This passage is meant to inform readers of the importance of our vocabulary and ways to enlarge it.
2. Paul T. Rankin found that incomes and vocabularies are closely related.
3. When concerning comprehension in reading, "Vocabulary in Context" is a factor more important than intelligence.
4. The size of one's vocabulary has a greater influence on his comprehension than his reading speed.
5. The dictionary doesn't tell the meaning of "fast color" because it is not so frequently used as other phrases.
6. The prefixes and roots in the 14 words are the components of more than 14,000 words in the dictionary.
7. All the three approaches introduced in the passage can lead to a better memory of both word and meaning.
8. According to linguistic scientists, new words make us better communicators and thinkers when _____.
9. We should use the CPD formula to enlarge our vocabulary because it can, just like the hybrid corn, bring us _____.
10. The CPD method refers to enlarging one's vocabulary by _____.

第三节 答案解析

参考译文划线点评

Passage One

美国的时间观念

苏珊·安东尼的上班时间是朝八晚五,期间有两次15分钟的喝咖啡休息时间和1小时的午餐时间。此外,她要定时赴约,并且每星期完成一定的工作任务。每次她进出办公楼,都要在打卡机上打卡。她的工作日深受美国人的时间观念影响——尽管她没有意识到这一点。

旅客在外国旅行时,如果不具备该国的时间观念,就会感觉到有点不知所措。因为大多数人觉得时间是理所当然的,所以价值观、风俗和社会礼节对时间观念的影响,很少为人所知。[1]一种重视成功和进步的文化,会让人不去浪费时间。深受这种文化影响的高效工作者,在工作节奏缓慢的国家中会有失落感。在信教的国度,习俗为信徒和宗教仪式规定了具体时间(年、月、日)。如果某人想在宗教节日里进行约会,他会不知不觉地冒犯了信徒。社会礼节决定了探访、会议、甚至是打电话的相应时间。[2]约会迟到两个小时,在某种文化里是可以接受的,但在其他文化中,让别人多等15分钟也会被认为是无礼的。

准时

在美国的商务、学术和社会场合中,守时是很重要的。孩子们在学校里就学习守时的重要性。迟到和铃声的运用告诉孩子们,守时和时间本身是应该尊重的。最近,报纸上刊登了一份有趣的报道,讲述了学童在时间方面的体验:

当我还小的时候,妈妈就常常告诉我,在学校第一声铃响的时候,要到达学校。这是极为重要的。为了能准时到校,准备工作在前一天晚上就开始了。我要按吩咐早点睡觉,以便第二天早上7点我能起床。这样,我会有足够的时间去准备。尽管我总能看上一会儿的电视卡通,但是我知道再过一小时,我就要穿上衣服,吃早餐,刷牙,梳头,然后走在上学的路上。否则,我会冒犯了妈妈的、学校的、或者是整个世界的规矩。究竟是哪一个,我也说不清楚。

[8]准时赴约的人被认为是可以信赖的。要是人们在面试、约会或上课的时候迟到,他们会被认为是不可靠和不负责任的。在商界,"时间就是金钱"。公司很可能因为主管人员在开会的时候迟到,就罚他们的款。当然,要我们总是守时是不可能的。社会和商务礼节同时也给我们定下了迟到的规则。如果要迟到几分钟才能赴约,要打电话通知对方。这样做是得体的,而且是必要的。要约会对象或朋友等上10到20分钟是无礼的。另一方面,如果你参加派对时迟到30分钟,那是可以接受的。

尊重最终期限,在学术和职业生涯中都是很重要的。课堂作业和商务汇报都要在最终期限前上交。[3]迟交作业的学生常感到惊讶的是教授们会降低作业的等级或拒绝批改他们的作业。不管是准时还是在最终期限内完成任务,人们控制时间时,都受到文化的影响。

时间的划分

时间是可以感知的。人们能"获得时间"、"花时间"、"浪费时间"、"节约时间",甚至是"消磨时间"。在美国英语中,常见的问题展示了时间作为"所有物"的具体本质。"你有空吗?""为此,你能腾出时间吗?""你有多少空余时间?"[9]把时间当做所有物,影响了我们细分时间的方式。

总的说来,美国人做事情要一次一件。一项活动要是受干扰而中断,他们会惴惴不安。在商界,仔细地安排时间和划分活动是常见的。约会日历簿都是根据15、30、60分钟的间隔来分行的。一个面试在2:30-3:00举行,一段小憩后,参加3:15-4:00的会议。[4]"凡事皆有时间和地点"的观念,延伸到美国社会生活的方方面面。突然来访的客人很可能会扰乱主人的个人安排。因此,人们更喜欢在拜访朋友前,给他们打个电话,而不是不期而至。为了适应他人的日程安排,美国人会提前几天或几周做出商务计划和社交安排。

将来

[5]各种文化在定位时间的时候,都倾向于选择过去、现在或未来中的一个作为参照点。以未来为参照点包括对变化的偏爱,是美国人的文化特色。美国社会鼓励人们向前看,而不是向后看。技术上、社会上、艺术上的潮流都快速地更新换代,同时影响着人民的生活方式和彼此之间的关系。

[10]考虑到美国人喜欢改变,传统在美国文化中地位不高,就显得不足为奇了。那些支持传统生活方式和思想方式的人会被认为是顽固的或落伍的。在这个变化迅速的社会里,每一代都经历了"代沟",这是很常见的。有时候,家长们千方百计地想了解孩子的价值观。就连宗教机构也必须适应信徒们的当代需求。[6]在教堂服务的民间歌手、宗教女领导、《圣经》的俚语版,都反映了传统机构希望能"与时俱进"。

快速的变化,尤其是在市区里,使我们着眼于未来,而非过去或现在。一些美国人相信未来象征着成功和进步,而胃溃疡是这种生活方式的结果。

身为文化中的一员,我们都对如何控制时间,有一种直觉的了解。通常,我们要与其他持不同时间观念的人打交道,才能懂得时间观念。[7]尽管来自两种不同文化的个体对时间的看法会相差无几,但我们总觉得在另一种文化中生活,节奏不是慢了,就是快了。我们知道了如何控制、划分和看待时间后,就能对个体和文化做出有意义的洞察。

1. 【答案】NG
   【题眼】Highly efficient business people are always from cultures that value achievement and progress.
   【定位】第2段第3、4句。

   [解析]原文第3句提到了信息点 A culture that values achievement and progress,第4句提到了信息点 Highly efficient business people,但不能从原文找到题目中两个信息点之间的关系,因此本题答案为NG。

2. 【答案】N

【题眼】Arriving two hours late for an appointment is considered rude in every culture.

【定位】第2段末句。

【解析】原文该句中第1个分句的内容与题目所述相反,因此本题答案为N。

3. 【答案】Y

【题眼】If a student hands in his assignments late, the professor may refuse to grade his work.

【定位】第1个小标题 **Promptness** 部分的末段第3句。

【解析】原文表明如果学生迟交作业,教授有两种对付的方法。题目表达了其中一种的可能,因此本题答案为Y。

4. 【答案】Y

【题眼】The idea that "there is a time and place for everything" is not only restrained in the business circle.

【定位】第2个小标题 **Division of Time** 部分的末段第5句。

【解析】原文该句表明"there is a time and place for everything"这种想法延伸到社会的各个方面,结合本段第2、3、4句,可以知道这种想法是从商业圈延伸开来的,因此题目说这种想法并不局限于商业圈是正确的。

5. 【答案】Y

【题眼】The American culture favors future orientation with regard to time.

【定位】最后一个小标题 **Future Time** 部分的首段第1、2句。

【解析】原文的... is characteristic of...表明美国文化崇尚以未来为参照点来定位,结合前面首句中提到的每个文化都以不同的时间为参照点来定位,可以推断出题目答案为Y。

6. 【答案】NG

【题眼】There are as many women leaders as men leaders now in the religious institutions.

【定位】最后一个小标题 **Future Time** 部分的第2段最后两句。

【解析】原文只提到了现在宗教团体里也有了女性领导人,但没有提到男女领导人的数量哪个比较大,因此本题答案为NG。

7. 【答案】N

【题眼】It is quite impossible for people from different cultures to have similar time orientation.

【定位】最后一个小标题 **Future Time** 部分的末段第3句。

【解析】原文指出了来自不同文化的人可能有相似的时间观念,这与题目所述相反,因此本题答案为N。

8. 【答案】undependable/unreliable; irresponsible

【题眼】People who do not keep appointment are often considered _____ or _____.

【定位】第1个小标题 **Promptness** 部分的第3段第1、2句。

【解析】空白处应为形容词。原文第2句中的 late to job interviews, appointments or classes 都是 do not keep appointment 的具体例子,题目中的定语从句表达的内容就相当于原文第2句中的 If 条件状语从句的内容,因此,本题的答案就是第2句主句中 viewed as 后的形容词。另外,根据第1句,答案中的 unreliable 也可同义改写成 undependable。

9. 【答案】the treatment of time as a possession

【题眼】The careful division of time is greatly influenced by _____.

【定位】第2个小标题 **Division of Time** 部分的首段末句。

【解析】空白处应为名词词组。题目中的 careful division of time 是对原文 the way time is carefully divided 的同义替换,原文是主动句,题目是被动句,所以它们的主语和宾语的位置是相反的,因此本题答案为原文句中的主语。

10. 【答案】the inclination toward(s) change

【题眼】Tradition plays a limited role in the American culture considering _____.

【定位】最后一个小标题 **Future Time** 部分的第2段首句。

[解析]空白处应为名词词组。题目要求找到导致传统在美国文化中地位不高的原因,解题的关键在于明白原文中 given 一词的功能等同于题目中的 considering(考虑到)。由此可见,本题答案就是 given 一词后的名词词组。

参考译文划线点评 **Passage Two**

国际货币基金组织

1944 年,来自 44 个国家的官员聚集在美国的布雷顿森林,召开了一次历史性的会议。他们希望能为二战结束后预计将会出现的经济问题早做打算。[1]这些努力促成了国际货币基金组织的成立,该组织于 1945 年 12 月 27 日正式成立,当时有 30 个成员国。所有的主权国家,只要愿意并且有能力承担义务,就可以成为基金组织成员国。该基金组织发展迅速,到 2000 年底已有 183 个成员国。中国于 1980 年 4 月重新获得成员国地位。

国际货币基金组织的目标

国际货币基金组织的成立,是为了促进国际货币合作以及外汇的稳定,防止竞争性汇率贬值,并为各国提供临时金融援助,帮助这些国家缓解贸易支付差额赤字。

[2]在布雷顿森林体系下,所有加入基金组织的成员国都要以黄金为基准来确定本国货币的汇率,当时一盎司黄金和 35 美元完全等值。

[3]布雷顿森林体系解体后,基金组织同意让各成员国自行选择本国货币汇率的决定方式。唯一的要求是成员国不再把本国货币的价值与黄金相挂钩,并且要把本国货币价值的决定方式通知其他成员国。

[3]在任何时候,基金组织都负责监督成员国的汇率,其方式是通过向成员国获得必要数据并搜集相关材料,这些材料用来讨论和评估全球主要的汇率政策。

基金组织的资金来源

然而,要实现这些目标,就要有大量的资金储备。基金组织有三个资金来源,分别是缴费、借贷和信托基金。

配额是国际货币基金组织的核心。配额大小由基金组织管理机构决定。它是根据国家的经济重要程度而定的,包括人口、国际贸易以及国民生产总值等指标。例如,中国在 2001 年 1 月 28 日的配额是 46 亿 8720 万美元的特别提款权。[4]成员国需要向基金组织缴费,也称作会费,这是成员国必须向基金组织缴纳的费用,就像持股人为加入股份公司而支付的股金一样。这以特别提款权形式体现出来,并且与成员国的配额等值。[5]75%的会费以成员国本国货币的形式支付,25%以特别提款权或者指定的储备货币形式支付。投票权和从基金组织提取资金的资格与配额大小息息相关。配额非常重要,因为它决定了成员国在困难时期最多可以提取多少资金。配额每五年评审一次,并进行相应调整。

从 1956 年开始,国际货币基金组织的活动迅速增多,主要原因是英国为了应对本国货币体系的各种危机而大量提款。从那时开始,基金组织开始采取措施充实自身资源。除增加了四种一般性配额外,基金组织还向重要成员国出售黄金来增加对这些国家货币的持有量。[6]基金组织于 1962 年订立"借款总安排"。这样,主要成员国同意向基金组织提供相当于 60 亿美元的借款。通过向成员国政府或货币管理部门借款,基金组织为有利于成员国的特别项目提供援助。

[7]在 1976 年,基金组织决定在四年内以市场价格出售其六分之一的黄金储备,并将所获利润用作信托基金。目的是为了向低收入国家提供优等贷款。

贷款和偿还

作为国际调控和资助机构,基金组织有权对成员国货币对黄金的政策,或者对基金组织或特别提款权认可的货币进行监督。

1. [8]普通信贷

[8]这是基金组织提供的最基本的贷款,用来解决成员国收支平衡的短期困难。其最大信贷额度为成员国缴费配额的 125%,借款期限是三至五年不等。

基金组织利用其金融资源,以有利于国际和国家繁荣稳定的方式,协助其成员国解决收支平衡问题。基金组织的项目对象只限于成员国的财政部、中央银行以及类似的金融机构。[9]提供贷款时,基金组织从储备中提供外汇或者特别提款权给借方,借方用等值的本国货币还款。因此被称作提款的借贷就相当于成员国用本国货币购买外汇或者特别提款权。

2. 特殊便利

为了帮助成员国解决一些特殊困难,基金组织为他们提供特殊便利,例如石油便利、信托基金便利和结构调整便利。每一项特殊便利都针对某个特定的货币问题。

3. 偿还

成员国最长要在三至五年内向基金组织还款,在某些情况下可以延长至十年。成员国经常提早还款,是以自愿形式,或是根据一项要求,即成员国的黄金或者外汇储备大量增加时需还款。

特别提款权

特别提款权是基金组织向成员国提供的,除已有的一般提款权外,可以从基金组织借贷或是提款的特别权利。特别提款权并不代表实际资金,而只是一种信贷形式。特别提款权可以在成员国之间,或是在成员国与基金组织之间交换。

[10]特别提款权在成员国之间的分配与其对基金组织缴费数量成正比。特别提款权的价值最初是以黄金的形式表现的。1974 年以后,特别提款权就建立在一揽子货币价值的基础上,这些货币的构成每五年评审一次。

---

1. 【答案】C

【题眼】What is true about the first members of the IMF?

【定位】首段第 3 句。

【解析】原文该句末的 with 30 members 表明选项 C 正确。选项 A 中的 China 在该段末句提及,但全文并无提及 China 是否是第一批 IMF 的成员;选项 B 中的 Bretton Woods 在该段首句提及,但这个会议发生在 IMF 成立之前;选项 D 的信息完全没有原文依据。

2. 【答案】C

【题眼】The Bretton Woods System required that the IMF members define the exchange rate of their currencies by means of _____.

【定位】第 1 个小标题 Objective of the IMF 下第 2 段。

【解析】原文该段中的 in terms of 与题目中的 by means of 为同义词,可见 in terms of 后的 gold 为本题答案,因此本题应选项 C。

3. 【答案】B

【题眼】After the Bretton Woods System was abandoned, the exchange rate of the member countries is monitored by _____.

【定位】第 1 个小标题 Objective of the IMF 下第 3 段首句和第 4 段。

【解析】该部分第 3 段首句首先提到 the Bretton Wood System 解体,第 4 段开头提到无论何时,IMF 都负责监督成员国的利率,结合两句可判断选项 B 为本题答案。

4. 【答案】A

【题眼】Which of the following is regarded as the membership fee of the IMF members?

【定位】第 2 个小标题 Finance Resources of the Fund 部分的第 2 段第 5 句。

【解析】原文该句中的... also called...表明 subscription 就是 membership fee,因此本题应选项 A。

5. 【答案】C

【题眼】The membership fee of the IMF members can be paid in SDRs up to _____.

【定位】第 2 个小标题 Finance Resources of the Fund 部分的第 2 段第 7 句。

【解析】原文该句表明 IMF 会员国的会费可分两部分缴纳,其中 25%(即四分之一)可以 SDRs 的形式缴纳,可见选项 C 为本题答案。

6. 【答案】B

【题眼】The IMF entered the "general arrangement to borrow" in _____.

【定位】第 2 个小标题 Finance Resources of the Fund 部分的第 3 段倒数第 3 句。

【解析】根据题眼定位后,或逐一查找四个选项的时间,可知只有选项 B 提到的时间与题目的内容相关。

7. 【答案】B

【题眼】The Trust Fund was established to help _____.

【定位】第 2 个小标题 **Finance Resources of the Fund** 部分的末段。

【解析】选项 B 与原文该段末句的 The purpose was to...后的内容相同,为本题答案。选项 C 中的 gold 和 market rate 在该段首句也有提及,但 stabilize 在原文并无提及。其他两个选项也没有原文依据。

8.【答案】balance of payments

【题眼】A <u>normal credit</u> is provided by the IMF to help the members that have problems with their _____.

【定位】第 3 个小标题 **Loan and Repayments** 部分的第 1 点 Normal credit 下第 1 段第 1 句。

【解析】空白处应为名词词组。本题考查 IMF 通过提供 normal credit 帮助成员国解决什么问题,原文该句 to solve...后的内容表明这个问题就是"balance of payments",因此 balance of payments 为本题答案。

9.【答案】foreign currencies or SDRs

【题眼】When the IMF makes a <u>loan</u> to a member, the <u>borrower</u> must exchange its own currency for equivalent amount of _____.

【定位】第 3 个小标题 **Loan and Repayments** 部分的第 1 点 Normal credit 下第 2 段倒数第 2 句。

【解析】空白处应为名词词组。原文该句表明 IMF 成员国可用本国货币换取外币或 SDRs,题目中的 exchange... for...就是"以……换取……"的意思,可见,"外币或 SDRs"(即 foreign currencies or SDRs)为本题答案。

10.【答案】their subscription to the IMF

【题眼】Each member's <u>SDRs</u> are determined in accordance with _____.

【定位】末段首句。

【解析】空白处应为名词词组。题目中的 in accordance with 是对原文 in proportion to 的近义改写,可见原文 in proportion to... 后的 their subscription to the IMF 为本题答案。

参考译文划线点评　　　　　　　　　　　　　　　Passage Three

应该如何扩充你的词汇量

确切地说,平常你都做些什么?你怎样打发时间?保罗·T.兰金非常想要知道答案。为了得到这个答案,他访问了 68 个人并对他们在除了睡觉以外的每分钟里做的事情都做了准确、详细的记录。在整理好他的访问资料后,[2]<u>他发现,平均说来,每个人除了睡觉以外的 70%的时间都花在了同一件事情上面——交流,即听、说、读、写。</u>

这个发现与人事管理实验室的研究结果不谋而合。[2]<u>在进行智能开发和职业培训等工作时,他们每年都会进行涉及 3 万个词汇的测试,从得来的数据中,他们发现高收入人群的词汇量相应也很大。</u>相较于迄今为止我们所知道的其他因素,词汇量更能预测经济上的成功。

这种说法是有道理的。每增加一个词汇都会使你在听、说、读、写方面有所提高。[8]<u>而且,语言学家已指出我们的思维实际上是依赖语言进行的。如果真是这样,那么词汇的增加也就会使我们的思维更灵活,更善于交流。</u>这就难怪更多的词汇也就可能意味着更多的金钱。现在立刻开始扩充你的词汇量吧,难道这还需要什么更好的理由吗?

就拿阅读来说吧。你读的到底是什么呢?按常理说,你读的是单词。研究也证实了这一点。[3]<u>"上下文词汇"对理解有 39%的帮助,超过了其他所研究过的任何一种独立因素——甚至智力因素。</u>而"词汇辨别"更有助于加快阅读速度——其贡献率高达 28%,高于任何其他因素。[4]<u>总之,你在增进词汇量方面所付出的努力会使你在阅读理解和阅读速度两方面得到回报。</u>

假定你在阅读过程中碰到了一个奇怪的单词 lumtebs。你发现你自己会停下来更仔细地分析 lumtebs 这个单词吗?不用在意这样的拼写错误。实际上这个单词是 stumble。只不过字母排列搞乱了。显然你现在知道生词确实让你减慢阅读速度了吧——或者甚至让你完全停了下来。而且,生词也妨碍理解。比如,"避免饶舌(Eschew garrulity)"和"避免说得太多(Avoiding talking too much)",哪个更容易理解呢?

你需要的是一种行之有效的、灵活的扩充词汇的方法。杂交玉米将几种最优玉米杂合起来就能保证最高产量。[9]<u>同样,将扩充词汇量的多种方法结合起来使用也会给你带来最大的收获。所以你应该使用 CPD 公式。</u>

通过上下文

当问到大学生在阅读时突然遇到一个不认识的单词该怎么办,84%的学生会说:"查字典。"然而,这么做,你就会打断最有效阅读所需的思维过程。

但是还有另一个原因。假定有人问你 fast 这个单词是什么意思。你回答"快速的或者迅速的"。[5]但是在"fast color"、"fast woman"或"fast friend"这些短语中的 fast 还是那个意思吗? 如果在"a horse is fast"这个小句中,fast 表示被牢牢系住还是以最快的速度飞驰呢? 它可以表示两者中任何一个意思。这要看情况而定。根据字典吗? 不,根据上下文——根据这个单词的实际使用情况。[5]毕竟,fast 这个单词在字典里有 20 多种不同的意思。但字典并不会告诉你具体是哪种意思。所以我们还是得从上下文入手。

通过构词成分

现在看看下一步。一些我们不熟悉的单词常常包含一个或多个组成成分,如果我们可以认出这些组成成分的话,它们就可以帮助我们明确单词的意思。假定你读到某人"had a predilection for reading mysteries"。对于这个句子,上下文当然不会有多大帮助。但是你看看有没有哪个前缀、后缀或是词根是你懂得的? 哦,有一个熟悉的前缀 pre-,是"之前"的意思。再回头看看上下文并且试着插入"之前"这个意思。读神话显然排在其他类型的阅读之前。是的,pre-dilection(偏爱)就是置于其他东西"之前"的东西。

再以单词 monolithic 为例。试着拆分一下这个单词的构词成分。这个单词有一个前缀 mono-,意思是"一",以及一个词根 lith,意为"石头"。最后,还有一个后缀-ic,意思是"由……组成"。这三个部分组合在一起意思就是:"由一块石头组成的"。

[6]为了加速你对单词成分的了解和运用,你首先要熟悉英语中 14 个最为重要的单词。这些为数不多的单词中的前缀和词根出现的频率非常高,在一般案头词典中我们可以发现超过 1.4 万个单词有这些前缀和词根。掌握了这些极其有用的捷径,你就能够扩充你的词汇量了,不是以蜗牛的速度来,一次增加一个单词,而是大踏步前进,一次就增加上千个单词。

第二步就是寻找熟悉的构词成分。这即使不能给你提供精确的意思,至少也会给你提供一些近似的信息。

通过字典

现在你该明白为什么你需要在最后而不是在一开始就查字典了。你已经仔细看过上下文了,也找过熟悉的构词成分。现在你可以扮演夏洛克·福尔摩斯——一个令人兴奋的角色了。你开始假设。尽量根据上下文或者单词的构词成分来解开一个秘密。那个生词到底是什么意思?只有在你经过一番脑力活动推测出一个释义后,才应该打开字典来看看你的猜测是否正确。

[7]总的说来,通过前两步或前面两种方法得出的意思比字典上提供的意思更令人感兴趣。因为你自己已经完全深入其中了。你明白单词的意思了吗?[7]兴趣的增加会使你更能记住单词及其意义,也可以鼓励你养成良好的学习习惯,进而不断取得进步。当你看到你所期待的释义清清楚楚地出现在字典里时,你会多么地有成就感啊!如此,CPD 公式能为你提供灵活、准确和互动的各种方法以达到最大的效果。

[10]好了,你的新公式就是——上下文(C)、构词成分(P)、字典(D)。运用它!随后的练习将具体地、循序渐进地帮你敏锐地辨别上下文提示,学会最有用的构词成分和越来越轻松准确地使用字典。其结果会像你在银行里存了一笔钱了。

---

1. 【答案】Y

【题眼】This passage is meant to inform readers of <u>the importance of our vocabulary and ways to enlarge it</u>.

【定位】文章标题、各个小标题及开头三段。

【解析】这是一道主旨题。由标题则可知文章讲述了扩大词汇量的方法,再通读文章开头几段,第 3 段第 2 句指出词汇量的增加使人成为更好的读者、作者、说话者和听者,由此可看出词汇量的重要性。因此题目概括了文章的主旨,故答案为 Y。

2. 【答案】N

【题眼】<u>Paul T. Rankin</u> found that <u>incomes and vocabularies</u> are closely related.

【定位】第 1 段倒数第 2 句和第 2 段第 2 句。

【解析】关于 Paul T. Rankin 的研究结果可在文章第 1 段找到,关于 incomes and vocabularies 关系的信息点在第 2 段第 2 句可以找到。由此可见,题目把 the Human Engineering Laboratories 的研究成果张冠李戴到 Paul T. Rankin 的名下,故答案为 N。

3. 【答案】Y

【题眼】When concerning comprehension in reading, "Vocabulary in Context" is a factor more important than intelligence.

【定位】第 4 段第 5、6 句。

【解析】原文说到"Vocabulary in Context"比所研究过的其他任何孤立的因素对理解的贡献都大,甚至比 intelligence 都大,故答案为 Y。

4. 【答案】NG

【题眼】The size of one's vocabulary has a greater <u>influence on his comprehension</u> than his <u>reading speed</u>.

【定位】第 4 段末句。

【解析】原文只提到增加词汇量对阅读理解和速度都有益,但没有比较词汇量的大小对理解和速度的影响哪个比较大,因此本题答案为 NG。

5. 【答案】NG

【题眼】The dictionary doesn't tell the meaning of <u>"fast color"</u> because it is not so frequently used as other phrases.

【定位】第 1 个小标题 Through Context 部分第 2 段第 4 句和倒数第 2、3 句。

【解析】结合原文两句,虽然可以确定题目主句的内容是真实的,但是造成这个现象的原因是否如题目中的原因状语从句所述的那样,根据原文难以确定,因此本题答案为 NG。

6. 【答案】Y

【题眼】The prefixes and roots in the <u>14 words</u> are the components of more than <u>14,000 words</u> in the dictionary.

【定位】第 2 个小标题 Through Word Parts 部分的第 3 段第 1、2 句。

【解析】原文第 2 句中的... are found in...表明在第 1 句中提到的 14 个重要单词里的前缀和词根可用于组成词典里 14000 多个单词,这也是题目表达的意思,因此本题答案为 Y。

7. 【答案】N

【题眼】All the three approaches introduced in the passage can lead to <u>a better memory</u> of both word and meaning.

【定位】倒数第 2 段第 1 句和第 4 句。

【解析】根据原文,只有前两种方法,即 Through context 和 Through word parts,可以激起读者更多的兴趣,而更多的兴趣能使我们把单词及意思记得更牢,而本题却说所有三种方法都可以,故答案为 N。

8. 【答案】we actually think with words

【题眼】According to linguistic scientists, new words make us better <u>communicators and thinkers</u> when _____.

【定位】第 3 段第 3、4 句。

【解析】空白处应为一个句子。原文第 4 句 if 引出的从句是使我们成为 better communicators and thinkers 的条件,由此可见,本题解题的关键就是要找出 if 引出的从句中 that 指的是什么。联系上一句话可以推断,that 指的是 we actually think with words,因此这就是答案。

9. 【答案】maximum results

【题眼】We should use the <u>CPD formula</u> to enlarge our vocabulary because it can, just like the <u>hybrid corn</u>, bring us _____.

【定位】第 6 段最后两句。

【解析】空白处应为名词词组,作 bring 的直接宾语。题目要求填入的部分属于使用 CPD 方法的原因,根据最后一句的 that's why,可知原因在倒数第 2 句。题目中的 bring us 与原文中的 ensure 意思类似,因此答案就是其后的名词词组。

10. 【答案】Context, Parts and Dictionary

【题眼】The <u>CPD</u> method refers to enlarging one's vocabulary by _____.

【定位】各小标题及末段首句。

【解析】空白处应为名词词组。第 6 段末句首次提到 CPD,但没有做出解释,从接下来的三个小标题可以推断 CPD 分别代表什么。另外,文章末段首句的破折号后明确指出 CPD 的定义。

第一节 灵机一动明辨是非

解题技巧1:主题定位和关键词定位巧妙结合

快速阅读的文章一般比较简单,但是篇幅相对较长,而另一方面,因为题目有 NG"未提及"的情况存在,所以我们也无法根据常识推断或猜测,而必须在文中找到相关证据。这就要求我们尽可能缩小寻读范围,在尽可能少的段落或句子里找到与考题相关的内容。

在解题时,考生应首先根据题目的主题大致确定相关信息可在文章哪个小标题部分寻找,然后根据关键词(题眼)在上述部分进行搜寻和定位。这样,通过主题定位和关键词定位,既可以缩短用时,又可以大幅度提高准确率。

[例1]**1. Do something new.**

Very little that's new occurs in our lives. The impact of this sameness on our emotional energy is gradual, but huge: It's like a tire with a slow leak. You don't notice it at first, but eventually you'll get a flat. It's up to you to plug the leak—even though there are always a dozen reasons to stay stuck in your dull routines of life. That's where Maura, 36, a waitress, found herself a year ago.

Fortunately, Maura had a lifeline—a group of women friends who meet regularly to discuss their lives. Their lively discussions spurred Maura to make small but nevertheless life-altering changes. She joined a gym in the next town. She changed her look with a short haircut and new black T-shirts. Eventually, Maura gathered the courage to quit her job and start her own business.

Here's a challenge: If it's something you wouldn't ordinarily do, do it. Try a dish you've never eaten. Listen to music you'd ordinarily tune out. You'll discover these small things add to your emotional energy.

2. Reclaim life's meaning.

...

3. Put yourself in the fun zone.

...

4. Bid farewell to guilt and regret.

...

5. Make up your mind.

...

6. Give to get.

...

[题目]Even small changes people make in their lives can help increase their emotional energy.　　　　　　　　　[2006.12/T5]

【解析】根据题目中的 changes 一词可推断本题应属于第 1 个小标题下的内容,再抓住 small, emotional energy 等词将信息源准确定位于第 1 个小标题下末句,然后可以判断题目和原文该句为同一表达,因此本题答案应为 Y。

解题技巧2:如何区分 N 和 NG

题目描述的内容与原文的相关内容明显矛盾、相反或不符,则答案为 N;而题目与原文之间是一种或然关系,即题目提到的内容可能发生,也可能不发生,根据原文难以求证是哪种可能性,则答案为 NG。

【例2】**2. Take advantage of site features.**

Lawful job search sites offer levels of privacy protection. Before posting your resume, carefully consider your job search objectives and the level of risk you are willing to assume.

CareerBuilder.com, for example, offers three levels of privacy from which job seekers can choose. The first is standard posting. This option gives job seekers who post their resumes the most visibility to the broadest employer audience possible.

The second is *anonymous* (匿名的) posting. This allows job seekers the same visibility as those in the standard posting category without any of their contact information being displayed. Job seekers who wish to remain anonymous but want to share some other information may choose which pieces of contact information to display.

The third is private posting. This option allows a job seeker to post a resume without having it searched by employers. Private posting allows job seekers to quickly and easily apply for jobs that appear on CareerBuilder.com without retyping their information.

【题目】Of the three options offered by CareerBuilder.com in Suggestion 2, the third one is apparently most strongly recommended. [2007.6/T5]

【解析】根据题目中的 Suggestion 2 直接定位原文该部分后,可知该部分第 2 段、第 3 段和末段分别用 the first, the second 和 the third 引出了三种做法,但要注意的是,文中只是客观介绍这三种做法,没有对比哪种做法最好。由此可见,因为题目所述的观点难以通过原文得到证实,这种观点已无所谓对还是错。这时,可以说题目所述与原文内容构成一种"或然"的关系,可判断本题答案为 NG。

一般判断 N 和 NG 的标准如下:

No 题:
(1)信息与原文相反
(2)将原文信息张冠李戴
(3)将原文中不确定的或未经证实的内容作为正确的或客观的来表述
(4)改变原文的条件、范围、频率、可能性等

NG 题:
(1)无中生有
(2)将原文具体化,即题目中涉及的范围小于原文涉及的范围
(3)以个别代替整体,即将原文所举例子的特殊现象推广为普遍现象
(4)随意比较原文中提到的两个事物
(5)原文中作者或某个人物的目标、目的、愿望、誓言等内容,在题目中作为客观事实陈述

解题技巧3:考题中的生词可帮助定位

有些考题含有超出考纲词汇的生词,但是考生不用害怕这些生词,因为生词常常都很能吸引读者的眼光,可以成为帮助定位信息源的工具。生词通常在原文中就有,命题者只是照搬该生词到题目里面,因此这些生词就是题目的题眼,只要在原文中找到这些生词,相关的信息就能找到。

【例3】There's an energy crisis in America, and it has nothing to do with fossil fuels. Millions of us get up each morning already weary over what the day holds. "I just can't get started," people say. But it's not physical energy that most of us lack. Sure, we could all use extra sleep and a better diet. But in truth, people are healthier today than at any time in history. I can almost guarantee that if you long for more energy, the problem is not with your body.

【题目】The energy crisis in America discussed here mainly refers to a shortage of fossil fuels. [2006.12/T1]

【解析】题目中的 fossil 是超纲词,以此为题眼可迅速将题目的信息源定位于上文首句,对比原文与题目就可确定本题答案为 N。

解题技巧4:出题有顺序性

通常来说,快速阅读的题目在原文中的出现是有一定顺序的,准确定位前一题后,便可顺着原文找到下一题的出处。但是非判断题7与句子填空题8之间不一定有顺序。

第二节 句子填空3种改写技巧

解题技巧1:明确考点

对考题进行分析,明确其考查的内容是时间、地点、人物、数量、方式或是原因等,继而在文中相关信息中查找该考题所考查的内容。以下信号词有助于判断考点要求:

> at, in, on 等后面的空白处考查的是时间或地点;
> after, before, during 等后面的空白处考查的是时间;
> by 后面的空白处考查的可能是方式或动作的施动者;
> by means of, through 后的空白处考查的是方法手段;
> to 后面的空白处考查的可能是目的、对象、程度;
> because, for, due to, owing to 后的空白处考查的是原因。

【例4】Identity theft and identity fraud are terms used to refer to all types of crime in which someone wrongfully obtains and uses another person's personal data in some way that involves fraud or deception, typically for economic gain.

【题目】According to the passage, identity theft is committed typically for _____.　　　　[2007.6/T10]

【解析】根据空白处前的 for 可判断本题需要查找的是一个"目的"。再以 identity theft 为题眼定位信息源后,可发现原文句末 for 引出的正好符合题目"目的"的要求,因此 economic gain 为本题答案。

解题技巧2:巧妙进行逻辑转换或微调,确保内容无误

明确考点后,考生应在所定位的一个或若干个句子中搜寻所需内容。原文中的相关信息在表达方式上可能和考题有所不同甚至大相径庭,但它们都只是同义替换,考生只要牢牢抓住原文和考题的逻辑,充分利用原文中的信号词(如某些介词、连词等),找出二者相对应的地方,就能找到与答案相关的信息。

> **考点往往涉及以下的转换形式:**
> (1)否定句与肯定句之间的转换,如原文为双重否定句,考题以肯定句式表达;
> (2)主动句与被动句之间的转换,如原文为主动句,考题以被动句式表达;
> (3)原因与结果之间的转换,如原文原因在前,结果在后,题目则把两者位置倒转;
> (4)条件与目的之间的转换,如原文目的在前,方式在后,题目则把两者位置倒转;
> (5)after 与 before 之间的转换,如原文用 after 表明两个事物的先后顺序,题目则以 before 考查两者顺序。

【例5】The interstate system has been an essential element of the nation's economic growth in terms of shipping and job creation: more than 75 percent of the nation's freight deliveries arrive by truck; and most products that arrive by rail or air use interstates for the last leg of the journey by vehicle.

【题目】Trucks using the interstate highways deliver more than _____.　　　　[2006.6/T9]

【解析】以题目中的 Truck, interstate highways 等词为题眼定位上文后,可发现在原文的 ... deliveries arrive by truck 与题目中的 Trucks deliver... 形成的主谓关系刚好相反,因此,本题答案(即题目的宾语部分信息)应在原文属于主语部分的 more than 75 percent of... deliveries 中寻找,最后根据 more than 这个在原文和题目共有的信号词确定本题答案为 75 percent of the nation's freight。

解题技巧3:确保语言形式无误

最后,考生必须用正确的语言形式(即语法形式)把与答案相关的信息表达出来。此时,考生应该明确需要作答的部分在整个句子中充当什么成分,是主语、谓语、宾语、定语或是状语等,继而决定所填入的内容应该是什么词性或时态、语态等。特别注意:

> 介词后需要名词或动名词短语充当宾语;
>
> to 后面可能接动词不定式短语,但如果 to 是介词,其后为名词或动名词短语;
>
> when, where, because, if 等从句联系词后接主谓从句。

【例6】Most Americans recognize that universities contribute to the nation's well-being through their scientific research, but many fear that foreign students threaten American competitiveness by taking their knowledge and skills back home.

【题目】Many Americans fear that American competitiveness may be threatened by foreign students who will _____.

[2007.12/T9]

【解析】根据空白处前的"will"确定本题答案应为原形动词开头的动词词组,然后以 competitiveness 为题眼定位相关信息息源于上文。对比原文与题目可以看到,题目的内容是对原文 but 引出的分句的同义改写,原文句末 by taking their knowledge and skills back home 与题目 who 引出的定语从句都是对 foreign students 的补充说明,由此可见,taking their knowledge and skills back home 在内容上符合题目的要求。因此 take their knowledge and skills back home 为本题答案。

第三节 选择题2种应试技巧

解题技巧1:见到什么选什么

快速阅读选择题的选项设置有一个显著的特点:正确选项照抄原文,干扰项无中生有、没有原文依据或只是原文的片言只字。因此,此种题型可以使用"见到什么选什么"的技巧,哪个选项与原文的语句重合最多,它就是正确选项。

【例7】Universities are also encouraging students to spend some of their undergraduate years in another country. In Europe, more than 140,000 students participate in the Erasmus program each year, taking courses for credit in one of 2,200 participating institutions across the continent. And in the United States, institutions are helping place students in summer *internships* (实习) abroad to prepare them for global careers. Yale and Harvard have led the way, offering every undergraduate at least one international study or internship opportunity—and providing the financial resources to make it possible.

[2007.12/T4]

【题目】How do Yale and Harvard prepare their undergraduates for global careers?

A) They organize a series of seminars on world economy.

B) They offer them various courses in international politics.

C) They arrange for them to participate in the Erasmus program.

D) They give them chances for international study or internship.

【解析】根据题干中的 Yale 和 Harvard 可定位上文末句,该句提到了 international study or internship opportunity,选项 D 重述了这些词,因此选项 D 就是本题答案。其他选项均没有原文依据。

解题技巧2:利用选项缩小答案的范围

快速阅读文章常引用数据,出题者通常会将位置相近、形态相同的数字、人名、地名设置为选项,题干则与其中一个相关。这种选择题的选项通常很简短,有些甚至只有一两个词,这时,我们可以选项为定位工具,在原文逐个查找选项的内容是否符合题意。一旦确定某个选项为正确答案,其他选项就无须再花时间查找。这样比仅靠题干关键词定位效率更高。

【例8】Of the forces shaping higher education none is more sweeping than the movement across borders. Over the past three decades the number of students leaving home each year to study abroad has grown at an annual rate of 3.9 percent, from 800,000 in 1975 to 2.5 million in 2004. Most travel from one developed nation to

another, but the flow from developing to developed countries is growing rapidly. The reverse flow, from developed to developing countries, is on the rise, too. Today foreign students earn 30 percent of the doctoral degrees awarded in the United States and 38 percent of those in the United Kingdom. And the number crossing borders for undergraduate study is growing as well, to 8 percent of the undergraduates at America's best institutions and 10 percent of all undergraduates in the U.K. In the United States, 20 percent of the newly hired professors in science and engineering are foreign-born, and in China many newly hired faculty members at the top research universities received their graduate education abroad.   [2007.12/T3]

【题目】In the United States, how many of the newly hired professors in science and engineering are foreign-born?

    A) 10%.   B) 20%.   C) 30%.   D) 38%.

【解析】原文该段有多个数字,而且段落较长,而题干中没有比较突出的关键词,这时不如先利用选项的数字将搜索范围缩小。上文前5行的数字中没有双位数的百分比,利用"数字缩小搜索范围"的方法,即可将范围缩小到原文的一半。接着,根据选项的数字定位选项A和选项B在倒数第三行,选项C在第6行,选项D在第7行。现在只要看第3行、第6行和第7行的数字前后的几个词就可以立刻确定选项B为本题答案。

第四节 历年典型真题突破训练

Passage One   07年12月真题

Universities Branch Out

As never before in their long history, universities have become instruments of national competition as well as instruments of peace. They are the place of the scientific discoveries that move economies forward, and the primary means of educating the talent required to obtain and maintain competitive advantage. But at the same time, the opening of national borders to the flow of goods, services, information and especially people has made universities a powerful force for global integration, mutual understanding and geopolitical stability.

In response to the same forces that have driven the world economy, universities have become more self-consciously global: seeking students from around the world who represent the entire range of cultures and values, sending their own students abroad to prepare them for global careers, offering courses of study that address the challenges of an interconnected world and *collaborative* (合作的) research programs to advance science for the benefit of all humanity.

Of the forces shaping higher education none is more sweeping than the movement across borders. Over the past three decades the number of students leaving home each year to study abroad has grown at an annual rate of 3.9 percent, from 800,000 in 1975 to 2.5 million in 2004. Most travel from one developed nation to another, but the flow from developing to developed countries is growing rapidly. The reverse flow, from developed to developing countries, is on the rise, too. Today foreign students earn 30 percent of the doctoral degrees awarded in the United States and 38 percent of those in the United Kingdom. And the number crossing borders for undergraduate study is growing as well, to 8 percent of the undergraduates at America's best institutions and 10 percent of all undergraduates in the U.K. In the United States, 20 percent of the newly hired professors in science and engineering are foreign-born, and in China many newly hired faculty members at the top research universities received their graduate education abroad.

Universities are also encouraging students to spend some of their undergraduate years in another country. In Europe, more than 140,000 students participate in the Erasmus program each year, taking courses for credit in one of 2,200 participating institutions across the continent. And in the United States, institutions are helping place students in summer *internships* (实习) abroad to prepare them for global careers. Yale and Harvard have led the way, offering every undergraduate at least one international study or internship opportunity—and providing the financial resources to make it possible.

Globalization is also reshaping the way research is done. One new trend involves sourcing portions of a research program to another country. Yale professor and Howard Hughes Medical Institute investigator Tian Xu directs a research center focused on the genetics of human disease at Shanghai's Fudan University, in collaboration with faculty colleagues from both schools. The Shanghai center has 95 employees and graduate students working in a 4,300-square-meter laboratory facility. Yale faculty, postdoctors and graduate students visit regularly and attend videoconference seminars with scientists from both campuses. The arrangement benefits both countries; Xu's Yale lab is more productive, thanks to the lower costs of conducting research in China, and Chinese graduate students, postdoctors and faculty get on-the-job training from a world-class scientist and his U.S. team.

As a result of its strength in science, the United States has consistently led the world in the commercialization of major new technologies, from the mainframe computer and the integrated circuit of the 1960s to the Internet *infrastructure* (基础设施) and applications software of the 1990s. The link between university-based science and industrial application is often indirect but sometimes highly visible: Silicon Valley was intentionally created by Stanford University, and Route 128 outside Boston has long housed companies spun off from MIT and Harvard. Around the world, governments have encouraged copying of this model, perhaps most successfully in Cambridge, England, where Microsoft and scores of other leading software and biotechnology companies have set up shop around the university.

For all its success, the United States remains deeply hesitant about sustaining the research-university model. Most politicians recognize the link between investment in science and national economic strength, but support for research funding has been unsteady. The budget of the National Institutes of Health doubled between 1998 and 2003, but has risen more slowly than inflation since then. Support for the physical sciences and engineering barely kept pace with inflation during that same period. The attempt to make up lost ground is welcome, but the nation would be better served by steady, predictable increases in science funding at the rate of long-term GDP growth, which is on the order of inflation plus 3 percent per year.

American politicians have great difficulty recognizing that admitting more foreign students can greatly promote the national interest by increasing international understanding. Adjusted for inflation, public funding for international exchanges and foreign-language study is well below the levels of 40 years ago. In the wake of September 11, changes in the visa process caused a dramatic decline in the number of foreign students seeking admission to U.S. universities, and a corresponding surge in enrollments in Australia, Singapore and the U.K. Objections from American university and business leaders led to improvements in the process and a reversal of the decline, but the United States is still seen by many as unwelcoming to international students.

Most Americans recognize that universities contribute to the nation's well-being through their scientific research, but many fear that foreign students threaten American competitiveness by taking their knowledge and skills back home. They fail to grasp that welcoming foreign students to the United States has two important positive effects: first, the very best of them stay in the States and—like immigrants throughout history—strengthen the nation; and second, foreign students who study in the United States become ambassadors for many of its most *cherished* (珍视) values when they return home. Or at least they understand them better. In America as elsewhere, few instruments of foreign policy are as effective in promoting peace and stability as welcoming international university students.

1. From the first paragraph we know that present-day universities have become _____.
   A) more and more research-oriented
   B) in-service training organizations
   C) more popularized than ever before
   D) a powerful force for global integration

2. Over the past three decades, the enrollment of overseas students has increased _____.
   A) by 2.5 million
   B) by 800,000
   C) at an annual rate of 3.9 percent
   D) at an annual rate of 8 percent

3. In the United States, how many of the newly hired professors in science and engineering are foreign-born?
   A) 10%.   B) 20%.   C) 30%.   D) 38%.

4. How do Yale and Harvard prepare their undergraduates for global careers?
   A) They organize a series of seminars on world economy.
   B) They offer them various courses in international politics.
   C) They arrange for them to participate in the Erasmus program.

D) They give them chances for international study or internship.

5. An example illustrating the general trend of universities' globalization is _____.

    A) Yale's collaboration with Fudan University on genetic research

    B) Yale's helping Chinese universities to launch research projects

    C) Yale's student exchange program with European institutions

    D) Yale's establishing branch campuses throughout the world

6. What do we learn about Silicon Valley from the passage?

    A) It houses many companies spun off from MIT and Harvard.

    B) It is known to be the birthplace of Microsoft Company.

    C) It was intentionally created by Stanford University.

    D) It is where the Internet infrastructure was built up.

7. What is said about the U.S. federal funding for research?

    A) It has increased by 3 percent.   B) It has been unsteady for years.

    C) It has been more than sufficient.   D) It doubled between 1998 and 2003.

8. The dramatic decline in the enrollment of foreign students in the U.S. after September 11 was caused by _____ _____.

9. Many Americans fear that American competitiveness may be threatened by foreign students who will _____ _____.

10. The policy of welcoming foreign students can benefit the U.S. in that the very best of them will stay and _____ _____.

Passage Two   07 年 6 月真题

Protect Your Privacy When Job-hunting Online

    Identity theft and identity fraud are terms used to refer to all types of crime in which someone wrongfully obtains and uses another person's personal data in some way that involves fraud or deception, typically for economic gain.

    The numbers associated with identity theft are beginning to add up fast these days. A recent General Accounting Office report estimates that as many as 750,000 Americans are victims of identity theft every year. And that number may be low, as many people choose not to report the crime even if they know they have been victimized.

    Identity theft is "an absolute epidemic," states Robert Ellis Smith, a respected author and advocate of privacy. "It's certainly picked up in the last four or five years. It's worldwide. It affects everybody, and there's very little you can do to prevent it and, worst of all, you can't detect it until it's probably too late."

    Unlike your fingerprints, which are unique to you and cannot be given to someone else for their use, your personal data, especially your social security number, your bank account or credit card number, your telephone calling card number, and other valuable identifying data, can be used, if they fall into the wrong hands, to personally profit at your expense. In the United States and Canada, for example, many people have reported that unauthorized persons have taken funds out of their bank or financial accounts, or, in the worst cases, taken over their identities altogether, running up vast debts and committing crimes while using the victims' names. In many cases, a victim's losses may include not only out-of-pocket financial losses, but substantial additional financial costs associated with trying to restore his reputation in the community and correcting erroneous information for which the criminal is responsible.

    According to the FBI, identity theft is the number one fraud committed on the Internet. So how do job seekers protect themselves while continuing to circulate their resumes online? The key to a successful online job search is learning to manage the risks. Here are some tips for staying safe while conducting a job search on the Internet.

1. Check for a privacy policy.

    If you are considering posting your resume online, make sure the job search site you are considering has a privacy policy, like CareerBuilder.com. The policy should spell out how your information will be used, stored and whether or not it will be shared. You may want to think twice about posting your resume on a site that automatically shares your information with others. You could be opening yourself up to unwanted calls from *solicitors* (推销员).

When reviewing the site's privacy policy, you'll be able to delete your resume just as easily as you posted it. You won't necessarily want your resume to remain out there on the Internet once you land a job. Remember, the longer your resume remains posted on a job board, the more exposure, both positive and not-so-positive, it will receive.

2. Take advantage of site features.

Lawful job search sites offer levels of privacy protection. Before posting your resume, carefully consider your job search objectives and the level of risk you are willing to assume.

CareerBuilder.com, for example, offers three levels of privacy from which job seekers can choose. The first is standard posting. This option gives job seekers who post their resumes the most visibility to the broadest employer audience possible.

The second is *anonymous* (匿名的) posting. This allows job seekers the same visibility as those in the standard posting category without any of their contact information being displayed. Job seekers who wish to remain anonymous but want to share some other information may choose which pieces of contact information to display.

The third is private posting. This option allows a job seeker to post a resume without having it searched by employers. Private posting allows job seekers to quickly and easily apply for jobs that appear on CareerBuilder.com without retyping their information.

3. Safeguard your identity.

Career experts say that one of the ways job seekers can stay safe while using the Internet to search out jobs is to conceal their identities. Replace your name on your resume with a *generic* (泛指的) identifier, such as "Intranet Developer Candidate," or "Experienced Marketing Representative."

You should also consider eliminating the name and location of your current employer. Depending on your title, it may not be all that difficult to determine who you are once the name of your company is provided. Use a general description of the company such as "Major auto manufacturer," or "International packaged goods supplier."

If your job title is unique, consider using the generic equivalent instead of the exact title assigned by your employer.

4. Establish an email address for your search.

Another way to protect your privacy while seeking employment online is to open up an email account specifically for your online job search. This will safeguard your existing email box in the event someone you don't know gets hold of your email address and shares it with others.

Using an email address specifically for your job search also eliminates the possibility that you will receive unwelcome emails in your primary mailbox. When naming your new email address, be sure that it doesn't contain references to your name or other information that will give away your identity. The best solution is an email address that is relevant to the job you are seeking such as salesmgr2004@provider.com.

5. Protect your references.

If your resume contains a section with the names and contact information of your references, take it out. There's no sense in safeguarding your information while sharing private contact information of your references.

6. Keep *confidential* (机密的) information confidential.

Do not, under any circumstances, share your social security, driver's license, and bank account numbers or other personal information, such as race or eye color. Honest employers do not need this information with an initial application. Don't provide this even if they say they need it in order to conduct a background check. This is one of the oldest tricks in the book—don't fall for it.

1. Robert Ellis Smith believes identity theft is difficult to detect and one can hardly do anything to prevent it.

2. In many cases, identity theft not only causes the victims' immediate financial losses but costs them a lot to restore their reputation.

3. Identity theft is a minor offence and its harm has been somewhat overestimated.

4. It is important that your resume not stay online longer than is necessary.

5. Of the three options offered by CareerBuilder.com in Suggestion 2, the third one is apparently most strongly recommended.

6. Employers require applicants to submit very personal information on background checks.

7. Applicants are advised to use generic names for themselves and their current employers when seeking employment online.

8. Using a special email address in the job search can help prevent you from receiving _____.

9. To protect your references, you should not post online their _____.

10. According to the passage, identity theft is committed typically for _____.

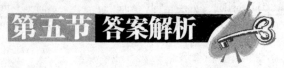

参考译文划线点评

Passage One

大学走出国门

大学不仅成为和平的工具,而且也成为国家竞争的工具,这在大学悠久的发展历史上是从未有过的局面。科学发现能够促进经济发展,而大学则是科学发现的孵化地;人才是获得和保持竞争优势的必要条件,而大学则是人才教育的主要手段。但与此同时,国门的开放使得货物、服务、信息、尤其是人才得以自由流通,[1]这将大学变成了一个巨大的动力,促进全球一体化进程,推动双边理解,保证地缘政治的稳定性。

为了因应促进世界经济发展的各种动力,大学也更加自觉地走向全球化:吸收全世界各地代表所有不同文化和价值观的学生;把自己的学生送到国外留学,让他们为将来全球性的职业生涯做好准备;提供研究性课程,应对内部彼此依存的世界所面临的挑战,也提供合作型研究项目,以推动科学进步,使全人类受益。

在塑造高等教育的种种影响力中,影响最大的莫过于国门内外的流动性。三十年来,[2]出国留学的学生人数以每年3.9%的速度增长,从1975年的80万人上升到2004年的250万人。虽然大多数学生是从一个发达国家前往另一个发达国家求学,但是,从发展中国家前往发达国家留学的学生人数正在迅速增加,而且与其相逆反的留学模式——发达国家的学生到发展中国家留学的人数也在上升。今天,在美国授予的博士学位中,有30%授予了外国学生;在英国,则有38%。到国外留学攻读本科学位的学生人数也在增加,美国最好的大学中,8%的本科学生是留学生,而在英国的大学里,留学生占所有本科生人数的10%。[3]美国有20%新聘的理工科教授是在外国出生的;中国名牌研究型大学的新聘教师中间,有很多人在国外接受了研究生教育。

大学也鼓励学生在就读本科学位期间拥有海外留学经验。在欧洲,每年有超过14万名学生参加Erasmus计划,他们在遍布欧洲大陆的、参加该计划的2200所大学中的一所选修功课,获得学分。美国的大学则帮助学生参加暑期海外实习,以为将来全球性的职业生涯做好准备。[4]耶鲁大学和哈佛大学就是这方面的领军者,它们为每一名本科生都安排至少一次国际研究或者实习的机会,同时还提供经费支持,使之真正可行。

全球化也改变着研究的操作方式。新的趋势是把研究项目的一部分拿到外国去做。[5]耶鲁大学教授、霍华德·休斯医学院研究员徐天(音译)在上海复旦大学领导着一个研究中心,关注人类疾病的基因研究,两校的教师合作完成研究内容。位于上海的研究中心有95名工作人员和研究生,在占地面积4300平方米的实验室中工作。耶鲁的教师、博士后和研究生会定期来访并与两校的科学家一起参加视频会议。这样的安排能使中美两国同时受益;因为在中国做研究成本较低,所以徐教授的耶鲁实验室能有更多研究成果;另一方面,中国的研究生、博士后和教师也得到了世界级科学家和他的美国团队的在职培训。

依靠其强大的科学力量,美国一直在重大新技术的产业化过程中引领着全世界,从20世纪60年代的大型计算机和集成电路到20世纪90年代的因特网基础设施和应用软件都是如此。高校科研和产业应用之间的关系往往不那么直接明了,但有时候却显而易见:[6]硅谷本来就是斯坦福大学有计划地建设起来的,波士顿市外的128号公路地区则一直公司林立,这些公司都是从麻省理工学院和哈佛大学分离出来的。世界各地的政府都在鼓励这种模式,也许最成功的要数英国的剑桥大学了,微软和其他几十家主要的软件和生物科技公司都在剑桥周围设有办事机构。

尽管有着这样的成功,美国却对于是否要保持这样的"研究—大学"模式犹豫不决。大多数政治人物都意识到科学投资和国家经济力量之间是彼此相关的,[7]但是对于研究经费上的支持却一直不稳定。国家卫生学院的预算在1998年到2003年间翻了一番,但是在那以后,其预算增长却赶不上通货膨胀。同期,对于自然科学和工程学的支持力度也几乎跟不上通货膨胀的强度。努力"收复失地"当然会受到欢迎,但是如果科研经费增长兼具稳定性和可预测性,能达到长期GDP的增长水平(目前大约是在扣除通货膨胀因素后每年增加3%),将会对美国更加有用。

美国政治人物很难意识到,录取更多的海外留学生能增进国际理解,从而大大地促进国家利益的实现。如果把通货膨胀考虑进来,如今对国际交流和外语研究的公共资金投入远低于40年前。[8]"9·11"事件发生之后,签证程序发生了变化,这使得想要赴美留学的外国学生人数骤减,而澳洲、新加坡和英国的外国留学生人数则相应剧增。尽管在美国大学和商界领袖的反对下,签证程序得到了改善,外国留学生人数有所上升,但是很多人仍然认为美国是一个不欢迎外国留学生的国家。

多数美国人都意识到,大学因为科研工作而对国家的繁荣贡献良多,[9]但是也有很多人害怕外国留学生会因为把学习到的知识和技能带回本国从而威胁到美国的竞争力。其实这些人没有认识到,录取外国留学生对美国有两个主要的好处:首先,[10]最好的留学生会留在美国,就像美国历史上的移民一样,会使美国更加强大;其次,在美国求学的外国留学生回国以后,可以成为美国最宝贵的价值观的宣传大使。至少,他们对这些价值观有更加深刻的认识。极少外交手段能像欢迎国际留学生一样有效地促进和平与稳定,在美国如此,在其他国家也一样。

1. 【答案】D

【题眼】From the first paragraph we know that present-day universities have become _____.

【定位】根据题干中的 present-day universities 查找到第 1 段最后一句。

【解析】第1段两次出现 universities,都说现代社会下大学的作用,instruments of national competition 等也可以作为正确选项。给出的四个选项中,只有 D 项 a powerful force for global integration 出现在最后一句中。

2. 【答案】C

【题眼】Over the past three decades, the enrollment of overseas students has increased _____.

【定位】根据题干中的 Over the past three decades 和 students 字眼查找到第 3 段第 2 句。

【解析】题干中的 increased 相当于第 3 段第 2 句中的 grown,之后的内容就是答案,即选项 C。要注意排除 A、B 两个选项的干扰。

3. 【答案】B

【题眼】In the United States, how many of the newly hired professors in science and engineering are foreign-born?

【定位】根据题干中的 United States, newly hired professors in science and engineering are foreign-born 查找到第 3 段最后一句。

【解析】选项为百分比,应该到出现百分比最多的第 3 段查找,其最后一句中很清楚地用数字 20% 表明此题答案为 B。

4. 【答案】D

【题眼】How do Yale and Harvard prepare their undergraduates for global careers?

【定位】根据题干中的 Yale and Harvard 和 undergraduates 查找到第 4 段最后一句。

【解析】从第 4 段最后一句可以得知,耶鲁大学和哈佛大学为了帮助学生将来从事 global careers,他们给每一名学生提供至少一次国际研究或者实习的机会,所以答案选 D。

5. 【答案】A

【题眼】An example illustrating the general trend of universities' globalization is _____.

【定位】根据题干中的 universities' globalization 查找到第 5 段第 1 句。

【解析】具体的 example 在之后的第 3 句中,即:耶鲁大学与复旦大学在基因研究方面合作。所以答案为 A。

6. 【答案】C

【题眼】What do we learn about Silicon Valley from the passage?

【定位】根据题干中的 Silicon Valley 查找到第 6 段第 2 句。

【解析】从第 6 段第 2 句中可以非常清楚地看出答案为 C。

7. 【答案】B

【题眼】What is said about the U.S. federal funding for research?

【定位】根据题干中的 U.S., funding, research 查找到第 7 段第 2 句。

【解析】第 7 段第 2 句中 but 后的关键词 unsteady 正是 B 中的核心词。

8. 【答案】changes in the visa process

【题眼】The dramatic decline in the enrollment of foreign students in the U.S after September 11 was caused by _____.

【定位】根据题干中的 September 11 和 dramatic decline 查找到第 8 段第 3 句。

【解析】第 8 段第 3 句中 in the wake of 意为"在……之后",即题干中的 after。文章原句的主语即为本题要填入的部分,原句是主动句,题目只是把它改成了被动句而已。

9. 【答案】take their knowledge and skills back home

【题眼】Many Americans fear that American competitiveness may be threatened by foreign students who will _____.

【定位】根据题干中的 American competitiveness, threatened, foreign students 查找到最后一段第 1 句。

【解析】本题和第 8 题极为相似,原句是主动句,题目把它改成了被动句,但考生还是要在完全理解句子意思的基础上填入正确答案,并同时要兼顾语法:will 后面要用动词原形。

10. 【答案】strengthen the nation

【题眼】The policy of welcoming foreign students can benefit the U.S. in that the very best of them will stay and _____.

【定位】根据题干中的 welcoming foreign students 和 the very best of them will stay 查找到最后一段第 2 句。

【解析】题目对原文进行了概括和简化,依照原文,and 后面与 stay 并列的谓语 strengthen the nation 即为本题答案。

参考译文划线点评

Passage Two

上网求职时保护你的隐私

[10]"盗用他人身份"和"利用他人身份行骗"是指有人主要是为了获得经济上的好处而以某种诈骗和欺骗的手段不正当地获取并使用他人的个人资料的种种犯罪行为。

与盗用他人身份有关的犯罪数量如今开始快速上升。总审计局最近的一份报告估计,每年有多达 75 万美国人都是身份盗用的受害者。而且这一数字可能偏低,因为许多人即使知道自己被侵害也不上报。

[3]Robert Ellis Smith 是一位受人尊敬的作者和个人隐私的倡导者。他说,身份盗用这一现象"太猖獗了"。"在过去的四五年里它变得越来越严重,现在世界各处无不存在。[1]这对每个人都有影响,而且对于如何预防你几乎是无能为力,最为糟糕的是当你发现受骗的时候很可能早已为时晚矣。"

你的指纹独一无二,也不可能被他人利用,可你的个人资料则不同,特别是你的社保号码、银行账户号码或者信用卡号码、电话卡号码以及其他有价值的能识别身份的资料,一旦落入歹人之手,就会让你蒙受损失,为他人获取个人利益。比如,在美国和加拿大,许多人都报告说未经授权的人从他们的银行或者金融账户里取走了钱,或者,最为糟糕的是,一并盗走了他们的身份,使用受害者的名字积累了巨额的债务并实施了犯罪。[2]在很多情况下,受害者的损失不仅仅是直接的经济损失,还有与设法恢复他们在社区里的名誉和更正由犯罪所导致的错误信息相关的大笔额外的花费。

根据 FBI,身份盗用是头号网络诈骗行为。那么,求职者继续在网上发布简历的同时该如何保护自己呢?成功的网上求职的关键是要学会控制风险。下面是网上求职时保护自我安全的一些建议。

1. 核实隐私规定。

如果你在考虑要把你的简历挂到网上去的话,那么要确保该求职网址具备隐私规定,比如像 CareerBuilder.com。该规定应该告知你,你的信息将如何使用、保存,是否会和他人共享。当你要把简历挂到一个会自动与他人共享你的个人信息的网址上去的时候,你可能要三思,因为这可能会使你自己暴露在推销电话的骚扰当中。

当你浏览该网址的隐私规定的时候,你要能够和挂简历一样容易删除简历。[4]你一旦找到工作后,就不一定想要你的简历继续挂在那里了。记住,你的简历挂在网上的时间越久,它就会暴露给越多的人,当然既有正面的也有负面的影响。

2. 利用网址特征。

合法的求职网址提供不同层次的隐私保护。[5]在发布你的简历之前,仔细考虑你的求职目标和你愿意承担的风险大小。

比如,CareerBuilder.com 就提供三个可供求职者选择的隐私层次。第一个层次是标准发布。这种选择使求职者发布的简历被尽可能多的招聘者看到。

第二个层次是匿名发布。该层次也可以使求职者被尽可能多的招聘者看到,但不显示求职者的联系信息。那些希望保持匿名但是同时又想与他人共享其余一些信息的求职者可以选择要显示哪些联系信息。

[5]第三个层次是秘密发布。这种选择可以让求职者发布简历,而他的简历不会被招聘者搜寻到。秘密发布可以让求职者快速便捷地申请出现在 CareerBuilder.com 上的工作,而不必重新输入他们的资料。

3. 保护你的身份。

职业专家说,求职者在使用网络进行求职时,保障安全的其中一个办法是隐藏他们的身份。[7]用一个泛指的称呼取代你简历上的名字,比如"局域网开发求职者",或者"经验丰富的市场营销代表"。

你也应该考虑把你当前雇主的名字和地址删除掉。一旦你所在公司的名字公开的话,根据你的头衔,也许并不难确定你的身份。[7]使用一个笼统的名字描述公司,比如"大型汽车生产商",或者,"国际包装商品供应商"。

如果你的头衔是独一无二的,考虑使用泛指的称呼而不要使用你的上司给你的确切的头衔。

4. 为网上求职申请一个电子邮箱。

网上求职时保护隐私的另一个办法是特别为此开通一个电子邮箱账户。这会保护你现有的电子邮箱,以防你不认识的人得到你的邮箱,并拿来与别人分享。

[8]为求职特别申请一个电子邮箱也排除了你的重要邮箱会收到垃圾邮件的可能性。为你的新邮箱命名时要确保邮箱地址当中不会影射到你的名字或者其他暴露你身份的信息。最好的办法就是使用一个和你正在寻找的工作相关的电子邮箱地址,比如 salesmgr2004@provider.com。

5. 保护你的证明人。

[9]如果你的简历有一部分提到了证明人的名字和联系信息的话,把它删掉。保护你自己的信息而暴露证明人的私人联系信息,这样做是毫无道理的。

6. 保持机密信息的机密性。

在任何情况下,都不要暴露你的社保号码、驾照号码、银行账户号码或者其他的个人信息,比如种族或者眼睛颜色。[6]有诚意的雇主在你应聘之初并不需要这些信息。即使他们说他们是为了进行背景调查才需要这些信息,也不要提供给他们。这是人人皆知的老把戏——不要轻信。

---

1. 【答案】Y

 【题眼】Robert Ellis Smith believes identity theft is difficult to detect and one can hardly do anything to prevent it.

 【定位】第 3 段最后一句。

 ···

 【解析】题目和原文虽然用词不同,但所表达的意思是一致的,所以答案为 Y。

2. 【答案】Y

 【题眼】In many cases, identity theft not only causes the victims' immediate financial losses but costs them a lot to restore their reputation.

 【定位】第 4 段最后一句。

 ···

 【解析】原文使用了较为复杂的句子结构、语法结构和词语表达,题目是对原文的高度概括,两者意思一致,所以答案为 Y。本题考查考生对于复杂长句的理解。

3. 【答案】N

 【题眼】Identity theft is a minor offence and its harm has been somewhat overestimated.

【定位】第3段第1句。

【解析】原文提到 Identity theft is "an absolute epidemic"(身份盗用这一现象太猖獗了),可见"身份盗用"绝不是一个 minor offence,其危害也是很大的。所以答案为 N。此外,原文第2段和第3段多处提到这一事实,都有助于做出正确判断。

4. 【答案】Y

【题眼】It is important that your resume not stay online longer than is necessary.

【定位】第1个小标题 **Check for a privacy policy** 部分的第2段最后两句。

【解析】原文提到"你一旦找到工作后,就不一定想把你的简历继续挂在那里了",接着后面一句又做了补充说明"挂得越久,暴露越多",可以判断题目与原文的意思是一致的。

5. 【答案】NG

【题眼】Of the three options offered by CareerBuilder.com in Suggestion 2, the third one is apparently most strongly recommended.

【定位】第2个小标题 **Take advantage of site features** 部分的第4段。

【解析】对应原文第二个小标题 Suggestion 2,选项直接给出定位点,该建议包括三项内容,但文中只是客观介绍,题干中 most strongly recommended 在文中并无依据,所以答案为 NG。

6. 【答案】N

【题眼】Employers require applicants to submit very personal information on background checks.

【定位】最后一个小标题 **Keep confidential information confidential**。

【解析】原文说雇主不需要你在求职时提交银行账号、社会保障号码等个人信息,而题目中的 submit very personal information 与此相矛盾。所以答案为 N。

7. 【答案】Y

【题眼】Applicants are advised to use generic names for themselves and their current employers when seeking employment online.

【定位】第3个小标题 **Safeguard your identity** 部分的第1段和第2段。

【解析】原文说得很详细,但总的意思是说网上求职不要用真名,而用 generic name。题目正是对原文的高度概括。所以答案为 Y。

8. 【答案】unwelcome emails

【题眼】Using a special email address in the job search can help prevent you from receiving _____.

【定位】第4个小标题 **Establish an email address for your search** 部分的第2段第1句。

【解析】空白处应该是名词或名词短语,作动名词 receiving 的宾语。原文中 eliminates the possibility 后用了一个由 that 引导的同位语从句,语法较为复杂,题目中直接用了短语 prevent sb. from doing sth.来表达了原文的这一意思,所以答案为 unwelcome emails。

9. 【答案】names and contact information

【题眼】To protect your references, you should not post online their _____.

【定位】第5个小标题 **Protect your references** 部分的第1句。

【解析】空白处应该是名词或名词短语。紧扣题目中的 references,对照原文,很容易得出答案 names and contact information。

10. 【答案】economic gain

【题眼】According to the passage, identity theft is committed typically for _____.

【定位】首段结尾处。

【解析】空白处应该是名词或动名词。快速阅读首尾段都要仔细阅读,即使最后一题的答案依据出现在首段,查找也不难。只要考生遵守了这一原则,本题就非常容易,可直接填入答案 economic gain。

第一节 突击训练

Passage One

Sun and Skin Cancer

When Ellen was a teenager, she loved to be out in the summer sun. She ran, she worked in her garden. She would swim and sit by the pool for hours soaking up the sunshine. And she never got tired of hearing people tell her how great her *tan* (古铜色) looked.

As Ellen got older, she continued to spend lots of time outdoors in the sun. By the time she was in her forties, Ellen's skin had developed a weathered look, with small *wrinkles* (皱纹). That was okay, but she also began to notice brown patches developing on her face and hands. Ellen saw a doctor and found out she had a relatively mild case of skin cancer. Ellen was lucky. Her cancer was detected early. With early treatment, she was completely cured. But Ellen had begun—late in life—to pay for all those years she had spent in the sun. Ellen isn't unusual. The athletic, bronzed bodies we see in magazine ads and TV commercials constantly sell the idea that a good tan means health, attractiveness, and fun. The result is that many people believe those ads. And they spend a lot of time in the sun—often just trying to get tan. That golden or bronze color may look nice, but skin doctors know that sitting in the sun until you are baked several shades darker is not such a hot idea.

According to the National Cancer Institute, over 400,000 Americans can expect to get some form of skin cancer this year. Most of these people will be 40 or older. However, skin cancer—especially skin cancer caused by exposure to the sun—can often take many years to develop. So it's never too early to protect yourself in the sun.

As soon as warm weather arrives, lots of people who don't already have dark skin want to start working on their tans. But a tan isn't really nature's way of making you look beautiful. A tan is your skin's defense against the sun's *ultraviolet* (紫外线的) radiation. UV rays damage skin cells. So when you decide to have a marathon roasting session in the sun, cells in your skin called *melanocytes* (黑素细胞) go to work overtime. They produce an extra supply of *melanin* (黑色素), the brown-black *pigment* (色素) that gives your skin its color. That extra melanin makes your skin darker, and that's why you "tan".

Think of your tan as a shield of melanin your body produces to block out the UV radiation. The problem is, it's a weak shield at best. There's no way for your body to protect itself fully against the sun's harmful rays-especially if you expose yourself to the sun hour after hour, day after day, year after year. As you get older, the buildup of many hours in the sun means more of a chance for skin damage—and possibly skin cancer.

This skin damage takes two general forms. Some UV attacks supporting cells in the lower layer of the skin, called the *dermis* (真皮). That causes skin to get dry, tough and wrinkled. Even more serious is the damage the sun's UV rays can do to the DNA of skin cells. DNA is the genetic blueprint that cells use to reproduce. With damaged DNA, the skin may produce *mutated* (变异) cells that start to grow in an uncontrolled way: skin cancer.

Nature gives you a clue about how much sun is enough by the color of your skin. If your skin is light, you don't have much built-in protection against the sun. You probably tan very little, if at all. So be very careful in the sun.

If you have dark skin and dark hair, you can probably stand a bit more sun exposure. Just don't be fooled into thinking you can stay out in the sun indefinitely. You can't. People with dark skin also get sunburned and can suffer skin damage. It just takes a bit longer for the damage to show up.

The three most common types of skin cancer are all connected with exposure to the sun. The most common of these is basal cell carcinoma. Basal cancers often look like wax-like growths or red, *scaly* (有鳞的) patches. They appear most often on the face, neck, or hands.

Squamous (有鳞片的) cell cancer is the second common type. This cancer spreads more quickly. Squamous cell cancers often appear on the head, hands, or other sun-exposed parts of the body. They show up as sharply outlined red, scaly patches.

The third type of skin cancer is called *melanoma* (黑素瘤). Melanoma is often caused by too much exposure to the sun, but it can be brought on by other things as well. Melanoma show up as brown or black *mole-like* (痣疮的) growths on the back and legs. They can also appear on the palms, fingers, and toes.

Melanoma is the rarest of these three kinds of skin caner, but it is the most serious form. While the overwhelming majority of basal and squamous cell cancer cases can be cured, many melanoma cases are fatal.

Since all of these forms of cancer can resemble harmless skin marks of irritations, be aware of marks of growths on your skin. And consult a doctor if you notice any changes.

"In general, look for anything new in your skin," advises skin doctor, Dr. Louis Vogel. "Pay attention to anything on your skin that grows rapidly, that bleeds or has irregular color. Also, suspect any mole that *itches* (发痒) or has some areas that are darker or higher than others."

Although skin cancer is the most common form of cancer, it is also the most treatable—if caught early. There are several methods of treatment. They include surgical removal, treatment with heat, extreme cold and freezing, as well as chemical treatment and use of X-rays. However, as with many other diseases, the most important "cure" is prevention. "Cover as much skin as possible when you are out in the sun," warns Dr. Vogel. "When you are at the beach, wear sun blocks. There are many things in life you can't prevent. But skin cancer is something you can often prevent if you take the proper precautions."

1. Ellen was told by doctor that she had a mild skin cancer in her _____.
   A) twenties   B) thirties   C) forties   D) fifties
2. Who are estimated as the most likely skin cancer victims by the National Cancer Institute?
   A) The male.   B) The female.
   C) Those work under the sun.   D) Those 40 years of age or above.
3. The shield of melanin protecting you against the UV radiation is actually _____.
   A) effective   B) weak   C) useless   D) harmful
4. What happens when the DNA of the skin cells are damaged?
   A) Skins get dry, tough and wrinkled.   B) Skins cells may become mutated.
   C) The supporting cells in the dermis die.   D) Skin cancer may get uncontrolled.
5. Compared with people with light skin, those with dark skin _____.
   A) get tanned more easily   B) are more likely to get skin cancer

C) have a strong built-in protection against the sun   D) don't get sunburned

6. What is the most common type of skin cancer?

A) Basal cancer.   B) Cell cancer.   C) Squamous cell cancer.   D) Melanoma.

7. Melanoma appears most often on _____.

A) head   B) hand   C) face   D) back

8. In magazines and TV commercials, a good tan has been promoted as _____.

9. Even serious skin cancers may not be easy to notice because they appear like _____.

10. The author believes that the best "cure" for skin cancer is _____.

Passage Two

The Role of Homepage

There are many *metaphors* (比喻) for the role of homepages in the user experience. All have some relevance because the homepage does play many roles. Not all metaphors are equally valid, however, and some of them can be misleading if they dominate your thinking. These are some of the more common metaphors for homepages:

Magazine cover

The primary business goal of a cover is to make you pick up the magazine from a sea of hundreds of them at the newsstand. In contrast, users don't see the homepage until they have already decided to pick out the website and visit it. Thus, homepages don't need to stand out and grab the user's attention because the user will already be looking at them. A secondary job of a magazine cover is to define by example the content, style, and so forth inside the magazine. This area is where you can learn the most lessons for web design.

Your face to the world

The old saying goes that you get only one chance to make a first impression. On the web you really get only one chance to make any impression. When the first impression isn't good, you don't get a second chance because the user will never return. At the same time, web design is interaction design, and the experience that follows after users enter the site is key. Contrary to a beauty contest, you can't be too superficial on a homepage; you need to carry out the promises.

Artwork

People look at artwork in two steps: they first give the piece a quick look to see whether it interests them at all. Then they take the time to really look at the piece and appreciate or analyze it. Many design teams think of their homepage as artwork and invest only in the visual rather than the interaction design of the page. Your homepage's visual design should, of course, be clean and professional since customers do take a first impression from this design. Unlike artwork, however, they are not going to just sit and enjoy the homepage after they've decided it's worth checking out. The homepage is just a stepping stone to their true destination inside your site. Therefore, always invest more in the interaction design of your site.

Building lobby

A lobby is not a destination in itself; you just pass through it. The homepage too is the entrance point and makes the traffic to pass in different directions. Thus every homepage needs good *signage* (标记) like the signs in a hospital lobby for the different *wards* (病房) and departments. Hospital signage gives proper priority for urgent destinations like the emergency room or labor and delivery, and your website should prioritize users' destinations, too.

Company receptionist

Related to the lobby metaphor is the idea of a human being who directs visitors to the right place, welcomes returning customers, provides friendly and helpful guidance, and makes people feel cared for. These are all valuable qualities for a homepage but can result in annoying and interruptive "assistants" if taken too literally.

Book table of contents

The design for the table of contents for a book focuses on getting you to one place and provides a *hierarchical*

(分等级的) overview. By giving you a list of choices, the table of contents gets you directly to your choice through page numbers. This metaphor is the one that comes closest to the mechanics of *hypertext* (超文本) link, which is the foundation of web use.

Newspaper front page

The front page of a newspaper presents a short, prioritized overview of most important news. Front pages have the advantage of being edited by an authority who selects the content from many contributors. Because of their regular publishing schedule, newspapers have time to focus on the front page to get it right. This metaphor should not be taken literally since a printed newspaper is a once-per-day product that is updated on a 24-hour schedule. Websites might need to be updated many times a day or just a few times a month. A newspaper also might have many other elements besides the news, but it doesn't have to represent them all on the front page, because the standard *format* (格式) for a newspaper is so recognizable. Websites need to represent many more services on the homepage because the style is less established than newspaper.

All these metaphors have some truth to them, but each has ways in which it differs from the true nature of homepages. Websites are not artwork, newspapers, building, or people. It is dangerous to take a single metaphor and use only that. Not only that, it is hard to design a homepage because it must have aspects of all the metaphors. Most designs go too far in one direction.

The homepage has multiple goals and the users also have multiple goals. Sometimes a user arrives at a homepage to find out what the company does—maybe to invest in it or perhaps to place in on a shortlist of possible *vendors* (卖主). Sometimes a user is researching a specific purchase, and sometimes a user needs to get service and support for products he or she already owns. Trouble is, it's often the same person who *flits* (突然掠过) between goals from one visit to the next. It's not possible to simply divide the users, fit them into neat little boxes, and provide a narrow range of choices to each type of user.

Inexperienced users often feel overwhelmed by homepages that don't clearly help them understand their options. When they can't understand a website, users may become embarrassed and blame themselves; you will rarely hear from them. They will just leave the site and turn to places that feel more welcoming.

1. This passage mainly discusses the different roles of homepage by analyzing several metaphors related to homepages.
2. In contrast to the homepage, a magazine cover needs to stand out and grab the reader's attention.
3. If the homepage doesn't make a good first impression on the visitors, it should try to impress them on their second visit.
4. More attention should be paid to the interaction design of the website.
5. Unlike the lobby of a building, many homepages don't have good signage that prioritizes user's destinations.
6. The homepage possessing the valuable qualities of a receptionist will become annoying to visitors.
7. Websites and newspapers are similar that they both need to be updated once 24 hours.
8. You can learn the most lessons for web design from magazine cover in its job of illustrating _____ inside the magazine.
9. The homepage needs to have _____ visual design so as to impress the customers at the first sight.
10. The _____ is usually regarded as the foundation of web use.

Passage Three

Renewable Energy

How does energy use affect the environment?

All forms of electricity generation have some level of environmental impact. However, clean energy technologies, including renewable energy and combined heat and power, have fewer impacts than other sources of electricity generation.

To learn about the environmental impacts of electricity generation technologies, click on an energy source below.

How clean is the electricity I use?

In the United States, electricity is generated in many different ways, with a wide variation in environmental impact. Traditional methods of electricity production contribute to air quality problems and the risk of global climate change.

With the advent of electric customer choice, many electricity customers can now choose the source of their electricity. In fact, you might now have the option of choosing cleaner, more environmentally friendly sources of energy.

How can I make a difference?

The energy decisions we make every day can encourage the development of new power sources, save natural resources, and help ensure that the quality of our environment is preserved. In many parts of the country, consumers now have the opportunity to choose the source of the power that is delivered to their home or business—including energy derived from renewable sources.

"Renewable energy" generally refers to electricity supplied from renewable energy sources, such as wind and solar power (energy supplied by the sun), geothermal (energy created from the extreme heat contained in liquid rock—called *magma* (岩浆)—within the Earth's core), hydropower (energy derived from the movement of water as it flows downstream), and various forms of biomass (fuel from sources such as trees, wood and agricultural wastes and fuel crops). These energy sources are considered renewable because they are continuously replenished on the Earth.

In addition, mobile sources of air pollution—such as cars, trucks, trains and lawnmowers—also contribute to air pollution nationwide and are an important source of air pollution in many urban areas.

Hydrogen Energy

Using hydrogen energy could help address many concerns facing our nation and our world. We believe hydrogen can contribute to resolving these issues for these reasons:

Firstly, hydrogen can be made from a variety of domestic feedstocks like water, biomass, coal and natural gas.

Second, hydrogen is *non-toxic* (无毒的), non-poisonous and will not contribute to groundwater pollution. It does not create "fumes" or other harmful emissions; in fact, using hydrogen in fuel cells produces only electricity and pure water.

Furthermore, hydrogen is a key enabler for the development and more widespread implementation of renewable energy technologies, resulting in cleaner and more efficient products in the marketplace.

Fifty million tons of hydrogen is produced each year worldwide, with nine million tons being consumed in the U.S. The challenge is to bring hydrogen into the everyday lives of customers as they begin to use hydrogen-powered vehicles and other applications.

Geothermal Energy

Our earth's interior—like the sun—provides heat energy from nature. This heat—geothermal energy-yields warmth and power that we can use without polluting the environment.

Geothermal heat originates from Earth's fiery consolidation of dust and gas over 4 billion years ago. At earth's core—4,000 miles deep—temperatures may reach over 9,000 degrees F.

Solar Energy

Sunlight, or solar energy, can be used directly for heating and lighting homes and other buildings, for generating electricity, and for hot water heating, solar cooling, and a variety of commercial and industrial uses. After the 1973 oil *embargo* (禁运), there was a *resurgence* (复苏) of interest in solar energy. Faced with a possibility of scarce oil resources, the United States government allocated $400 million per year, from a mere $1 million per year, for solar energy research. The expenditure is small compared to the expenditure on nuclear research. Currently, there is a need for allocating increased resources in solar research. Compared to the old forms of reducible energy (coal, oil, nuclear), solar energy offers a clean renewable form of energy. This presentation will provide an overview of the past, present and future of solar energy.

Wind Energy

We have been harnessing the wind's energy for hundreds of years. From old Holland to farms in the United States, windmills have been used for pumping water or grinding grain. Today, the windmill's modern equivalent—a wind *turbine* (涡轮机)—can use the wind's energy to generate electricity.

Wind turbines, like windmills, are mounted on a tower to capture the most energy. At 100 feet (30 meters) or more aboveground, they can take advantage of the faster and less turbulent wind. Turbines catch the wind's energy with their propeller-like blades. Usually, two or three blades are mounted on a shaft to form a *rotor* (旋转器).

A blade acts much like an airplane wing. When the wind blows, a pocket of low-pressure air forms on the downwind side of the blade. The low-pressure air pocket then pulls the blade toward it, causing the rotor to turn. This is called lift. The force of the lift is actually much stronger than the wind's force against the front side of the blade, which is called drag. The combination of lift and drag causes the rotor to spin like a propeller, and the turning shaft spins a generator to make electricity.

Wind turbines can be used as stand-alone applications, or they can be connected to a utility *power grid* (蓄电池 电极板) or even combined with a *photovoltaic* (光电的) (solar cell) system. For utility-scale sources of wind energy, a large number of wind turbines are usually built close together to form a wind plant. Several electricity providers today use wind plants to supply power to their customers.

Ocean Energy Basics

The ocean can produce two types of energy: thermal energy from the sun's heat, and mechanical energy from the tides and waves.

Oceans cover more than 70% of Earth's surface, making them the world's largest solar collector. The sun's heat warms the surface water a lot more than the deep ocean water, and this temperature difference creates thermal energy. Just a small portion of the heat trapped in the ocean could power the world.

Ocean thermal energy is used for many applications, including electricity generation. There are three types of electricity conversion systems: closed-cycle, open-cycle, and *hybrid* (混合的). Closed-cycle systems use the ocean's warm surface water to vaporize a working fluid, which has a low-boiling point, such as *ammonia* (氨). The vapor expands and turns a turbine. The turbine then activates a generator to produce electricity. Open-cycle systems actually boil the seawater by operating at low pressures. This produces steam that passes through a turbine/generator. And hybrid systems combine both closed-cycle and open-cycle systems.

Ocean mechanical energy is quite different from ocean thermal energy. Even though the sun affects all ocean activities, tides are driven primarily by the gravitational pull of the moon, and waves are driven primarily by the winds. As a result, tides and waves are *intermittent* (断断续续的) sources of energy, while ocean thermal energy is fairly constant. Also, unlike thermal energy, the electricity conversion of both tidal and wave energy usually involves mechanical devices.

1. Using renewable energy to produce electricity doesn't influence the environment.
2. In the United States, only energy produced from renewable sources can be delivered to consumers' home.
3. The air pollution contributed by mobile sources in suburban areas is as serious as that in urban areas.
4. When hydrogen is used in fuel cells, only electricity and pure water are produced.
5. The US government advocates that hydrogen-powered vehicles be used instead of fuel-powered vehicles.
6. Before 1973, the US government spent only 1 million dollars every year in solar energy research.
7. Oceans are the biggest solar energy collectors because they take up most of the earth's surface.
8. _____ is a renewable source that produces energy by using plant material, vegetation, or agricultural waste as a fuel.
9. _____, which is the windmill's modern form, can be used to transfer wind energy into electricity.
10. In the ocean, tides and waves can generate _____ energy.

第二节 答案解析

参考译文划线点评

阳光和皮肤癌

少年时期的埃伦喜欢顶着炎炎夏日在外玩耍。她会在自家的花园里奔跑玩耍,拨弄花园的花花草草,也会在水池里游游泳,然后在池边静静地坐上几个小时,享受阳光的沐浴。人们对她那晒得古铜色的皮肤的称赞,对她来说是百听不厌。

再大一点儿的时候,埃伦仍然喜欢在户外的阳光下度过大部分时光。[1]到了40多岁的时候,她的皮肤开始变得衰老,长出了细小的皱纹。这还没什么,麻烦的是她还发现她的脸上和手上有了褐色的斑点。[1]埃伦去找了医生检查后发现自己患上了一种较为温和的皮肤癌。她算是幸运的。癌症发现得早,治疗及时,才得以痊愈。但埃伦也在她的后半生开始为她在阳光下度过的日子付出代价。埃伦的情况并不是一个特例。[8]我们在杂志广告和电视广告上看到的健壮的古铜色肌肤不断向我们传递这样的信息,即晒成古铜色的皮肤意味着健康、有吸引力、有活力。结果很多人相信了那些广告而长时间在阳光下曝晒——经常仅仅就是为了把皮肤晒黑。那种金色或者古铜色的皮肤可能看起来很健美,但皮肤科医生知道坐在太阳下将几处皮肤晒黑并不是什么好主意。

[2]根据美国国家癌症研究所的调查,今年有超过40万名美国人可能会患上某种形式的皮肤癌。其中40或40岁以上的人占了大多数。不过,皮肤癌——特别是因太阳曝晒引起的皮肤癌——经常要很多年后才会被发现。因此越早在阳光下保护自己越好。

天气一变暖,很多皮肤已经变白的人就开始想办法把自己晒黑。但是晒黑并不是一种使你看起来健美的自然的方式。皮肤变黑是你的皮肤对太阳紫外线辐射的一种抵御性反应。紫外线会损坏皮肤细胞。因此当你决定在阳光下来一场"马拉松式炙烤"时,你皮肤中的黑素细胞就会超时工作,产生出额外的黑色素,即一种能影响你皮肤颜色的棕黑色的色素。那种额外的黑色素使你的皮肤变得更黑,这就是你为什么会被"晒黑"的原因了。

[3]你可以将皮肤变黑看做是身体产生出黑色素来抵挡紫外线辐射。但问题是它的抵御能力并不强。你没有办法使自己的身体完全不受到紫外线的伤害——特别是你还要日复一日、年复一年地长期把自己暴露在太阳下。随着年龄的增长,暴露在阳光下的时间越久对皮肤造成伤害的可能性就越大——也就有可能导致皮肤癌。

对皮肤的伤害主要有两种形式。一些紫外线会伤害被称为"真皮"的皮肤较底层的支持细胞,导致皮肤变得干燥、粗糙、起皱。更严重的是太阳紫外线会对皮肤细胞的DNA造成伤害。DNA是细胞得以再生的基因蓝图。[4]DNA受到损坏,皮肤就可能产生出变异的细胞并以一种不受控制的方式增长,最终导致皮肤癌。

你可以根据自身皮肤的颜色自然地判断出大约承受多少阳光是合适的。[5]如果你的肤色浅,你对阳光就不会有多少内在的防御能力,就算能晒黑一点儿,你的皮肤也不会变得很黑。因此在阳光下要格外小心。

[5]如果你的皮肤和头发的颜色较深,你就可能能够忍受更多的阳光曝晒。但不要傻傻地以为你就能不受限制地待在阳光下。你不能。深色皮肤的人也会被太阳晒伤并有可能患上皮肤癌,只不过出现症状的时间晚一点儿而已。

三种最常见的皮肤癌都与在阳光下晒有关。[6]最常见的一种是基底细胞癌。患基底细胞癌的皮肤常常有呈蜡样光泽的肿块或红色鳞屑性斑点,常出现在脸、颈或者手等部位。

排在第二位的最常见的皮肤癌是鳞状细胞癌。这种癌症扩散更快,经常在头、手或者其他暴露在阳光下的部位发作,感染部位呈明显的红色鳞状斑块。

第三种皮肤癌是恶性黑素瘤。黑素瘤通常是由于皮肤长期暴露在太阳下引起的,但其他因素也可能引起黑素瘤。[7]黑素瘤长在背部和腿上,是呈棕色或黑色的痣状隆起。它们也可能长在手掌、手指和脚趾上。

黑素瘤是这三种皮肤癌中最不常见的,但也是最严重的。绝大多数的基底细胞癌和鳞状细胞癌都可以治疗,而很多黑素瘤则是致命的。

[9]因为癌症的所有这些形式都很像无害的发炎症状,因此要小心你皮肤上隆起的痕迹。如果发现任何不正常的变化,就赶紧找医生检查。

"总的说来,寻找你皮肤上所有的新东西",皮肤科医生路易斯·沃格尔博士建议道。"关注在你皮肤上快速生长的

东西,那些出血或者有不规则颜色的东西。此外,对发痒的或者有些部分比其他部分颜色深或有隆起的色素痣都不要掉以轻心。"

　　皮肤癌是一种最常见的癌症,但如果发现早的话它也是最易治疗的癌症。皮肤癌有几种治疗方法。包括手术切除、热疗、冷冻治疗以及化疗和 X 光放射治疗。[10]不过,和很多其他疾病一样,最重要的"治疗"是预防。"当外出暴露在阳光下时,要尽可能地遮盖住皮肤,"沃格尔博士警告说,"在海滩上时,要使用防晒用品。生命中有很多东西是你无法预防的。但如果你采取适当的预防措施,皮肤癌却是你通常能够预防的疾病。"

1. 【答案】C
　　【题眼】Ellen was told by doctor that she had a mild skin cancer in her _____.
　　【定位】第 2 段第 2 句和第 4 句。

　　【解析】原文该段第 2 句开始讲述 Ellen 到了 40 来岁时发生的事,其中一件事就是第 4 句提到的她得了皮肤癌,由此可见,选项C为本题答案。

2. 【答案】D
　　【题眼】Who are estimated as the most likely skin cancer victims by the National Cancer Institute?
　　【定位】第 3 段首句和第 2 句。

　　【解析】根据原文,National Cancer Institute 预计今年将有超过 40 万美国人会得某种皮肤癌,而其中大部分都在 40 岁或以上,也就是说 40 岁或以上的人比其他年龄段的人更可能得皮肤癌,因此选项 D 为本题答案。其他选项均无原文依据。

3. 【答案】B
　　【题眼】The shield of melanin protecting you against the UV radiation is actually _____.
　　【定位】第 5 段第 1 句和第 2 句。

　　【解析】原文该段第 2 句中的 a weak shield 表明本题应选选项 B。选项 D 的 harmful 一词可在该段第 3 句找到,但原文是说太阳光有害,并非黑色素的防御有害身体,因此选项 D 不符合题意;选项 A 与原文相反,选项 C 没有原文依据。

4. 【答案】B
　　【题眼】What happens when the DNA of the skin cells are damaged?
　　【定位】第 6 段末句。

　　【解析】原文该句表明 DNA 受损后,皮肤就会产生变异细胞,也就说,"皮肤细胞会变异",这就是选项 B 的意思,因此选项 B 为本题答案。选项 A 是真皮受损的结果,并非 DNA 受损的结果;选项 C 中的 dermis 在原文该段也有提及,但该段没有提及真皮细胞什么情况下会死亡,因此选项 C 也不符合题意。选项 D 只是将原文的某些词语连接起来,表达的意思根本没有原文依据。

5. 【答案】C
　　【题眼】Compared with people with light skin, those with dark skin _____.
　　【定位】第 7 段第 2 句和第 8 段第 1 句。

　　【解析】第 7 段第 2 句指出肤色浅的人对阳光伤害有内在的保护机能,虽然这种机能并不强大;每 8 段第 1 句里的 stand a bit more 表明肤色深的人能对抗更多阳光的伤害,即他们内在的保护机能比肤色浅的人更强,因此选项 C 为本题答案。选项 A 和选项 B 应该是肤色浅的人的特点,选项 D 与原文该部分末段末句的内容相反。

6. 【答案】A
　　【题眼】What is the most common type of skin cancer?
　　【定位】第 9 段第 2 句。

　　【解析】第 9 段第 2 句指出 basal cell carcinoma 是最常见的皮肤癌类型,可见选项 A 为本题答案。选项 C 和选项 D 是其他两类皮肤癌,不符合题意;选项 B 属于无中生有,原文并无提及这一类型的皮肤癌。

7. 【答案】D

【题眼】Melanoma appears most often on _____.

【定位】倒数第五段最后两句。

【解析】原文该段最后两句指出 Melanoma 最常生长的地方,选项 D 就是这里提到的其中一个地方,其他选项是另外两种皮肤癌生长的地方,而非 Melanoma 生长的地方。

8.【答案】health, attractiveness, and fun

【题眼】In magazines and TV commercials, a good tan has been promoted as _____.

【定位】第 2 段第 10 句。

【解析】空白处应为名词词组。虽然原文是主动句式,题目是被动句式,但原文中的 sell the idea 与题目中的 promote 意思相同,对照两句的意思可以知道 a good tan 在媒体中被等同于"health, attractiveness, and fun",因此 health, attractiveness, and fun 为本题答案。

9.【答案】harmless skin marks of irritations

【题眼】Even serious skin cancers may not be easy to notice because they appear like _____.

【定位】倒数第三段首句。

【解析】空白处应为名词词组。原文该句指出各种类型的皮肤癌看起来都只是像皮肤发炎,所以一发现异常应立刻看医生。暗示皮肤癌难以察觉的原因就是它们看起来只像皮肤发炎,因此原文该句中的 harmless skin marks of irritations 为本题答案。

10.【答案】prevention

【题眼】The author believes that the best "cure" for skin cancer is _____.

【定位】末段第 4 句。

【解析】空白处应为表语,可为名词词组或形容词词组。原文该段第 2 句和第 3 句列举了各种医学上医治皮肤癌的方法,第 4 句开头的 However 表明该句陈述的方法才是最"重要"的,也就是"最好"的,因此该句中提到的 prevention 是最好的方法,也就是本题答案。

参考译文划线点评

Passage Two

主页的作用

有很多关于主页的比喻可以说明主页在用户体验中的作用。所有的比喻都有一定的相关性,因为主页确实发挥着多种作用。但是,并非所有比喻都一样贴切、合理,有些比喻如果主导了你的思维的话它们就会有一定的误导性。[1]下面是一些最常见的关于主页的比喻:

杂志封面

[2]封面的首要商业目的就是使该杂志在报亭的大量杂志中脱颖而出,吸引读者的注意。与此相反,用户是在已经决定点击并访问某些网站后才会看到主页。因此,主页并不需要非常显眼来引起用户的注意,因为用户一点击站点就自然会看见主页。[8]杂志封面的第二个作用是举例描述杂志的内容、风格等等。这方面则是我们在网页设计课程上学得最多的地方。

面对世界的脸

俗话说你给人留下第一印象的机会只有一次。在网上你真的也只有一次机会给人留下印象。[3]第一印象不好,你也就没有第二次机会了,因为用户将永远不会再访问你的网页。同时,网页设计是互动设计,用户进入网站后得到的体验才是最关键的。与选美比赛相反,主页上的东西不能太肤浅,你需要使你的网页有名副其实的内容。

艺术品

人们一般分两步来观赏艺术品:首先是快速地浏览一下物品看它能否引起自己的兴趣,然后再花时间真正地观察、欣赏和研究。很多设计人员都将他们的主页看做是艺术品,因此非常注重其视觉效果而不是页面的互动设计。[9]主页的视觉设计当然要清楚并显得专业化,因为顾客对主页的第一印象确实源于页面设计。但与艺术品不同,顾客不会在决定主页值得一看后就坐下来欣赏。主页只是一块进入网站的跳板,网站里面的内容才是人们浏览网页的真正目的所在。[4]因此,一定要注意在网站的互动设计上多下功夫。

大楼前厅

　　前厅本身并不是目的地;它只是你刚好要通过的地方。主页也是一个使浏览者进入到不同板块的入口。[5]因此每个主页也都需要清楚的标记,就像医院大厅通向不同病房和科室的指示牌一样。医院的指示牌会优先突出急救室或者产房等紧急救治场所,你的网站也应该突出用户关注的重点。

公司接待员

　　与"前厅"隐喻有关的是公司的接待人员,他们为客人带路,接待返回的顾客,友好地提供咨询和帮助,伴客人感利宾至如归。[6]这些都是主页具有的宝贵特质。但是如果这些服务显得太机械的话,反而会导致顾客不快并变成碍手碍脚的"助手"。

书的目录

　　一本书的目录设计重点在于集中在一处给出全书内容的层次结构。通过给你提供一系列的选项,目录可以让你通过它提供的页码直接翻到你想看的部分。[10]这个比喻是与超文本链接的作用最相近的,超文本链接是网页使用的基础。

报纸头版

　　一份报纸的头版会为你提供简短的重要新闻的梗概,按新闻的重要性排序。头版是由负责从众多来稿中挑选文章的权威人员编辑,具有一种特别的优势。因为报纸的发行在时间上是有规律的,因此有足够的时间来编辑头版。[7]这个比喻不能从字面上理解,因为一份印刷的报纸是按天生产的产品,24小时更新一次。而网站可能需要一天更新多次或一个月只更新几次。一份报纸除新闻以外还可以有很多其他的内容,但不必都在头版上显示出来,因为报纸有明确的标准格式。网站则需要在主页上提供更多的服务,因为相较于报纸,网页的风格不那么固定。

　　所有这些比喻的使用都不无道理,但是每一个比喻都在有些方面与主页有本质的不同。网站不是艺术品、报纸、大楼,也不是人。仅仅使用某一个比喻中说明了他们有属于了真的时代仅如此,设计主页也不是件容易的事,因为它必须包含所有这些比喻的方方面面,而大多数设计都太偏向于某一个方面。

　　主页有多个目标,用户也是如此。有时用户访问某个主页是想看看公司是做什么的——也许准备投资或将其列入可能做交易的卖主名单。有时用户会为购买某样产品而上网找信息和资料,有时用户则是需要得到对他或她购买的产品的服务和支持。麻烦的是,在访问一个又一个网站时,往往同一个人也会突然改变他的目标。我们不可能简单地将用户分类,将他们整齐地划为一个个小组,然后给每种类型的用户提供狭窄的选择。

　　对于没有经验的用户,那些不能正确地帮助他们弄清楚选项的主页常常会使他们不知所措。当用户无法弄清楚某个网站时,他们可能会变得非常地窘迫和自惭;你几乎收不到他们的任何询问求助。他们只会放弃这个网站转向让他们觉得更容易进入、更易操作的网站。

1.【答案】Y

　　【题眼】This passage mainly discusses the <u>different roles of homepage</u> by analyzing <u>several metaphors</u> related to homepages.

　　【定位】标题及文章第1段末句。

　　【解析】由第1段末句可知文章讲述了一些关于主页的常见比喻,目的是说明文章标题的内容,即主页的作用。由此可知题目概括了文章的主题,故答案为Y。

2.【答案】Y

　　【题眼】In contrast to the homepage, <u>a magazine cover</u> needs to <u>stand out</u> and <u>grab the reader's attention</u>.

　　【定位】第1个小标题 **Magazine cover** 部分的开头三句。

　　【解析】原文该部分第2句的 In contrast 表明 magazine cover 和 homepage 具有相反的性质,第3句是 homepage 不必具有的特性,结合这两句可以推断,题目所述是正确的,因此本题答案为Y。

3.【答案】N

　　【题眼】If the homepage doesn't make a good <u>first impression</u> on the visitors, it should try to impress them on their <u>second visit</u>.

　　【定位】第2个小标题 **Your face to the world** 部分的第3句。

【解析】根据原文,如果顾客对主页的第一印象不好,他们不会再次访问这个主页,也就没有第二次机会给他们留下好印象了,因此本题答案为 N。

4. 【答案】Y

【题眼】More attention should be paid to the <u>interaction design</u> of the website.

【定位】第 3 个小标题 **Artwork** 部分的末句。

【解析】本题中的 More attention should be paid to 与原文中的 invest more 意思相当,因此答案为 Y。

5. 【答案】NG

【题眼】Unlike the <u>lobby</u> of a building, many homepages don't have <u>good signage</u> that <u>prioritizes</u> user's destinations.

【定位】第 4 个小标题 **Building lobby** 部分。

【解析】题目中提到的 lobby, good signage 和 prioritize user's destinations 等信息点都在原文中提及,但是原文只是指出主页"必须"有 good signage,且能够 prioritize user's destinations,并未评论有多少主页做到了这些,因此难以判断题目所说的 many homepages 的情况是否正确,由此可见,本题答案为 NG。

6. 【答案】N

【题眼】The homepage possessing the <u>valuable qualities</u> of a receptionist will become <u>annoying</u> to visitors.

【定位】第 5 个小标题 **Company receptionist** 部分的末句。

【解析】题目只表达了原文主句的意思,舍弃了原文句中的条件状语从句 if taken too literally,在没有假设条件的情况下题目所描述的事情就不会发生,因此本题答案应为 N。

7. 【答案】N

【题眼】Websites and <u>newspapers</u> are similar that they both need to be <u>updated once 24 hours</u>.

【定位】最后一个小标题 **Newspaper front page** 部分的首段第 4、5 句。

【解析】原文第 5 句明确提到网站可能一天内要更新很多次,也可能一个月才更新几次,结合第 4 句,可知网站更新的时间间隔与报纸不相同,题目的陈述与此相反,因此本题答案为 N。

8. 【答案】the content, style, and so forth

【题眼】You can learn the <u>most lessons</u> for <u>web design</u> from <u>magazine cover</u> in its job of illustrating _____ inside the magazine.

【定位】第 1 个小标题 **Magazine cover** 部分的最后两句。

【解析】空白处应为名词词组。题目中的 illustrating 与原文中的 define by example 的意思相当,因此答案就在原文 example 之后。

9. 【答案】clean and professional

【题眼】The homepage needs to have _____ <u>visual design</u> so as to impress the customers at the first sight.

【定位】第 3 个小标题 **Artwork** 部分的第 4 句。

【解析】空白处应为形容词词组。本题要求找到表明 visual design 的特性的词,在原文中,"visual design should, ... , be clean and professional"明确指出了 visual design 必须具有的特性,因此,原文中的表语即为本题答案。

10. 【答案】mechanics of hypertext link

【题眼】The _____ is usually regarded as the <u>foundation of web use</u>.

【定位】第 6 个小标题 **Book table of contents** 部分的末句。

【解析】空白处应为名词词组。原文中的非限制性定语从句修饰的是相隔最近的名词词组,因此本题答案应为 mechanics of hypertext link,而不是句子的主语 metaphor。

可再生能源

能源应用怎样影响环境？

[1]所有的发电方式都在某种程度上影响环境。然而，清洁能源技术，包括可再生能源、热电联产，比起其他发电方式，对环境造成的影响更小。

想知道发电技术对环境影响的更多信息，请点击以下关于能源的原材料。

我所用的电有多洁净？

在美国，电力是通过许多不同方式产生的，而它们对环境的影响也各有不同。传统发电方式引起空气质量问题并威胁到全球气候的改变。

随着电力消费者选择时代的到来，许多消费者现在可以选择他们的电力来源。实际上，你可以选择更干净、更环保的能源。

我能做出哪些贡献？

每天，我们所做出的能源选择能促进新能源的发展、节省自然资源、确保环境质量。[2]在美国的大部分地区，消费者现在可以选择传送到住家或公司的能源——可再生能源就是其中一种。

可再生能源通常指由可再生能（如：风力、太阳能、地热能、水力和其他形式的生物质能）所提供的能源。其中，太阳能指由太阳提供的能量；地热能指地球核心的岩浆所蕴藏的大量热能；水力指水往下冲击时所产生的能量；[8]生物质能指那些从树木、农业废品得到的燃料或燃烧农作物的热量。这些能源被认为是可再生的，因为它们在地球上可以不断地得以更新、补充。

[5][20]，空气的移动污染源（例如：汽车、卡车、火车和剪草机）对全国的污染都有所影响，也成为众多城市空气污染的主要来源。

氢能

氢能的应用能帮助我们解决许多全国和全球性的问题。我们相信氢能解决这些问题，是基于以下几点：

首先，氢能可以从许多国内现有的原料中产生——如水、生物质、煤和天然气。

其次，氢能无毒无害，且不会造成地下水污染。它不会产生浓烟或其他有害气体。[4]实际上，氢能用作燃料电池仅产生电力和纯净水。

此外，氢能为可再生能源的推广与发展起到重要的作用。这样，在市场上会出现更干净、更有效的能源产品。

每年全国能生产五千万吨氢，九百万吨是在美国本土消耗的。[5]困难的是要把氢能带到消费者的日常生活中去，比如，让消费者开始使用氢能发电的交通工具和其他用途。

地热能

我们地球的内部像太阳一样，在不断地产生热量。这种地热可以给我们带来热量和能量，而不会对环境造成影响。

地热能源于40亿年前地球尘埃和气体的炽热聚集。地核（即地下4000英里深）的温度可达到华氏9000度。

太阳能

太阳光或太阳能可直接应用于供热或室内照明，也可用于发电、热水供暖、太阳能制冷和其他多种商务和工业用途。[6]在1973年石油禁运后，人们又开始对太阳能感兴趣起来。因为石油可能稀缺，美国政府每年花4亿美元进行太阳能研究，而过去每年的资金只有100万美元。这一花费，相对花在核能研究上的经费而言，却还是小巫见大巫。现在，有必要对太阳能的研究投入更多。比起不可再生能源（煤、石油、核能），太阳能是一种清洁且可更新的能源形式。本次论述将对太阳能的过去、现在和将来做一个总括的介绍。

风能

上百年以来，我们都一直利用风能。从古荷兰到美国农场，风车一直用作泵水和磨碾谷物。[9]今天，风车的现代版是风轮机，该机器能利用风能发电。

风轮机，像风车一样，都放置在塔的高处，以获得最多的能量。在100英尺（即30米）或以上的高度，它们可以利用更快但更和顺的风。风轮机以推进器式的轮叶捕捉风能。通常，两三块轮叶安装在一个轮轴上，形成一个旋转器。

轮叶像飞机的机翼那样工作。风吹动时，一股低压气阱在轮叶的顺风侧形成。这股低压气阱推着轮叶和转子转动。这叫做推力。实际上，这股推力比拉力（即：风力撞向轮叶前侧的力）要强。推力与拉力相结合，使转子像推进器一样旋转,而旋转轴继而让发动机生电。

　　风轮机能单独使用,也可与蓄电池电极板相连接而使用,甚至还可以与光电系统结合使用。为了大规模地应用风能,大批的风轮机通常会紧挨着一并建造,形成风力发电厂。今天,几家电力供应商都应用了风力发电的技术,向客户提供电力。

海洋能源原理

　　[10]海洋能产生两类能源:来自太阳的热能和来自潮汐和海浪的机械能。

　　[7]海洋占地球面积的70%,使海洋汇集了地球上最多的太阳能。太阳热使海水表面的温度比深水的温度要高很多,这种温差导致了热能的产生。蕴藏在海洋里的一小部分能量就能为整个世界发电。

　　海洋热能应用于许多领域——包括发电。有三种电能转换系统:封闭式、开放式、混合式。封闭式系统利用海洋温暖的表面来蒸发受压流体。这种受压流体(如:氨水)的沸点较低。蒸汽不断生成,形成漩涡。漩涡激活发电机来发电。开放式系统以低压运转汽化海水,产生蒸汽经过涡轮机和发电机。混合系统是由封闭系统和开放式系统组合而成。

　　海洋机械能与地热能有所不同。尽管太阳影响所有的海洋活动,但是潮汐主要是由月亮的地心引力而产生,而海浪则由风吹动而引起。因此,潮汐与海浪所产生的能量均是断断续续的,而海洋热能则是比较稳定的。此外,与热能不同的是,潮汐与海浪能量的电能转换,通常需要机械装置。

---

1. 【答案】N

　　【题眼】Using <u>renewable energy</u> to produce electricity doesn't influence the environment.

　　【定位】第1个小标题 **How does energy use affect the environment?** 部分的首段。

　　[解析]原文表明所有发电的方式,包括可再生能源,都会对环境造成某种程度的影响,然而可再生能源的影响较小,题目所述与此相反,由此可见,本题答案为N。

2. 【答案】N

　　【题眼】In the <u>United States</u>, only energy produced from renewable sources can be delivered to consumers' home.

　　【定位】第3个小标题 **How can I make a difference?** 部分的首段末句。

　　[解析]原文该句破折号后的 including...暗示可再生能源只是传送到消费者家中的多种能源之一,并不是如题目所说的 only,因此本题答案为N。

3. 【答案】NG

　　【题眼】The air pollution contributed by <u>mobile sources</u> in <u>suburban areas</u> is as serious as that in urban areas.

　　【定位】第3个小标题 **How can I make a difference?** 部分的末段。

　　[解析]原文只是说移动污染源成为众多城市(urban)空气污染的主要来源,并没有提到移动污染源对 suburban areas 空气的影响,也没有对比移动污染源对市区和郊区的影响哪个更严重,因此本题答案为NG。

4. 【答案】Y

　　【题眼】When <u>hydrogen</u> is used in <u>fuel cells</u>, only electricity and pure water are produced.

　　【定位】第4个小标题 **Hydrogen Energy** 部分的第3段末句。

　　[解析]原文句末 in fact 开始的分句表达的内容与题目是相同的,因此本题答案为Y。

5. 【答案】NG

　　【题眼】The US government advocates that <u>hydrogen-powered</u> vehicles be used instead of <u>fuel-powered</u> vehicles.

　　【定位】第4个小标题 **Hydrogen Energy** 部分的末段末句。

　　[解析]原文只提到了人们致力于把氢能用作交通工具的动力,但没有提到美国政府对此的态度,也没有提到美国政府认为 fuel-powered vehicles 要被替代,因此本题答案为NG。

6. 【答案】Y

　　【题眼】Before <u>1973</u>, the US government spent only <u>1 million dollars</u> every year in <u>solar energy research</u>.

　　【定位】第6个小标题 **Solar Energy** 部分的第2、3句。

【解析】原文第 3 句表明美国太阳能研究的花费从每年 100 万上升到 4 亿,结合第 2 句,可以推断这发生在 1973 年的石油禁运以后,也就是说,1973 年以前,太阳能的研究费用每年只有 100 万,因此本题答案为 Y。

7.【答案】Y

【题眼】Oceans are the biggest solar energy collectors because they take up most of the earth's surface.

【定位】最后一个小标题 Ocean Energy Basics 部分的第 2 段首句。

【解析】原文的分词结构 making...表明了上下文的因果关系,题目表明的因果关系与此一致,因此本题答案为 Y。

8.【答案】Biomass

【题眼】_____ is a renewable source that produces energy by using plant material, vegetation, or agricultural waste as a fuel.

【定位】第 3 个小标题 How can I make a difference?部分的第 2 段倒数第 2 行。

【解析】空白处应为名词词组。原文该句提到了多种再生能源,每种能源的定义都在其名称后的括号里说明了,只要细心按照题眼查找到相应的能源名称即可。

9.【答案】A wind turbine

【题眼】_____, which is the windmill's modern form, can be used to transfer wind energy into electricity.

【定位】第 7 个小标题 Wind Energy 部分的首段末句。

【解析】空白处应为名词词组。原文句中的破折号表明 windmill's modern equivalent 和 a wind turbine 是相同的东西,题目中定语从句里的 which 与原文的破折号,因此 a wind turbine 就是答案。

10.【答案】mechanical

【题眼】In the ocean, tides and waves can generate _____ energy.

【定位】最后一个小标题 Ocean Energy Basics 部分的首段。

【解析】空白处应为形容词词组。原文中的...from...这一结构表明其前面是结果,而其后是来源,题目中 generate 一词表明要求寻找的是结果,因此答案就在原文 from 一词前面。

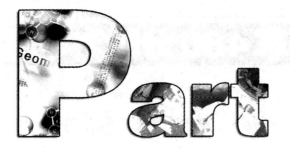

第二篇

听力理解

稳拿 480 分听力考点突破

2006 年 6 月开始,大学英语四级考试采用新题型。其中,听力理解部分共 36 题,考试时间 35 分钟,占总分的 35%。听力部分试题结构如下:

Section A:对话理解题。共 15 题,前 8 题是 8 个短对话,每个对话 1 题;后面 7 题对应两篇长对话,每个对话有 3~4 题。共占总分的 15%。

Section B:短文理解题。3 篇短文 (也可能用小篇幅 (不十分太复杂的故事、讲话、叙述等) 每篇短文之后有 3 4 个问题,共 10 题,占总分的 10%。

Section C:复合式听写题。一篇短文听三遍,要求补全短文中空缺的 8 个单词 (每个占总分的 0.5%) 和 3 个句子 (每个占总分的 2%)。

那么,英语听力部分应如何备考呢?

熟悉题型,找到主攻方向

通过大量做题(尤其是历年考试真题),适应并习惯四级听力测试语音语调;对所有题目,尤其是做错了的题目,认真分析、总结,探求其中的题型特点和规律;对照本书中提到的各种解题技巧,体会解答的要领,力求在艰苦的学习过程中找到成功的乐趣,并通过成功树立信心。

泛听和精听相结合

把四级考试真题作为精听材料。要在完全听懂的基础上做听写练习;还要对原文的语音、语调进行跟读和模仿。对四级真题要像对自己的生日一样熟悉。

泛听着眼于量大,只求掌握大意,不必了解每个细节。如今网络资源丰富,资讯发达,各种英语电影、电视节目(包括新闻节目)都可以成为泛听的好材料。不少人喜欢观看 *Friends*, *Break Jail* 等电视节目,并从中提高了英语的听说能力。泛听时要注意字幕带来的好处及弊病:初学时,它有助于理解原文;但到后来,它会导致人们的懒惰习性,阻碍听力水平的进一步提高。

听力训练(精听)时间以每天精神最佳时候为宜

每天都安排一段时间练习精听,但时间不宜过长,每次最多连续一小时。

培训扎实的语言基本功

听力理解水平包括记忆和回想的能力、选择要点的能力、推断演绎的能力、判断和得出结论的能力以及运用背景知识的能力。语音、语调、词汇、语法是语言的基本要素,对它们的熟练掌握是打好语言基本功的关键。

培养听力中的预测、综合判断能力

听力技巧包括听前、听中和听后的准备、实施过程和相应的预测、记忆以及综合判断能力。

从所给的文字材料和题目选项等线索中发现一些背景信息,缩小谈话者的话题范围。

听的过程中要强化记忆,对所听的内容进行联想,并对所听到的内容进行适当的加工,对整体和细节不可偏废。

第一节 短对话题型应试技巧

一、4 种必备技巧

1. 区分语音和语调

(1)区分语音

四级听力试题常利用单词间相同或相似的发音形成干扰。

在平时学习中考生应做到发音准确,并注意区分易混单词的读音。考生还应熟悉单词的重读、弱读、连读、同化等变化。但如果在考试中实在没听清,就应充分调动自己的词汇知识、语法知识、背景知识,借助话题的语域以及上下文的逻辑关系等做出最合情合理的推测。

【例 1】A) She will help the man to catch up.   B) She is worried about the man's health.

C) She has bought the man an up-to-date map.   D) She's bought the man a pair of glasses today.

M: I am worried about those classes I missed when I was sick.

W: I will try to bring you up-to-date on what we've done.

Q: What does the woman mean?

[2001.1/T3]

【解析】第二个说话者说到 bring you up-to-date on...表示"使你了解关于……最新情况",所以选 A,即她会帮他补课的。很多考生不熟悉连读,把其中的 up-to-date 误听成 today,影响了对全句的理解。第一个说话者(S1)谈到:"我很担心生病时落下的课。"第二个说话者(S2)的回答必然是对这句话的反应。即使没有听清第二句话,也可以猜到可能是一句安慰或者鼓励的话。[答案:A]

另外,纯粹以解题技巧来分析一下这道题,我们发现,原文中容易听懂、听到的词有 worry about, classes, bring up-to-date 等,而四个选项中,B 的 worried about,C 的 bought... up-to-date 以及 D 的 bought, glasses, today,都构成了典型的"音近迷惑项"。换言之,对这样的听力题,其解题技巧是:听到什么,就不选什么。其暗含的出题规则就是:正确答案往往是原文"意义"的再现,而且这种再现,均经过句型、词汇的重建。而迷惑项则注重从语音相近角度出现。

【例 2】A) She can tell Joan when she sees her at noon.

B) She should tell Joan's brother about the reception.

C) She must call on Joan after the reception.

D) She may see Joan's brother at lunch.

W: I ought to call Joan and tell her about the reception this evening.

M: Why bother, you'll see her at lunch.

Q: What does the man mean?

[1999.6/T10]

【解析】选项 B 和 D 中的 brother 和男士回答中的 bother 读音相近。男士的意思是"不要麻烦了,午饭时你会见到她",即建议女士不要打电话了。考生如果不清楚这是一种不赞同题型,那么就会被 brother 所迷惑而误选。[答案:A]

> **四级听力(包括选项)中的音近词**:paper–newspaper; collect–correct; bother–brother; long–longer; shine–sunny; last–lost; table for four–timetable; for some time–four times; weak–week; hat–hut; rain–ruin; class–glass; lesson–lessen; too–to; tired–tied; patience–patient; assistant–assistance; too much trouble–take the trouble
>
> **其他易混单词包括**:praise–price; scatter–shatter; walk–work; fourteen–forty; task–tax; hospital–hospitable; appear–appeal; strict–strait; reward–award; mail–male; wait–weight; bear–bare; brake–break; fair–fare; sent(send 的过去式)–scent; dew–due; pleasure–pressure

(2)区分语调

英语语调具有表意功能。相同的词句,用不同的语音、语调表达,其内涵意义也会不同。听力测试中常用不同的语音、语调来表达说话人的怀疑、否定、厌烦或肯定、赞叹等。如:陈述句若用升调可表示怀疑;问句用降调则表示肯定;当一方提出一个问题时,另一方立即用升调重复这句话中的某一关键词语,通常表示答话人对这一关键性词语所表达意

义的否定。

【例3】A) Go on with the game
B) Draw pictures on the computer
C) Review his lessons
D) Have a good rest.

W: Mark is playing computer games.

M: Should he do that when the final exam is drawing near?

Q: What does the man think Mark should do?

[2002.6/T6]

【解析】S2 的话语 Should he do that when the final exam is drawing near?为高降低升语调,表明说话者不赞成"考试临近还玩电脑游戏"。[答案:C]

2. 掌握常用语境关键词

四级听力中涉及的常见生活场景很有限,而且重复率很高。它们必然是学生的日常学习生活中最为常见的场景。所以只要考生抓住了这些固定的内容和相关的固定词汇、句型,就抓住了出奇制胜的技巧。

(1)校园生活场景

借书:library, book for reading assignment, close, open, weekend, weekday, check out, volume, the upper shelf, a book hard to identify, has been misplaced

教授和学生关系:do research, professor, semester, work as one's assistant, I have a class at ten, come in one's office hours, research report, revise, publish, read some books he recommended, correct all the typing errors in it, read it through again

同学之间的交流:briefings (lectures, presentations) seem to go on forever, more attentive, topic, hard to follow, yet on with one's essay, have a real hard time, be through with, finish the assignment, political science class, each presents a different theory, get a full mark in math exam, help sb. to catch up, find quality paper to type essays, have one's hands full with, make progress, well worth the time and trouble, rewarding, take five classes, a large selection of books

(2)家庭生活场景

外出活动:go to the movies, go out for dinner, see a different type of movie for a change, be tired of movies about romantic stories, love stories, detective stories, royal theater, what to wear to the party, cannot afford something new, attend a party

外出游玩:the holiday, be on the plane, travel by air, fly somewhere for one's vacation, we'll have another fine day, go to the seaside, leave very early, set off early, go sightseeing, take a half-day tour of the city, spend more time on sightseeing, catch the flight, get one's flight changed, switch to a different flight

家居生活、休闲:sit out in the backyard to enjoy the beautiful day, there is a lot of laundry to do, wash clothes, why did sb. call, pick up the magazine, paint the house, have the house painted, climb the ladder, go home for the summer, count the days, on one's way home, pack for the summer vacation, the apple pie tastes very good

(3)其他场景

买票、在机场:sell out, attend a show, a seat available, all the morning flights have been booked out, return one's ticket, change one's destination, this area is for the airport staff only, fly over to see, keep in touch, see sb. off

约会:could arrange it for me, rather busy these days, to arrange an appointment for sb. with sb. else, going to contact sb., confirm my appointment with sb., expect sb., will you please get me through to sb., be with sb.

预订:a table for four, a corner table, a table near the window, reserve a table, book a room with a bath, a single/double room on the second floor, make reservation for one's journey

购物:the newest model, represent the latest technology, we sell nothing but the best, be of the same brand, have a good sale, nice-looking straw hat, you can wear it rain or shine

> **邮局**:I'm going to send the parcel to London, what's the postage for it
> **银行**:cash a check, open an account, savings account, traveler's check, credit card, interest, withdraw money, deposit money
> **火车站**:platform, one-way ticket, round-trip ticket, express
> **医院**:emergency room, operation, ward, tablets, medicine, drugs, injection, surgeon, recover

3. 速读选择项

考生要善于抓住空隙时间(如放指令的时间)抢先阅读选择项,以便预测谈话或短文的内容和提问形式。这样,在听音时才能做到有目的地听、有选择地记。

对待选择项应采取快速阅读的方法。选择项的长短、简繁不一,具体处理方法也要有所不同。选择项都比较短时,可采用扫视法。用眼光扫视选择项,大体了解其内容。当选择项较长时(短文理解的选择项往往较长),可分两步处理。第一步,整体看,发现其共同成分;第二步,采用竖读方法,着重看区别。选择项(尤其是较长的选择项)各项之间往往有相同的内容。应先整体扫视选择项,很快发现其共同处,然后将视线移到各项不同之处进行竖读(即由上向下看,而不是由左向右看)。

掌握这种技巧,能对选择项的相同与不同部分印象更深刻,这对确定听音重点十分重要。虽然在听音之前很难确定题目的确切内容,但选择项的结构和内容往往暗示问题的类型和大致内容。有些题的选择项很有特点,非常明显地反映出其问题的类型。例如看到这样的选择项时:

A) At the airport.　　　B) In a restaurant.　　　C) At the railway station.　　　D) In a department store.
完全可以肯定此问题问的是地点。

虽然不是所有的选择项都会像以上这个例子这样明显地反映问题的类型,但提前做到心中有数,采取主动肯定是有帮助的。总之,**快速(区别)是原则,预测(主题)是目的**。

4. 掌握常用口语词组和表达

听力部分常考习惯表达,考生必须对常用口语短语和表达全面复习,做到胸中有数。

【例4】A) It is no longer available.　　　B) It has been reprinted four times.
C) The store doesn't have it now, but will have it soon.　　　D) The information in the book is out of date.
W: I'd like to buy a copy of Professor Franklin's book on seashells.
M: I'm sorry, Ms. That book has been out of print for some time.
Q: What does the man say about the book?　　　[1998.6/T8]
【解析】本题中的关键是对词组 out of print 的理解。out of print 相当于 no longer available,表示已绝版,不再印刷。考生如果不懂 out of print 的意思,就会落入出题者设下的圈套而误选其他选项。[答案:A]

> **对下列词组,要耳熟能详**:
>
> at the risk of, account for, a case in point, at ease with,
>
> back up, beyond hope, beyond reach, board the train, be booked up, break the ice, break through, break into tears/laughter, bring about, by means of, but for,
>
> call it a day, for sale, fall back on, as follows,
>
> get along well with, give in, give up, give sb. a lift, give sb. a ring, on guard against, give birth to, go Dutch, go into detail, go hungry,
>
> hang up, have one's hands full, hold one's breath, hold up, heart and soul, hand on, hand out, hang about, head for, hold water, hold true,
>
> if only, in particular, ill at ease, in advance, in person, in search of, in addition, in season, in spite of, in broad daylight, in theory, in disguise, in vain, in high spirits, in the habit of, in question,
>
> keep an eye on, keep track of, keep body and soul together, keep in touch with, keep one's promise, know for sure, keep company, kill time, keep in mind, keep secret,
>
> last but not least, lay down, lay off, leave alone, lead to, leave behind, leave out, throw light on, live on, lose face, lose weight, let down, look out,
>
> make ends meet, make sure, make a fuss over, make use of, make no difference, mistake... for, make ef-

forts, make fun of, make sense, mind one's own business,

no matter, no wonder, nothing but, now that, nothing serious,

on one's own, on purpose, on sale, on schedule, on the contrary, on the spot, on vacation, out of date, out of place, out of fashion, out of stock, out of work, out of breath, out of sight, out of tune, out of question, out of the question, out of order, out of print,

pass on to, pass away, pick up, point out, prior to, put forward, put up with,

rain or shine, read between the lines, run for, recover from, result in, ring sb. up,

stand by, stand for, stick to, see to it that, safe and sound, on second thoughts, set aside, show off, shut up, slip one's mind, be sold out, strike the hour,

take after, take pride in, take shelter, take... seriously, take into consideration, lose one's temper, turn out, turn to, ahead of time, from time to time,

use up, under arrest, under the weather, upside down,

when it comes to, wait in line, white lie, white elephant, walks of life, without doubt, may as well, without exception, with regard to.

二、10 种短对话题型应试技巧

对话题型的备考训练必须抓住竖听和横听两点结合来进行。所谓竖听,是指一套题目从头听到尾。所谓横听,是指把相同考点和类型的题目放在一起比较着听,从而迅速抓住同类对话的规律,真正做到以不变应万变。以下介绍对话题型的分类、不同题型的特点、难点及对策。

对话最枯燥, 但多数情况下, 往往不能从听到的内容中找到与选择项内容完全相同的部分, 即对话中一般没有现成的答案。因此, 在听的时候要注意抓住选择项的同义或反义词(组)用辨别法答题(解答活动类的题多用此法), 或根据对话内容采用归纳、推论或辨别的方法回答。

1. 时间副词题

S2 中出现的时间副词是解题的关键。特别注意 S2 中表达快、慢、逐步、偶尔等概念的时间副词,并到选项中找相应的替换词。

时间副词小结:

(1)第一组(表示"逐步,逐渐地"):
one step at a time, step by step, bit by bit, little by little, word by word, piece by piece, line by line, inch by inch

(2)第二组(表示"否定"):
hardly, barely, rarely, scarcely, little, seldom

(3)第三组(表示"很快地"):
in no time, in next to no time, by and by, do sth. on short notice, in two or three minutes, right now, right away, right off, in a minute, in a moment, in a second

(4)第四组(表示"偶尔地,有时候"):
at certain time, on certain occasion, at times, from time to time, every once in a while, every so often, every now and then, on and off

(5)第五组(表示"提前"):
before hand, in advance, ahead of time

(6)第六组(表示"间隔"):
weekly, yearly, monthly

[例5] A) The man should stop his voyage at sea and concentrate on studies.

B) The man should do it step by step.

C) She could help the man with his studies.

D) The man should get out of his studies for a while.

【录音】**M:** I am really worried about my graduation papers. I am completely at sea what to do next.

　　W: You should do it one step at a time. Once you get started, you can get it done.

　　Q: What does the woman mean?

【解析】one step at a time 与选项 B 中的 step by step 相替换。[答案:B]

2. S2 是中间带 but 的转折题

题型规律如下:

> (1)第一个人的话尽量听懂。
> (2)第二个人的回答有两部分,并且两者间有一个 BUT 连接,这个 BUT 是最根本的标志。
> (3)BUT 后面是答案。如果听不出后面的内容,可否定其前面一句的内容,记住 BUT 表示转折。

【例6】A) The man hates to lend his tools to other people.

　　B) The man hasn't finished working on the bookshelf.

　　C) The tools have already been returned to the woman.

　　D) The tools the man borrowed from the woman are missing.

【录音】**W:** Simon, could you return the tools I lend you for building the book-shelf last month?

　　M: Oh, well, I hate to tell you this, but I can't seem to find them.

　　Q: What do we learn from the conversation?　　　　　　　　　　　　　　[2005.6/T1]

【解析】can't find 表明已经 missing。[答案:D]

3. 虚拟语气题

在大学英语四级听力考试中,虚拟语气出现频率较高,解答这类试题的关键是:

> **(1)了解和辨别虚拟语气的基本结构:**
> 　　If we had..., we would (might, could) have...
> 　　If only...
> 　　I wish...
> 　　I should (would, could) have...
> 　　Had she come in for an interview, I would've...
> **(2)理解虚拟语气句中所包含的假设含义。**
> **(3)选项答案的特点:**
> 　　①否定掉虚拟语气中所表达的含义——反着选答案。
> 　　②虚拟语气间的内部替换。
> 　　③与真实条件句相替换。

【例7】A) He is not very enthusiastic about his English lessons.

　　B) He has made great progress in his English.

　　C) He is a student of the music department.

　　D) He is not very interested in English songs.

【录音】**W:** Mr. Jones, your student Bill shows great enthusiasm for musical instruments.

　　M: I only wish he showed half as much for his English lessons.

　　Q: What do we learn from the conversation about Bill?　　　　　　　　[2001.6/T4]

【解析】关键词:enthusiasm。否定 he showed half as much enthusiasm 即是:he didn't show much enthusiasm,同义转换即成选项 A。

4. 惊讶语气 How could you...题

题型规律:

> (1)S1 通常是对自己关于某一事情的想法进行陈述,语气较平稳。

(2)S2 则以 How could you...(你怎么可以……)句型对 S1 说的话表示质疑。

(3)Q 一般询问 S2 说的话是什么意思。

(4)答案应选择与 S1 意思相反的选项,或者否定 how could you 的后半句话。

【例 8】A) Mr. Long's briefing was unnecessarily long.

  B) The woman should have been more attentive.

  C) Mr. Long's briefing was not relevant to the mission.

  D) The woman needn't have attended the briefing.

【录音】W: Mr. Long's briefing seemed to go on forever. I was barely able to stay awake.

  M: How could you sleep through that? It was very important to the mission we're going to carry out.

  Q: What does the man imply?   [2002.1/T9]

【解析】原文到选项的语义转换关系是:How could you sleep...? → You should not have slept. → You should have been more attentive. 首先否定 how could you 的后半句,然后改用正面表达,即得出答案。[答案:B]

5. 建议题

  题型规律:

(1)解题关键:

  建议句型在 S2 中出现必为考点,平时应该注意建议句型的积累。大家只要熟悉这一类句型,由此来把握做题的正确思路,就容易选出正确答案。

(2)常见的建议句型归纳如下:

  ①Maybe you should... ; Let's... ; You'd better... , You'd be better off doing ?

  ②How about... ? What about... ?

  ③Why not... ? Why don't you... ? Why... ? What if... ?

  ④标准一般疑问句,如:Shall we... ? Have you tried... ? Have you checked sth./checked with sb.?

  ⑤反问句,如:Hadn't you better... ? Shouldn't you... ? Wouldn't... ? Couldn't you... ?

  ⑥How does... sound?

  ⑦Why don't you do?

  ⑧It doesn't hurt if you do... ?

  ⑨If I were you...

(3)答案特征:

  正确选项的动词,就是建议句中的主要动词或其同义替换。

【例 9】A) Give the ring to a policeman.

  B) Wait for the owner of the ring in the rest room.

  C) Hand in the ring to the security office.

  D) Take the ring to the administration building.

【录音】W: I found an expensive diamond ring in the rest room this morning.

  M: If I were you, I would turn it in to the security office. It is behind the administration building.

  Q: What does the man suggest the woman do?   [2005.6/T2]

【解析】本题 If I were you, I would...是典型的提出建议的句型,该句型紧接的动词(或者同义替换)就是正确答案。听到 turn it in,理解到其含义是 hand in,即可轻松选出答案。[答案:C]

6. 不赞同题

  题型规律:

(1)S2 的语气和语调有明显的怀疑口吻。

(2)用来表示不赞同的句型:

  Do you mean that? Do you think so? Is that true? You think it's right! I couldn't agree less! Who told you that! What makes you say so? That's not saying much! Don't look at me! Are you kidding/joking? You don't say so! So you say! Who says that! 以 how/why 开头的反问句,如:How did she know? How can we get there on time? Why run? Why waste our money? Why bother?

(3)选项答案:

①以 disagree, ridiculous, unbelievable 等否定词作为标志词。

②否定 S1 的话,意思与之相反的选项是答案。答案选项中往往有与 S1 的关键词相对立的词。

③不赞同的原因。

【例 10】A) She can tell Joan when she sees her at noon.

B) She should tell Joan's brother about the reception.

C) She must call on Joan after the reception.

D) She may see Joan's brother at lunch.

【录音】W: I ought to call Joan, and tell her about the reception this evening.

M: Why bother? You will see her at lunch.

Q: What does the man mean? [1999.6/T10]

【解析】本题属于推理题,要求判断的实际上是"不赞同的原因"。注意这道题中的"语音相似陷阱":B 项和 D 项中的 brother,都是由 S2 中的 bother 衍生而来的干扰因素。看穿了其中戏法的眼睛雪亮的读者,是不会上这种当的。[答案:A]。

7. 数字计算题

数字计算题最常见的就是时间与价格的运算,也有少数日期和人数方面的运算题。考生应把重点放在听懂数字之间的关系上,听音的同时在相应的选项上做记号或笔记,以便听到题目以后做简单的运算。对话中已经提到的数字一般不会是答案,答案往往是对话中的数字经过简单运算后的结果。

常见的有关数字的词汇和词组有:

易混单词辨音:-teen 和-ty 等;

表示单位的词:pair, couple, quarter, a dozen of, score, decade, hundred, thousand, million 等;

倍数:half, double, twice, times, twice as much as, three times as much as 等;

分数:one third, two eighths(百分比:percentage, percent);

加减乘除:plus, minus, multiply, divide;

相关词汇:fare, ticket, discount, sale price, on sale, on special, special price, garage sale, change 等。

【例 11】A) 5:00   B) 5:15   C) 5:30   D) 5:45

M: What's the time of departure?

W: 5:30. That only leaves us 15 minutes to go through the customs and check our baggage.

Q: At what time did the conversation take place?

【解析】此题中的考点在于能否听懂 That only leaves us 15 minutes to go,从而判断与 5:30 的前后关系。从男士的回答中得知,现在只剩下 15 分钟办理通关、行李检查手续了,而出发时间是 5:30,那么谈话发生的时间应该是两个数字相减,即 5:15。另外,还要注意的是 5:30 与 5:13 的区别,15 分钟和 50 分钟的区别。带有-ty 的单词的重音在第一个音节,第二个音节弱读,是短音/i/。带有-teen 的单词是双重音,第一和第二个音节都重读,第二个音节是长音/iː/。数字计算题的关键在于听懂数字之间的关系并进行运算。[答案:B]

8. 地点场景题

听力测试中,考查地点的题目也是常考题。这些地点有些是对话中直接提到的,有些则需要根据对话细节来进行推断。四级听力常见的场景有校园、餐厅、图书馆、银行、邮局、机场、火车站等。

常见的有关地点的问题有:

Where does this conversation most probably/likely take place?

Where is the man/woman probably going?

Where are the man and woman at the moment?

可能出现的地点和场景及其标志性单词。请参考第 48 页"掌握常用语境关键词"。

地点题的特点决定了关键是找出标志性单词,并由此做出判断。

【例 12】A) At a bookstore.　　　B) In a workshop.　　　C) At an art gallery.　　　D) In a department store.

M: Can you tell me the title of this oil painting?

W: Sorry, I don't know for sure. But I guess it's an early 18th century work. Let me look it up in the catalogue.

Q: Where does this conversation most probably take place?　　　　　　　　　　　　　[2001.1/T2]

【解析】本题中的关键词是 oil painting 油画,work 作品,catalogue 目录,所以对话应该发生在美术馆。[答案:C]

9. 身份与关系题

这类考题考查学生通过对话内容猜测说话者职业、身份或说话者之间关系的能力。如果抓住与职业和身份相关的标志性词语,问题也就迎刃而解了。

考题中经常出现的职业有:

> ad visor, carpenter, dentist, driver, doctor, electrician, landlady, librarian, manager, nurse, physician, plumber, policeman, professor, receptionist, repairman, salesman, secretary, shop assistant, surgeon, tutor, waiter, waitress

考题中经常述及到的表示人物关系的标志性词语有:

> ***Teacher and Student:*** term (semester), research, assignment, homework, paper, thesis, lecture, teaching assistant, professor, class, course, office hour, grade, test, quiz, exam, score, mark, grade, fail, pass, scholarship, library, text book, reference book
>
> ***Librarian and Reader:*** library, check out, book for the reading assignment, on the upper shelf, volume, close, open, on the weekend, weekday
>
> ***Doctor and Patient:*** fever, pain, cold, cough, headache, stomachache, sore throat, fractured ankle, diagnose, diagnosis, prescription, injection
>
> ***Salesman and Customer:*** sale, reduction, discount, bargain, cashier, shop-assistant, attendant
>
> ***Waiter and Customer:*** menu, steak, lobster, ham, soup, salad, dessert, coffee, juice, reserve, book, order, table by the window, table for two
>
> ***Husband and Wife:*** anniversary, spend the weekend, spend the holiday, go to the cinema, go to the theatre, fix the shower pipe, the electricity bill, the babysitter

只要抓住关键词,联想对话发生的场景,这类题型是很容易拿分的。

【例 13】A) A math teacher and his colleague.　　　　B) A teacher and his student.

C) A student and his classmate.　　　　　　D) A librarian and a student.

W: I heard you got full marks in the math exam. Congratulations!

M: Thanks. I'm sure you also did a good job.

Q: What's the probable relationship between the two speakers?　　　　　　　　　[2001.6/T1]

【解析】第一句话当中的标志性词语为 mark 和 exam,由此可见对话肯定是关于校园生活的。第二句话当中的关键词是 also,说明两名说话者之间有某种相同之处,那么答案肯定是 C,即两人都是学生。[答案:C]

10. 否定关系题

否定关系题是考生失分比较多的题。

首先,考生应注意区分助动词的肯定和否定形式在读音上的不同,尤其是情态动词的肯定和否定形式的不同,如 can 和 can't。表肯定的情态动词一般弱读,如 can 读成 /kən/,表否定的情态动词一般重读,如 can't 读成 /kænt/或/kɑːnt/。

考生还应特别留意那些"伪敌人/伪朋友"。有时否定的形式却表示肯定的意思,如:

I can't agree with you more. 我完全赞同你的说法。

I can never find a more suitable person for this job. 我找不到更适合做这份工作的人选了(你是最适合这份工作的)。

Not a single person is absent. 没有一个人缺席。

I never fail to write home once a month. 我每个月都写信回家。

有时肯定的形式却表达否定的意思,如:含有 fail to do, absence, denial, refusal, miss, hardly, scarcely, barely, seldom, rarely 等表示否定意思的单词的句子,或是含有表示否定语法意义结构的句子,如 little, few, too... to, rather than, prefer to 等。

【例 14】A) He played his part quite well.　　　　B) He was not dramatic enough.

　　　　C) He performed better than the secretary.　D) He exaggerated his part.

　　M: How did you like yesterday's play?

　　W: Generally speaking, it was quite good. The part of secretary was played wonderfully, but I think the man
　　　　who played the boss was too dramatic to be realistic.

　　Q: How does the woman feel about the man?　　　　　　　　　　　　　　[2001.6/T10]

【解析】本题的难点在于对词组 too... to 的理解。too... to 是一个暗含否定语法意义的词组。too dramatic to be realistic
　　　　表示"太戏剧化了,以至于不够真实",这与选项 D"他夸大了他的角色"意思相符。[答案:D]

　　另外,考试中考完全否定(neither, nor, nobody, never, none)的题并不多见,而部分否定(如 all, every, many, always 等与 not 连用,表示"不是全都、并非所有"),双重否定(句中多含 too, not either, also 等词),否定转移和暗示否定等题倒是考试的重点。这类题应引起考生足够的重视。

第二节 长对话题型应试技巧

　　长对话是短对话的延伸,两人就某一个话题进行多个回合的交流、讨论。与短对话相比,长对话提供的信息量更大,背景更丰富,因而更便于理解对话的场景。

　　长对话共两篇,每篇在 200 词左右,共 7 道题。一般说来,长对话听力题主要包括主旨大意题、细节题以及逻辑推理题,考查考生对时间、地点、数字和人物行为、观点的理解,也考查学生的逻辑推理能力。

一、长对话听力理解的读题技巧

1. 主动出击,在听音之前快速浏览选项

　　浏览选项的主要目的是:(1)预测谈话内容;(2)扫除生僻单词、易混淆词对听力理解造成的障碍。

【例 1-1】A) The benefits of strong business competition.

　　　　B) A proposal to lower the cost of production.

　　　　C) Complaints about the expense of modernization.

　　　　D) Suggestions concerning new business strategies.

【例 1-2】A) It cost much more than its worth.　　B) It should be brought up-to-date.

　　　　C) It calls for immediate repairs.　　　　D) It can still be used for a long time.

【例 1-3】A) The personnel manager should be fired for inefficiency.

　　　　B) A few engineers should be employed to modernize the factory.

　　　　C) The entire staff should be retrained.

　　　　D) Better-educated employees should be promoted.

【例 1-4】A) Their competitors have long been advertising on TV.

　　　　B) TV commercials are less expensive.

　　　　C) Advertising in newspapers alone is not sufficient.

　　　　D) TV commercials attract more investments.

[新题型样卷]

　　浏览选项后可知,这段对话讨论有关业务问题,涉及到的关键词有:business, competition, cost of production, expense of modernization, business strategies, personnel manager, staff, retrain, advertising on TV 等。

2. 选择项都比较短时,通过扫读了解问题

上面例1-2各选项较短,主语都是It,谓语部分各不相同:A) 花费超过价值;B) 应当更新;C) 需要立即维修;D) 还可以用很长时间。考虑到问题中的It是适合所有四个选项的,所以,它的含义最有可能是"机器,设备"。相应地,本题的问题就是"机器怎么样?"

3. 选择项较长时,要善于注意发现各选项间的共同成分,着重理解其间的区别

一般来说,特别长的选项往往含有很多共同成分,只有一些小地方不一致,而不一致之处就是答题的关键所在,所以需要特别关注。

总之,浏览选择项都要以"了解对话话题、熟悉关键词"为目的,尽可能地归纳出该题目的问题。

二、长对话题的听音技巧

读选项、猜问题后,下一步就是听对话。此时,最重要的就是:全神贯注,全力以赴!决不可以开小差、分神!

在准确读题的基础上听录音,是有的放矢的,可以边听边做笔记。尤其是长对话中的数字题,人名、地名题等,在选项旁边做简短的笔记可以帮助记忆。如果问题猜测准确,一边听一边就可以选择答案。

听音时注意下面几点:

> (1)开头部分引入对话,结尾部分总结对话,往往说明了对话的背景,揭示对话的主题,要重点对待。
> (2)长对话有它的基本套路,往往其中一个人总是发问,另一个人总是作答,在问答中层层递进,说明问题、解释
> 现象或者提出观点等。带着通过读题而得到的问题来听,可以区分哪些是有效的信息,哪些是冗余的信息。

三、长对话题的笔记技巧

听录音时做笔记,因人而异。每个人的习惯不同,做笔记的方法也不一样。但总的原则是:简洁明了!要充分利用缩略语和各种符号来表示相关含义。

四、3种题型分析

1. 主旨题

主旨题考查对长对话大意的把握,一般是对话的第一题或最后一题。在长对话中,很多时候主题是直接点明的,一般在前几轮对话中就会得到体现;也有些对话到中间才给出主题,需要考生认真抓住主题词;少数对话不直接点明话题,这就需要考生在听懂整篇对话的基础上自己概括出主题以及主旨大意。主旨题针对的是整篇对话,所以即使听的时候漏掉了一些细枝末节,对理解整个对话的主旨也没有大碍。

(1)提问方式

> What is the major concern of...?
> What is the conversation mainly about?
> What's the major topic of the conversation?
> What's sb.'s opinion of...?
> Why does sb. call sb.?
> What are the two speakers discussing?

(2)实例分析

【例1-1】A) The benefits of strong business competition.
B) A proposal to lower the cost of production.
C) Complaints about the expense of modernization.
D) Suggestions concerning new business strategies.

[新题型样卷]

【读题】四个选项的中心词都是名词:benefits, proposal, complaints, suggestions。相应的修饰语界定了它们的范围。A) 激烈商业竞争的好处;B) 降低生产成本的建议;C) 有关现代化开支的投诉;D) 有关新的商业战略的建议。作为长对话的第一题,这几个名词词义较泛,所以这很可能是一道主旨题。

【听音】**W:** Hello, Gary. How're you?

M: Fine. And yourself?

W: Can't complain.【前面属于 Greetings, 即寒暄语】Did you have time to look at my proposal?

M: No, not really. Can we go over it now?

W: Sure. I've been trying to come up with some new production and advertising strategies.【主题在这个话轮中揭示出来】First of all...

Q: What are the two speakers talking about?

【解析】注意,女士在回答时说 Can't complain. Did you have time to look at my proposal? complain 对应于 C 中的 complaints 有迷惑性,my proposal 对应于 B 也有迷惑性。可是,答案不能选 C 和 B。完整的归纳是 D,正好与女士说的 I've been trying to come up with some new production and advertising strategies. 含义一致。

【总结】主旨题考查对整篇对话的把握能力,要关注的是整体,而不是细枝末节。长对话的主旨题中,特别不能不加辨别地听到什么就选什么,因为错误的干扰项往往也是对话中提到的词语,但却不是主题。

2. 细节题

细节题关注对细节的把握和描述。一般即常说的 what, when, where, how, why 等。通常没有固定的提问方式,它可以涉及到对话的方方面面,比如人物的特征,事情的过程或先后顺序,做事的喜好,个人的观点态度等等。细节题包罗万象,需要考生注意力高度集中。

【例 1-2】A) It cost much more than its worth.

B) It should be brought up-to-date.

C) It calls for immediate repairs.

D) It can still be used for a long time.

【例 1-3】A) The personnel manager should be fired for inefficiency.

B) A few engineers should be employed to modernize the factory.

C) The entire staff should be retrained.

D) Better-educated employees should be promoted.   [新题型样卷]

【读题】正如前面讨论过的,例 1-2 的问题可能是"机器怎么样?"例 1-3 中,A) 人事经理效率低,应当解雇;B) 应该聘几个工程师来改造工厂;C) 所有人员都应当再接受培训;D) 应该提拔受过更好教育的员工。可以看出,这些选项都围绕"人员,员工"展开,本题的问题与"人事"有关。

【听音】**W:** First of all, if we want to stay competitive, we need to modernize our factory. New equipment should've been installed long ago【第一个话题】.

M: How much will that cost?

W: We have several options ranging from one hundred thousand dollars all the way up to half a million.

M: OK. We'll have to discuss these costs with finance.

W: We should also consider human resources【第二个话题】. I've been talking to personnel as well as our staff at the factory.

M: And what's the picture?

W: We'll probably have to hire a couple of engineers to help us modernize the factory【答题处】.

Q2: What does the woman say about the equipment of their factory?

Q3: What does the woman suggest about human resources?

【解析】解答听力理解题时,在段落录音结束后才听到问题,所以在听清楚题目之前的所有工作都具有预测性。这一节中,first of all 和 also 表明谈论两个不同话题,即"安装设备以改进工厂"以及"人力资源",分别对应于例 1-2 和例 1-3。例 1-2 中与题意最接近的选项是 B(干扰项是 C),例 1-3 中与原文一致的选项是 B。

【总结】在"读题猜答案"的环节,区分各选项的差别为迅速选定答案奠定基础。听录音时,重点在听懂,记忆的内容应该与答题有关。切不可因为没有记录下某一句话而心情大乱,以致后文都没有听清,造成恶性循环。实在没有听懂的,可以姑且不理,它很可能与题目无关,也有可能在下文的提示下而得到明确。

3. 原因推理题

长对话中的原因推理题目考查简单的逻辑推理能力，它提到的逻辑关系也是对话中明确地用 since, as, lead to, result from 等说明了的，因而这实际上与"事实细节题"大同小异。

(1)提问方式

> What leads to...?
> What's the reason for...?
> Why...?
> What happened to... that...?
> What are the causes for...?

表示原因的提示词有：as, since, because of, due to, as a result, so, this leads to the result that, consequently, therefore, thus...

(2)实例分析

【例 2-1】A) He wanted to buy one from Japan.
B) He wasn't sure about its quality.
C) He thought it was for business use.
D) He thought it was expensive.

【听音】**M:** You see the first video phones, were made in Japan, and they can only show a still black-and-white image. So this video phone is much better than that. Mind you, I'm not sure if I'd want one. Would you?

　　　W: Well, no, I don't think I would. I bet it costs a lot of money. Does it say how much it costs?

　　　M: Yes, the early black-and-white ones cost several hundred pounds, but this one costs several thousand pounds.

　　　W: Mm. Why does anybody want one, do you think?

　　　M: Business organizations that need to frequently contact the overseas organizations would want it. It's like a face-to-face conversation, so maybe a lot of overseas travel can be avoided.

　　　Q: Why didn't the man want one of them?

【解析】对话中，男士说："So this video phone is much better than that. Mind you, I'm not sure if I'd want one. Would you?"他承认这种电话很好，却又说自己不想要。这就卖了个关子，让女士马上得出这种电话可能很贵的结论。男士说这种电话要几千英镑一部，这时女士说："Why does anybody want one?"男士解释说这种电话尽管很贵，但对跨国大公司来说，还是合算的。因此，"贵"是他们不想买的主要原因。

第三节 短文理解应试技巧

短文理解部分通常有三篇听力材料，要求能听懂大意、抓住要点、记住主要情节。

一、3 种常用技巧

1. 预测内容与问题

预测内容与问题对于做好短文理解意义重大。听音之前迅速浏览选项，可对短文的内容有个大概的了解与推测。由于很多问题都是考查有关细节的，且问题与原文的顺序基本一致，考生可边听录音，边看选项，听到什么选什么，避免"听到的没记住，记住的没有考"的现象。对那些不太重要的词句或没有听清的个别单词，可置之不理。

2. 抓主题句

在听短文时应尽快抓住能概括短文中心思想的主题句和关键词，这样有助于短文的理解。主题句通常是文章的第一句话或最后一句话，对全篇文章的内容起到概括和提示的作用，往往是文章的中心论点，表达了说话人对所谈内容的观点和态度。

3. 边听边记

用简单的文字或符号记下主要信息或情节。记录时要有针对性和选择性。遇到与选项相关的数字、人名、地名、时间等应重点作笔记,否则可能会忘掉或者混淆。由于答案多与原文相似、相同或者是原文的同义替换,因此应尽量记下原话,以作比较。对那些出现频率较高的词要特别留心,它们对全篇的理解至关重要。

关于做笔记我们强调以下几点:

第一,听为主记为辅,做笔记一定不能影响听,要做到听记两不误。

第二,速记不同于听写,目的是自己能够识别,所以要在最短的时间内用英语、字母、汉字、图形或其他符号把重要信息的细节记录下来。

第三,因为有预测为基础,如果精力允许的话,做笔记时最好同时看选项,在相关选项的旁边做必要记录,这样才能实现预测中提到的"边听边选"。

当然,有些时候选项没有干扰性,对问题的预测也很准确,听到相关信息就能够选出答案了,这时就不必做笔记。

二、3 种常考题型分析

短文部分的题型主要可分为以下几类:

1. 主旨大意题

解答这类题的关键是抓住关键句。有的文章在开头明确主题,有的文章在结尾总结文章的主题,有的需要结合整篇文章,特别是结合首尾两句得出。

【例1】A) The difference between classical music and rock music.

B) Why classical music is popular with math students.

C) The effects of music on the results of math tests.

D) How to improve your reasoning ability.

Do you have a tough math test coming up? Then listen to some classical piano music just before the test. You might come up with a higher score.

Q：What is the passage mainly about? [1999.1/Passage Two]

【解析】本题开门见山地指出数学测验前听古典钢琴曲能提高成绩。因此很容易就能回答关于文章主要内容的提问。

[答案:C]

2. 细节事实题

这种题考查的是考生对短文细节部分的把握。由于答案比较直接、明确,在听文章时应做好笔记。

【例2】11. A) A car outside the supermarket. B) A car at the bottom of the hill.

　　 C) Paul's car. D) The sports car.

12. A) Inside the car. B) At the foot of the hill. C) In the garage. D) In the supermarket.

13. A) The driver of the sports car. B) The two girls inside the car.

　　 C) The man standing nearby. D) The salesman from London.

14. A) Nobody. B) The two girls. C) The bus driver. D) Paul.

　　 Paul, a salesman from London, was driving past a sports car parked outside a supermarket when he saw it start to roll slowly down the hill. Inside the car were two young girls on the passenger seat but no driver. Paul stopped quickly, jumped in front of the sports car and tried to stop it, pushing against the front of the car. Another man, who was standing nearby, got into the car and put on the hand brake, saving the girls from injury. It was at this point that Paul noticed his own car rolling slowly down the hill and going too fast for him to stop it. It crashed into a bus at the bottom of the hill and was so badly damaged that it had to be pulled away to a garage. As if this was not bad enough, Paul now found he had no one to blame. He was so busy chasing his car that he did not get the name of the driver of the sports car who just came out of the supermarket and drove away without realizing what had happened.

Q11: Which car was badly damaged?

Q12: Where was the driver of the sports car when the accident happened?

Q13: Who did Paul think was to blame for the accident?

Q14: Who was injured in the accident? [2000.1/Passage One]

【解析】11. C   12. D   13. A   14. A

3. 推理题

此类题要求考生依据听到的信息做出合理推测和正确的判断。由于没有明示信息,答案并非显而易见,所以更需要领会暗含的意思,更需要综合能力。

【例3】A) To help solve their psychological problems.   B) To play games with them.

C) To send them to the hospital.   D) To make them aware of its harmfulness.

    The first step in stopping drug abuse is knowing why people start to use drugs. The reasons people abuse drugs are as different as people are from one another. But there seems to be one common thread: people seem to take drugs to change the way they feel. They want to feel better or to feel happy or to feel nothing. Sometimes they want to forget or to remember. People often feel better about themselves when they are under the influence of drugs. But the effects don't last long. Drugs don't solve problems. They just postpone them. No matter how far drugs may take you, it's always a round trip. After a while people who misuse drugs may feel worse about themselves and then they will use more and more drugs. If someone you know is using or abusing drugs, you can help. *The most important part you can play is to be there. You can let your friend know that you care. You can listen and try to solve the problem behind your friend's need to use drugs. Two people together can often solve a problem that seems too big for one person alone.* Studies of heavy drug users in the United States show that they felt unloved and unwanted. They didn't have close friends to talk to. When you or your friends take the time to care for each other, you are all helping to stop drug abuse. After all, what are friends for?

    Q: According to the passage, what is the best way to stop friends from abusing drugs?

【解析】从斜体字部分(最重要的就是在你朋友的身边陪伴他,让他知道你关心他,倾听并尽力解决隐藏在朋友需要毒品后面的问题。两个人在一起可以解决对一个人来说很困难的问题)可以看出,这些都表明,帮助朋友戒毒最好的方法就是解决他的心理问题。[答案:A]

第四节 复合式听写高分技巧

    复合式听写综合考核考生听的能力、拼写能力、做笔记的能力和书面表达能力。它要求学生在听完一篇约250词的文章三遍后,把文章中空缺的内容(新题型中单词8处,句子3处)补充完整。

> **第一遍**是全文朗读,没有停顿,要求考生听懂大致内容。
>
> **第二遍**朗读时,单词听写部分每个空格后略有停顿,考生需要边听边填入所缺单词;句子听写部分后有较长时间的停顿,让考生根据所听到的内容写出主要意思。
>
> **第三遍**与第一遍一样,没有停顿,供考生核对所填内容。

    对考生应考而言,要注意合理利用这三遍录音:听读第一遍时,听为主、记为辅,着重整体的理解。考生可以在听的同时,顺便填写有把握的单词和做些笔记。这时的重点是借助文字材料,理解和把握全篇内容和脉络。第二遍时,记为主、听为辅。考生应抓紧时间,写下言简意赅的笔记。第三遍时,着重细节,目的在于查漏补缺。

    复合式听写最能通过练习而见成效。

一、给分标准

    1. S1 至 S8 每题为 0.5 分。拼写完全正确的单词给 0.5 分,凡有错不给分,大小写错误忽略不计;

    2. S9 满分为 2 分,答出第一和第二部分内容且语言正确各得 1 分;

3. S10 满分为 2 分,答出第一和第二部分内容且语言正确各得 1 分;

4. S11 满分为 2 分,答出第一部分内容且语言正确得 0.5 分,答出第二部分内容且语言正确得 0.5 分,答出第三部分内容且语言正确得 1 分;

5. 没有答对问题得 0 分。

二、扣分标准

1. S9 至 S11 题中有语言错误扣 0.5 分,每题语言错误扣分不超过 0.5 分,凡不得分部分如有语言错误不再重复扣分;

2. S9 至 S11 题中凡有与问题无关的内容扣 0.5 分。

3. S9 至 S11 题中如出现明显属于笔误造成的拼写错误和大小写、标点符号错误,不扣分;

4. 用汉语回答问题不给分。

三、预览全文,预测空缺信息

有些考生在听写开始之前,根本就不看卷面上的文字。等到放音开始以后,才匆忙浏览。可是又要听、又要看、又要记,顾此失彼,一样都没做好。这就是"匆忙上阵、不做准备"的恶果。

正确的做法是考生应利用考前空隙以及播放考试指令时间,浏览试卷该项下的文字,尤其是主题句,根据主题句预测文章发展线索和大意,并预测空格处信息,在听写时就可以有的放矢。

那么如何预测空格处信息呢? 可以依靠的只有上下文内容线索和语法形式线索两种。

首先,内容线索。不同体裁的文本,有不同的篇章组织形式。复合式听写材料多为说明文,往往主题突出,条理分明,逻辑严谨。文章的开头或段首多半有主题句,之后的段、句进一步扩展、说明或论证主题句。通过识别作者如何组织文章中词、短句、句子以及文本,可以更好地解读文章的意义。作者在组织篇章时,常常会使用一些语篇标记语,来标记语篇衔接关系。因此,考生可以借助语篇标记语去推断句、段之间的逻辑关系及文章的内容。比如,当读到 however 时,就会知道下面的信息是和上文不同或相反的情况;therefore 说明结果,furthermore 提供进一步的信息等等。由此,不仅可以判断有关单词的意义,也可以判断空白处句子的意义。

其次,形式线索。语篇中句子的语法结构为判断空白处的文字在句中的作用提供依据,我们可以根据其句子成分判断空白处单词的词性(名词?动词?形容词?等)和形式(单数、复数?分词、原形?比较级?等),从而以准确填空。

下面我们以 2005 年 1 月的试题为例,分析一下如何根据已知卷面信息来做预测:

【例 1】 There are a lot of good cameras available at the moment—most of these are made in Japan, but there are also good (S1) _____ models from Germany and the USA. We have (S2) _____ a range of different models to see which is the best (S3) _____ for money. After a number of different tests and interviews with people who are (S4) _____ with the different cameras being assessed, our researchers (S5) _____ the Olympic BY model as the best auto-focus camera available at the moment. It costs $200 although you may well want to spend more—(S6) _____ as much as another $200—on buying (S7) _____ lenses and other equipment. It is a good Japanese camera, easy to use. (S8) _____
_____ whereas the American versions are considerably more expensive.

　　The Olympic BY model weighs only 320 grams, which is quite a bit less than other cameras of a similar type. Indeed one of the other models we looked at weighed almost twice as much. (S9) _____
_____. All the people we interviewed expressed almost total satisfaction with it. (S10) _____.

【读题预测】通过听前的快速阅读,很容易知道这篇文章的内容是介绍 Olympic BY model 的照相机的性能和价格。下面我们具体看一看每一个要填写信息的部分:

S1 于形容词(good)和名词(models)之间,又根据上下文的意思,这里很可能是要填"质量"或另外一个形容词。

S2 位于助动词 have 后,此处缺少谓语动词(要用过去分词)。从意义上看,它应该表示"调查"。

S3 "the best _____ for money",空格处需要填名词。可能用"value for money(性价比)"的搭配。

S4 "be _____ with the cameras",空格处需要一个形容词,可能是 familiar。

S5 前后都是名词词组,它应该是句子的谓语动词。时态上应当是一般现在时,意义上应该可以用于"_____ the model as the best camera"结构,因此相当"choose"之类。

S6 属于插入语,在插入成分中修饰"as... as"结构,应当是副词,比如 just。

S7 是用来修饰名词"lenses"的,故需要一个形容词。

S8 填分句,意义上与后面的 whereas 引导的分句形成对照,应当是描述日式相机的内容。

S9 是独立的句子。前文谈到 BY 相机很轻,几乎是其他品牌的一半重,后文说消费者对它表示满意。这里应该是陈述这种相机的好处。

S10 同样应该是关于这种相机质量的论述。

【答案】S1. quality(不要误写成 qualify 或 quantity)　　　　S2. investigated(拼写时注意用-ed)

S3. value　　　　　　　　　　　　　　　　　S4. familiar(拼写时容易写成 familliar 等错误形式)

S5. recommend(拼写是两个 m)　　　　　　　S6. perhaps(拼写时不要在 s 后面再加 e)

S7. additional(拼写是两个 d;1 个 t)

S8. Equivalent German models tend to be heavier and slightly less easy to use(and 前后各值1分)

S9. Similarly (0.5分), it is smaller than most of its competitors (1分), thus fitting easily into a pocket or handbag(1分)

S10. The only problem was a slight awkwardness in loading the film

由此可见,有效的预测可以帮助正确确定答案。

四、单词听写,注重准确

复合式听写中的单词是在一定的上下文中出现的,因此要听写的单词不仅要求意义上符合语境,而且形式上也要完全准确。要确保得分,一要准确辨音,二要准确书写。

1. 准确拼音

准确辨音是听力理解最基本的技能。如果不能分辨出每个词的正确发音,词义的理解上就会出现偏差,甚至跟原意完全相反。上下文语境以及语音规则为准确辨音提供有益的参考。研究表明,即使词汇和句子结构都很简单,如果对某个语音现象或语音规则缺乏理解或者不完全掌握,仍会造成听力理解的困难,致使听不懂句子的意思或者听错句子的意思。那么,有哪些语音现象和语音规则是考生必须掌握的呢?

(1)连读

主要是指前一个单词结尾的辅音与后一个单词开头的元音连起来发音,如:first_of_all;look_at_it;tell_us;all_about it;fill_in;stop_it;put_it_off;call_a spade_a spade 等。另外,还有增加元音之间的过渡的/ w /、/ j /、/ r /等音构成连读的,如:see_off;hurry_up;too_easy;Asia_and_Africa;stay_up;my_uncle; after_all; clear_up; for_a moment 等。

(2)弱读

即音的弱化,指在口语中某些元音由于语速快或在句中处于次要位置而不发标准读音,变为弱化元音的语音现象。在日常口语中,这种弱化现象具有不确定性,它完全取决于说话人当时的语气、情绪、习惯等因素。一般而言,学单个词的弱读不难,但如果将弱读放到句子中,并与前面或后面的单词发生连读时,学生常会遇到辨音困难,往往会把实词与虚词的连音部分听成别的单词。可见,掌握好弱读对听力理解有很大帮助。

　　常见的弱化方式如下:

长元音被读成短元音,例如,been /biːn/ 读成 /bin/,me /miː/ 读成 /mi/。
省掉一个元音或一个辅音,例如,and /ænd/ 省略读成 /ən/,have /hæv/ 省略读成 /v/。
把元音弱化成 /ə/,例如,are /ɑː/ 读成 /ə/,were /wəː/ 读成 /wə/,shall /ʃæl/ 读成 /ʃəl/。

(3)同化

一个音在连贯发音中由于受邻近音的影响而发生读音变化,这种语音现象是同化。音的同化可能是受前面一个词发音的影响,也有可能是受后面一个词发音的影响,或者是相邻两个词发音互相影响。

　　音的同化有几种常见的方式:

(1) / t / + / j / = / tʃ /: Couldn't_you do it by yourself?

(2) / d / + / j / = / dʒ /: Did you understand?　Should you need help, just call.
(3) / s / + / j / = / ʃ /: In case you need it.　Does your uncle live here?

（4）新词的发音

英语作为网络时代的语言,其变化的步伐更是日新月异。在大学英语四、六级考试委员会提供的新四级考试复合式听写的样卷上,赫然出现了 Kyoto Protocol(京都议定书)这样生僻的词汇。可见,为了拿高分,考生极有必要吸收新的词汇和新的表达法。

下面是一些常见的英语新词,请注意它们的读音:

email	mobile phone	surf the Internet
IT	log in	log off
browser	online	offline
mouse	modem	browser
hacker	clone/cloning	lay off/layoff
virus	AIDS	stem cells
multicultural society	show business	multinational corporation
China's WTO accession	CEO	MBA (Master of Business Administration)
IQ, EQ, CQ, FIQ		

2. 准确书写

听写单词时,如果听不懂要听写的词,那自然怪我们的能力不够,下的功夫还太少;但如果单词听懂了,又隐隐约约写得出一点点,结果却拿不到分,岂不太可惜?因此,如何把能够写对的单词写准确,确保拿分,就是我们努力的方向。为此,必须注意如下几点:

（1）单词各音节之间的辅音字母,注意是否双写

很多考生因为辅音字母的单、双写问题而丢了分,所以需要引起注意。比如,success, value, focused, necessary, recommend 等词,音节之间的辅音,有的是一个字母,有的是两个字母,平时记忆时要根据发音规律记牢。还有的与词形变化有关,比如,有的学生常常把 write 的现在分词和过去分词错写成 writting, writen 等。

（2）一个音节之中,注意元音的拼写

包括某个元音(比如/ i /),该用哪一个元音字母?在不同的单词中,a, e, i, o, u 都可以发/ i /,如 language, college, dolphin, business。是否含有元音重出(指拼写中有 ia, ie, io 等两个元音字母连在一起)?比如,diary, experience, couple, variety, ruining, species, mysterious 等词,错误往往就在元音部分。

（3）注意不发音的字母

不可漏写不发音的字母,比如,island, exhausted, isle, comb 等词中的 s, h, b。

（4）词尾的变形

因为有上下文,单词的形态受到语义、语法等各方面因素的制约,写单词时要特别留意词尾的变化。这其实就是考查语言基本功。大体说来,涉及词形变化的有如下几个方面的考虑:

名词:单数与复数、抽象名词的常用后缀、所有格。如 2004 年 6 月的听写中,art, prints, musical, instruments,都用了复数;2003 年 1 月的听写中,fish, species 也用了复数,不过 species 一词单、复数同形;1998 年 1 月听写了 experiences,也用复数,同年听写中,the world's (youngest college graduate),用的是名词的所有格形式。至于-ure, -ty, -ment, -ity 等名词后缀,更是备考名词拼写时要注意的重点。

动词:非谓语动词与谓语动词的形式。过去式、过去分词、现在分词是考查重点,也有要求填写动词原形的,不过比较少见。

形容词:注意词尾的写法,是否用比较级等。主要是一些以-al 结尾的形容词,如 typical, additional, historical, normal 等,还有些从动词的分词形式变化而来的形容词,也是考查的重点。

副词:注意副词结尾的-ly。

（5）容易拼写错误的词

每个人都会有自己的盲点，存在一些容易写错的单词，在平时学习过程中，就应该注意总结，发现问题，采取相应的对策。

五、长句听写，听记要点，扩充成句，注重句型变换的技巧

对于长句的听写，播放第二遍录音时，空格后留有较长时间的停顿，只要精力集中，完全有可能把原句听写出来，但要想一字不拉照搬原句谈何容易！实际上，我们写下来的内容往往会有些节略。此时，听写的核心问题就在于：第一，句子中的各个要点是否记录完整；第二，由要点扩充成完整的句子是否句子结构合理、语义完整。所以，长句子的听写技巧，可以概括为两点：听记要点的技巧与句型变换的技巧。

1. 听记要点的技巧

足够信息量的笔记是写好要点的重要条件。但有听必记，在有限的放音时间里不仅是不可能做到的，而且还会顾此失彼，丢了西瓜，拣了芝麻。那么我们该如何提高记笔记的效率呢？

首先，要善用缩略语、缩略词和各种符号。字母较多的单词只写该词前几个字母，字母较少的单词，可完整写出该词要快速、省时，并能表达含义。所记内容不要求完整，只要能起到提示的作用，自己能看懂就行了。

其次，要有选择地记笔记。所记词应以实词为主，定语、状语可略去不记。听时应以意群为单位，先记下句子的主要结构，留待第三遍再去补全句子。文章要点显然不可缺漏，但也无需有闻必录，而应分清主次，有所取舍。

通过这两种方法，考生大大压缩了所记的词语，赢得了时间，精炼了内容，增大了笔记的信息量，为写好内容要点创造了条件。

2. 句型变换的技巧

在不能完全照抄原句的时候，在不改变原句意义的前提下进行句型变换成了唯一的出路。其要点是：按照意群，用关键词把每个意群的大意记下来，然后整合成完整的句子。意群之间的关联成分，可以留在最后句子整合时补充。为了表明意群之间的关系，可以使用自己设计的符号，如用箭头、星号等表示先后顺序或并列的要点。具体的句型变换技巧主要有如下几种：

（1）词汇层面上的同义替换

指的是当句子中出现写不出的单词时，可以直接用同义词或近义词替换，不涉及句子结构的改变。这种替换，主要发生在名词、动词、形容词等之间。

【例2】Let's calm down and try to <u>figure things out</u>.　　　　　　　　　　　　　　[2003.9]

　　Let's try to <u>think of a solution</u>.

用短语动词 think of a solution 替换 figure things out，词义相同，整个句子的结构没有变动。

【例3】I've got to <u>go over my notes</u> for tomorrow's midterm.　　　　　　　　　　　[2005.1]

　　I've got to <u>study</u> for tomorrow's midterm.

【例4】We'll have to <u>leave</u> very early.　　　　　　　　　　　　　　　　　　　[2001.1]

　　We'll <u>set off</u> early.

【例5】I <u>call</u> my parents <u>at every weekend</u>.　　　　　　　　　　　　　　　　[2003.1]

　　I <u>phone</u> my parents <u>regularly at weekends</u>.

【例6】It looks like he <u>bought out the bookshelf</u>.　　　　　　　　　　　　　　[2000.1]

　　He <u>bought a lot of books</u>.

【例7】I'll have to <u>get</u> my ticket of the flight <u>changed</u>.　　　　　　　　　　[2000.1]

　　I'll have to <u>switch</u> to a different flight.

【例8】Jane <u>is counting the days to</u> go home for the summer.　　　　　　　　　[1999.6]

　　Jane <u>is eager to</u> go home for the vacation.

【例9】The apple pie <u>is very delicious</u> indeed.　　　　　　　　　　　　　　[2000.1]

　　The apple pie <u>tastes very good</u>.

【例10】The speech was extremely <u>moving</u>.　　　　　　　　　　　　　　　　[1997.1]

　　The speech was <u>touching</u>.

(2)句子层面上的句型转换

有时仅仅替换相应单词不能解决问题,就必须另外搭建句子的架构,用自己熟悉的句型从容改写。比如,不仅肯定句、否定句可以相互替换,句子与短语也可以相互替换。

[例11] I should bring the book to you , but it completely <u>slipped my mind</u>.

<u>I had forgotten</u> to bring the book.

[例12] Great. I am doing a report on the rain forest. <u>Maybe I can get some new information to add to it.</u>   [2005.6]

<u>She thinks the lecture might be informative.</u>

[例13] Although she won the English speech contest, <u>she didn't think it's such a big deal.</u>   [2005.1]

<u>She is modest about her success in the contest.</u>

[例14] <u>I turned down the offer</u> because it would mean frequent business trips away from my family.   [2000.6]

I wanted to spend more time with my family, so <u>I didn't accept the job.</u>

[例15] The banana pie is incredible but <u>Mike doesn't care much for desert.</u>   [2004.1]

<u>The banana pie doesn't appeal to Mike.</u>

第五节 考点突破专项扫雷训练

Unit One

Section A

11. A) They are both anxious to try Chinese food.　　B) They are likely to have dinner together.
    C) The man will treat the woman to dinner tonight.　　D) The woman refused to have dinner with the man.

12. A) It's only for rent, not for sale.　　B) It's not as good as advertised.
    C) It's being redecorated.　　D) It's no longer available.

13. A) The next subway train is coming soon.
    B) The subway train will wait a few minutes at the stop.
    C) There are only one or two passengers waiting for the subway train.
    D) They can catch this subway train without running.

14. A) The assignment looks easy but actually it's quite difficult.
    B) The assignment is too difficult for them to complete on time.
    C) They cannot finish the assignment until Friday.
    D) They have plenty of time to work on the assignment.

15. A) The man will go to meet the woman this evening.
    B) The man and the woman have an appointment at 8 o'clock.
    C) The woman can't finish making the jam before 8 o'clock.
    D) The woman won't be able to see the man this evening.

16. A) The interview was easier than the previous one.
    B) Joe is sure that he will do better in the next interview.
    C) Joe probably failed in the interview.
    D) The oral part of the interview was easier than the written part.

17. A) She is not interested in the article.
    B) She has given the man much trouble.
    C) She would like to have a copy of the article.
    D) She doesn't want to take the trouble to read the article.

18. A) He saw the big tower he visited on TV.　　B) He has visited the TV tower twice.
    C) He has visited the TV tower once.　　D) He will visit the TV tower in July.

Questions 19 to 22 are based on the conversation you have just heard.

19. A) They're classmates.
    C) They're cousins.
    B) They're roommates.
    D) They're lab partners.

20. A) He couldn't decide on a topic for his paper.
    C) He hadn't heard from his family for a while.
    B) He thought his paper was late.
    D) He thought the woman had been ill.

21. A) To find their way back to the nest.
    C) To identify kinds of honey.
    B) To locate plant fibers.
    D) To identify relatives.

22. A) Visit his parents.
    C) Observe how bees build nests.
    B) Write a paper.
    D) Plan a family reunion.

Questions 23 to 25 are based on the conversation you have just heard.

23. A) Salt Lake City, USA.
    C) Helsinki, Finland.
    B) New York City, USA.
    D) Stockholm, Sweden.

24. A) The twenty-ninth.
    C) The twenty-third.
    B) The twenty-second.
    D) The twenty-fourth.

25. A) He asked for a specially-prepared dinner.
    B) He wanted an aisle seat.
    C) He requested some milk for his baby.
    D) He asked for a seat near the front of the plane.

Section B

Passage One

Questions 26 to 28 are based on the passage you have just heard.

26. A) Grocery store.　　B) Supermarket.　　C) Fast-food restaurant.　　D) Hotels and bars.

27. A) After they order their food, the customers usually wait just a few minutes.
    B) The customers carry the food to a table themselves.
    C) For many people the service at the fast-food restaurant is more important than the quality of food.
    D) Customers can't take the hamburgers away.

28. A) At the fast-food restaurant, the service is fast and the food is inexpensive.
    B) At the fast-food restaurant, the food has the best quality.
    C) The fast-food restaurants are more beautiful and cleaner than the ordinary ones.
    D) The fast-food restaurant provides different food.

Passage Two

Questions 29 to 31 are based on the passage you have just heard.

29. A) Two groups of people participated in an experiment.
    B) Light-colored rooms make students do better on the exam.
    C) People in the nice-looking rooms tend to be biased in their opinion.
    D) The effects of a room's general appearance and its wall color on visitors.

30. A) They will make the visitors walk faster.
    B) They will make the visitors cover more area.
    C) They will make the visitors appreciate the exhibits more.
    D) They will make visitors find the subjects on display less beautiful.

31. A) Darkness stimulated more and sooner activity.
    B) Different environments will lead to different performances.
    C) Students should take an exam in a comfortable room painted dark brown.

D) Beautiful decorations cause people to react slowly to objects in a room.

Passage Three

Questions 32 to 35 are based on the passage you have just heard.

32. A) To make recommendations on dieting.
    B) To report the latest advances in brain surgery.
    C) To relate an experiment combining sleep and exercise.
    D) To advise ways of dealing with sleep difficulties.

33. A) Your heart rate is lowered.　　　　　B) It becomes harder to relax.
    C) You become too tired to sleep.　　　D) Sleep rhythms are disturbed.

34. A) Failure to rest during the day.　　　B) Lack of sleep on weekends.
    C) Vigorous exercise in the evening.　　D) Eating cheese before going to sleep.

35. A) At a radio station.　　　　　　　　B) In a lecture hall.
    C) In a biology lab.　　　　　　　　　D) At the doctor's office.

Section C

Robert Edwards was blinded in an automobile accident nine years ago. He was also (36) _____ deaf because of old age. Last week, he was (37) _____ near his home when a thunderstorm was coming. He took (38) _____ under a tree and was (39) _____ by lightning.

He was (40) _____ to the ground and woke up some 20 minutes later, (41) _____ face down in water (42) _____ a tree. He went into the house and (43) _____ down in bed. (44) _____ _____ and when he opened his eyes, he could see the clock across the room fading in and out in front of him. (45) _____. The only one possible explanation by one doctor was that, (46) _____.

Unit Two

Section A

11. A) He is going to give a talk on golf.　　　B) He is eager to meet Jane's parents.
    C) He has the same hobby as Jane's father.　D) He thinks playing golf is a good way to kill time.

12. A) She will help the man to catch up.　　　B) She is worried about the man's health.
    C) She has bought the man an up-to-date map.　D) She has bought the man a pair of glasses today.

13. A) A bookshelf.　　B) A pencil.　　　　　C) Some stocks.　　　D) A pencil-sharpener.

14. A) He liked to show off in class.　　　　B) He was the first person she met at school.
    C) He had a funny face.　　　　　　　　D) He was late for school on the first day.

15. A) She is too busy to go.　　　　　　　B) She is willing to go.
    C) She doesn't want to wait long.　　　　D) She enjoys the wonderful weather.

16. A) They set off early.　　　　　　　　B) They wait for the right time.
    C) They go sightseeing.　　　　　　　　D) They go to the cinema.

17. A) Susan spent a lot of time in preparing for the exam.
    B) Susan couldn't pass the exam.
    C) Susan thought she did quite well in the exam.
    D) Susan had expected the exam to be easier.

18. A) He is not enthusiastic about his chemistry lessons.　B) He has made great progress in his study.
    C) He is a student of chemistry.　　　　　　　　　　D) He is not interested in chemical experiments.

Questions 19 to 22 are based on the conversation you have just heard.

19. A) Play basketball with friends from work.　　B) Try out for the company baseball team.

C) Compete in a weight-lifting race.   D) Go on a diet as his wife suggests.

20. A) Her husband stays too much time away from home.   B) Her husband's fitness instructor is not qualified.
    C) Her husband is not strong enough for the sport.   D) Her husband's diet is not healthy for his age.

21. A) Her husband should keep diet.   B) Her husband should start with a light workout.
    C) Her husband needs to visit a fitness trainer.   D) He should see a doctor.

22. A) It helps improve the strength of his muscle.   B) It helps strengthen his heart.
    C) It helps develop mental toughness.   D) It helps improve the quality of his sleep.

Questions 23 to 25 are based on the conversation you have just heard.

23. A) She wants to buy all that she likes.   B) She wants to buy things at a discount with the card.
    C) She doesn't want to borrow money from her parents.   D) She hopes to establish a good credit rating.

24. A) People generally have a difficult time getting out of debt.
    B) Students often apply for more credit cards than they need.
    C) The interest rates on student cards are very high.
    D) Students usually spend too much money.

25. A) Find a better paying job for her to cover her expenses.
    B) Teach her how to make a financial management plan.
    C) Show her how she can apply for low-interest student credit cards.
    D) Persuade her to cancel the credit card.

Section D

Passage One

Questions 26 to 28 are based on the passage you have just heard.

26. A) In the blue pages.   B) In the white pages.
    C) In the yellow pages.   D) In a special section.

27. A) On the first page of the telephone book.   B) At the end of the telephone book.
    C) In the front of the white pages.   D) Right after the white pages.

28. A) Check your number and call again.   B) Ask the operator what has happened.
    C) Ask the operator to put you through.   D) Tell the operator what has happened.

Passage Two

Questions 29 to 32 are based on the passage you have just heard.

29. A) Because they wanted something harder for their children to play.
    B) Because they wanted something softer for their children to play.
    C) Because they wanted something less heavy for their children to play.
    D) Because they wanted something more interesting for their children to play.

30. A) Animal skins stuffed with grass or leaves.   B) Animal skins stuffed with feathers or hay.
    C) Grass or hay held together by vines.   D) Grass or leaves held together by vines.

31. A) They thought ball playing was only for fun.
    B) They thought ball playing was like fighting.
    C) They thought ball playing could prepare people for war.
    D) They thought ball playing was difficult.

32. A) The first balls and ball games.   B) Egyptian sports.
    C) How Egyptian children played Games.   D) How ball games were played in ancient Egypt.

Passage Three

Questions 33 to 35 are based on the passage you have just heard.

33. A) It enables other birds to see the crow easily.　　B) It makes men want to catch the crow for a pet.

　　C) It enables the crow to hide in gardens.　　D) It makes men think that the crow is evil and mean.

34. A) Birds.　　　　B) Grain.　　　　C) Insects.　　　　D) Fruits.

35. A) He thinks they are harmful and should be put under control.

　　B) He thinks their voices are interesting and should be trained.

　　C) He enjoys studying them and their habits.

　　D) He likes them and wants to protect them.

Section C

　　Packaging is an important form of　(36)_____. A package can sometimes motivate someone to buy a product. For example, a small child might ask for a breakfast food that comes in a box with a picture of a TV　(37)_____. The child is more interested in the picture than in breakfast food. Pictures for children to　(38)_____or cut out, games printed on a package, or small　(39)_____ inside a box also motivate many children to buy products—or to ask their parents for them.

　　Some packages suggest that a buyer will get something for nothing. Food products sold in reusable containers are examples of this. Although a (40)_____ product in a plain container might cost (41)_____, people often prefer to buy the product in a reusable glass or dish, because they believe the container is free. However, the cost of the container is (42)_____ to the cost of the product.

　　The size of a package also motivates a buyer. Maybe the package has "(43)_____ size" or "family size" printed on it. (44)_____. But that is not always true. (45)_____.

　　The information on the package should provide some answers. (46)_____
_____. The words and pictures do not tell the whole story. Only the product inside can do that.

Unit Three

Section A

11. A) Celebrate her birthday.　　　　　　　　B) Attend a meeting.

　　C) Look for a birthday present for her husband.　　D) Wear a red silk dress.

12. A) The man needs help.　　　　　　　　B) The man is complaining.

　　C) The man enjoys the work.　　　　　　D) The man is talking with the professor.

13. A) She didn't get the film.　　　　　　　B) She had no idea where the film was.

　　C) The supermarket closed after she left.　　D) She went to see a film.

14. A) In a school.　　　B) In a hospital.　　　C) In a clothing store.　　　D) In a barber's shop.

15. A) Mr. Power's speech was unnecessarily long.

　　B) The woman should have been more attentive.

　　C) Mr. Power's speech was not relevant to the experiment.

　　D) The woman needn't have gone to the lecture.

16. A) She plans to return to her present job.　　B) She will stop working and concentrate on her kids.

　　C) She will work full-time.　　　　　　　　D) She will take a part-time job.

17. A) The woman is meeting the man at the railway station.

　　B) They are complaining about the poor service in the railway station.

　　C) They are discussing their plans for Christmas.

　　D) The man is seeing the woman off.

18. A) She was to write a letter herself.　　　　B) She can't type the letter right now.

　　C) She has to turn down the man's request.　　D) She is not sure if the computer is fixed.

Questions 19 to 22 are based on the conversation you have just heard.

19. A) Places the woman has visited.
    C) School activities they enjoy.
    B) A paper the man is writing for a class.
    D) The woman's plan for the summer.

20. A) She has never been to Gettysburg.
    C) Her family still goes on vacation together.
    B) She took a political science course.
    D) She's interested in the United States Civil War.

21. A) Why her parents wanted to go to Gettysburg.
    C) Where her family went for a vacation ten years ago.
    B) Why her family's vacation plans changed ten years ago.
    D) Where her family went on their last vacation.

22. A) It's far from where she lives.
    C) She doesn't know a lot about it.
    B) Her family went there without her.
    D) She's excited about going there.

Questions 23 to 25 are based on the conversation you have just heard.

23. A) He happened to pass by Dr. Carter's office.
    B) A friend referred him to Dr. Carter's office.
    C) He found Dr. Carter's number in the phone book.
    D) He saw the office on his way home from work the day before.

24. A) He hurt his knee when a tall ladder fell on him.
    B) He injured his ankle when he fell from a ladder.
    C) He broke his hand when he fell off the roof of his house.
    D) He cut his fingers when painting his house.

25. A) The man should put some ice on his injury.
    C) The man ought to take it easy for a few days.
    B) The man needs treatment right away.
    D) The man should not move while waiting.

Section B

Passage One

Questions 26 to 28 are based on the passage you have just heard.

26. A) An adult stranger.   B) An infant.   C) Teenage children.   D) A servant.

27. A) He writes books about babies.
    C) He is a professor.
    B) He recommends babysitters.
    D) He is in charge of a testing center.

28. A) How to Test Infants.
    C) Choosing a Specialist.
    B) Parents and Children.
    D) Day Care for Babies.

Passage Two

Questions 29 to 31 are based on the passage you have just heard.

29. A) To make people sleep better.
    C) To help people to avoid falling.
    B) To record people's walking on a slippery surface.
    D) To strengthen people's feet and legs.

30. A) By getting inputs from one's eyes, ears and limb sensations.
    B) By planting one's feet on the ground at the same time.
    C) By shortening one's pace and slowing one down.
    D) By preventing people from getting old.

31. A) When people have a right state of mind, they can succeed.
    B) When people are watching amusing TV programs, they tend to laugh.
    C) When people realize the risk of falling, they will control their movement.
    D) When people are getting old, they should have a happy heart.

Passage Three

Questions 32 to 35 are based on the passage you have just heard.

32. A) A musical instrument.   B) A multi-functional digital product.

C) Teenager-parent relationship.   D) An even simpler MP3 player.

33. A) It looks like a photo album.   B) It is the only program by the Apple Company.
    C) It has a bigger screen than most cell phones.   D) It is smaller than a cigarette-box.

34. A) Attend classes without going to school.   B) Go to Disneyland for free.
    C) Find a job with television stations.   D) Download the latest TV shows at a low price.

35. A) The high price of it.   B) Most parents' dislike of it.
    C) Its doubtful quality.   D) Its puzzling usage.

Section C

If parents bring up a child with the aim of turning the child into a (36) _____ they will cause a disaster. According to several leading educational (37) _____ this is one of the biggest mistakes which ambitious parents make. Generally, the child will be only too (38) _____ of what the parent expects, and will fail. Unrealistic parental expectations can cause great (39) _____ to children. However, if parents are not too (40) _____ about what they expect their children to do, but are ambitious in a (41) _____ way, the child may succeed in doing well— (42) _____ if the parents are very (43) _____ of the child.

Michael Li is very lucky. He is crazy about music, (44) _____. Although Michael's mother knows very little about music, Michael's father plays the trumpet in a large orchestra. (45) _____.

Michael's friend, Winston, however, is not so lucky. Both his parents are successful musicians, and they set too high a standard for Winston. (46) _____. Winston is always afraid that he will disappoint his parents and now he seems quiet and unhappy.

第六节 答案解析

Unit One

Section A

11. M: Jennifer, would you join me for dinner tonight?
    W: You treated me last weekend. Now it's my turn. Shall we try something Chinese?
    Q: What do we learn from the conversation?

[B]【解析】推理判断题。S1 是一个简单疑问句:你今晚愿意和我一起吃饭吗? 按理 S2 应该用 Yes 或者 No 回答。但是,我们并没有听到 Yes 或者 No,由此可以判定,S2 的回答要么是强烈的否定,要么是带条件的肯定。实际上,女士说:"上个周末你请了我,这次该我请你了。我们吃中餐吧。"这是带条件的肯定回答。故 B 正确。

[点睛]选项 B 和 D 意义相反,一般而言,其中有一个是答案。女士说"我们吃中餐吧。"这只是一个提议,并不是选项 A 所说的那样 anxious。C 将人物颠倒。

12. W: Good morning. I'm calling to inquire about the two-bedroom house you advertised in the evening newspaper.
    M: I'm sorry, but it's already sold.
    Q: What do we learn about the house from the conversation?

[D]【解析】听懂男士说的 but 后面的内容"房子已经卖掉了",就很容易选出答案 D。

[点睛]本题是 S2 中间带 but 的转折题,but 后面是答案。A 是含有 sale 的干扰项,for rent 意为"供租用",for sale 意为"待售";B 有比较含义,而对话中没有比较;C 在录音中根本没有提到。

13. M: Hurry, there's a subway train coming.
    W: Why run? There will be another one in a minute or two.

Q: What does the woman mean?

[A]【解析】听懂女士所说的"何必跑呢？一两分钟后还会有一趟地铁"，就很容易选出 A。

> 【点睛】本题为不赞同题，why do sth. 意即不必这么做。B 在录音中并未提及；C 是利用只言片语进行干扰；D 错在 this，应该是 the next。

14. M: Wow, that's a big assignment we've got for the psychology class.

W: Well, it's not as bad as it looks. It isn't due until Friday evening.

Q: What does the woman mean?

[D]【解析】关键在于听懂比较结构"not as bad as it looks 不像看上去那么糟"以及否定结构"not due until 直到……才截止"。说明不难，而且时间充裕，所以答案为 D。

> 【点睛】此题为事实细节题，应注意把握说话者的语气。A 正好把难度颠倒；B 中的 too difficult 也不对；作业的上交日期截止到星期五晚上，这并不等于 C"他们直到截止日才能完成"，故 C 不正确。

15. W: Hello, is that Larry? I'm stuck in a traffic jam. I'm afraid I can't make it before 8 o'clock.

M: Never mind. I'll be here waiting for you.

Q: What do we learn from the conversation?

[B]【解析】推断题。女士说她在 8 点以前可能赶不到了，由此可推断他们原本约定在 8 点见面。所以选 B。

> 【点睛】男士说他会等待女士的到来，故 A、D 均不正确；对话中的 jam 表示"交通堵塞"而不是"果酱"，make it 在对话中意为"及时抵达"而不是"制作"，故 C 错。

16. W: Listen to me, Joe. The interview is already a thing of the past. Just forget about it.

M: That's easier said than done.

Q: What can we infer from the conversation?

[C]【解析】推理题。关键在于听懂女士所说的"是过去的事了，忘了它吧"，由此可推断这不是什么好事，浏览四个选项，C 是正确答案。

> 【点睛】easier said than done 意为"说起来容易做起来难"。A、D 是含有 easier 的干扰项；Joe 没有对 interview 一事发表乐观的看法或期望，故 B 不正确。

17. M: Would you like to have a copy of Professor Anderson's article?

W: Thanks, if it's not too much trouble.

Q: What does the woman imply?

[C]【解析】女士说"谢谢，如果不是太麻烦的话"，言下之意，她想要一份复印件，因此选 C。

> 【点睛】S1 是一般疑问句，因此，S2 应给出 Yes 或 No 的回答。正确理解 S2"带条件的肯定回答"，即可得出答案。

18. W: Did you visit the television tower when you had vacation in Shanghai last summer?

M: I couldn't make it last July, but I finally visited it three months later. I plan to visit it again sometime next year.

Q: What do we learn about the man?

[C]【解析】关键在于听懂男士所说的"不过我三个月后去了"，所以选 C。

> 【点睛】本题是 S2 中间带 but 的转折题，男士说的 but 后面的内容是直接答题之处。另外，读题也是一个重要环节，若未能读清各选项的含义，往往会误选答案。选项 A 即是利用 visit, TV, tower 等词组合成极具迷惑性的干扰项。

Now you'll hear two long conversations.

Conversation One

M: Hi, Sue. Where have you been?

W: Oh. Hi, [19] I was just at the library. I have to hand in my biology paper tomorrow.

M: [19]/[20] Tomorrow? Oh, no, I thought it wasn't due till Monday.

W: [20] Oh, don't worry. It is due Monday. But I'm going away for the weekend and won't be back till Monday night.

M: Oh, where are you going?

W: California. We're having a family reunion. It's my grandmother's ninetieth birthday. So all the cousins and aunts and uncles are going. She planned the whole thing herself.

M: Wow. That's great. How many people will be there?

W: Around sixty. My family is big and spread up, but we're pretty close. So have you started working on your biology paper?

M: Yeah. I'm doing it on bees and [21] how they're able to recognize whether another bee is related to them.

W: How can they tell?

M: [21] They use their sense of smell. The sweat bees guard their nests this way. If another bee approaches the nest, the guard determines if the new bee is familiar. If it is, it's allowed to enter.

W: Interesting. Can other insects do this?

M: Well, the paper wasps can. Each wasp nest has a special combination of plant fibers and so the wasps that live there have a unique smell. Those two are the only kinds I've read about so far.

W: Well, you've still got time. It sounds like the bees are picky about who comes to their family reunion.

19. What is the relationship between the speakers?

[A]【解析】人物关系题。根据"明天得上交我的生物论文"及"明天?哦,不,我还以为星期一才截止。"断定二者是同学关系。

 【点睛】解答人物关系题的关键在于,抓住关键词,把握人物谈话时的语气。本题从对话开头就提到的 library 可立刻判断出是校园场景。

20. Why was the man worried at first?

[B]【解析】细节题。本题的信息可以在对话中直接听到,因此可边听边选答案。根据男士说的"我还以为星期一才截止"及女士说的"别担心。截止日期是星期一。"得出答案 B。

 【点睛】其中的"don't worry"暗示担心的事就是前面提到的内容。

21. According to the man, for what do some bees use their sense of smell?

[D]【解析】细节题。可边听边将选项中的实义词与听到的信息进行匹配。男士说:"我在研究蜜蜂,以及它们怎样识别另一只蜜蜂是不是它们的亲戚。……它们用嗅觉做到这一点。"由此得出答案 D。

 【点睛】考查对话中的重点细节。符合"同义替换"的原则。

22. What will the man probably do over the weekend?

[B]【解析】推理题。注意区分题目询问的是男士还是女士周末所做的事。本题问的是男士,虽然没有明说男士周末打算做什么事情,但是根据一开始男士表现出的担忧,应该为 B。

 【点睛】分别记录双方的信息很关键,否则在答题时容易出现"张冠李戴"的现象。

Conversation Two

W: Freedom Travel. How may I help you?

M: Yes, [24] I'd like to make a flight reservation for the twenty-third of this month.

W: Okay. What is your destination?

M: Well. [23] I'm flying to Helsinki, Finland.

W: Okay. Let me check what flights are available. And when will you be returning?

M: Uh, well, I'd like to catch a return flight on the twenty-ninth. Oh, and I'd like the cheapest flight available.

W: [24] Well, the price for the flight is almost double the price you would pay if you leave the day before.

M: Whoo. [24] Let's go with the cheaper flight. By the way, how much is it?

W: It's only $980.

M: Alright. Well, let's go with that.

W: Okay. That's Flight 1070 from Salt Lake City to New York, Kennedy Airport, transferring to Flight 90 from Kennedy to Helsinki.

M: And what are the departure and arrival times for each of those flights?

W: It leaves Salt Lake City at 10:00 AM, arriving in New York at 4:35 PM, transfers to Flight 90 at 5:55 PM, and arrives at Helsinki at 8:30 AM the next day.

M: Alright. And, uh, [25] I'd like to request a vegetarian meal.

W: Sure, no problem. And could I have your name, please?

23. What is the man's destination?

[C]【解析】细节题。由选项可预知本题可能考查地点,原文直接点明,符合"听到什么选什么"的原则。可得出答案C。

【点睛】可边听边记录与选项相关的信息,听到C时应该记下destination或flying to字眼,听到A、B时记录航班号和时间,听完问题自然可以选对答案。D在对话中并未提及。

24. What is the man's departure date?

[B]【解析】细节、推理题。对话中有三处提到出发日期。客户先说,他打算订这个月23日的航班。旅行社业务员在说到价格时提到,"这个票价几乎是提前一天走的两倍",于是客户说,"那就让我订便宜的航班吧"。由此推断,该男士的出发日期是22日。

【点睛】本题的难点在于,对话一开始男士就说出了自己想要出行的日期,因而容易使人误选强干扰项B。在听到题目之前,所有选项的数字都应该加以标注,用符号说明其对应的事件。

25. What request did the man make regarding his flight?

[A]【解析】细节题。根据"我想要一顿素餐",可知答案为A。

【点睛】答案往往是原文的同义转换或概括,排除B、C、D在对话中均小提及。

Section B

Passage One

Most Americans eat breakfast and lunch quickly unless it is a business luncheon or family occasion. And the favorite fast food in the United States is the hamburger. It seems impossible but 3,400,000,000 hamburgers are eaten each year. This is enough to make a line of hamburgers around the world four times.

[26] The favorite place to buy a hamburger is a fast-food restaurant. In these restaurants people stand at the counter, order their food, wait just a few minutes and carry the food to a table themselves. [27] They can eat it in the restaurant or take the food out and eat it at home, at work, or in a park.

[28] Fast-food restaurants are very popular because the service is fast and the food is inexpensive. For many people, this is more important than the quality of the food. These restaurants are popular because the food is always the same. People know that if they eat at a certain company's restaurant in the north or south of the city, the food will be the same; if they eat it in New York or San Francisco, it will still be the same.

26. Where do people usually buy hamburgers?

[C]【解析】细节题。关键在于抓听到"最受人们欢迎的买汉堡包的地方是快餐厅",与题目中的people usually buy相符。因此选C。

【点睛】符合"听到什么选什么"的原则。本题的另一个解题小窍门:由于文中出现频率最高的词是hamburger和fast-food restaurant,因此可推断C正确。

27. Which of the following statements is not true?

[D]【解析】细节题。关键在于听到"他们可以在快餐厅吃或者带走",所以选D。

【点睛】众多事实,可边听边匹配或排除。此外,依据生活常识也可以轻松地选出正确答案。

28. What makes the fast-food restaurant more popular than the ordinary restaurants?

[A]【解析】浏览选项,预测题目可能询问快餐厅的优势所在,因此在听录音时要格外注意这方面的信息。本题关键在于听到"快餐厅之所以受欢迎是因为服务很快、食物便宜",所以选A。

【点睛】本题符合"听到什么选什么"的原则。根据常识也可推断,本题的答案应该是A。

Passage Two

  [29] Investigators were testing the effects of different colored walls on two groups of visitors to an exhibit of paintings. For the first group the room was painted white, for the second, dark brown. Movement of each group was followed by an electrical system under the carpet. The experiment revealed that those who entered the dark brown room walked more quickly, covered more area, and spent less time in the room than the people in the white environment. Dark brown stimulated more activity, but the activity ended sooner. Another experiment presented three groups of subjects with the same photographs, but each group was in a different kind of room—an "ugly" room like a messy storeroom, an average room, such as a nice office, and a tastefully designed living room with carpeting. [30]Results showed that the subjects in the beautiful room tended to give higher mark to the faces than did those in the ugly room. [31] Other studies suggest that students do better on tests taken in comfortable, attractive rooms than in ordinary-looking or ugly rooms.

29. What is the main idea of the passage?

[D]【解析】主旨题。关键在于听懂短文第一句话"不同的墙面颜色对参观者造成的不同影响",其中关键词是 effects"影响"。

  [点睛]短文的开头或结尾部分往往是出主旨题的重点。

30. How will a beautiful room influence visitors at an exhibition?

[C]【解析】细节题。关键在于听到"结果表明,在漂亮的房间里的受试者给这些面孔打出来的分数比在难看的房间里的受试者打出的分数高",意即"漂亮的房间会使参观者更加欣赏展品",故选 C。

  [点睛]正确选项往往是原文的概括或同义表达。选项 A、B 是在深褐色房间里的受试者的表现,而 D 是在难看的房间里受试者的表现。

31. What can be concluded from the two experiments?

[B]【解析】本题根据两个试验进行总结或直接根据最后一句话都可以得出答案为 B。

  [点睛]结论题的依据一般在结尾处。选项 A、C、D 都属于具体描述,而只有 B 才是概括性的话语,本题也可从这种角度来解答。

Passage Three

  [32] Do you have trouble sleeping at night? Then maybe this is for you. When you worry about needing sleep and [33] twist around to find the comfortable position, you are probably only making matters worse.

  [33] What happened in this case is that your heart rate actually increases, making it more difficult to relax. You may also have some bad habits that contribute to the problem. [34] Do you rest frequently during the day? Do you get virtually no exercise or do you exercise strenuously late in the day? Do you sleep late on weekends?

  Any or all of these factors might be leading to your sleeplessness by disrupting your body's natural rhythm. What should you do, then, on sleepless nights?

  Don't bother sleeping pills. The best thing to do is drink milk or eat cheese or tuna fish—they'll help to produce the brain signal that induces sleep.

  [35] Until tomorrow's broadcast, this has been another in the series, *Hints For Good Health*.

32. What is the purpose of the talk?

[D]【解析】预读选项猜测,这可能是一道主旨题。短文第一句话"你有睡眠问题吗?"表明全文谈论的是睡眠问题。因此选 D。

  [点睛]解答主旨题的关键在于对文章有个整体的理解,抓住主题词和文章脉络。

33. According to the speaker, what happens when you toss and turn to get the comfortable position?

[B]【解析】细节题。关键在于听到"翻来覆去调整睡姿会让你的心跳加速,从而更难放松",所以选 B。

  [点睛]问题中的 toss and turn 是原文 twist 的同义表达。选项 A 与原文意思相悖。

34. According to the speaker, what sometimes causes people to have trouble sleeping?

[C]【解析】细节题。文中用"Do you... Do you..."结构列举了许多会导致失眠的因素,其中包括晚上过度运动,即选项 C。

> 【点睛】列举结构往往是出题点,此时应将选项一一与原文信息进行匹配。对于此类题,往往要边听边在选项旁做适当的记录。

35. Where is the talk most probably being given?

[A]【解析】顶读选项可以猜测,本题可能询问文中提到的某个具体地点,也可能是问短文的出处。短文最后提到"直到明天的广播……"。由此可见,这段话是从广播电台播出的。故 A 正确。

> 【点睛】其他选项具有一定的迷惑性,但只要抓住了关键词 broadcast,就不会选错答案。

Section C

36.【答案】partially
　　【解析】此处需要一个副词修饰形容词 deaf,从语义上可以猜出这是一个表示 deaf 程度的词。partially 中的 t 不要写成 c,因为此词由 part 派生而来。

37.【答案】strolling
　　【解析】此处需要一个现在分词,表示过去正在进行的一个动作。注意双写 l。

38.【答案】refuge
　　【解析】take refuge 是固定搭配,意为"寻求庇护,避难"。

39.【答案】struck
　　【解析】根据前面的 was 和后面的 by 可知,此处需要一个动词的被动作使词,struck 是 strike 的过去分词。

40.【答案】knocked
　　【解析】根据前面的 was 可知,此处需要一个动词的过去分词,即使听不清楚 -ed,依据语法知识也要加上。

41.【答案】lying
　　【解析】根据句子结构,此处需要一个现在分词作伴随状语,lying 是 lie 的现在分词。

42.【答案】below
　　【解析】此处指方位,需要一个介词,注意 below 不可写成 blow。

43.【答案】lay
　　【解析】此处需要一个与 went 并列的动词过去式作谓语,lay 为 lie 的过去式。

44.【答案】A short time later, he awoke; his legs were numb
　　【听音关键】short time, awoke, legs, numb
　　【答案重构】Soon, he came around, but his legs were numb

> 【画龙点睛】此句要抓住时间状语和两个主谓结构。由于 he awoke 和 his legs were numb 是两个独立的分句,其间不可用逗号,应该用分号或句号,否则就要加连词。

45.【答案】Doctors make certain that he has got back his sight and hearing from the flash of lightning, but they are unable to explain the cause
　　【听音关键】certain, back, sight, hearing, lightning, unable, explain
　　【答案重构】Although doctors are sure that he has recovered his sight and hearing due to the flash of lightning, they cannot explain why

> 【画龙点睛】此句较长,但比较好懂。要听清主从句的结构,并记录其中的形容词、名词、动词。

46.【答案】since Robert lost his sight as a result of a terrible accident, perhaps it could only be regained by another accident
　　【听音关键】lost, sight, accident, regain, another
　　【答案重构】since Robert lost his sight in a terrible accident, perhaps he could only regain it in another accident

> 【画龙点睛】此句要抓住因果关系和具有对比含义的 lost 和 regain。

Unit Two

Section A

11. W: Hey, Simon. I hear you're meeting Jane's parents for the first time.

   M: Yeah. Next weekend. Fortunately her father loves to play golf, so we will have something to talk about.

   Q: What can be inferred about Simon?

[C]【解析】推断题。男士提到"幸好她父亲喜欢打高尔夫,这样我们就有东西可聊了",所以推断他与简的父亲有同样的嗜好。故 C 正确。

[点睛]听到 fortunately, unfortunately 等表达评论的词语后,一定要注意后面的信息。选项 A 利用对话中出现过的原词拼凑成一个具有一定迷惑性的选项,但要注意 give a talk on...意为"做一次关于……的演讲";B 中的 eager 没有依据,从 fortunately 只能猜出 Simon 的紧张;Simon 没有对 playing golf 进行评论,故排除 D。

12. M: I am worried about those classes I missed when I was away.

   W: I will try to bring you up-to-date on what we've done.

   Q: What does the woman mean?

[A]【解析】细节题。关键在于听懂"我会尽力把到最近所学的内容都告诉你",言下之意,女士会帮助男士赶上上课的进度。A 中的 help... catch up 表达了此义,故 A 正确。

[点睛]up-to-date 意为"直至目前的,最新的",熟练掌握习惯表达对于听力很有帮助。B 偏离主题;C 中的 up-to-date 属于原词干扰,map 为无关信息;D 中的 glasses 属于语音干扰。

13. W: I am looking for a pencil-sharpener. I don't see any on the shelf.

   M: I saw some in the stock room this morning. I'll go and check.

   Q: What does the woman want to buy?

[D]【解析】关键在于听懂开头第一句话"我在找卷笔刀",因此选 D。其他选项均为原词或语音干扰。

[点睛]一般而言,在听力题中 S2 的话才是考查的重点。像本题借 S1 中的某个词发难,差不多算是"放冷枪"。但对于习惯了先读选项再等着听录音的老兵来说,这样的题就是送礼来了:哈哈,笑纳!

14. M: Do you know Dan? He is in your class.

   W: Certainly. In fact he was the first person I got to know in my class. I still remember the look on his face when he showed up late on the first day of school.

   Q: Why did the woman remember Dan so well?

[D]【解析】关键是要听到女士说的"我还记得第一天上学他迟到的时候脸上的表情"。即他开学第一天就迟到了,所以女士记住了他。D 中的 was late 对应录音中的 showed up late,因此选 D。

[点睛]the first, the last 等处出现的信息往往很重要。对话中出现的词组是 show up"出现,露面",而 show off 是"炫耀,卖弄"的意思,A 是用 show off 来混淆视听。B 错在 met,录音中是 know;而且 at school 也错了,应该是 in class。录音中的 the look on his face 指的是脸上的表情,而不是 C 所说的 had a funny face。

15. M: Wonderful day, isn't it? Want to join me for a ride?

   W: If you don't mind waiting while I get prepared.

   Q: What does the woman mean?

[B]【解析】当男士提出邀请时,女士回答说,"如果你不介意等我准备好",可见她已接受了邀请,所以选 B。

[点睛]S1 提出邀请或建议时(一般疑问句),要特别注意 S2 的反应(往往不直接用 Yes 或 No 回答!),条件句传达的信息往往表示接受或部分地(有条件地)接受。

16. M: Let's go to the cinema.

   W: OK. But we'll have to leave early, or else we'll get caught in the traffic.

   Q: What does the woman suggest?

[A]【解析】女士的建议是"我们要早点动身,否则会碰上交通堵塞",A 中的 set off 对应录音中的 leave,因此选 A。

【点睛】本题是 S2 中间带 but 的转折题。转折词后面的信息很重要,答案中的实义词往往是对话中使用的原词或其同义词。B、C 在录音中没有提到,D 是男士的建议。

17. M: Hi, Susan. How did your exam go yesterday?

W: Well, it wasn't as easy as I had thought. I should have spent more time in preparing for it.

Q: What do we learn from the conversation?

[D]【解析】女士提到"考试并不像我原先想的那么简单"。因此 D 正确,而 C 错误。should have 后接动词的过去分词表示"本该做而没有做某事",即"我本该花更多时间做准备"。A 恰好与女士的本意相反,故不正确。

【点睛】比较句型是重要考查点。B 属于过度推测,故不可选。

18. W: Mr. Jones, your student Michael shows great enthusiasm for sports.

M: I only wish he showed half as much for his chemistry class.

Q: What do we learn from the conversation about Michael?

[A]【解析】女士提到迈克尔对运动很有热情,男士则说要是他对化学课有那热情的一半就好了。由此可知迈克尔对化学课不感兴趣,所以选 A。

【点睛】本题主要考查虚拟语气。虚拟语气在大学英语四级听力考试中出现频率较高,因此应了解和辨别虚拟语气的基本结构。此类题的选项答案有如下特点:①否定掉虚拟语气中所表达的含义——反着选答案;②虚拟语气间的内部替换;③与真实条件句相替换。本题的正确选项符合第一种特点。

Now you'll hear two long conversations

Conversation One

M: Honey, the basketball game is about to start. And could you bring some chips and a bowl of ice cream? And... uh... a slice of pizza from the fridge.

W: Anything else?

M: Nope, that's all for now. Hey, honey, you know, [19] they're organizing a company basketball team, and I'm thinking about joining. What do you think?

W: Humph.

M: "Humph"? What do you mean by "Humph"? I was the star player in high school.

W: Yeah, twenty-five years ago. Look, [20] I just don't want you to have a heart attack, running up and down the court.

M: So, what are you suggesting? Should I just abandon the idea? I'm not that out of shape.

W: Well... [21] you ought to at least have a physical examination before you begin. I mean, it HAS been at least five years since you played at all.

M: Well, okay, but...

W: And you need to watch your diet and cut back on the fatty foods, like ice cream. And you should try eating more fresh fruits and vegetables.

M: Yeah, you're probably right.

W: And you should take up a little weight training to strengthen your muscles or [22] perhaps try cycling to build up your heart and blood system. Oh, and you need to go to bed early instead of watching TV half the night.

M: Hey, you're starting to sound like my personal fitness instructor!

W: No, I just love you, and I want you to be around for a long, long time.

19. What does the man want to do?

[A]【解析】细节题。由选项可预知此题可能考某人要做什么,可边听边选答案。对话开始,男士说到:"他们要组织一支公司篮球队,我考虑参加。"由此得出答案 A。

【点睛】选项 B 是强干扰项:稍微不慎,未看清选项中的形似词 baseball"棒球"或未听到对话中的 basketball,都会带来麻烦。区分各选项的含义，至关重要！C 中的 weight-lifting 是原文中 weight training 的形似干扰；D 中的 go on a diet 是男士妻子的建议,但不是男士的打算。

20. What is the woman's main concern?

[C]【解析】推理题。根据"我只是不想你患有心脏病还要在球场上跑来跑去"可判断出妻子担心丈夫的身体状况不适合篮球这项剧烈运动。故选 C。

【点睛】A 属于未提及的信息;B 中的 instructor 根本不存在,而是男士对女士的调侃,原文用的是"你就像是我的私人健康顾问";D 中的 diet 也是女士的建议,unhealthy 不是事实。

21. What is the woman's first suggestion to her husband?

[D]【解析】细节题。根据"至少在开始前你得先体检"可知答案是去看医生,即 D。其中,a physical examination 等同于 a medical examination,意即"体检"。

【点睛】同义替换是重要出题手段。选项 A、B 是女士后来提出的建议;C 在录音中没有提到,属于个别原词胡乱拼凑。

22. Why does the man's wife recommend cycling?

[B]【解析】细节题。对话中女士说:"……或许你该试试骑车,使你的心脏和血液系统得到加强。"不定式作目的状语,很容易选出答案 B。

【点睛】通过读题,区分各选项的差异(四个选项分别说及"肌肉"、"心脏"、"心理"、"睡眠"),然后边听边记,很容易就可以捕捉到相关细节,得到正确答案。

Conversation Two

M: Hi, Sis. I just came over to drop off the DVDs , and... Hey, wow! ? Where did you get all of this stuff?

W: I bought it. So, what do you think of my new entertainment center? And the widescreen TV...

M: Bought it?

W: ... and my new DVD player. Here, let me show you my stereo. You can really rock the house with this one.

M: But where did you get the dough to buy all this? You didn't borrow money from Mom and Dad again, did you?

W: Of course not. I got it with this!

M: This? Let me see that... Have you been using Dad's credit card again?

W: No, silly. It's mine. It's a student credit card.

M: A student credit card? How in the world did you get one of these?

W: I got an application in the mail.

M: Well, why did you get one in the first place?

W: Listen. [23] Times are changing, and having a credit card helps you build a credit rating, control spending, and even buy things that you can't pay for with cash... like the plane ticket I got recently.

M: What plane ticket?

W: Oh yeah, my roommate and I are going to Hawaii over the school break, and of course, I need some new clothes for that, so...

M: I don't want to hear it. How does having a student credit card control spending? It sounds like you've spent yourself into a hole. Anyway, student credit cards just lead to impulse spending... as I can see here. [24] And the interest rates of student credit cards are usually sky high, and if you miss a payment, the rates, well, just jump!

W: Ah. The credit card has a credit limit...

M: ... of $20,000?

W: No, not quite that high. Anyway, ...

M: I've heard enough.

W: Did I tell you we now get digital cable with over 100 channels? Oh, and here's your birthday present. A new MP3 player...

M: Yeah. Oh, don't tell me. Charged on the credit card. Listen. Hey, I don't think having a student credit card is a bad idea, but this is ridiculous. And how in the world are you going to pay your credit card bill?

W: Um, with my birthday money! It's coming up in a week.

M: [25] Hey, let's sit down and talk about how you're going to pay things back, and maybe we can come up with a budget that will help you get out of this mess. That's the least I can do.

23. Why did the woman want to obtain a student credit card?

[D]【解析】细节题。浏览选项,预测题目可能询问女士使用信用卡的原因,因此听的时候要特别留意相关信息。本题关键在于听到女士说的"时代不同了,拥有信用卡有助于建立个人信用,控制消费……"。因此选 D。

【点睛】本题答案可直接听到,关键在于记录相关细节,可边听边选答案。

24. According to the man, what is one reason for not having credit cards?

[C]【解析】细节题。关键是要听到男士说的"学生信用卡的利率高得离谱,要是不能及时偿还,利率还会飚升!"因此选 C。

【点睛】此题关键在于抓住话题,结合同义表达。

25. What is the man going to do to help the woman manage her money?

[B]【解析】推断题。在对话快结束时,男士说:"我们坐下来讨论一下你该怎样偿还你的信用贷款,或许这样我们可以做出预算,帮你摆脱这种困境。"这与选项 B 含义相同。

【点睛】由选项四个原形动词可以推断出,本题应该是询问对话最后提出的行动计划或建议。女士只是一名学生,况且对话中未提及 job 之类的话题,故 A 错误;选项 C、D 在对话中均未提及。

Section B

Passage One

Telephone books in the United States have white, blue and yellow pages. The white pages list people with phones by last name. [26] The blue pages contain numbers of city services, government agencies and public schools. Businesses and professional services are listed in a special section, the yellow pages. To make a long distance call, you need an area code. Each area in the U.S. has an area code. The area covered by an area code may be small or large. For example, New York City has one area code. But so does the whole State of Oregon. [27] If you want to know the area code of a place, you can look it up in the area code map printed in the front of the white pages. There are a lot of public telephones in the U.S. They have their own numbers. If you are making a long distance call on a public telephone and run out of money, give the number on your phone to the person you're talking to. Then hang up the receiver and he can call you back. [28] If you make a long distance call and get a wrong number, call the operator and explain what happened. This means that you can make the call again to the right number without having to pay more money.

26. Where can you find the telephone number of a city council in a telephone book?

[A]【解析】细节、推理题。预读选项猜测,本题可能询问某类电话号码会在电话簿的哪个部分找到。a city council 属于城市服务、政府机构这一类,所以可以在 the blue pages 中找到。故选 A。

【点睛】开头句如果列举了几个并列的东西,接下来肯定是分别介绍,因此一一记录与选项相关的信息(可记录在考题各选项旁边)可以保证考查其中任何一条都不会出错。

27. Where can you find the area code map of the U.S.?

[C]【解析】细节题。通过浏览选项可知,本题应该也是询问在电话簿的哪个部分能查找到某信息。短文中提到,在白页前面印有区号地图,因此选 C。

【点睛】符合"听到什么选什么"的原则。

28. What are you advised to do when you get a wrong number in making a long distance call?

[D]【解析】细节题。关键在于听到"如果打长途电话时拨错了号码,应该打电话给接线员说明情况。"D 表达的即是此义,所以选 D。

【点睛】符合"听到什么选什么"的原则。B 与短文原意相悖。

Passage Two

The first true piece of sports equipment that man invented was the ball. [29] In ancient Egypt, as in anywhere else, pitching stones was a favorite children's game. But a badly thrown rock could hurt a child. While looking for something less dangerous to throw, the Egyptians made what were probably the first balls. [30] At first, balls were made of grass or leaves held together by vines. Later they were made of pieces of animal skins sewn together and stuffed with feathers or hay. Even though the Egyptians were warlike, they found time for peaceful games. Before long they had developed a number of ball games, each with its own set of rules. Perhaps they played ball more for training than for fun. [31] Ball playing was thought of mainly as a way to teach young men the speed and skill they would need for war.

29. Why did the Egyptians invent the ball?
[B]【解析】推理题。文中提到,他们想有一种更安全的玩具,不像石头那么危险,那么肯定应是一种更软的玩具。故选 B。

[点睛]选项之间的差异主要是形容词,因此要特别注意短文中描述玩具的形容词,在选项中找出意义一致的,less dangerous 只能对应其中的 softer。

30. What was the first ball made of?
[D]【解析】细节题。最早的球是由用藤条缠在一起的草或树叶做成的。即 D。

[点睛]读题、区分各选项,然后捕捉关键词,是解答这种细节题的要诀。选项 A、B 的共同之处是 Animal skins,不同之处在于,一个是草或树叶,一个是羽绒或干草。C、D 的共同之处是 vines,不同之处在于,一个是草或干草,一个是草或树叶。认真地听,很容易捕捉到 grass, leaves, vines 等关键词,答案自然就显露出来了。

31. What did the Egyptians think of ball playing according to the speaker?
[C]【解析】细节题。预读选项可知,本题询问某些人对 ball playing 的看法。文章多次提到,埃及人好战,而打球可以训练战斗中所需要的速度和技巧。故 C 正确。

[点睛]捕捉高频词汇和首尾句很重要。

32. What is the main idea of the passage?
[A]【解析】由选项猜测,这是一道主旨大意题。文章的主题词是 balls 和 ball games,出现频率很高。所以选 A。

[点睛]主旨大意题考查考生对短文的主旨大意的概括理解,一般出现在短文的第一题或者最后一题。正确选项中应该含有主题词、高频词。

Passage Three

The bird known in the United States as the crow is all black—wings, body, head, feet and beak. [33] It looks mean and evil, and some people say that it has a character to match its looks. [34] Crows have the bad habit of robbing cornfields. They are accused of attacking the nests and eating the eggs and [34] the young of smaller birds. This crime is probably attempted more than it is carried out, however, for crows are often seen being driven away from the nests of angry smaller birds.

Some farmers put up scarecrows to keep crows out of their cornfields, and others organize "crow shoots" to try to get rid of the crows. But crows continue to grow just the same. Crows can sound their call in a dozen different ways, and each version has a special meaning. They can make other sounds, too. Some crows, if they are caught young, can even be taught to say words.

Crows are not completely bad, for [34] they eat some birds and insects that do damage to the gardens, cornfields and grainfields. [35] Whether crows are helpful or harmful, it is a subject of debate, but what is certain is that they are very interesting birds.

33. According to the author, what is the effect of the crow's all-black appearance?
[D]【解析】细节题。短文前两句话提到,乌鸦一身黑,"它看起来卑劣邪恶,有人说,其性格也与其外形相配"。因此选 D。

【点睛】符合短文听力"听到什么选什么"的原则。选项 A、B、C 在文中均未提及。

34. According to the passage, which of the following does the crow not eat?
[D]【解析】细节题。文中分别提到,乌鸦吃谷类、吃幼鸟、吃某些害虫,所以答案应选 D。

【点睛】三个选项都听到了,则选另类——没有听到的那个。

35. What is the author's feeling about crows?
[C]【解析】推理题。文中最后一句话提到,乌鸦到底是益虫还是害虫仍有待讨论,但乌鸦确实是一种很有趣的鸟。所以应选 C。

【点睛】正确总结结尾句。A 是文中提到的部分人的观点,并非作者的观点;作者是说乌鸦有趣,而不是指它们的声音,故 B 错误;D 中的 wants to protect them 于原文无据可依。

Section C

36. 【答案】advertising
   【解析】①形式上,此处需要一个名词作介词 of 的宾语;②意义上,该词应能总结下文(激发人们购买商品);③在听清该词后,注意拼写,不要把 s 写成 z。

37. 【答案】character
   【解析】①此处需要一个单数名词;②"一个电视____的图片",从意义与搭配上,此处大体应考虑"建筑、画面、场景、人物"等词;③character 在此处表示"人物"。注意第二个 a 不可写成 e 或 i,也不要将词尾 er 拼写成 or。

38. 【答案】color/colour
   【解析】根据前面的不定式 to 可知,此处需要一个动词且使用原形,该动词可以与 pictures 搭配。color 意为"结……涂色"。

39. 【答案】gifts
   【解析】此处需要一个复数名词,与 pictures, games 并列。

40. 【答案】similar
   【解析】本句由 although 引导让步从句,两个分句前后具有转折关系。主句中的 prefer to 暗含对比关系,比较的一方是 the product in a reusable glass or dish,另一方是本题所在的 a _____ product in a plain container。这种由"普通容器"包装的产品,理应便宜些,故 41 空处要填比较级形式的指示代词 less。这两种产品应相似才会有此比较,故 40 空处应填表达"相似、相同"含义的词。

41. 【答案】less
   【解析】参见 40 题的"解析"。

42. 【答案】added
   【解析】add to 是固定搭配,根据句意"容器的价格已经包含在了产品的价格之中",add 应使用其被动式 added。注意不可写成 adding。

43. 【答案】economy
   【解析】根据后面的 or 及 family 可知,此处需要一个名词。economy 在此处表示"经济实惠"。

44. 【答案】This suggests that the large size has the most products for the least money
   【听音关键】suggests, large size, most products, least money
   【答案重构】This means the large size costs the least money for the most products // This indicates that the large size has the best value for money

   【画龙点睛】此句的宾语从句中含有一个完整的主谓宾结构。注意具有对比含义的 most 与 least。

45. 【答案】To find out a buyer has to know how the product is sold and the price of the basic unit
   【听音关键】find, buyer, how, sold, price, basic unit
   【答案重构】To have a customer should learn how the product is sold and how much the basic unit is

   【画龙点睛】不定式 to 作主语,谓语动词用单数形式;此句的宾语部分含有两个并列的成分,而且其中一个并列成分还是个特殊疑问句。在重构答案时,可将第二个并列成分也改写成特殊疑问句。

46.【答案】But the important thing for any buyer to remember is that a package is often an advertisement

【听音关键】important, buyer, remember, package, advertisement

【答案重构】But it's important for buyers to remember that a package is often an ad

【画龙点睛】此句是系表结构,主语有后置修饰词,表语是一个完整的句子。可将此句改写成 it's... for sb. to do sth. 结构。

Unit Three

Section A

11. W: I don't know what I should give my husband on his birthday. Nothing seems to please him.

M: Why not a red silk tie?

Q: What is the woman going to do?

[C]【解析】本题需格外注意的是,题目询问的是女士打算做什么。女士提到丈夫的生日自己不知道该送点什么,所以选 C。

[点睛]S1 提出话题,注意实义词 husband, birthday。针对 S1 提问。小心! 选项 A 中的 her 明显错误,B 在录音中未提及,D 是利用个别原词进行干扰。

12. W: When will you be through with your work, John?

M: Who knows? The professor always has something for me to do at the last minute.

Q: What do we learn from the conversation?

[B]【解析】本题考查考生对语气的把握。男士提到"教授老是在最后时刻还找些事给我做",这分明是抱怨及不满的口气。故 B 正确。

[点睛]对语气的感悟能力往往决定听力理解的正确率。本题的关键词是 usually 和 the last minute,表明了他的怨气。

13. M: Did you get the film for your camera in the supermarket?

W: It was closed before I got there. I had no idea that it closes so early in the evening.

Q: What does the woman mean?

[A]【解析】女士提到"我还没到超市,它就已经关门了。"因此推断出她没买到胶卷,即 A。

[点睛]S1 是一般疑问句,S2 没有用 Yes 或 No 回答,所以 S2 的回答要么是否定,要么是带条件的肯定。本题中,S2 做出的是否定回答。女士要去超市买胶片,即她知道哪里有胶片,故 B 错误;C 错在 after,应是 before;D 中的 film 指的是"电影"而不是对话中的含义"胶片"。

14. W: You seem very confident about your interview, don't you?

M: Yes, I feel ready for it. I bought a good suit in a clothing store; I had my hair cut; I have studied almost everything about medicine.

Q: Where is the man probably going to work?

[B]【解析】关键词出现在对话末尾,即"我学习了有关医药的所有知识",因此他应该是在医院求职,选 B。

[点睛]地点题的读题重点在于理解相应的地点名词所确立的语境,以及在该语境下的关键词。本题要区分关键词和干扰信息:bought a good suit, hair cut 都是外表上为 interview 做的准备,而 medicine 才是真正的专业方向。

15. W: Mr. Power's speech seems to go on forever. I was barely able to stay awake.

M: How could you sleep through that? It was very important to the experiment we're going to carry out.

Q: What does the man imply?

[B]【解析】女士认为演讲没完了,自己听着都快睡着了。男士则说,你怎么能睡大觉呢?这对我们的实验很重要。言下之意,你本该认认真真地听讲才对。所以选 B。

[点睛]惊讶语气 How could you...。此类题的答案应选择与 S1 意思相反的选项,或者否定 How could you 的后半句话。本题中,原文到选项的语义转换关系是:How could you sleep...? →You should not have slept.→You should have been more attentive.首先否定 how could you 的后半句,然后改用正面表达,即得出答案。

16. M: Are you going to return to your present job after the vacation?

W: No. I plan to stay with the kids. That means I will be a full-time mother.

Q: What will the woman do?

[B]【解析】对话中的 full-time mother 即全职妈妈,只有 B 符合此义,故正确。

[点睛]其实 no 就否定了 A。而 C、D 与 full-time mother 显然矛盾。

17. W: Railway stations are sad places.

M: Sometimes, I guess. But we'll keep in touch and I'll go and see you at Christmas.

Q: What are the speakers doing?

[D]【解析】女士说"火车站是个令人伤感的地方。"男士说"我想有时是这样。但我们会保持联系,而且圣诞节我会去看你。"因此这是一段送别的对话。即 D。

[点睛]变相场景题,抓关键实义词。其实他们所说的"Railway stations are sad places.""keep in touch"和"I'll go and see you"都是典型的告别用语。本题的另一种解法:听到什么就不选什么。这也是短对话题的常用解题原则之一。

18. M: Jessica, could you type this letter for me?

W: Sorry. The computer broke down this morning. I'll do it for you as soon as I fix it.

Q: What does the woman imply?

[B]【解析】女士说,一修好电脑,我就为你打这封信。因此选 B。

[点睛]sorry 就暗示出了"现在不能打"的意思。S2 的回答属于"有条件的答应",从 C"拒绝帮助他们的请求"不正确。A 错在 write,应是 type;女士不能立刻为男士打这封信,原因就是电脑坏了且还没修好,故 D 不正确。

Now you'll hear two long conversations.

Conversation One

M: Hi, Janet, you are so lucky to be done with your final exams and term papers. I still have 2 more finals to take.

W: Really?

M: Yeah. [19] So what are you doing this summer, anything special?

W: Well, actually, yeah. My parents have always liked taking my sister and me to different places in the United States. You know, places with historical significance. I guess they wanted to reinforce the stuff we learned in school about history. And so even though we are older now, they still do once in a while.

M: Oh, [19] so where are you going this summer?

W: Well, [19] this summer it's finally going to be Gettysburg.

M: [20] Finally? You mean they never took you yet? I mean Gettysburg. It's probably the most famous civil war site in the country. It's only a couple of hours away. I think that would be one of the first places that they've taken you. I have been there a couple of times.

W: [21] We were going to go about ten, well, no, it was exactly ten years ago, but I don't know, something happened, I cannot remember what.

M: Something changed your plans?

W: Yeah, don't ask me what it was, but we ended up not going anywhere that year. I hope that doesn't happen again this year. I wrote a paper about Gettysburg last semester for a history class. I was talking well about the political situation in the United States right after the battle at Gettysburg, so [22] I'm eager to see the place.

19. What are the students mainly discussing?

[D]【解析】主旨题。对话开头,男士问今年夏天你有什么打算?接着他们一直在谈论女士的打算,所以选 D。

[点睛]对话或短文的的第一题各选项若是名词性词组,则很可能是问主旨、话题,此时,要特别留意起始段落。

20. What does the man find surprising about the woman?

[A]【解析】对话中,常出现这样的情况:一方重复另一方话中的某一个成分,以示对该部分内容迷惑不解,表示意外、惊

奇、感叹等强烈语气。"终于要去了？你的意思是他们还从来没有带你去过？我说的是葛底斯堡……"答案自然是A。

【点睛】特殊语气处要留神。可对比短对话题中的"重复反问题"。

---

21. What is the woman unable to remember?

[B]【解析】细节题。女士说，十年前他们本来打算去葛底斯堡旅游，可后来发生了某件事没去成。究竟发生了什么事她却不记得了。所以选B。

【点睛】本题也可根据其他线索得出答案：其间男士说"Something changed your plans?"女士回答说"Yeah"，由此也可以得出B。

---

22. What does the woman imply about Gettysburg?

[D]【解析】推断题。女士最后一句话明确表明她很渴望去葛底斯堡，故答案为D。

【点睛】即使听不懂或记不住每句话，也一定要记住对话或短文的尾句，因为这句话往往起到总结主旨或再次点题的作用。

Conversation Two

W: Dr. Carter's Office.

M: Yes, I'd like to make an appointment to see Dr. Carter, please.

W: Is this your first visit?

M: Yes, it is.

W: Okay. Could I have your name, please?

M: Yes. My name is Ronald Schuller.

W: And may I ask who referred you to our office?

M: Uh, [23] I drove past your office yesterday.

W: Okay. How about the day after tomorrow on Wednesday at 4 o'clock?

M: Uh. Do you happen to have an opening in the morning? I usually pick my kids up from school around that time.

W: Okay. Um... how about Tuesday at 8:00 A.M. or Thursday at 8:15 A.M.?

M: Uh, do you have anything earlier, like 7:30?

W: No. I'm sorry.

M: Well, in that case, Thursday would be fine.

W: Okay. Could I have your phone number please?

M: It's 643-0547.

W: Alright. And what's the nature of your visit?

M: Well, to tell you the truth, I fell from a ladder two days ago while painting my house, and I twisted my ankle when my foot landed in a paint can. I suffered a few scratches on my hands and knees, [24] but I'm most concerned that the swelling in my ankle hasn't gone down yet.

W: Well, did you put ice on it immediately after this happened?

M: Well yeah. I just filled the paint can with ice and...

W: And so after you removed the paint can...

M: Well, that's part of the problem. Uh, the paint can is still on my foot.

W: Look, Mr. Schuller. [25] Please come in today. I don't think your case can wait.

23. From the conversation, how did the man probably find Dr. Carter?

[A]【解析】细节题。问题"how did the man probably find Dr. Carter?"是对话中"And may I ask who referred you to our office?"的重述。这一点确定后，就不难做出判断，根据"我昨天开车经过你们的办公室"得出答案A。

【点睛】D是强干扰项，但是，选项中的内容 on his way home 在对话中并未提及。

---

24. Why does the man want to see the doctor?

[B]【解析】细节题。各选项提到的受伤部位不同,且受伤的原因也各异。谈到自己的伤病时,男士说:"我最担心的是,我脚踝上的淤肿还没有消。"说明是男士的脚踝受了伤,故答案选 B。

【点睛】预读选项并区分各选项间的异同,将有助于快速挑选到与所听信息相符的选项。除了 D 中的"在油漆房间时"属正确信息,A、C、D 中的其他信息均属无中生有。

25. What does the woman suggest at the end of the conversation?

[B]【解析】细节题。女士最后说:"请今天就来,我想你的病情不能等。"由此得出答案 B。

【点睛】"Please come in today."这句话很容易理解,因而可顺理成章地推出答案 B"该男士的伤病需立即治疗"。A 是女士最初向男士提出的建议,C 在原文中并未提及,D 利用原词 wait 进行干扰。

Section B

Passage One

A four-year study conducted by the Infant Testing Center in San Francisco, California, suggests that [26] babies feel more comfortable around other babies than with strange adults. According to the study, babies benefit by being with their fellow infants daily. Whereas a baby might show fear of an adult stranger, he is likely to smile and reach out to an unfamiliar infant. By the time the babies were one year old, they had begun to form friendships.

The above findings, based on the observation of 100 babies aged three months to three years might prove interesting to working parents who must find day care for their babies. Family care in a private home, with several babies together, is probably the ideal way to care for babies under three. [27] Dr. Benjamin Spock, a well-known specialist on children's disease and author of several books about babies, supports the idea. He says that [28] family day care is better for children than hiring a housekeeper or a babysitter.

26. With which of the following is a baby likely to feel most at ease?

[B]【解析】细节题。文章开头就提到"相比与陌生的成人在一起,婴儿在别的婴儿周围时会感觉更轻松自在。"而且之后的几句话也是围绕着这一话题展开的。C 中的 infant 指的就是文中的 other babies,故 B 正确。

【点睛】A"成年陌生人"令婴儿感觉更不自在,故不正确;C、D 在文中均未提及。

27. What does Dr. Benjamin Spock do?

[A]【解析】细节题。根据"Dr. Benjamin Spock 是一位著名的儿童疾病专家,而且也是多本婴儿书籍的作者"可知 A 正确。

【点睛】正确选项常常是原文的同义替换。B、D 利用原文的只言片语进行干扰,C 在文中并未提及。

28. What would be a good title for the passage?

[D]【解析】预读选项可知,这是一道主旨大意题。整篇文章主要是讲怎么看护婴儿的问题;尤其是文中的最后一句,不仅表达了专家的观点,而且也对全文的中心思想作了暗示。因此选 D。

【点睛】解答主旨大意题的关键是要对文章有一个宏观的理解,抓住主题词和文章脉络。主旨大意常体现于文章的开头、结尾处。

Passage Two

[29] If Mickey Mouse slips on a banana peel on TV, viewers laugh. But for ordinary people, falling is not amusing. If you fall off your bike, you can take days to heal. For old people, the result of a fall can be worse.

[29] Scientists at the University of Pittsburgh, US, wanted to know why some people are more likely to fall than others. They found that [30] balance involves more than planting your feet on the ground and standing tall. Your brain keeps your sense of balance with inputs from your eyes and inner ears and sensations from your feet and legs. If something goes wrong with any of these, you're likely to fall. People tend to fall more often as they grow older because their senses are less acute.

[31] State of mind is important too. When people know they're walking on a slippery surface, they shorten their pace and walk with more care. As a result, they fall less often.

"We actually make people slip and fall," researcher Mark Redfern said. People of different ages fall on purpose in his lab. Cameras record their falls and a computer analyzes the data. [29] Scientists then can train people who fall often how to be on the alert.

29. What is the main purpose of the research mentioned?

[C]【解析】选项以不定式 To 开头表示目的。本题询问的是文中提到的研究,其主要目的是什么。本文话题是 falling,开头就说"米老鼠摔跤会令观众开怀大笑。但普通人摔跟头并不好玩。"紧接着介绍了美国匹兹堡大学科学家的研究,目的自然是帮助人们避免摔倒。文章最后一句也重申了此目的。故 C 正确。

【点睛】主旨题要归纳,首尾句很重要。A 中的 sleep 是 slip 的近音干扰词,B 与实验无关,D 未提及。

30. According to the speaker, how does the brain keep one's sense of balance?

[A]【解析】通过选项可知,本题询问做某事的方式。A 中的大半部分字眼都能听到,其中的 limb 是对原文 your feet and legs 的概括。故选 A。

【点睛】B 中的 at the same time 属于无中生有,而 planting one's feet on the ground 在原文中是被部分否定的;C 在文中用来说明 state of mind,而不是本题的"如何保持平衡";D 在文中未提及。

31. What does the speaker mean by saying "state of mind is important"?

[C]【解析】C 是对原文的概括,而其他选项均与此话无关。此外,由于 state of mind is important 是本文的一个分话题,而本文的主要话题是 falling,因此也可大胆地推断 C 正确。其他选项均与本文的主题不大相关。

【点睛】选项 A 中有 state of mind 字眼,听到 state of mind is important 时,应该注意后文的解释,所以观察选项有助于捕捉信息。

Passage Three

Do you know what is the most wanted high-tech gift for teenagers in the US? It is the iPod. The small cigarette-box-shaped player provides hours of music, videos and audio books.

When the Apple Computer Company introduced the iPod on October 23, four years ago, users found it was very different from just a simple MP3 player. [32] As the brand grew, more and more new features were introduced. The iPod, as well as playing music and videos, can also store your address book, keep your appointments, hold text notes, and display your photo albums. It is big enough for you to take a whole library of music in your pocket.

[33] Its color screen is bigger than the screens on many hand-held televisions and most cell phones that show videos. When you travel on trains, planes, buses and wait in waiting rooms, the iPod seems to be a good companion.

Working with television stations and companies, the Apple Computer Company provides TV programs for iPod users. [34] You can download the newest TV shows from ABC and the Disney Channel, for only US$1.99 each.

[35] It seems the iPod is the perfect [32] digital friend for every teenager except for its price. Each costs up to US$399, which is enough to [35] make parents think twice about buying this gift for their children.

32. What is the main topic of this passage?

[B]【解析】预读选项猜测,这可能是一道主旨题。文章主要介绍的是 iPod,使用了大量篇幅来说明它的功能,结尾处提到 digital 一词,因此应该是 B 最具概括性。

【点睛】主旨题答案的特征是概括性。其他选项均为断章取义或原词胡乱拼凑。

33. Which of the following correctly describes the iPod?

[C]【解析】本题考查对细节的记忆。关键在于听到"它的彩屏比许多便携式电视及大多数能播放视频的手机的更大。"因此选 C。

【点睛】其他选项中的名词主体也都有提及,但 iPod 是用于播放 photo album 的,而不是看似 photo album,故 A 不对;B 说 iPod 是 program,也不对;文章开头说 iPod 是 small cigarette-box-shaped player,D 属于偷梁换柱。

34. What can users do with the iPod?

[D]【解析】D 中的 latest 是原文"你可以从 ABC 及迪斯尼频道下载最新的电视节目,每个节目只需 1.99 美元。"中 newest 的同义词,at a low price 是对原文中 for only US$1.99 each 的概括。

【点睛】A属于无中生有,B利用原词Disney进行干扰,C是对前一句话"苹果计算机公司与电视台、电视公司携手合作,为iPod用户提供电视节目。"的误解。

35. What makes it impossible for all kids to get their most wanted gift?

[A]【解析】文章最后两句只提到price, cost这样的信息,主要是用于说明iPod价格高昂。因此A正确。

【点睛】父母犹豫再三(parents think twice)是因为价格高,而不是不喜欢,故B错;C、D两项在文中均未提及。

Section C

36. 【答案】genius

【解析】根据预读可知此处需要一个名词,意思是父母期望孩子成为什么样的人。注意第一个/iː/音是e发出的,元音字母及组合要扎实地掌握。

37. 【答案】psychologists

【解析】此处需要复数名词,尽管p不发音,但不可漏写。h也不可漏写。

38. 【答案】aware

【解析】根据系动词及介词of,此处需要形容词。

39. 【答案】damage

【解析】cause damage to为固定搭配。

40. 【答案】unrealistic

【解析】根据语义,应该填贬义词。不要误填成两个词an realistic。根据语音知识,realistic前面也不应该是an。而且前一个句子中就出现了unrealistic这个词,故可参照着写下来。

41. 【答案】sensible

【解析】sensible是四级核心词汇,应该从语义、用法、拼写等方面全面掌握。

42. 【答案】especially

【解析】此词常考,不要漏写开头的e,且要双写l。

43. 【答案】supportive

【解析】根据前面的are可知此处需要形容词。遇到不熟悉的词,可根据发音结合熟词加前后缀拼写。

44. 【答案】and his parents help him a lot by taking him to concerts and arranging private piano and violin lessons for him

【听音关键】parents, take, concerts, arrange, lessons

【答案重构】and his parents help him a lot—they take him to concerts and arrange private piano and violin lessons for him

【画龙点睛】可以化长句为短句以降低错误率。标点符号要正确使用。

45. 【答案】However, he never makes Michael enter music competitions if he is unwilling

【听音关键】never, enter competition, unwilling

【答案重构】But he never forces Michael to enter music competitions if he doesn't want to

【画龙点睛】注意转折和否定。另外,此句中谓语如果用make,则宾补用不带to的不定式;而如果用force或ask,则需要加to。

46. 【答案】They want their son to be as successful as they are and so they enter him in every piano competition held

【听音关键】want, as successful as, enter, every competition

【答案重构】They want their son to be as successful as they are and so they make him enter every piano competition

【画龙点睛】注意比较结构和因果关系。根据上下文,两家父母的做法截然相反,因此听懂一种做法,另一种就明白了。

第二章

550分听力难点突破

　　这里介绍的是一些具有普遍意义的急中生智猜答案技巧,涉及的面很广,熟练掌握,必能有效地提高对话听力理解的答题能力。

第一节 短对话的4种猜答案技巧

解题技巧1:听到什么就不选什么

　　"听到什么就不选什么"是一个非常有风险的"技巧",可是,正如风险投资一样,风险越高,其回报率也就越大。如果所听的内容实在太难,你根本就没有听到具体在说什么,而只是听到了片言只语,那么,对于短对话题来说,你还有什么办法能起死回生? 这时能够救命的只有这条计策了。

　　严格来说,所有的听力理解、阅读理解等选择题,其基本点都在于选择与原文含义相同的选项。换言之,正确答案就是原文的同义替换。由此,对于听力题目来说,也应该是"听到什么就选什么",而不应该是"听到什么就不选什么"。那么,本"计策"又何以能够成立? 其依据是什么? 理解了这一点,我们才不会机械地套用它,以免铸成大错。

　　听力理解的短对话题型,只有一个话轮,然后就这个话轮提问,因而相对来说难度不大。为此,命题者必然就要在选项上做文章。他们能够做的,就是用对话中的原词、原句来做干扰项,而实际上,这些选项的含义却与原文相距甚远。因为这样的选项与原文具有"貌合神离"的色彩,因而被认定是具有难度的干扰项。如果随便从《大话西游》、《天龙八部》中抽几句话就充当干扰项,那样的选项显然不会具有干扰性,也就失去了作为干扰项的意义。所以,出题的人可以沾沾自喜地用原文中的词汇加以组合,编凑成与原文实际上并不相符的选项,希望没有听懂原文、只是听懂原文个别词句的考生上当受骗。

　　然而,道高一尺,魔高一丈,这种伎俩是早已经被火眼金睛的广大考生识破了的! 人们总结出这么一条计策,来专门对付相关的出题策略。听到什么就不选什么! 这尤其适用于一切比较简单一点的短对话和长对话题目中!

【例1】A) She has to study for the exam.　　　　B) She is particularly interested in plays.
　　　　C) She's eager to watch the new play.　　　D) She can lend her notes to the man.

【录音】**M:** If you aren't doing anything particular, shall we see the new play at the Grand Theater tonight?

　　　　W: Sounds great, but I've got to go over my notes for tomorrow's midterm.

　　　　Q: What does the woman imply?　　　　　　　　　　　　　　　　　　[2005.1/T3]

【解析】如果从解题的正路来分析,本题属于"中but题",S2的话中,but后的内容是考查要点。如果听懂了 go over my

notes for tomorrow's midterm(为明天的期中考试复习笔记),那么这道题肯定要"听到什么就选什么"。可是,对于没有听明白原文意思的考生来说,就只能用"听到什么就不选什么"的绝技了。干扰项 B、C、D 都用 play,notes 来设置陷阱,当然难不到我们。[答案:A]

解题技巧2:答非所问,必有弦外之音

在对话中,如果 S1 说了一个一般疑问句,S2 应该怎样回答呢?我们想,S2 应该回答 Yes 或 No——最开始学英语的时候,老师就教过我们这一点了。然而,在听力对话中,我们经常听到的却是 yes/no 的变体。回答中不仅没有出现 yes 或 no,而且有时候还会用问句来回答问句!这时,出题人往往就会考查对 S2 的回答的理解。一般说来,如果 S2 对 S1 的一般疑问句不作直接回答,表示 S2 是一种强烈的否定态度,或者是一种带条件的肯定态度。正确答案即可由此选定。

【例2】A) The woman is watching an exciting film with the man.

B) The woman can't take a photo of the man.

C) The woman is running toward the lake.

D) The woman is filming the lake.

【录音】M: Look, the view is fantastic. Could you take a picture of me with the lake in the background?

W: I am afraid I just ran out of film.

Q: What do we learn from the conversation?   [2004.1/T2]

【解析】S1 说:"风景美极了,以湖为背景给我照张相好吗?"S2 没有回答 yes 或 no,只是啰唆了一通"恐怕我没有底片了"。其含义当然是说"No",但其效果就比单纯的"No"好得多:我不给你照相是因为客观原因,而不是我不想。这就免得对方生气了。这也正是"答非所问"的功能之一。另外,本题也可以用"听到什么就不选什么"的策略。听力原文中,film 指照相用的"胶卷、底片",而错误选项中的 film 都是指"电影"。正确选项 D 中的 take a photo 正是原文中 take a picture 的同义替换。[答案:B]

【例3】A) She can find the right person to help the man.

B) She can help the man out.

C) She's also in need of a textbook.

D) She picked up the book from the bus floor.

【录音】M: Can I borrow your math textbook? I lost mine on the bus.

W: You've asked the right person. I happen to have an extra copy.

Q: What does the woman mean?   [2004.6/T7]

【解析】①如果没有听懂,选最不像的选项。本题也适用"听到什么不选什么"的原则。②对于 S1 的一般疑问句"我可以借你的数学课本吗?",S2 的预期的回答应该是"可以"或者"不可以"。从选项的助动词来看,可以简单地排除 C、D(C、D 中没有可以回答 S1 的助动词 can)。如果在 A、B 中选择,显然可以凭"the right person"排除 A。S2 的回答是:"你算是问对人了,我恰好多了一本。"[答案:B]

对于"答非所问"题,我们给出了几种情形的例子,是想表明,不同形式的回答实际上说明了说话人的不同意图,它具有灵活性。

解题技巧3:S2 简短回答不简单

> **题型特征:**对于 S1 的问话或者声明,S2 的回答分为"简短回答+详细解说"两部分。简短回答部分是日常口语,很容易听懂;然而后面紧跟着的解说部分充满了种种艰深的词汇,很长、很费解。
>
> **理解要点:**①若详细解说前没有 but,则解说部分是对前面简短回答的补充与说明;②若详细解说前有 but,则属于"中but题",解说部分含义与简短回答部分相反。由此可以推出答案。

在这种题型中,S2 的简短回答部分是其整个回答的"先遣部队",对于理解对话、解答问题具有重要的价值。因此,尽管它相对容易听懂,但也必须予以高度重视,力求凭借它正确答题。

【例4】A) They will be replaced by on-line education sooner or later.

B) They will attract fewer kids as on-line education expands.

C) They will continue to exist along with on-line education.

D) They will limit their teaching to certain subjects only.

[录音]**M:** What do you think of the prospects for on-line education? Is it going to replace the traditional school?

    W: I doubt it. ****(听不懂)

    Q: What does the woman think of conventional school?   [2005.1/T4]

[解析]S2 的后半句话非常长 (Schools are here to stay, because they are much more than just book learning. Even though more and more kids are going online, I believe few of them will quit school altogether.),"很难"听懂。那么,根据听到的内容,可以选择答案吗? 分析听懂了的部分可知,S1 问:on-line education (通过读题,这个词组应该听懂了)会替代传统的学校教育吗? 预期中的回答应该是"会"或者"不会"。而 S2 回答:我对此表示怀疑。由此,可以不犹豫地排除选项 A。至于剩下的选项中,能回答"会不会替代"的,只有 C 表示二者将会共存。B、D 都与 S1 的问题无关。[答案:C]

上例表明,尽管 S2 的后半部分构成了"听力"障碍,可是运用本答题技巧,难题就能迎刃而解。

解题技巧 4:强烈语气题

什么叫"强烈语气"? 真是难以说清楚。如果正常情况下用正常的语法、句型可以表达某个意思,而实际又没有用这样的句型,而是用了特殊的语法结构、语音、语调表达特殊含义,其间必然附带产生特殊的语气,尤其是表示强烈情感特征的语气。

在短对话听力题目中,具有强烈语气的结构主要有:

> 带升调的肯定句,表示疑问,例如:And I do?
>
> 否定疑问句,表示感叹,例如:Isn't it fantastic?
>
> 一般疑问句,表示建议与不满,例如:Are you kidding?
>
> 虚拟条件句,表示遗憾或愿望。
>
> 简短的回答语,如:Really? Oh, no! Terrible!
>
> 用疑问语气重复 S1 话语中的核心词组,表示怀疑、不赞同或者对 S1 的进一步论述。
>
> 特殊的重读词汇,表示对比。
>
> 肯定形式的反问句,表示强烈的否定语气,而否定形式的反问句,表示强烈的肯定语气,例如:由"Why (not)+动词原形"构成的建议句。

对于包含这类强烈语气的对话题目,其考查的重点往往就是这些特殊话语结构的含义。如果能准确理解它们,这些题也就可以轻松解答。万一未能听懂相关话语,只是听出了这样的特殊语气,那么,该如何理解对话,从而解题呢? 基本原则是:这样的强烈语气,是针对前面 S1 的话而来的。它要么表示对 S1 的强烈的肯定与支持,要么表示对 S1 的强烈否定。因此,不是正面选答案,就是反面选答案。

【例 5】A) She thought there were no tickets left for the show.

    B) She thought the seats on the left side were fully occupied.

    C) The show was planned a long time ago.

    D) The audience were deeply impressed by the show.

[录音]**M:** I heard there are a few seats left for the show tonight.

    W: Really? I was under the impression that the tickets were sold out a long time ago.

    Q: What do we know from the woman's reply?   [2002.1/T5]

[解析]S2 的 really 表明了一种强烈不赞同的语气,对 S1 的话表示否定。题目问 S2 的话意,我们只要看哪个选项否定了 S1 的话,那就是正确答案。[答案:A]

第二节 长对话题的 3 种猜答案技巧

解题技巧 1:话题与场景的判断——第一句话中的核心词汇揭示答案

在长对话中,寒暄语过后的第一句话往往引出话题,很可能是对话的主题所在,也是回答主旨、话题以及场景题的依据所在。简而言之,即:**首句所包含的(核心)单词就是答案的依据**。正确的答案往往是:①该单词的重现;②该单词的同义替换;③由该单词所能得出的自然的推论。

【例1】A) A popular television program.　　B) A breakthrough in technology.

　　　C) A recent purchase.　　　　　　D) A new electronics store.

【录音】Hey! You've got a new television.

　　　Q: What is the main topic of the conversation?

【解析】通读选项可知,本题问的是"话题",可归于"主旨大意题"。读题时要把握各选项间的差异:四个选项的中心词分别是 programme, breakthrough, purchase 和 store。带着这些内容听对话,并要特别关注对话的第一个话轮。本对话的第一句说:"嘿,你买了一台新电视!"由此可以推断出正确答案。[答案:C]

【例2】A) From a special seminar.　　　　B) From her professor.

　　　C) From a magazine.　　　　　　D) From her Canadian friend.

【录音】Hey, Sam! You should take a look at this article about Canadian scorpion.

　　　Q: How did the woman learn about the scorpion?

【解析】长对话题中,经常出现的一种题目是,要求判断话题资料的来源。这种题目的答案通常包括:(专业、学术)杂志、报纸、电视、电台、课本(教材)、演讲等。本题若听到了第一句话中的 article,就可以迅速判定答案。[答案:C]

> 　　由上面这些题目可以看出,长对话的第一题很可能就会针对对话的第一句话提问,涉及整个对话的主题或者话题。换言之,只要听懂了第一句话(或者第一个话轮),长对话题的第一题基本上就有把握了。

解题技巧2:问答中的细节——听到什么选什么

　　长对话细节题具有与短文、短对话都不一样的特点。短对话也考查细节题,但是,选项与对话中的内容往往是同义替换的关系,而原词或与原词发音相近的词常常被用来充作干扰项,也就是说,一般不能"听到什么就选什么",反而要"听到什么就不选什么"。而在长对话中,其细节题出题原则稍有变化,正确选项一般都是对话中的原词(语汇)再现,很少有用同音、音近词作干扰项的情形。虽然从这一点来看,长对话与短文听力考试都是一样的,但是,长对话与短文相比又另有优势:在长对话中,对话双方往往是一问一答,而且考试题目常常与对话中的问题一致。只要在读题阶段能够准确地判断出问题,那么就很有可能在对话中听到预期中的问题,从而对即将到来的应答语也就是答案做选择性地听取。当然,并非长对话题中所有细节题都是一一与对话中的问题一样的;实际上,其细节考查大多数同短文一样,也是融于对话双方的话语之中的。

　　简而言之,**在长对话中,包含实际意义的问答内容(尤其是特殊疑问句)往往是细节题的考查要点。**答题的基本原则是听到什么选什么。

【例3】A) To read four books.　　　　　B) To read four chapters.

　　　C) To read ten chapters.　　　　　D) To read for forty minutes.

【录音】**M:** Do you know what the assignment is for tomorrow's psychology class?

　　　W: Yes. We have to read four chapters in the textbook.

　　　Q: What is the psychology assignment?

【解析】问题与对话中的问题完全一致。听到什么选什么。[答案:B]

【例4】1. A) It's rather expensive.　　　　B) It's too small for the man.

　　　　C) It has plenty of light.　　　　D) It doesn't have many closets.

　　　2. A) Each tenant is given a parking space.　B) It's difficult to find a parking place.

　　　　C) The tenant has to pay to park.　　D) The tenant can use any space in the parking area.

【录音】**M:** I was only interested in the two-bedroom. Can you tell me what it's like?

　　　W: Well it is quite spacious and has sun most of the day. It's really cheerful. It also has an eating kitchen and there's plenty of closet space...

　　　M: I see, and what about parking?

　　　W: That's no problem at all. Each tenant is assigned a particular space, and that space is theirs as long as they stay in the apartment.

　　　Q1: What does the woman say about the two-bedroom apartment?

　　　Q2: What does the woman say about parking?

【解析】问题与对话中的问题完全一致。没有出现音近干扰的选项,因此,尽管正确答案与原文的实际用词不完全一致,也属于"听到什么就选什么"。Q1 用 has plenty of light 代替原文中的 has sun most of the day;Q2 中,is assigned a particular space 被替换成 is given a parking space。[答案:C, A]

解题技巧 3:由结尾处的核心词锁定答案

在长对话的最后一题中,如果四个选项都是动词原形、动词不定式或者现在分词,往往涉及到对话者的建议、正在或将要采取的行动。一般来说,对话结尾处的建议句型是考查要点。对于这种建议题,**解题的关键在于抓住建议句型中的谓语动词,理解其含义。**该动词原形或者其同义替换词组就是正确答案。

对话结尾处当然并不都是在提建议,但是,结尾处的核心词有助于揭示对话场景,可以回答有关下一步行动以及对话主旨等题目。这样的词汇往往令人记忆深刻,是答案所在。换言之,做题时要相信第一感觉,若无确切把握,最好不轻易改动答案。

【例5】A) Return early the next day.　　　　　B) Photocopy the articles he needs.
　　　　C) Ask Professor Gills for a copy of the articles.　　D) Wait until the girl is finished with her article.

【录音】M: Oh, great!　And here I went out of my way to free out the whole afternoon to read.
　　　　W: I'm sorry, but there is not much I can do about it. All I can suggest is that you come in first thing tomorrow morning and try again. We open at eight.
　　　　Q: What does the woman suggest that the man do?

【解析】作为长对话最后一题,四个选项是极有可能把前文的有关信息包括进来的,所以,读这道题目,也许会觉得有些选项显得不可思议。但是,本题颇能说明问题:对话结尾处的建议,成为解题的关键。"明天一早就来"也就是"return early the next day"。注意,本题还揭示了另一个重要的答题技巧:凭借时间副词直接判断答案。由 tomorrow 与 the next day 构成最直接的判断答案的信号。[答案:A]

【例6】A) Make extra money while taking classes.
　　　　B) Work in the clothing store.
　　　　C) Visit the hotel.
　　　　D) Continue her job search for a while.

【录音】M: *(After learning that the woman has been offered a job to manage a clothing store, and also been offered to intern in a hotel)* Well, if I were you, I would take the internship anyway. You could always get a job during the school year next year to make a few extra bucks.
　　　　Q: What does the man suggest the woman do?

【解析】"我要是你,我就参加实习。下一个学年里你随时可以找个工作赚钱。"与此含义相同的选项是 A。注意这里的干扰项 C。男士的建议是让女士去酒店实习,而不仅仅是"拜访"一下。[答案:A]

第三节 短文题的2种猜答案技巧

短文听力理解题特别注重对细节的考查。所谓细节,从提问的角度来看,就是常说的几个特殊疑问词:what, when, why, who, how, where。在 2001 年 1 月至 2006 年 1 月期间,共有 7 次考过短文听力,其中出现 what 问句 52 次,why 问句 10 次,when 问句 4 次,who 问句、where 问句各 2 次。由此可以看出,"短文究竟说了什么"是这种试题的主要考查目的。前面我们谈到过读题预测问题、在听的过程中记录关键信息等应试策略,还分别讨论过短文听力的细节题、主旨题以及推断题的解答要点。这里,我们就短文听力理解的两个具有普遍意义的问题做进一步说明。

解题技巧 1:一头一尾,决定成败

如果说,短文听力只要听懂短文的开头与结尾就能得到较好的成绩,这一点也不令人意外。为了进一步说明短文听力理解题头尾句的作用,我们先看几个例子。

【例1】1. A) The art of saying thank you.
　　　　B) The secret of staying pretty.
　　　　C) The importance of good manners.
　　　　D) The difference between elegance and good manners.

2. A) They were nicer and gentler.

 B) They paid more attention to their appearance.

 C) They were willing to spend more money on clothes.

 D) They were more aware of changes in fashion.

3. A) By decorating our homes.　　　B) By being kind and generous.

 C) By wearing fashionable clothes.　　D) By putting on a little make-up.

【录音】Do you remember a time when people were a little nicer and gentler with each other? I certainly do. ... (中间的大段话都没有听懂) Good manners add to your image, while an angry face makes the best dressed person look ugly.

Q1: What is the passage mainly about?

Q2: What does the speaker say about people of the past?

Q3: According to the speaker, how can we best improve our image? [2004.1/Passage One]

【解析】Q1:四个选项都是名词性词组。这是一道主旨大意题。"听到什么选什么"。manners 在原文中反复出现,应该能够听到;如果没有幻听,应该不会听到 elegance 吧?[答案:C]

Q2:短文第一句话原词再现,听到什么选什么。[答案:A]

Q3:如果不是选择题,而是问答题,我们会毫不犹豫地回答说:Good manners。似乎没有用上"听到什么选什么"的技巧,不过,同义替换也没有什么可怕的。——记住,短文听力理解中,一般不会有同音干扰,所以不会有问题的。[答案:B]

做了上面这篇短文听力理解,读者也许会吓一跳:啊!短文的听力理解原来这么……(都不知该用什么语言表达了!)不是说很难吗?其实也不尽然啊!听懂两句话,就解决问题了!

> **短文听力魔力法宝**:短文开头与结尾的关键词揭示主题内容,是解题的重要依据。与"听到什么选什么"的原则相结合,这些核心词就成为正确答题的钥匙。

解题技巧2:语义突出之处,必是出题关键

在听力理解题目中,语义突出的方式颇多。

首先而且主要的语义突出方式就是通过语音现象来加强语气。这一点,稍加注意便可体会到:关键之处,往往前后停顿时间稍长;重要单词,往往读得响亮又清晰。

其次,为与这种语义突出作用相匹配,在词汇上也会有一些特点。比如:the only, the first, the perfect setting 等等。这些词的共同特点是,对所修饰的对象起着突出的作用。

第三,在语法上,语义突出的方式也令人侧目:because, but, however 都能带来新的信息;最高级形式的形容词,表示目的的不定式,都会获得句子重音。

第四,在篇章结构上,起承转合之处,排序列举之处,均为显"耳"之处,万万不可忽视。这些语义突出之处,必有题目考查。

【例2】1. A) Beauty.　　 B) Loyalty.　　 C) Luck.　　 D) Durability.

2. A) He wanted to follow the tradition of his country.

 B) He believed that it symbolized an everlasting marriage.

 C) It was thought a blood vessel in that finger led directly to the heart.

 D) It was supposed that the diamond on that finger would bring good luck.

3. A) The two people can learn about each other's likes and dislikes.

 B) The two people can have time to decide if they are a good match.

 C) The two people can have time to shop for their new home.

 D) The two people can earn enough money for their wedding.

【录音】The period of engagement is the time between the marriage proposal and the wedding ceremony... The diamond represented beauty; he placed it on the third finger of her left hand. He chose that finger because it was thought that the blood vessel in that finger went directly to the heart... Many people say the purpose of the engagement period is to permit enough time to plan the wedding. But the main purpose is to let enough time pass so the two people are sure that they want to marry each other...

Q1: What was the diamond ring said to represent?

Q2: Why did the Austrian man place the diamond ring on the third finger of the left hand of his would-be wife?

Q3: What is the chief advantage of having the engagement period?　　　　[2005.6/Passage Three]

【解析】Q1:听到什么选什么。只有思想开小差的人才听不到这个词。短文中的 beauty 必定重读,它后面有稍许停顿,显得异常响亮。[答案:A]

Q2:如果作为阅读理解题,问题中的 why 与短文中的 because 当然很显目。但是,在听力理解过程中,要听清楚转瞬即逝的 because,平时还是要多加练习。不错,它是一个很有用的信号词,告诉我们答案之所在,但是,如果耳朵不好使,好计策也会落空的! [答案:C]

Q3:本题的答案,短文中也有显著的标志 engagement period。训练耳朵敏锐捕捉"重点"信息的能力,何其重要!我们实在不必完全听懂全文,但绝对付不起听不到如此响亮的关键词的代价! [答案:B]

小结:本例所有题目,都完全符合"听到什么选什么"的战术原则。

第四节 历年典型真题突破训练

Unit One　　07 年 12 月

Section A

11. A) She used to be in poor health.
    C) She was somewhat overweight.
    B) She was popular among boys.
    D) She didn't do well at high school.

12. A) At the airport.
    C) In a booking office.
    B) In a restaurant.
    D) At the hotel reception.

13. A) Teaching her son by herself.
    C) Asking the teacher for extra help.
    B) Having confidence in her son.
    D) Telling her son not to worry.

14. A) Have a short break.
    C) Continue her work outdoors.
    B) Take two weeks off.
    D) Go on vacation with the man.

15. A) He is taking care of his twin brother.
    C) He is worried about Rod's health.
    B) He has been feeling ill all week.
    D) He has been in perfect condition.

16. A) She sold all her furniture before she moved house.
    B) She still keeps some old furniture in her new house.
    C) She plans to put all her old furniture in the basement.
    D) She bought a new set of furniture from Italy last month.

17. A) The woman wondered why the man didn't return the book.
    B) The woman doesn't seem to know what the book is about.
    C) The woman doesn't find the book useful any more.
    D) The woman forgot lending the book to the man.

18. A) Most of the man's friends are athletes.
    C) The man doesn't look like a sportsman.
    B) Few people share the woman's opinion.
    D) The woman doubts the man's athletic ability.

Questions 19 to 22 are based on the conversation you have just heard.

19. A) She has packed it in one of her bags.
    C) She has probably left it in a taxi.
    B) She is going to get it at the airport.
    D) She is afraid that she has lost it.

20. A) It ends in winter.
    C) It will last one week.
    B) It will cost her a lot.
    D) It depends on the weather.

21. A) The plane is taking off soon.
    B) The taxi is waiting for them.

C) There might be a traffic jam. D) There is a lot of stuff to pack.
22. A) At home. B) At the airport.
    C) In the man's car. D) By the side of a taxi.

Questions 23 to 25 are based on the conversation you have just heard.

23. A) She is thirsty for promotion. B) She wants a much higher salary.
    C) She is tired of her present work. D) She wants to save travel expenses.
24. A) Translator. B) Travel agent.
    C) Language instructor. D) Environmental engineer.
25. A) Lively personality and inquiring mind. B) Communication skills and team spirit.
    C) Devotion and work efficiency. D) Education and experience.

Section B

Passage One

Questions 26 to 29 are based on the passage you have just heard.

26. A) They care a lot about children. B) They need looking after in their old age.
    C) They want to enrich their life experience. D) They want children to keep them company.
27. A) They are usually adopted from distant places.
    B) Their birth information is usually kept secret.
    C) Their birth parents often try to conceal their birth information.
    D) Their adoptive parents don't want them to know their birth parents.
28. A) They generally hold bad feelings towards their birth parents.
    B) They do not want to hurt the feelings of their adoptive parents.
    C) They have mixed feelings about finding their natural parents.
    D) They are fully aware of the expenses involved in the search.
29. A) Early adoption makes for closer parent-child relationship.
    B) Most people prefer to adopt children from overseas.
    C) Understanding is the key to successful adoption.
    D) Adoption has much to do with love.

Passage Two

Questions 30 to 32 are based on the passage you have just heard.

30. A) He suffered from mental illness.
    B) He bought The Washington Post.
    C) He turned a failing newspaper into a success.
    D) He was once a reporter for a major newspaper.
31. A) She was the first woman to lead a big U.S. publishing company.
    B) She got her first job as a teacher at the University of Chicago.
    C) She committed suicide because of her mental disorder.
    D) She took over her father's position when he died.
32. A) People came to see the role of women in the business world.
    B) Katharine played a major part in reshaping Americans' mind.
    C) American media would be quite different without Katharine.
    D) Katharine had exerted an important influence on the world.

Passage Three

Questions 33 to 35 are based on the passage you have just heard.

33. A) It'll enable them to enjoy the best medical care.
    B) It'll allow them to receive free medical treatment.
    C) It'll protect them from possible financial crises.
    D) It'll prevent the doctors from overcharging them.

34. A) They can't immediately get back the money paid for their medical cost.
    B) They have to go through very complicated application procedures.
    C) They can only visit doctors who speak their native languages.
    D) They may not be able to receive timely medical treatment.

35. A) They don't have to pay for the medical services.
    B) They needn't pay the entire medical bill at once.
    C) They must send the receipts to the insurance company promptly.
    D) They have to pay a much higher price to get an insurance policy.

Section C

More and more of the world's population are living in towns or cities. The speed at which cities are growing in the less developed countries is (36) _____. Between 1920 and 1960 big cities in developed countries (37) _____ two and a half times in size, but in other parts of the world the growth was eight times their size.

The (38) _____ size of growth is bad enough, but there are now also very (39) _____ signs of trouble in the (40) _____ of percentages of people living in towns and percentages of people working in industry. During the nineteenth century cities grew as a result of the growth of industry. In Europe the (41) _____ of people living in cities was always smaller than that of the (42) _____ working in factories. Now, however, the (43) _____ is almost always true in the newly industrialised world: (44) _____.

Without a base of people working in industry, these cities cannot pay for their growth; (45) _____. There has been little opportunity to build water supplies or other facilities. (46) _____, a growth in the number of hopeless and despairing parents and starving children.

Unit Two   07 年 6 月

Section A

11. A) It was mainly meant for cancer patients.
    B) It might appeal more to viewers over 40.
    C) It was frequently interrupted by commercials.
    D) It could help people of all ages to avoid cancer.

12. A) The man admires the woman's talent in writing.
    B) The woman took a lot of pictures at the contest.
    C) The woman is a photographer.
    D) The man is fond of traveling.

13. A) The man placed the reading list on a desk.   B) The man regrets being absent-minded.
    C) The woman saved the man some trouble.   D) The woman emptied the waste paper basket.

14. A) He has left the army recently.   B) He quit teaching in June.
    C) He has taken over his brother's business.   D) He opened a restaurant near the school.

15. A) She read only part of the book.
    B) She is interested in reading novels.
    C) She seldom reads books from cover to cover.

D) She was eager to know what the book was about.

16. A) She called to say that her husband had been hospitalized.
    B) She was absent all week owing to sickness.
    C) She was seriously injured in a car accident.
    D) She had to be away from school to attend to her husband.

17. A) The man lives two blocks away from the Smiths.
    B) The woman is not sure if she is on the right street.
    C) The Smiths' new house is not far from their old one.
    D) The speakers want to rent the Smiths' old house.

18. A) The man couldn't find his car in the parking lot.
    B) The man had a hard time finding a parking space.
    C) The woman found they had got to the wrong spot.
    D) The woman was offended by the man's late arrival.

Questions 19 to 22 are based on the conversation you have just heard.

19. A) The hotel clerk couldn't find his reservation for that night.
    B) The hotel clerk tried to take advantage of his inexperience.
    C) The hotel clerk had put his reservation under another name.
    D) The hotel clerk insisted that he didn't make any reservation.

20. A) A grand wedding was being held in the hotel.   B) It was a busy season for holiday makers.
    C) The hotel was undergoing major repairs.   D) There was a conference going on in the city.

21. A) It was free of charge on weekends.   B) It was offered to frequent guests only.
    C) It had a 15% discount on weekdays.   D) It was 10% cheaper than in other hotels.

22. A) Demand compensation from the hotel.   B) Find a cheaper room in another hotel.
    C) Ask for an additional discount.   D) Complain to the hotel manager.

Questions 23 to 25 are based on the conversation you have just heard.

23. A) Secretary of Birmingham Medical School.
    B) Head of the Overseas Students Office.
    C) Assistant Director of the Admissions Office.
    D) An employee in the city council at Birmingham.

24. A) A small number are from the Far East.   B) A large majority are from Latin America.
    C) About fifteen percent are from Africa.   D) Nearly fifty percent are foreigners.

25. A) She will have more contact with students.   B) She will be more involved in policy-making.
    C) It will be less demanding than her present job.   D) It will bring her capability into fuller play.

Section B

Passage One

Questions 26 to 28 are based on the passage you have just heard.

26. A) Her parents immigrated to America.   B) Her parents set up an ice-cream store.
    C) Her parents left Chicago to work on a farm.   D) Her parents thrived in the urban environment.

27. A) He was born with a limp.   B) He taught English in Chicago.
    C) He worked to become an executive.   D) He was crippled in a car accident.

28. A) She was fascinated by American culture.   B) She was very generous in offering help.
    C) She was highly devoted to her family.   D) She was fond of living an isolated life.

Passage Two

Questions 29 to 32 are based on the passage you have just heard.

29. A) He was seriously injured.
    C) He developed a strange disease.
    B) He was wrongly diagnosed.
    D) He suffered a nervous breakdown.

30. A) He raced to the nursing home.
    C) He could tell red and blue apart.
    B) He was able to talk again.
    D) He could not recognize his wife.

31. A) Two and a half months.
    C) Fourteen hours.
    B) Twenty-nine days.
    D) Several minutes.

32. A) They released a video of his progress.
    B) They avoided appearing on television.
    C) They welcomed the publicity in the media.
    D) They declined to give details of his condition.

Passage Three

Questions 33 to 35 are based on the passage you have just heard.

33. A) For farmers to exchange their daily necessities.
    B) For people to share ideas and show farm products.
    C) For officials to educate the farming community.
    D) For farmers to celebrate their harvests.

34. A) By offering to do volunteer work at the fair.
    B) By bringing an animal rarely seen on nearby farms.
    C) By bringing a bag of grain in exchange for a ticket.
    D) By performing a special skill at the entrance.

35. A) They help to increase the state governments' revenue.
    B) They contribute to the modernization of American farms.
    C) They remind Americans of the importance of agriculture.
    D) They provide a stage for people to give performances.

Section C

Students' pressure sometimes comes from their parents. Most parents are well (36) _____, but some of them aren't very helpful with the problems their sons and daughters have in (37) _____ to college, and a few of them seem to go out of their way to add to their children's difficulties.

For one thing, parents are often not (38) _____ of the kinds of problems their children face. They don't realize that the (39) _____ is keener, that the required (40) _____ of work are higher, and that their children may not be prepared for the change. (41) _____ to seeing A's and B's on high school report cards, they may be upset when their children's first (42) _____ college grades are below that level. At their kindest, they may gently (43) _____ why John or Mary isn't doing better, whether he or she is trying as hard as he or she should, and so on. (44) _____.

Sometimes parents regard their children as extensions of themselves and (45) _____. In their involvement and identification with their children, they forget that everyone is different and that each person must develop in his or her own way. They forget that their children, (46) _____
_____.

第五节 答案解析

Unit One 07年12月

Section A

11. W: I ran into Sally the other day. I could hardly recognize her. Do you remember her from high school?

M: Yeah. She was a little <u>out of shape</u> back then. Well, <u>has she lost a lot of weight</u>?

Q: What does the man remember of Sally?

[C]【解析】男士说 Sally 当时体形有点不成样子,随后问"她是不是减肥了",说明她当时体重超重,即 C。

【点睛】①She 选项题,一般问对话中的女士,可本题问对话中谈到的 Sally,需区分。②选项关键词位于表语(或谓语)部分,poor health, popular, overweight 和(do)well 等修饰词提供依据。③听到 out of shape, a lot of weight,即可迅速解题。

12. W: We don't seem to have a reservation for you, sir. I'm sorry.

M: But my secretary said that <u>she had reserved a room for me here</u>. I phoned her from the airport this morning just before I got on board the plane.

Q: Where does the conversation most probably take place?

[D]【解析】根据 reserved a room here 可知对话发生在宾馆前台。

【点睛】①介词选项,要求判断对话发生的地点。②要根据对话关键词解题。

13. W: What would you do if you were in my place?

M: <u>If Paul were my son, I'd just not worry.</u> Now that his teacher is giving him extra help and he is working harder himself, <u>he's sure to do well in the next exam.</u>

Q: What's the man's suggestion to the woman?

[B]【解析】女士问男士有什么建议,男士说"不用担心",她儿子下次会考好的。即建议女士要对自己的儿子有信心,故选 B。

【点睛】①动词的现在分词选项,涉及 her son,应当问"女士如何做"。②C、D 分别利用单词 extra help, not worry 混淆视听。

14. M: You've had your hands full and have been overworked during the last two weeks. I think you really need to <u>go out and get some fresh air and sunshine.</u>

W: You are right. <u>That's just what I'm thinking about.</u>

Q: What is the woman most probably going to do?

[A]【解析】男士建议女士"出去呼吸一下新鲜空气,晒晒太阳",即 A"稍微休息一下"。

【点睛】①动词原形选项,多问建议、将来的打算,重点是听懂对话中的建议句型。②不可根据对话中的片言只语 two weeks, go out 选 B、C。

15. W: Hello, John. How are you feeling now? I hear you've been ill.

M: They must have confused me with my twin brother Rod. He's been sick all week, <u>but I've never felt better in my life.</u>

Q: What do we learn about the man?

[D]【解析】男士明确说:我一辈子从来没有感觉到比现在更好的。意即他身体状况很好,故 D 正确。

【点睛】①He 选项,ill, health, perfect condition 表明对话涉及健康状况,需关注有关男士的描述。②本题若问男士的孪生兄弟 Rod 的健康状况,则应选 B。③否定词 never 和比较级 better 连用,表达最高级含义,与选项 D 中的 perfect 一致。④but 之后的内容往往是考点。

16. M: Did you really give away <u>all your furniture</u> when you moved into the new house last month?

W: <u>Just</u> the useless pieces, as I'm planning to <u>purchase a new set from Italy for the sitting room only</u>.

Q: What does the woman mean?

[B]【解析】男士问女士是否把全部旧家具都扔了,女士用了 just,only 说明没有全部扔掉,因此答案为 B。

【点睛】①选项均提及 She 如何处理 furniture,听对话时可预期相应内容。②A、C 选项中的 all 具有绝对化的含义,一般不会是答案。B 含 some,极可能是正确答案。③D 具有一定的迷惑性,但时态不对。

17. M: I've brought back your <u>Oxford Companion to English Literature</u>. I thought you might use it for your paper. Sorry not to have returned it earlier.

W: <u>I was wondering where the book was.</u>

Q: What can we infer from the conversation?

[D]【解析】男士还女士书时,女士说"我还在纳闷书到哪里去了呢",说明她忘了曾把书借给男士,即 D。

【点睛】①以 The woman 开头的选项,都带否定含义,核心词是 book,相关词有 return, about, useful, lend,可猜测对话内容。②听懂女士的回答,不难做出正确推理。

18. W: To tell the truth, Tony, <u>it never occurred to me that you are an athlete</u>.

M: Oh, really? <u>Most people</u> who meet me, including some friends of mine, <u>don't think so either</u>.

Q: What do we learn from the conversation?

[C]【解析】女士及大多数认识男士的人都不觉得男士是运动员,说明 C 正确。

【点睛】①各选项主语均不一致,在听力题中比较少见,可以看做是"哪个选项正确"的问题。②关键词是 athletes, sportsman,另外涉及到 friends, few people。辨明这些词之间的关系,就能解题。③对话中的关键句型值得学习:it never occurred to me that...虽然是否定句,表达的却是肯定含义;not... either(也不)表示"观点相同",故 B、D 均错误。

Now you'll hear the two long conversations.

Conversation One

M: Mary, [22] <u>I hope you are packed and ready to leave.</u>

W: Yes, I'm packed, but not quite ready. [19] <u>I can't find my passport.</u>

M: Your passport? That's the one thing you mustn't leave behind.

W: I know. I haven't lost it. [19] <u>I've packed it, but I can't remember which bag it's in.</u>

M: Well, you'll have to find it at the airport. [21] <u>Come on, the taxi is waiting.</u>

W: [22] <u>Did you say taxi? I thought we were going in your car.</u>

M: Yes, well, I have planned to, but I'll explain later. You've got to be there in an hour.

W: The plane doesn't leave for two hours. Anyway, I'm ready to go now.

M: Now, you are taking just one case, is that right?

W: No, [22] <u>there is one in the hall as well.</u>

M: Gosh, what a lot of stuff! [20] <u>You are taking enough for a month instead of a week.</u>

W: Well, you can't depend on the weather. It might be cold.

M: It's never cold in Rome. Certainly not in May. Come on, we really must go.

W: Right, we are ready. We've got the bags. I'm sure there is no need to rush.

M: There is. [21] <u>I asked the taxi driver to wait two minutes, not twenty.</u>

W: Look, I'm supposed to be going away to relax. You are making me nervous.

M: Well, I want you to relax on holiday, but you can't relax yet.

W: OK. I promise not to relax, at least not until we get to the airport and I find my passport.

19. What does the woman say about her passport?

[A]【解析】对话开头,女士说找不到护照,并说"我拿了的,只是不记得放在哪一个袋子里了",故 A 正确。

【点睛】①选项均讨论 She 把 it 怎么样了。由动词 packed, get, left, lost 不难对各选项予以区别。②对话开头的 passport 由男士重复反问过，是信息重点，猜测即是选项中的 it。女士否认"遗失(lost)"，排除 D。③由原文中的 pack 即可选定答案。

20. What do we know about the woman's trip?

[C]【解析】根据男士的讽刺"你带的东西都够一个月而不是一周用了"，可见女士计划外出一周。

【点睛】①难点是判断选项主语 it 的含义，必须根据对话来理解。②选项关键词是 winter, cost a lot, one week, weather。录音提到 a week 和 weather，但说到 weather 时用的是否定句，故可排除 D，选 C。A、B 均未提及。

21. Why does the man urge the woman to hurry?

[B]【解析】男士两次提及 taxi 在等，故答案为 B。

【点睛】①由 plane, taxi, traffic jam 猜测，本题可能与交通有关。②离飞机起飞还有两个小时，时间充裕，A 不对；C 未提及；尽管东西多，但都已经打好包了，D 也不准确。B 是对话中重复出现的信息，是正确答案。③可以根据听到的提问方式确认答案。

22. Where does the conversation most probably take place?

[A]【解析】根据"离开"、"厅里(还有一个箱子)"、"你的车"等关键词可知二人准备离开家外出旅游。

【点睛】显然问"对话发生在何处"。根据对话中的关键词(信息)推理判断。

Conversation Two

W: Oh, [23] I'm fed up with my job.

M: Hey, there is a perfect job for you in the paper today. You might be interested.

W: Oh? What is it? What do they want?

M: Wait a minute. Eh, here it is. [24] The European Space Agency is recruiting translators.

W: The European Space Agency?

M: Well, that's what it says. They need an English translator to work from French or German.

W: So they need a degree in French or German, I suppose. Well, I've got that. What's more, I have plenty of experience. What else are they asking for?

M: Just that. A university degree and three or four years of experience as [24] a translator in a professional environment. They also say the person should have a lively and inquiring mind, effective communication skills and the ability to work individually or as a part of the team.

W: Well, if I stay at my present job much longer, I won't have any mind or skills left. By the way, what about salary? I just hope it isn't lower than what I get now.

M: It's said to be negotiable. [25] It depends on the applicant's education and experience. In addition to basic salary, there is a list of extra benefits. Have a look yourself.

W: Hmm, travel and social security plus relocation expenses are paid. Hey, this isn't bad. I really want the job.

23. Why is the woman trying to find a new job?

[C]【解析】对话第 1 句女士就说自己厌倦了自己的工作，故答案为 C。

【点睛】①选项涉及 She 对工作的态度、期望。②对话首尾处是出题重点。③答案中的 be tired of 是原文 be fed up with 的同义表达。

24. What position is being advertised in the paper?

[A]【解析】对话多次提到所招聘职位是"翻译"，故选 A。

【点睛】①表示职业、职务的名词选项，只需听到原文"对号入座"即可。②关键信息是考点，往往在对话中多次出现。

25. What are the key factors that determine the salary of the new position?

[D]【解析】对话中男士说，工资待遇"取决于求职者的教育背景和工作经历"，D 是原文再现，正确。

【点睛】①名词选项。不仅需理解各选项的含义,还需在录音中听到有关信息,并做相应记录。②A、B 的内容在对话中同时出现,作并列成分,故可同时排除。C 未提及。

Section B
Passage One

When couples get married, they usually plan to have children. Sometimes however, a couple cannot have a child of their own. In this case, they may decide to adopt a child. In fact, adoption is very common today. There are about 60,000 adoptions each year in the United States alone. Some people prefer to adopt infants. Others adopt older children. Some couples adopt children from their own countries. Others adopt children from foreign countries. In any case, they all adopt children for the same reason: [26] they care about children and want to give their adopted child a happy life. Most adopted children know that they are adopted. Psychologists and childcare experts generally think this is a good idea. However, many adopted children or adoptees have very little information about their biological parents. [27] As a matter of fact, it is often very difficult for adoptees to find out about their birth parents, because the birth records of most adoptees are usually sealed. The information is secret, so no one can see it. Naturally, adopted children have different feelings about their birth parents. Many adoptees want to search for them, but others do not. The decision to search for birth parents is a difficult one to make. [28] Most adoptees have mixed feelings about finding their biological parents. Even though adoptees do not know about their natural parents, [29] they do know that their adoptive parents want them, love them and will care for them.

26. According to the speaker, why do some couples adopt children?
[A]【解析】短文先介绍了种种收养孩子的行为,然后总结说:不管是什么样的情形,人们收养孩子都出于同一个理由:他们喜欢孩子。故 A 正确。

【点睛】①由选项中的 need, want 可知,本题问"他们"的目的、打算。内容上涉及 children, old age 和 life experience,可重点关注有关内容。②care about children 是原词再现。③说明理由的内容常是考点。

27. Why is it difficult for adoptees to find out about their birth parents?
[B]【解析】短文说到:大多数被收养者的出生记录往往不对外公开,相关资料是保密的,因此没有人能看到。B 与此相符。

【点睛】①四个选项主语均不相同,但都涉及"收养"关系;distant, secret, conceal 等都有"遮蔽信息"的含义。②考点内容由 because 引导出来,也是语义重心所在,应不难作答。

28. Why do many adoptees find it hard to make the decision to search for the birth parents?
[C]【解析】短文提到:被收养者很难做出要寻找生身父母的决定;大多数人对寻找自己的生身父母感情复杂。mixed feelings 是解题关键词。答案选 C。

【点睛】①A、B、C 中均提到 feelings,只是各自的修饰语不同;听到录音中相应的修饰语 mixed,即可作答。②不可仅凭常识自以为是地选 B。实际上,A 与短文内容不符,B、D 则未提及。

29. What can we infer from the passage?
[D]【解析】短文开头提到,人们收养孩子是因为他们喜欢(care about)孩子;最后又说,被收养者知道,其养父母需要他们,爱(love)他们,会照顾他们。因此,D 正确。

【点睛】①各选项均讨论"收养"关系,只是各有侧重。A、B 显然不符合文章内容;C 貌似正确,但短文没有讨论 understanding 的问题。②推理题要依据文章的主旨、多次重复的信息解答。

Passage Two

Katharine Graham graduated from the University of Chicago in 1938 and got a job as a news reporter in San Francisco. [30] Katharine's father used to be a successful investment banker. In 1933 he bought a failing newspaper—The Washington Post. Then Katharine returned to Washington and got a job, editing letters in her father's newspaper. She married Philip Graham who took over his father-in-law's position shortly after and became publisher of The Washington Post. But for many years her husband suffered from mental illness and he killed himself in 1963. After her husband's death, Katharine operated the newspaper. In the 1970s, the newspaper became famous around the world. And Katharine was also recognized as an important leader in newspaper publishing. [31] She was the first woman to head a major American publishing company—The Washington Post Company. In a few years, she successfully expanded the company to include newspaper, magazine, broadcast and cable companies. She died of head injuries after a fall when she was 84. More than 3,000 people attended her funeral including many government and business leaders. [32] Her friends said she would be remembered as a woman who had an important influence on events in the United States and the world. Katharine once wrote: "The world without newspapers would not be the same kind of world." After her death, the employees of The Washington Post wrote: [32] "The world without Katharine would not be the same at all."

30. What do we learn from the passage about Katha-rine's father?

[B]【解析】短文说,Katharine 的父亲于 1933 年买下了陷入困境的《华盛顿邮报》。故 B 正确。

【点睛】①选项主语是 He,要注意区分短文中听到的不同人物及其所作所为。有精神疾病的是 Katharine 的丈夫;做过记者的是 Katharine;邮报是 20 世纪 70 年代闻名天下的,当时由 Katharine 负责。②要根据问题选择答案。

31. What does the speaker tell us about Katharine Graham?

[A]【解析】原文提到:Katharine 是担任美国主要出版公司领导人的第一位女性。故 A 正确。

【点睛】①考点含 the first woman 这种强调性字眼,是文章的语义重心所在,应能听到、记住。②选项 A 用 lead a big... company 解释原文中的 to head a major... company,是典型的同义替换选项。③其他选项,要么文章未提及,要么人物和事件弄混。

32. What does the comment by employees of The Washington Post suggest?

[D]【解析】文章结尾的几句都是对 Katharine 的评价。"她将作为一个对美国以及全世界的事件产生过重要影响的女性为世人所怀念……没有 Katharine 的世界将是一个完全不同的世界。"这些表述含义相同,D 与此一致。

【点睛】①各选项均谈到 Katharine 的影响,分析各选项的区别,主要是影响的范围不一致。A 说 business world,C 说 media,范围都太窄。B 在短文中未提及。若能记住 world 一词,即可准确无误答题。②文章结尾句若是对前文的重复强调,是明白无误的语义重心,则往往是出题考点。

Passage Three

Obtaining [33] good health insurance is a real necessity while you are studying overseas. It protects you from minor and major medical expenses that can wipe out not only your savings but your dreams of an education abroad. There are often two different types of health insurance you can consider buying: international travel insurance and student insurance in the country where you will be going. An international travel insurance policy is usually purchased in your home country before you go abroad. It generally covers a wide variety of medical services and you are often given a list of doctors in the area where you will travel who may even speak your native language. [34] The drawback might be that you may not get your money back immediately. In other words, you may have to pay all your medical expenses and then later submit your receipts to the insurance company. On the other hand, [35] getting student health insurance in the country where you will study might allow you to only pay a certain percentage of the medical cost at the time of service and thus you don't have to have sufficient cash to pay the entire bill at once. Whatever you decide, obtaining some form of health insurance is something you should consider before you go overseas. You shouldn't wait until you are sick with major medical bills to pay off.

33. Why does the speaker advise overseas students to buy health insurance?

[C]【解析】短文开头说,好的健康保险可以使你免受大大小小的医疗费用的困扰;这些费用不仅会耗尽你的积蓄,而且还会让你的留学梦破灭。C 正确。

【点睛】①选项中的关键信息是"就医"(medical care/treatment)、"钱"(free, financial crises, overcharge)。可据此听取有关信息。②考点是第 2 句,它是对第 1 句(主题句)的解释说明。

34. What is the drawback of students' buying international travel insurance?

[A]【解析】短文提到,购买国际旅行保险的缺点是你不能马上拿回你支付的钱。A与此完全一致,是答案。

【点睛】①各选项要么是否定句,要么有only, very complicated 等修饰语,都具有负面含义,涉及返款、申请程序、就医限制等。②可一边听录音一边对相关选项作正误判断,不难推知,B、C、D均不正确。

35. What does the speaker say about students' getting health insurance in the country where they will study?

[B]【解析】短文说,在留学国购买健康保险可以在就医时只支付部分医疗费,而不必一下子支付所有费用。选项B与原文一致。

【点睛】①A、B是好处,C、D说局限("不得不……")。其中,A是全盘的否定,B是部分否定。注意这些细微差别,便于在听到相应信息时判断、辨别。②短文先概述两种健康险(对应第33题),然后分别介绍两种保险的特点(对应第34题和第35题),出题点和文章结构一一对应。

Section C

36. 【答案】alarming
    【解析】此处需要一个形容词作表语,说明城市增长的速度。alarming 意为"惊人的"。

37. 【答案】increased
    【解析】此处需要过去时态的谓语动词,increased 不要漏掉词尾 d。

38. 【答案】sheer
    【解析】此处需要一个形容词作定语,修饰 size。sheer 意为"绝对的,纯粹的",不要写成动词 shear"修剪,剪切"。

39. 【答案】disturbing
    【解析】此处需要一个形容词作定语,修饰 signs。disturbing"烦扰的",注意 dis 和 ur 的拼写。

40. 【答案】comparison
    【解析】此处需要一个名词,其后有介词短语 of percentages... and percentages...,是两个百分数之间的对比。comparison 意为"比较,对照"。

41. 【答案】proportion
    【解析】此处需要一个名词,proportion 意为"比例"。

42. 【答案】workforce
    【解析】此处需要一个表示某类"人"的名词,作为定语 working in factories 的中心词,workforce 意为"劳动力,工人总数"。

43. 【答案】reverse
    【解析】此处需要一个名词,语义与前文形成转折,the reverse 意为"相反情况,对立面"。

44. 【答案】the percentage of people living in cities is much higher than the percentage working in industry
    【听音关键】percentage, living in cities, higher, industry
    【答案重构】there are much more people living in cities than those working in industry

【画龙点睛】只要抓住比较句型,听写时可利用第 40 题所在句子中的 percentages of people living in towns and percentages of people working in industry 进行修改,不必盲目地听记。考试中利用上下文听写起来更简单,所以本题不建议改写。

45. 【答案】there is not enough money to build adequate houses for the people that live there, let alone the new arrivals
    【听音关键】not enough money, adequate houses, people that live there, new arrivals
    【答案重构】there isn't money to build enough houses for the people living there, let alone the new arrivals

【画龙点睛】将难词用同义词代替,将从句用分词代替。

46. 【答案】So, the figures for the growth of towns and cities represent proportional growth of unemployment and underemployment
    【听音关键】figures, growth of towns and cities, represent, proportional growth of unemployment and underemployment
    【答案重构】So, the growth of towns and cities stands for proportional growth of unemployment and underemployment

【画龙点睛】根据尾句的后半部分，可以判断它是最后一个要听写的句子尾部的同位语，因此听写句子中的中心词应该是 growth。

Unit Two　　07年6月

Section A

11. W: Did you watch the 7 o'clock program on Channel 2 yesterday evening? I was about to watch it when someone came to see me.

M: Yeah! It reported some major breakthrough in cancer research. People over 40 would find the program worth watching.

Q: What do we learn from the conversation about the TV program?

[B]【解析】男士说，"40 岁以上的人会觉得这个节目值得看"，故选 B。选项 B"这个节目对 40 岁以上的观众更具有吸引力"是对原文的同义改写，该选项中的 appeal to sb. 意为"对某人有吸引力"。

【点睛】①选项都以 it 作主语。由 viewers, commercials 等关键词推断,it 是个电视节目。A, B, D 中的关键词 patients, viewers, people 指人,可推测,本题问 it 对哪种人有益或受什么人欢迎？②选项中出现数字时,该数字必然是关键词,注意在录音中辨别,并可用作选择答案的依据。

12. W: I won the first prize in the National Writing Contest and I got this camera as an award.

M: It's a good camera! You can take it when you travel. I had no idea you were a marvelous writer.

Q: What do we learn from the conversation?

[A]【解析】男士说"我不知道原来你是这么棒的作家"，由此可以推断出答案选 A"男士钦佩女士的写作才华"。

【点睛】①B, C 都以 the woman 开头,说女士爱好摄影,几乎是同义选项,一般都是干扰项。②A, D 都说男士的心理(关键词 admire, fond),并涉及到 writing, traveling,应注意听录音内容。应不难听到男士说的 when you travel,可排除 D。

13. M: I wish I hadn't thrown away that reading list!

W: I thought you might regret it. That's why I picked it up from the waste paper basket and left it on the desk.

Q: What do we learn from the conversation?

[C]【解析】男士说:"我真希望没有扔掉那张阅读书单。"女士回答说:"我估计你会后悔的,所以就把它从废纸篓里捡出来,放在书桌上了。"故 C"女士给男士省去了许多麻烦"正确。

【点睛】①A, B 以 the man 为主语,C, D 以 the woman 为主语,本题应该就整个对话的理解出题,问对话中两人各自做了些什么事情。②选项关键词有 reading list, regrets, save trouble, waste paper basket 等,这些词可能在对话中出现。本题符合短对话听力"听到什么就不选什么"的解题原则。

14. W: Are you still teaching at the junior high school?

M: Not since June. My brother and I opened a restaurant as soon as he got out of the army.

Q: What do we learn about the man from the conversation?

[B]【解析】女士问:"你还在教初中吗？"男士说:"6 月以来就没有了……"可见 B 正确。

【点睛】①都是以 he 开头的句子选项,本题必然问男士如何。②关键词有 left army, quit teaching, take over business, open a restaurant,相关内容很可能在对话中提及(听到什么不能随意选什么！)。③可以根据时间副词答题,容易听清 June 这样的明显的时间状语。A 中的 recently 是由原文 as soon as 中的 soon 转化而来的干扰项。④短对话中第二个说话人的简短回答部分极其重要！

15. M: Hi, Susan! Have you finished reading the book Professor Johnson recommended?

W: Oh, I haven't read it through the way I'd read a novel. I just read a few chapters which interested me.

Q: What does the woman mean?

[A]【解析】女士说:"我只读了我感兴趣的几章。"故 A 正确。

【点睛】①she 选项,关键信息是"读书",故本题问女士如何读书。②A, D 说的是 the book, B, C 说的是泛指的

books/novels。A，C 意义相近，都有否定含义，B，D 中的 interested，eager 表示肯定含义。③对话结构：男士提出一个简单疑问句；女士没有用 yes 或 no 回答，其回答分两部分，前半段语法结构复杂，难以听懂，后半段是补充说明，容易听懂。解答技巧：首先，正确选项往往表示对男士问题的否定回答或带条件的肯定回答；其次，女士答语中容易听懂的补充说明部分即可充分解题。

16. M: Jane missed class again, didn't she? I wonder why?

   W: Well, I knew she had been absent all week. So I called her this morning to see if she was sick. <u>It turned out that her husband was badly injured in a car accident.</u>

   Q: What does the woman say about Jane?

[D]【解析】双方讨论 Jane 为什么缺课，女士说："她丈夫在车祸中受了重伤。"与此相符的是 D。

【点睛】①she 选项，一般可能就对话中的女士一方提问，但由选项知，选项中的 she 已经缺课一个星期，应该指对话中提到的某个人。②内容上，hospitalized, sickness, injured, attend to 都表明有人受伤住院，只不过，A，D 说的是 her husband 住院，B，C 说的是她自己。此外，B，D 还表明"她"缺了课。③不难根据对选项的分析听到短文的有关内容，从而准确答题。注意排除 A：打电话的不是 she(Jane)，而是对话中的女士。

17. W: I'm sure the Smiths' new house is somewhere on the street, but I don't know exactly where it is.

   M: But <u>I'm told it's two blocks from their old home.</u>

   Q: What do we learn from the conversation?

[C]【解析】男士说："可是他们跟我说，他们的新家距离旧房子才两个街区。"故 C 正确。

【点睛】①选项的主语各不相同，应该是就对话整体的理解提问。②内容上，选项提到 Smith 夫妇的新居、旧家，提到 two blocks away 和 not far，还提到 right street, rent，听录音时，注意听辨相关信息。③经典的"but"题。不可选 A！

18. W: I've been waiting here almost half an hour! How come it took you so long?

   M: Sorry, honey! <u>I had to drive two blocks before I spotted a place to park the car.</u>

   Q: What do we learn from the conversation?

[B]【解析】男士说他开车转了两个街区才找到一个停车的地方，B 与此相符。

【点睛】①A，B 说男士，find 动作的宾语不同（car 和 parking space）；C，D 说女士，关键信息是 wrong spot，offended。预计对话内容涉及"停车"、"迟到"，与对话内容一致的选项就是答案。②find a parking space 是 spot a place to park the car 的同义表达。③A 具有迷惑性，offend 语义太重，C 利用 spot 做干扰（spot n. 地点 v. 看见）。

Now you'll hear the two long conversations.
Conversation One
M: Hello, [19] <u>I have a reservation for tonight.</u>

W: Your name, please.

M: Nelson, Charles Nelson.

W: OK, Mr. Nelson. That's a room for five and...

M: Excuse me, you mean a room for five pounds? I didn't know the special was so good.

W: No, no, no—according to our records, a room for 5 guests was booked under your name.

M: No, no—hold on. You must have two guests under the name.

W: OK, [19] <u>let me check this again.</u> Oh, here we are.

M: Yeah?

W: [19] <u>Charles Nelson, a room for one for the 19th...</u>

M: Wait, wait. [19] <u>It was for tonight, not tomorrow night.</u>

W: Em..., em..., I don't think we have any rooms for tonight. [20] <u>There's a conference going on in town</u> and—er, let's see... yeah, no rooms.

M: Oh, come on! You must have something, anything!

W: Well, let—let me check my computer here... Ah!

M: What?

W: There has been a cancellation for this evening. A honeymoon suite is now available.

M: Great, I'll take it.

W: But, I'll have to charge you 150 pounds for the night.

M: What? I should get a discount for the inconvenience!

W: Well, the best I can give you is a 10% discount plus a ticket for a free continental breakfast.

M: Hey, isn't the breakfast free anyway?

W: Well, [21] only on weekends.

M: [22] I want to talk to the manager.

W: Wait, wait, wait... Mr. Nelson, I think I can give you an additional 15% discount...

19. What is the man's problem?

[A]【解析】对话一开头男士就提到了 reservation,但女士多次提供的所谓相关信息都是错的,事实上就是她找不到男士预订的当晚房间。所以答案选A。

【点睛】①本题都是以 hotel clerk 开头的选项,宾语部分含有 his/he 等指示代词,A、C、D 都说 his reservation 出现意外状况。由此推断:本对话发生在酒店职员(女性)和客户(男性)之间;本题大概是问"男士的 reservation 究竟怎么了"。②由对话前半部分可以轻松判断 A 正确。③B 具有一定的迷惑性,但其中的 his inexperience 没有依据。

20. Why did the hotel clerk say they didn't have any rooms for that night?

[D]【解析】对话中女士说:"我想我们今天晚上没有房间了。城里正在开一个大会……"故 D 正确。

【点睛】①四个陈述句选项,似乎各不相关,实际上都会影响到 hotel 的经营。不妨猜测,本题问:什么因素影响着这家酒店的经营? ③听到什么选什么。

21. What did the clerk say about breakfast in the hotel?

[A]【解析】女士说早餐只在周末免费,A 与之一致。

【点睛】①选项都涉及 it 的免费、打折,考虑到对话与入住酒店有关,it 应该是酒店提供的一种服务。②根据选项中出现的 free, weekend, 15%, 10%, weekdays 等关键词,留意对话中提到的酒店服务内容,不难获得相应信息。

22. What did the man imply he would do at the end of the conversation?

[D]【解析】对话结尾处男士说:"我要见你们的经理。"也就是说,他要向酒店经理投诉,故 D 正确。

【点睛】①原形动词选项,一般问对话中的一方将要采取什么行动或提出什么建议。②内容上,它们都表示某种要求或威胁。听录音时要重点理解男士的意图。③对话结尾处经常出题。

Conversation Two

M: [23] Sarah, you work in the admissions office, don't you?

W: [23] Yes, I, mmm, I've been here ten years as an assistant director.

M: Really? What does that involve?

W: Well, I'm in charge of all the admissions of postgraduate students in the university.

M: Only postgraduates?

W: Yes, postgraduates only. I have nothing at all to do with undergraduates.

M: Do you find that you get a particular sort of... different national groups? I mean, do you get larger numbers from Latin America or...?

W: Yes. Well, [24] of all the students enrolled last year, nearly half were from overseas. They were from African countries, the Far East, the Middle East, and Latin America.

M: Em. But have you been doing just that for the last 10 years, or, have you done other things?

W: Well, I've been doing the same job. Er, before that, I was secretary of the Medical School at Birmingham, and further back, I worked in the local government.

M: Oh, I see.

W: So I've done different types of things.

M: Yes, indeed. How do you imagine your job might develop in the future? Can you imagine shifting into a different kind of responsibility or doing something...?

W: Oh, yeah, from October 1, I'll be doing an entirely different job. There's going to be more committee work. I mean, [25] more policy work, and less dealing with students, unfortunately—I'll miss my contact with students.

23. What is the woman's present position?

[C]【解析】对话一开始就提到,女士是招生办的副主任,故 C 正确。

> 【点睛】①名词选项题,可以判断,本题问某个人的身份。专有名词容易区分。②长对话首尾处常常出题。

24. What do we learn about the postgraduates enrolled last year in the woman's university?

[D]【解析】对话中女士提到:"去年招收的所有学生中,近乎一半来自海外。"故 D 正确。

> 【点睛】①每个选项都可以分成两部分:数量(具体的百分比或者大略的数量)、地区。本题肯定问有多少人来自什么地方。②听清楚对话中涉及到的任何一部分都可以正确作答。D 中的 foreigners 是原文 from overseas 的同义表达。

25. What will the woman's new job be like?

[B]【解析】对话结尾处(常考点!)女士说,10 月 1 日开始她就要做完全不同的工作,会有更多政策性工作,而学生工作会减少。B 与此相符。

> 【点睛】①A, B 选项以 she 开头,说"她"将要"更多地"(more)做什么工作;C, D 以 it 开头,说"它"将更容易做,或将更充分发挥她的才能。由 C 的比较句来看,it 应该也是指 job,甚至是 future job(与 present job 相对,用将来时态)。可见,本题问女士将要从事的工作的内容、情况。②听到什么选什么。

Section B

Passage One

My mother was born in a small town in northern Italy. [26] She was three when her parents immigrated to America in 1926. They lived in Chicago when my grandfather worked making ice cream. Mama thrived in the urban environment. At 16, she graduated first in her high school class, went onto secretarial school, and finally worked as an executive secretary for a railroad company. She was beautiful too. When a local photographer used her pictures in his monthly window display, she felt pleased. Her favorite portrait showed her sitting by Lake Michigan, her hair went blown, her gaze reaching toward the horizon. My parents were married in 1944. Dad was a quiet and intelligent man. He was 17 when he left Italy. Soon after, [27] a hit-and-run accident left him with a permanent limp. Dad worked hard selling candy to Chicago office workers on their break. He had little formal schooling. His English was self-taught. Yet he eventually built a small successful wholesale candy business. Dad was generous and handsome. Mama was devoted to him. After she married, [28] my mother quit her job and gave herself to her family. In 1950, with three small children, dad moved the family to a farm 40 miles from Chicago. He worked the land and commuted to the city to run his business. Mama said good-bye to her parents and friends, and traded her busy city neighborhood for a more isolated life. But she never complained.

26. What does the speaker tell us about his mother's early childhood?

[A]【解析】文章开头就提到了母亲的童年时代,说"母亲出生在意大利,3 岁时就随其父母移民到了美国",所以答案选 A。

> 【点睛】①选项主语都是 her parents,关键词有 immigrated (to America), set up (a store), work (on a farm), thrived (in the urban environment)。内容各不相关。只能判断,本题问 her parents 做了什么事情?②短文第 2 句就出现了 her parents,听起来必定清晰可辨吧!答案是原文再现的选项,本题要错都难。③不妨体会一下其他选项(干扰项)中提到的关键词是如何在短文中一一出现的。

27. What do we learn about the speaker's father?

[D]【解析】文章中间部分提到,"一场肇事逃逸的交通事故使父亲瘸腿,留下永久残疾",可知正确答案为 D。

> 【点睛】①选项主语都是 he,关键词有 limp/crippled, taught English, become an executive,仅 A, D 语义上关联。本题问"他"的情况。②听录音时,要注意短文中提到的男性,并根据选项中的关键词(若短文提及的话)逐项判断。

28. What does the speaker say about his mother?

[C]【解析】文章结尾部分说母亲是如何为家庭做出牺牲的,提到"母亲结婚后辞去工作,把一生奉献给了家人",C 与此含义相同。

【点睛】①显然本题问"she"怎么样,选项讲她"迷恋美国文化"、"乐于助人"、"奉献给家庭"、"喜欢与世隔绝的生活",听录音时,可以根据相应信息——辨别、判断。②文章曾提到,母亲"thrived in the urban environment",结婚后随丈夫搬家到农场生活,毫无怨言(never complained),并不表示她就喜欢。故不可选 D。

Passage Two

During a 1995 roof collapse, [29] a firefighter named Donald Herbert was left brain damaged. For ten years, he was unable to speak. Then, [30] one Saturday morning, he did something that shocked his family and doctors. He started speaking. "I want to talk to my wife." Donald Herbert said out of the blue. Staff members of the nursing home where he had lived for more than seven years raced to get Linda Herbert on the telephone. "It was the first of many conversations the 44-year-old patient had with his family and friends during the 14-hour stretch", Herbert's uncle Simon Menka said. "How long have I been away?" Herbert asked. "We told him almost ten years," the uncle said, "he thought it was only three months." Herbert was fighting a house fire December 29, 1995, when the roof collapsed, burying him underneath. After going without air for several minutes, [31] Herbert was unconscious for two and a half months and has undergone therapy ever since. News accounts in the days and years after his injury described Herbert as blind and with little if any memory. A video shows him receiving physical therapy but apparently unable to communicate and with little awareness of his surroundings. [32] Menka declined to discuss his nephew's current condition or whether the apparent progress is continuing. "The family was seeking privacy while doctors evaluated Herbert," he said. As word of Herbert's progress spread, visitors streamed into the nursing home. "He's resting comfortably," the uncle told them.

29. What happened to Herbert ten years ago?

[A]【解析】文章刚开头就提到了 Herbert 十年前的遭遇"屋顶倒塌,身为消防员他大脑损伤,丧失了语言能力",所以答案选 A。

【点睛】①seriously injured, wrongly diagnosed, strange disease, nervous breakdown 这些关键词都描述身体上的不良状况,故本题问"he"遭受了什么不幸? ②seriously injured 是对 brain damaged 的概述性表达。

30. What surprised Donald Herbert's family and doctors one Saturday?

[B]【解析】文章说到,一个周六的早上,他做了一件令其家人和医生震惊的事情:他开口说话了。所以答案选 B。

【点睛】选项都描述 he(能够)做什么事情。选项谓语部分的动词都是关键词,只要听到与这些关键词意义一致的内容,即可断定答案。

31. How long did Herbert remain unconscious?

[A]【解析】短文提到,Herbert 昏迷了两个半月,此后一直接受治疗。故 A 正确。

【点睛】①由选项可知,这是表示时间的数字题,短文中与选项一致的时间数字都需要做笔记,以便根据问题做出选择。②文章提到的相关数字:连续 14 小时与亲友交谈;29日发生火灾;缺氧几分钟;昏迷两个半月。

32. How did Herbert's family react to the public attention?

[D]【解析】文章结尾部分提到"Herbert 的叔叔拒绝谈论他侄子目前的状况",因此答案选 D。

【点睛】①选项都以 they 作主语,本题问"they"做了什么。②A,D 的宾语涉及到"他"的情况,与短文主旨相关,而 B,C 仅说 they 的情况,因此,答案很可能在 A,D 之中。③短文结尾处常出题。

Passage Three

Almost all states in America have a state fair. They last for one, two or three weeks. The Indiana State Fair is one of the largest and oldest state fairs in the United States. It is held every summer. It started in 1852. [33] Its goals were to educate, share ideas, and present Indiana's best products. The cost of a single ticket to enter the fair was 20 cents. During the early 1930's, officials of the fair ruled that the people could attend by paying with something other than money. For example, [34] farmers brought a bag of grain in exchange for a ticket. With the passage of time, the fair has grown and changed a lot, but it is still one of Indiana's most celebrated events. People from all over Indiana and from many other states attend the fair. They can do many things at the fair. They can watch the judging of the price: cows, pigs, and other animals; they can see sheep getting their wool cut, and they can learn how that wool is made into clothing; they can watch cows giving birth. In fact, people can learn about animals they would never see except at a fair. The fair provides a chance for the farming community to show its skills and farm products. For example, visitors might see the world's largest apple, or the tallest sunflower plant. Today, children and adults at the fair can play new computer games, or attend more traditional games of skill. They can watch performances put on by famous entertainers. [35] Experts say such fairs are important, because people need to remember that they're connected to the earth and its products, and they depend on animals for many things.

33. What were the main goals of the Indiana's state fair when it started?

[B]【解析】短文提到印第安纳州农贸市场(fair 即"集市")的目的时说,其目的是"教育、交流观点、展示印第安纳州最好的产品"。因此 B 正确。

【点睛】①选项都是 for... to do...结构,表示目的。For 的宾语以及不定式成分的内容是解题关键。②预测出问题与目的有关,则不会错过短文中的 Its goals were...,因而可以找准答案。③C 中的 educate 与原文一致,干扰性强。根据后文可以判断,该农贸市场是为农民而不是为官员服务的,由此排除C。

34. How did some farmers gain entrance to the fair in the early 1930's?

[C]【解析】短文明确提到,在 20 世纪 30 年代初,农贸市场的官员规定,人们可以用物而不是钱来买它的入场门票。短文举例说,农民可以用一袋谷子换门票。所以 C 正确。

【点睛】①表示方式的介词短语选项。②预测出问题(问方式)后,听到短文中的 could attend by paying...,就应该全神贯注,由此不难听到 for example 带出来的内容。举例说明的内容属于"语义重心",常常成为考点。

35. Why are state fairs important events in America?

[C]【解析】文章结尾最后一句话说:"农贸市场很重要,因为人们需要记住,他们与地球以及地球上出产的物品密切相关,他们依靠动物来获取很多东西。"选项 C 是对这句话的高度概括,即农贸市场使美国人民意识到农业的重要性,所以是正确答案。

【点睛】①选项主语都是 they,动词 help, contribute, remind, provide 都有"起……作用"的含义,推测本题问"they"的作用。②区分各选项的关键词是宾语部分的中心名词,revenue (财政收入), modernization (of farms), importance of agriculture, stage (for performances)含义各不相同。当选项含义差异较大时,应该容易根据听到的信息做出正确判断。

Section C

36.【答案】meaning

【解析】①空格处作表语,有修饰语 well,应该是个形容词,或者动词的非谓语形式。②意义上,well 和空格的内容一起,应该与 but 后面的 helpful 一致。③meaning 作形容词,意为"怀有什么特定意图的"。

37.【答案】adjusting

【解析】①空格处充当介词 in 的宾语,而且与 to 连用后接了自己的宾语 college,应该是个动名词。②adjusting 意为"适应"。③注意拼写。不可漏写 d,要在词尾加 ing。

38.【答案】aware

【解析】①空格处是表语,后面可以接 of 短语。一般应该是形容词,或者动词的过去分词。②语义上,"父母不_____子女的问题",比较合理的内容应该是"了解",与下一句中的 realize 一致。③aware 的拼写较为简单。

39.【答案】competition

【解析】①三个 that 从句作 realize 的宾语,空格处是从句的主语,应该填名词(凡名词,均须注意单复数问题),第 39 题与第 40 题语义相关。②从句中的比较结构以及单词 change 表明对比;根据下一句中的 high school,考虑到本句中的 college,可以推断,此处是说大学与中学的不同之处。③根据录音,本题与下一题分别填 competition 和 standards。前者是单数,后者是复数。注意拼写,尤其是元音字母的写法。

40. 【答案】standards

【解析】见第 39 题解析。

41. 【答案】Accustomed

【解析】①空格处引导状语,应该是动词的非谓语形式,且后面接 to+动名词(由此可以缩小范围,如 devoted, used,等)。②内容上应该表示原因,与"父母发火"有关系。③accustomed to 意为"习惯于做某事"。注意要双写 c,句首字母大写,词尾有 ed。

42. 【答案】semester

【解析】①空格处是名词短语的修饰语,一般是形容词或名词(名词作定语时用单数形式的较多,有的用所有格)。②semester 一词较简单,注意元音字母的拼写。

43. 【答案】inquire

【解析】①空格处是谓语动词,在情态动词 may 后面,用原形。②该动词可以接宾语从句。③此处也可拼写成 enquire。

44. 【答案】At their worst, they may threaten to take their children out of college, or cut off funds

【听音关键】worst, threaten, take children out of college, cut off funds

【答案重构】At their worst, they may threaten to take their children out of college or not to give them money any longer

【画龙点睛】本句和上一句在结构和意思上形成对比,可以上一句作为参考。简单句的句型和用词都可以不必改变。

45. 【答案】think it only right and natural that they determine what their children do with their lives

【听音关键】right, natural, determine, do with their lives

【答案重构】regard/consider it right and natural for them to decide what their children do with their lives

【画龙点睛】注意 it 作形式宾语,真正的宾语由 that 引导。句中词汇可以用同义词替换,但是句子的基本结构不能出错。

46. 【答案】who are now young adults, must be the ones responsible for what they do and what they are

【听音关键】young adults, responsible

【答案重构】who are now young adults, should be (the ones who are) responsible for themselves

【画龙点睛】注意 responsible 的拼写;此外,复杂句式尽量简化。

第三章

610分听力突击训练

第一节 突击训练

Unit One

Section A

11. A) By car.   B) By bus.   C) By bike.   D) On foot.

12. A) Because they are alike.

    B) Because the man's briefcase has a lock.

    C) Because the man's briefcase is smaller.

    D) Because she doesn't have one.

13. A) She is worried about something.   B) She has a headache.

    C) She is suffering physically.   D) She wants to write something.

14. A) The best of Jazz.   B) Christmas carols.

    C) Rock music collection.   D) Classical albums.

15. A) 7:30.   B) 8:00.   C) 8:30.   D) 9:00.

16. A) He ran a red light.   B) He was speeding.

    C) He went through a stop sign.   D) He turned a corner too fast.

17. A) A bus station.   B) A highway.   C) An airport.   D) A railway station.

18. A) She spent a large sum of money on the coat.

    B) It was a birthday gift from her husband.

    C) She bought the coat on her husband's birthday.

    D) Her friend sent it to her at a party.

Questions 19 to 21 are based on the conversation you have just heard.

19. A) In a fabulous train.   B) In a wooden cottage.   C) In an American car.   D) In a big tent.

20. A) Steve was disappointed because he didn't catch any fish.

    B) The man found his camping trip disastrous and silly.

    C) The two speakers are enjoying their traveling by train.

    D) The woman was admiring the man's photos taken on his tour.

21. A) When fishing in the center of the lake.

    B) When canoeing on the lake.

C) When swimming in the lake.

D) When cutting trees on the edge of the lake.

Questions 22 to 25 are based on the conversation you have just heard.

22. A) Absurd.　　　　　　　B) Sad.　　　　　　C) Exciting.　　　　　D) Fantastic.

23. A) The father thinks that the special effects and the acting were terrific.

   D) The daughter doesn't like the ship's doctor.

   C) The conversation is taking place in the theatre.

   D) The movie they are talking about is a science fiction movie.

24. A) The captain.　　　　　　　　　　　B) The communications officer.

   C) The doctor.　　　　　　　　　　　　D) The frog people.

25. A) The photography.　　　　　　　　　B) The communications officer.

   C) The doctor.　　　　　　　　　　　　D) The plot.

Section B

Passage One

Questions 26 to 28 are based on the passage you have just heard.

26. A) Meat and rice.　　　　　　　　　　B) Bread and butter.

   C) Water and soup.　　　　　　　　　　D) Candy and ice cream.

27. A) When our work is over.　　　　　　B) At regular intervals each day.

   C) When we are in the best mood.　　　D) When we feel hungry.

28. A) If he swallows dry bread easily.　　B) If he eats a lot of dry bread.

   C) If he drinks milk or hot water.　　D) If he could hardly swallow dry bread.

Passage Two

Questions 29 to 31 are based on the passage you have just heard.

29. A) Because the world is becoming more and more noisy.

   B) Because they have learned that noise is also a kind of pollution.

   C) Because noise is an unwanted waste for human beings.

   D) Because people knew little about noise before.

30. A) We may forget what we have thought about.

   B) Our thoughts may be disturbed.

   C) Our mind might be harmed.

   D) We may have difficulty finding the right words.

31. A) Sometimes we have to shout loudly so that others can hear us.

   B) Noise pollution is the worst kind of pollution we suffer from.

   C) We can put noise under control if we take effective measures.

   D) Our environment is getting much better except for the pollution.

Passage Three

Questions 32 to 35 are based on the passage you have just heard.

32. A) Be very persuasive and believable.

   B) Maintain direct eye contact with listeners.

   C) "Sell" his or her ideas to an audience.

   D) Be exceptionally well-disposed.

33. A) Confidence.　　　　　　　　　　　B) Speaking interest.

   C) Audience's interest and esteem.　　D) Speaking chance.

34. A) Smile to each other.
    B) Feel annoyed and glare at each other.
    C) Try to make a conversation with each other.
    D) Feel indifferent to each other.

35. A) Get information what we want.
    B) Make a certain link with the listener.
    C) Make friends with others.
    D) Get others' comments on one's speaking.

Section C

Nowadays, dieting is a popular practice in many countries. However, of the nearly 50% American adults (36) _____ dieting, only less than 10% will be able to (37) _____ their weight loss for at least a year. (38) _____ in the Framingham Heart Study pointed out that losing and gaining weight again might be (39) _____ to your heart. Over a 14-year (40) _____, they analyzed the weight changes and health of 3,130 people. They found that those adults whose weight (41) _____ the most had about a 50% (42) _____ risk of developing heart disease than those whose weight (43) _____ more stable. (44) _____, but they think that people who diet frequently may prefer high-fat foods. (45) _____ _____. Dieters may lose pounds from their legs (46) _____ _____.

Unit Two

Section A

11. A) Do whatever the committee asks of him.
    B) Make decisions in agreement with the committee.
    C) Run the committee according to his own will.
    D) Elect the committee chairman himself.

12. A) Her back hurt during the meeting.
    B) She agreed that it was a good meeting.
    C) She will take back what she has said.
    D) His support would have helped this morning.

13. A) To make an arrangement for dealing with the problems.
    B) To help her solve the problem.
    C) To deal with the hardest problem.
    D) To deal with the most important problem.

14. A) He agrees with the woman about the watermelons.
    B) The watermelons aren't grown here.
    C) There aren't any watermelons today.
    D) He wants to know if the watermelons are really good.

15. A) Three women were killed.
    B) Only one child was badly injured.
    C) No one survived.
    D) No one was killed.

16. A) She doesn't intend to give him her notes.
    B) She thinks he should read the history books himself.
    C) The new teacher did not want anyone to take notes.
    D) She did not think anything important was discussed.

17. A) San Francisco has many unexplored areas.
    B) Lawrence would probably be a good person to ask.
    C) The campers should try to get a lot of information.
    D) Lawrence will help if he's there this summer.

18. A) Student and professor.
    B) Athlete and coach.

C) Patient and doctor.   D) Customer and salesperson.

Questions 19 to 21 are based on the conversation you have just heard.

19. A) She blushed when talking to a group of people.
    B) She couldn't help looking at a sign when she gave a presentation.
    C) She didn't know the answer to the professor's question.
    D) She felt embarrassed talking to the man.

20. A) She could forget about people, so she won't blush.
    B) She could know where to exit, which makes her feel safe.
    C) She could know how many people have left the room.
    D) She could get more confidence because the professor is standing there.

21. A) To give Sarah an exceptional example.
    B) To support his idea that women blush more than men.
    C) To introduce Brian to Sarah.
    D) To tell Sarah men also blush a lot.

Questions 22 to 25 are based on the conversation you have just heard.

22. A) He was watching a game on TV with some friends.
    B) He was seeing his wife off at the airport.
    C) He was having a barbeque with some friends.
    D) He was playing a game with some friends.

23. A) Henry's friends kicked it because they were very excited.
    B) Henry accidentally dropped it.
    C) One of Henry's friends bumped into it with his arm.
    D) One of Henry's friends was too excited to hold the vase.

24. A) It burned up in a fire.
    B) Hot water damaged the entire copy.
    C) Someone mistakenly threw it into the trash.
    D) It was soaked in blue ink.

25. A) Disappointed.   B) Furious.   C) Satisfied.   D) Unhelpful.

Section B

Passage One

Questions 26 to 28 are based on the passage you have just heard.

26. A) It is obviously a mental process.
    B) It is more of a physical process than a mental action.
    C) It is a process that involves one's entire body.
    D) It involves the muscles as well as the brain.

27. A) Because they are natural conductors of concerts.
    B) Because they want to show that they understand the music.
    C) Because only in this way can they enjoy it fully.
    D) Because they cannot grasp it if they don't perform it.

28. A) An Ear for Music.   B) Music Appreciation.
    C) Muscle Participation in Mental Acts.   D) A Definition of the Thinking Process.

Passage Two

Questions 29 to 32 are based on the passage you have just heard.

29. A) To tell campus personnel of the new library services.

B) To announce the new movies on campus this summer.

C) To notify university people of important schedule changes.

D) To remind the students to validate their identification cards.

30. A) Athletic and recreational.　　　　B) Food and transportation.

C) Bookstore and post office.　　　　D) Medical and audio-visual.

31. A) It has special summer hours only on weekends.

B) It has special summer hours both weekdays and weekends.

C) It has no special summer hours at all.

D) The information is not available.

32. A) To ride on intercampus buses.

B) To read announcements in the cafeteria.

C) To make use of the infirmary.

D) To check books out of the library.

Passage Three

Questions 33 to 35 are based on the passage you have just heard.

33. A) To make Chinese companies more competitive.

B) To improve the competitiveness of European companies in China.

C) To improve Sino-EU friendship.

D) To make Sino-EU joint ventures more competitive.

34. A) It will bring a lot of business experience to China.

B) It will greatly improve the financial situation of Chinese education.

C) New techniques in teaching will be introduced to China.

D) Chinese teachers will be trained and become better qualified in the program.

35. A) Chinese Central government.

B) The local government in Hubei Province.

C) Both the Central government and Hubei Province.

D) Both Hubei province and EU Commission.

Section C

　　Alfred Nobel, a Swedish chemist and the inventor, left more than 9 million dollars of his　(36) ＿＿＿＿　to found the Nobel prizes. Under his will, (37) ＿＿＿＿　in 1895, the income from this fund was to be (38) ＿＿＿＿　yearly in five equal parts as prizes to those who had most helped humankind. A prize was to be awarded in each of five fields: (39) ＿＿＿＿, chemistry, physiology (or medicine), literature, and peace. A prize in (40) ＿＿＿＿　was established in 1968. The Nobel Foundation is the　(41) ＿＿＿＿　owner and administrator of the prize funds, though it is not (42) ＿＿＿＿　in awarding the prizes. A prize may be omitted in any year. The peace prize has been omitted most (43) ＿＿＿＿.

　　Nominations of candidates are submitted to the prize-awarding institutions before February 1 of each year. (44) ＿＿＿＿ ＿＿＿＿＿＿＿＿＿＿＿＿＿＿＿＿＿＿＿＿＿＿＿＿. No person may apply directly. (45) ＿＿＿＿＿＿＿＿＿＿＿ ＿＿＿＿＿＿＿＿＿＿＿＿＿＿＿＿＿＿＿. Prizes have been refused at times—generally because of political pressure. (46) ＿＿＿＿＿＿＿＿＿＿＿＿＿＿＿＿＿＿＿＿＿＿＿＿＿.

Unit Three

Section A

11. A) Someone has taken away her luggage.
    B) Her flight is 50 minutes late.
    C) Her luggage has been delayed.
    D) She can't find the man she's been waiting for.

12. A) Because she doesn't feel cold outside.
    B) Because she finds no room to stand inside.
    C) Because she wants to smoke outside.
    D) Because she doesn't like the smell inside.

13. A) In a paint shop.   B) At an art museum.
    C) In a swimming pool.   D) At a restaurant.

14. A) She is washing her hair.   B) She is having her hair dyed.
    C) She is drying her hair.   D) She is having her hair cut.

15. A) Because all the brown shirts are too big.
    B) Because the size she wants is not available.
    C) Because she does not care for the style.
    D) Because all the shoes are sold out.

16. A) She disagrees with the man.   B) Jim will have a bright future.
    C) She is indifferent about Jim.   D) Jim never promises anything.

17. A) It is a total failure.
    B) It is so awful that she wants to hit him.
    C) It is a great success.
    D) She would appreciate it more if he hadn't been so nervous.

18. A) Hosting a program.   B) Designing a studio.
    C) Painting a picture.   D) Taking a photograph.

Questions 19 to 21 are based on the conversation you have just heard.

19. A) The matter is the owner's responsibility and she doesn't care about it.
    B) The man in 4B is the apartment owner's son and it's beyond her responsibility.
    C) She is afraid that the musician might get annoyed and move out.
    D) She cares more about other tenants' problems.

20. A) She cannot do anything because the landowners are enjoying their rights.
    B) She has discussed this with the landlords, but his request has fallen on deaf ears.
    C) She has livestock as well, so she sympathizes with the neighbor's situation.
    D) She thinks the tenant is very annoying and his request is unjustified.

21. A) The manager hasn't told the tenant anything about the noise.
    B) The military activity takes place every week.
    C) The manager has done nothing about the noise.
    D) Probably the activity will go on in the next two years.

Questions 22 to 25 are based on the conversation you have just heard.

22. A) How to get Jack out of the office.
    B) How to improve the situation in the office.
    C) How to move to another office.
    D) How to work in a noisy environment.

23. A) They want to get some help from Jack.

B) They want to talk to Jack about everything.

C) Jack is a very popular teacher.

D) Jack wants to show he's a good teacher.

24. A) Report this to the school administrator.

B) They talk to Jack about it together.

C) Forbid students to come to teachers' office at will.

D) Change the storage room into a meeting room.

25. A) His suggestion might work.   B) His suggestion is pointless.

C) She is disappointed by his suggestion.   D) She thinks Stan is joking.

Section B

Passage One

Questions 26 to 28 are based on the passage you have just heard.

26. A) Each worker is only concerned with his own work.

B) Different businesses produce different products.

C) Each worker plays a certain role in finishing a certain product.

D) The workers are very specialized experts in their field.

27. A) It will reduce the labor.

B) It will raise the productivity.

C) It's easy for the workers to become experts.

D) It will make the workers satisfied with their work.

28. A) Ironical.   B) Objective.   C) Enthusiastic.   D) Critical.

Passage Two

Questions 29 to 31 are based on the passage you have just heard.

29. A) By producing pressure waves going in the opposite direction.

B) By mixing high frequency sound waves with low frequency sound waves.

C) By making copies of the unwanted sound waves and letting them out a little later.

D) By mixing new sound waves with the noise and sending them out together.

30. A) Make a car quieter.   B) Make a car lighter.

C) Reduce the cost of a silencer.   D) Improve the performance of a silencer.

31. A) It increases the cost of car production.

B) Carmakers are not sure if it is necessary.

C) It is still being tried out by experts.

D) Most people still have doubts about its function.

Passage Three

Questions 32 to 35 are based on the passage you have just heard.

32. A) Men spend more nights in their friends' home than women.

B) Women are much more talkative than men.

C) Women enjoy more and better friendships than men.

D) Men have more difficulty remembering names than women.

33. A) A male friend.   B) A female friend.   C) Her parents.   D) Her husband.

34. A) Men tend to keep their innermost feelings to themselves.

B) Women are more serious than men about marriage.

C) Men often take sudden action to end their marriage.

D) Women depend on others in making decisions.

35. A) Happy and successful marriages.　　　B) Friendships of men and women.

C) Emotional problems in marriage.　　　D) Interactions between men and women.

Section C

Good manners and etiquette are not complicated. Anyone can (36) _____ courtesy and consideration for others—the (37) _____ of which good manners are made—without knowing the (38) _____ rules of etiquette. And no one is (39) _____ knowing these rules. They are learned (40) _____—at home, in school, at work, and in everyday (41) _____ with both friends and strangers. To (42) _____ their knowledge of good (43) _____, many people continue to read etiquette books as adults.

(44) _____. Good manners help win friends. Naturally,

(45) _____.

Good manners also help please members of the family, special friends, teachers, employers, and strangers like salespeople and law officers. (46) _____.

People who practice good manners and understand the rules of etiquette also make themselves happy. Knowing how to behave properly, in familiar as well as in strange situations, builds self-confidence. Meeting new people and visiting new places become pleasurable instead of frightening experiences.

第二节 答案解析

Unit One

Section A

11. W: If I were you I'd take the <u>bus</u> to work. <u>Driving</u> in that rush-hour traffic is <u>terrible</u>.

M: <u>But</u> by the time the bus gets to my stop, there aren't any seats left.

Q: How does the man prefer to go to work?

[A]【解析】四个选项都是交通方式。女士说交通高峰期自己开车太可怕,还是坐巴士好;而男士的话以 But 开头,男士说等巴士开到他所在的站点时,已经没有座位了。可见他更愿意自己开车,所以选 A。

【点睛】本题是 S2 以 But 开头的转折题。But 表明,S2 不同意 S1 的观点,通常把 S1 的意见否定掉就是答案。本题中,S1(即女士)宁愿坐巴士而不愿开车去上班,那么 S2(即男士)的观点则是否定女士的看法,也就是宁愿开车去上班。故 A 正确。选项 C、D 在录音中均未提及。

12. M: My briefcase is just like yours, isn't it?

W: Almost. Mine is smaller, <u>but it doesn't have a lock.</u> I think I'd rather have one like yours.

Q: Why would the woman rather have a briefcase like the one the man has?

[B]【解析】女士说,她的公文包没有锁,她宁愿要一个像男士那样的公文包。由此可知男士的公文包有一把锁。所以选 B。

【点睛】本题属于 S2 中间带 but 的转折题,but 后面是答案。注意比较对象的异同点。女士宁愿要像男士那样的公文包,说明两个包肯定有区别,故排除 A;对话中女士提到自己的公文包更小,C 与其意思相反,而且这也不是重点所在;D 中的 one 指代的是 one briefcase,D 与对话内容不符。

13. W: <u>Could you give me something for the pain?</u> I didn't get to sleep until three o'clock this morning.

M: I think <u>aspirin</u> is just what you need.

Q: What is wrong with the woman?

[C]【解析】女士由于疼痛而难以入睡,男士说她需要阿司匹林。本题的关键词是 pain, aspirin,由此可知 C"她身体很不舒服"正确,而 A"担心某事"错误。

【点睛】B 属于过度推测,对话中没有明确说明是头痛,故 B 错;D 是错将 pain 听成 pen 后可能造成的误解,因此辨音也是听力考点之一。

14. M: Have you bought a Christmas gift for your brother?

　　W: Not yet, but I've been thinking about getting him a record. <u>He likes classical music best.</u>

　　Q: Which record would the woman's brother like most?

[D]【解析】关键在于听到女士说的 but 之后的话,即她弟弟最喜欢的是 classical music,所以选 D。此处的 albums 指的是"唱片"而不是"相册"。

【点睛】中 but 题,对 but 后面的内容要格外注意。A、B 和 C 分别是含有 best, Christmas 和 music 的干扰项。

15. M: Hurry up, <u>the game starts at nine</u> and we have a long way to go.

　　W: Take it easy. We need half an hour to get there and <u>there's still one left.</u>

　　Q: What time is it now?

[B]【解析】预读选项可知,这是一道时间题,而且逐个选项之间相隔半小时。预测题目可能会涉及增减计算,因而对录音中出现的时间表达及相应信息要用心细听。比赛 9 点开始,现在还剩一个小时(there's still one left 中省略了 hour),所以现在应该是 8 点,即 B。

【点睛】对于此类时间题,可边听边在选项旁做适当的记录。注意本题要用减法。赶去看比赛只需要半个小时,属于干扰信息,不要因此而误选 C。

16. W: I don't understand how you got a ticket. I always thought you were a careful driver.

　　M: I usually am, <u>but I thought I could make it before the light turned.</u>

　　Q: Why did the man get a ticket?

[A]【解析】预读选项可知,四个选项均与驾驶不当有关。本题关键是要听到男士说的 but 之后的话"我原以为自己可以在交通信号灯变色之前开过去",可见他闯红灯了。故选 A。常用短语 make it 意为"办成,做到",get a ticket 在此处意为"得到一张罚款单"。

【点睛】本题属于 S2 中间带 but 的转折题,but 后面往往是直接答题之处。本题的关键词是 light"交通信号灯"。而选项 A 中的 speeding,C 中的 stop sign,及 D 中的 corner, fast 在对话中均未提及,故这三个选项均错误。

17. M: How do Jane and Bill like their new house?

　　W: It's really comfortable, but they're tired of having to hear the <u>jets go over their house</u> at all hours.

　　Q: What is located close to Jane and Bill's new house?

[C]【解析】四个选项都是地点名词,听音时要善于抓住关键词。本题的关键词是 jets,而且女士提到"喷气式飞机在他们家上空飞行",可见他们住在机场附近。因此选 C。

【点睛】中 but 题,答案在 but 之后。体现地点、身份的经典词汇要积累,听到时才能迅速做出反应。

18. M: That's a lovely coat you're wearing.

　　W: Oh, thank you. <u>My husband gave it to me for my birthday.</u>

　　Q: What did the woman say about the coat?

[B]【解析】预读选项猜测,问题与 coat 有关。女士提到,这件大衣是她丈夫送给她的生日礼物,所以选 B。

【点睛】正确选项往往是原文的同义表达。选项 A、D 在录音中均未提及;C 与对话内容完全相悖,故错误。

Now you'll hear two long conversations.

Conversation One

M: [20] <u>Have you seen our holiday pictures?</u>

W: No, I haven't. <u>I'd like to, though.</u>

M: <u>Look.</u> This is the train that took us there. It's fabulous. You could all sit up here and see out from the observation window.

W: Oh, have they got stairs in the train then?

M: Oh, yes. Fully equipped. [19] And here's the house we stayed in. One of those wooden built cottages.

W: Yes, that's really pretty. And look at that fabulous car in front.

M: Oh, what a car! Typical massive, American car. It was just lovely.

W: Yes, it does look nice.

M: [20] And here we are on a fishing trip.

W: Uh, yes. And that was a big fish, too.

M: Well, that's Steve looking pretty pleased with himself.

W: Mm. [20] Did you catch anything?

M: No, I was a disaster. But it's really nice being out there.

W: Looks nice.

M: And then we went up to a camp on the lake. Don't you love the way the trees come down to the edge of the lake there?

W: Looks really peaceful and lovely. Are you having a meal there?

M: Yes. That's us having one of our cook-ups.

W: Mm, the tent looks a bit small.

M: Well it was, but you don't spend much time in the tent, do you?

W: I suppose not.

M: [21] Here we are on the lake again. This was a canoeing trip.

W: Yes, do you know how to paddle?

M: Wasn't hard to learn at all. Picked it up very quickly.

W: Well, what worried me was you were wearing those life-jackets.

M: Yes, [21] we all had to wear those silly life-jackets, but nobody minded very much. It was really good fun.

19. Where did the man stay during his holiday?

[B]【解析】听到 the house we stayed in 之后，紧接着听到 wooden built cottages，信息可转换为 we stayed in a wooden cottage。

【点睛】在选项中四个地点都提到的情况下，应该一一记录每个地点发生的相应事件，然后听清问题再作答。

20. Which of the following is true according to the conversation?

[D]【解析】整个对话是男士在给女士边看自己拍的照片，边介绍旅行的过程。开头第一个回合的对话就有说明。男士说"你看过我假期拍的照片吗？"女士说"没有。"男士介绍说"看！这是……"。从女士的话语中(如：really pretty, nice, lovely)可看出女士在称赞男士拍的照片，故选 D。

【点睛】开头句往往交待背景。其他选项的话题在对话中均有提及，但是信息不完全正确。对话中提到，Steve 看起来很得意，所以 A 错；男士提到过 disaster 和 silly 这两个词，但并不是用来评价整个旅程，所以 B 错；两个人并没有一起乘火车去旅游，只有男士去了，所以 C 错。

21. When did the tourists wear the life-jackets?

[B]【解析】四个选项的动词都不相同，而且地点也有一定的区别，因此在听到选项的内容时，应把相关的信息记录在选项旁边。男士说在湖上划木舟(canoeing)时，还必须穿上救生衣。所以 B 正确。

【点睛】符合"听到什么选什么"的原则。其他选项的动作在对话中也均有提及，但都跟穿救生衣无关，故排除。对于细节题，尤其是多个选项在对话中都出现过的情况，一定要边听边作记录，以免张冠李戴。

Conversation Two

W: Dad, Dad, Dad!

M: Uh, what, what, uh, uh! ?! ?

W: The movie is over. You slept through the best part.

M: Ah, ah, I must have dozed off during the last few minutes.

W: Right. You were gone for so long you should have brought your pillow and blanket. So, what did you think about it?

M: Well, overall, I'm a little disappointed with the movie. I mean, [22] the story was a little strange, you have to admit. I mean, really. [25] How believable is a plot about a captain who navigates his spaceship to the far reaches of the galaxy and encounters a race of frog people? I mean, come on.

W: Ah, I thought it was fantastic. I mean, you have to admit that [23] the special effects were awesome, and the acting wasn't bad either.

M: Ah, come on. What about the ship's [25] communications officer? I mean, what did you think about him? Wasn't he a little strange to you? He was always talking to himself, and he had that funny hairdo.

W: Well, he was a little... unusual but [23]/[24] the ship's doctor was amazing. It was so cool when he brought the captain back to life during one of the battles.

M: [24]/[25] That was pretty realistic, but then the rest of the movie just went from bad to worse. And [25] the photography was so fake!

W: How do you know? [23] You were snoring so loud the neighbors probably had to close their windows.

22. What is the father's opinion about the movie's storyline?

[A]【解析】父亲几乎一直都在抱怨电影的不好,所以可以排除 C 和 D 这两个表达积极意义的选项,而父亲说过,"这个故事有点奇怪",所以选 A"荒谬的"。

　【点睛】观察选项可知,本题询问的是观点或情绪,听对话时应该注意表达态度的用词和语气。此外,本题也可依据父亲的用词(如 strange, How believable, from bad to worse, fake 等)推断答案为 A。

23. Which of the following statements is true?

[D]【解析】细节辨认题。由 spaceship, galaxy, a race of frog people, special effects 等标志词可推断出这是科幻电影,答案为 D。

　【点睛】此题涉及的内容比较分散,需要事先多花些时间浏览选项,找到关键信息。A 错在 father,应该是 daughter,在对话中女儿评价说"特技很棒,而且演技也不赖",而父亲的反应是"Ah, come on. (得了吧!)";在对话中,女儿说"宇宙飞船的医生很了不起",B 与之意思相反;根据女儿所说的"你的鼾声那么响,邻居们很可能得关上窗户。"可知是在家里,故 C 错。

24. Whose performance do the father and daughter agree upon in the movie?

[C]【解析】父女俩只对那个医生有一致的评价,女儿说"宇宙飞船的医生很了不起……"之后,父亲肯定她的说法:"非常逼真",所以选 C。

　【点睛】听到有关选项中的四个人物的描述时,可以边听边做笔记,再根据问题回答,就不会混淆了。其余三项均未有明确的统一意见。

25. What seems to be the thing the father likes about the movie?

[C]【解析】父亲认为摄影很假,通讯官有点奇怪,故事情节也不可信,所以只有 C 是正确的。

　【点睛】选项为四个实义词时,可边听边做笔记。另外,父亲连连使用 come on"得了吧"这个口语中常用的表达,表示不同意或不屑一顾的意思。在对话中,父亲除了对医生的评价是"That was pretty realistic",对其他的评价几乎都是含否定意味的。也可由此得出答案是 C。

Section B

Passage One

　Our eating habits are very important for good health and a strong body. There are times when most of us would rather eat sweets and ice cream than meat and rice. [26] Sweets and ice cream are not bad for the stomach if we eat them at the end of a meal. If we eat them before a meal, they may take away our appetite. [27] It is important for us to eat our meal at the same time each day. When we feel hungry, it is a sign that our bodies need food. When we feel angry or excited, we may not want to eat. When we are worried, we may not want to eat, either.

A long time ago, in England, [28] some judges used to decide whether a man was telling the truth by giving him some dry bread. If the man could not swallow the bread, it was a sign that he wasn't telling the truth. He was telling a lie. Although this seems very strange and rather foolish, it is indeed an excellent way of finding out the truth. [28] A man who is worrying about something has difficulty in swallowing anything dry. Because when he is worrying, he loses his appetite and does not want to eat.

26. Which of the following may take away our appetite before we have our meal?

[D]【解析】四个选项均是食物,在听音的过程中若听到了选项中的词,则要在选项旁稍做记录。文章主要讲的是饮食习惯与健康的问题。文中提到,饭前吃 sweets and ice cream 会影响胃口,D 将其中的 sweets 换成了同义词 candy。故选 D。

【点睛】A 在文中提到了,但与本题的提问无关,故排除;B 中的 butter 和 C 在文中均未提及。本题也可从另一种角度来解答:根据生活常识,A、B、C 都有可能是正餐的内容;只有 D 属于零食范畴,若在饭前食用容易影响胃口。故可判断 D 正确。

27. When had we better have our meals?

[B]【解析】四个选项描述的都是时间。文中提到,每天在同一时间吃饭很重要。选项 B 中的 at regular intevals 就是文中 at the same time 的同义表达,所以 B 正确。

【点睛】A、C 在文中均未提及,D 在文中虽有提及,但不是吃饭时间的建议,只是表明我们的身体需要食物。此外,本题也可依据生活常识轻松地选出正确答案 B。

28. How could the judges in old England tell that a man had told a lie?

[D]【解析】预读选项时要注意辨别各选项间的异同。文章的后半部分讲了很久以前英格兰法官判断嫌疑人是否说谎的方法:给他吃干面包。吃不下就是说谎了,因为人在不安的时候难以咽下任何干的食物。故选 D。

【点睛】英语的习惯是先说结果,再说原因。文中也是先说法官的做法,然后解释为什么他们会这样做。A、B 表达的均是肯定含义,与文中的否定含义(如 could not, has difficulty 等)相违背,故可同时排除;C 在文中未提及。

Passage Two

The sense of sound is one of our most important means of knowing what is going on around us. Sound has a waste product, too, in the form of noise. Noise is growing and it may get much worse before it gets any better.

Scientists have been studying how noise affects people and animals. They are surprised by what they have learned. [29] Peace and quiet are becoming harder to find.

Noise pollution is a threat that should be looked at carefully.

There is a saying that it is so noisy that you can't hear yourself think. Doctors who study noise believe that we must sometimes hear ourselves think. [30] If we don't, we may have headaches, other aches and pains, or even worse mental problems.

Ways of making less noise are now being tested. There are even laws controlling noise. We cannot return to the "good old days" of peace and quiet. [31] But we can reduce noise, if we shout loudly enough about it.

29. Why are scientists surprised by the findings in their noise study?

[A]【解析】四个选项描述的都是原因,而且可预测问题与 noise 有关。关键在于听到"和平与安宁正变得愈发难寻",A 是其同义表达,故正确。

【点睛】正确选项往往是原文的同义表达。文中提到科学发现等特殊信息时应该特别注意细节。选项 B、C 都是利用原词进行语音干扰,D 在录音中未提及。

30. What may happen if we cannot hear ourselves think?

[C]【解析】预读选项可知，题目询问如果……可能会发生什么事。因此，在听音时要特别注意由 if 之类的词引导的条件句及这样做会导致什么后果。关键在于听到"如果我们听不见自己思考，可能会有头痛、其他的疼痛，甚至更糟的是会出现心理问题。"选项 C 就是原文中 mental problems 的同义表达，故正确。

【点睛】符合"同义替换"的原则。在听到 we must sometimes hear ourselves think 后面的 If we don't 时，要留意细听这样做将导致的不良后果。

31. Which of the following is true according to the passage?

[C]【解析】本题属于是非筛选型细节题。C 是对文章最后一句深层意义的解释，原文中的 shout 并非表示"大喊大叫"，而是"呼吁"的意思。因此选 C。

【点睛】A 利用 shout loudly 进行语音干扰；B 错在 worst，文中只提到噪音污染是我们应该认真看待的一种威胁；D 在文中并未提及。本题的另一种解法：从常识及逻辑的角度来看，只有 C 最合情合理；而 A、D 不是太合情理，B 的表述过于绝对。由此推断，答案为 C。

Passage Three

Eye contact is a nonverbal technique that helps the speaker "sell" his or her ideas to an audience. Besides its persuasive powers, eye contact helps hold listener interest. [32] A successful speaker must maintain eye contact with an audience. To have good rapport with listeners, a speaker should maintain direct eye contact for at least 75 percent of the time. Some speakers focus exclusively on their notes. Others gaze over the heads of their listeners. [33] Both are likely to lose audience's interest and esteem. People who maintain eye contact while speaking, whether from a podium or from across the table, are "regarded not only as exceptionally well-disposed by their target but also as much more believable and earnest."

To show the potency of eye contact in daily life, we have only to consider how passers-by behave when their glances happen to meet on the street. [34] At one extreme are those people who feel obliged to smile when they make eye contact. At the other extreme are those who feel awkward and immediately look away. [35] To make eye contact, it seems to make a certain link with someone.

32. What should a good speaker do according to this talk?

[B]【解析】细节题。关键在于听到"一位成功的演讲者必须与听众保持目光接触。"B 中的 listeners 对应文中的 an audience，因此选 B。

【点睛】选项 A、D 利用文中原词进行语音干扰；文章开头提到"目光接触是一种非语言技巧，它有助于演讲者把自己的想法'出售'给听众。"由此可知，C 不是本题的答案。本题也可从另一角度进行解答：如果没有听到关键句，考生也可根据录音中多次出现的 eye contact 大胆推测答案为 B。

33. What will the speaker lose if he or she cannot keep eye contact?

[C]【解析】简单推理题。关键是要听到"两种情况都可能失去听众的兴趣与尊重。"并且明白 both 指代的是什么。"一些演讲者只专注于他们的笔记"，"另一些演讲者凝视听众的头顶上方"，这两种情况都属于演讲者与听众之间缺乏目光接触。由此可推断，C 正确。

【点睛】符合"听到什么选什么"的原则。选项 A、B、D 在录音中均未提及。本题的另一种解法：如果没有听到关键句，但听到了文章开头提到的"目光接触有助于保持听众的兴趣"，也可进行逆向思维，即缺少目光接触会失去听众的兴趣，故选 C。

34. In daily life, what will happen when two passers-by make eye contact?

[A]【解析】隐含细节题。文中使用"At one extreme are... At the other extreme are..."的结构列举了路人在目光接触时可能出现的两种极端行为，即"当目光接触时有些人觉得有必要笑一笑"，"有些人觉得尴尬并立刻把脸转过去"。由第一种极端行为可推测出答案是 A"互相微笑"。

【点睛】B、C、D 三项在文中均未提及。解题小窍门:如果听清了问题,根据生活常识,我们也能轻松地选出本题的正确答案。

35. What benefits do we get from eye contact?
[B]【解析】细节题。关键是要听到文章末句"进行目光接触,似乎就与某人有了某种联系"。文中多次提到了 speaker, listener, audience,末句中的 someone 其实就是指代 the listener/audience,故 B 正确。

【点睛】文章的首、尾句往往是出题的重点,因此在听音时要格外注意。选项 A、D 在文中均未提及;文中并没有表达"有目光接触就能与其他人交朋友"这样的信息,C 属于过度猜测,故错误。

Section C

36. 【答案】currently
【解析】根据预读可知此处不缺主要句子成分,很可能需要一个修饰 dieting 的副词。要注意双写 r。

37. 【答案】maintain
【解析】根据上下文猜测,此句可能意为"只有不到 10% 的人能够在至少一年的时间内'保持'减轻后的体重"。be able to 后需要动词原形。注意别漏掉字母 i。

38. 【答案】Researchers
【解析】此处缺少主语,根据空格后的修饰词 Heart Study 可知,此处应填表示"研究人员"之类含义的复数名词。由于位于句首,要注意大写字母 R。

39. 【答案】harmful
【解析】根据句意"减肥后体重再次反弹也许会对你的心脏_____",推测此处应填入表示"有害的、不利的"之义的形容词。be harmful to 为固定搭配。

40. 【答案】period
【解析】根据前面的 Over a 14-year 可知,此处需要一个表示时间概念的单数名词。注意 e 与 io 的拼写。

41. 【答案】shifted
【解析】根据前一句中的 weight changes,猜测此处应填入表示"变化、波动"的词,形式为动词过去式。shift 是四级常考词汇。

42. 【答案】increased
【解析】此处为动词过去分词作定语,不可写成原形。注意不要拼写错了 ea。

43. 【答案】remained
【解析】此处需要系动词过去式,后接形容词 stable,语义应该与前面的 shifted 相反。

44. 【答案】For now the researchers are not sure how weight changes are linked to health problems
【听音关键】not sure, weight changes, linked, health problems
【答案重构】Researchers are not yet sure how weight changes and health problems are linked

【画龙点睛】只要表达出研究者不明确体重变化和健康之间的关系即可,句型可灵活变换。

45. 【答案】Losing and regaining weight may also cause an unhealthy distribution of body weight
【听音关键】losing, regaining, weight, unhealthy distribution
【答案重构】Weight loss and regain may also lead to an imbalanced distribution of body weight

【画龙点睛】动名词跟名词之间往往可以转换,实义词可以用同义词替换。

46. 【答案】only to regain weight in an area such as their stomach, which increases the risk of developing heart disease
【听音关键】only to, regain weight, increases, risk, heart disease
【答案重构】but might regain weight in other areas such as their stomach, which increases the risk of developing heart disease

【画龙点睛】这个句子比较复杂,only to 是固定结构,此处表达"结果……",也可用转折词加情态动词 but might 替换它。which 指代 weight regain 这一结果。

Unit Two

Section A

11. W: Was Michael elected to the committee?

M: Yes, in fact he was made chairman <u>but only agreed to take the job if they let him make all the decisions himself.</u>

Q: What does Michael intend to do?

[C]【解析】男士说的 but 后面提到，只有在让他自己做主的条件下，他才会当这个主席。所以选 C。

【点睛】本题属于 S2 中间带 but 的转折题，but 后面的信息往往是解题的关键。本题的"小偏方"：A 与 B 意思相近，都是指男士听命于委员会；而 C 与 A、B 两项却又意思相反，C 是指男士要按自己的意愿来掌管委员会。四个选项中，如果其中的两个选项之间是矛盾关系，那么正确答案常常来自有矛盾关系的一组选项之中。而如果有两个选项意思相近，则可同时排除这两项。由此可得出答案为 C。而 D 只是利用原词胡乱拼凑。

12. M: I agree with what you said at the meeting this morning. It was very good.

W: <u>You should have backed me up then, when I needed it.</u>

Q: What does the woman mean?

[D]【解析】女士说"你应该在我最需要支持的时候支持我。"所以选 D。

【点睛】虚拟语气在大学英语四级听力考试中出现的频率较高。"虚拟语气的内部替换"是此类题选项答案的特点之一，本题的答案 D 即具有此特点。

13. W: These problems are too hard to handle. Will you give me some advice?

M: There are many ways to deal with them, <u>but the most important is to have a careful plan.</u>

Q: What is the man's suggestion?

[A]【解析】男士提到，最重要的是要有一个(解决问题的)详细的计划。A 中的 make an arrangement 对应对话中的 have a careful plan，所以选 A。

【点睛】中 but 转折题，转折词后的信息很重要。其余选项均是利用原词进行干扰。

14. W: The watermelons grown here are <u>delicious</u>.

M: <u>Aren't they?</u>

Q: What do we learn from the man's response?

[A]【解析】男士说了一个反意问句的尾巴，且用降调，表示强烈支持女士的观点，他的意思是"西瓜的确很好吃"。所以选 A。

【点睛】本题属于反意问句尾巴题。也即 S1(陈述句)+S2(反意问意的尾巴)构成一个完整的反意疑问句。此类题的答案标记之一是：含 agree，即表示 S2 赞同 S1 观点的选项是答案。选项 A 符合此特点。

15. W: How could anyone <u>survive</u> the accident?

M: It's a <u>miracle</u>. There were two men in the truck and three women with a child in the car, <u>but no one was badly hurt.</u>

Q: What was the result of the accident?

[D]【解析】四个选项描述的都是意外事故的伤亡情况。本题的关键词(或表达)是：survive"从……中逃生"，miracle"奇迹"和"没有人受重伤"。所以选 D。

【点睛】其他选项都是原词的错误拼凑。其实，只要听懂了女士说的话或听到了 miracle 这个词，或者"没有人受重伤"这句话，都可做出正确的回答。

16. M: Can I borrow your history notes? I didn't attend the class yesterday.

W: I didn't take any notes. <u>The teacher just read dates from her notes to us, and I thought I could find them in any history book.</u>

Q: What is the woman trying to say?

[D]【解析】女士说她没有记笔记，因为老师光是讲一些书上都有的东西，所以选 D。

【点睛】正确选项往往是原文的概括或同义表达。听清"我没有做任何笔记"就不会选 A。B 和 C 都是原词胡乱拼凑。

17. M: Do you think Lawrence could help us plan the camping trip to San Francisco?

W: Well, since he spends every summer there, he might know a thing or two about it.

Q: What does the woman mean?

[B]【解析】女士说，既然 Lawrence 每年夏天都去那儿，那他可能对旧金山会有所了解。言下之意，向他咨询肯定错不了。所以选 B。

【点睛】符合短对话听力"同义替换"的原则。选项 B 中的 ask 呼应原文中的 know，这也是一个线索。而且答案和原文用的都是猜测语气：would probably 和 might。

18. W: I had such a bad start in the last race. It was hard to catch up.

M: We'll work on your start. The most important thing is concentration.

Q: What is the probable relationship between the two speakers?

[B]【解析】女士说"我在最后一场比赛中起跑就不好。"男士说"我们会抓紧训练你的起跑。"因此可断定二者是运动员和教练的关系，即 B。

【点睛】身份关系题。抓住关键词，把握他们的语气，就能准确答题。本题的关键词是 start, race, catch up，由此可判断 B 正确。

Now you'll hear two long conversations.

Conversation One

M: Hi, Sarah. What's up?

W: Oh, hi, I just got out of a history class. I had to give a presentation.

M: How did it go?

W: Terribly. I'm sure I made a fool of myself.

M: Why? Weren't you prepared?

W: No, it was not that. [19] I just get so embarrassed and nervous whenever I have to speak in front of a group of people. I stand up and my face gets red and then I get even more nervous because I know everyone can see me blushing.

M: It's not so bad to blush.

W: [19] But it happens all the time. If the professor asks a question and I know the answer, I blush like crazy if he calls on me. Doesn't that ever happen to you?

M: No, not really. [20] Maybe you should just try to forget about the people. Look at something else in the room like the exit sign.

W: I guess I could try that but I doubt it'll help.

M: You know, we talked about it in psychology class. Blushing, even thought it's involuntary, is more or less a learned behavior.

W: What do you mean?

M: Oh, children hardly ever blush at all. And among adults, supposedly, [21] women blush more than men.

W: I wonder why?

M: I don't know, [21] but I have a friend at high school, Brian Smith. It was really easy to make him blush. He turned red whenever a waitress would ask him for his order.

W: I'm not that bad. Well, I've got to get going for my next class. I'll talk to you later.

19. What was the woman's problem?

[A]【解析】对话开头女士就说自己"像傻瓜"，说明她有问题，紧接着谈论的是她在众人面前说话会脸红。所以她最大的问题是 A。

【点睛】选项都是一些问题的体现,可以预测题目询问女士的问题是什么。对话中提到脸红、上课做报告以及与人交谈,听时注意对相关内容做记录,进行正确信息的匹配。

20. Why might looking at the exit sign help the woman according to the man?

[A]【解析】根据对话思路,女士说完自己的问题,男士很可能会提出建议。根据"也许你应该努力忽略他人的存在。"选A。

【点睛】符合"听到什么选什么"的原则。B 中的 exit 及 D 中的 professor 均属语音干扰,实际上 B、C、D 三个选项的内容在对话中均未提及。本题"小偏方":如果没听到关键句,只听见了问题,那么从常理的角度来看,应该是 A 最合适。

21. Why does the man mention his friend Brian?

[A]【解析】四个选项均以 To 开头表示目的。之前女士提到女人比男人更容易脸红,女士想知道原因,男士补充说,"我不知道,不过我有个高中同学 Brian,他特别容易脸红。"所以 Brian 是个特例,故选 A;而男士并不是想以此告诉 Sarah 男人也常脸红,故 D 错。

【点睛】转折词 but 后的信息很重要。Brian 是男性,所以 B 不可能是正确的;男士并没有提及要介绍 Brian 给 Sarah 认识,故 C 也不对。

Conversation Two

W: Hey, Henry, how's everything going, and what's with the flowers?

M: They're for my wife.

W: Oh, a wedding anniversary or something?

M: To tell the truth, it couldn't be worse. You see, I have to pick my wife up from the airport this evening, but while she was gone, there were a few minor mishaps.

W: Oh really? What happened?

M: [22] Well, I had some of the guys over Friday night to watch a basketball game on TV, [23] but one of them got all excited, and started horsing around, waving his arms, and he accidentally knocked over my wife's 250-year-old Chinese porcelain vase given to her by her grandmother, and broke it beyond repair.

W: Oh no! You're in hot water now.

M: If it had only been that.

W: Oh, there's more?

M: Yeah, you see, the water from the vase spilled all over the manuscript of a book my wife has been writing for the past two years. It blurred the ink over many of the pages.

W: Oh no!

M: And so one of the guys had the bright idea of drying the pages by the fire while we watched, uh, the rest of game, [24] but a spark from the fire must have blown out and burned the manuscript to a crisp.

W: Ah, so I get it now. You're buying the flowers for her as a part of some kind of peace offering, right?

M: No, not at all. [25] They're for my funeral.

22. What was Henry doing Friday night when his problems started?

[A]【解析】选项讲的是男士当时在干什么。听到女士问"哦,是吗?发生什么事了?"时,就该预测到后面讲的是事情的经过。男士随即说道,"我有几个朋友周五晚上过来看篮球赛。"所以选 A。

【点睛】通过选项预测问题有助于迅速捕捉答案。男士将要去机场接妻子,而不是 B;C 中的 barbeque 在录音中未提及;对话中出现过 game,但它是 basketball game 的省略表达,D 利用 game 进行语音干扰。

23. How was the vase broken?

[C]【解析】根据选项可以预测问题是 vase 被谁怎样弄坏了。对话中提到,一个朋友看球赛看得很兴奋,手舞足蹈,不小心把 Henry 妻子一只 250 年历史的中国陶瓷花瓶打翻了。其中的 he 不是 Henry,而是他的朋友,答案为 C。

【点睛】可以利用有交叉信息的选项缩小选择范围:B 和 C 的差异主要是主语不同,C 和 D 的差异主要是动词不同,而 C 正是答案。

24. How did the manuscript of the book become totally ruined?

[A]【解析】选项讲的是一件东西怎么被毁坏的。在说完花瓶被打破之后,Henry 又说"如果仅仅如此也就好了。"可见还有更糟糕的事发生,紧接着,他提到了书稿的遭遇,根据"但肯定是有火星进出来,把书稿给烧焦了"可知书最终是被火焚毁的,因此选 A。

【点睛】B、D 都是含有原词的干扰项,C 在对话中根本没提到。这里的 spark, blow out 和 crisp 可能考生不太熟悉,但只要听到 fire 或 burn,估计就能猜出书是被烧毁的。

25. How will his wife feel when she got the whole story?

[B]【解析】选项中的形容词表示的是四种情感。此题是推理题,妻子最后会怎么表现在对话中并未提及,但从丈夫谈话的口气中可以很明显感觉到事情的严重性,最后丈夫说道:"我死定了。"可以推测妻子知道后会非常愤怒,所以选 B。

【点睛】根据用词和语气判断态度是必须掌握的能力。解题"小窍门":如果大致听懂了所发生的事情,按照人之常情,Herry 的妻子在了解了整个情况之后肯定会大发雷霆,故选 B。

Section B

Passage One

[26] Some psychologists maintain that mental acts such as thinking are not performed in the brain alone, but that one's [28] muscles also participate. It may be said that we think with our muscles in somewhat the same way as we listen to music with our bodies.

You surely are not surprised to be told that you usually listen to music not only with your ears but with your whole body. [27] Few people can listen to music that is more or less familiar without moving their body or more specifically, some part of their body. Often when one listens to a concert on the radio, he is tempted to direct the orchestra even though he knows there is a competent conductor on the job.

Strange as this behavior may be, there is a very good reason for it. [27] One cannot derive all possible enjoyment from music unless he participates, so to speak, in its performance. The listener "feels" himself into the music with more or less noticeable motions of his body.

[26] The muscles of the body actually participate in the mental process of thinking in the same way, but this participation is less obvious because it is less noticeable.

26. According to this passage, what do some psychologists maintain about thinking?

[D]【解析】文章首尾句均提到了 thinking, muscles, brain 的关系,答案为 D。

【点睛】短文的开头与结尾部分往往成为出题的重点。A、B 只是利用原词胡乱拼凑,干扰性较上;C 是听音乐时的情况,不要误选。

27. Why do people move their body while listening to music that is familiar?

[C]【解析】根据选项中的 because 可知题目问的是原因。文章中间部分主要讲述人体参与音乐欣赏的事实和原因,英文的习惯一般是先说事实,后说原因,因此听到"几乎没有谁会在听到或多或少有些熟悉的音乐时身体不会动,或者更明确些,身体的某个部位"后就应该预测到后面要讲原因。后文提到,一个人如果不参与到音乐的演奏中去,他就无法完全地享受音乐。故选 C。

【点睛】正确答案往往是原文的同义表达或概括。其余选项均为无中生有。

28. What is the talk mainly about?

[C]【解析】预读选项可知,这是一道主旨大意题。标题应该概括最主要的信息,可利用主题句中的核心词和全文高频实义词做出选择或缩小选择范围。本文的高频词有:thinking, muscles, brain, body, 等。本文主要讲的是肌肉参

与思维过程,而不是在给思维下定义,故选 C 而非 D。

【点睛】A、B 均与 music 有关,它们只是用来证明主题的具体例子,不能概括全文。

Passage Two

[29] During the summer session there will be a revised schedule of services for the university community. Specific changes for intercampus bus services, summer hours for the cafeteria and recreational and athletic facilities will be posted on the bulletin board outside the cafeteria. Weekly movie and concert schedules which are in the process of being arranged will be posted each Wednesday outside the cafeteria.

[30] Intercampus buses will leave the main hall every hour on the half hour and make all of the regular stops on their route around campus. [30] The cafeteria will serve breakfast, lunch, and early dinner from 7 a.m. to 7 p.m. during the week and from noon to 7 p.m. on weekends. [31] The library will maintain regular hours during the week, but shorter hours on Saturdays and Sundays. The weekend hours are from noon to 7 p.m.

[32] All students who want to use the library borrowing services and recreational athletic, and entertainment facilities must have a valid summer identification card. This announcement will also appear in the next issue of the student newspaper.

29. Which of the following is the main purpose of this announcement?
[C]【解析】四个选项均以 To 开头表示目的。开头句就交待了主题,其中的核心词是 revised schedule,C 中的 change 是文中 revise 的同义词,答案为 C。

【点睛】主旨题要有概括性。其他选项都是具体项目的通知,不是该通知的总目的。故均可排除。

30. Specific schedule revisions for which of the following facilities are listed in this announcement?
[B]【解析】文中详细通知了 intercampus buses, cafeteria 和 library 的变更安排,B 对应前两者。

【点睛】选项为短语的题目往往需要记笔记并进行同义匹配。

31. According to the announcement, which of the following is true of special summer hours for the library?
[A]【解析】文中提到 library 时有 hour 的信息,shorter hours on Saturdays and Sundays 对应的是 A。

【点睛】浏览选项可知与 special summer hours 有关,听短文时应该记录相关信息。本题符合"同义替换"的原则。

32. According to the announcement, when is a validated identification card needed?
[D]【解析】文章结尾提到 card,前面提到办卡的目的是"使用图书馆借阅服务,使用运动设施及娱乐设施",只有 D 符合。

【点睛】浏览选项可知与目的、用途有关,听到 who want to use 时应该警惕。其他选项均属无关信息。

Passage Three

The nationwide EU-China Training Project for Clerical Staff recently started in Beijing following the launch of a piloting program in Wuhan, Hubei Province.

[33] The project is designed to improve the competitiveness of Sino-EU joint ventures. Any enterprise in any region will be able to discuss training requests with foreign experts and jointly devise training programs. Helped by European and Chinese experts the project will not only train clerical staff, but also [34] benefit the Chinese education system by employing the latest European training methods. Most of the project's services will be free.

[35] The piloting program in Wuhan, funded with 15 million euros from the EU Commission and Hubei Province, will improve staff in Sino-EU joint ventures over the next five years. Another 40 projects will go in other provinces and in different companies.

33. What's the purpose of the project?

[D]【解析】文章先介绍了一个项目,然后说明其目的。文中提到"此项目旨在提高中欧合资企业的竞争力",D表达的正是此义,故正确。

【点睛】根据选项可以预测题目问的是目的;A、B、D三项之间有共同点,但更要注意它们的不同之处,而C和D之间也存在异同点。因此,听的时候就会有针对性且能迅速捕捉信息。

34. How can the project benefit the Chinese education system?

[C]【解析】文章在叙述了目的之后接着讲好处,根据"通过引进欧洲最新的教育方法,使中国的教育系统受益",可知C正确。

【点睛】根据选项可以预测话题是某事带来的影响或好处。本题符合"同义替换"的原则。

35. Who supported the piloting program in Wuhan?

[D]【解析】文章结尾主要介绍武汉的项目,其中的定语 funded with 15 million euros from the EU Commission and Hubei Province 说明是两个机构出资的,问题中的 support 对应文中的 fund,故答案为 D。

【点睛】选项是结构名称,可以预测是某种行为的执行者或承受者。本题符合"听到什么选什么"的原则。

Section C

36.【答案】fortune

【解析】根据预读可知此处需要一个名词。注意字母组合 or 和 tune。该词的派生词 fortunately, unfortunately 是四级高频词汇。

37.【答案】signed

【解析】此处需要过去分词或形容词作定语。与 will"遗嘱"搭配的动词往往是 sign"签署"。

38.【答案】distributed

【解析】此处需要过去分词。上下文的意思是,fund"基金"被 distributed"分配成"五部分。dis 不是 des。

39.【答案】physics

【解析】此处应该是一个表示学科的名词。字母组合 ph 发 / f /音,y 发 / i /音,第一个 s 发 / z /音,c 发 / k /音。

40.【答案】economics

【解析】根据语义,此处应该是表达另外一个学科奖项的名词。注意 economy, economic, economics 的重音和语义区别:economy,重音在第 2 音节,*n.* "经济";economic,重音在第 3 音节,*adj.* "经济的";economics,重音在第 3 音节,*n.* "经济学"。

41.【答案】legal

【解析】此处需要形容词作定语。词根 leg 是 law 的意思,其派生词多与法律有关,如 legal"合法的,法定的"。

42.【答案】involved

【解析】be involved in 为固定搭配,意为"涉及"。

43.【答案】frequently

【解析】此处需要一个频率副词。frequently 意为"频繁地"。

44.【答案】The nominations are made by individuals and institutions qualified according to the regulations of the appropriate awarding body

【听音关键】nominations, by individuals and institutions, regulations, awarding body

【答案重构】Qualified individuals and institutions make the nominations following the rules of the appropriate awarding body

【画龙点睛】被动句可以变成主动句,但要注意主语和宾语不要混淆。

45.【答案】Besides the cash prize, each award consists of a gold medal and a diploma

【听音关键】cash, gold medal, diploma

【答案重构】Each award consists of a cash prize, a gold medal and a diploma

【画龙点睛】把所有包含的内容列举清楚,其顺序符合表达习惯。

46. 【答案】Prizewinners who are unwilling or unable to accept the prize may apply for and receive the medal and diploma later

【听音关键】Prizewinners, may apply, medal and diploma later

【答案重构】Prizewinners may apply for and receive the medal and diploma later if they are unwilling or unable to accept the prize at the moment

【画龙点睛】定语从句可以变成状语从句,准确表达主句更加重要。

Unit Three

Section A

11. W: Could you help me, sir? My flight got in 15 minutes ago. <u>Everyone else has picked up the luggage but mine hasn't come through.</u>

M: I'm sorry, Madam. I'll go and find out if there is any more to come.

Q: What's the woman's problem?

[C]【解析】女士抱怨:"我乘坐的航班 15 分钟前就到了,别人的行李都拿到了,就是我的行李还没来。"可知女士的行李被耽搁了。所以选 C。

【点睛】观察选项可知不是找不到行李或人,就是行李或航班被延误了,因此听时要抓住话题,如果说的是行李,只要听动词是被人取走还是耽搁了即可。

12. M: Don't you feel cold outside, Jenny?

W: A little bit. <u>But I can't stand the terrible smoke inside.</u> I'd rather stay here if you don't mind.

Q: Why does the woman want to stay outside?

[D]【解析】预读选项可知,题目询问女士做某事的原因,其中两个选项与 inside 有关,另外两个选项与 outside 有关。女士提到"我受不了里面的烟味",这才是她出去的原因。D 是其同义表达。

【点睛】本题是中间带 but 的转折题,女士说的 but 后面的内容是直接答题之处。另外,要理解 stand 在此意为"忍受",也可以从 terrible 一词推断出女士对 smoke 的反感。其他选项均是利用原词进行语音干扰。

13. M: This is an interesting <u>exhibit</u>. Have you seen the big <u>oil painting</u> by Grant Wood?

W: Yes, it's nice, but I like the <u>watercolors</u> by Wyath better. They are in the next room.

Q: Where did the conversation most probably take place?

[B]【解析】从标志性单词 exhibit, oil painting, watercolors 可推断出对话地点应该是在美术馆,故选 B。

【点睛】解读地点题的重点在于理解相应的地点名词所确立的语境,以及在该语境下的关键词。选项 A 是含有 paint 的迷惑项,但 paint shop 是指油漆店,故 A 不正确;可能也会有考生因为听到 water 而选 C,但只要听到了 exhibit, oil painting 等词就可排除 C;D 为无关信息。

14. M: Excuse me, Madam. Your husband is on the phone.

W: I can't possibly talk to him now. <u>Tell him my hair is being dried.</u>

Q: What is the woman probably doing?

[C]【解析】辨音题。注意易混读音:have one's hair dried 吹干头发;have one's hair dyed 染头发。C 将原文的被动语态变成了同义的主动表达。B 具有一定的迷惑性,而且如果考生看题时较粗心,误把形似词 dyed 看成了 dried,那也可能会错选 B;A、D 的干扰性较小。

【点睛】四个选项描述的动作不相同,因此在听音时要格外注意相关动词。

15. W: Could I see a pair of shoes like the brown ones in the window? I need a size 6 and a half.

M: I'm sorry, <u>but that style doesn't come in half sizes.</u> Can I show you a seven?

Q: Why can't the woman get what she wants?

[B]【解析】女士需要 6.5 码的鞋,而男士说,这种款式的鞋没有半码。也就是说,没有女士想要的码数,所以选 B。

【点睛】中 but 题,转折词 but 后的信息很重要。答案往往是原文的同义表达。

16. M: Everyone thinks Jim is a very <u>promising</u> student.

   W: <u>It goes without saying.</u> He has shown his <u>intelligence</u> since early childhood.

   Q: What's the woman's opinion about Jim?

[B]【解析】男士用 promising"有前途的"形容 Jim,女士说 It goes without saying"当然,不言自明",说明她完全同意男士的说法,故排除 A。B 中的 a bright future 是对话中的 promising 的同义表达。

【点睛】听懂短语很关键。平时应注意积累一些口语词组、惯用语、易产生歧义短语、常用表达及句型等。如果不懂"It goes without saying."的含义,则有可能误选 C;D 是对 promising 的误解。

17. M: How did you like my performance this evening? I was awfully nervous.

   W: <u>I couldn't appreciate it more. You really made a hit.</u>

   Q: What does the woman say about the man's performance?

[C]【解析】女士说"我非常欣赏你的表演。你引起了轰动。"说明男士的演出非常成功。故选 C。

【点睛】考查 not... more/better 构成的特殊句型。此句型表示不可能有比这更好的情况发生了,也就是指这样很好,所以表达的是肯定的意思。如:I couldn't agree with you more.意为"我完全同意你的观点。"A 和 C 意思是相反,一般而言,其中有一个就是答案。B、D 均是利用原词进行干扰,而实际上与对话内容是风马牛不相及。

18. W: Well, <u>tonight we have Professor Pitt in studio to talk about his recent book *Fashion Images*.</u> Good evening, professor.

   M: Good evening, and <u>thank you for inviting me here this evening.</u>

   Q: What is the woman doing?

[A]【解析】女士说,今晚 Pitt 教授来到演播室谈论他的新作。男士说,谢谢你对我的邀请。可见女士是在主持节目,因此选 A。

【点睛】正确选项往往是对原文的同义表达或概括。听到 studio,可知对话发生在演播室。选项 B 是含有 studio 的干扰项;选项 C、D 均与对话无关。

Now you'll hear two long conversations.

Conversation One

W: Well, hi, Mr. Brown. How's your apartment working out for you?

M: Well, Miss Nelson. That's what I would like to talk to you about. Well, I want to talk to you about that noise! You see. Would you mind talking to the tenant in 4B and asking him to keep his music down, especially after 10:00 p.m.?

W: Ohhh. Who? Me?

M: Why, yes. The music is blaring almost every night, and it should be your job as manager to take care of things.

W: Hey, [19] I just collect the rent. Besides, the man living there is the owner's son... OK, I'll see what I can do. Anything else?

M: Well, yes. Could you talk to the owners of the property next door about the bad smell drifting this way?

W: Well, [20] the area is zoned for agricultural and livestock use, so there's nothing much I can do about that.

M: Well, what about that, that noise?

W: Oh, that noise. I guess the military has resumed its exercises.

M: You have to be kidding. Can't anything be done about it?

W: Why, certainly. [21] I've protested this activity, and these weekly activities should cease within... the next three to five years.

M: Hey, [21] you never told me about these problems before I signed the rental agreement.

19. Why is the woman hesitant about meeting the man's first request for a quieter environment?

[B]【解析】根据选项可预测问题很可能是关于女士为什么不管某件事的。当男士问女士能否去管一下 4B 房间传出的音乐噪音时,女士说"我只是来收房租的,再说,那个房间住的是房东的儿子",B 正好符合此意。

[点睛]A 错在 doesn't care about it,根据女士犹像之后说的"好吧,我看看我能做点什么。"可知她并非不关心;C 属于无中生有,制造噪音的人根本不是什么音乐家;D 说她更关心其他房客的问题,这就更加荒谬了。

20. How does the manager respond when the tenant complained about the bad smell?

[A]【解析】当谈到隔壁传过来的异味时,经理(女士)说"该区域是农牧区,我无能为力",即邻近地产所有人有权对自己的地方做出规划和处理,故选 A。

[点睛]选项大致描述对某个问题的处理情况,而且文字较多,加上每个选项之间没有什么类似之处,所以浏览时只要粗略掌握每一选项的大意即可。本题符合"同义替换"的原则。

21. What's not true concerning the military exercises?

[C]【解析】本题属于是非筛选型细节题。根据女士的话"我已经抗议过了,这些每周一次的活动应该会在接下来的三至五年内结束。"所以 B、D 正确,C 错误。男士说"在我签租约前你从没告诉过我这些问题。"故 A 也正确。因此答案为 C。

[点睛]预读选项可知,题目可能与 noise, military activity 有关。对于此类细节题,最好边听边在选项旁作记录。注意别漏听了问题中的 not。

Conversation Two

W: Stan, do you have a minute?

M: Oh, hi, Cathy, sure. What's up?

W: [22] I've been meaning to talk to you about the situation in the office.

M: I'm not there very often. It's so noisy that I can't work.

W: That's exactly what I'm getting at. We're supposed to be able to do our preparation and marking in that office. But have you noticed? [23] Jack constantly has students coming in to get help with his course. A lot of people are going in and out.

M: Has anybody spoken to him about it?

W: No, not yet. But someone's going to have to.

M: We can't really ask him to stop having students come in for help, can we?

W: No, of course not. But I'm not able to do my work and neither are you. I imagine it's the same for the others in the office.

M: Hum... [24] could we ask for a kind of meeting room? When teaching assistants have to talk with the students, they could go to the meeting room and not use the office. You know, there's a room down the hall, a rather small room that we could ask to use. It's only for storing supplies.

W: You mean that little storage room? Oh, that would be too small.

M: Are you sure? With the cabinets taken out, it might be bigger than it looks.

W: [25] Come to think of it, you may be on to something. I'd like to have a look at that room. Can we go there now?

M: Sure, let's go.

22. What problem at the office are Cathy and Stan discussing?

[B]【解析】选项是四个相关性不大的话题,预测可能是主旨题。根据女士的话"我想和你谈一下办公室环境的问题。"可知,对话主要和办公环境有关,答案为 B。

[点睛]主旨大意题一般是对话的第一题或最后一题。在长对话中,很多时候主题是直接点明的,一般在前几轮对话中就会体现,本题就是此种情况。

23. Why do Jack's students come to see him?

[A]【解析】可边听边做记录。根据"Jack 经常有学生来请教。"可知选 A。

【点睛】选项围绕 Jack 展开,所以听到 Jack 这个名字时,要特别注意。本题的另一种解法:学生去教师办公室找老师,较多情况下是想向老师请教。四个选项中只有 A 最合适。

24. What does Stan suggest they do?

[D]【解析】选项是一些可以采取的措施。根据男士说的"我们能不能要求有会议室呢?"选 D。

【点睛】A 和 C 未提及;B 只是男士询问女士的内容,并非建议,所以不选 B。本题也可依据常识大胆推测答案:学生进出办公室向老师请教问题,老师肯定不可能将学生拒之门外,故 C 不合理;其他教师即使和 Jack 谈论此问题,也还是不大可能完美地解决这个问题,故 B 也不大合适;A"向上级打报告"也不是明智之举;只有 D"将贮藏室改为办公室"才可能较好地解决此问题,既不打击学生的学习积极性,也不影响教师办公。

25. What does Cathy say about Stan's suggestion?

[A]【解析】选项是女士对男士的建议所持的看法。当男士告诉女士那个房间并不小时,女士说,"细想一下,也许你言之有理。我想去看看那个房间。我们可以现在去那儿吗?"可知女士认为 Stan 的建议或许可行,所以选 A。

【点睛】正确选项往往是原文的同义表达或概括。B、C、D 都是持否定观点,只有 A 属于肯定看法。

Section B

Passage One

In all economic systems today, most businesses of any size rely on one system of organization: the division of labor. This means that the workers are specialized. [26] Each worker has a particular duty to perform as one part of the whole operation.

A good example of the division of labor is an assembly line in an automobile factory. One worker may install a door while another adds lights. Normally, workers stay in one place, and a conveyor belt moves the product to them. [27] If one worker had the responsibility of producing an entire car, he or she might be able to complete one each year. By comparison, factories with assembly lines may produce an average of about thirty-five cars a year per worker.

The division of labor permits mass production, [28] but it does have some disadvantages. For one thing, few people know or understand all aspects of an operation. In addition, mass production may be more efficient, but many workers complain that they get little job satisfaction from working on one small duty, day after day. To them, there is much more satisfaction in doing a job from beginning to end.

26. What does the speaker mean by the division of labor?

[C]【解析】文章提到 division of labor 后就解释道:This means...,此后就是答案所在。C 是原文的同义表达。

【点睛】文章主要介绍了一个概念"劳动分工",开头是定义,然后举例说明其优缺点。本题的另一种解法:即使没听清关键句,只要听清了问题,也可依据常识轻易地从四个选项中选出,C 用于表示"劳动分工"。

27. What is the advantage of using an assembly line in an automobile factory?

[B]【解析】通过对比:一个工人负责整车生产的话,一年生产一辆;而分工合作的话,平均每人每年生产 35 辆。由此可概括出 B"提高生产力"。

【点睛】数据和对比结构是为了说明"生产流水作业有助于大大提高生产力"这一思想。

28. What is the speaker's attitude towards the division of labor?

[B]【解析】预读选项可知,题目询问的是某人所持的观点或态度。文章不仅说了"劳动分工"的好处,而且承认它有不足之处。因此是客观的,答案为 B。

【点睛】态度题可以结合用词和文章结构来回答。

Passage Two

The idea of fighting a noise by making more noise sounds strange, but that's exactly what motor engineers are doing. Carmakers' research and development laboratories have already proved that mixing in more noise with the help of loudspeakers can reduce the unwanted noise.

Sound is made up of pressure waves in the air. If two sound waves of the same frequency mix so that the highest point of one wave happens at the same time with the lowest point of the other wave, the result is no sound. [29] Therefore, by producing a perfect copy of the noise and delaying it by half a wave cycle, we can kill the unwanted noise. Using this technique many carmakers are racing to develop noise-killing systems both inside and outside the cars.

Another good thing about the use of noise-killing systems is that it saves the need for a silencer, [30] which not only reduces the weight of a car, but also makes the motor burn less oil and work better.

Some engineers believe that the noise-killing system will be used in most cars in the near future. [31] But the carmakers haven't decided if they will put it into production because it would add several hundred dollars to the cost of their cars.

29. Which of the following gives a general idea of how the noise-killing system works?
[C]【解析】文章开头主要介绍利用噪音减少噪音的想法和原理,之后用 therefore 引出具体做法。文中提到,"因而,通过复制噪音并延迟半个声波周期将其释放出来,我们就能够消除多余的噪音。"C 是其同义表达,其中 let out later 准确对应原文中的 delay。

[点睛]把握文章思路有助于捕捉题目信息源。表示结论的线索词后面的信息往往是考点。

30. Besides its main function, what else can the noise-killing system do?
[B]【解析】文章前半部分介绍完减少噪音系统的主要功能后,用 Another good thing 引出另一好处:不仅能减轻车身的重量,而且能降低耗油量,并提高工作性能。B 对应其中的 not only 部分。

[点睛]表示列举、转折等的线索词后面的信息往往是考点。A 是减少噪音系统的主要功能,故不符合题意;如果使用了此系统,汽车就不必再安装消音器(silencer)了,故 C、D 也不正确。

31. Why isn't the noise-killing system popular yet?
[A]【解析】文章尾句指出,该系统尚未普遍使用的原因是"会增加几百美元的成本"。即 A。

[点睛]文章首尾句很重要。表示因果关系的信号词后面的信息往往是考点。

Passage Three

[35] Researching friendship, psychologist Lillian Rubin spent two years interviewing more than two hundred women and men. No matter what their age, their job, their sex, the results were completely clear: [32] women have more friendships than men, and the difference in the content and the quality of those friendships is "marked and unmistakable."

More than two-thirds of the single men, Rubin interviewed, could not name a best friend. Those who could were likely to name a woman. [33] Yet three-quarters of the single women had no problem naming a best friend, and almost always it was a woman. More married men than women named their wife/husband as a best friend, most trusted person, or the one they would turn to in time of emotional distress. [33] "Most women," says Rubin, "identified at least one, usually more, trusted friends to whom they could turn in a troubled moment, and they spoke openly about the importance of these relationships in their lives."

"In general," Rubin writes in her new book, "women's friendships with each other rest on shared emotions and support, but men's relationships are marked by shared activities."

"Even when a man is said to be a best friend," Rubin writes, "[34] the two share little about their innermost feelings. Whereas a woman's closest female friend might be the first to tell her to leave a failing marriage, it wasn't unusual to hear a man say he didn't know his friend's marriage was in serious trouble until he appeared one night asking if he could sleep on the sofa."

32. What is one of the psychologist Rubin's findings?

[C]【解析】C 是原文开头重要信息的概括。其他选项属于无中生有或信息胡乱拼凑。

【点睛】选项是男女之间的差异,听时要捕捉所比较的信息点,听到 the results were completely clear 就应该知道后面是此题信息源。

33. According to Rubin's study, to whom is a married woman more likely to turn for emotional support?

[D]【解析】文章在进行总的比较之后具体介绍差异。B 中的 female 是原文中 woman 的同义词,故选 B。

【点睛】数据常被用来支持或证明某一观点,因而出现数据处往往值得注意。

34. Which of the following statements might Rubin support?

[A]【解析】文章采用了大量引语,接近结尾处 Rubin 讲到 men 时说"这两个人在内心最深处的情感方面几乎没有什么共同之处。"即 A。

【点睛】文中人物的观点应该一一简单记录并与选项进行匹配。B、C 中的 marriage 虽有提及,但只是用来说明 A;D 属于未提及信息。

35. What does the research done by psychologist Rubin center around?

[B]【解析】文章开头第 2 个单词就是 friendship,后文又比较 men 和 women 在这方面的差别,所以研究的核心为 B。

【点睛】捕捉核心词和文章结构的能力必须具备。文中多次提到 marriage 这个词,但它只是用来例证 friendship 这个主题的,故 A、C 错误;Rubin 主要是研究男女在友谊方面的差别,而不是男女之间的互动,故 D 不对。

Section C

36. 【答案】demonstrate

【解析】情态动词 can 后面接动词原形。此词尽管较长,但根据发音规则很好拼写。

37. 【答案】stuff

【解析】此处需要名词,正常语序是 good manners are made of...。根据语义应该是 stuff "东西"而不是近音词 staff "人员"。

38. 【答案】specific

【解析】此处需要形容词。specific 是四级常考词汇,与 special 形似,意思是"具体的,特定的",反义词是 general "笼统的,大概的"。

39. 【答案】born

【解析】be born doing sth. 为固定表达,意为"天生就……"。

40. 【答案】gradually

【解析】根据前一句话及破折号后面的语义,应该填副词 gradually "逐渐地、日积月累地"。注意要双写 l。

41. 【答案】contact

【解析】此处需要能够与介词 with 搭配的名词;根据上下文预测,此处的语义应表示"接触,联系"。contact 作名词时常用于 in contact with sb. 结构中;作动词时是及物动词,直接接宾语,无须接 with。

42. 【答案】expand

【解析】不定式 to 之后接动词原形;根据后半句的内容,此处在语义上应填表示"扩大,拓展"的词。expand one's knowledge 为习惯搭配。此处不要错写成 expend "花费,消耗"。

43. 【答案】conduct

【解析】good 修饰名词。good conduct 为本文 good manner 的同一范畴词。

44. 【答案】There are a number of reasons why people want to learn good manners and the rules of etiquette

【听音关键】reasons, learn good manners, rules of etiquette

【答案重构】People have a lot of reasons to learn good manners and the rules of etiquette

【画龙点睛】复杂句可以简化,但要保证句意不变。

45. 【答案】people who treat other people with kindness and sympathy are most likely to become popular because they are considered good companions

【听音关键】treat other people, kindness, sympathy, popular, considered good companions

【答案重构】those treating others kindly and sympathetically arc most likely to be popular because they are considered good companions

【画龙点睛】从句可简化成分词作定语,介词短语可以转换成副词表达。

46. 【答案】Good manners help put people at ease, make them cooperative and just plain happy

【听音关键】put people at ease, cooperative, happy

【答案重构】Good manners help make people feel at ease, cooperative and very happy.

【画龙点睛】此句属于简单并列句。

第三篇

篇章词汇理解

稳拿480分篇章词汇考点突破

篇章词汇理解(即选词填空)的测试形式为一篇与传统阅读题型长短相当的文章,其中有10个空白处,要求考生从所提供的由15个单词构成的词库(word bank)里选出最合适的词分别填入各空白处,每个单词只能选择一次,也就是说,这15个单词里有且只有10个单词会被选中。

篇章词汇理解所考查的范围不针对冠词、介词或虚词进行出题,而只会对名词、动词、形容词、副词等实词进行考查。其测试形式表面上看起来是对词汇的考查,其实是对考生综合语言能力和篇章理解能力的测试。虽然该题型不以语法现象为考点,但是因为所选择的单词不需要在时态和语态等方面进行形式转换,故解题时对一些语法现象加以利用往往会取得事半功倍的效果。另外,该题型所提供的选项里,除了纯干扰项外,各选项之间也互相干扰,一个空白处的误填会引起连锁反应,造成其他空白处难以正确解答。

选词填空题解题步骤

(1)先将词库(word bank)中的15个词的词性大致分类。

(2)快速浏览全文。努力寻找文中的主题句(topic sentence),弄清楚文章的主旨大意。一般来说,命题者不会在文章的首句设立考点。

(3)边阅读文章边解题。阅读时,考生首先应该充分运用自己掌握的语法等语言知识将可选范围缩小到最小,然后根据上下文、文章的主旨大意或各部分之间的逻辑关系等进行判断并最终做出选择。

(4)把所选单词放进文章并通读全文。通读全文的时候,考生应该从整体的角度来检验填入所选单词后各部分的语法是否正确,逻辑是否合理,上下文是否连贯。

第一节 语法知识是解题基础

考生在解答选词填空题时,需要根据语法知识确定词性和词形。考生应该首先对含有命题点即空白处的句子进行结构分析,找出空白处所需的单词在整个句子里充当什么成分,是作主语、谓语还是定语、状语等,进而决定此处所缺单词的词性和词形。这个时候我们就需要知道什么词性的单词可以充当什么具体成分。

解题技巧1:如何确定空白处为动词

以下五种情况,空白处可为动词:

(1)**n./pron.** ___ **vt.** ___ **n./pron.** 即空白处前已有名词/代词作主语,则空白处应为及物动词作谓语,空白处后的名词/代词是该动词的宾语;

(2)**n./pron.** ___ **vi.** 即空白处前是名词/代词,空白处后不带宾语,则空白处为不及物动词;

(3)**n./pron.** ___ **vi.** ___ **adv./prep.** 即空白处前是名词/代词作主语,空白处后是副词/介词,则空白处为不及物动词,与该副词/介词构成固定搭配；

(4)*n./pron.* __link v./be__ *adj.* 即空白处前已有名词/代词作主语,空白处后为形容词,则空白处为系动词或 be 动词;

(5)*to* ___*v.* 即空白处前有不定式标志 to,则可考虑空白处为动词原形。

另外,空白处还有可能为动词分词形式,请参考解题技巧 2 的详解。

确定了空白处为动词之后,还要判断空白处应为动词原形还是动词过去式或分词、第三人称单数形式,这根据上下文提供的语境及语义即可判断。

【例 1】El Nino usually lasts for about 18 months. The 1982-83 El Nino brought the most (destructive) weather in modern history. Its effect was worldwide and it left more than 2,000 people dead and caused over eight billion pounds (worth) of damage. The 1990 El Nino lasted until June 1995. Scientists _____ this to be the longest El Nino for 2,000 years.   [2006.6/T54]

【解析】本句主语是 Scientists,宾语是 this,因此空白处应为及物动词,作本句的谓语。结合上文的句子时态和内容,可进一步判断该及物动词为一般现在时。

【例 2】We know that *chronic* (慢性的) pain can *disrupt* (扰乱) a person's life, causing problems that _____ from missed work to depression.   [2007.6/T50]

【解析】空白处位于修饰 problems 的定语从句中,从其前面的 that 及其后面的介词 from 可确定从句缺少了谓语动词,因此空白处应填入动词。另外,从句的逻辑主语为"problems"而非"that",由此可判断空白处的动词应为动词的原形,而非第三人称单数动词。

解题技巧 2:如何确定空白处为分词

在以下三种情况中,空白处可为过去分词:

(1)has/have/had __*p.p.*__ 如果句子是现在完成时或过去完成时,has, have 或 had 后的空白处就应该填写动词的过去分词;

(2)be __*p.p.*__ 在被动语态的句子里,过去分词与助动词 be 构成句子的谓语;

(3)__*p.p.*__ *n.* 或 *n.* __*p.p.*__ 过去分词可以作形容词,表示其修饰的名词为被动或已发生的事件。

在以下两种情况中,空白处可为现在分词:

(1)*be* __-ing__ 如果句子为进行时态,在 be 动词后的空白处应填写动词的现在分词;

(2)__-ing__ *n.* 或 *n.* __-ing__ 现在分词也可充当形容词,表示其修饰的名词为主动的或正在发生的事件。

分词充当形容词时,也可以被副词修饰,因此,在副词后的空白处也可以为分词。

【例 3】The rainfall is increased across South America, _____ floods to Peru.   [2006.6/T50]

【解析】在上句中,前半段已经是一个完整的主谓句,在这种情况下,后半段应以一个动词的分词开头,整个分词结构起到对主句补充说明的作用。而根据空白处后的名词 floods 可推断该分词应为一个及物动词的分词形式。

【例 4】Groups of children _____ as peacemakers studied human rights and poverty issues in Colombia, eventually forming a group with five other schools in Bogotá known as The Schools of Peace.   [2007.12/T49]

【解析】上句的主谓为 groups of children... studied,由此可见,空白处所需的应为定语或状语之类的辅助成分。因为空白处位于主语(名词)之后,可推断空白处为主语的后置定语,结合空白处后的 as... 可推断答案最可能是一个动词的分词形式。

解题技巧 3:如何确定空白处为名词

名词在句子当中通常作主语或宾语(包括动词的宾语和介词的宾语)。

在以下情况下,空白处应为名词:

(1)a/an/the __*n.*__, *adj.* __*n.*__, *vt.* __*n.*__ 即空白处前面是冠词、形容词或及物动词;

(2)__*n.*__ *v.* 即空白处后面是动词谓语,空白处则是该动词的主语;

(3)*prep.* __*n.*__ 即空白处前面是介词,空白处充当介词宾语,在这种情况下,空白处也可能是一个动名词。

在确定空白处为名词后,还要确定该名词是单数还是复数,除了可以根据上下文的内容做出判断外,还可根据修饰该名词的冠词判断单复数。如果空白处后面是动词,则要根据主谓一致的原则判断名词的单复数。

【例5】This modern _____ for pain management has led to a wealth of innovative treatments which are more effective and with fewer side effects than ever before. [2007.6/T54]

【解析】根据空白处前的形容词modern及空白处后的介词for可判断空白处应为名词,作句子的主语,再根据句子的谓语has led to...可确定该名词应为单数名词。

【例6】The World Centers of Compassion for Children International call attention to children's rights and how to help the _____ of war. [2007.12/T55]

【解析】空白处前的冠词the和空白处后的介词of提示空白处应填写一个名词,作help的宾语。

解题技巧4:如何确定空白处为形容词

在以下情况中,空白处可为形容词:

(1) *adj.* **n.** 或 **n.** *adj.* 形容词是修饰名词的,可以前置或后置,因此,如果空白处前或后是名词,则应考虑空白处是否为形容词;

(2) *adv.* *adj.* 副词可以修饰形容词,因此如果空白处前面是副词,可以考虑空白处是否为形容词;

(3) *be/link v.* *adj.* 形容词可以作be动词或系动词的表语,因此在be动词或系动词后,可考虑是否需要一个形容词作表语。

【例7】Decades ago, there were only a _____ number of drugs available, and many of them caused _____ side effects in older people, including dizziness and fatigue. [2007.6/T55,56]

【解析】在上句中,第一个空白处前为冠词a,后为名词number,由此可推断此处应填写形容词;第二个空白处虽位于动词caused后,但其后已有名词side effects作动词caused的宾语,由此可见,空白处应为修饰side effects的形容词。

解题技巧5:如何确定空白处为副词

在以下情况中,空白处可为副词:

(1) *adv.* *v.* 或 *v.* *adv.* 副词通常修饰动词,因此,如果在空白处前后可以找到句子的主语和谓语,则应考虑空白处是否为副词,用于修饰该动词的程度状态;

(2) *adv.* *adj.* 副词也可修饰形容词,因此在形容词前的空白处也可能是副词;

(3) *adv.* 从句 有些副词作句子的状语,表达转折、因果等逻辑关系,这可以通过上下文的语义关系做出判断。

【例8】Today, we take pain _____. [2007.6/T48]

【解析】分析句子结构可知,主谓宾都齐全,但句子意思却不完整,缺少一个表示观点、态度的副词。

第二节 上下文是解题关键

根据语法知识把可选范围缩小后,往往还有几个可选的单词。这时,需要利用上下文作进一步的判断。上下文包括篇章主题和句间的逻辑关系。

解题技巧1:利用篇章主题确定词义范围与色彩

一篇文章,一个话题,都要求与之相关的词汇。单词意义的差别、所使用的语域不同,所适应的上下文也各有别。考点所要求的单词往往与文章的主题有关,只要明白了文章的主题,在词库中选择与该主题相关的单词,就可以找到答案了。

【例9】 As war spreads to many corners of the globe, children sadly have been drawn into the center of conflicts.

...

... The World Centers of Compassion for Children International call attention to children's rights and how to help the _____ of war.

[2007.12/T55]

【解析】根据全文首句中的 war, conflicts 等词及上下文的内容,可知本文的话题与"帮助饱受战祸的儿童"等有关,在词库提供的名词 images, information, projects, role, technology 和 victims 中,很明显,与主题密切相关的为 victims。

解题技巧2:利用句间逻辑关系确定词义范围与色彩

仅靠考点所在的句子往往很难判断考点单词的词义范围与色彩,但是联系句间的逻辑关系,问题就能迎刃而解。

句间逻辑关系包括:

(1)并列关系,通常由 and, or, as well as 等表示;

(2)对比关系,通常以 but, however, on the contrary, by contrast, rather than 等表示;

(3)比较关系,通常以 as... as, like, similar, parallel 等表示;

(4)因果关系,通常以 because, for, as, since, as a result of, so that, therefore, thus, hence, consequently 等表示;

(5)举例关系,通常以 for example, for instance, like, such as, and so on, that is 等表示;

(6)补充递进关系,通常以 and, furthermore, what is more, moreover, in addition 等表示。

【例10】So while some parts of the world prepare for heavy rains and floods, other parts face drought, poor crops and _____.

[2006.6/T51]

【解析】空白处前的 and 表明此处需要一个名词与前面的 drought, poor crops 并列作动词 face 的宾语,而且该名词还必须是与这两个概念一样带有消极意义,并意为某种"灾祸",因此在提供的名词 strength, phenomenon, attraction, starvation, exhaustion 和 worth 中,应选择 starvation。

第三节 巧用词汇关系事半功倍

常见的词汇关系包括:(1)固定搭配;(2)复现。

解题技巧1:巧用固定搭配中的简单虚词

英语中的固定搭配通常是动词、名词、形容词与副词、介词构成的词组。虽然搭配中的副词和介词通常是含义简单的虚词,如 to, in, for, about, up, above 等,但每一个都有其固定的搭配对象,这对考点词汇的选择起到巧妙的提示作用。

【例11】Years ago, doctors often said that pain was a normal part of life. In particular, when older patients _____ of pain, they were told it was a natural part of aging and they would have to learn to live with it. [2007.6/T47]

【解析】通过句子成份分析可判断空白处应为可与 of 搭配的动词,作从句的谓语。根据上下文的内容和时态可以推断空白处应为动词的过去时形式。这样,在提供的过去式动词 relieved, limited 和 complained 中,只有 relieved 可与 of 搭配,由此就可确定本题答案应为 relieved。

解题技巧2:巧用词汇的复现关系

词的复现指的是某一词以原词、同义词、近义词、上义词、下义词、概括词或其他形式重复出现在语篇中,语篇中的句子通过这种复现关系达到相互衔接,意义统一完整。因此,考点所要求填写的单词往往在考点之前或之后出现,但注意的是,答案大多是以复现词的方式出现,而通常不会是原词复现。

【例12】El Nino is the name given to the mysterious and often unpredictable change in the climate of the world. This strange _____ happens every five to eight years.

[2006.6/T47]

【解析】通过对句子成分的分析可以知道空白处应为名词,作句子的主语。根据考点所在句子开头的 this 可以知道考点的名词应该是对上一句提到的内容的概括,由此可见,该名词应为抽象名词,并且是 change 的上义词,在词库的名词 strength, phenomenon, attraction, starvation, exhaustion 和 worth 中,轻易就能确定只有 phenomenon 符合上下文的要求。

第四节 考点突破专项扫雷训练

Passage One

This is a holiday widely celebrated with different names in many countries. Although it __1__ as a religious holiday, it has lost its religious connections in the United States. It is now celebrated largely as a children's day, and many American children look forward to it for days and weeks __2__.

The orange pumpkin is harvested at this time of year and is __3__ out, a funny face cut into it, and a candle placed inside as a decoration in the window. City folks, nowadays, sometimes use paper pumpkins for decorations.

Some years ago, the holiday was celebrated by __4__ up in strange and frightening costumes and playing tricks on one's neighbors and friends, such as ringing door bells, throwing bits of corn on the window panes, and in other ways making minor __5__.

More recently, children come to the door to have friends and neighbors admire their costumes and guess who they are behind the false faces and receive treats of candy, fruit or cookies. They say, "Trick or Treat", meaning, "I will __6__ a trick on you if you will not give me a treat." This practice has even more recently developed into a __7__ international activity. Instead of candy, the children collect money for UNICEF (United Nations International Children's Emergency Fund). This __8__ collection of money by children for __9__ children throughout the world is known as "UNICEF Trick or Treat". Begun only recently, it results in several million dollars each year __10__ to UNICEF. The collection box is orange, reminiscent of the pumpkin.

A) needy	B) concentrated	C) disturbance	D) hollowed
E) concerned	F) play	G) critical	H) beforehand
I) significant	J) contributed	K) dressing	L) special
M) originated	N) generated	O) prediction	

Passage Two

As the plane circled over the airport, everyone sensed that something was wrong. The plane was moving __1__ through the air, and although the passengers had __2__ their seat belts, they were suddenly thrown forward. At that moment, the airhostess appeared. She looked very pale, but was quite calm. Speaking quickly but almost in a whisper, she __3__ everyone that the pilot had fainted and asked if any of the passengers knew anything about machines—or at least how to drive a car. After a moment's __4__, a man got up and followed the hostess into the pilot's cabin.

Moving the pilot aside, the man took his seat and listened carefully to the __5__ instructions that were being sent by radio from the airport below. The plane was now dangerously __6__ the ground, but to everyone's __7__, it soon began to climb. The man had to circle the airport several times in order to become __8__ with the controls of the plane. But the danger had not yet passed. The __9__ moment came when he had to land. Following instructions, the man guided the plane toward the airfield. It shook __10__ as it touched the ground and then moved rapidly along the runway and after a long run it stopped safely.

A) informed	B) familiar	C) hesitation	D) violently
E) challenge	F) unsteadily	G) charming	H) approaching
I) slightly	J) urgent	K) reminded	L) horrible
M) relief	N) fastened	O) instant	

Passage Three

People's attitudes toward drugs vary from person to person. Some see them as __1__; others think of them as dangerous. Then what is the __2__ attitude toward drugs?

I think the first thing to think about is the difference between drugs and wonder drugs. The *antibiotics* (抗生素) can really __3__ certain bacterial diseases. On the other hand, the major diseases __4__ Americans today are cancer, stroke, high blood pressure, *coronary diseases* (冠心病), etc. Against them, the doctor's bag of tricks is __5__. He has no wonder drugs.

So the first important lesson is not to expect too much from drugs. If you can accept the fact that the war against many of our most destructive diseases is, at best, a *holding operation* (防御战) rather than an inevitable __6__, it will do a great deal to ease your own life as well as that of your doctor. Too many patients __7__ great pressures on doctors to prescribe for every small symptom, even when such treatment is __8__ dangerous.

Unfortunately, the medical profession is guilty of taking part, to a certain __9__, in the wrongful action. The patient who demands a shot of penicillin for every cough may be given the injection by a __10__ doctor because he is certain that if he does not, the patient will search until he finds a doctor who will.

A) cure	B) consistently	C) exert	D) sensible
E) cancel	F) extent	G) threatening	H) defense
I) miraculous	J) limited	K) awfully	L) boundless
M) triumph	N) attracting	O) reluctant	

第五节 答案解析

参考译文   Passage One

在许多国家,人们以不同的名字庆祝这一节日。尽管它起源于一个宗教节日,但是,在当代的美国它已经和宗教没有什么关系了。现在,它主要是孩子们庆祝的一个节日,许多美国孩子在万圣节前几天或几个星期前就开始翘首企盼了。

人们在一年中的这个时候收获橙色的南瓜。他们把南瓜挖空,刻出一个滑稽的面孔,再在里面点上一根蜡烛作为窗户的装饰。现在,城镇居民有时候会用纸南瓜作为装饰。

在过去的一些年里,为了庆祝这一节日,人们穿上奇怪吓人的服装,对邻居、朋友搞些恶作剧。例如按门铃、往窗户玻璃上扔小块的玉米,或以其他方式来制造小混乱。

如今,孩子们挨家挨户敲响大门,让他们的朋友或邻居欣赏他们的万圣节服装,并猜猜面具后面的真面目。他们还会收到糖果、水果或曲奇饼。孩子们会说"Trick or Treat",意思是:如果你不款待我的话,我就搞出些恶作剧。这一做法最近发展成为一项意义深远的国际活动。孩子们不再要糖果,而是为"联合国国际儿童紧急救援基金"筹款。孩子们在为全世界贫困儿童筹款,这项活动被称为"UNICEF(联合国国际儿童紧急救援基金)的 Trick or Treat"。虽然该活动开始不久,但每年都为 UNICEF 筹得几百万美元善款。筹款箱的颜色是橙色的,这让人联想起万圣节的南瓜。

[词性分析]

名 词:disturbance 扰乱;骚乱;烦恼 play 剧本;游戏 dressing (食物)调料;敷料 special 特价,特刊 prediction 预言,预测

动 词:concentrated 全神贯注;集中;浓缩[过去式或过去分词] hollowed 挖空[过去式或过去分词] concerned 涉及;

使关心[过去式或过去分词]　play 玩;演奏;扮演　contributed 捐款;有助于;投稿[过去式或过去分词]　dressing 穿衣;包扎伤口;加作料[现在分词]　originated 起源于,产生;创始[过去式或过去分词]　generated 产生;引起[过去式或过去分词]

形容词:needy 贫困的　critical 决定性的,危急的;批评的　significant 相当数量的;重要的;意味深长的　special 特殊的;专门的

副　词:beforehand 事先

1. [M]此处需要不及物动词,作谓语。根据下文 has lost its religious connections,可以推断该半句指它"起源于"宗教节日。词库中 generated 和 originated 都表达此义,但 generated 为及物动词,只能用于 be generated 或 generate sth.,故答案为 originated。

2. [H]此处需填副词。look forward to 的动作只可能在节日到来之前发生,由此可知答案为 beforehand(事先)。

3. [D]此处需要及物动词过去分词,且能跟 out 连用,与前半句中的 is harvested 语态一致。根据下文 cut into it 及 a candle placed inside,可知南瓜要被"挖空",因此答案为 hollowed。hollow... out 意为"把……挖空"。

4. [K]此处需要不及物动词与 up 连用,而且在 by 之后,所以是动名词。根据其后的 in... costumes,可知该动词应表达"穿着"或"打扮"之义,故答案为 dressing。dress up 意为"穿上"。

5. [C]此处需填入名词。上一句提到孩子们对邻居和朋友搞恶作剧,空白处的名词应与此相关,是"按门铃"和"扔玉米"造成的结果,由此可知该词表消极意义,因此 disturbance(扰乱)正确。

6. [F]此处需要及物动词,且为原形,宾语是 a trick。前文第 3 段已出现过 playing tricks,因此可知答案为 play。

7. [I]此处需要一个描述性的形容词,与 international 一起修饰 activity。根据谓语动词 developed into,可知该词表积极意义,故 significant 比较合适,意为"重要的"。

8. [L]此处需要填入形容词。由前一句可知这是一种孩子们在万圣节时筹钱的方式,而且用于 UNICEF,所以不同于普通的方式,由此可知 special 正确。

9. [A]此处需形容词,修饰 children。前文括号里 UNICEF 的全称表明筹集的资金用于儿童的紧急救援(emergency),因此找出与 emergency 语义相关的词即是答案,即 needy,意为"贫困的"。

10. [J]此处需要及物动词分词形式,与 to 连用,作后置定语修饰 several million dollars。由上文所说孩子们为 UNICEF 筹钱,可知此处应指钱"捐"给 UNICEF,因此 contributed 正确。contribute to 意为"捐献"。

参考译文　　　　　　　　　　　　　　　　　　Passage Two

　　飞机在机场上方盘旋的时候,大家都觉察到有些不对劲。飞机在空中摇摇摆摆地飞行着。尽管乘客们扣紧了安全带,他们还是猛地被甩向前方。就在那时,乘务员出现了。她看上去面色苍白,但神色镇定。她以飞快而近乎耳语的声音告诉大家,飞行员晕倒了,并询问乘客中有没有人擅长操作机器,或者至少会开车。经过片刻的犹豫之后,一位男士站了起来,随后跟着那位乘务员走进驾驶舱。

　　这位男士把飞行员移到一旁,然后坐下来,仔细聆听机场发来的无线电紧急指令。飞机正逼近地面,险象环生,但是,让大家欣慰的是,飞机很快又爬升起来了。为了熟悉操控飞机,这位男士不得不驾驶飞机绕着机场飞了好几圈。但他们并没有脱离危险。当他不得不降落的时候,可怕的时刻到了。根据指挥,那名男士要把飞机驶向飞机场。着陆的时候飞机猛烈地摇晃,然后沿着跑道疾驰。在滑行了很长一段距离后,飞机安全地停了下来。

[词性分析]

名　词:hesitation 犹豫　challenge 挑战　relief 轻松,解脱

动　词:informed 通知[过去式或过去分词]　challenge 挑战　charming 迷人[现在分词]　approaching 逼近[现在分词]　reminded 提醒,使想起[过去式或过去分词]　fastened 扎牢,扣紧[过去式或过去分词]

形容词:informed 见闻广的　familiar 熟悉的　charming 迷人的　urgent 紧急的　horrible 可怕的　instant 立即的,直接的

副　词:violently 剧烈地　unsteadily 不稳定地,摇摆地　slightly 轻微地

1. [F]本句不缺任何必要成分,而且动词 move 在这里用作不及物动词,故此处需要一个副词作状语。首句说到 there

was something wrong 可判断该副词带有消极意义,而且三个可选副词中只有 unsteadily 可以表示 move 的方式,故为答案。

2. [N]此处需要动词的过去分词,与 had 一起构成谓语,seat belt 作其宾语。根据语义搭配可判断答案为 fastened,也可根据信号词 although 判断该动词与 thrown forward 语义相反,因此答案为 fastened。

3. [A]此处需要动词,作句子的谓语。而且因为整篇文章用的是过去时态,故这个动词还必须是及物动词的过去式。从该句开头的分词 Speaking 这个信号词入手,可判断空白处需要的是一个与说有关的单词,故答案为 informed。

4. [C]这里需要名词,作 after 的宾语。而且既然有了 after a moment,那就说明这位男士并没有立刻站起来,而是有点犹豫,故答案为 hesitation。

5. [J]此处需要形容词,作 instructions 的定语。根据本文对当时危急形势的描述,及修饰 instructions 的定语从句,可判断此处答案为 urgent。

6. [H]此处需要动词的现在分词,与 was 一起构成谓语。根据下文的转折句 but... it soon began to climb 可判断本句表达的意思与 climb 相反,即本句谓语为"……接近地面",故答案为 approaching。

7. [M]此处需要一个表达心情的名词,与 to one's 构成搭配。后面的转折分句暗示该名词应表达与前一个分句中的 dangerously 相对的意思,应具有积极意义,故答案为 relief。

8. [B]此处需要名词或形容词,作 become 的表语。因为有信号词 with,我们可以优先考虑能和 with 搭配的形容词或名词。根据上文可知,该男士本身并非飞行员,他在驾驶飞机之前必须先"熟悉"飞机的操作,故答案为 familiar。

9. [L]此处需要形容词作定语,修饰 moment。根据前一句"But the danger had not yet passed."可判断此处需要一个表示更强烈的消极意义的形容词,故答案为 horrible。

10. [D]本句结构比较完整,空白处需要副词作状语修饰 shook。根据上文"But the danger had not yet passed."可判断此处应填入一个表示消极意义的副词,词库中的 violently 和 unsteadily 都具有消极意义,但相比之下,unsteadily 表达的危险程度不如 violently,故答案为 violently。

参考译文　　　　　　　　　　　　　　　　Passage Three

对待药物的态度因人而异。有人觉得它们像奇迹一般;有人认为它们很危险。那么什么才是对待药物的明智态度呢?

我想我们首先要思考一下药物和灵丹妙药之间的区别。抗生素类药物确实能治疗某些细菌疾病。但另一方面,当今威胁美国人的主要疾病是癌症、中风、高血压和冠心病等。而对付这些疾病,医生的药葫芦十分有限。他并没有灵丹妙药。

所以我们首先应学会不要对药物期望过高。我们与众多极具危害性的疾病之间的战争,充其量只是一场防御战,并不会取得必然的胜利。如果你能接受这个事实的话,就会让你自己和你医生的生活变得大为轻松。太多的病人对医生施加巨大的压力,要他们为每一个小小的症状都开出处方治疗,尽管有时这种疗法十分危险,人们还是这么做。

遗憾的是,医务人员在某种程度上也有处理不当之嫌。如果病人一咳嗽就要求注射青霉素,那么医生就可能会勉强同意,因为他很清楚,如果他不照做的话,病人也会想方设法找到愿意这么做的医生。

[词性分析]

名　词:cure 治疗,疗法　extent 程度,范围　defense 防卫　triumph 胜利,成功

动　词:cure 治疗　exert 发挥,施加　cancel 取消　threatening 威胁[现在分词]　limited 限制,限定[过去式或过去分词]　triumph 获胜,成功　attracting 吸引[现在分词]

形容词:sensible 明智的　threatening 胁迫的,危险的　miraculous 奇迹般的,非凡的　limited 有限的　boundless 无边无际的　reluctant 勉强的

副　词:consistently 一贯地,始终如一地　awfully 非常,十分

1. [I]此处需要形容词或名词。后半句的 dangerous 一词表明此处需要相同成分的形容词,而且根据 some... others 的用法以及分号的使用可判断此处需要一个意义与 dangerous 相反的褒义词,故答案为 miraculous。

2. [D]此处需要形容词作 attitude 的定语。根据文章的主题(对待药物的正确态度)以及下文作者在这方面的介绍可判断此处需要一个表示积极意义的形容词,故答案为 sensible。

3. [A]此处需要及物动词,而且是原形,diseases 作其宾语。根据本文的主题及 diseases 的动词搭配可确定答案为 cure。

4. [G]根据 diseases 与后面的种种疾病的对应关系可确定本句主语核心词为 diseases,故_____ Americans 这个部分应该是修饰 diseases 的,所以此处需要一个现在分词,和 Americans 一起作 diseases 的后置定语。根据句子的基调可确定此处需要一个表示消极意义的词,故答案为 threatening。

5. [J]此处需要形容词、名词或动词的分词形式。结合下一句可推断本句谓语表明医生没有灵丹妙药对付癌症等主要疾病,因此可确定答案为 limited。

6. [M]这里需要可数名词,继而根据信号词组 rather than,可判断此处需要填入一个与 holding operation 相对的单词,另外,该单词的词义应表明与疾病作战的结果,故答案为 triumph。

7. [C]此处需要动词原形作谓语,以 pressures 为其宾语,而且应该可与介词 on 搭配,故答案为 exert。

8. [K]此处需要副词修饰 dangerous。该句中的 even 引出的让步从句应表明疗法"很"危险,因此空白处应为表示危险程度的副词,由此可判断答案为 awfully。

9. [F]根据句子结构分析可确定 to a certain _____与句子主要结构无关,此时可优先考虑这是一个介词 to 的固定短语,词库中适合该搭配的只有 extent。to a certain extent 意为"某种程度上"。

10. [O]这里需要形容词或相当于形容词功能的词。根据 because 引导的从句可知这个医生这么做并非心甘情愿,故答案为 reluctant。

第一节 急中生智巧猜答案

解题技巧 1：确定积极还是消极意义，缩小选择范围

　　辨认词的积极意义和消极意义包括两方面：(1)根据上下文辨认考点需要积极意义还是消极意义的词；(2)辨认词库中的词是积极意义还是消极意义。考点的上下文常常可提供线索，根据这些线索可以判断考点说的是某事物的优点还是缺点，优势还是劣势等，进而确定空白处的单词应该是积极意义还是消极意义，再到词库中寻找相应词义色彩的词，就可以大大缩小选择范围，节省大量时间。

【例1】The classroom (offers) opportunities for children to replace angry, violent behaviors with _____, peaceful ones.　　　　　　　　　　　　　　　　[2007.12/T51]

【解析】根据语法知识可判断空白处应为形容词，与 peaceful 并列修饰 ones，根据句中的 replace... with... 可知该形容词应与 peaceful 一样具有积极的词义，与前文的 angry 和 violent 的词义色彩相反，这样，在词库的形容词 comprehensive, cooperative 和 entire 中，不难确定 cooperative 为本题答案。

解题技巧 2：介词后一定是名词或动名词充当介词宾语

　　若空白处前为介词，介词就成为信号词，提示空白处应为名词或动名词。在所有介词中，特别要注意 to，因为 to 除了可充当介词外，它还可以充当引出不定式的信号词，如果考点在 to 后，就要注意判断空白处属于以上哪种情况，应填入名词还是动词。

> 　　以下为带介词to 的短语，后接动名词：abandon oneself to, adhere to, stick to, cling to, admit to, confess to, contribute to, feel up to, get down to, give one's mind to, give way to, yield to, keep to, lead to, look forward to, object to, take to, turn to, succumb to, point to, see to, be/get used to, be accustomed to, be addicted to, be committed to, be dedicated to, be devoted to, be opposed to, be reduced to, be subject to, submit to 等。

【例2】Indeed, pain is now considered the fifth vital sign, as important as blood pressure, temperature, breathing rate and pulse in _____ a person's well-being.　　　　　　　　　　　　[2007.6/T49]

【解析】根据空白处前的介词 in 可初步确定本题答案应为名词或动名词，再根据空白处后的名词词组 a person's well-being 可进一步确定空白处为动名词，a person's well-being 为其宾语，词库中只有两个动名词 prompting 和 determining，这样分析之下，选择的范围一下子从 15 个选项缩小到了两个选项，再根据上下文语义可最终确定本题答案为 determining。

解题技巧 3：不定冠词帮助判断考点是否为元音开头的单词

　　若词库中混杂了元音开头和辅音开头的单词，考点前的不定冠词(a/an)可帮助缩小选择的范围。

【例3】Husbands and children now do some of these jobs, a _____ that has changed the target market for many products. [2006.12/T49]

【解析】词库中有六个名词 scale, potential, gap, extreme, purchase 和 situation,因为考点在不定冠词 a 之后,此名词应为辅音开头,因此首先可排除元音开头的单词 extreme。根据上下文的意思来看,所填入的名词应是对前一个分句意思的概括,最合适的词应该是 situation。

解题技巧4:利用词库中的近义词或反义词

若词库中出现一对近义词或一对反义词,其中一个必定是干扰项。反义词考查考生对文章语境色彩的辨析,只要辨析考点所填单词是积极意义还是消极意义,就不难排除干扰项。近义词考查考生对词汇搭配用法的掌握,这需要考生牢记近义词的各种用法及搭配。

【例4】A) gravely   B) respect   C) limited   D) specialize
E) seriously   F) prompting   G) involves   H) relieved
I) significant   J) magnificent   K) range   L) issues
M) result   N) determining   O) complained

【题目】Today, we take pain _____. [2007.6/T48]

【解析】上句的主谓宾齐全,因此空白处应为做状语的副词。在词库中,只有两个副词:gravely 和 seriously,这两个副词是近义词,都有"严肃","严重"的意思,但与 take 搭配的必须是 seriously,take sth. seriously 是正确的搭配,而 take sth. gravely 是不正确的。因此,碰到 seriously 和 gravely 这两个极其相近的近义词时,两者不同的搭配情况就是作出正确选择的关键。

解题技巧5:英文单词往往一词多性

词库提供的单词具有一词多性的特点,如有些单词既是名词又是动词,有些动词的分词也可以充当形容词,确定空白处所需单词的词性后要全面考虑词库中的单词词性,不能遗漏。

【例5】A) gravely   B) respect   C) limited   D) specialize
E) seriously   F) prompting   G) involves   H) relieved
I) significant   J) magnificent   K) range   L) issues
M) result   N) determining   O) complained [2007.6]

【解析】在选项当中,respect, range, issues, result 既是动词也是名词,需要归入不同的词库。另外,limited, relieved, complained 既可能是动词的过去式,也可能是过去分词,虽然不必将分词与动词分开归类,但是要注意这些词既可以作动词谓语,也可以作形容词修饰语。

第二节 历年典型真题突破训练

Passage One   07年12月真题

As war spreads to many corners of the globe, children sadly have been drawn into the center of conflicts. In Afghanistan, Bosnia, and Colombia, however, groups of children have been taking part in peace education ___47___. The children, after learning to resolve conflicts, took on the ___48___ of peacemakers. The Children's Movement for Peace in Colombia was even *nominated* (提名) for the Nobel Peace Prize in 1998. Groups of children ___49___ as peacemakers studied human rights and poverty issues in Colombia, eventually forming a group with five other schools in Bogotá known as The Schools of Peace.

The classroom ___50___ opportunities for children to replace angry, violent behaviors with ___51___, peaceful ones. It is in the classroom that caring and respect for each person empowers children to take a step ___52___ toward becoming peacemakers. Fortunately, educators have access to many online resources that are ___53___ useful when helping children along the path to peace. The Young Peacemakers Club, started in 1992, provides a Website with resources for teachers and ___54___ on starting a Kindness Campaign. The World Centers of Compassion for Children International call attention to children's rights and how to help the ___55___ of war. Starting a Peacemakers' Club is a praiseworthy venture for a class and one that could spread to other classrooms and ideally affect the culture of the __56__ school.

A) acting	B) assuming	C) comprehensive	D) cooperative
E) entire	F) especially	G) forward	H) images
I) information	J) offers	K) projects	L) respectively
M) role	N) technology	O) victims	

Passage Two　　07 年 6 月真题

Years ago, doctors often said that pain was a normal part of life. In particular, when older patients __47__ of pain, they were told it was a natural part of aging and they would have to learn to live with it.

Times have changed. Today, we take pain __48__. Indeed, pain is now considered the fifth vital sign, as important as blood pressure, temperature, breathing rate and pulse in __49__ a person's well-being. We know that *chronic* (慢性的) pain can *disrupt* (扰乱) a person's life, causing problems that __50__ from missed work to depression.

That's why a growing number of hospitals now depend upon physicians who __51__ in pain medicine. Not only do we evaluate the cause of the pain, which can help us treat the pain better, but we also help provide comprehensive therapy for depression and other psychological and social __52__ related to chronic pain. Such comprehensive therapy often __53__ the work of social workers, *psychiatrists* (心理医生) and psychologists, as well as specialists in pain medicine.

This modern __54__ for pain management has led to a wealth of innovative treatments which are more effective and with fewer side effects than ever before. Decades ago, there were only a __55__ number of drugs available, and many of them caused __56__ side effects in older people, including dizziness and fatigue. This created a double-edged sword: the medications helped relieve the pain but caused other problems that could be worse than the pain itself.

A) gravely	B) respect	C) limited	D) specialize
E) seriously	F) prompting	G) involves	H) relieved
I) significant	J) magnificent	K) range	L) issues
M) result	N) determining	O) complained	

第三节　答案解析

参考译文　　　　　　　　　　　　　　　　　　Passage One

　　战争扩散到地球的许多角落,不幸把儿童也卷入冲突的中心。然而,在阿富汗、波斯尼亚和哥伦比亚等地,成群的孩子们正在参与各种和平教育项目。在学会了如何解决冲突后,这些孩子就承担起和平使者的角色。1998 年,哥伦比亚的儿童和平运动甚至被提名为诺贝尔和平奖的候选人。几群充当和平使者的儿童研究哥伦比亚的人权问题和贫困问题,并最终和首都波哥大的另外五所学校一起组成了一个名叫"和平学校"的团体。

　　学校教室为孩子们提供了用合作、和平的行为取代愤怒、暴力的行为的机会。正是在教室里,对每一个人的关心和尊敬使学生能够朝着成为和平使者迈进一步。幸运的是,教育者们可以利用许多网络资源,它们对帮助孩子们走向和平之路尤为有用。1992 年创建的少年和平使者协会提供了一个网站,上面有教师需要的教学资料,还有有关启动善心计划的资料。世界国际儿童关怀中心呼吁人们关注儿童权利、关注如何帮助战争中的受害者。对一个班级来说,组建一个和平使者协会是值得赞赏的事情,它可以影响并扩展到别的班级,并有望影响到全校的风气。

【词性分析】

名　词：acting 行为；演出，演技　images 形象[复数]　information 信息　projects 工程，项目[复数]　role 角色；作用　technology 技术　victims 受害者；牺牲者[复数]

动　词：acting 行为；表演[现在分词]　assuming 认为；假设[现在分词]　offers 提供[第三人称单数]　projects 投影[第三人称单数]

形容词：acting 代理的　comprehensive 综合的；理解的　cooperative 合作的　entire 整个的，全部的

副　词：especially 尤其，特别地　forward 向前　respectively 分别地，各自地

47. [K]空白处缺名词。根据句子意思，特别是谓语 take part in，可以比较容易地确定答案为 projects。

48. [M]空白处缺名词。构成搭配 take on the role of..."承担⋯⋯的角色"。

49. [A]分析句子结构，句子已有谓语动词 studied，此处所填入的词应该作主语的后置定语。再结合句子意思，groups of children 与 peacemakers 应该指同一群人，填入 acting 正好可以与 as 构成固定搭配，所以答案为 acting。

50. [J]本句缺谓语动词。句子主语是单数第三人称，再结合句子意思，不难选出正确答案 offers。

51. [D]空白处缺形容词。此形容词在语义上应该与 peaceful 一致，表示正面和积极意义，而与前面的 angry 以及 violent 表示负面意义的词相对。由此，可以比较容易地选出正确答案 cooperative。

52. [G]观察句子结构，不缺主谓宾成分，可知此处缺一个副词，把词库中的三个副词进行对比，可以发现只有 forward 符合句意：take a step forward 意为"朝前迈了一步"。

53. [F]空白处之前的系动词和之后的形容词 useful 之间要填入的应该是一个副词，在 especially 和 respectively 之间，不难选定 especially。

54. [I]根据句子结构，可以断定 and 之后的部分应该是与之前的(a Website with) resources 并列的同类名词，可以确定答案是 information。

55. [O]空白处要填入的应该是一个名词，根据上下文的意思，特别是空白处之后的修饰成分 of war，可以选出正确答案 victims。

56. [E]首先判定空白处需要一个形容词来修饰名词 school，再根据句子意思，尤其是本句中 a class 与 spread to other classrooms，可以锁定要填入的词是 entire。

参考译文　　　　　　　　　　　　　　　　　　　Passage Two

多年以前，医生经常说疼痛在生活中是很正常的。特别是当年纪大的病人抱怨疼痛的时候，医生会告诉他们这是变老的自然过程，他们得学会容忍疼痛。

时代变了。如今，我们以认真而严肃的态度对待疼痛。在判断一个人的健康程度的时候，疼痛现在的确被认为是第五个重要的迹象了，和血压、体温、呼吸速度以及脉搏同样重要。我们知道慢性疼痛会扰乱一个人的生活，引起一系列问题，比如休假在家甚至抑郁症等。

这就是为什么如今越来越多的医院依靠专攻疼痛医学的医生的原因了。我们不仅分析疼痛的原因，这可以帮助我们更好地治疗疼痛，而且我们为抑郁症和其他与慢性疼痛相关的心理和社会问题提供综合性治疗。这样的综合性治疗除了经常需要疼痛医学方面的专家的协作外，还需要社会工作者、心理医生和心理学家的协作。

这种现代的对于疼痛处理的重视导致了许多创新性的治疗，这些治疗比以前更加有效，而且副作用更小。几十年前，只有有限的几种药物，而且其中许多药物在老人身上会引起很大的副作用，包括眩晕和疲劳。这是一把双刃剑：药物治疗有助于减轻疼痛，但是却引起了其他的问题，这些问题可能比疼痛本身更糟糕。

【词性分析】

名　词：respect 重视，关心，考虑；方面；尊敬　prompting 敦促，促使，催促，推动　range 范围，射程　issues 问题；发行；发出，流出[复数]　result 结果

动　词：respect 尊敬　limited 限制，限定[过去时或过去分词]　specialize 专长，专攻　prompting 敦促，促使，催促，推动[现在分词]　involves 包含，涉及[第三人称单数]　relieved 援助；减轻或解除(痛苦或困难)[过去时或过去分词]　range 在⋯范围内变动　issues 发行；发出，流出[第三人称单数]　result 导致　determining 决定[现在分词]　complained 抱怨[过去时或过去分词]

形容词：limited 有限的　relieved 感到宽慰的,放心的　significant 重要的,有重大意义的,有相当数量的,不可忽略的　magnificent 宏伟的,壮丽的

副　词：gravely 严峻地,严肃地　seriously 严重地,重大地,严肃地,认真地

47. **[O]** 空白处缺谓语动词,用一般过去时。根据上下文意思和空白处紧跟的介词 of 搭配,可以比较容易地确定答案为 complained。

48. **[E]** 分析句子结构可知,主谓宾都齐全,但句子意思却不完整,尚缺少一个表示观点、态度的实义副词。备选的两个副词 seriously 和 gravely 中,只有前者可与 take 构成词组 take sth. seriously,表示"认真对待某事",符合句意。

49. **[N]** 空白处位于介词 in 之后,且又带名词词组作其宾语,故应该填入动名词。从备选的两个 -ing 结构中,只有 determining 合适,该处表示"在判断或决定一个人的健康程度的时候"。

50. **[K]** 很明显,空白处前的 that 引导的是一个定语从句,修饰 problems,而且可以看出 that 在句中作主语,所以此处填入的应该是定语从句的谓语动词。根据时态,该动词应是动词原形,再根据 from... to 的搭配,不难选出正确答案 range。

51. **[D]** 此处要填入的应该是定语从句的谓语动词,而且用一般现在时。再根据句意,以及空白处后面的介词 in 的搭配,可选出正确答案 specialize。

52. **[L]** 根据空白前的修饰成分 other psychological and social 断定,此处要填入一个复数名词;再根据句意,可以锁定正确答案 issues。

53. **[G]** 空白处要填入的应该是句子的谓语动词,而且是第三人称单数形式,只有 involves 符合,而且也贴合句意。

54. **[B]** 空白处要填入的应该是一个名词,根据前文的意思及与空格后介词 for 的搭配,可以断定正确答案应该是 respect "重视"。（如果没有意识到 respect for 有"对……的重视"的含义,就会轻率地否定 respect,从而误选 prompting。）

55. **[C]** 空白处要填入的应该是一个形容词,而且根据副词 only 可以很快选出正确答案 limited。

56. **[I]** 空白处后的 side effects 意为"副作用",此处需要一个形容词,根据前后句意义的对比,从词库可供选择的两个形容词 significant 和 magnificent 中,很容易选出与前句中 few 意思相反的 significant 作为答案。

第三章

610分篇章词汇突击训练

第一节 突击训练

Passage One

An investigator into the drug *overdose* (服药过量) death of Marilyn Monroe 43 years ago Friday still is not convinced she killed herself.

John W. Miner, who investigated Monroe's death as a Los Angeles County prosecutor, claims Monroe's psychologist, Dr. Ralph Greenson, played him secret audiotapes made by the star during one of her therapy sessions __1__ before her death. A key __2__ of the *alleged* (所谓的) tapes, according to Miner, is that Monroe was not __3__ and was actively planning to become a serious, Shakespearean actress.

Miner says he took careful, hand-written notes of the tapes and later produced a near-exact transcript. There is no __4__ Miner's claims are true, since Dr. Greenson is now dead and no one else claims to have heard the tape.

"You are the only person who will ever know the most __5__ thoughts of Marilyn Monroe," she allegedly told her doctor.

In Miner's transcript, Monroe discussed her plans to __6__ Shakespeare.

"No __7__ person could possibly think that the person who made those tapes killed herself," Miner said.

She also may have recorded her feelings about having to __8__ off her *romance* (罗曼史) with Robert Kennedy.

"There is no room in my life for him," she allegedly said. "I guess I don't have the __9__ to face up to it and hurt him. I want someone else to tell him it's over. I tried to get the president to do it, but I couldn't __10__ him."

A) proof	B) reasonable	C) postpone	D) secret
E) bold	F) break	G) optimistic	H) shortly
I) revelation	J) pursue	K) courage	L) constantly
M) depressed	N) assignment	O) reach	

Passage Two

Drumming (打鼓), shouting and men dressed up in wedding dresses. African football crowds are mad in showing their __1__ in their own special way.

"Some people had painted football shirts onto their bodies," says English fan Claire Zakiewicz, who __2__ a man in a wedding dress at a game in Senegal last year. "Everyone was shouting—it was like England, everyone in the crowd wants to be the manager."

With dancing and singing such a big part of African culture it's no surprise that African stars are as ___3___ for their victory dances as their crowds are for their cheering. Cote d'Ivoire *striker* (射手) Didier Drogba is well-loved for doing the "fouka fouka", a special African dance, after he ___4___.

Others see football as something more serious: a ___5___ to the continent's problems. After war-torn Cote d'Ivoire ___6___ for this year's World Cup, many hoped it could help unite the warring North and South.

One ___7___ fan declared: Our players have put an end to the war. The time for ___8___ has come.

Four of the continent's five World Cup 2006 teams are newcomers. But all share similar ___9___: to improve their lives with victories on the world stage. With fighting in Angola, political ___10___ in Togo, and Ghana in financial trouble, African fans hope their footballers can bring them some joy.

A) scores	B) qualified	C) reunion	D) intense
E) spotted	F) disagreements	G) similarity	H) solution
I) emotional	J) famed	K) flees	L) passion
M) longed	N) ambitions	O) accidentally	

Passage Three

If an animal is moved from its home in the *tropics* (热带地区) to a cold climate, it will die if it is not kept warm. And animals ___1___ to cold climates will die if they are moved to the tropics. Many plants, too, will die if they are removed from the place where they ___2___ grow and are *transplanted* (移植) into an unfamiliar soil. Almost every species is adapted to life in a particular place by its organs and their functions and by ___3___ habits. The specialized adaptation has great advantages, for it ___4___ many organisms to survive under different conditions. It also has disadvantages, for it means that the life of most species is controlled by ___5___ conditions.

Living things are not ___6___ over the earth freely; most species have definite habits for living places. Ecology is the study of how organisms live in their environment. This means finding out how an organism survives and ___7___ in certain surroundings. By environment we mean not only the soil and the climate but the living things of the same species and other species, plant or animal. Most living things are ___8___ to their environment. Some can ___9___ certain features of their environment to suit themselves; a *beaver* (海狸), for example, can make ponds by building dams, many birds and insects can build elaborate nests to provide ___10___ for their young. But these skills are restricted and highly specialized. Most organisms must adapt their bodies to fit in with their surroundings, and since they can adapt only for particular surroundings, they are found only in places where they can live successfully with the least effort.

A) normally	B) shelter	C) assigned	D) accustomed
E) scattered	F) abundant	G) surely	H) alter
I) reproduces	J) permanent	K) slaves	L) approach
M) enables	N) alternative	O) local	

第二节 答案解析

参考译文 **Passage One**

43 年前，玛丽莲·梦露因服用过量安眠药而离开人世。上周五，一位调查人员经过调查仍然相信她不是自杀的。

曾调查梦露死因的前洛杉矶检察官约翰·W.米诺声称,梦露的心理咨询师拉尔夫·格林森医生给他听了些秘密的录音带。录音带是在梦露去世前不久接受心理治疗时录制的。按照米诺的说法,从这些所谓的录音带中找到了一项重要发现——梦露没有沮丧,而且还在积极地筹划,希望自己成为一名真正的莎士比亚戏剧演员。

米诺说,他听磁带时做了详细的笔记,稍后还整理出几近完整的录音文字。由于格林森医生已不在人世,而且没有其他人声称听过这些录音带,因而米诺这一说法的真实性没有得到证实。

"你是唯一一个知晓玛丽莲·梦露最隐蔽想法的人。"她这样跟她的医生说过。

在米诺的录音稿中,梦露讲述了她准备出演莎士比亚剧的计划。

"任何有理智的人都不会相信录音的这个人会自杀。"米诺说。

她可能还录下了她与罗伯特·肯尼迪不得不分手的心情。

"我的生命中已不再有他的位置,"她这样说,"我想我没有勇气面对这件事,去伤害他。我想让别人告诉他我们已经结束了。我试图让总统告诉罗伯特·肯尼迪这件事,但是我联系不到他。"

[词性分析]

名 词:proof 证据;校样 secret 秘密 break 休息;破裂 revelation 揭示 courage 勇气 assignment 任务;分派 reach 能达到的范围

动 词:postpone 推迟,延期 break 打破;损坏;折断 pursue 从事;追赶;追求 reach 到达;延伸;够到;与……取得联系;达成(协议等)

形容词:proof 防……的 reasonable 讲道理的;合理的 secret 秘密的 bold 大胆的 optimistic 乐观的 depressed 沮丧的

副 词:shortly 立刻,不久 constantly 经常地

1. [H]本句不缺任何必须成分,故可优先考虑副词作状语。本句中的 during one of her therapy sessions 表明该副词其后的时间状语应为一次性的,在词库的两个副词中,constantly 是一个表示持续性的副词,故可排除,答案为shortly。

2. [I]此处需要名词作句子的主语核心词,本句是为了进一步说明上一句提到的磁带揭示了什么秘密,词库中的 revelation 和 secret 在语义上都与此有关。根据本句的谓语部分可知该秘密已经揭开,而 secret 一词含有"不为人知、尚未揭晓"的意思,不妥当,因此答案为 revelation。

3. [M]此处需要形容词、名词或动词的分词作表语。根据 and 这个表示并列关系的信号词可判断空白处需要一个表示消极意义的词,故答案为 depressed。

4. [A]此处需要名词,可以是不可数名词,也可是单数可数名词。根据后面 since 引导的从句以及前文所说是 Dr. Greenson 把录音带放给 Miner 听的,可推断主句暗示"死无对证",故答案为 proof。

5. [D]此处需要形容词作 thoughts 的定语。该句话是梦露对她的医生说的,结合该句中的 only person 等可推断 secret 最适合,表明只有医生一个人知道她的秘密。

6. [J]由不定式信号词 to 可推断,此处需要动词。第 2 段末句提到梦露曾经 planning to become a serious, Shakespearean actress,本句同样讲到了梦露和莎士比亚,由此可判断本题答案为 pursue(追求)。

7. [B]此处需要形容词或分词作定语。根据文中所述 Miner 的调查和发现以及他的观点可判断他认为梦露并不是自杀的,由此可决定此处需要一个表示积极意义的词,故答案为 reasonable。

8. [F]此处需要动词,且可与 off 搭配,根据空白处后的内容可以推断该动词表明梦露和肯尼迪"结束"恋情,故 break 最适合。

9. [K]此处需要名词,作 have 的宾语。根据 face up to 这个信号词组以及下文 I want someone else to tell him it's over,可判断此处答案为 courage,表明梦露没有勇气来面对这件事情。

10. [O]此处需要动词原形,根据 but 一词的作用可推断该动词表明的动作与前面分句中 get 的意思相同,在该句中表明没能"联系到"总统,故答案为 reach。

参考译文

Passage Two

打鼓、呐喊还有穿着婚礼服的男士。非洲足球迷们用自己特有的疯狂方式来表达他们的热情。

"有些人把球衣画到自己身上,"英国球迷克莱尔·萨吉维斯说。她去年在塞内加尔的一场比赛上看见了一个穿着结

婚礼服的男士。"每个人都在大喊大叫,情况就像在英格兰那样,每个人都想成为足球队的经理。"

又唱又跳是非洲文化很重要的一部分。难怪非洲球迷以他们的呐喊声而出名,非洲足球明星则以他们获胜后所跳的舞蹈而著名。科特迪瓦队射手迪迪尔·德罗巴因射门得分后跳 fouka fouka 舞(一种非洲独有的舞蹈)而广受人们的喜爱。

其他人把足球看成一种更为严肃的事物——足球能解决非洲问题。饱受战争之苦的科特迪瓦能参加今年的世界杯之后,很多人希望足球也能帮忙,把南北敌对双方统一起来。

一个激动的球迷宣称:我们的运动员结束了战争,统一的时候到了。

参加 2006 年世界杯的五支非洲球队中,有四支是新队伍。但是这几支球队都拥有相似的雄心壮志:在世界舞台上用胜利来改善生活状况。尽管安哥拉爆发内战,多哥出现政治分歧,加纳陷入金融危机,非洲球迷们还是希望他们的足球运动员能给他们带来些许欢乐。

[词性分析]

名 词:scores 得分;二十;刻痕 [复数] reunion 统一,团聚;(久别后的) 聚会 disagreements 不和,争执 [复数] solution 解决方案;解决;溶液 passion 激情,热情;酷爱 ambitions 雄心,野心[复数]

动 词:scores 得分;给……评分;刻痕于[第三人称单数] qualified 具有资格[过去式或过去分词] spotted 认出,发现;玷污[过去式或过去分词] flees 逃跑,逃走[第三人称单数] longed 渴望,热望[过去式或过去分词]

形容词:qualified 有资格的 intense 强烈的,剧烈的;认真的;热情的 spotted 有斑点的,有污点的 emotional 易动感情的 famed 著名的,闻名的

副 词:accidentally 偶然地,意外地

1. [L]此处需要名词,作 show 的宾语核心词。根据第 1 句所描述的非洲球迷们大喊呐喊的情况,可推断出他们表达了对足球的"热情",故答案为 passion。

2. [E]此处需要动词,且为及物动词,作 who 引导的从句的谓语。根据时间信号词 last year,可确定该动词必须是过去式,结合上下文可推断该动词意为"看到,认出",故答案为 spotted。

3. [J]此处需要形容词或相当于形容词功能的词作表语,并可与介词 for 搭配。下一句关于科特迪瓦球员的例子是为了具体说明本句提到的现象,因此可推断空白处需要与 well-loved for 意义相近的词,故答案为 famed。

4. [A]此处需要动词,作 after 从句的谓语。根据整个句子的时态可确定该动词必须是现在时,且为第三人称单数形式,本句是举例说明上一句的,由此可推断该从句与上一句中的 victory 语义相关,故答案为 scores。

5. [H]这里需要单数可数名词作同位语。根据下文非洲人对足球能制止战争等的描述以及该词与 to the... problems 的搭配,可判断本题答案为 solution。

6. [B]此处需要动词,作 after 从句的谓语,且为过去式的形式,可与介词 for 搭配。根据上下文的内容,可判断此句表明科特迪瓦"有资格"参加世界杯,因此 qualified 最合适。

7. [I]此处需要形容词或分词作定语。根据本文对球迷的基调(mad, passion)可确定答案为 emotional。

8. [C]此处需要名词,作介词 for 的宾语。本句是对上一句 put an end to the war 的进一步说明和总结,因此可推断答案为 reunion,表明统一是战争结束带来的结果。

9. [N]此处需要名词,作 share 的宾语。本句中的不定式结构 to improve...表明该句指所有的人怀着相似的"愿望、目标",故答案为 ambitions。

10. [F]此处需要名词,与 fighting 一起作介词 with 的宾语。根据同一句中的 fighting 和 financial trouble,可判断此处需要的是一个具有消极意义的名词,故答案为 disagreements。

参考译文 Passage Three

生长在热带地区的动物要是被带到寒冷地区而且不能保暖的话,它很快就会死亡。同样,习惯了寒冷气候的动物如果被放到热带地区也会死亡。许多植物要是从它们的生长地被移走,移植到陌生的土壤环境中,也会死亡。几乎每个物种都会因其器官、功能以及一直以来习惯的特性而适存于某个特定地方。这种特别的适应性有很多好处,因为它使很多生物在不同的环境下都能存活。但这也有缺点,因为这就意味着大多数物种的生命会受制于当地的环境。

生物并非随意地散落在地球上的,大部分物种都有特定的习惯来适应它们的生存环境。生态学是研究生物体如何

适应环境而生存的。这就意味着要找出生物如何在某种环境下生存并繁衍的规律。所谓环境,不仅是指土壤和气候,还包括相同物种和不同物种的生物体,如动植物。大多数生物都对它们生存的环境有强烈的依赖性。有些生物能够改变环境的某些特点,以适应自己的生活。例如,一只海狸能筑堤围塘;许多鸟类和昆虫能筑起巢穴为它们的孩子提供住所。但这些技能很受限制而且专业性很强。大部分的生物体必须改变自身来适应环境,而且由于它们只能适应特定的环境,所以它们只会生活在最容易存活的地方。

[词性分析]

名　词:shelter 庇护物,住所　slaves 奴隶[复数]　approach 方法;靠近;途经　alternative 可供选择的方法或事物

动　词:shelter 掩蔽,庇护　assigned 分配,指派[过去式或过去分词]　accustomed 使……习惯于[过去式或过去分词]　scattered 分散,分布;撒播[过去式或过去分词]　alter 改变　reproduces 繁殖,复制[第三人称单数]　staves 苦干,拼命干[第三人称单数]　approaches 接近,靠近　enables 使能够[第三人称单数]

形容词:accustomed 习惯的　scattered 分散的　abundant 丰富的,充裕的　permanent 永久的,持久的　alternative 选择性的　local 当地的,局部的

副　词:normally 通常地　surely 的确地

1. [D]此处需要形容词或动词的分词来构成 animals 的后置定语,且可与介词 to 搭配。本句与上一句的内容相反,对比两句的结构和内容,可以推断空白处应为 accustomed 一词。
2. [A]此处需要副词,作 where 从句里的状语。removed from... into...结构表明定语从句里的内容与 into 后的 unfamiliar 相反,由此可确定本题答案为 normally。
3. [J]此处需要形容词或相当于形容词功能的词,作 habits 的定语。本句是对前三句提到的例子的概括,结合前三句的内容可确定答案为 permanent。
4. [M]此处需要动词,充当 if 从句中的谓语,而且该动词应该是第三人称单数形式,并可与 to 搭配,词库中只有 enables 合适。
5. [O]此处需要形容词或相当于形容词功能的词,作 conditions 的定语。本句作为末句,与本段的主题密切相关,指出物种的生命受制于它们生长所在地的条件,词库中只有 local 可表达这个意思。
6. [E]此处需要形容词或动词的分词形式。分号后面的分句是对前一个分句的进一步说明,空白处前已有 not,因此可推断空白处的单词与第 2 个分句中的 have definite habits 意思相反,由此可确定答案为 scattered。
7. [I]此处需要一个第三人称单数的不及物动词,与 survives 作 how 引导的从句的谓语,它应该是与 survive 类似的动词,用于描述生物的习性,故答案为 reproduces。
8. [K]此处可能需要形容词或名词,作 are 的表语;也可能需要动词分词作谓语。前文第 1 段最后一句提到大部分物种的生命受制于环境,此句属于前文的复现,所填词应与第 1 段最后一句中的 controlled 同义,词库中只有 slaves 可表达这个意思。
9. [H]此处需要动词原形,作句子的谓语。下文海狸筑坝等例子是为了说明本考点所在句子的观点的,因此根据例子的内容可确定答案为 alter,表明生物改变环境来适应自己。
10. [B]此处需要名词,作 provide 的宾语。句中的不定式 to provide _____ for their young 是 build nests(筑巢)的目的,由此可判断答案为 shelter。

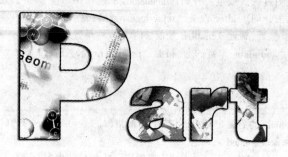

第四篇

篇章阅读理解

稳拿480分阅读考点突破

大学英语四级考试的篇章阅读理解题由 2 篇篇幅在 250~300 词之间,内容、难度和体裁不同的短文构成,每篇各有 5 个相关的多项选择题。文章的题材通常包括历史、文化、人物传记、科技、地理、生物、化学、医学、电子、常识、文学等,体裁有叙述文、议论文、说明文等,通过对历年试题的分析可以发现,四级篇章阅读文章主要是议论文和说明文。

阅读理解的题型主要包括主旨型、推理型、作者语气或态度型、结论型等主观题和事实型、推测词义型、指代关系型等客观题。

阅读题的解题步骤

(1)迅速浏览一下文章。通常只要看看每段的第 1 句话就够了,目的是先对文章的体裁做出判断。

(2)迅速浏览问题。

(3)通读全文并答题。

基本应试技巧

(1)注意解题顺序:应先回答与细节和事实有关的问题,然后回答与文章大意有关的题目,最后再完成推理性的题目。

(2)灵活采用解题方法:一定要认真阅读每个选项,找出它们之间的不同点。

(3)做完一篇文章所有的题目后,把 5 个题的答案连接起来,看看与文章的大意是否相符。

第一节 主旨大意题的 3 种命题规律

主旨类试题的目的在于考查考生对文章的主题、中心思想的理解以及区别主要信息和次要信息的能力。所谓主旨,即中心思想,是一篇文章或一个段落的核心,是作者在文章中要表达的主要内容,是作者写作意图的具体体现。作者通常都在文章中努力通过各种支持细节(Supporting Details)来进行阐明。

根据问题内容的不同,这类问题可分为主题型、标题型和目的型。主题型一目了然,就是找中心思想(Main Idea);标题型是为文章选择标题(Title);目的型就是推断作者的写作意图(Purpose)。

主旨大意题的主要命题方式如下:

The passage is mainly about _____.

The main idea of the passage is that _____.

The best title for this passage would be _____.

What is the subject of the passage?

Which of the following best summarizes/reflects the main idea of the passage?

The main purpose of this passage is to _____.

主旨大意题通常有以下 3 种命题规律。

命题规律 1:段首段尾处常出题

在四级考试中,文章或段落的主旨常以主题句的形式出现。文章的第 1 段段首段尾或最后一段段尾处往往是整篇文章主题的所在;每一段的段首或段尾句有时是该段的主题句,因此命题者常常围绕此处出题。

在演绎类的文章中,语篇主题句一般位于篇章的开头部分;在归纳总结类文章中,多出现在段末或篇末;不过有时主题句也出现在文章中间。找到了主题句,就等于找到了此类题的答案。

【例 1】 So long as teachers fail to distinguish between teaching and learning, they will continue to undertake to do for children that which only children can do for themselves. Teaching children to read is not passing reading on to them. It is certainly not endless hours spent in activities about reading. Douglas insists that "reading cannot be taught directly and schools should stop trying to do the impossible".

Teaching and learning are two entirely different processes. They differ in kind and function. The function of teaching is to create the conditions and the climate that will make it possible for children to devise the most efficient system for teaching themselves to read. Teaching is also a public activity: it can be seen and observed.

Learning to read involves all that each individual does to make sense of the world of printed language. Almost all of it is private, for learning is an occupation of the mind, and that process is not open to public scrutiny.

If teacher and learner roles are not interchangeable, what then can be done through teaching that will aid the child in the *quest* (探索) for knowledge? Smith has one principal rule for all teaching instructions. "Make learning to read easy, which means making reading a meaningful, enjoyable and frequent experience for children."

When the roles of teacher and learner are seen for what they are, and when both teachers and learners fulfill them appropriately, then much of the pressure and feeling of failure for both is eliminated. Learning to read is made easier when teachers create an environment where children are given the opportunity to solve the problem of learning to read by reading.

[1999.1/第 4 篇]

【题目】The main idea of the passage is that _____.

A) teachers should do as little as possible in helping students learn to read

B) teachers should encourage students to read as widely as possible

C) reading ability is something acquired rather than taught

D) reading is more complicated than generally believed

【解析】此题的主题句出现在首段末句,该句引用了道格拉斯的观点:reading cannot be taught directly(阅读不能直接被教会)。这实际上也是作者全文想要论证的观点,也就是文章的主题。[答案:C]

命题规律 2:归纳文中未出现的主题句

因为文章体裁的原因,或是由于短文是节选的,有的文章是没有主题句的。这时就要靠考生自己概括或归纳文章的主题思想了。概括主题可以从归纳每段的要点开始,最后将各段要点集中概括,进而归纳出全文的主题思想。

【例 2】 It is hard to track the blue whale, the ocean's largest creature, which has almost been killed off by commercial whaling and is now listed as an endangered species. Attaching radio devices to it is difficult, and visual sightings are too unreliable to give real insight into its behavior.

So biologists were delighted early this year when, with the help of the Navy, they were able to track a particular blue whale for 43 days, monitoring its sounds. This was possible because of the Navy's formerly top-secret system of underwater listening devices spanning the oceans.

Tracking whales is but one example of an exciting new world just opening to civilian scientists after the cold war as the Navy starts to share and partly uncover its global network of underwater listening system built over the decades to track the ships of potential enemies.

Earth scientists announced at a news conference recently that they had used the system for closely monitoring a deep-sea volcanic *eruption* (爆发) for the first time and that they plan similar studies.

Other scientists have proposed to use the network for tracking ocean currents and measuring changes in ocean and global temperatures.

The speed of sound in water is roughly one mile a second—slower than through land but faster than through air. What is most important, different layers of ocean water can act as channels for sounds, focusing them in the same way a *stethoscope* (听诊器) does when it carries faint noises from a patient's chest to a doctor's ear. This focusing is the main reason that even relatively weak sounds in the ocean, especially low-frequency ones, can often travel thousands of miles. [2002.6/第 3 篇]

【题目】The passage is chiefly about _____.

A) an effort to protect an endangered marine species

B) the civilian use of a military detection system

C) the exposure of a U.S. Navy top-secret weapon

D) a new way to look into the behavior of blue whales

【解析】本文没有明显的语篇主题句。第 1、2 段以追踪蓝鲸为例引出话题,即军事技术(水下监听)在非军事领域的应用。第 3 段进一步加以明确,指出追踪蓝鲸仅仅是这一技术应用的一个例子。第 4 段说的是水下监听技术在 monitoring deep-sea volcanic eruption 方面的应用。第 5 段说的是水下监听技术在 tracking ocean currents and measuring changes in ocean and global temperatures 方面的应用。最后一段是作了原理性的说明。综上所述,本文的话题是水下监听技术,主题则是这一技术在非军事领域的广泛应用。[答案:B]

命题规律 3:概括文章的标题

　　文章标题的选择就是主题的选择,所不同的是,主题或中心思想一般以句子的形式表达,而标题则以短语的形式表达。因此,文章标题的选择必须建立在对文章充分了解的基础上,因此考生应先归纳全文中心大意,而后选出最能完整概括全文的标题。

【例 3】　Americans are proud of their variety and individuality, yet they love and respect few things more than a uniform, whether it is the uniform of an elevator operator or the uniform of a five-star general. Why are uniforms so popular in the United States?

Among the arguments for uniforms, one of the first is that in the eyes of most people they look more professional than *civilian* (百姓的) clothes. People have become conditioned to expect superior quality from a man who wears a uniform. The television repairman who wears a uniform tends to inspire more trust than one who appears in civilian clothes. Faith in the skill of a garage mechanic is increased by a uniform. What easier way is there for a nurse, a policeman, a barber, or a waiter to lose professional *identity* (身份) than to step out of uniform?

Uniforms also have many practical benefits. They save on other clothes. They save on laundry bills. They are *tax-deductible* (可减税的). They are often more comfortable and more durable than civilian clothes.

Primary among the arguments against uniforms is their lack of variety and the consequent loss of individuality experienced by people who must wear them. Though there are many types of uniforms, the wearer of any particular type is generally stuck with it, without change, until retirement. When people look alike, they tend to think, speak, and act similarly, on the job at least.

Uniforms also give rise to some practical problems. Though they are long-lasting, often their initial expense is greater than the cost of civilian clothes. Some uniforms are also expensive to maintain, requiring professional dry cleaning rather than the home laundering possible with many types of civilian clothes. [2000.6/第 3 篇]

【题目】The best title for this passage would be _____.

A) Uniforms and Society 　　　　　　B) The Importance of Wearing a Uniform

C) Practical Benefits of Wearing a Uniform 　　D) Advantages and Disadvantages of Uniforms

【解析】本文可分为三个部分。第 1 段提出话题:uniform。以下的四段中,每段的第 1 句都是该段的主题句。第 2、3 段说明了制服的好处,第 4、5 段说的是制服的不利方面。因此,这篇文章的主题是:制服的利与弊。[答案:D]

第二节 事实细节题/推理判断题的 10 种命题规律

事实细节题和推理判断题在历年考题中比例几乎是最大的,虽然它们的提问方式并不相同,但是它们的命题规律是一致的,都是针对文章的某句话、某个对象等细节事实而出题。

事实细节题的命题方式通常有以下几种:

Which of the following is (NOT) true when talking about...?

What is the example of... as described in the passage?

The reason for... is _____.

According to the passage, when (where, why, how, who, etc.)...?

The following statements about... are true EXCEPT _____.

推理判断题的命题方式通常有:

The writer implies but not directly states that _____.

It can be inferred from the passage that... is _____.

The author strongly suggests that _____.

It can be concluded from the passage that _____.

What do we learn about... from Paragraph X?

The study/research/example of... indicates that _____.

以下为 10 种命题规律。

命题规律 1:例子常考

举例子是作者说明某种观点时常用的一种写作手法,就例子的细节或目的提问则是考试的一项常见内容。提问细节时当然对号入座就可以了,提问目的时则要结合段落的主题来回答。请看下面这段文字及相关的两个问题。

【例 4】 (... Exposed to higher standards of service everywhere, Israelis are returning home expecting the same...)

Privatization, or the threat of it, is a motivation as well. *Monopolies* (垄断者) that until recently have been free to take their customers for granted now fear what Michael Perry, a marketing professor, calls "the revengeful consumer." When the government opened up competition with Bezaq, the phone company, its international branch lost 40% of its market share, even while offering competitive rates. Says Perry, "People wanted revenge for all the years of bad service." The electric company, whose monopoly may be short-lived, has suddenly stopped requiring users to wait half a day for a repairman. Now, appointments are scheduled to the half-hour. The graceless EI AI Airlines, which is already at auction, has retrained its employees to emphasize service and is boasting about the results in an ad campaign with the slogan, "You can feel the change in the air." For the first time, praise outnumbers complaints on customer survey sheets. [2003.1/第 4 篇]

【题目】1. If someone in Israel today needs a repairman in case of a power failure, _____.

A) they can have it fixed in no time

B) it's no longer necessary to make an appointment

C) the appointment takes only half a day to make

D) they only have to wait half an hour at most

2. The example of EI AI Airlines shows that _____.

A) revengeful customers are a threat to the monopoly of enterprises

B) an ad campaign is a way out for enterprises in financial difficulty

C) a good slogan has great potential for improving service

D) staff retraining is essential for better service

【解析】本段共举了三个例子来说明"私有化的威胁使服务质量改善"的主题,提问涉及后两个例子:电力公司和航空公司。第 1 题为事实细节题,只涉及第二个例子内部的内容,从原文中的 scheduled to the half-hour 可知答案为 D。第 2 题属于推理判断题,询问第三个例子支持什么观点。值得注意的是,例子支持的观点通常会在例子前后提到。根据原文最后两句,再联系本段第 4 句"人们想报复这些年来的差劲服务",可知其后所举的例子都与 service 这个观点有关,即"怎样改善差劲的服务"。四个选项中只有 C 和 D 提到了这一点,但选项 C 中的 slogan 是 improving service 的结果,故不正确,因此答案为 D。[答案:D, D]

命题规律 2:引文常考

使用引文,尤其是名人名言,是作者证明自己观点的一种行之有效的方法。提问一般会针对引文的意思、目的、立场或作者对引文的态度。请看下例。

【例 5】All work and no play could make for some very messed-up kids. "Play is the most powerful way a child explores the world and learns about himself," says T. Berry Brazelton, professor at Harvard Medical School. Unstructured play encourages independent thinking and allows the young to negotiate their relationships with their peers, but kids aged 3 to 12 spent only 12 hours a week engaged in it.　　　　　　　　[2003.6/第 1 篇]

【题目】According to the author a child develops better if _____.

A) he has plenty of time reading and studying

B) he is left to play with his peers in his own way

C) he has more time participating in school activities

D) he is free to interact with his working parents

【解析】原文第 1、2 句分别转借谚语和他人之口从反、正两方面说明玩耍是儿童发展的最佳途径。[答案:B]

命题规律 3:转折处常考

转折一般指由 however, but, in fact, nevertheless, nonetheless, yet 等引导的句子,这些词前面的内容一般只是起铺垫的作用,后面才是语义和信息的焦点所在,是命题者的兴趣所在,也是答案所在。由 though 或 although 引导的让步状语从句,焦点同样是主句。对转折处的考查在四级考试中随处可见。

【例 6】Historically, most physical-fitness tests have usually included measures of muscular strength and endurance, not for health-related reasons, but primarily because such fitness components have been related to performance in athletics. However, in recent years, evidence has shown that training programs designed primarily to improve muscular strength and endurance might also offer some health benefits as well.　　　　[2002.6/第 4 篇]

【题目】People were given physical fitness tests in order to find out _____.

A) how well they could do in athletics

B) what their health condition was like

C) what kind of fitness center was suitable for them

D) whether they were fit for aerobic exercise

【解析】第 1 句内部有由 but 引导的一个转折句,而解答的关键就是转折词后面的内容,因此,本题选 A(how well they could do in athletics 是对 related to performance in athletics 的解释)。[答案:A]

命题规律 4:对比处常考

对比处常见的标志是:in/by contrast (with), in opposition (to), on the contrary, not... but..., rather than, while, on the other hand 等词或词组。这些地方涉及到两种事物、观点、情况等的对比,有的还体现出作者的态度和观点,因此也容易成为考试的兴趣点。

【例 7】Cold symptoms such as stuffy nose, runny nose and scratchy throat typically develop gradually, and adults and teens often do not get a fever. On the other hand, fever is one of the characteristic features of the flu for all ages. And in general, flu symptoms including fever and chills, sore throat and body aches come on suddenly and are more severe than cold symptoms.　　　　[2005.1/第 1 篇]

【题目】Which of the following symptoms will distinguish the flu from a cold?

A) A stuffy nose.　　　　　　　　　　B) A high temperature.

C) A sore throat.　　　　　　　　　　D) A dry cough.

【解析】本段先讲感冒的症状,接下来 On the other hand 笔锋一转,引出流感的典型特征,最后一句则是流感的症状与感冒的区别。本题的答案就在 On the other hand 一句中,选项 high temperature 是对 fever 的解释,为正确答案。
[答案:B]

命题规律 5:因果关系常考

因果关系可以用不同的词汇和结构来表达,如:

> 连词:because, since, for, as, so, therefore, consequently, as a result 等;
>
> 动词或动词词组:cause, result in(接结果), result from(接原因), owe... to, attribute... to, originate from, arise
> from 等;
>
> 名词:basis, cause, result, consequence 等。

做题时特别要注意那些表示隐含因果关系的词、短语或结构。

【例 8】Women have slightly better memories than men, possibly because they pay more attention to their environment, and memory relies on just that. [2002.6/第 2 篇]

【题目】One possible reason why women have better memories than men is that _____.

A) they have a wider range of interests

B) they are more reliant on the environment

C) they have an unusual power of focusing their attention

D) they are more interested in what's happening around them

【解析】如果找准了答案在文章中的出处,那么不难看出:选项 D 是对原文的解释,为正确答案。选项 B 是对原文的曲解(原文说女性更注意周围的环境,其记忆依赖于对环境的关注),选项 C 则对原文断章取义,都不可。[答案:D]

命题规律 6:从句常考

经验告诉我们:英语文章中较长、结构较复杂的句子经常会吸引命题者的注意,成为考点。其中特别要注意定语从句和同位语从句。

【例 9】When the auto enters the highway system, a retractable arm will drop from the auto and make contact with a rail, which is similar to those powering subway trains electrically. Once attached to the rail, the car will become electrically powered from the system, and control of the vehicle will pass to a central computer. [2002.1/第 1 篇]

【题目】What provides autos with electrical power in an automated highway system?

A) A rail. B) The engine.

C) A retractable arm. D) A computer controller.

【解析】第 1 句中的 which 从句和第 2 句中的 once 从句告诉我们:是 rail 给车提供电能。[答案:A]

命题规律 7:分词结构常考

英语中用从句表达的内容也可以简化成分词结构,包括现在分词(结构)和过去分词(结构)。分词结构在句中可以充当各类状语,如表示伴随、原因、条件等的状语。分词不像从句,没有明确的引导词,因此,可能被误认为是主句的一部分,并使考生对整个句子的意思产生误解。因此,对分词结构的理解也常出现在四级考试中。

【例 10】Tracking whales is but one example of an exciting new world just opening to civilian scientists after the cold war as the Navy starts to share and partly uncover its global network of underwater listening system built over the decades to track the ships of potential enemies. [2002.6/第 3 篇]

【题目】The underwater listening system was originally designed _____.

A) to trace and locate enemy vessels

B) to end the cold war

C) to open to civilian use

D) to build a new world

【解析】本题考查对过去分词结构 built over the decades...的理解。该分词结构修饰的就是与题目相关的 underwater listening system,分词结构里的不定式结构表明了 underwater listening system 的用途,由此不难选出正确答案 A。[答案:A]

命题规律8:特殊标点符号处常考

一些标点符号与篇章结构或句间关系有密切联系,也常常成为考点。这些标点符号包括:

> 破折号:对前面的内容进行解释说明、或补充,常考细节性问题;
> 引号:表示引用、强调或讽刺,常考细节、语义或态度性问题;
> 冒号:对前面的内容进行解释,常考细节性问题;
> 括号:表示解释,常考细节性问题。

[例11]　Henry Ford, the famous U.S. inventor and car manufacturer, once said, "The business of America is business."...

The negative side of Henry Ford's statement, however, can be seen when the word business is taken to mean big business. And the term big business—referring to the biggest companies, is seen in opposition to labor. Throughout U.S. history working people have had to fight hard for higher wages, better working conditions, and the right to form unions. Today, many of the old labor disputes are over, but there is still some employee anxiety. Downsizing—the laying off of thousands of workers to keep expenses low and profits high—creates feelings of insecurity for many.
[2003.6/第2篇]

[题目]Henry Ford's statement can be taken negatively because _____.

A) working people are discouraged to fight for their rights

B) there are many industries controlled by a few big capitalists

C) there is a conflicting relationship between big corporations and labor

D) public services are not run by the federal government

[解析]本题的答案在第2段第1、2句,解答关键在于理解破折号之后的内容。[答案:C]

命题规律9:最高级常考

> first, last, most, least 等词表示的最高级,因为意义绝对,答案唯一,也常出现在考试提问中。

[例12]Business sees huge opportunities in the elder market because the baby boomers, 74 million strong, are likely to be the wealthiest group of retirees in human history.
[2002.1/第3篇]

[题目]Why can businessmen make money in the emerging elder market?

A) Retirees are more generous in spending money.

B) They can employ more gerontologists.

C) The elderly possess an enormous purchasing power.

D) There are more elderly people working than before.

[解析]在原文中,wealthiest这个表示最高级的词汇成为了命题焦点,"富裕"意味着"购买力"。[答案:C]

命题规律10:First/Firstly... Second/Secondly... Finally 等并列关系词出现的地方常考

解答此类题时,只要把细节考点(First/firstly... Second/Secondly...)找到,对照选项内容,跟事实细节不一致的就不是选项。考生只需细心一点都能辨清真伪。

[例13]Why is America lagging behind in the global PR race? First, Americans as a whole tend to be fairly provincial and take more of an interest in local affairs. Knowledge of world geography, for example, has never been strong in this country. Secondly, Americans lag behind their European and Asian *counterparts* (相对应的人) in knowing a second language. Less than 5 percent of Burson Marshall's U.S. employees know two languages. Ogilvy and Mather has about the same percentage. Conversely, some European firms have half or more of their employees fluent in a second language. Finally, people involved in PR abroad tend to keep a closer eye on international affairs. In the financial PR area, for instance, most Americans read the *Wall Street Journal*. Overseas, their counterparts read the *Journal* as well as the *Financial Times of London* and *The Economist*, publications not often read in this country.
[1999.6/第2篇]

[题目]We learn from the paragraph that employees in the American PR industry _____.

A) speak at least one foreign language fluently

B) are ignorant about world geography

C) are not as sophisticated as their European counterparts

D) enjoy reading a great variety of English business publications

【解析】该段以 First, Secondly 和 Finally 分别引出美国在全球公共竞赛中落后于其欧洲对手的三个主要原因:美国人视野较窄,只关心本地的事务,关于世界地理的知识了解不多(但并不是一无所知,因此 B 不正确);外语流利的人很少(可见 A 是不正确的);阅读面很窄,只读《华尔街日报》(可见 D 也不正确)。由此可推断出美国人与欧洲对手相比,没有那么老练。[答案:C]

第三节 词义推断题的 2 种命题规律

　　词义推断题必须结合上下文提供的各种线索,找出句与句之间的内在关系,如因果关系、解释关系、呼应关系等,然后根据不同关系辨别词义。

　　词义推断题的命题方式主要有下列几种:

> According to the author, the word "..." means _____.
>
> Which of the following is the closest in meaning to "_____"?
>
> The phrase "..." in Paragraph X can be best replaced by _____.
>
> What's the meaning of "..." in Line X, Paragraph X?
>
> As used in Line X, the word "..." most probably refers to _____.

　　词义推断题常涉及以下命题规律。

命题规律 1:代词常考

　　对此类题,一定要理解句中代词(例如:they, it, he, she, this, that, these, those 等)的所指(代词的所指一般在上文出现),以及句中不同的时态和语态的功用。

【例 14】The reality that has blocked my path to become the typical successful student is that engineering and the liberal arts simply don't mix as easily as I assumed in high school. Individually they shape a person in very different ways; together they threaten to confuse. The struggle to reconcile the two fields of study is difficult.

[2001.1/第 2 篇]

【题目】The word "they" in "... together they threaten to confuse." (Line 3) refers to _____.

A) practicality and rationality　　　　　　B) engineering and the liberal arts

C) reality and noble ideals　　　　　　　D) flexibility and a value system

【解析】第 2 句里面有两个 they,它们的所指是一样的。因为代词都是有前指的,因此 they 的所指应该回到上一句去寻找。另一方面,they 是复数,它应指上一句中的某两个(或以上的)事物,由此可推断,they 指的是上一句话中提到过的 engineering and the liberal arts。[答案:B]

命题规律 2:生词和一词多义词常考

　　此种题型涉及生词辨义和熟词生义两种,一般说来,所考单词的含义可通过以下两种方法进行推测:

> (1)根据上下文提供的定义或解释说明。其标志有:①or, that is, in other words, namely 等词或词组;②破折号、冒号、括号等;③定语从句。
>
> (2)根据上下文的逻辑关系。包括因果关系、转折关系、对比关系等。

【例15】The researcher then studied the videotapes to analyze the matches in detail. Surprisingly, he found that errors were more likely when the referees were close to the incident. When the officials got it right, they were, on average, 17 meters away from the action. The average distance in the case of errors was 12 meters. The research shows the *optimum* (最佳的) distance is about 20 meters.

[2000.6/第 1 篇]

[题目] The word "officials" (Line 2) most probably refers to _____.

　　A) the researchers involved in the experiment　　B) the inspectors of the football tournament

　　C) the referees of the football tournament　　D) the observers at the site of the experiment

[解析] 题目询问 officials 的意思是什么。officials 属于一词多义，可以指任何的官员或公务员，在没有上下文的情况下，四个选项的理解都是正确的，但根据上下文可知，officials 指的应是上句中提及的 the referees，其他选项中的 researchers, inspectors 和 observers 在文中并未提及。[答案：C]

第四节 观点态度题的2种命题规律

　　观点态度题主要要求考生运用综合分析和归纳能力，判断作者(或文中提及人物)对文章中某一问题的态度(Attitude)及全文的基调(Tone)。

观点态度题的命题方式通常有以下几种：

> How does the author feel about...?
>
> In the author's opinion, ...?
>
> What's the author's attitude towards...?
>
> The author seems to be against/in favor of _____.
>
> Which of the following can best describe the author's attitude towards...?
>
> The tone of the author is _____.

　　解答这类题应从篇章的体裁着手。一般来说，说明文体裁客观，所以作者的态度应是客观的(objective)或中立的(neutral)；而在议论文中，作者往往会体现自己的观点，但文章主旨句一般暗示作者的态度，所以需要特别注意；在描述性文章中，作者的观点往往不直接提出，但在其写作时常带有某种倾向，考生应细心捕捉表达或暗示其情感态度的词、短语或句子。

> 　　文章中的衔接词(如 but，however，on the contrary 等)或特殊句式，如虚拟语气，往往体现了作者的观点态度。可帮助判断态度的词有：形容词、副词、情态动词(如 must, may, should 等)。

观点态度题的选项常用词有：

> (1)褒义词：positive(肯定的), enthusiastic(热情的), optimistic(乐观的), concerned(关心的), sympathetic(同情的), supportive(支持的), cautious(审慎的), approving(满意的), favorable(赞成的), etc.
>
> (2)贬义词：doubtful(怀疑的), negative(否定的), indifferent(漠不关心的), pessimistic(悲观的), critical(批评的), cynical(玩世不恭的), depressed(沮丧的), ironic(讽刺的), arbitrary(武断的), disappointed(失望的), contradictory(反对的), etc.
>
> (3)中性词：subjective(主观的), objective(客观的), neutral(中立的), matter-of-fact(事实的), personal(针对个人的), impersonal(非个人的), informative(提供信息的), descriptive(描述性的), etc.

命题规律1：作者提出观点处常考

　　若题目只是问作者对某一问题的态度和观点，应注意篇章中起连接作用的那些词语，如 in my opinion, my view is..., as I see it 等等；其次应注意表明作者观点和态度的关键词，如形容词、动词等。

[例16]　　New technology links the world as never before. Our planet has shrunk. It's now a "global village" where countries are only seconds away be fax or phone or satellite link. And, of course, our ability to benefit from this high-tech communications equipment is greatly enhanced by foreign language skills.

　　　　Deeply involved with this new technology is a breed of modern business people who have a growing respect for the economic value of doing business abroad. In modern markets, success overseas often helps support domestic business efforts.

　　　　Overseas assignments are becoming increasingly important to advancement within executive ranks. The

executive stationed in another country no longer need fear being "out of sight and out of mind." He or she can be sure that the overseas effort is central to the company's plan for success, and that promotions often follow or accompany an assignment abroad. If an employee can succeed in a difficult assignment overseas, superior will have greater confidence in his or her ability to cope back in the United States where cross-cultural considerations and foreign language issues are becoming more and more *prevalent* (普遍的).

Thanks to a variety of relatively inexpensive communications devices with business applications, even small businesses in the United States are able to get into international markets.

English is still the international language of business. But there is an ever-growing need for people who can speak another language. A second language isn't generally required to get a job in business, but having language skills gives a candidate the edge when other qualifications appear to be equal.

The employee posted abroad who speaks the country's principal language has an opportunity to fast-forward certain negotiations, and can have the cultural insight to know when it is better to move more slowly. The employee at the home office who can communicate well with foreign clients over the telephone or by fax machine is an obvious asset to the firm.

[2003.1/第 3 篇]

【题目】What is the author's attitude toward high-tech communications equipment?

A) Critical.　　　　B) Indifferent.　　　　C) Prejudiced.　　　　D) Positive.

【解析】本题的基调是比较鲜明的。从首段首句及首段末句中的 benefit 一词,可以判断作者是持肯定态度的,因此选项 D 为正确答案。[答案:D]

命题规律 2:文中提及的某个人或某个群体的态度常考

此类题应抓住题干中的线索词进行准确定位,找到相应的段落和句子,从析他 他能反映人物的观点态度,有时文章涉及过去和现在人们的观点,此时应注意问题问的是人们什么时候的态度。

【例 17】These fitness spas did not seem to benefit financially from the aerobic fitness movement to better health since medical opinion suggested that weight-training programs offered few, if any, health benefits.　　[2002.6/第 4 篇]

【题目】What was the attitude of doctors towards weight training in health improvement?

A) Positive.　　　　B) Indifferent.　　　　C) Negative.　　　　D) Cautious.

【解析】原文中由 since 引出的原因状语从句表明医学界认为重力训练无助于增进健康,即使有帮助,也很少,由此可见,医生对此类运动持否定态度。[答案:C]

第五节 考点突破专项扫雷训练

Passage One

The next big breakthrough in artificial intelligence could come from giving machines not just more logical capacity, but emotional capacity as well.

Feelings aren't usually associated with *inanimate* (无生命的) machines, but Posalind Picard, a professor of computer technology at MIT, believes emotion may be just the thing computers need to work effectively. Computers need artificial emotion both to understand their human users better and to achieve self-analysis and self-improvement, says Picard.

"If we want computers to be genuinely intelligent, to adapt to us, and to interact naturally with us, then they will need the ability to recognize and express emotions, to have emotions, and to have what has come to be called emotional intelligence," Picard says.

One way that emotions can help computers, she suggests, is by helping keep them from crashing. Today's computers produce error messages, but they do not have a "gut feeling" of knowing when something is wrong or doesn't make sense. A healthy fear of death could motivate a computer to stop trouble as soon as it starts. On the other hand, self-preservation would need to be subordinate to service to humans. It was fear of its own death that prompted RAL, the fictional computer in the film *2002: A Space Odyssey*, to *exterminate* (消灭) most of its human associates.

Similarly, computers that could "read" their users would accumulate a store of highly personal information about us—not just what we said and did, but what we likely thought and felt.

"Emotions not only contribute to a richer quality of interaction, but they directly impact a person's ability to interact in an intelligent way," Picard says. "Emotional skills, especially the ability to recognize and express emotions, are essential for natural communication with humans."

1. According to Picard, emotional intelligence is necessary to computers because _____.
   A) it can make computers analyze the information more efficiently
   B) it can help to eliminate the computers' innate problems
   C) it can improve the mechanic capacity of computers
   D) it can make computers achieve a better understanding of human users

2. An emotionally intelligent computer is likely to _____.
   A) have a successful interaction with human beings by adapting to their needs
   B) enable human beings to enhance their ability to express emotions in daily life
   C) automatically produce correct messages
   D) be free from producing meaningless messages in its operation

3. The phrase "gut feeling" (Line 2, Para. 4) most probably means _____.
   A) intuitive feelings   B) guilty feelings
   C) confusing feelings   D) unpleasant feelings

4. The film *2002: A Space Odyssey* (Line 5, Para. 4) is mentioned to illustrate _____.
   A) a typical case of a fictional computer with emotions
   B) the necessity of bringing computers with emotions under control
   C) the possibility that computers with emotions might kill human associates
   D) the troubles that might be caused by computers with emotions

5. What does the author think about the computers with emotions?
   A) The author has high expectation for its potential in the future.
   B) The author worries that it will threaten the security of human beings.
   C) The author doubts its capacity to interact with human beings.
   D) The author believes that it will take the place of human beings in many aspects.

Passage Two

A recent study, published in last week's *Journal of the American Medical Association*, offers a picture of how risky it is to get a lift from a teenage driver. Indeed, a 16-year-old driver with three or more passengers is three times as likely to have a fatal accident as a teenager driving alone, by contrast, the risk of death for drivers between 30 and 59 decreases with each additional passenger.

The author also found that the death rates for teenage drivers increased dramatically after 10 pm, and especially after midnight. With passengers in the car, the driver was even more likely to die in a late-night accident.

Robert Foss, a scientist at the University of North Carolina Highway Safety Research Center, says the higher death rates for teenage drivers have less to do with "really stupid behavior" than with just a lack of driving experience. "The basic issue," he says, "is that adults who are responsible for issuing licenses fail to recognize how complex and skilled a task driving is."

Both he and the author of the study believe that the way to *mitigate* (使……缓解) the problem is to have states institute so-called graduated licensing systems, in which getting a license is a multistage process. A graduated license requires that a teenager first prove himself capable of driving in the presence of an adult, followed by a period of driving with passenger restrictions, before graduating to full driving privileges.

Graduated licensing systems have reduced teenage driver crashes, according to recent studies. About half of the states now have some sort of graduated licensing system in place, but only 10 of those states have restrictions on passengers. California is the strictest, with a *novice* (新手) driver prohibited from carrying any passenger under 20 (without the presence of an adult over 25) for the first six months.

1. Which of the following situations is most dangerous according to the passage?

A) Adults giving a lift to teenagers on the highway after 10 pm.

B) A teenager driving after midnight with passengers in the car.

C) Adults driving with three or more teenage passengers late at night.

D) A teenager getting a lift from a stranger on the highway at midnight.

2. According to Paragraph 3, which of the following statements is true?

A) Teenagers should spend more time learning to drive.

B) Driving is a skill too complicated for teenagers to learn.

C) Restrictions should be imposed on teenagers applying to take driving lessons.

D) The licensing authorities are partly responsible for teenagers' driving accidents.

3. A suggested measure to be taken to reduce teenagers' driving accidents is that _____.

A) driving in the presence of an adult should be made a rule

B) they should be prohibited from taking on passengers

C) they should not be allowed to drive after 10 pm

D) the licensing system should be improved

4. A graduated license is issued to a driver who _____.

A) is at least a middle school graduate   B) has learned driving at a driving school

C) gains full driving rights step by step   D) has a driving experience long enough

5. The present situation in about half of the states is that the graduated licensing system _____.

A) is under discussion   B) is about to be set up

C) has been put into effect   D) has been perfected

Passage Three

The National Trust in Britain plays an increasingly important part in the preservation for public enjoyment of the best that is left unspoiled of the British countryside. Although the Trust has received practical and moral support from the Government, it is not a rich Government department. It is a charity which depends for its existence on voluntary support from members of the public.

The attention of the public was first drawn to the dangers threatening the great old houses and castles of Britain by the death of Lord Lothian, who left his great seventeenth-century house to the Trust together with the 4,500-acre park and estate surrounding it. This gift attracted wide publicity and started the Trust's "Country House Scheme". Under this scheme, with the help of the Government and the general public, the Trust has been able to save and open to the public about one hundred and fifty of these old houses. Last year about one and three quarters of a million people paid to visit these historic houses, usually at a very small charge.

In addition to country houses and open spaces the Trust now owns some examples of ancient wind and water mills, nature reserves, five hundred and forty farms and nearly two thousand five hundred cottages or small village houses, as well as some complete villages. In these villages no one is allowed to build, develop or disturb the old village environment in any way and all the houses are maintained in their original sixteenth-century style. Over four hundred thousand acres of coastline, woodland, and hill country are protected by the Trust and no development or disturbances of any kind are permitted. The public has free access to these areas and is only asked to respect the peace, beauty and wildlife.

So it is that over the past eighty years the Trust has become a big and important organization and an essential and respected part of national life, preserving all that is of great natural beauty and of historical significance not only for future generations of Britons but also for the millions of tourists who each year invade Britain in search of a great historic and cultural heritage.

1. The National Trust is _____.

   A) a rich government department

   B) a charity supported mainly by the public

   C) a group of areas of great natural beauty

   D) an organization supported by public taxes

2. The "Country House Scheme" was started _____.

   A) with the founding of the National Trust

   B) as the first project of the National Trust

   C) after Lord Lothian's donation

   D) to protect Lord Lothian's house

3. Land protected by the National Trust _____.

   A) can be developed and modernized

   B) includes naturally and historically valuable sites

   C) consists of country houses and nature reserves

   D) is primarily for tourists to Britain

4. The word "invade" in the last paragraph is used to emphasize that _____.

   A) the British do not like tourists

   B) tourists to Britain are unfriendly

   C) tourists come to Britain in large numbers

   D) Britain is attacked by masses of tourists

5. The main purpose of this passage is to _____.

   A) inform the readers about the National Trust

   B) promote the National Trust's membership

   C) make people aware of the natural beauty of Britain

   D let the general public share the views of the National Trust

Passage Four

Only special plants can survive the terrible climate of a desert, for these are regions where the annual range of the soil temperature can be over 75°C. Furthermore, during the summer there are few clouds in the sky to protect plants from the sun's ray. Another problem is the fact that there are frequently strong winds which drive small-sharp particles of sand into the plants, tearing and damaging them. The most difficult problem for all forms of plant life, however, is the fact that the entire annual rainfall occurs during a few days or weeks in spring.

Grasses and flowers in desert survive from one year to the next by existing through the long, hot, dry season in the form of seeds. These seeds remain inactive unless the right amount of rain falls. If no rain falls, or if insufficient rain falls, they wait until the next year, or even still the next. Another factor that helps these plants to survive is the fact that their life cycles are short. By the time that the water from the spring rains disappears—just a few weeks after it falls—such plants no longer need any.

The *perennials* (多年生植物) have special features which enable them to survive as plants for several years. Thus, nearly all desert perennials have extensive root systems below ground and a small shoot system above ground. The large root network enables the plant to absorb as much water as possible in a short time. The small shoot system, on the other hand, considerably limits water loss by *evaporation* (蒸发).

Another feature of many desert perennials is that after the rainy season they lose their leaves in preparation for the long, dry season, just as trees in wetter climates lose theirs in preparation for the winter. This reduces their water loss by evaporation during the dry season. Then, in the next rainy reason, they come fully alive once more, and grow new branches, leaves and flowers, just as the grasses and flowers in desert do.

1. Ordinary plants can not survive the desert weather as a result of the following EXCEPT for _____.

   A) the strong winds

   B) the strong sun's ray

   C) the long summer days

   D) the high soil temperature

2. Some grasses and flowers can survive in the desert because _____.

   A) they need little water for their survival

   B) they bear long roots and the seeds are fit for dry weather

C) they stay in the form of seeds to wait for the right amount of water

D) with long roots, they do not depend on the rain to get enough water

3. We can learn from the passage that the shoot system of the perennials _____.

A) can help the perennials absorb less of the sun's ray

B) decides the appearance of the perennials in desert

C) limits the function of the perennials' branches

D) may prevent the perennials from losing much water

4. According to the passage, spring is the best time for plants in desert _____.

A) to find a shady place   B) to get water for their growth

C) to reduce water loss   D) to enjoy the sunshine

5. The last paragraph is mainly about _____.

A) the comparison between plants in different areas

B) the growth of new leaves in the rainy season

C) water loss by evaporation in the dry season

D) the changes in the leaves of the perennials

Passage Five

Despite the fact that advertisers spend $44 billion on the major television networks and cable TV advertising, a new study shows that consumers consider print ads more entertaining and less offensive than television commercials. The study, conducted by Video Storyboard Tests in New York, showed that more consumers considered print ads "artistic" and "enjoyable."

The 2,000 consumers surveyed blasted TV ads compared to their print counterparts: 34 percent of respondents thought print ads were artistic, compared with 15 percent for television ads; 35 percent thought print ads were enjoyable, compared to 13 percent for television; and, most surprising, 33 percent of consumers felt print ads were entertaining, compared to only 18 percent for TV ads. Much of the artistic impact and positive reaction to print ads comes from the illustrations used. The illustration is primary in creating the mood for a print ad, which ultimately affects consumers' feelings about the image of a brand.

While the study's sponsors were somewhat surprised by the survey results, some industry executives felt that print ads were finally getting the credit they deserve. Richard Kirshenbaum, chair and chief creative officer of Kirshenbaum, Bond & Partners, a New York advertising and public relations firm, is one such believer. In fact, Kirshenbaum says that when he looks to hire a new person for a creative position in his agency, "I always look at the print book first because I think it is harder to come up with a great idea on a single piece of paper."

But as impressed as consumers say they are by the *aesthetics* (美学) and style of print ads, television executives (as you might expect) dismiss the findings. One network official said, "Nothing will replace the reach and magnitude of an elaborately produced television spot. TV ads get talked about. Print ads don't."

1. The sponsors of the concerned study are _____.

A) advertisers   B) Video Story Tests   C) television executives   D) not specified

2. Consumers' feelings about print ads mainly derive from _____.

A) the pictures used   B) their cheapness

C) their positive image   D) their artistic value

3. What had the study's organizers expected of the survey results?

A) More consumers would prefer TV ads to print ads.

B) More consumers would prefer print ads to TV ads.

C) Both TV ads and print ads should have their fans.

D) Print ads should get the credit they deserve.

4. What are television executives' response to the survey results?

A) They accept the results unwillingly.

B) They insist on the superiority of TV ads.

C) They are impressed by the study.

D) They are encouraged by the study.

5. What seems to be the author's attitude to print ads?

A) Favorable.　　　　B) Critical.　　　　C) Neutral.　　　　D) Suspicious.

Passage Six

　　Irradiating (照射) fruits, vegetables, pork and chicken to kill insects and bacteria has been approved by the Food and Drug Administration over the past decade or so. Irradiation of other meats, such as beef and lamb, is being reviewed. Federal approval does not require that industry adopt the process, and few food processors presently offer irradiated products.

　　Market studies have shown that many consumers are afraid that eating irradiated foods may cause cancer, despite scientific studies that prove the safety of treated foods. Some people argue that more severe government inspection, higher food-safety standards, and more careful food-preparation practices by consumers are all that is needed to ensure that food is safe. Consequently, companies currently see no need to spend millions of dollars *outfitting* (配备) processing plants with the equipment necessary for a process that very few shoppers are in favor of.

　　All supermarkets that sell irradiated food must label that food either directly on the packaging or in the case of bulk items like fruits and vegetables by placing a sign nearby. There is no requirement for the labeling of irradiated food served by chain restaurants or hospitals that buy directly from distributors, nor any regulations for products that contain irradiated ingredients.

　　Presently, the FDA allows food to be treated with three types of radiation—gamma rays, high-energy electrons, and X-rays—and sets limits on *doses* (辐射量) depending on the type of food. The principle is that the dose to be used for a certain type of food should not exceed the amount that is sufficient to kill most harmful insects and bacteria present in it. Different types of food, because of their different *molecular* (分子) compositions, may require different doses of radiation.

1. According to the passage, killing insects and bacteria present in food by irradiating _____.

A) has been completely approved by the FDA

B) is being reviewed by the FDA

C) is not completely approved by the U.S. government

D) has been widely adopted in the U.S.

2. Which of the following statements about the consumers' attitudes toward irradiated foods is NOT true?

A) Many consumers are afraid that irradiated foods may cause cancer.

B) Some consumers are doubtful of the safety of irradiated foods.

C) Some consumers suggest a more severe government inspection be taken.

D) Most consumers welcome the food processing companies outfitted with irradiating equipment.

3. What does "processing plants" in the second paragraph most probably refer to?

A) Market information processors.　　　　B) Food-processing factories.

C) Business companies.　　　　D) Supermarkets.

4. Irradiated food has to be labeled when _____.

A) it is sold at the supermarket　　　　B) it is served at the restaurants

C) it is provided in the hospitals　　　　D) it is produced at the factories

5. Which of the following best reflects the content of the passage?

A) Although FDA does not approve irradiating food, consumers accept irradiated food.

B) Neither FDA approves irradiating food, nor do consumers accept irradiated food.

C) FDA approves irradiating food to some extent, but irradiated food is not widely accepted.

D) Both FDA and consumers think that irradiated food is not safe.

第六节 答案解析

参考译文划线点评　　　　　　　　　　　　　　　　　　　　**Passage One**

[5]既赋予机器更多逻辑能力也赋予它们情感能力可能是在人工智能方面的下一个重大突破。

通常情感与没有生命的机器扯不上关系,但是麻省理工学院的计算机科学教授珀萨琳·皮卡德相信,为了有效地工作,机器也需要情感。[1]皮卡德说,机器既需要人工情感来更好地了解其人类使用者,也需要它来完成自我分析和自我提高。

[2]"如果我们希望计算机具备真正的智能,可以适应我们,可以自然地与我们进行互动,那它们就会需要识别与表达情感的能力、拥有情感的能力以及拥有最终被称为情感智能的能力,"皮卡德如是说。

她提出,情感帮助计算机的途径之一是让它们免于瘫痪。[3]当今计算机产生许多错误信息却因为不具备"本能的情感"而无法知道何时出了毛病或某些东西含义不明。出于对死亡的正常害怕心理可能会推动计算机一出现故障就立即将其中止。[4]但是另一方面,自卫的本能应该服从于为人类服务。在电影《2002:太空奥德赛》里,正是对自我毁灭的恐惧促使那台虚构的计算机 RAL 去消灭它的大多数人类同僚。

同样,能为人攻读、认使用者的计算机亦征需我们大量的非常个性化的信息——既有我们的情感和行为,也有我们可能的思考和感觉。

"情感不仅对更高效的互动有益,而且直接影响一个人以一种聪明的方式进行互动的能力,"皮卡德说,"情感能力,尤其是识别与表达情感的能力,对于与人类的正常交流是必不可少的。"

1. [D]事实细节题。本题考查文中人物的观点。可从第 2 段的结尾句中找到答案,选项 A 和 C 无依据,选项 B 与本句中的 self-improvement 不符,improve 不等同于 eliminate。

2. [A]推理判断题。在第 3 段开头的条件状语从句中,"to adapt to us, and to interact naturally with us"既是与"to be genuinely intelligent"并列的结构,也是对其的补充解释,由此可以推断出答案。选项 B 无合理的依据。根据第 4 段第 2 句,情感只是让计算机知道什么时候出了毛病或指令不明,并可对此做出修正,但这并不意味着选项 C 或 D。

3. [A]词义推断题。在原句中,有了 gut feeling,计算机就能知道何时出了毛病,由此可以推断 gut feeling 应该是一个好的特性,不带有任何贬义,从而排除选项 B、C、D。

4. [B]推理判断题。本题考查例子与观点的关系。该例子支持的观点是例子的前一句,即第 4 段第 4 句。其他选项虽然属实但并非作者在本文要阐明的目的。

5. [A]推理判断题,也是观点态度题。根据文章开头以及纵观全文可知,作者对改进被赋予情感的计算机的功能寄予了很高的期望。本题最具干扰性的是选项 B,计算机对人类的威胁在第 4 段"太空奥德赛"的例子里有显示,但这并非作者的主要想法,作者认为只要控制得好,情感计算机就能更高效(如最后一段所述)。

参考译文划线点评　　　　　　　　　　　　　　　　　　　　**Passage Two**

一项发表在上周的《美国医学会杂志》的最新研究向人们展示了搭乘由青少年驾驶的车辆的危险性。[1]的确,一个年仅 16 岁的驾车者搭载三个或以上乘客时发生致命车祸的可能性是青少年单独驾驶车辆时的三倍,相反,对于年龄介于 30 至 59 岁之间的驾车者来说,每多一个乘客,车祸致死的可能性就降低一些。

[1]这篇文章的作者还发现,在晚上 10 点以后尤其是午夜以后青少年驾车者的死亡率急剧上升。如果车里有乘客,则驾车者死于深夜交通事故的可能性更大。

北卡罗莱纳大学高速公路安全研究中心的科学家罗伯特·福斯说,青少年驾车者较高的死亡率不是与"十足愚蠢的行为"而是与缺乏驾驶经验有较大关系。[2]"根本的问题，"他说，"是负责发放驾驶执照的成年人没有认识到驾驶汽车是一项多么复杂和需要技术的任务。"

[3]他和那份研究报告的作者都相信，缓解这个问题的办法是让各个州建立所谓的渐进式驾驶执照发放制度，[4]即获得驾驶执照将是一个多阶段的过程。渐进式的驾驶执照发放制度要求青少年首先须证明自己能在一个成年人在场的情况下驾驶，随后在一段时间在限制乘员的条件下驾驶，最后逐渐取得全部驾驶权利。

根据最新的研究成果，渐进式驾驶执照发放制度已经减少了青少年驾车者的车祸数量。[5]现在约有半数的州已经实施了某种渐进式驾驶执照发放制度，但是只有其中的 10 个州规定了乘员限制。加利福尼亚州是最严格的：除非有一名年满 25 岁的成年人在场，初学驾驶的人在头 6 个月内禁止搭载任何未满 20 岁的乘客。

1. [B]事实细节题。本题考查对比处。第 1 段第 2 句的 by contrast 表明青少年驾车者比成年驾车者造成的危险性更高。另外，从第 2 段可知，青少年驾车者在晚上 10 点后驾车危险性上升，而且当车里有乘客的时候，危险性最高，综合以上两段，就可判断 B 为正确选项。

2. [D]推理判断题。第 3 段结尾句暗示负责发放驾驶执照的成年人轻率地将驾驶执照发放给经验不足的青少年，这是青少年车祸的部分原因。本文讨论的重点是青少年学会开车后的驾驶执照发放制度，并未讨论青少年学习驾驶的问题，因此其他选项都不是该段的推论。

3. [D]事实细节题。答案在第 4 段的首句。选项 A 和 B 在第 4 段最后一句皆有提及，但它们是渐进式发放制度的一些具体的做法，不如选项 D 有概括性。文中并未就青少年驾驶的时间给予限制的建议，因此选项 C 不正确。

4. [C]词义推断题。本题考查对 graduated 一词的理解。根据第 4 段第 1 句中的 "... is a multistage process" 及第 2 句中的 "... first... followed... before" 等词，可以看出 graduated 一词表示的是一个渐进的过程，选项 C 中的 step by step 与此同义，因此 C 正确。选项 A 将 graduated 曲解为"毕业"；文中未提及获得驾照的人必须进入驾驶学校学习，因此选项 B 不对；文中也没提到要有多长时间的驾驶经验才算足够长，所以以选项 D 不正确。

5. [C]事实细节题。本题考查对动词词组的理解。在结尾段的第 2 句中，短语 have... in place 意为"具备，拥有"，选项 C 为其近义表达。

参考译文划线点评

英国的国家托管会在为了让公众分享而保护英国乡村尚未被破坏的最美好的东西方面发挥着越来越重要的作用。尽管托管会得到政府的实际和精神上的支持，但它并不是一个有钱的政府部门，[1]它是一个慈善机构，其生存依赖于公众成员的自愿支持。

威胁英国那些巨大的老房子和城堡的危险第一次引起公众的注意是洛锡安勋爵的去世。这位勋爵把他那座 17 世纪的大宅连同 4500 英亩的园子及其周围的物业都留给了托管会。[2]这次遗赠吸引了公众的广泛注意，也使托管会启动了"乡村房屋计划"。通过这个计划，托管会在政府和公众的帮助下已经挽救了大约 150 座这样的老房子并将它们向公众开放。去年大约有 175 万人付费参观了这些有历史意义的房子，通常门票都非常便宜。

除了乡村房屋和空地以外，托管会现在还掌管了一些典型的古代风力和水力磨坊、自然保护区、540 个农庄、将近2500 座乡村别墅和小村舍以及一些完整的村庄。在这些村庄里不允许任何人以任何方式修建、开发或破坏古村落的环境，所有的房屋都按其原有的 16 世纪的风格保留。超过 40 万英亩的海岸线、林地和坡地都由托管会保护，不允许任何开发和破坏。公众可以免费进入这些地方，唯一的要求是尊重当地宁静的气氛、美丽的景色和野生动植物。

80 年过去了，托管会已经成为一个重要而庞大的组织，成为英国国民生活中举足轻重和受人尊敬的一部分，[3]它保护所有的自然美景和历史胜地不仅是为了英国人的后代，也是为了每年造访英国历史和文化遗产的数以百万计的外国游客。

1. [B]事实细节题。从文章第 1 段末句可找到答案。选项 A 显然与原文意思相反，选项 C 和 D 则无原文依据。

2. [C]推理判断题。第 2 段第 2 句表明洛锡安勋爵捐赠了他的房产后，这个计划才启动起来，因此选项 C 正确，也由此可以否定选项 A。根据第 2 段最后两句可知这个计划是为了保护具有历史价值的房子，而不仅仅是为了保护洛锡安勋爵的房子，因此选项 D 不对。

3. [B]事实细节题。最后一段从 preserving 开始的部分指出了本题的答案。第 3 段倒数第 2 句所说的 "no development or

disturbances of any kind are permitted"可帮助排除选项 A;选项 C 内容不完整;选项 D 中的限制词 primarily 使用不妥,无原文依据。

4. [C]词义推断题。由 invade 所在的句子"for the millions of tourists who each year invade..."可知这是托管会保护自然美景和历史胜地的原因所在。从而可以推断出 invade 强调来英国游玩的游客之多,因此选项 C 为正确答案。

5. [A]主旨大意题。纵观全文可发现 the National Trust 和 the Trust 在文章开头以及文中反复出现,文章是一篇说明文,主要目的是介绍 the National Trust 的机构性质及其功能,因此选项 A 正确。文章未讨论托管会的成员问题,因此选项 D 不正确。最后两段虽然提到英国的自然景色很美,但这并非文章的主题思想,因此选项 C 不对。本题最具干扰性的是选项 D,但是本文并不是一篇议论文,其目的不是让读者认同其中的观点,文章更多的是用说明性的语言来说明托管会的一些做法。

参考译文划线点评　　　　　　　　　　　　Passage Four

[1]因为沙漠地区的土壤温度在全年的变化可以超过75℃,所以只有特殊的植物才能在沙漠的恶劣气候条件下存活。而且,夏季的天空中也几乎没有云保护植物不受阳光的照射。另一个问题是经常有强风把尖锐的小沙粒吹进植物体内,把它们撕裂、摧毁。不过,对于植物的各种生命形态来说,[4]最严峻的问题是全年的降雨都集中在春季的几天或几个星期。

[2]沙漠里的花和草要从一年活到下一年,靠的是以种子的形态熬过那漫长、炎热的旱季。除非有足量的降雨,这些种子都保持着不活跃的状态。如果没有降雨,或者降雨量不够,它们就等到下一年,甚至再下一年。另一个帮助这些植物存活的因素是它们短暂的生活周期。到春季的雨水消失的时候——降雨后仅仅几周——这些植物就不再需要任何水了……对于植物的……这则是收……也能够……只生存几年的植物一样方法。几乎所有的多年生植物的地下根系都很大而地表的枝叶系统都很小。庞大的根系使植物在短时间内尽可能多地吸收水分。[3]另一方面,小的枝叶系统在相当程度上限制了由蒸发带来的水分流失。

[5]许多沙漠多年生植物的另一特点是,在雨季过后,它们会用落叶来迎接漫长的旱季,正如湿润气候条件下的树木用落叶来迎接冬季一样。这在旱季减少了它们因蒸发造成的水分流失。然后,就像沙漠中的花草一样,在下一个雨季,它们会再次焕发生机,长出新的枝、叶和花。

1. [C]事实细节题。本题考查列举处。第 1 段前三句分别列举了影响植物在沙漠生长的三个因素:soil temperature(选项 D),sun's rays(选项 B),strong winds(选项 A),只有选项 C 没有提及。

2. [C]推理判断题。可根据第 2 段前 3 句推断出答案。选项 A 无原文依据,选项 B 前半句不对,选项 D 则有悖常理。

3. [D]事实细节题。本题的解题的关键是注意题干是关于 shoot system 的提问,而不是 root system,在第 3 段末句可找到相关的信息,并由此可确定 D 为正确选项。

4. [B]推理判断题。第 1 段的最后一句谈到降雨量集中在春天,第 2 段第 2 句谈到种子在下雨季节才发芽生长,由此可推断出选项 B。其余三项均无原文依据。

5. [D]主旨大意题。第 4 段第 1 句通过 Another feature 引出本段的主题句,本句的中心词是 perennials 和 leaves,据此可以判断选项 D 正确。其他选项均没有关注这两个中心词。

参考译文划线点评　　　　　　　　　　　　Passage Five

尽管广告商们在各大电视网及有线电视台的广告费高达440亿美元,但是一项新的研究表明,消费者认为平面广告比电视广告更具娱乐性和更少令人不快。这项由纽约"电视故事板测试"调查公司主持的研究表明,更多消费者认为平面广告"有艺术性"以及"令人愉快"。

与平面广告相比,电视广告遭到接受调查的 2000 名消费者的强烈批评:34%的人认为平面广告而15%的人认为电视广告有艺术性;35%的人认为平面广告而13%的人认为电视广告是令人愉快的;最让人吃惊的是,33%的消费者觉得平面广告而只有18%的人觉得电视广告具有娱乐性。[2]平面广告带给消费者的艺术性印象及其引起的正面反应很大程度上是因为其使用的画面。在为一个平面广告营造气氛方面,画面是第一位的,它最终将影响消费者对一个品牌形象的感觉。

[1]/[3]这项研究的赞助商对调查结果略感惊讶，而该行业的一些经理们却觉得平面广告终于赢得了它应得的荣誉。纽约的一家广告和公共关系公司——"基尔欣鲍姆、邦德及其合伙人"公司的主席及首席创意官理查德·基尔欣鲍姆是持这种信念的人之一。事实上，基尔欣鲍姆说，当他为公司的创作职位聘用新人时，"我总是先看他的平面作品集，因为我认为单单在一张纸上表现一个绝妙的想法会更加困难。"

[4]尽管消费者说他们被平面广告的美感和时尚所打动，但是不出所料，电视业的经理们却拒不接受这种研究结果。一位电视网的管理人员说，"什么也不能代替一个精心制作的电视广告的巨大影响范围和影响力。电视广告是人们议论的焦点，而平面广告却不是。"

1. [D]事实细节题。原文第 3 段第 1 句提及 sponsors，但该句并没有指明赞助商是谁，因此选项 D 正确。其他三个选项在文中虽有提到，但均无依据表明与 sponsor 有关。

2. [A]事实细节题。本题题干中的 derive from 与第 2 段第 2 句中的 come from 近义，所以本题关键在于 illustration 一词的理解，picture 与之近义，因此选项 A 正确。

3. [A]推理判断题。第 3 段的首句中的 the survey result 指的是第 1 段和第 2 段的调查结果：平面广告比电视广告更受欢迎，而该句表明该项研究的组织者预计的是与此调查相反的结果，因此选项 A 正确，也因此可否定选项 B。根据同一句，选项 D 虽在文中出现但并非他们预料的结果，而是行业经理们的观点。选项 C 无依据。

4. [B]推理判断题。本题考查转折处。结尾段首句由 But 引出，由此可知电视业的经理们拒绝接受调查结果，也就是说，他们仍然认为电视广告优于平面广告，因此选项 B 正确。

5. [C]观点态度题。纵观全文，作者以客观的口吻和态度报告调查结果、消费者的反应，研究赞助商们的态度以及电视业经理们的反应，并未使用任何表明个人观点或看法的字眼。

参考译文划线点评 **Passage Six**

[1]用射线照射水果、蔬菜、猪肉和鸡肉从而杀死虫子和细菌在大约十年前就已经被食品与药物管理局(FDA)批准了。对牛肉和羊肉等其他肉类的照射正在接受评估。联邦政府的批准并不意味着生产商必须采用这道工序，而且目前也没有几家食品加工企业提供照射过的产品。

市场研究表明，尽管科学研究证明照射处理过的食物是安全的，许多消费者仍然担心这些食物有致癌的可能。有些人认为，要保证食物的安全，政府更加严格的检查、更高的食品安全标准以及消费者对食物进行更加仔细的预先处理都是必不可少的。[2]/[3]结果，商家普遍觉得花几百万美元为加工厂配备这些加工设备毫无必要，因为没有几个顾客赞成这样做。

[4]所有出售照射食品的超市都必须直接在食品包装上贴一个标签，如果是像水果和蔬菜那样的散装食品则在旁边放置一个标识。对于直接从批发商进货的连锁餐厅或者医院所提供的照射食品则没有强制要求贴上标签，对含有照射过的成分的产品也没有任何规定。

目前，食品与药物管理局(FDA)允许用三种射线对食品进行处理——伽马射线、高能电子射线和 X 射线，而且根据食品种类的不同对辐射量设立了限制。其原则是，施用于某种食品的辐射量不应超过足够杀灭该食品中大多数害虫和细菌的辐射量。不同种类的食品因其不同的分子结构而对辐射量会有不同的要求。

1. [C]推理判断题。本题考查对 review 一词的理解。从文章第 1 段第 1 句可知，有些经过照射处理的食品已被 FDA 认可；从第 2 句的 being reviewed 可知，有些食物仍然正在评估中。所以选项 A、B、D 都太绝对或概括过度，均不正确。

2. [D]推理判断题。本题考查对复合句的理解。本题解题的关键是找出第 2 段结尾句中的 that 引导的定语从句修饰的是 process，从该定语从句可推断出消费者对其持不认同的态度，由此可见，选项 D 是本题的答案。选项 A、B、C 在第 2 段中都先后有明确提及。

3. [B]词义推断题。根据上下文，特别是 outfit 和 equipment 两个词，可知是为 processing plants 配备设备，因此，可推断出 processing plants 指的是食品加工厂。

4. [A]事实细节题。第 3 段指出食物在哪些情况下要贴上被照射过的标签，其中第 1 句提到在 supermarket 一定要标明哪些食品被照射过，但在医院或餐厅并无规定，选项 D 在文章中没有提及。

5. [C]主旨大意题。第 1 段提及 FDA 认可部分食品可以用辐射方法进行处理，第 2 段谈到消费者对 irradiated food 持怀疑态度，同时符合这两条的只有选项 C。

第二章 550分篇章阅读难点突破

第一节 正确选项的4种设置规律

正确选项的设置有四大规律:(1)同义替换,(2)概括或归纳,(3)反着说,(4)关键词。

命题规律1:同义替换

在历年四级阅读题中,正确选项从来都不会直接采用原文的表达方式,即使采用了原文的部分词句,关键词也一定会换用其他同义的表达方式,语义题是这一规律的极端体现。

【例1】First, pruning may be done to make sure that trees have a desired shape or size.

【题目】Pruning may be done to _____.

    A) make the tree grow taller   B) improve the shape of the tree

    C) get rid of the small branches   D) make the small branches thicker

【解析】选项B是对原文have a desired shape的同义替换,为正确答案。

> 由这一规律可知:照抄原文的选项一定不是正确答案。这一规律还提醒我们:平时学习时应注意词汇量和表达方法的积累,尽量用不同的说法来表达同样的意思。

命题规律2:概括或归纳

另一种最为常见的命题规律是:正确选项是对原文内容的概括或归纳,主旨大意题自然要遵守这一规律,观点态度题和推理判断题大多符合这一规律,甚至事实细节题也常常通过这种方式给出正确答案。

【例2】To prepare children for successful careers in first grade and beyond, Japanese schools do not teach reading, writing and mathematics, but rather skill such as persistence, concentration, and the ability to function as a member of a group.   [2005.1/第2篇]

【题目】In Japan's preschool education, the focus is on _____.

    A) preparing children academically

    B) developing children's artistic interests

    C) tapping children's potential

    D) shaping children's character

【解析】原文说,为了给学生一年级及以后的成功做好准备,日本学校教的是毅力、专注和团队合作能力。这几点都是性格方面的培养,因此,日本学前教育的重点可以归纳为"塑造性格"。[答案:D]

要答对这类题目,平时必须培养概括和归纳的能力,能够用一个词或词组、简单的句子来概括阅读材料的大段描写或叙述。这一规律提醒我们:含义具体的选项一般不是正确答案,而概括、抽象的选项多是正确答案。

命题规律3:反着说

反着说主要有以下几种情况:

(1)原文说"A 是 B",问"非 A 是什么?",答"非 B"。
(2)原文说"A 是非 B",问"非 A 是什么",答"B"。
(3)原文说"A 比 B 重要/大/好(或其他比较级)",问"B 和 A 相比怎样",答"次要/小/低劣(或其他的相反)"。
(4)原文说"A would rather B than C"或"A prefer B to C",问"C 如何",答"不受 A 重视"。

这一规律虽不及前两条规律普遍,但只要文章中出现了这类句子,提问的可能性就很大,而且由于很多学生不太适应这种逻辑思维方式,失分率很高。

[例3]In fact, the analysis showed, normal children aged 9 to 17 exhibit a higher level of anxiety today than children who were treated for mental illness 50 years ago. [2004.1/第 1 篇]

[题目]According to an analysis, compared with normal children today, children treated as mentally ill 50 years ago _____.

　　A) were less isolated physically 　　　　B) were probably less self-centered
　　C) probably suffered less from anxiety 　　D) were considered less individualistic

[解析]在原句中,normal children today 是主语,children 50 years ago 是参照物,而在问题中,他们的角色正好相反;原句中提到现在的小孩焦虑程度较高,反过来,可理解成 50 年前被视为有心理疾病的小孩焦虑程度较低,据此,就能找到正确答案了。[答案:C]

命题规律4:关键词

所谓的关键词,指的就是段落或文章的主题词。因为相当一部分阅读理解题考查的是段落或文章的中心大意,因此,正确答案必须是关键词、包含关键词或对关键词的解释。

[例4]In the recent comparison of Japanese and American preschool education, 91 percent of Japanese respondents chose providing children with a group experience as one of their top reasons for a society to have preschools. Sixty-two percent of the more *individually oriented* (强调个性发展的) Americans listed group experience as one of their top three choices. [2005.1/第 2 篇]

[题目]Most Americans surveyed believe that preschools should also attach importance to _____.

　　A) problem solving 　　　　　　　　　B) group experience
　　C) parental guidance 　　　　　　　　D) individually-oriented development

[解析]从原文可以看出,虽然强调集体体验的美国人远远少于日本人,但强调的人还是占了多数,达到 62%。因此,本题的正确选项就是本段的关键词 group experience。[答案:B]

这一规律对于选择正确选项很有帮助,因为很多事实细节题会考查段落或文章的中心大意,掌握了关键词就等于掌握了一把钥匙。

第二节 干扰项的6种设置规律

干扰项的设置有六大规律:(1)轻重异位;(2)曲解原意、偷换概念;(3)张冠李戴;(4)答非所问;(5)字面意义;(6)缺少依据。

命题规律1:轻重异位

选项虽然提及,但不是重点所在。

【例5】Another common episode of absent-mindedness: walking into a room and wondering why you're there. Most likely, you were thinking about something else. "Everyone does this from time to time," says Zelinski. The best thing to do is to return to where you were before entering the room, and you'll likely remember. [2002.6/第2篇]

【题目】What do we learn from the last paragraph?

A) If we focus our attention on one thing, we might forget another.

B) Memory depends to a certain extent on the environment.

C) Repetition helps improve our memory.

D) If we keep forgetting things, we'd better return to where we were.

【解析】这是一篇关于记忆的文章,本段中,作者先列举了心不在焉的一种表现:进入房间却忘了想干什么。原因是你可能在想其他事,作者提出的解决办法是:回到进房间以前所在的地方。问题是"从最后一段可以知道什么?"D干扰性很强,因为作者在分析原因时提到了这一点,但这只是表面化的答案,并非重点所在,重点是记忆和环境的关系:回到以前的环境中就可以记起为什么要进房间了,即环境对记忆具有一定程度的影响。[答案:B]

命题规律2:曲解原意、偷换概念

选项一般不会完全重复原文文字,要注意所用文字与原文的意义是否一致,特别是对原文断章取义或歪曲、偷换原文某些词的意思时。

【例6】In my fridgeless Fifties childhood, I was fed well and healthily. [1997.6/第1篇]

【题目】The statement "In my fridgeless Fifties childhood, I was fed well and healthily." suggests that _____.

A) the author was well-fed and healthy even without a fridge in his fifties

B) the author was not accustomed to use fridges even in his fifties

C) there was no fridge in the author's home in the 1950s

D) the fridge was in its early stage of development in the 1950s

【解析】本题的关键在于Fifties的理解:是50年代还是50多岁?childhood这个词排除了后一种可能,应理解为50年代。很多同学被A项的前半部分所迷惑,没注意该选项最后几个单词改变了原文的意思。正确答案C是对fridgeless的同义替换。[答案:C]

命题规律3:张冠李戴

把文中对A的叙述、评价或描写套用于B。

【例7】   "The first thing people are usually judged on is their ability to perform well on a consistent basis," says Neil P. Lewis, a management psychologist. "But if two or three candidates are up for a promotion, each of whom has reasonably similar ability, a manager is going to promote the person he or she likes best. It's simple human nature."

Yet, psychologists say, many employees and employers have trouble with the concept of politics in the office. Some people, they say, have an idealistic vision of work and what it takes to succeed. Still others associate politics with flattery, fearful that, if they speak up for themselves, they may appear to be flattering their boss for favors.

Experts suggest altering this negative picture by recognizing the need for some self-promotion. [2004.6/第1篇]

【题目】It's the author's view that _____.

A) speaking up for oneself is part of human nature

B) self-promotion does not necessarily mean flattery

C) hard work contributes very little to one's promotion

D) many employees fail to recognize the need of flattery

【解析】本题问的是作者的观点,从文章来看,作者主张利用office politics,与老板和同事处好关系,谋取个人的发展,这并不等于奉承,B正确。A将"提拔能力接近、自己喜欢的人是人的本性"同"为自己说话看起来像在奉承"两件事混淆,属于典型的张冠李戴。作者并不认为能力完全不重要,C错误;D前半部分和文章结尾一致,但却把最后一个单词self-promotion换成flattery,属于偷换概念,也能迷惑部分不够细心的考生。[答案:B]

命题规律 4:答非所问

选项在文中虽有提及,但不能正确回答问题;或逻辑关系不对。

[例 8]Consequently, most of the world's fridges are to be found, not in the tropics where they might prove useful, but in the wealthy countries with mild temperature where they are climatically almost unnecessary. Every winter, millions of fridges hum away continuously, and at vast expense, busily maintaining an artificially-cooled space inside an artificially-heated house—while outside, nature provides the desired temperature free of charge.

[1997.6/第 1 篇]

[题目]Which of the following phrases in the fifth paragraph indicates the fridge's negative effect on the environment?

    A) Hum away continuously.   B) Climatically almost unnecessary.

    C) Artificially-cooled space.   D) With mild temperature.

[解析]四个选项都是从文中摘录出的,而且都表明了作者对冰箱的否定态度,但题目问的是冰箱对环境的负面影响,分析四个选项,只有 A(不停地嗡嗡响)构成噪音污染,是对环境的影响,其他选项并非冰箱对环境的影响,全部排除。[答案:A]

命题规律 5:字面意义

答案给出的是某关键词句的字面意义、表面意义或肤浅意义。

[例9]   A is for always getting to work on time.

        B is for extremely busy.

        C is for the conscientious way you do your job.

      You may be all these things at the office, and more. But when it comes to getting ahead, experts say, the ABCs of business should include a P, for politics, as in office politics.

      ...

      In fact, today, experts define office politics as proper behavior used to pursue one's own self-interest in the workplace. In many cases, this involves some form of socializing within the office environment—not just in large companies, but in small workplaces as well.

[2004.6/第 1 篇]

[题目]"Office politics" (Para. 4) is used in the passage to refer to _____.

    A) the code of behavior for company staff

    B) the political views and beliefs of office workers

    C) the interpersonal relationships within a company

    D) the various qualities required for a successful career

[解析]题目针对的是文章的一个核心概念:office politics。选项 B 取的是 politic 一词的字面意义,予以排除;A 和 D 过泛,不符合文意;C 才是文章集中论述的内容,为正确答案。[答案:C]

> 这一命题规律提示我们:字面意义、表面意义、肤浅意义不是正确选项,同文章主题有关的深刻含义才是正确选项。

命题规律 6:缺少依据

选项与常识相符,但文中并未提及或虽有提及,但不足以推断出该观点。

[例 10]   Even dinner parties, if they happen at all, have gone casual. In a time of long work hours and demanding family schedules, busy hosts insist, rightly, that it's better to share a takeout pizza on paper plates in the family room than to wait for the perfect moment or a "real" dinner party. Too often, the perfect moment never comes. Iron a fine-patterned tablecloth? Forget it. Polish the silver? Who has time?

      Yet the loss of formality has its down side. The fine points of etiquette that children might once have learned at the table by observation or instruction from parents and grandparents ("Chew with your mouth closed." "Keep your elbows off the table.") must be picked up elsewhere. Some companies now offer etiquette seminars for employees who may be competent professionally but clueless socially.

[2004.1/第 3 篇]

[题目]Which of the following may be the best reason for casual dining?

A) Family members need more time to relax.

B) Busy schedules leave people no time for formality.

C) People want to practice economy in times of scarcity.

D) Young people won't follow the etiquette of the older generation.

【解析】如果不看原文,四个选项都有道理,但 A、C、D 在文中没有提到,缺少依据,予以排除,根据上述第 1 段的内容,选 B。[答案:B]

总结起来,做篇章阅读理解叶必须细心、冷静、沉着,避免误入命题者精心设计的圈套。

进行选择时一般有以下答题技巧:

主旨大意题:中心思想是解;概括性的是解;包括正反两面的是解;肤浅的不是解;片面的不是解;

词义理解题:字面意思一般不是解,深刻含义一般是解;

照抄原文不是解,同义替换是解;

绝对的不是解,相对的是解;

具体的不是解,抽象的是解;

符合常识的不是解,看似合理的不是解,看似反常的往往是解。

四个选项中确定两个可能选项的方法:反义项可能是解;形似项可能是解;近义项可能是解。

第三节 历年典型真题突破训练

Passage One 07 年 12 月真题

By almost any measure, there is a boom in Internet-based instruction. In just a few years, 34 percent of American universities have begun offering some form of distance learning (DL), and among the larger schools, it's closer to 90 percent. If you doubt the popularity of the trend, you probably haven't heard of the University of Phoenix. It grants degrees entirely on the basis of online instruction. It enrolls 90,000 students, a statistic used to support its claim to be the largest private university in the country.

While the kinds of instruction offered in these programs will differ, DL usually signifies a course in which the instructors post *syllabi* (课程大纲), reading assignments, and schedules on Websites, and students send in their assignments by e-mail. Generally speaking, face-to-face communication with an instructor is minimized or eliminated altogether.

The attraction for students might at first seem obvious. Primarily, there's the convenience promised by courses on the Net: you can do the work, as they say, in your *pajamas* (睡衣). But figures indicate that the reduced effort results in a reduced commitment to the course. While drop-out rates for all freshmen at American universities is around 20 percent, the rate for online students is 35 percent. Students themselves seem to understand the weaknesses inherent in the setup. In a survey conducted for eCornell, the DL division of Cornell University, less than a third of the respondents expected the quality of the online course to be as good as the classroom course.

Clearly, from the schools' perspective, there's a lot of money to be saved. Although some of the more ambitious programs require new investments in servers and networks to support collaborative software, most DL courses can run on existing or minimally *upgraded* (升级) systems. The more students who enroll in a course but don't come to campus, the more the school saves on keeping the lights on in the classrooms, paying doorkeepers, and maintaining parking lots. And, while there's evidence that instructors must work harder to run a DL course for a variety of reasons, they won't be paid any more, and might well be paid less.

57. What is the most striking feature of the University of Phoenix?

A) All its courses are offered online.

B) Its online courses are of the best quality.

C) It boasts the largest number of students on campus.

D) Anyone taking its online courses is sure to get a degree.

58. According to the passage, distance learning is basically characterized by _____.

A) a considerable flexibility in its academic requirements

B) the great diversity of students' academic backgrounds

C) a minimum or total absence of face-to-face instruction

D) the casual relationship between students and professors

59. Many students take Internet-based courses mainly because they can _____.

A) earn their academic degrees with much less effort

B) save a great deal on traveling and boarding expenses

C) select courses from various colleges and universities

D) work on the required courses whenever and wherever

60. What accounts for the high drop-out rates for online students?

A) There is no strict control over the academic standards of the courses.

B) The evaluation system used by online universities is inherently weak.

C) There is no mechanism to ensure that they make the required effort.

D) Lack of classroom interaction reduces the effectiveness of instruction.

61. According to the passage, universities show great enthusiasm for DL programs for the purpose of _____.

A) building up their reputation   B) cutting down on their expenses

C) upgrading their teaching facilities   D) providing convenience for students

Passage Two   07 年 12 月真题

In this age of Internet chat, videogames and reality television, there is no shortage of mindless activities to keep a child occupied. Yet, despite the competition, my 8-year-old daughter Rebecca wants to spend her leisure time writing short stories. She wants to enter one of her stories into a writing contest, a competition she won last year.

As a writer I know about winning contests, and about losing them. I know what it is like to work hard on a story only to receive a rejection slip from the publisher. I also know the pressures of trying to live up to a reputation created by previous victories. What if she doesn't win the contest again? That's the strange thing about being a parent. So many of our own past scars and dashed hopes can surface.

A *revelation* (启示) came last week when I asked her, "Don't you want to win again?" "No," she replied, "I just want to tell the story of an angel going to first grade."

I had just spent weeks correcting her stories as she *spontaneously* (自发地) told them. Telling myself that I was merely an experienced writer guiding the young writer across the hall, I offered suggestions for characters, conflicts and endings for her tales. The story about a fearful angel starting first grade was quickly "guided" by me into the tale of a little girl with a wild imagination taking her first music lesson. I had turned her contest into my contest without even realizing it.

Staying back and giving kids space to grow is not as easy as it looks. Because I know very little about farm animals who use tools or angels who go to first grade, I had to accept the fact that I was *co-opting* (借用) my daughter's experience.

While stepping back was difficult for me, it was certainly a good first step that I will quickly follow with more steps, putting myself far enough away to give her room but close enough to help if asked. All the while I will be reminding myself that children need room to experiment, grow and find their own voices.

62. What do we learn from the first paragraph?

A) Children do find lots of fun in many mindless activities.

B) Rebecca is much too occupied to enjoy her leisure time.

C) Rebecca draws on a lot of online materials for her writing.

D) A lot of distractions compete for children's time nowadays.

63. What did the author say about her own writing experience?

A) She did not quite live up to her reputation as a writer.

B) Her way to success was full of pains and frustrations.

C) She was constantly under pressure of writing more.

D) Most of her stories had been rejected by publishers.

64. Why did Rebecca want to enter this year's writing contest?

A) She believed she possessed real talent for writing.

B) She was sure of winning with her mother's help.

C) She wanted to share her stories with readers.

D) She had won a prize in the previous contest.

65. The author took great pains to refine her daughter's stories because _____.

A) she believed she had the knowledge and experience to offer guidance

B) she did not want to disappoint Rebecca who needed her help so much

C) she wanted to help Rebecca realize her dream of becoming a writer

D) she was afraid Rebecca's imagination might run wild while writing

66. What's the author's advice for parents?

A) A writing career, though attractive, is not for every child to pursue.

B) Children should be allowed freedom to grow through experience.

C) Parents should keep an eye on the activities their kids engage in.

D) Children should be given every chance to voice their opinions.

Passage Three   07 年 6 月真题

I don't ever want to talk about being a woman scientist again. There was a time in my life when people asked constantly for stories about what it's like to work in a field dominated by men. I was never very good at telling those stories because truthfully I never found them interesting. What I do find interesting is the origin of the universe, the shape of space-time and the nature of black holes.

At 19, when I began studying astrophysics, it did not bother me in the least to be the only woman in the classroom. But while earning my Ph.D. at MIT and then as a post-doctor doing space research, the issue started to bother me. My every achievement—jobs, research papers, awards—was viewed through the lens of *gender* (性别) politics. So were my failures. Sometimes, when I was pushed into an argument on left brain *versus* (相对于) right brain, or nature versus *nurture* (培育), I would instantly fight fiercely on my behalf and all womankind.

Then one day a few years ago, out of my mouth came a sentence that would eventually become my reply to any and all provocations: I don't talk about that anymore. It took me 10 years to get back the confidence I had at 19 and to realize that I didn't want to deal with gender issues. Why should curing sexism be yet another terrible burden on every female scientist? After all, I don't study sociology or political theory.

Today I research and teach at Barnard, a women's college in New York City. Recently, someone asked me how many of the 45 students in my class were women. You cannot imagine my satisfaction at being able to answer, 45. I know some of my students worry how they will manage their scientific research and a desire for children. And I don't dismiss those concerns. Still, I don't tell them "war" stories. Instead, I have given them this: the visual of their physics professor heavily pregnant doing physics experiments. And in turn they have given me the image of 45 women driven by a love of science. And that's a sight worth talking about.

57. Why doesn't the author want to talk about being a woman scientist again?

A) She feels unhappy working in male-dominated fields.

B) She is not good at telling stories of the kind.

C) She finds space research more important.

D) She is fed up with the issue of gender discrimination.

58. From Paragraph 2, we can infer that people would attribute the author's failures to _____.

A) her over-confidence as a female astrophysicist

B) the very fact that she is a woman

C) her involvement in gender politics

D) the burden she bears in a male-dominated society

59. What did the author constantly fight against while doing her Ph.D. and post-doctoral research?

    A) Widespread misconceptions about nature and nurture.

    B) People's stereotyped attitude towards female scientists.

    C) Unfair accusations from both inside and outside her circle.

    D) Lack of confidence in succeeding in space science.

60. Why does the author feel great satisfaction when talking about her class?

    A) Her students' performance has brought back her confidence.

    B) Her female students can do just as well as male students.

    C) More female students are pursuing science than before.

    D) Female students no longer have to bother about gender issues.

61. What does the image the author presents to her students suggest?

    A) Women students needn't have the concerns of her generation.

    B) Women have more barriers on their way to academic success.

    C) Women now have fewer problems pursuing a science career.

    D) Women can balance a career in science and having a family.

Passage Four   07 年 6 月真题

I've been writing for most of my life. The book *Writing Without Teachers* introduced me to one distinction and one practice that has helped my writing processes tremendously. The distinction is between the creative mind and the critical mind. While you need to employ both to get to a finished result, they cannot work in parallel no matter how much we might like to think so.

Trying to criticize writing on the fly is possibly the single greatest barrier to writing that most of us encounter. If you are listening to that 5th grade English teacher correct your grammar while you are trying to capture a *fleeting* (稍纵即逝的) thought, the thought will die. If you capture the fleeting thought and simply share it with the world in raw form, no one is likely to understand. You must learn to create first and then criticize if you want to make writing the tool for thinking that it is.

The practice that can help you past your learned bad habits of trying to edit as you write is what Elbow calls "free writing." In free writing, the objective is to get words down on paper non-stop, usually for 15-20 minutes. No stopping, no going back, no criticizing. The goal is to get the words flowing. As the words begin to flow, the ideas will come out from the shadows and let themselves be captured on your notepad or your screen.

Now you have raw materials that you can begin to work with using the critical mind that you've persuaded to sit on the side and watch quietly. Most likely, you will believe that this will take more time than you actually have and you will end up staring blankly at the page as the deadline draws near.

Instead of staring at a blank screen start filling it with words no matter how bad. Halfway through your available time, stop and rework your raw writing into something closer to finished product. Move back and forth until you run out of time and the final result will most likely be far better than your current practices.

62. When the author says the creative mind and the critical mind "cannot work in parallel" (Line 3, Para. 1) in the writing process, he means _____.

    A) one cannot use them at the same time   B) no one can be both creative and critical

    C) they are in constant conflict with each other   D) they cannot be regarded as equally important

63. What prevents people from writing on is _____.

    A) putting their ideas in raw form   B) trying to capture fleeting thoughts

    C) attempting to edit as they write   D) ignoring grammatical soundness

64. What is the chief objective of the first stage of writing?

A) To get one's ideas down.　　　　　B) To collect raw materials.

C) To choose an appropriate topic.　　D) To organize one's thoughts logically.

65. One common concern of writers about "free writing" is that _____.

A) it does not help them to think clearly　B) it takes too much time to edit afterwards

C) it overstresses the role of the creative mind　D) it may bring about too much criticism

66. In what way does the critical mind help the writer in the writing process?

A) It allows him to sit on the side and observe.　B) It saves the writing time available to him.

C) It helps him to come up with new ideas.　D) It refines his writing into better shape.

第四节　答案解析

参考译文划线点评　　　　　　　　　　　　　　　**Passage One**

　　不管用什么标准来衡量,网络教育都在快速发展。短短几年间,美国34%的大学都已开始提供某种形式的远程学习。而在那些规模较大的学校里,提供网络教育的占几近90%。如果你还不相信网络教育如此火爆,那你可能没有听说过[57]凤凰城大学。该大学颁发的学位完全是通过网络教学提供的。学校招生人数达9万,这个数字使其号称是美国最大的私立大学。

　　虽然网络课程提供的教学形式会各不相同,但远程学习通常都表现为这样一种课程:教师将课程大纲、阅读作业及课程进度安排在网站上公布,学生通过电子邮件提交作业。[58]一般来说,学生与教师面对面的交流降低到最低程度,甚至完全没有。

　　初看起来,这种教育形式[59]吸引学生之处似乎显而易见。首先,网络课程声称可以给学生带来一大方便:就像有人说的那样,你可以穿着睡衣学习。[60]但也有数字显示,由于要求学生付出的努力减少,导致学生对学习不够用心投入。美国大学一年级学生辍学率为20%左右,而网络学生辍学率为35%。学生自己似乎也了解这种教育形式本身固有的一些欠缺。在为康奈尔在线(康奈尔大学远程教育学院)做的一次调查中,预计在线课程的质量与在校课程的质量一样好的受访者不到三分之一。

　　显然,[61]从学校的角度来说,远程教育可以节省大笔资金。虽然一些规模更大的课程需要斥资增加新的服务器、扩建网络来支持配套的软件,但大部分远程教育课程可以在现有的或稍加升级的系统上运行。报考该课却不来校园上课的学生越多,学校在用于教室照明、支付看门人及维护停车场的费用上就可以节省越多。而且,虽然有证据显示,因各种原因,为了开设远程教育课程教师更辛苦地工作,但是,他们得到的报酬并不会更多,而可能会更少。

57. [A]【定位】根据题干中的 University of Phoenix 查找到第1段第3句。

　　【解析】文章第3句提到 University of Phoenix,随后的第4句具体说明了它的特色,其中的 entirely on the basis of online…与选项 A 中的 all… online 一致。

　　【点睛】C 中的 on campus 是明显的错误信息。B 中的 best 和 D 中的 sure to get 无据可依。

58. [C]【定位】根据题干中的 distance learning 和 characterized 查找到第2段。

　　【解析】第2段最后一句简要总结 DL 的特征。句中 face-to-face communication 对应选项 C 中的 face-to-face instruction, minimized or eliminated altogether 对应 a minimum or total absence, general speaking 对应题干中的 basically。

　　【点睛】答案往往含有原文实义词的同义词或同根词。其余各项尽管可能也正确,但短文中未提及,而且并非基本特征(basically characterized)。

59. [D]【定位】根据题干中的 students, Internet-based courses 查找到第3段第1~2句。

　　【解析】题目问原因,第1句总述这种教育形式吸引学生之处似乎显而易见,第2句具体解释原因,关键词是

convenience。而 in your pajamas(可以穿着睡衣听课)说明随时随地可以学习。

【点睛】此段并未提及获得学位是否很容易的信息,故 A 错。节省交通和住宿费也无据可依,故 B 错。

60. [C]【定位】根据题干中的 drop-out rates 查找到第 3 段第 4 句。

【解析】第 4 句谈到网络学生退学率高,是为了说明学生对课程缺乏责任心,由第 3 句可知,the reduced effort results in a reduced commitment,因而答案是 C。题干中的 accounts for 与第 3 句中的 results in 语义相当。

【点睛】B 是用第 5–6 句中不相干的词拼凑出来的干扰项;其他各项与文章内容不符,或未在文中提及。

61. [B]【定位】根据题干中的 universities, enthusiasm 查找到最后一段第 1 句。

【解析】最后一段第 1 句的关键词是 money saved,对应选项 B。该段说明大学是如何通过远程教育节省开支的。

【点睛】在文中找不到题干中的原词时要找同义信息,选择时也主要根据同义替换原则。尽管网络教学客观上为学生提供方便(D),有可能为学校带来声望(A),也迫使学校购置相应设备(C),但这些都不是大学热心远程教育的目的。

参考译文划线点评   Passage Two

[62]在今天这个充斥着网络聊天、电子游戏和真人电视秀的时代,占据孩子们空闲时间的无聊活动并不缺乏。但是,尽管这些活动都在尽力争宠,我 8 岁的女儿丽贝卡却愿意在空闲时间里写些短篇故事。她希望将其中的一个故事投去参加一个写作比赛。去年她曾在这个比赛中获奖。

[63]作为一个作家,我很了解赢得比赛或输掉比赛是怎么回事,我了解辛辛苦苦写出的故事却只换来出版社的退稿单时的心情,我也了解要竭力保持以往的荣耀带来的名声时的压力。如果她不能再次获奖该怎么办?这就是为人父母让人不可思议的地方。我们自己过去遭受的种种创伤和破灭的希望可能又会冒出来。

上周我问她:"你难道不想再次得奖吗?""不想,"[64]她回答说,"我只想讲一个上一年级的天使的故事。"这让我顿悟。

那时,我刚花了几周时间修改她即兴讲出来的故事,我对自己说,[65]我只是一个有经验的作家,在指导身边的一位年轻作家。我对她的那些故事中的人物、冲突及结局提出建议。在我的指导下,故事中刚上一年级的胆怯天使立刻变成了第一次上音乐课、爱胡思乱想的小女孩。我已将她的比赛变成了我的比赛,而我自己却甚至没有意识到这一点。

走到一旁、还孩子成长的空间,并不像看起来那么简单。因为我对会使用工具的家畜和上一年级的天使一无所知,所以我得承认这样的事实:我在借用我女儿的经验。

虽然走到一旁对我来说并非易事,但这确实是一个不错的开始。我会继续这样做,让自己离她远远的,给她足够的空间;但同时又离她很近,在她寻求帮助的时候,可以伸出援手。我会一直提醒自己,[66]孩子们需要空间去尝试、去成长、去找到他们自己的表达方式。

62. [D]【定位】第 1 段。

【解析】此题考查段落主旨,根据第 1 句中的关键信息"占据孩子们空闲时间的无聊活动并不缺乏"和第 2 句中的"尽管这些活动都在尽力争宠",可知 D"很多娱乐活动竞相占据孩子们的时间"是最佳概括。

【点睛】A 错在主观判断 do find fun,文中并未提及孩子们的反应。

63. [B]【定位】根据题干中的 her own writing experience 查找到第 2 段第 1 句。

【解析】第 2 段开头连续 3 句都是以 I 作主语,说明作者本身的写作经历及感受,B 中的 pains and frustrations 概括了其中的关键词 losing, work hard, rejection slip 和 pressures。

【点睛】其他选项均为片面信息甚至是扭曲事实。

64. [C]【定位】根据题干中的 Rebecca 和 writing contest 查找到文章第 1 段尾句及第 3 段。

【解析】文章第 1 段尾句虽然提到了 Rebecca wants to enter this year's writing contest,但原因是在第 3 段用引语说明的:"我只想讲一个上一年级的天使的故事。"根据关键词"讲故事",答案为 C。

【点睛】把握文章整体结构有助于快速查找到具体题目的解题依据。

65. [A]【定位】根据题干中的 refine her daughter's stories 查找到第4段第1句。

　　【解析】第1句说明现象，第2-3句解释原因，关键词是 experience, guide,对应 A 中的 experience, guidance。

【点睛】把握句子之间的逻辑关系很重要。像这种可在文中找到相应答题点的细节题,不可凭主观想象答题,一定要校对原文细节,找出相应用词,确定答案。

66. [B]【定位】根据题干中的 advice 查找到最后一段。

　　【解析】文章最后一句关键词是 experiment, grow,对应 B 中的 grow through experience。

【点睛】建议、结论一般都会在末段提出,因此可以直接在末段寻找作者的建议。

参考译文划线点评　　　　　　　　　　　　　Passage Three

　　[57]我再也不想谈论当女科学家这个话题了。我生活中有那么一段时间人们老是问我,供职于一个男性占主导地位的领域感觉如何?我从来就不擅长讲述那些经历,因为我真的觉得它们很没意思。我真正感兴趣的是宇宙的起源,时空的形状和黑洞的性质。

　　在我19岁开始学习天体物理学的时候,作为教室里唯一的女生我一点儿也没有感到不自在。但是当我取得麻省理工学院的博士学位,然后以博士后的身份做太空研究的时候,这个问题开始困扰我了。[58/59]我所取得的每一个成绩,无论是工作,还是研究论文,抑或是获奖,别人都是通过性别政治的透镜来看待的。对我的失败也是如此。有时候,当我与别人争论左脑与右脑的问题,或者是先天天赋与后天固有的问题呢,[5?]~~我 ⋯⋯⋯⋯⋯⋯⋯⋯⋯⋯⋯⋯~~ 同胞的立场上给了狠狠的反驳。

　　于是,几年前的一天,从我的嘴里冒出了一句最终成为我对所有挑衅的回应的话:我再也不想谈论这个话题了。我花了10年的时间才找回了我19岁时的自信,才意识到我本不想谈论性别问题。为什么消除性别歧视就应该是加在每一位女科学家身上的另一个不堪忍受的负担呢?毕竟,我不是学社会学或者政治理论的。

　　如今,我在纽约市一所名叫 Barnard 的女子大学搞科研,也教书。我的班级里一共有45名学生。[60]近来,有人问我其中女生有多少。我得意地回答说45,你无法想象我这样回答时的自豪与满足。我知道其中一些学生担心他们以后又搞科研又想要小孩怎么顾得过来。我不回避这个问题,但我并没有说这两者之间是矛盾的。[61]相反,我给他们的是这么一幅画面:她们的物理学教授挺着大肚子做物理试验。反过来,她们给我展现了一幅45名女生献身于科学事业的画面。这是一幅值得讨论的画面。

57. [D]【定位】第1段第1-3句。

　　【解析】文章开头即说:我再也不想谈论当女科学家这个话题了。这与本题题干一致。紧接着,作者就解释原因:别人不断地问及这个问题;作者觉得这个问题没有意思。选项 D 中的"fed up with"意思是"因受够了感到厌倦",和文中的 constantly, never found them interesting 含义一致,是正确答案。

【点睛】①第1段结尾,作者说她喜欢自己的工作,而第2句表明,该工作男性占主导,所以 A 错。②B 似乎与原文一致,但原文说的是"was never very good",并不是"is not good";而且 B 也不是作者不想谈论这个话题的根本原因。③作者说自己的工作很 interesting,没有谈及它是否 important;作者并没有就性别歧视问题和自己的科学研究的重要性进行比较,故 C 没有根据。

58. [B]【定位】第2段第3句和第4句。

　　【解析】第2段第3-4句提到:"我所取得的每一个成绩,无论是工作,还是研究论文,抑或是获奖,别人都是通过性别政治的透镜来看待的。对我的失败也是如此。"由此可见,人们把她的失败也归因于她是一名女性这个事实。所以答案选 B。

【点睛】①围绕文章主题进行选择是捷径,与主题无关的不可能是答案。②如果对 C 理解错误,容易误选。C 的含义是"她参与到了性别政治之中",事实上,原文是说别人用性别政治的眼光看待她的成就与失败,而不是说她参与了性别政治活动。本段未提及 A 与 D 的内容。

59. [B]【定位】由题干中的 Ph.D. and post-doctoral research 定位到第2段第2句及其上下文。

【解析】本句由 But 引导,说作者在读博士、攻读博士后期间,the issue 开始影响她。理解 the issue 的含义,即可回答本题"作者 fight against 什么东西"的问题。根据前一句可知,the issue 指的是"她是唯一的女性"这个问题;后文则提到,很多人都在"透过性别政治的透镜"看待她的成败。所以 B"人们对女性科学家的成见"正确。

【点睛】①答案应该与文章主题一致。②C 和 D 完全没有提及,A 中的 misconceptions 也没有根据。

60. [C]【定位】由题干中的 satisfaction 和 talking about her class 定位到第 4 段的 2~3 句。

【解析】原文用 at 引导出 satisfaction 的原因:"being able to answer, 45."她班上 45 名学习物理的学生都是女生,这让她很得意(因为她自己上大学时,班上只有她一个女生)。联系到本文的主旨,可以判断 C 正确。

【点睛】短文没有提到学生如何使她恢复自信,也没有提到她的男学生,故 A 与 B 错误。短文提到有些女学生担心搞研究与生小孩的矛盾,可见她们也要考虑 gender issues,故 D 错。

61. [D]【定位】由题干中的 image the author presents to her students 定位到最后一段倒数第 3 句。

【解析】短文提到,有些学生对怎样 manage scientific research and a desire for children 有顾虑,作者一方面承认这种顾虑有道理,另一方面则以身示范,向学生展示了挺着肚子做实验的形象(文中的 their physics professor 即是作者自己),说明在工作和家庭之间是可以达到平衡的。故选 D。

【点睛】①A 与短文内容矛盾(作者承认这些顾虑是存在的)。B 中的 more barriers 没有根据(一定要根据短文内容回答,不可根据自己的常识回答)。C 中的 fewer 没有根据。②围绕段落主题选择答案。

参考译文划线点评   **Passage Four**

　　我一生中大部分时间都在写作。一本名叫《写作——无师自通》的书使我知道了一种区别和一种做法。这种做法使我的写作大受裨益。这种区别就是创造性思维与批判性思维之间的区别。[62]尽管要完成定稿这两种思维都不可或缺,可是它们却不能并行着参与写作过程——无论我们多么认为原本如此。

　　试图匆匆忙忙地就对你的写作加以批判可能是我们大多数人在写作中所碰到的最大的障碍。如果你在听五年级的英文老师纠正你的语法,而同时你又尽力在捕捉一个稍纵即逝的想法,那么,你的想法就会消失得无影无踪。如果你捕捉到了这种稍纵即逝的想法,并且想以未经润色的形式把它拿来与人分享,那么没有人会明白你的意思。如果你想使写作成为你思考的工具的话,那么你一定要学会先创作,再批判。

　　[63]这种可以帮助你克服在写作的同时就试图编辑的坏习惯的做法便是 Elbow 所称作的"自由式写作"。[64]自由式写作的目的就是不停地把想说的话付诸笔端,通常连续写作 15 到 20 分钟。不停止,不回头复查,不批判。目的就是把想说的话不停地写下去。随着话语开始流淌,思想也会逐渐明朗化,使自己呈现在你的笔记本或者屏幕上。

　　[66]现在你拥有了可以用批判性思维加以整理的素材。刚才创作的时候,你设法使批判性思维只在一旁坐着静心观察,现在则可以发挥其用武之地了。[65]你很有可能会以为这样加工整理素材会让你时间不够用,结果是最后随着交稿日期的逐渐临近,你将只是盯着稿件发呆。

　　不要再盯着空屏幕发呆了,无论文字有多糟糕,都开始动手写吧。在有限的时间过了一半的时候,[66]停下来,把原始素材加工,使它离最后的完工稿更接近一点。这样不断地反复,到交稿的时候,最终的结果很可能会比现在的办法写出来的稿子要好得多。

62. [A]【定位】第 1 段最后一句。

【解析】本句话的意思是:"尽管要完成定稿这两种思维都不可或缺,但是,它们却不能同时并行着参与写作过程……"理解的难点是 in parallel,即"并行、平行、同时进行"。如果对这个句子的确切含义不明确,就要参考下文作者给出的解释。第 2 段结束时提到,"一定要学会先创作后批判",也就是说这两种思维活动有先后之分,"不能同时进行"。故 A 正确。

【点睛】①B 是对原文的误读。原文明确提到,要写作两种思维都不可缺少,因此 B"没有人可以同时具有创造性思维和批判性思维"错误。②C 强调两种思维的冲突,也与原文含义不一致。③原文没有说哪种思维更重要,D 没有根据。

63. [C]【定位】第3段第1句。

【解析】第3段第1句说"这种可以帮助你克服在写作的同时就试图编辑的坏习惯的做法便是Elbow所称作的'自由式写作'"。由此可知,边写作边编辑是一种坏习惯,它会阻碍"自由式写作",所以答案应为C。

【点睛】①本题难在找准原文出题点。题干中的"使人不能往下写"暗示出"不良的写作习惯",若由此找到考点所在句子,则容易解题。②也可以用排除法解题。理解到其余三个选项都是"自由式写作"的方法,则可选出正确答案。

64. [A]【定位】由题干中的objective查到第3段第2句。

【解析】第3段第2句说得很清楚"自由式写作的目的就是不停地把想说的话付诸笔端",而根据文章,自由式写作就是写作的第一个阶段。所以答案选A。

【点睛】①本题答案直接,难度不大。②B中的raw materials来自第4段开头。原文指批判性思维加工用的"原材料",是一种比喻的说法,B用它作干扰项,注意排除。③C,D原文没有提到。

65. [B]【定位】第4段第2句。

【解析】①由题干中的common concern找到考点所说的Most likely引导的句子。Most likely"很有可能",表明下面提到的问题是较常见的。②对believe引导的宾语从句的理解是本题的考点与难点,其中this will take more time than you actually have中的this的指代关系是理解的关键。根据前一句,它指to work with (raw materials) using critical mind,也就是B所说的to edit afterwards。故答案是B。

【点睛】①关键是找对考点,然后根据上下文和语法关系正确理解原文。②如果找对考点,仅仅根据原文中的time一词即可正确作答。

66. [D]【定位】第4段第1句和第5段第2句。

【解析】第4段第1句说,批判性思维在写作过程中的作用就是对"原材料进行加工"。怎样加工的呢？第5段第2句说,写到中途要停下来,对初稿加工,使之离最终稿更接近一点,也就是说,对初稿润色。故D正确。

【点睛】①A曲解原文;作者任何时候都要投入精力,或者忙于创造,或者忙于润色修改,不可能"坐在一边看"。②由上题可知,批判性思维不一定会节约时间,故B错。③使作者涌现新想法的是创造性思维,而不是批判性思维,故C错。

Passage One

Not all sounds made by animals serve as language, and we have only to turn to that extraordinary discovery of *echolocation* (回声定位) in bats to see a case in which the voice plays a strictly practical role.

To get a full appreciation of what this means we must turn first to some recent human inventions. Everyone knows that if he shouts near a wall or a mountainside, an echo will come back. The further off this solid obstacle, the longer time it will take for the return of the echo. A sound made by tapping on the main body of a ship will be reflected from the sea bottom, and by measuring the time interval between the taps and the receipt of the echoes the depth of the sea at that point can be calculated. So was born the echo-sounding equipment, now in general use in ships. Every solid object will reflect a sound, varying according to the size and nature of the object. A shoal of fish will do this. So it is a comparatively simple step from locating the sea bottom to locating a shoal of fish. With experience, and with improved equipment, it is now possible not only to locate fish but to tell if it is herring, cod, or other well-known fish, by the pattern of its echo.

A few years ago it was found that certain bats emit *squeaks* (吱吱声) and by receiving the echoes they could locate and steer clear of obstacles—or locate flying insects on which they feed. This echolocation in bats is often compared with radar, the principle of which is similar.

1. The main purpose of this passage is to _____.

    A) describe that animals can make different sounds

    B) prove that animals' voices can play practical roles

    C) inspire the readers to make more inventions

    D) startle the readers with some shocking facts

2. The discovery of echolocation may help with all of the following EXCEPT _____.

    A) measuring the depth of the sea

    B) distinguishing different kinds of fish

    C) improving the functions of radar

    D) varying the size and nature of an object

3. By saying "A shoal of fish will do this"(Lines 6–7, Para. 2), the author means _____.

    A) only one special kind of fish can reflect sounds

B) only one special kind of fish can be used to help locate a ship

C) a large group of fish can reflect sounds

D) a large group of fish can be used to help locate a ship

4. As it is discussed in the passage, the squeaks of bats can be functionally compared with _____.

A) human languages   B) a mountainside   C) a shoal of fish   D) taps on a ship

5. Which of the following statements can be inferred from the passage?

A) Animals are more intelligent than humans.

B) Humans are more intelligent than animals.

C) Animals are often compared with human inventions.

D) Humans are often inspired by animals.

Passage Two

Real policemen hardly recognize any resemblance between their lives and what they see on TV—if they ever get home in time. There are similarities, of course, but the cops don't think much of them.

The first difference is that a policeman's real life revolves round the law. Most of his training is in criminal law. He has to know exactly what actions are crimes and what evidence can be used to prove them in court. He has to know nearly as much law as a professional lawyer, and what is more, he has to apply it on his feet, in the dark and rain, running down an alley after someone he wants to talk to.

Little of his time is spent in chatting to *scantily-clad* (衣着暴露的) ladies or in dramatic confrontations with desperate criminals. He will spend most of his working life typing millions of words on thousands of forms about hundreds of sad, unimportant people who are guilty—or not—of stupid, petty crimes.

Most television crime drama is about finding the criminals: as soon as he's arrested, the story is over. In real life, finding criminals is seldom much of a problem. Except in very serious cases like murders and terrorist attack—where failure to produce results reflects on the standing of the police—little effort is spent on searching.

Having made an arrest, a detective really starts to work. He has to prove his case in court and to do that he often has to gather a lot of different evidence. So, as well as being overworked, a detective has to be out at all hours of the day and night interviewing his witnesses and persuading them, usually against their own best interests, to help him.

1. The first sentence implies that _____.

A) the life of the real policemen and that of the policemen on TV are entirely different

B) the real policemen will find the similarities if they can get home in time

C) the real policemen seldom can get home in time to watch TV

D) the policemen shown on TV can always get home in time

2. It is essential for a policeman to be trained in criminal law _____.

A) so that he can catch criminals in the streets

B) because many of the criminals he has to catch are dangerous

C) so that he can justify his arrests in court

D) because he has to know nearly as much about law as a professional lawyer

3. The everyday life of a policeman or detective is _____.

A) exciting and glamorous   B) full of danger

C) devoted mostly to routine matters   D) wasted on unimportant matters

4. When murders and terrorist attacks occur, the police _____.

A) prefer to wait for the criminal to give himself away

B) make great efforts to try to track down their man

C) try to make a quick arrest in order to keep up their reputation

D) usually fail to produce results

5. What's the best title for the passage?

A) Policemen and Detectives B) Detectives'Life—Fact and Fantasy
C) The Reality of Being a Detective D) Drama and Reality

Passage Three

In a moment of personal crisis, how much help can you expect from a New York taxi driver? I began studying this question and found the answers interesting.

One morning I got into three different taxis and announced, "Well, it's my first day back in New York in seven years. I've been in prison." Not a single driver replied, so I tried again. "Yeah, I shot a man in Reno." I explained, hoping the driver would ask me why, but nobody asked. The only response came from a Ghanaian driver, "Reno? That is in Nevada?"

Taxi drivers were uniformly sympathetic when I said I'd just been fired. "This is America," a Haitian driver said. "One door is closed. Another is open." He argued against my plan to burn down my boss's house. A Pakistani driver even turned down a chance to profit from my loss of hope; he refused to take me to the middle of the George Washington Bridge—a $20 trip. "Why you want to go there? Go home and relax. Don't worry. Take a new job."

One very hot weekday in July, while wearing a red ski mask and holding a stuffed pillowcase with the word "BANK" on it, I tried calling a taxi five times outside different banks. The driver picked me up every time. My ride with a Haitian driver was typical of the superb assistance I received.

"Let's go across the park." I said. "I just robbed the bank there. I got $25,000."

"$25,000?" he asked.

"Yeah, you think it was wrong to take it?"

"No, man. I work 8 hours and I don't make almost $70. If I can do that, I do it too."

As we approached 86th and Lexington, I pointed to the Chemical Bank.

"Hey, there's another bank," I said, "Could you wait here a minute while I go inside?"

"No, I can't wait. Pay me now." His reluctance may have had something to do with money—taxi drivers think the rate for waiting time is too low—but I think he wanted me to learn that even a bank robber can't expect unconditional support.

1. From the Ghanaian driver's response, we can infer that _____.
   A) he was indifferent to the killing
   B) he was afraid of the author
   C) he looked down upon the author
   D) he thought the author was crazy

2. Why did the Pakistani driver refuse to take the author to the middle of the George Washington Bridge?
   A) Because he was able to help the author to find a new job.
   B) Because he wanted to go home and relax.
   C) Because it was far away from his home.
   D) Because he thought that the author would commit suicide.

3. What is the author's interpretation of the driver's reluctance "to wait outside the Chemical Bank"?
   A) The driver thought that the rate for waiting time was too low.
   B) The driver thought it wrong to support a taxi rider unconditionally.
   C) The driver was frightened and wanted to leave him as soon as possible.
   D) The driver did not want to help a suspect to escape from a bank robbery.

4. Which of the following statements is true about New York taxi drivers?
   A) They are ready to help you do whatever you want to.
   B) They refuse to pick up those who would kill themselves.
   C) They are sympathetic with those who are out of work.
   D) They work only for money.

5. The passage mainly discusses _____ .

A) how to please taxi riders

B) how to deal with taxi riders

C) the attitudes of taxi drivers towards riders in personal trouble

D) the attitudes of taxi drivers towards troublesome taxi riders

Passage Four

The publishing of management books is unceasing. But are they teaching us the right lessons?

They promise to reveal the secrets of being a great change agent. Their prescriptions are usually pretty similar and seem sensible. They tell us successful managers set ambitious goals, build a sense of purpose, trust their people, invest in the future, and so on. They are also alike in tone, favoring the missionary, you-can-do-it style, pioneered by Dale Carnegie's *How to Win Friends and Influence People*.

But if there is one cause of skepticism, it is how bad these books have been in their choice of examples. The most famous example of this was the Peters and Waterman book, *In Search of Excellence*, which triggered the current publishing boom. They carefully chose the 40 firms that had been the most outstanding performers in the past decade and from this sample identified 12 golden rules of management. Unfortunately, a decade later, two-thirds of these excellent companies had gone bankrupt or been taken over.

It is a trap that all these books have fallen into. For decades Peter Drucker held up British retailer Marks & Spencer as the world's best managed company. Past books have admired the greatness of Saatchi & Saatchi, IBM, Hanson, GEC, or, until the recent crash in internet stocks, the virtues of Amazon, Priceline and Lastminute.com. Why is success so fast? Why do the books get it so wrong?

One problem is that they all ignore luck. Over time, virtually all gamblers lose. However, once in a while, some one will still have an amazing *streak* (一连串) of luck. But studying how this gambler plans and thinks is completely purposeless—his run of luck is pure chance. So it is with many companies that have had a run of success. Often there is little to be learned, because as with M&S, their luck will run out tomorrow.

1. What does the author say about the management books?

A) They are published endlessly.　　B) They teach us the right lessons.

C) They are distinct from each other.　　D) They chose their examples carefully.

2. The phrase "a great change agent" in Line 1, Para. 2 refers to _____ .

A) a great company that is always changing

B) a great company that favors change

C) a company that is good at adapting to new situations

D) a company that has undergone great changes

3. The book *In Search of Excellence* _____ .

A) used 40 good examples in it　　B) is a well-known book on business management

C) made many companies go bankrupt　　D) should have been written a decade later

4. In the author's opinion, internet companies _____ .

A) can serve as good examples for management books

B) are really great companies with a bright future

C) succeeded fast simply because of good fortune

D) made no profits from the very beginning

5. What will the next paragraph most probably talk about?

A) Some other reasons why gamblers lose.　　B) Reasons why some companies are lucky.

C) Reasons why people ignore luck.　　D) What can be learned from lucky companies.

Passage Five

Faces, like fingerprints, are unique. Did you ever wonder how it is possible for us to recognize people? Even a skilled writer probably could not describe all the features that make one face different from another. Yet a very young child—or even an animal, such as a pigeon—can learn to recognize faces. We all take this ability for granted.

We also tell people apart by how they behave. When we talk about someone's personality, we mean the ways in which he or she acts, speaks, thinks and feels that make that individual different from others.

Like the human face, human personality is very complex. But describing someone's personality in words is somewhat easier than describing his face. If you were asked to describe what a "nice face" looked like, you probably would have a difficult time doing so. But if you were asked to describe a "nice person," you might begin to think about someone who was kind, considerate, friendly, warm, and so forth.

There are many words to describe how a person thinks, feels and acts. Gordon Allports, an American psychologist, found nearly 18,000 English words characterizing differences in people's behavior. And many of us use this information as a basis for describing, or typing, his personality. Bookworms, conservatives, military types—people are described with such terms.

People have always tried to "type" each other. Actors in early Greek drama wore masks to show the audience whether they played the *villain*'s (坏人) or the hero's role. In fact, the words "person" and "personality" come from the Latin persona, meaning "mask". Today, most television and movie actors do not wear masks. But we can easily tell the "good guys" from the "bad guys" because the two types differ in appearance as well as in actions.

1. The main idea of this passage is _____.
   A) how to distinguish people's faces
   B) how to describe people's personality
   C) how to distinguish people both inward and outward
   D) how to differ good persons from bad persons

2. The author is most probably a _____.
   A) behaviorist   B) psychologist   C) writer   D) sociologist

3. The reason why it is easier to describe a person's personality in words than his face is that _____.
   A) a person's face is more complex than his personality
   B) a person's personality is easily distinguished
   C) people's personalities are very alike
   D) many words are available when people try to describe one's personality

4. We learn from the passage that people classify a person into certain type according to _____.
   A) his way of acting and thinking
   B) his way of speaking and behaving
   C) his learning and behavior
   D) his physical appearance and his personality

5. The word "type" in the first sentence of the last paragraph is closest in meaning to _____.
   A) classify   B) distinguish   C) describe   D) recognize

Passage Six

More and more, the operations of our business, governments, and financial institutions are controlled by information that exists only inside computer memories. Anyone clever enough to modify this information for his own purposes can get substantial rewards. Even worse, a number of people who have done this and been caught at it have managed to get away without punishment.

It's easy for computer crimes to go undetected if no one checks up on what the computer is doing. But even if the crime is detected, the criminal may walk away not only unpunished but with a glowing recommendation from his former employers.

Of course, we have no statistics on crimes that go undetected. But it's disturbing to note how many of the crimes we do know about were detected by accident, not by systematic inspections or other security procedures. The computer criminals who have been caught may be the victims of uncommonly bad luck.

For example, a certain *keypunch* (键盘打孔) operator complained of having to stay overtime to punch extra cards. Investigation revealed that the extra cards she was being asked to punch were for dishonest transactions. In another case, dissatisfied employees of the thief *tipped off* (向······透露) the company that was being robbed.

Unlike other lawbreakers, who must leave the country, commit suicide, or go to jail, computer criminals sometimes escape punishment, demanding not only that they not be charged but that they be given good recommendations and perhaps other benefits. All too often, their demands have been met.

Why? Because company executives are afraid of the bad publicity that would result if the public found out that their computer had been misused. They hesitate at the thought of a criminal boasting in open court of how he *juggled* (要弄) the most confidential records right under the noses of the company's executives, accountants, and security staff. And so another computer criminal departs with just the recommendations he needs to continue his crimes elsewhere.

1. Computer crimes can be better detected to a certain degree if _____.
   A) less information is put into the computer
   B) what the computer is doing can be monitored
   C) computer criminals are more seriously punished
   D) people's dependence on computer is not so much

2. It is implied in the third paragraph that _____.
   A) many more computer crimes go undetected than are discovered
   B) the rapid increase of computer crimes is a troublesome problem
   C) most computer criminals are smart enough to cover up their crimes
   D) most computer criminals who are caught blame their bad luck

3. The fourth paragraph wants to support the idea that _____.
   A) computer crimes are seldom serious
   B) computer criminals are seldom punished
   C) computer criminals are usually unfortunate
   D) computer crimes are usually found accidentally

4. What may happen to computer criminals once they are caught?
   A) With a bad reputation they can hardly find another job.
   B) They will be denied access to confidential records.
   C) They may walk away and easily find another job.
   D) They must leave the country or go to jail.

5. The passage is mainly about _____.
   A) why computer crimes are difficult to detect by systematic inspection
   B) why computer criminals are often able to escape punishment
   C) how computer criminals manage to get good recommendation from their former employees
   D) why computer crimes can't be eliminated

第二节 答案解析

参考译文划线点评

Passage One

并非动物发出的所有声音都充当语言，[1]我们只要把目光转向在蝙蝠身上发现的奇特的回声定位法，就可以从中看到声音确实在发挥着实际效用的一个例子。

要完全弄懂这意味着什么，我们必须首先看看人类最近的一些发明。谁都知道如果在一堵墙旁边或山腰上喊叫，就会听到回音。离这个固体障碍越远，回音传回来的时间就越长。如果轻敲一艘船的船体，声音会从海底反射回来，

[2]通过测量敲击与接收到回声之间的时间差就可以算出海水在那一点的深度。今天广泛应用于船舶的回声探测仪就是由此而诞生的。[2]/[3]每一个固体都能反射声音,因其尺寸和性质的差异而有所不同。[3]一群鱼也可以充当这个角色。既然能测出海水的深度,那么要测出一群鱼的位置相对来说就轻而易举了。如今,凭借经验和经过改良的仪器不仅能测出一群鱼的位置,[2]还能通过不同的回声类型辨别出这是青鱼、鳕鱼还是其他众所周知的鱼类。

　　几年前人们发现某些蝙蝠会发出吱吱的叫声,并通过回声判断出障碍物的位置从而避开障碍,或者发现它们的食物——飞过的昆虫。蝙蝠的这种回声定位法经常被比作原理近似的雷达。

1. [B]主旨大意题。文章第1段就点明主题,明确指出以蝙蝠为例,动物发出的声音有实际作用,只有选项B可以概括文章的这个写作目的。

2. [C]事实细节题。本题考查列举处,可用排除法解答。选项A、B、D在第2段中都有相关提及。只有选项C在文中并未提到。

3. [C]词义推断题。本题考查shoal的词义推测及代词this的理解。依据第2段结尾几句话,可推测出a shoal of fish指的是"海里的一群鱼";this则是指上一句提到的固体可以反射声音的这种功能,因此这句话表明一大群鱼就能像一个固体物件一样反射声音。

4. [D]推理判断题。根据最后一段可知,蝙蝠发出吱吱声可以探测障碍物的距离,而第2段也指出轻敲船体可测知海底的距离,因此在功能上,选项D与蝙蝠的吱吱声相同。选项A中的human languages在文中尚未提到。选项B和C在文中各自的例子中充当的都是障碍物的角色,因此都不正确。

5. [D]推理判断题。文章先说动物的回音定位功能,再说到回声定位探测仪的发明,由此可见,是动物的某些能力启示了人类的创造,因此只有选项D可从文中推测。文章并没有从智力方面比较人类和动物,因此可以排除选项A和B;而文章也没有比较动物和人类发明之间的异同,因此可排除选项C。

参考译文划线点评　　　　　Passage Two

　　[1]真正的警察很少承认他们的生活与他们在电视上所看到的——如果他们能按时回家的话——有什么相似之处。相似之处当然有,但是警察们认为寥寥无几。

　　第一个不同之处在于一个警察的真实生活是与法律密不可分的。他所受的培训大部分都是关于刑法的。[2]他必须准确地知道什么行为是犯罪、什么证据可以用来在法庭上证实这些罪行。他必须了解的法律知识几乎和一个职业律师所了解的一样多,更有甚者,他还必须靠自己的双脚去实践这些法律知识——在雨夜,在小巷里穷追某个问话对象。

　　他几乎不会有时间去跟衣着暴露的女郎闲扯,也不会跟什么亡命之徒戏剧性地正面交锋。[3]他的大部分工作时间都会花在填写那些连篇累牍的报告上,而这些报告里的主角尽是些犯了——或是没犯——愚蠢而轻微的罪行的可怜而微不足道的人。

　　电视上的刑事剧大多讲的是如何追捕罪犯;罪犯一朝被抓获,故事就结束了。[4]在现实生活里,追捕罪犯通常都不是问题的关键。除非是诸如谋杀以及恐怖袭击等特别严重的犯罪——在此类犯罪中,如果警方未能交差,将影响其声誉——否则他们一般不会花多大力气去搜捕犯人。

　　进行了逮捕之后,侦探的工作实际上才刚开始。他必须在法庭上证实犯罪事实,而为了这个目的他通常必须去搜罗一大堆五花八门的证据。因此,一个侦探除了要超时工作以外,还得夜以继日地在外奔波,向证人了解情况,并且说服他们帮助自己——而这通常都与他们的最大利益相抵触。

1. [C]推理判断题。本题考查对第1句的理解,if引出的条件状语从句前的破折号表明这个假设是相对于之前的看电视来说的,而不是相对于整句话的,因此,这个句子只是给予一些附加的信息:真实生活中的警察没有时间回家,连看电视都赶不上。由此可见,选项C是正确的理解。选项A说法过于绝对,与原文的hardly不符。

2. [C]推理判断题。本题考查内在的因果关系。从第2段的第3句可以推断出答案,选项A毫无原文依据,原文中也并没有暗示选项B和D这两种因果关系。

3. [C]推理判断题。本题考查对长句的理解。根据第3段第2句可以推断出答案。本题最具干扰性的是选项B,按照常识,警察的工作通常都被认为很危险,但是第3段首句由little引出的倒装句表明了他们并不是时时都与罪犯交锋,处于危险之中,因此选项B不对。

4. [B]推理判断题。本题考查对复合句的理解。答题关键在于正确理解第4段最后一句,except引出的句子暗示警方只有在遇到特别严重的犯罪时才会尽力破案,选项B是对这个意思的归纳。本题最具干扰性的是选项D,文章虽有failure to produce results出现,但只是为了说明警方没破案会影响其声誉,选项D涉及的是其结果,文章并未提及破案的结果。

5. [B]主旨大意题。由全文第1段可知本文是一篇对比的文章,第2段首句的The first difference更确定了本文的主题,表明全文将会对比真实的警察生活与电视上的刑事剧,因此只有选项B能概括文中对比的双方。

参考译文划线点评   Passage Three

在一个人窘迫之际,能指望从纽约的一个出租车司机那里得到多少帮助呢?我开始研究这个问题,而且发现答案非常有趣。

一天早上,我坐进三辆不同的出租车,声称:"嗯,这是我七年来第一天回纽约。我一直在坐牢。"没有一个司机吭声,于是我接着再试,"是的,我在雷诺用枪打死了一个人。"我解释道,希望司机能问我原因,可没人问。[1]唯一的反应来自一个加纳司机:"雷诺?那是在内华达州?"

[4]当我说我刚被解雇了时,司机们无一例外地表示了同情。"这就是美国,"一个海地司机说,"一扇门关上了,另一扇还开着。"他反对我想烧掉我老板房子的计划。[2]一个巴基斯坦司机甚至拒绝了从我的绝望上挣钱的机会;他拒绝挣20美元把我送到乔治·华盛顿桥的中央去。"你干吗去那儿?回家吧,放松一下。别担心,重新找个工作就是了。"

7月的一天,很热,不是周末。我戴着一个红色滑雪面罩,手里举着一个塞满东西的枕头套,上面写着"银行"的字样。我五次想在不同的银行外面叫一辆出租车。每次司机都让我上了车。其中跟一个海地司机的一段路,堪称我所受到过的最热情的帮助。

"我们穿过公园,"我说,"我刚抢了银行。我抢了25000美元。"

"25000美元?"他问道。

"对呀,你觉得这样做不对吗?"

"不,老兄。我干8个小时还挣不到70美元。如果我能,我也会这样做。"

当我们经过第86街和来克辛顿街的时候,我指着化学银行。

"喂,这儿还有一家银行,"我说,"我进去的时候你能不能在这儿等我一会儿?"

"不行,我不能等。现在给钱吧。"他之所以不愿意可能与钱有关——出租车司机们认为等人的收费太低了——[3]但我觉得他是想让我明白,即使是银行劫匪也别指望得到无条件的帮助。

1. [A]推理判断题。从第2段最后一句的only response可以看出这个司机只问了一个与杀人无多大关系的问题,由此可见,司机对此事毫不关心,态度冷漠。

2. [D]推理判断题。本题的关键在于必须知道在美国,高耸的大桥通常是人们自杀的场所,有了这个背景知识,就能从第3段最后两句推断出司机以为作者要到华盛顿桥去自杀。

3. [B]事实细节题。本题考查对复杂句的理解。答案可以在文章的最后一句话中找到,破折号后面but引出的转折句才是作者对司机不愿等人的解释。选项A是一般出租车司机的想法,选项C和D都无原文依据。

4. [C]推理判断题。答案可从第3段第1句话中找到,选项C是该句的同义替换。选项A中的do whatever you want to过于绝对。选项B不符合逻辑,因为司机不可能先问乘客是否要自杀才决定要不要载这个乘客。巴基斯坦司机的例子表明司机不都是只为了钱,因此选项D不正确。

5. [C]主旨大意题。文章开篇第1句话就是整篇文章的主题句,接下来的各段内容都是围绕此主题展开的。本题最具干扰性的是选项D,事实上,该选项中的troublesome意为"烦人的",而不是"陷入麻烦的",因此不能用该词形容文中的乘客,这样就可以排除选项D了。

参考译文划线点评   **Passage Four**

[1]关于管理方面的书一直不停地出版。可是这些书真的让我们获益匪浅吗?

[2]这些书都一定会揭示那些麻雀变凤凰的公司的成功秘诀。它们开的药方大同小异,而且似乎都很有道理。它们告诉我们,成功的经理人总是制定雄心勃勃的计划,树立一种使命感,相信部下,投资于未来等等。它们的腔调也差不多,喜欢采用由戴尔·卡耐基在《如何赢得友谊及影响别人》一书中首创的传教士式的励志风格。

但是,如果说有什么值得怀疑的理由的话,那就是这些书所选的案例的确很糟。[3]最有名的一个例子是曾经掀起出版热潮的彼得斯和沃特曼所写的《追求杰出》一书。他们仔细地挑选了40家过去十年表现最优秀的公司,并以此为样总结出12条管理方面的金科玉律。但不幸的是,十年过去了,这些杰出公司中的三分之二要么已经破产,要么遭到兼并。

所有这些书都落入了一个陷阱。数十年来,彼得·杜拉克一直把英国零售商玛莎百货列为世界经营最佳的公司。以前书本上都对盛世、IBM、汉森、通用电气这些公司推崇备至,在最近网络股票急剧下跌之前还包括亚马孙、价格在线以及Lastminute.com。为什么成功来得如此迅速?为什么这些书会犯下这么严重的错误?

[4]它们都有一个问题:忽视运气。如果日复一日地赌,实际上所有的赌徒都会输。但是,偶尔有人也会有短时间惊人的运气。只不过研究这个赌徒的计划和思维方式却是完全无意义的——他的一连串运气纯粹是偶然。那些取得过一连串成功的公司也不过如此。通常没有什么值得一学,因为正如玛莎百货一样,运气也是会在来日用完的。

1. [A]事实细节题。本题考查对 unceasing 一词的理解。若能根据构词法分析第一段首句 unceasing 的词义,就能知道它与选项 A 中的 endless 同义。选项 B 和 D 显然与原意相悖,作者明显对这些书持批判态度,第 1 段第 2 句对它们的价值提出质疑。选项 C 与第 2 段第 2 句中的 similar 和末句中的 alike 相反。

2. [D]词义推断题。关于管理方面的书通常都是告诉读者成功的方法的,因此,结合考点所在的句子及其所在的段落,可以看出句中的 secrets(秘诀)一词是指成功的秘诀,由此可以推断 a great change agent 应是指一些经历巨大转变(并获得成功)的公司,因为只有这样的公司才能成为关于管理的书籍中的好例子。

3. [B]推理判断题。本题考查复合句的理解。第 3 段第 2 句是一个定语从句,从由 which 引出的定语从句可推断该书是管理方面书籍的经典之作,因此可确定选项 B 为正确答案。第 3 段最后一句可证明选项 A 不准确;选项 C 对原文有曲解,并不是这本书使许多公司破产;选项 D 毫无合理的推断依据。

4. [C]推理判断题。第 4 段最后两句指出了这些公司的问题,最后一段的首句回答了这些问题,表明他们忽视了运气的影响,暗示他们的成功是偶然的好运所至,由此可以肯定地推断出答案应为选项 C。

5. [A]推理判断题。本段将成功的公司与好运的赌徒做了生动有趣的类比,如果接下来分析赌徒为什么会失败则可以帮助理解公司失败的原因,所以选项 A 是合理可能的。运气是偶然的,无法解释的,所以选项 B 不可能;选项 C 与本文无关;作者对所出版的管理书籍是持批判态度的,认为它们根本没有教会读者有用的东西,选项 D 有悖原意。

参考译文划线点评   **Passage Five**

和指纹一样,面容也是独一无二的。你是否想过我们为什么能识别人?即使是一个技巧娴熟的作家多半也无法描绘出使一张面孔与众不同的所有特征。但是一个非常年幼的孩子——或是动物,譬如一只鸽子——却能学会识别不同的面孔。大家都认为这种能力是理所当然的。

另外我们也通过行为来识别人。当谈到某人的个性的时候,实际上是在谈论他或她使自己区别于他人的行为、言语、思考和感觉方式。

正如人的面孔一样,人的个性也是非常复杂的,但是用语言描述一个人的个性比描述他的面孔容易一些。如果有人要求你描述一张"漂亮的脸"应该是什么样的,你多半会感到很棘手。[3]但是如果让你描述一个"好人",你或许马上就会想到一个善良、体贴、友好、热情或诸如此类的人。

有很多词藻可以用来描述一个人的思考、感觉和行为方式。[3]美国心理学家戈登·欧珀茨发现,有将近 1.8 万个英语单词可用来形容人的行为方式的不同,而且许多人都以此信息作为描述自己个性的基础,或在此基础上把自己的个性归入某个类别。书呆子、保守派、好战分子——描述一个人的时候总是会用到这样的字眼。

[5]人们总是尽量把彼此归入到某个类别里。早期的希腊戏剧里的演员靠戴面具来告诉观众自己所扮演的角色是坏蛋还是英雄。实际上,"person(人)"和"personality(个性)"这两个词都来自于拉丁文"persona",就是"面具"的意思。今天的大多数电视和电影演员都不再戴面具。[4]但是我们还是能够轻易地分出"好人"和"坏人",其原因是这两种人不管是外表还是行为都有所不同。

1. [C]主旨大意题。全文从人的 face"面孔"(即外表)和 personality"个性"(即内在)这两方面来讨论如何区分不同的人,每一段都有明显的主题句即开头句揭示各自的大意,它们都是围绕着共同的主题展开的,只有选项 C 把这两方面都概括了。

2. [B]推理判断题。根据本文的主题"如何识别不同的人",以及文中的诸多与心理学有关的关键词如 personality, think, act, feel, nice person, good guys, bad guys 等,可推断本文作者最可能是选项 B(心理学家)。本题最具干扰性的是选项 A(行为主义者),虽然第2段第1句有提到 behave,但本文的重点不是讨论人们具体的行为,而是讨论抽象的个性,因此选项 A 不对。本文为一篇较具科普性的文章,应该是有一定专业知识的人写的,而不是普通作家写的,因此选项 C 不对。选项 D(社会学家)研究的是社会问题。

3. [D]推理判断题。本题考查对比关系。从第3段末句中可以发现,描述人的个性可以轻易列出一些词,而上一句说到描述人的面貌时,却找不到一个合适的词,再根据第4段的"nearly 18,000 English words characterizing differences in people's behavior",可推断出答案应为选项 D。其他选项明显与原意相悖。

4. [D]推理判断题。本题考查因果关系。根据全文主题以及结尾段的由 because 引导的原因状语从句可以推断出答案,其他选项概括得都不完整。

5. [A]词义推断题。type 所在的句子是本段的主题句,因此,type 的词义可从其后分说的句子推断。根据同一段第2句及最后一句中说到在戏剧中"好人"和"坏人"的分类,可知道 type 是指"归类,分类"之意,因此选项 A 正确。其他选项虽然放回原句中也符合语法,但都不能表达"分类"的意思。

参考译文划线点评   **Passage Six**

我们的工商业、政府以及金融机构的运作越来越多地受到仅存于计算机存储器中的信息的控制。只要足够聪明,任何为了自己的目的而更改这些信息的人都会得到丰厚的回报。更有甚者,为数不少干过这种事并被捉住的人设法逃脱了惩罚。

[1]如果无人检查计算机处理的信息内容,计算机犯罪便不容易被发现。[4]但是,即便罪行被发现,罪犯不仅可能会逃脱惩罚,而且还可能从他的前任老板那里拿到一份光彩的推荐信。

当然,我们没有统计过有多少罪行未被发现。[2]/[3]但是如果数一数有多少我们已知的罪行是靠侥幸而不是通过系统的检查或其他保安程序发现的,就会让人头痛不已。至于有些计算机罪犯被捉拿归案,得归因于他们少有的倒霉。

例如,某个操作键盘打孔机的人抱怨说必须加班给额外的卡片打孔。调查显示,让她打孔的额外卡片所处理的是不诚实的交易。在另外一宗案子里,窃贼的手下因为不满而向被盗的公司透露了消息。

其他的人犯了法不是被驱逐出境就是自杀身亡,或者被关进监狱。计算机罪犯则不然,有时能逃脱惩罚。他们不仅要求免于起诉,还想要得到光彩的推荐信或是其他好处。而他们的要求往往大都能得到满足。

为什么?因为公司高层害怕如果公众发现他们的计算机被误用会带来不良的公共形象。一想到罪犯会在法庭上吹嘘自己是如何易如反掌地盗窃那些最机密的记录——而且是在公司的高层、会计和保安人员的鼻子底下,他们就犹豫不决了。[4]就这样,又一个计算机罪犯带着他在其他地方继续犯罪时用得着的推荐信逃之夭夭。

1. [B]推理判断题。首先,本题要求找到如何较好地 detect(发现)计算机犯罪,不是问如何防止计算机犯罪,因此,选项 C 不正确。只要将第2段第1句反过来理解,就能知道若要发现计算机犯罪,就要时常检查计算机处理的信息内容,因此选项 B 正确。另外,选项 A 和 D 说的做法不现实,而且文中也没有指出我们应该这样做。

2. [A]推理判断题。第3段第2句中的 detected by accident 暗示了答案。其他选项都没有合理的推断依据。本题最具干扰性的是选项 D,本段最后一句又提到与选项相关的内容,但并没有如选项 D 那样用 most 限定范围,因此选项 D 不准确。

3. [D]推理判断题。例子都是支持出现在其前后的观点的。第4段举了两个例子,分别为了说明上一段第2句和第3句的观点,将这两句的观点综合来看,就可知道作者想要说明计算机犯罪的发现极具偶然性,因此选项 D 为正确答案。本题最具干扰性的是选项 C,虽然第 3 段末句提到计算机罪犯被抓是因为他们运气不好,但事实上,作者这样写是表示其幽默感,真正的目的是为了说明计算机犯罪很少被发现或被惩罚,因此选项 C 不是作者的真正想法。

4. [C]事实细节题。根据第 2 段末句以及第 5 段末句都可以明确地找出答案。

5. [B]主旨大意题。纵观全文各个段落(除第 4 段举例外),可以明确地判断出它们都是围绕一个主题展开讨论:为什么计算机罪犯得以成功逃脱惩罚。选项 A 所述的"很难通过系统的检查发现计算机罪犯"并不完全属实,原文并未指出这样做 difficult(很难);选项 C 所述的"计算机罪犯想法从前任老板那里得到好推荐"虽然属实,但文章并没有详细解释 how(怎么样);本文也并没有讨论如何消除计算机犯罪及其结果,因此选项 D 也并非本文的中心论题。

第五篇

中译英

稳拿480分语法考点突破

第一节 中译英语法要点归纳

纵观历年四级考题语法部分,必考语法点为:虚拟语气、非谓语动词的用法、谓语动词的时态和语态、主谓一致、情态动词、关联词、倒装结构、比较结构、强调结构、从句等。下面以真题为例,结合四级中采纳的翻译新题型,逐一详细解析各重点语法部分的常考点。

一、虚拟语气

(一)虚拟语气用于非真实条件句

英语中的条件句可分为真实条件句与非真实条件句。由 if 引导的非真实条件句表示对现在、过去、将来的事实进行假设时,主、从句的谓语动词形式如下表所示:

表虚拟的时间	if 从句谓语形式	主句谓语形式
现在	过去时/were	would/should/could/might+动词原形
过去	had+过去分词	would/should/could/might+have+过去分词
将来	一般过去时 were to+动词原形 should+动词原形	would/should/could/might+动词原形

【例 1】Jean doesn't want to work right away because she thinks that if she _____ (要是找到工作) she probably wouldn't be able to see her friends very often. 　　　　　　　　　　　　　　　　　[1996.1]

【答案】were to get a job

【译文】吉恩不想马上参加工作,因为她觉得要是找到工作,可能就无法常常去看望朋友。

【解析】考查对将来的虚拟。

【例 2】If I hadn't stood under the ladder to catch you when you fell you _____ (现在就不能这样笑了). 　　　　　　　　　　　　　　　　　　　　　　　　　　　　　[1999.1]

【答案】couldn't be smiling like this now

【译文】你摔下来的时候如果我没有站在梯子下接住你,你现在就不能这样笑了。

【解析】从句是对过去的虚拟,但主句是对现在的虚拟,主句谓语动词用 could+动词原形。此句考查虚拟语气在错综时间条件句中的用法,即条件从句中的动作发生的时间与主句不一致,这时就需要根据句意选择适当的虚拟形式。

(二)虚拟语气用于宾语从句中

> wish 后的宾语从句可用三种谓语动词形式表示虚拟:
> (1)一般过去时(即 were 型虚拟)表示对现在情况的假设;
> (2)过去完成时表示对过去情况的假设;
> (3)"would+动词原形"表示对将来的愿望。

【例 3】Sometimes I wish I _____ (生活在) in a different time and a different place. [2000.1]

【答案】were living

【译文】有时候我希望自己生活在一个不同的时间和空间。

【解析】此题考查 wish 后的宾语从句表示对现在情况的假设。

【例 4】He didn't go to the party, but he does wish he _____ (当时在那里). [1992.6]

【答案】had been there

【译文】他没有去舞会,不过他很希望自己当时在那里。

【解析】此题考查 wish 后的宾语从句表示对过去情况的假设。

(三)虚拟语气用于 It is+*adj./n.*+that 结构中

> 此结构的形容词和名词包括:advisable, appropriate, basic, desirable, elementary, essential, fitting, fundamental, imperative, important, impossible, incredible, natural, necessary, obligatory, proper, strange, urgent, vital, a pity, a shame, no wonder that...,其虚拟形式是从句的谓语动词为(should)+动词原形。

【例 5】It is highly desirable that a new president _____ (被任命) for this college. [1990.6]

【答案】be appointed

【译文】大家非常希望任命一位新校长来管理这所大学。

【解析】it 为形式主语,主句中的表语是 desirable,谓语动词形式用(should)+动词原形。

【例 6】It is essential that these application forms _____ (尽早寄出去). [2000.1]

【答案】be sent as early as possible

【译文】重要的是把这些申请表尽早寄出去。

【解析】主句中的表语是 essential,谓语动词用"(should)+动词原形"虚拟式,此题还要注意使用被动语态。

(四)虚拟语气用于表语从句及同位语从句中

> 以下这些名词后的表语从句及同位语从句中应该用虚拟语气,谓语动词的形式为(should)+动词原形:advice, decision, desire, demand, idea, importance, instruction, necessity, motion, order, preference, proposal, recommendation, resolution, request, requirement, suggestion。

【例 7】It is Harold's desire that he _____ (和妻子合葬).

【答案】(should) be buried next to his wife

【译文】Harold 希望死后和妻子合葬。

【解析】本题考查的是 desire 后面的表语从句,句中谓语动词应该用 should 型虚拟语气,should 可省略。

【例 8】The suggestion that the mayor _____ (颁奖) was accepted by everyone. [2000.6]

【答案】(should) present the prizes

【译文】每个人都接受了让市长来颁奖的建议。

【解析】此题考查的是 suggestion 后的同位语从句,句中谓语动词要采用 should 型虚拟式。

(五)虚拟语气用于某些特定结构中

> 用于 if only, would rather+从句, as if/though, It is (high) time that...等结构中,与 if 引导的虚拟结构形式

　　一样。

【例 9】Look at the terrible situation I am in! If only I ＿＿＿＿＿＿＿＿＿ (听从了你的建议).　　　　[1993.6]

【答案】had followed your advice

【译文】看看我所处的糟糕情形! 我要是听从了你的建议就好了。

【解析】if only 表示"要是……该多好",此句表示对过去情况的假设,用"had+过去分词"虚拟式。在 if only 引导的简单
　　　　句中,表示对现在和将来的虚拟,动词用一般过去时或"would+动词原形"虚拟式;表示对过去情况的假设,动词
　　　　用过去完成式虚拟式。

【例 10】I'd rather you ＿＿＿＿＿＿＿＿＿ (不带那些重要文件) with you.　　　　[1993.6]

【答案】didn't take those important documents

【译文】我宁愿你不带那些重要文件在身上。

【解析】此题考查 would rather 后的宾语从句中对将来情况的虚拟,谓语动词用一般过去时。

(六)虚拟语气用于状语从句中

> 　　状语从句中谓语动词用(should)+动词原形,这种虚拟形式仅限于 lest, in case 或 for fear that 引导的目的
> 状语从句中。在 as if 或 as though 引导的方式状语从句中,谓语动词虚拟式的变化就要依据对过去、现在、将来
> 的假设选择适当的动词虚拟式了。

【例 11】The mad man was put in the soft-padded cell lest he ＿＿＿＿＿＿＿＿＿ (伤害自己).　　　　[1998.1]

【答案】injure himself

【译文】那个疯子被安置在有软垫的房间以免他伤害自己。

【解析】lest/in case/for fear that 引导的目的状语从句中谓语动词用(should)+动词原形。

【例 12】Take your raincoat in case ＿＿＿＿＿＿＿＿＿ (以防下雨).

【答案】it should rain

【译文】带上雨衣,以防下雨。

【解析】in case 引导的目的状语从句中谓语动词用(should)+动词原形。

二、非谓语动词

(一)现在分词

1. 现在分词作状语,可以表示时间、原因、结果、条件、让步、伴随状况等。

【例 13】＿＿＿＿＿＿＿＿＿ (在求职面试之后), you will be required to take a language test.　　　　[1993.6]

【答案】After being interviewed for the job

【译文】在求职面试之后,你会被要求参加一项语言测试。

【解析】现在分词作状语,表示时间;此题还要注意使用被动语态。

【例 14】He wasn't asked to take on the chairmanship of the society, ＿＿＿＿＿＿＿＿＿ (人们认为他人缘不够广).

【答案】being considered insufficiently popular with all members

【译文】他没有被要求担任社团主席,因为人们认为他人缘不够广。

【解析】此题用现在分词的被动式表原因,因为分词的逻辑主语 he 是分词动作 consider 的承受者。分词被动式的一般
　　　　式是 being done,完成式是 having been done。

2. 现在分词短语作宾补

> 　　此类分词短语主要出现在感官动词之后,如:feel, hear, notice, observe, perceive, see, smell, watch, listen
> to, look at 等,强调动作正在发生;或出现在使役动词之后,如:get, have, bring, keep, leave, send, set, start
> 等。

【例 15】"I was late for the laboratory yesterday." "I know. I saw you ＿＿＿＿＿＿＿＿＿ (拼命地跑)."

【答案】running madly

【译文】"我昨天的实验迟到了。""我知道。我看见你拼命地跑。"

【解析】由于前面有感官动词 see,因此用现在分词强调当时 run 这个动作正在发生。

【例 16】His remarks left me _____ (想知道他的真实目的). [1999.6]

【答案】wondering about his real purpose

【译文】他的评论令我想知道他的真实目的。

【解析】现在分词出现在使役动词 leave 后。

3. 现在分词的完成式和被动式

【例 17】The children went there to watch the _____ (铁塔被竖起). [1990.1]

【答案】iron tower being erected

【译文】孩子们去那里观看铁塔被竖起。

【解析】现在分词被动式的一般式是 being done,完成式是 having been done。

【例 18】Corn originated in the New World and thus was not known in Europe until Columbus found it _____ (被种植) in Cuba. [2000.1]

【答案】being cultivated

【译文】玉米来自新大陆,因此在哥伦布发现它在古巴被种植之前,欧洲人并不知道它。

【解析】当分词动作(种植)和其逻辑主语(玉米)是动宾关系时使用现在分词的被动式。

4. 现在分词的复合结构

> 分词复合结构也称独立主格结构,形式是名词/代词+分词。其中名词或代词与现在分词是逻辑上的主谓关系,与过去分词是动宾关系,在句中作状语。现在分词复合结构有时可由介词 with 或 without 引导。

【例 19】_____ (由于这么多董事缺席), the board meeting had to be put off. [2001.1]

【答案】So many directors being absent

【译文】由于这么多董事缺席,只好推迟董事会议。

【解析】由于逗号隔开,只能译成从句或现在分词复合结构。

【例 20】_____ (演讲发表之后), a lively discussion started. [1995.1]

【答案】The speech having been delivered

【译文】演讲发表之后,活跃的讨论开始了。

【解析】speech 与 deliver 是动宾关系,故用过去分词,且 delivered 发生在主句谓语动词 started 之前,故用完成时。

(二)动名词

1. 动名词作动词宾语

> 有些动词只可接动名词而不可接不定式, 这些动词包括:abandon, admit, advice, advocate, anticipate, appreciate, avoid, complete, consider, delay, deny, deserve, discuss, dislike, enjoy, escape, excuse, fancy, favor, finish, forgive, imagine, include, involve, keep, mention, mind, miss, pardon, postpone, practise, quit, recall, recommend, resist, risk, save, suggest, tolerate, understand 等。

【例 21】That young man still denies _____ (在商店后面放了火). [2000.1]

【答案】having started the fire behind the store

【译文】那个年轻人仍然否认在商店后面放了火。

【解析】deny 后接动名词,注意本题要使用动名词的完成式,其形式是 having done,表示动作或状态(放火)在谓语动词(否认)之前完成。

【例 22】People appreciate _____ (与他一起工作) because he has a good sense of humor. [1998.1]

【答案】working with him

【译文】人们喜欢与他一起工作,因为他很有幽默感。

【解析】appreciate 后接动名词。

2. 动名词作介词宾语

介词后接动名词作宾语很普遍,其中特别要记住一些含有介词 to 的短语:

> 以下带介词 to 的短语后面接动名词:abandon oneself to, adhere to, stick to, cling to, admit to, confess to, contribute to, feel up to, get down to, give one's mind to, give way to, yield to, keep to, lead to, look forward to, object to, take to, turn to, succumb to, point to, see to, be/get used to, be accustomed to, be addicted to, be committed to, be dedicated to, be devoted to, be opposed to, be reduced to, be subject to, resort to, submit to 等。

【例 23】The man in the corner confessed to _____ (对经理说了谎) of the company.　　　　[1997.6]

【答案】having told a lie to the manager

【译文】角落里的那个人承认对公司经理说了谎。

【解析】短语 confess to 后面要接动名词,而"撒谎"这一动作发生在"承认"之前,所以要用完成时。

3. 动名词用在固定结构之后

> 下列固定结构只可接动名词而不可接不定式:be busy/engaged (in), burst out, can't help/stand/resist, feel like, give up, have a good time (in), have difficulty/trouble (in), keep from, leave off, look like, put off, spend/waste time (in), It's no use, There's no point in 等。

【例 24】She was so angry that she felt like _____ (扔东西打他).　　　　[1992.6]

【答案】throwing something at him

【译文】她如此生气以至想扔东西打他。

【解析】feel like 后面要用动名词。

4. 动名词的主动表被动

> 在 need, want, require, deserve, bear 等动词及 be worth 后面的动名词以主动形式表达被动意义。

【例 25】What a lovely party! It's worth _____ (我终生铭记).　　　　[2002.6]

【答案】remembering all my life

【译文】多么有趣的舞会!值得我终生铭记。

【解析】worth 后面的动名词以主动形式表达被动意义。

5. 动名词的被动时和完成时

【例 26】The police accused him of setting fire to the building but he denied _____ (在起火当晚在那个地区).　　　　[1996.1]

【答案】having been in the area on the night of the fire

【译文】警察起诉他纵火焚烧那座大厦,但他否认在起火当晚在那个地区。

【解析】由于指的是过去已经发生的事,因此要用动名词的完成时。

(三)不定式

1. 不定式作动词宾语

> 有些动词只可接不定式而不可接动名词, 这些动词包括:afford, aim, appear, attempt, beg, choose, claim, dare, decide, deserve, desire, determine, except, expect, happen, hesitate, hope, learn, neglect, offer, prepare, pretend, proceed, promise, resolve, seek, seem, threaten, volunteer, wish 等。

【例 27】With a large family to support, Mr. Johnson can't _____ (连生病都生不起).

【答案】afford to be sick

【译文】约翰逊先生要养活一大家子人,他连生病都生不起。

【解析】"做不起某事,承受不了某事带来的后果"往往用 can't afford to do sth.。afford 之后也可以接名词作宾语。

2. 不定式作宾语补足语

> 不定式作宾语补足语时，不定式符号 to 在感官动词（如 see, watch, observe, notice, hear, listen to, feel 等）和使役动词（如 let, make, have 等）的宾语后面可以省略。

【例 28】I have heard both teachers and students ＿＿＿＿＿＿＿＿ (都说他不错).　　[1999.6]

【答案】speak well of him

【译文】我听到过老师和学生都说他不错。

【解析】感官动词 hear 后面接不定式作宾语补足语时，不定式符号 to 可以省略，表示"听到过，经常听到"；说某人不错，常用短语 speak well of sb.来表达。

【例 29】With the development in science and technology man can make various flowers ＿＿＿＿＿＿＿ (提前开放).　　[2001.6]

【答案】bloom before their time

【译文】由于科技的发展，人类可以使各种花卉提前开放。

【解析】花的"开放"用 bloom 一词，此处的"提前"指在正常花期之前，最简单明了的表达是 before their time。

3. 不定式作被动句中的主语补足语

【例 30】As a public relations officer, he is said ＿＿＿＿＿＿＿＿ (认识一些很有影响力的人).　　[2001.6]

【答案】to know some very influential people

【译文】作为一名公共关系官员，据说他认识一些非常有影响力的人。

【解析】he is said 后面需要不定式作主语补足语。

4. 不定式用于 but, except 之后

【例 31】Lots of empty bottles were found under the old man's bed. He ＿＿＿＿＿＿＿＿ (肯定除了喝酒什么也没做).

【答案】must have done nothing but drink

【译文】在老人的床底下找到了很多空瓶子。他肯定除了喝酒什么也没做。

【解析】根据前一句的时态，后一句是对过去的肯定猜测，用 must have done；由于 but 前面有动词 do，其后的不定式就不带 to 了。

5. 不定式的进行、完成和被动式

【例 32】If the building project ＿＿＿＿＿＿＿ (需要在月底前完工的) is delayed, the construction company will be fined.　　[2001.6]

【答案】to be completed by the end of this month

【译文】如果这项需要在月底前完工的建筑工程被拖延的话，建筑公司将被罚款。

【解析】空白处需要填一个表示将来时态的非谓语动词形式，作定语修饰名词 the building project,应该用不定式；且 complete 和 project 是动宾关系，所以用被动语态。

6. 既可接动名词，又可接不定式的动词

> 下列动词后面接动名词和不定式均可:begin, cease, continue, dread, forget, hate, intend, learn, like, dislike, omit, prefer, regret, remember, need, neglect, start, stop, try 等。但应注意区分接动名词和接不定式时的用法差异,一般说来,不定式表具体的或未完成的动作;动名词则表示笼统的、经常性的或已成为过去的动作。

【例 33】John regretted ＿＿＿＿＿＿＿ (上周没去参加那个会议).　　[1990.1]

【答案】not going to the meeting last week

【译文】约翰很后悔上周没去参加那个会议。

【解析】regret 后接动名词表示已成为过去的动作。

【例 34】We ＿＿＿＿＿＿＿ (很遗憾地通知你) that the materials you ordered are out of stock.　　[1988.6]

【答案】regret to inform you

【译文】我们很遗憾地通知你:你所订购的材料已脱销。
【解析】regret 后接不定式表示具体的动作。

三、从句(名词性从句、定语从句、状语从句)

(一)名词性从句

【例35】We agreed to accept ＿＿＿＿＿＿＿ (任何一位他们认为最好的) tourist guide. [2000.1]
【答案】whoever they thought was the best
【译文】我们同意接受任何一位他们认为最好的导游。
【解析】引导从句的关系词在从句中作主语,而且是"任何一位",应该用 whoever,而不是 whomever 或 who。

【例36】In some countries, ＿＿＿＿＿＿＿ (所谓的平等) does not really mean equal rights for all people. [1995.6]
【答案】what is called "equality"
【译文】在有些国家,所谓的平等并不真正意味着人人享有平等权利。
【解析】"所谓的……"即"被称为……的",汉语中的"的"字结构往往用 what 引导的主语从句表达。

(二)定语从句

引导定语从句的有关系代词 as, who, whom, whose, which, that 和关系副词 when, where, why 等。

1. as 引导定语从句

as 作为关系代词来引导定语从句是常考的考点,故单独详细讲解如下:

> (1)as 可引导非限制性定语从句,相当于 which 引导的非限制性定语从句,如:I am from Beijing, as you know. 相当于 I am from Beijing, which you know. 但 as 引导的非限制性定语从句可以放在句首:As you know, I am from Beijing. 而 which 引导的非限制性定语从句不能放在句首。
> (2)as 可作为关系代词来引导定语从句,既可以单独引导定语从句,又可以与主句中的 the same 或 such 相呼应,从句中的谓语动词常省略。

【例37】＿＿＿＿＿＿＿ (正如所料), the response to the question was very mixed. [1996.6]
【答案】As (had been) expected
【译文】正如所料,对该问题的反应是各种各样的。
【解析】as 引导的非限制性定语从句可以放在句首。As had been expected 可简略为分词形式 As expected。

【例38】The British are not so familiar with different cultures and other ways of doing things, ＿＿＿＿＿＿＿ (正如经常发生在其他国家的情形一样). [1998.6]
【答案】as is often the case in other countries
【译文】正如经常发生在其他国家的情形一样,英国人不熟悉外国文化和习俗。
【解析】as 引导的非限制性定语从句,代替前半句所说的内容。as is often the case 已经约定俗成为固定表达"情况也是如此"。

2. 关系代词 that 与 which 用法的区别

which可以引导一个非限制性定语从句,that 则不能。
which 之前可以有介词,that 之前则不能。

> **只能用 that,而不能用 which 的主要情况:**
> (1)当先行词是 all, anything, everything, few, little, much, none, nothing, something 等不定代词时。
> (2)当先行词被序数词或形容词最高级所修饰时。
> (3)当先行词被 the very, the only 等词修饰时。

【例39】All ＿＿＿＿＿＿ (合理的) is not necessarily practicable.
【答案】that is reasonable
【译文】合理的事情未必都可行。

【解析】当先行词是 all 时,定语从句用 that 引导。

【例 40】There is hardly an environment on earth _____ (动物种群尚未成功适应).   [1990.6]

【答案】to which some species of animal or other has not adapted successfully

【译文】地球上几乎没有什么环境动物种群尚未成功适应的。

【解析】environment 是先行词,adapt to 是固定搭配。介词的选择取决于它与先行词的搭配或与从句中谓语动词的搭配。"尚未"用现在完成时表达。

(三)状语从句

1. hardly/barely/scarcely... when 和 no sooner... than 引导的时间状语从句

这两个短语置于句首时,从句主谓需要部分倒装,其中谓语动词用过去完成时。

【例 41】No sooner _____ (我们一到山顶) than we all sat down to rest.   [1991.6]

【答案】had we reached the top of the hill

【译文】我们一到山顶就全部坐下来休息。

【解析】no sooner 后面的主谓需要部分倒装,其中谓语动词用过去完成时。

2. as 引导的让步状语从句

【例 42】_____ (家也许很简陋), there's no place like home, wherever he may go.

【答案】Humble as it may be

【译文】家也许很简陋,但是无论一个人走到哪里,没有任何地方像家一样(温暖)。

【解析】as 也可转换为 though，as 在引导让步状语从句时必须倒装到句首，在它前面的可以是形容词、名词、副词，翻译中"家"可以用 it 代替，因为后文使用的是名词。

3. 状语从句特殊的引导词

now that 既然,由于

【例 43】Now _____ (既然你熟悉了作者的观点), try reading all the sections as quickly as you possibly can.   [1992.6]

【答案】that you are familiar with the author's ideas

【译文】既然你熟悉了作者的观点,尽快读完所有章节。

【解析】由于句首是 now,显然考查的是 now that 引导的原因状语从句。

in that 因为,由于

【例 44】Criticism and self-criticism is necessary in _____ (原因是这有助于) find and correct our mistakes.   [1998.6]

【答案】that it helps to

【译文】批评与自我批评有必要的原因是这有助于发现和改正我们的错误。

【解析】空格前出现 in,根据中文分析,显然是考查 in that 引导的原因状语从句。

in case/for fear that/lest 以防,万一,以免

【例 45】He was punished lest _____ (再犯同样错误).   [2001.6]

【答案】he should make the same mistake again

【译文】他受到了惩罚,以防再犯同样的错误。

【解析】lest 后面需用 should 型虚拟语气结构。"同样的"用 the same 表达。

【例 46】Give me your telephone number _____ (以防万一我需要你的帮助).

【答案】in case/for fear that I need your help

【译文】把你的电话号码告诉我,以防万一我需要你的帮助。

【解析】"以防万一"用 in case 或 for fear that。

so... that/such... that 如此……以至于……

【例 47】The radio was of _____ (这么差的质量) that I took it back and asked for a better one.

【答案】such inferior quality

【译文】这台收音机的质量太差,所以我回去要求换台好的。

【解析】由于空格前有 of,所以只能用 such+名词结构。

as long as/so long as 只要

【例 48】He will surely finish the job on time as _____ (只要让他以自己的方式去做). [2001.1]

【答案】long as he's left to do it in his own way

【译文】只要让他以自己的方式去做,他肯定会按时完成工作。

【解析】as 提示需要 as long as 短语引导条件状语从句。be left to do sth. "被允许自行做某事"。

unless 除非,只要不

【例 49】_____ (政府才能有效运行) unless it is free from such interference. [1994.1]

【答案】Government cannot operate effectively

【译文】政府只有摆脱了这样的干扰,才能有效运行。

【解析】由于 unless 表示 if... not 的含义,所以译成否定句。

if only 只要

【例 50】I'm sure he is up to the job if _____ (只要他肯用心). [1998.1]

【答案】only he would give his mind to it

【译文】我相信,只要他肯用心,他是可以胜任此工作的。

【解析】if only 引导的从句中要注意使用虚拟语气。

provided/providing (that) 如果

【例 51】We should be able to do the job quickly, _____ that _____ (如果你给我们所有必需的信息). [1999.6]

【答案】provided/providing; you give us all the necessary information

【译文】如果你给我们所有必需的信息,我们应该可以做得很快。

【解析】空格之间出现 that,显然考查 provided/providing that 引导的条件状语从句。若没有 that 限制,也可用 if 从句。

even if 即使

【例 52】Rod is determined to get a seat for the concert _____ (即使那意味着要排一整夜队). [2001.6]

【答案】even if it means standing in a queue all night

【译文】Rod 下决心要买到一张音乐会的票,即使那意味着要排一整夜队。

【解析】"即使"用 even if,"意味着做某事"用 mean doing sth.,而 sb. means/meant to do sth.表示"某人打算/有意做某事"。

even though 尽管,虽然

【例 53】Even _____ (虽然惩罚是不公平的), Helen accepted it without complaint. [1990.6]

【答案】though the punishment was unjust

【译文】虽然惩罚是不公平的,Helen 还是毫无怨言地接受了。

【解析】开头的 even 提示此处的"虽然"是短语 even though 的一部分,否则也可用 Although, Though。

> "no matter+wh-疑问词"和"wh-疑问词+ever"引导的让步状语从句可以互换。
> 但"wh-疑问词+ever"引导的名词从句,则不可用"no matter"替换。
> No matter whether... or... 结构中也可将 no matter 省略,因而形成 whether... or...或 whether or not...引导选择条件句。

【例 54】_____ (不论遇到什么困难), we'll help one another to overcome them. [2001.1]

【答案】Whatever difficulties/No matter what difficulties we may come across/meet

【译文】不论遇到什么困难,我们都会相互帮助来克服。

【解析】"不论什么"可用 Whatever 或 No matter what 表达。"遇到"可用 come across 或 meet。

【例 55】The substance does not dissolve in water _____ (不管是否加热).

【答案】whether (it is) heated or not

【译文】不管是否加热,这种物质都不会溶解于水。

【解析】主要考查让步状语从句"no matter+wh-疑问词"句型,表示"不论、不管……"。凭四级词汇知识可以理解 substance(物质)和 dissolve(溶解)的意义。另外要考虑对"加热"的处理,是主动还是被动,从上下文推断出 water 被加热,所以采用被动语态,即 whether (it is) heated or not,其中 it is 可以省略。

四、时态

(一)一般现在时在状语从句中表示将来的动作和状态

【例 56】The article suggests that when a person _____ (处于超常压力下) he should be especially careful to have a well-balanced diet.　　　　　　　　　　　　　　　[2002.1]

【答案】is under unusual stress

【译文】这篇文章建议当一个人处于超常压力之下时,他应该特别注意饮食的均衡。

【解析】"处于压力下"用 under stress,"超常"即"不寻常",用 unusual。

(二)一般过去时在状语从句中表示将来的动作和状态

【例 57】I decided to go to the library as soon as I _____ (一做完我正在做的事).　　　　[1991.6]

【答案】finished what I was doing

【译文】我决定一做完我正在做的事就去图书馆。

【解析】主句谓语是过去时,所以从句也应该是过去时。

(三)过去进行时

【例 58】While Jane _____ (提着牛奶到厨房时), she spilled some of it on her skirt.

【答案】was carrying milk to the kitchen

【译文】当 Jane 提着一桶牛奶到厨房时,她洒了一些在裙子上。

【解析】提重物的"提"往往用 carry。主句为一般过去时,而从句以 while 引导,应该用过去进行时。

(四)将来进行时

【例 59】We _____ (这个时候将在旅行) next year.

【答案】shall be traveling this time

【译文】明年这个时候我们将在旅行。

【解析】此处用将来进行时,表示将来某一刻正发生的事情。

(五)过去将来时

【例 60】He refused to tell us whether he _____ (是否愿意承担这项工作).

【答案】would (like to) undertake the job

【译文】他拒绝告诉我们他是否愿意承担这项工作。

【解析】"愿意"可用 would 或 would like to。

(六)过去完成时

【例 61】A thief who broke into a church was caught because traces of wax, found on his clothes, _____ (来自) the sort of the candles used only in churches.　　　　　　　　　　[1999.6]

【答案】had come from

【译文】闯入教堂的贼被抓住了,因为在他衣服上发现的蜡痕来自那种教堂所专用的蜡烛。

【解析】come 是在过去的动作 found 之前发生,所以用过去完成时。

(七)将来完成时

表示到将来某时已结束的动作

【例 62】"May I speak to your manager Mr. Williams at five o'clock tonight?"　"I'm sorry. Mr. Williams _____ (早已经开会去了) long before then."　　　　　　　　　　　　　　　[2000.6]

【答案】will have gone to a conference

【译文】"今晚 5 点我能和你们经理威廉姆斯先生谈谈吗?""很抱歉。到那时威廉姆斯先生早已去开会了。"

【解析】根据句中的时间状语 long before then(then 指的是 five o'clock tonight)可知,本题应用将来完成时。

表示持续到将来某时的动作

【例 63】By the time he arrives in Beijing, we _____ (就在这里住了两天了).　　　　　[2001.6]

【答案】will have stayed here for two days

【译文】等他到达北京时,我们将已经在这儿逗留两天了。

【解析】by the time 引导的状语从句若用一般现在时,其主句动词应该用将来完成时,表示在将来某段时间前已经完成的动作。

(八)过去完成进行时

【例 64】After searching for half an hour, she realized that her glasses _____ (在桌子上) all the time.

[1990.6]

【答案】had been (lying) on the table

【译文】找了半小时后她意识到自己的眼镜一直就在桌子上。

【解析】"在桌子上"是"意识到"之前一直持续的动作,用过去完成进行时。

五、主谓一致

(一)意义一致原则

指根据意思确定动词谓语是用单数还是复数。

【例 65】How close parents are to their children _____ (有很强的影响) the character of the children.

[1991.6]

【答案】has a strong influence on

【译文】父母与孩子的关系密切程度对孩子的性格有很强的影响。

【解析】名词性从句作主语,其表示的是单数意义,谓语动词用单数形式。

(二)就近一致原则

【例 66】Neither tears nor protest _____ (不能影响他们父母的决定).

【答案】affects their parents' decision

【译文】泪水和抗议都不能影响他们父母的决定。

【解析】not only... but also..., or, nor, either... or..., neither... nor..., whether... or...连接两个主语时,谓语动词与最邻近的主语保持一致。

(三)两个特殊短语

【例 67】Neither of the young men who had applied for a position in the university _____ (得以录取).

[1998.1]

【答案】was accepted

【译文】那两位申请过该大学的一个职位的年轻人都没被录取。

【解析】由 either/neither of+复数名词或代词作主语时,谓语用单数。

【例 68】Many a famous pop singer _____ (被毒品毁掉了).

【答案】has been ruined by drugs

【译文】好多知名的流行歌手都被毒品毁掉了。

【解析】many a+*n.*/more than one+*n.*,意义是复数,谓语用单数。

六、特殊结构

(一)强调结构

> It is/was+被强调部分+that/who+原句中的其他部分。在使用强调句型时要注意,指人时可以用 who 或 that,其他情况下一律用 that。

【例 69】It _____ (直到天黑) she realized it was too late to go home. [2000.1]

【答案】was not until dark that

【译文】直到天黑,她才意识到太晚了,无法回家。

【解析】"直到"与瞬间动词(如 realize)连用时要用否定 not until。It 提示此处要用强调结构。

(二)倒装结构

倒装结构分为部分倒装和全部倒装。部分倒装指谓语中的一部分,如助动词 do, does, did, have, has, had,情态动词 can, could, may, might, should, would, ought to, must, need 等,系动词 be(am, is, are, was, were)等放在主语前面,其余部分包括谓语动词仍在主语后面。

部分倒装应用于下列情况中:

(1)有否定含义的副词或短语位于句首作状语

这类词有:neither, never, no, nor, not, seldom, rarely, hardly, barely, scarcely, little, few, under no circumstances, by no means, in no case, in no way, on no account, on no condition, no sooner 等。

【例 70】The organization had broken no rules, but _____ (但是它也没有负责任地行动). [1996.1]

【答案】neither had it acted responsibly

【译文】该组织没有违反任何规定,但是它也没有负责任地行动。

【解析】否定副词 neither 引出的句子要部分倒装。注意时态。

【例 71】I could not persuade him to accept it, _____ (也无法使他看到其重要性). [1995.1]

【答案】nor could I make him see the importance of it

【译文】我没能说服他接受此事,也无法使他看到其重要性。

【解析】否定副词 nor 引出的句子要部分倒装。

(2)only 位于句首修饰状语或宾语

【例72】Only under special circumstances _____ (允许大学一年级学生) to take make-up tests. [1997.6]

【答案】are freshmen permitted

【译文】只有在特殊情况下才允许大一新生补考。

【解析】only 位于该句句首,并且修饰句中状语,主谓要部分倒装。only 位于句首修饰主语时,句子则不倒装。

(3)虚拟倒装

虚拟语气的让步状语从句中,在省略了 if 的情况下主谓部分倒装。

【例73】Had _____ (我如果听了你的话), all this misery might have been avoided.

【答案】I taken your advice

【译文】我如果听了你的话,就可能会避免这一切痛苦了。

【解析】句首是 Had,结合需要翻译的部分,本句是使用虚拟语气的让步状语从句,且省略了 if,所以从句主谓部分倒装。Had I taken your advice=If I had taken your advice。

(三)比较结构

常考的考点包括原级和比较级结构,特别是 as+形容词/副词原级(+n.)+as, more+形容词/副词比较级+than, no+形容词/副词比较级+than, a bit/a little/a lot/even/far/greatly/many/much/slightly/still+形容词/副词比较级这些结构。

【例74】"Anne acts quite unfriendly." "I think she's _____ (与其说是不友好,不如说是腼腆)."

【答案】more shy than unfriendly

【译文】"Anne 表现得很不友好。""我认为与其说她是不友好,不如说她是腼腆。"

【解析】表达"与其说……不如说……"用 more... than...,表示同一个人或物在不同性质上的对比。如:He is more brave than wise. 他有勇无谋。在这种特殊结构中,more 是必不可少的,即使形容词是单音节的。

【例75】"This cake is delicious." "Well, at least it's _____ (和……一样好吃) than the one I baked last week."

【答案】no worse

【译文】"这个蛋糕真好吃。""是的,至少和我上周做的那个一样好吃。"

【解析】than 和句意要求用"no+形容词/副词比较级+than"结构,意思是"同……一样……",因此这里虽然表示"好吃",但要用 no worse。

七、情态动词

情态动词完成式所表达的意义:

> can't/couldn't have done 不可能做过(表示对过去情况的断然否定);could have done 本可能(强调有某种能力,表示对过去情况的一种遗憾);may/might (not) have done 也许(没)做了(表示对过去情况各种可能性的猜测);must have done 肯定做过 (表示对过去情况十分肯定的猜测);needn't have done 本不必;should (not) have done 本(不)应做(表达后悔、责备语气);would (not) have done(表示按照正常规律)将(不)会。

【例76】Some women _____ (本来能够挣一份可观的工资) in a job instead of staying home, but they decided not to work for the sake of the family. [2000.1]

【答案】could have made a good salary

【译文】如果不是待在家里,一些妇女本来能够挣一份可观的工资。但考虑到家庭,她们才决定不去工作。

【解析】这句话表示说话人对过去情况的一种遗憾,用 could have done 表示。

【例77】Research findings show that we spend about two hours, dreaming every night, no matter what we _____ (可能做过什么) during the day. [1999.1]

【答案】may have done

【译文】研究表明,无论我们白天可能做过什么,每天晚上都会做大约两个小时的梦。

【解析】"may+动词完成式"表示对过去情况各种可能性的猜测。

八、关联词

【例78】I think I was at school, _____ (要不然就是正在跟一个朋友度假) when I heard the news. [2000.6]

【答案】or else I was staying with a friend during the vacation/or else I was on vacation with a friend

【译文】我认为当我听到这个消息的时候是在学校,要不然就是正和一个朋友一起度假。

【解析】考查状语从句关连词。"要不然"可用 or else, otherwise 表示。

【例79】Prof. Ward hardly ever went to _____ (看电影或看戏).

【答案】either the cinema or the theater

【译文】Ward 教授几乎从不看电影或看戏。

【解析】可用否定词加 either... or...表示"既不……也不……"。

第二节 考点突破专项扫雷训练

1. _____ (多亏了一系列的新发明), doctors can treat this disease successfully. [2007.12]

2. In my sixties, one change I notice is that _____ (我比以前更容易累了). [2007.12]

3. I am going to pursue this course, _____ (无论我要作出什么样的牺牲). [2007.12]

4. I would prefer shopping online to shopping in a department store because _____ (它更加方便和省时). [2007.12]

5. Many Americans live on credit, and their quality of life _____ (是用他们能够借到多少

来衡量的), not how much they can earn. [2007.12]

6. The finding of this study failed to _____ (将人们的睡眠质量考虑在内). [2007.6]

7. Because of the leg injury, the athlete _____ (决定退出比赛). [2007.6]

8. Please come here at ten tomorrow morning _____ (如果你方便的话). [2007.6]

9. Specialists in intercultural studies say that it is not easy to _____ (适应不同文化中的生活). [2006.12]

10. Since my childhood I have found that _____ (没有什么比读书对我更有吸引力). [2006.12]

11. The victim _____ (本来会有机会活下来) if he had been taken to hospital in time. [2006.12]

12. Some psychologists claim that people _____ (出门在外时可能会感到孤独). [2006.12]

13. The nation's population continues to rise _____ (以每年 1200 万人的速度). [2006.12]

14. _____ (为了挣钱供我上学), Mother often takes on more work than is good for her. [2006.6]

15. The professor required that _____ (我们交研究报告) by Wednesday. [2006.6]

16. The more you explain, _____ (我愈糊涂). [2006.6]

17. Though a skilled worker, _____ (他被公司解雇了) last week because of the economic crisis. [2006.6]

18. I don't mind your _____ (你延期做出决定) the decision as long as it is not too late. [2006.1]

19. I suggested he _____ (使自己适应) his new conditions. [2006.1]

20. I have no objection _____ (再听听你的故事). [2006.1]

21. This popular sports car _____ (正在生产出来) out at the rate of a thousand a week. [2006.1]

22. _____ (请你找张空白纸) and write your name at the top? [2006.1]

23. Though you stay in the sea for weeks, you will not _____ (失去联系) the outside world. [2005.6]

24. It is a pity that we should stay at home when we have _____ (这么好的天气). [2005.6]

25. I would _____ (不会诉诸法律) a court of law if I hadn't been so desperate. [2005.6]

26. John cannot afford to go to university, _____ (更不用说出国了). [2005.6]

27. Frankly speaking, I'd rather you _____ (不采取任何措施) about it for the time being. [2005.1]

28. In the Chinese household, grandparents and other relatives _____ (起着不可缺少的作用) in raising children. [2005.1]

29. The fifth generation computers, with artificial intelligence, _____ (正在研制) and perfected now. [2005.1]

30. If you won't agree to our plan, _____ (他们也不会同意). [2004.6]

31. I should say Henry is _____ (与其说是个作家不如说是) as a reporter. [2004.6]

32. Please be careful when you are drinking coffee in case you _____ (弄脏了新地毯). [2004.6]

33. If this can't be settled reasonably, it may be necessary to _____ (诉诸武力). [2004.1]

34. The room is in a terrible mess; it _____ (肯定没打扫过). [2004.1]

35. Everybody knows he _____ (受到了冤枉指控). [2004.1]

36. He wears a pair of sunglasses _____ (唯恐被别人认出来). [2004.1]

37. She never dreams of _____ (被派到国外) for further study soon. [2004.1]

38. I _____ (将在做实验) from three to five this afternoon. [2003.6]

39. How close parents are to their children _____ (有很强的影响) the character of the children. [2003.6]

40. But for his help, I _____ (我不可能这么早完成). [2003.6]

41. His remarks left me _____ (想知道他的真实目的). [2003.6]

42. Mark often _____ (试图逃脱罚款) whenever he breaks traffic regulations. [2003.6]

43. There was a knock at the door. It was the second time someone _____ (打扰我) that
    evening. [2003.1]

44. _____ (正是由于她太没有经验) that she does not know how to deal with the situation. [2003.1]

45. When I _____ (发现他骗我) I stopped buying things there and started dealing with
    another shop. [2003.1]

46. The manager would rather his daughter _____ (不在一个办公室内工作). [2003.1]

47. The sports meet originally due to be held last Friday _____ (最终因天气不好而取消
    了). [2003.1]

48. Not only _____ (他向我收费过高), but he didn't do a good repair job either.

49. On average, it is said, visitors spend only _____ (一半的钱) in a day in Leeds as in London.

50. Though a skilled worker, _____ (他被公司解雇了).

51. If the whole operation _____ (没有提前计划), a great deal of time and money would
    have been lost. [1999.6]

52. It is unlikely that a nation would choose war if its goals _____ (能够实现) peacefully.

53. He must have had an accident, or he _____ (早就应该在这儿了) then. [1990.1]

54. We didn't know his telephone number, otherwise we _____ (早就给他打电话了) him. [1995.6]

55. But for his help, I _____ (我不可能这么早完成作业).

56. I would rather you _____ (当初没把一切都告诉我).

57. As Commander-in-Chief of the armed forces I have directed that _____ (采取所有措施)
    for our defence. [1993.6]

58. It is vital that enough money _____ (筹集到来资助这个项目). [1997.1]

59. It is of the utmost importance that you _____ (按时到这儿). [1995.6]

60. It is recommended that the project _____ (不启动) until all the preparations have
    been made. [1995.6]

61. It is essential that _____ (把所有这些数字检查两遍).

62. Many a delegate was in favor of his proposal that _____ (建立特别委员会) to investi-
    gate the incident. [2002.1]

63. This crop has similar qualities to the previous one, _____. (不仅抗风，而且适应) the
    same type of soil. [1999.6]

64. If I correct someone, I will do it with as much good humor and self-restraint as if I _____
    (就是那个正在被纠正的人). [1996.6]

65. After the Arab states won independence, great emphasis was laid on education, with _____
    (男孩女孩都被鼓励去上学). [1997.1]

66. I'll never forget _____ (第一次遇到你的情形). [2001.1]

67. If I _____ (记住关窗), the thief would not have got in. [1996.1]

68. Mark often attempts to _____ (逃避罚款) whenever he breaks traffic regulations. [1995.6]

69. The bank is reported in the local newspaper _____ (被抢劫) in broad daylight
    yesterday. [2001.4]

70. All flights _____ (由于风暴而被取消), they decided to take the train. [1991.6]

71. You are just the same _____ (跟我第一次遇到你的那一天).

72. It is useful to be able to predict the extent _____ (价格变化影响供求的程度). [1997.1]

73. Much _____ (虽然他喜欢她), he does get annoyed with her sometimes. [2000.6]

74. Buying clothes _____ (是一件很耗时的事), because those clothes that a person likes
    are rarely the ones that fit him or her.

75. The owner and editor of the newspaper _____ (将参加这次会议). [2002.6]

76. Not until the game had begun _____ (他才到达) the sports ground.

77. We have been told that under no circumstances _____ (用办公室的电话) for personal affairs.　　　　　　　　　　　　　　　　　　　　　　　　　　　　　　　　　　　　　　　[1999.6]

78. He knows little of mathematics, and _____ (就更谈不上) chemistry.

79. Mary's score on the test is the highest in her class, she _____ (肯定学习很努力). [1989.1]

80. You _____ (本来不必进行) all those calculations. We have a computer to do that sort of thing.　　　　　　　　　　　　　　　　　　　　　　　　　　　　　　　　　　　　　　[1991.6]

第三节 答案解析

1. 【答案】Thanks to a series of new inventions
   【解析】①待译内容是原因状语。②"多亏了"一般译作 thanks to。owing to"由于",用于此处也可以接受。③"一系列的"可译作 a series of, a succession of, a chain of, a string of 或 a sequence of。

   【点睛】注意短语的选择和正确使用。

2. 【答案】I'm more inclined/liable/prone to tiredness/to get tired than before
   【解析】①待译内容是主谓结构的句子,作整个句子的表语从句。②"某人容易做某事"一般用(sb.) be inclined/liable/prone to (do) sth.的结构。③使用比较结构。

   【点睛】"我容易……"不要译为 I'm easy……

3. 【答案】no matter what sacrifice I will have to make/whatever sacrifice I will make/no matter how much I will sacrifice
   【解析】①待译内容是让步状语(从句)。②"无论什么"可以译作 no matter what 或 whatever。"作出牺牲"译作 make sacrifice。sacrifice 也可以作动词,故整句还可译作 no matter how much I will sacrifice。

   【点睛】多义、多词性的词要灵活使用。

4. 【答案】it/the former is more convenient and time-saving
   【解析】①待译内容是原因状语从句。②虽然"省时"可以译作 it saves time,但"方便"(convenient)和"省时"(time-saving)是并列的表语,最好都使用形容词形式。

   【点睛】此处的"它"根据上下文指的是前者 shopping online。

5. 【答案】is measured by how much they can borrow
   【解析】①待译内容是谓语,用一般现在时、被动语态。②"他们能够借到"作"多少"的定语从句。

   【点睛】表示金钱的多少用 how much。

6. 【答案】consider the quality of people's sleep/ take people's sleep quality into account/consideration
   【解析】①"把……考虑在内"用 take... into consideration/account 或者 consider 都可以,直接用动词原形。②"人们的"一般译作 people's。③"睡眠质量"说成 sleep quality 或 the quality of (people's) sleep 均可。

   【点睛】动词不定式后直接跟动词原形,所以不用变换形式。

7. 【答案】decided/decides to quit the match
   【解析】①待译内容是句子的谓语,要注意人称、时态等。用一般过去时即可。②"决定"译作 decide, determine, make up one's mind 均可。其后可以接从句、不定式。③"退出比赛"即 to quit the match/contest/game。如果一时想不起 quit,可以说成 not to go on with the match。用不定式最方便。

   【点睛】若译作从句,即:decided that he would quit the match。

8. 【答案】if it is convenient for you/ at your convenience
   【解析】①待译内容是条件状语从句,用 if 引导;主句是祈使句,相当于将来时态,故从句应该用一般现在时。②"你方便"的表达要注意。如果用 available,可以说成 if you are available then。如果用 convenient,则只能够说成 if it is convenient for you。

[点睛]还可以用介词短语表示条件,译成 at your convenience。

9. 【答案】adapt oneself to life/living in different cultures
   【解析】"适应……"的英文表达为 adapt oneself to sth./doing sth.。

   [点睛]adapt 需要一个反身代词 oneself 作泛指宾语,to 后面应该跟一个名词或者动名词, 不可以直接跟动词原形作不定式。

10. 【答案】nothing is more attractive to me than reading
    【解析】否定(nothing)+比较(more)=最高级。

    [点睛]也可以是:nothing appeals to me more than reading。主句是现在完成时,从句所说内容为现在的事实、状态,用一般现在时即可。

11. 【答案】would have/stand a chance to survive (of survival)
    【解析】根据条件从句,可以看出本句要用虚拟语气来表达。

    [点睛]与过去相反的虚拟语气,从句要用过去完成时,主句用 would + have done。"有机会做……"用"stand/have a chance to do/of..."。

12. 【答案】may/might feel lonely when they are away from home
    【解析】本题的词汇考点是 lonely(孤独)和 alone(独自)的辨析,而"出门在外"的表达方法则比较多样化。

    [点睛]也可以是:may/might feel lonely when they are not in their hometown/are traveling。

13. 【答案】at a speed/rate of 12 million per year
    【解析】注意词组"以……的速度"的表达是 at a speed of...。表示准确数字时,million 后面不能加 s。

    [点睛]也可以是:at an annual speed of 12 million。

14. 【答案】In order to make/earn/get money for my education/schooling/study
    【解析】此题考查要点有二:"挣钱"与"上学"。汉语中的"(我)上学"是动词,英语中最好译成名词。"供"可译成介词 for。

    [点睛]本句还有多种译法。比如,上面的 for my education 改作 for me to go to school。另外一些译法有:In order to pay for my tuition (fee); In order to cover the cost/expenses of my schooling; In order to support my study/to finance my education;等。support 意为"供养,维持",finance 意为"为……提供资金,为……筹措资金"。

15. 【答案】we hand in/turn in/submit our research reports
    【解析】此题考查虚拟语气特殊句型。require 等词后跟 that 引导的宾语从句时,从句的谓语动词要用(should)+动词原形。

    [点睛]表示命令、建议、要求、请求、提议、重要性等的动词、名词、形容词后面的 that 从句的谓语动词都应该用虚拟语气:(should)+动词原形。

16. 【答案】the more confused I am/become/get
    【解析】此题考查"愈来愈……"的译法。这种句型的译法是:the+比较级+句子,the+比较级+句子。

    [点睛]"糊涂的"还可以说成 puzzled 或 muddled。本句也可以倒过来译作:the less I understand。

17. 【答案】he was laid off/fired/sacked/dismissed kicked out by his company
    【解析】此题考查被动语态和时态。被动语态的结构为 be+动词的过去分词。

    [点睛]本句应该使用一般过去时,所以系动词用 was。

18. 【答案】delaying making
    【解析】mind 后接动名词作宾语。"推迟,延期"可用 delay, postpone 或 put off。"做决定"用动宾搭配 make a deci-

sion。空格前的 your 是动名词的逻辑主语。

【点睛】delay 和 mind 都可后接名词作宾语,此类动词还有:admit, avoid, anticipate, consider, contemplate, deny, dislike, fancy, finish, involve, permit, practice, quit, risk 等。

19.【答案】should adapt himself to

【解析】suggest 引导的宾语从句中,谓语用(should)+动词原形的虚拟语气。adapt oneself to sth.意为"使自己适应……"。

【点睛】主句的谓语为表示建议、要求、命令等类动词时,从句中的谓语动词要用虚拟式。这类动词还有 order, ask, demand, command, request, require 等。

20.【答案】to hearing your story again

【解析】have no objection to doing sth.意为"不反对做某事"。

【点睛】要注意积累含介词 to 的固定搭配。常考的有:be/get used to, confess to, contribute to, devote to, object to, be opposed to, look forward to, see to, resort to, stick to, take to。

21.【答案】is now being turned

【解析】空格后的 out 提示用短语 turn out 表达"生产"之义;语法上要用被动语态的进行时。

【点睛】翻译时语法和词汇表达要全面考虑。

22.【答案】Could you take a blank sheet of paper

【解析】"一张纸"译为 a sheet of paper;blank"空白的,未录音的",常修饰 paper(纸张)、cassette(磁带)、form(表格)等。

【点睛】该句为问句,应用 could/would you... 句型表示请求。注意 blank 的近义词 empty 表示"空无一物的",vacant 表示"无人占用的";bare 表示"光秃秃的"。

23.【答案】lose contact with

【解析】"与……失去联系"用 lose contact with,注意不要漏了介词 with。

【点睛】①"保持联系"可以用 keep in contact/touch with。②同一个词用作不同词性时,要注意其用法,如 contact 作动词时为及物动词,后面不需要跟介词 with。

24.【答案】such fine weather

【解析】weather 为不可数名词,用 such 修饰。

【点睛】such 作为指定限定词,既可修饰可数名词又可修饰不可数名词。so 直接修饰形容词或副词。

25.【答案】have never resorted to

【解析】"诉诸……"用动词短语 resort to 表达。对过去的虚拟,主句谓语用 would have done 结构。

【点睛】情态动词后接完成时是重要考点。

26.【答案】not to speak of/not to mention/let alone going abroad

【解析】"更不用说"有好几种习惯表达,后面都接名词、代词或动名词。

【点睛】对于词组,不仅要记住词义,还要记准用法。

27.【答案】didn't do anything

【解析】"would rather+从句"结构中,从句动词需用过去时。

【点睛】would/had rather 的用法要注意:如果后接从句,从句谓语动词用过去式表虚拟;如果直接接动词,则为动词原形。

28.【答案】play indispensable roles

【解析】play a role in sth./doing sth. 意为"在……中起作用"。

【点睛】role 在这个短语中可以用 part 代替。

29.【答案】are being developed

【解析】根据后面的 now 判断是现在时,故其后并列的 perfected 应该是过去分词,所以用现在进行时的被动语态翻译。

【点睛】要仔细分析和利用上下文的线索。

30. 【答案】neither will they

【解析】有否定含义的词位于句首引起主谓部分倒装。

【点睛】引起主谓部分倒装的否定词还有:never, seldom, rarely, hardly, barely, scarcely, little, few 等。

31. 【答案】not so much a writer

【解析】not so much... as 意为"与其说……不如说……"。

【点睛】比较结构是翻译的重要考点。

32. 【答案】stain the new carpet

【解析】此处"弄脏"指弄上污渍,常用四级核心词 stain 表达。

【点睛】传统题型中的"词汇与结构"部分的核心词和重要语法点往往在新题型的翻译中考查。

33. 【答案】resort to force

【解析】resort to sth."求助于或诉诸某事物"为常考短语,resort 作名词时常表示"度假胜地"。

【点睛】多义词需要利用上下文牢固掌握。

34. 【答案】can't have been cleaned

【解析】如果是对过去事实的肯定推测,表示"一定是做了……",用 must have done,对此类意义的否定用 can't have done。

【点睛】其他情态动词完成式所表达的意义:should (not)/ought (not) to have done 本(不)应做(表达后悔、责备语气);may (not)/might (not) have done 也许(没)做(表示对过去事实的推测);would have done 表示按照正常规律"将会做";needn't have done 本不必做(但却做了)。

35. 【答案】was wrongly accused/charged

【解析】"指控"有两种表达,如果是主动语态,可表达为 charge sb. with sth.或 accuse sb. of sth.;本句显然要译成被动语态,由于 accuse 和 charge 都有"指控"之义,都可用。

【点睛】另一个关键是时态:主从句时态不一致,从句中所述为过去发生之事,用一般过去时。

36. 【答案】for fear that he should be recognized

【解析】"唯恐"、"以免"、"以防"等否定含义的目的状语从句由连词 for fear that..., lest..., in case...引导时,从句中的谓语动词常用 should+动词原形构成。

【点睛】虚拟语气是重要考点。

37. 【答案】being sent abroad

【解析】考查被动语态的动名词作介词宾语。由于她与"派"是动宾关系,所以此处用被动语态,而空格前是介词 of,要求用动名词作宾语,故将 be 变为 being。

【点睛】翻译时要注意上下文语法衔接。

38. 【答案】will be doing the experiment

【解析】在将来某段时间内将持续进行的动作用将来进行时。

【点睛】略微复杂一些的时态常考,要根据上下文的线索判断。

39. 【答案】has a strong influence on

【解析】名词性从句作主语,表示单数意思,谓语动词用单数形式。influence 与 on 搭配。

【点睛】介词与实义词的搭配常考。

40. 【答案】would not have finished so early

【解析】but for 表示"要不是……",隐含了非真实条件从句,用了这个介词短语,主句中的动词要用虚拟式。

【点睛】这是一个简单句形式的含蓄条件句,表示虚拟条件的有 but for, without 等介词。

41. 【答案】wondering about his real purpose

【解析】leave 的宾语补足语如果是宾语发出的动作,用动词的-ing 分词形式;如果是宾语承受的动作,用动词的-ed 分词形式。

【点睛】非谓语动词的各种用法是重要考点。

42. 【答案】attempts to escape being fined

【解析】attempt to do sth.和 escape doing sth.均为固定用法。此句中的 doing 要用被动语态。

【点睛】被动语态是此题隐含的考点,汉语往往看不出被动,但英语中如果主语是某个动作的承受者,就要用被动语态。

43. 【答案】had interrupted me

【解析】在 it was the first (second,...) time 后面的定语从句中,谓语动词用过去完成时。

【点睛】遇到该结构时,要分清是 it was 还是 it is。在 It is the first (second,...) time 后面的从句中,谓语动词要用现在完成时。

44. 【答案】It is because she is too inexperienced

【解析】考查强调结构和实义词 inexperienced。

【点睛】强调结构 it is 或 it was 后面几乎可接各种句子成分,此处强调原因,后接原因状语从句。

45. 【答案】caught him cheating me

【解析】考查 catch obj. doing sth.结构。

【点睛】分词作宾语补足语时可根据其中涉及的动词和宾语的关系判断用-ing 还是-ed 分词:如果宾语是动作发出者,用-ing 分词;若是承受者,则用-ed 分词。

46. 【答案】did not work in the same office

【解析】考查虚拟语气的特殊结构:would rather 的宾语从句中谓语动词用过去时。

【点睛】虚拟语气的特殊结构有多种,应该全面准确掌握。

47. 【答案】was finally called off/cancelled because of the bad weather

【解析】主要考查"取消"的表达,用 call off 或 cancel。

【点睛】sports meet 是"被取消",故用被动语态,不要因为汉语中没体现而忽略。

48. 【答案】did he charge me too much/did he overcharge me

【解析】本题有两个考点:倒装句和前缀 over-。动词"收费"的对应词为"charge"。"过高"可用 too much 表达,但更加巧妙的用词是"overcharge"。另外本句中否定词 not only 前置于句首,是倒装句的标志。结合后半句的一般过去时形式,翻译成"Not only did he charge me too much"或者"Not only did he overcharge me"。

【点睛】类似的知识点还要注意 Never/Neither/Hardly/Scarcely 等否定词在句首的倒装情况。

49. 【答案】half as much money

【解析】考查 as... as...结构表示倍数关系,细读原句,后半句有明确的"as"一词,空缺部分是要"as"。

【点睛】根据比较结构中的倍数原则,倍数词放在最开始,接下去有关于量的 as much+*n.*+as,如 twice as much/many as,因此本句可填入"half as much money"。

50. 【答案】he was fired by the company

【解析】本题考查被动语态和时态,被动语态的基本结构为 be+done(动词的过去分词)。

【点睛】本句应该使用一般过去时。

51. 【答案】had not been planned beforehand

【解析】考查对过去的虚拟。

【点睛】同时要使用被动语态。

52. 【答案】could be achieved/met
【解析】考查对将来的虚拟,同时要使用被动语态。注意从句中谓语动词的形式。

【点睛】"实现目标"的动词可以用 achieved, met 等。

53. 【答案】would have been here
【解析】or 引导的是一个并列的含蓄条件句,暗含着虚拟条件,而且表示的是对过去的假设。

【点睛】含蓄条件句是指那些没有条件却暗含虚拟条件的句子。在含蓄条件句中,如果表示对现在或将来情况的假设,谓语动词用"should/would+动词原形"虚拟式,如果表示对过去情况的假设,谓语动词用"should/would have+过去分词"虚拟式。

54. 【答案】would have telephoned
【解析】并列的含蓄条件句,由 otherwise(否则)引导。

【点睛】并列句形式的含蓄条件句,表示虚拟条件的有 or, otherwise 等。

55. 【答案】would not have finished my assignment/homework so early
【解析】but for 表示"要不是……",用了这个介词短语,主句中的谓语动词要用虚拟式。

【点睛】这是一个简单句形式的含蓄条件句,表示虚拟条件的有 but for, without 等介词。

56. 【答案】hadn't told me all this
【解析】此题考查 would rather 后的宾语从句中对过去情况的虚拟。

【点睛】谓语动词用过去完成时。

57. 【答案】all measures be taken
【解析】direct 后的宾语从句中,谓语动词形式用(should)+动词原形。

【点睛】此句中注意还要使用被动语态。

58. 【答案】be collected to fund the project
【解析】主句中的表语是 vital,所以从句中谓语动词用"(should)+动词原形"虚拟式。

【点睛】此题还要注意使用被动语态。

59. 【答案】be here on time
【解析】主句中的表语是短语 of the utmost importance,谓语动词用"(should)+动词原形"表虚拟。

【点睛】属于主语从句中要用虚拟语气的第二种情况,主句的表语为一些表示建议、要求、命令等的名词短语。

60. 【答案】not be started
【解析】如果主句的谓语是表示建议、要求、命令等类动词的被动语态,从句中的谓语动词要使用虚拟式。

【点睛】由于后面有 until,空格处应该用否定形式。此题另外还要注意应译成被动语态。

61. 【答案】all these figures (should) be checked twice
【解析】主句中的表语是 essential,谓语动词用"(should)+动词原形"虚拟式。

【点睛】还要注意使用被动语态。

62. 【答案】a special committee be set up
【解析】此题考查的是 proposal 的同位语从句。

【点睛】还要注意使用被动语态。

63. 【答案】being both wind-resistant and adapted to
【解析】分词作伴随状语。

【点睛】both... and...表示"不仅……而且……"。

64. 【答案】were the one being corrected
【解析】as if 后面往往需要虚拟语气。

【点睛】注意"正在被"的表达。

65. 【答案】girls as well as boys being encouraged to go to school
【解析】现在分词复合结构由介词 with 引导。

【点睛】此题同时注意被动语态。

66. 【答案】meeting you for the first time
【解析】英语中有些动词后面既可接动词不定式,又可接动名词,但是含义不同,如本题中 forget doing sth."忘记自己做过了某事",而 forget to do sth. 是"忘了去做某事"。

【点睛】这类动词还有 stop, try, remember, regret 等:stop to do sth."停下来去做某事",stop doing sth."停止做某事";try to do sth."努力做某事;试图做某事",try doing sth."试一试做某事";remember to do sth."记得要做某事",remember doing sth."记得做过某事";regret to do sth.表示对要去做的事表示遗憾,含有"很遗憾不得不这样做"的意思;regret doing sth.表示对已经做过的事后悔。

67. 【答案】had remembered to close the window
【解析】remember to do sth."记得要做某事"。

【点睛】remember doing sth."记得做过某事"。

68. 【答案】escape being fined
【解析】"逃避"用 escape,其后接现在分词作宾语。

【点睛】注意被动语态。

69. 【答案】to have been robbed
【解析】不定式作主语补足语。

【点睛】注意被动语态的完成时。

70. 【答案】having been canceled because of the storm
【解析】考查独立主格结构。

【点睛】注意要用完成时态。

71. 【答案】as you were the day when I first met you
【解析】the same 与 as 连用,表示"同……一样"。

【点睛】注意固定搭配。

72. 【答案】to which a price change will affect supply and demand
【解析】to some extent 固定搭配意为"某种程度上"。

【点睛】注意固定搭配。

73. 【答案】as he likes her
【解析】根据空格前的 much 和要求翻译的句意,显然是考查 as 引导的让步状语从句。

【点睛】as 在此处表示"虽然,尽管"。

74. 【答案】is often a very time-consuming job
【解析】非谓语动词短语作主语时谓语动词用单数形式。

【点睛】"耗时的"表达成 time-consuming。

75. 【答案】is to attend the conference
【解析】the owner and editor of the newspaper 意思是"该报的所有者兼编辑",是单数含义。

【点睛】用 and 连接的成分表单一概念时谓语动词用单数。

76. 【答案】did he arrive at

【解析】not until"直到……才……"位于句首,主谓部分倒装。

【点睛】表示否定含义的状语从句前置时,主谓部分要倒装。

77. 【答案】may we use the telephone in the office

【解析】under no circumstances"无论如何不"位于宾语从句句首,所以从句主谓部分倒装。

【点睛】表示否定含义的状语从句前置时,主谓部分要倒装。

78. 【答案】still less of

【解析】still less 用在否定句之后,其意思是"更不用说,何况"。

【点睛】同样的还有 much less。

79. 【答案】must have studied very hard

【解析】表示对过去情况有把握的猜测,用"must+动词完成式"表示。

【点睛】must have done 这个用法仅限于肯定句。

80. 【答案】needn't have done

【解析】这句话表示对过去情况温和的责备。

【点睛】"本不必"用 needn't have done sth.。这个用法仅限于否定句。

第二章 550分中译英词汇突破

第一节 中译英词汇要点归纳

中译英的解题基础是对词汇的理解和辨析。考生平时要注意弄清楚词的内涵,并了解名词、动词、形容词等实词之间以及实词与介词或副词之间的搭配关系,同时要记住一些惯用法,如"步行",要说 on foot,不说 by foot,而"乘车"要说 by bus,不说 on bus。再如,anything but 的基本意思是 not at all,而 nothing but 的基本意思是 only。中译英考查考生对常用词组的理解和运用能力。

改革后的中译英测试可归纳为以下几个要点:动词短语、名词短语、形容词短语、介词短语和固定搭配。

一、动词短语

> 动词与虚词的搭配是中译英的考查重点,其中包括:动词+副词、动词+介词、动词+副词+介词。这类动词主要有:break, bring, call, come, count, get, go, hand, hold, keep, lay, let, make, put, run, set, take, turn 等。

【例 1】Computer technology ＿＿＿＿＿＿＿＿＿ (会给工商管理带来革命).　　　　　　[2004.1]

【答案】will bring about a revolution in business administration

【译文】计算机技术会给工商管理带来革命。

【解析】表达"带来"的常用短语为 bring about;情态动词 will 表示将来的趋势"会"。常考的含 bring 的动词短语还有:bring around/round"说服,使信服;使恢复知觉(或健康)";bring back"带回;使想起";bring forth"生(孩子);开(花);结(果)";bring off"圆满完成";bring out"出版,推出;使显出;激起,引起";bring up"养育,教养;提出"。

【例 2】We have ＿＿＿＿＿＿＿＿＿ (得尝试各种方式以降低) down the costs of the construction project.　　[1994.1]

【答案】to try every means to bring

【译文】我们得尝试各种方式以降低建筑工程的费用。

【解析】have to do sth.意为"不得不/必须做某事";短语 bring down 可表达"降低;打倒"。在解答该题时,空格前后的提示对正确翻译很重要。

二、名词短语

【例 3】Niagara Falls is ＿＿＿＿＿＿＿＿＿ (一个绝好的旅游胜地) drawing millions of visitors every year. [2000.1]

【答案】a great tourist attraction

【译文】尼亚加拉瀑布是一个绝好的旅游胜地,每年都吸引上百万的游人。

【解析】固定短语。tourist attraction"旅游胜地"。

【例 4】The traditional approach ＿＿＿＿＿＿＿＿＿ (处理复杂问题) is to break them down into smaller, more easily managed problems. [1996.6]

【答案】to dealing with complex problems

【译文】传统的处理复杂问题的方法是把它们分解成更小的、更易解决的问题。

【解析】空格前的 approach 提示用固定搭配 approach to doing sth.。牢记与名词搭配的介词及其用法是翻译名词短语的关键。

三、形容词短语

【例 5】It's very ＿＿＿＿＿＿＿＿＿ (你很体谅人) not to talk aloud while the baby is asleep. [2004.1]

【答案】considerate of you

【译文】你很体谅人,在孩子睡觉时不大声说话。

【解析】同源形近词 considerable 表示"(程度、数量等)相当大(或多)的"。

【例 6】Young people ＿＿＿＿＿＿＿＿＿ (不满足于) stand and look at works of art, they want art they can participate in. [2000.6]

【答案】are not content to

【译文】年轻人不满足于只站在那里观看艺术品,他们还希望自己能参与其中。

【解析】content 表示"满足的",常用以下搭配:be content with sth., be content to do sth.。联系句子前后,用后者。

四、介词短语

【例 7】Finding a job in such a big company has always been ＿＿＿＿＿＿＿＿＿ (做梦也想不到的). [1997.1]

【答案】beyond his wildest dreams

【译文】在这样一个大公司里找到工作一直是他做梦也想不到的。

【解析】介词固定搭配 beyond one's wildest dreams,beyond 表示"超出……";beyond one's means"入不敷出"。

【例 8】＿＿＿＿＿＿＿＿＿ (如果没有帮助) of their group, we would not have succeeded in the investigation. [2003.1]

【答案】But for the help

【译文】如果没有他们组的帮助,我们的调查不会成功。

【解析】介词固定搭配 but for 含虚拟语气,符合句意。另外也可使用 Without the help。

五、固定搭配

【例 9】Not only the professionals but also the amateurs ＿＿＿＿＿＿＿＿＿ (将受益于) the new training facilities. [2003.6]

【答案】will benefit from

【译文】专业运动员和业余选手都将受益于新的训练设施。

【解析】benefit from"受益于"。benefit 作及物动词时表示"使受益",后接受益者。

【例 10】Having spent some time in the city, he had no trouble ＿＿＿＿＿＿＿＿＿ (找到了去历史博物馆的路).

【答案】finding the way to the history museum

【译文】在该市住了一段时间后,他毫不费力地找到了去历史博物馆的路。

【解析】本题考查的是 have no trouble (in) doing sth.结构,同时又需兼顾 the way to...的表达。

第二节 词汇突破训练

1. The prevention and treatment of AIDS is ＿＿＿＿＿＿＿＿＿ (我们可以合作的领域). [2007.6]

2. To make donations or for more information, please ＿＿＿＿＿＿＿＿＿ (按以下地址和我们联系). [2007.6]

3. Having spent some time in the city, he had no trouble ＿＿＿＿＿＿＿＿＿ (找到去历史博物馆的
   路). [2006.6]

4. Cancer is ＿＿＿＿＿＿＿＿＿ (仅次于) heart disease as a cause of death. [2005.6]

5. If you don't like to swim, you _____ (不妨待在家里). [2004.6]

6. The car _____ (中途抛锚) for no reason. [1998.1]

7. A well-written composition calls _____ (要求用词恰当) and clear organization among other things. [1996.6]

8. That was so serious a matter that I had no choice _____ (只好叫来警察). [1996.1]

9. The sports meet originally due to be held last Friday _____ (最终因天气不好而取消了). [1996.1]

10. She's fainted. Throw some water on her face _____ (她就会苏醒过来). [2004.1]

11. One day I _____ (偶然看到一篇报纸文章) about the retirement of an English professor at a nearby state college. [1998.1]

12. I'm very sorry to _____ (打扰你) with so many questions on such an occasion. [1999.6]

13. The early pioneers had to go _____ (历尽艰辛,以在新的土地上定居). [2000.6]

14. There are other problems which I don't propose to _____ (在这个时候深入探讨). [1996.1]

15. When I was very young, I was terribly frightened of school, but I soon _____ (克服了这种心理). [1991.6]

16. There was a big hole in the road which _____ (阻塞了交通). [2002.1]

17. What he told us about the affair simply doesn't _____ (毫无意义). [1993.1]

18. Her fluency in English gives _____ (更有优势) other girls for the job. [1993.1]

19. _____ (请你找张空白纸) and write your name at the top? [2003.6]

20. The police _____ (设下圈套) to catch the thieves. [1994.1]

21. In a sudden _____ (盛怒之下) the man tore up everything within reach. [2000.1]

22. The doctor told Penny _____ (过多目晒) to the sun is bad for the skin. [1995.1]

23. The British Constitution is _____ (在很大程度上) a product of the historical events described above. [2000.6]

24. I have no _____ (不反对共度) the evening with them. [1995.1]

25. I cannot give you _____ (这种车的订单) you sell because there is no demand for it in the market. [1993.6]

26. Every culture has developed _____ (偏好) certain kinds of food and drink and equally strong negative attitudes toward others. [2004.1]

27. The shy girl _____ (感到尴尬不安) when she could not answer her teacher's questions. [1998.6]

28. She _____ (非常专心) in her job that she didn't hear anybody knocking at the door. [1996.1]

29. Improved consumer confidence _____ (具有关键性的作用) an economic recovery. [2000.1]

30. The director _____ (很挑剔) the way we were doing the work. [2000.1]

31. Tony _____ (感到很失望) the results of the exam. [1999.6]

32. The committee is _____ (一致反对) to any changes being made in the plan. [1999.1]

33. He is _____ (十分乐观) his chances of winning a gold medal in the Olympics next year. [2000.1]

34. As a mother, she is too _____ (护着女儿了). She should let her see more of the world. [1993.1]

35. A dark suit _____ (更适合) to a light one for evening wear. [2003.6]

36. For _____ (尽管这对恋人之间有差异), the couple were developing an obvious and genuine affection for each other. [1998.1]

37. _____ (尽管向前发展) of science, the discomforts of old age will no doubt always be with us. [1991.6]

38. I left for the office earlier than usual this morning _____ (以免遇上交通阻塞).

39. What he said just now had little to do with _____ discussion (正在讨论的问题). [1998.6]

40. The rest of the day was entirely _____ (任凭他支配) for reading or recreation. [2003.6]

41. The older New England villages have changed relatively little _____ (除了) a gas station or two in recent decades. [2001.6]

32. All the students in this class passed the English exam with _____ (除了) Li Ming. [1996.6]

43. In my opinion, he's by _____ (显然是最富有想象力) of all the contemporary poets. [2002.6]

44. Students or teachers can participate in excursions to lovely beaches around the island at _____ (每隔一段时间). [1997.1]

45. He decided to make further improvements on the computer's design in the _____ (根据客户的要求). [1995.1]

46. Remember that customers don't _____ (讨价还价) in that city. [1999.1]

47. I suggested he _____ (使自己适应新的环境). [2001.1]

48. The old couple decided to _____ (收养一儿一女) though they had three children of their own. [1997.6]

49. It has been revealed that some government leaders _____ (滥用职权) to get illegal profits for themselves. [1996.6]

50. It was in the United States that I made _____ (结识) Professor Jones. [2003.6]

第三节 答案解析

1. 【答案】the field (where) we can cooperate/ the field in which we can cooperate/ one field of our cooperation
【译文】防治艾滋病是我们可以合作的领域。

【解析】①待译内容是个名词词组,中心词是"领域",译作 field/area 均可,前面用 a 或 the 都行。②名词词组的修饰语"我们可以合作的"包含主语和谓语动词,应该译成定语从句。首先确定关系词,用 where 或 in which 均可;"可以"用情态动词can 表示;"合作"即 cooperate。

2. 【答案】contact us at the following address
【译文】捐赠或更多信息,请按以下地址和我们联系。

【解析】①待译内容是祈使句的主干部分,动词短语,用动词原形。②"联系"即 contact,及物动词,汉语中的状语"和我们"译作contact 的宾语,用宾格 us。③状语成分"按以下地址"译作 at the following address,注意介词用at。

3. 【答案】finding his/the way to the History Museum
【译文】在这座城市待了一段时间后,他对找到去历史博物馆的路没有问题。

【解析】此题考查 have (no) trouble (in) doing sth.这一结构,同时注意 find one's way to...的表达。

4. 【答案】second only to
【译文】癌症是仅次于心脏病的死亡杀手。

【解析】考查习惯用语"be second only to(仅次于)"。

5. 【答案】may as well stay at home
【译文】如果你不喜欢去游泳,不妨待在家里。

【解析】may as well 为固定表达,意为"不妨",后接动词原形。

6. 【答案】broke down halfway
【译文】这辆车在中途无缘无故地抛锚了。

【解析】break down 意为"崩溃,瓦解;(机器等)出毛病,坏掉"。含 break 的常用短语还有:break off"中断,突然停止";break out "(火灾、疾病、战争、暴动等)突然发生;逃脱";break up"破碎,碎裂,瓦解;学期结束;分开"。

7. 【答案】for good choice of words
【译文】一篇好作文要求用词恰当、结构清晰。

【解析】表达"要求"可用 call for。含 call 的其他常考短语有:call on/upon"访问,拜访;号召,要求";call up"召集,动员;打电话;使人想起";call off"取消";call in"叫……进来,召来"。

8. 【答案】but to call in the police
   【译文】事态实在严重,我别无选择,只好叫来警察。

   【解析】表达"叫来"用 call in;but 后用不定式表示"只能做……;只好做……"的含义。

9. 【答案】was finally called off/cancelled because of the bad weather
   【译文】原定于上周五举行的运动会最终因天气不好而取消了。

   【解析】表达"取消"用 call off 或 cancel。"v.+off"型常考动词短语还有:set off"出发;引起";break off"停止,中断";wear off"逐渐减少,逐渐消失"。

10. 【答案】and she'll come around/round
    【译文】她昏过去了。往她脸上泼点水她就会苏醒过来。

    【解析】"苏醒"表达为 come around/round。祈使句+and 并列的简单句,表示"如果……就会……"。含 come 的常考动词短语还有:come along"出现,发生;进步,进展";come out"出现,显露;出版,发表;结果是";come on"(表示鼓励、催促等)快,走吧;进步,进展;发生,开始";come about"发生";come after"查找(某人)";come at"达到,了解";come across"偶然看到"。

11. 【答案】came across a newspaper article
    【译文】大我偶然看到报纸上有一篇关于一所国有大学的一位单身语教授很体味的文章。

    【解析】"偶然看到"可表达为 come across。

12. 【答案】have bothered you
    【译文】在这个时候问这么多问题来打扰您,实在不好意思。

    【解析】考查动词搭配关系。bother sb. with sth. 意为"以某事打扰某人"。本句用动词不定式的完成时态。

13. 【答案】through many hardships to settle on the new land
    【译文】为了在新的土地上定居,早期的开拓者不得不历尽艰辛。

    【解析】go through"经历;获得通过;详细讨论"。含 go 的常考动词短语还有:go along with"同意";go back on"违背,背弃";go into"进入,调查,审查;深入探讨";go up"烧毁;兴建;上升,增长"。

14. 【答案】go into at the moment
    【译文】还有其他一些问题我不打算在这个时候深入探讨。

    【解析】go into"深入探讨";"在这个时候,眼下"表达为 at/for the moment。

15. 【答案】got over it
    【译文】我还很小的时候十分害怕上学,但很快就克服了这种心理。

    【解析】"克服"表达为 get over 或 overcome。含 get 的动词短语还有:get off"动身";get across"使……被理解,沟通";get away"逃脱"。

16. 【答案】held up the traffic
    【译文】马路上有个大洞阻塞了交通。

    【解析】"阻塞(交通)"常用表达是 hold up。含 hold 的其他常考动词短语有:hold back"抑制,阻碍;退缩;隐瞒";hold on"继续,坚持,保持;不挂断电话"。

17. 【答案】make any sense
    【译文】他跟我们说的那件事毫无意义。

【解析】固定短语。make sense"有意义;合理"。

18. 【答案】her an advantage over
【译文】她英语流利,和其他女孩相比,更有优势得到这份工作。

【解析】"相较他人的优势"为 an advantage over sb.。含 advantage 的短语还有:take advantage of"利用"。

19. 【答案】Could you take a blank sheet of paper
【译文】请你找张空白纸把名字写在顶上好吗?

【解析】"一张纸"为 a sheet of paper;blank 意为"空白的,未录音的",常修饰纸张、磁带、表格等。由于句尾用的是问号,故应用 Could you.../Would you please... 句型。blank 的近义词 empty 表示"空无一物的";vacant"无人占用的";bare"光秃秃的"。

20. 【答案】set a trap
【译文】警方设下圈套捉拿窃贼。

【解析】固定搭配。set a trap"设圈套";动词的时态是一般过去时。

21. 【答案】burst of anger
【译文】盛怒之下,这个男人只要抓到东西就撕碎。

【解析】a burst of 指感情的一时冲动。

22. 【答案】that too much exposure
【译文】医生告诉潘妮过多日晒会对皮肤有坏处。

【解析】空格后的 to 表明用短语 exposure to"显露,暴露,曝光"。

23. 【答案】to a large extent/degree
【译文】英国的宪法是上述历史事件的产物。

【解析】表示"在……程度上"用 to a... extent/degree。

24. 【答案】objection to spending
【译文】与他们共度今宵,我没意见。

【解析】objection to 后跟动名词。

25. 【答案】an order for the type of car
【译文】我不能向你订购这种车,因为市场对它没有需求。

【解析】an order for sth.为固定搭配,意为"……的订单"。

26. 【答案】its preferences for
【译文】每种文化都有自己偏爱的饮食类型,并且对其他文化的饮食有同样强烈的否定态度。

【解析】固定搭配。preference for sth./doing sth."偏好"。

27. 【答案】felt awkward/embarrassed and uncomfortable/uneasy
【译文】那害羞的女孩回答不出老师的问题时,感到尴尬不安。

【解析】feel 后接形容词或及物动词的过去分词。

28. 【答案】was so absorbed
【译文】她工作非常专心,以至于有人敲门也没有听到。

【解析】形容词固定搭配,be absorbed in 意为"全神贯注于";so... that...句型表示"如此……以至"。

29. 【答案】is crucial to/plays a key role in

【译文】增强消费者的信心对于经济复苏具有关键性的作用。

【解析】"对……具有关键性的作用"可用 be crucial to 或者 play a key role in。不同搭配中的介词不同。

30. 【答案】was critical of
【译文】主任对我们的工作方法很挑剔。

【解析】固定搭配 be critical of"对某人或某事提出批评,对……挑剔",注意介词用 of。

31. 【答案】is very disappointed with
【译文】托尼对考试成绩感到很失望。

【解析】形容词固定搭配 be disappointed with"对……感到失望"。

32. 【答案】totally opposed
【译文】委员会一致反对计划的任何变动。

【解析】空格后的 to 和空格前的 is 说明用 be opposed to 短语。如果没有 is 的限制,也可用 objects to 来表达。

33. 【答案】optimistic about
【译文】他对自己明年能否在奥运会上赢得金牌这一问题十分乐观。

【解析】be optimistic/pessimistic about "对……感到乐观/悲观"。

34. 【答案】protective towards her daughter
【译文】作为母亲,她太帮着女儿了。其实她应该让孩子了了见见世面。

【解析】"对……过于爱护的"可用 be protective towards/of。

35. 【答案】is preferable
【译文】深色衣服比浅色衣服更适合作晚装。

【解析】固定搭配。A is preferable to B 表示"A 比 B 更可取,更好,更合意"。suitable 也有"适合"之义,但没有比较含义,且与介词 for 搭配。

36. 【答案】all their differences
【译文】尽管这对恋人之间有差异,但他们之间却正在产生明显的、真挚的爱情。

【解析】介词固定搭配。for all"虽然;尽管"。同义的表达还有 despite, in spite of。

37. 【答案】Despite the advances
【译文】尽管科学向前发展,老年的病痛无疑仍将伴随着我们。

【解析】也可以用 for all 或 in spite of 表达"尽管"之义。

38. 【答案】in case of traffic jam
【译文】今天早晨我比平常提前动身去办公室,以免遇上交通阻塞。

【解析】介词固定搭配。in case of "假如;万一;如果……发生"。

39. 【答案】the question under
【译文】他刚才所说的话与正在讨论的问题关系不大。

【解析】介词固定搭配。空格后的名词 discussion 表明需要用介词 under,表示"正在……"。

40. 【答案】at his disposal
【译文】那天剩下的时间完全任凭他支配——读书也好,娱乐也行。

【解析】介词固定搭配。at sb.'s disposal"任某人处理,供某人使用"。

41. 【答案】except for

【译文】除了最近几十年修建了一两个加油站之外,古老的新英格兰村庄几乎没有什么变化。

【解析】介词固定搭配。except for "除……之外,除去",后接名词(短语),符合句子需要。表示"除了"还有 in addition to "除……之外(还)";besides "除……外(还)"着重"另外还有";except "从整体里减去一部分",着重于"排除在外"。

42. 【答案】the exception of
【译文】除了李明之外,全班同学都通过了英语考试。

【解析】介词固定搭配。空格前的 with 提示只能用介词搭配 with the exception of,表示"除了"。

43. 【答案】far the most imaginative
【译文】我认为,他显然是当今最富有想象力的诗人。

【解析】介词固定搭配。空格前的 by 和需译部分提示要用 by far;它可放在最高级前作程度副词,表示"显然"。辨析易混淆短语:so far "迄今为止"。

44. 【答案】regular intervals
【译文】每隔一段时间,老师或学生们都可以到美丽的环岛海滨去集体旅游。

【解析】介词固定搭配。at intervals 意为"每隔一段(时间或距离)";辨析易混淆短语:at length 相当于 in the end/at last,意为"终于,最后;详细地";at a/the rate of 可表示"以……比率";at this/that rate 表示"照这/那样的话;照这/那种情形"。

45. 【答案】light of the requirements of customers
【译文】根据客户的要求,他决定进一步改进计算机的设计。

【解析】空格前的 in the 提示只能用固定短语 in the light of,意为"根据"。in accordance with "根据",是一个正式的表达。

46. 【答案】bargain about prices
【译文】记住,在那个城市顾客买东西时不讨价还价。

【解析】bargain about sth. 意为"就……讨价还价"。

47. 【答案】should adapt himself to his new conditions
【译文】我建议他应该使自己适应新的环境。

【解析】本句中应用"(should)+动词原形"表示虚拟。

48. 【答案】adopt a boy and a girl
【译文】虽然自己已有了三个孩子,这对老夫妇仍决定收养一儿一女。

【解析】考查动宾搭配。adopt "收养"。辨析形近词:adapt 意为"使适应"。

49. 【答案】abuse their authority and position
【译文】据透露,一些政府领导滥用职权,非法谋利。

【解析】abuse 后接人或动物表示"虐待,谩骂"。

50. 【答案】the acquaintance of
【译文】我是在美国结识琼斯教授的。

【解析】空格前的 made 提示用 make the acquaintance of sb.,意为"结识某人"。

第一节 突击训练

1. In fact, Peter would rather have left for San Francisco _____ (而不愿待在纽约).

2. This article _____ (呼吁人们多关注) to the problem of cultural interference in foreign language teaching and learning.

3. It was essential that the application forms _____ (必须退还) before the deadline.

4. Not that John doesn't want to help you, _____ (而是他没有这个能力).

5. A good many proposals were raised by the delegates, _____ (正如预料的那样).

6. In the advanced course students must take performance tests at _____ (每隔一月).

7. Mark often attempts to escape _____ (罚款) whenever he breaks traffic regulations.

8. A man escaped from the prison last night. It was a long time _____ (之后警卫才发现).

9. In no country _____ (除了在英国), it has been said, can one experience four seasons in the course of a single day.

10. While crossing the mountain area, all the men carried guns lest they _____ (受到袭击) by wild animals.

11. I don't mind your _____ (你延期做出决定) as long as it is not too late.

12. I suggested he _____ (使自己适应) his new conditions.

13. I have no objection _____ (再听听你的故事).

14. _____ (这两本书都不认为) the opinion that the danger of nuclear war is increasing.

15. "You are very selfish. It's high time _____ (你认识到) you are not the most important person in the world." Edgar said to his boss angrily.

16. You see the lightning the _____ (闪电一发生), but you hear the thunder later.

17. Mr. Johnson preferred _____ (别人给他重活干).

18. When he arrived, _____ (发现只有) but the aged and the sick at home.

19. Housewives who do not go out to work often feel they are not working _____ (充分发挥自己的能力).

20. _____ (即使计算是正确的), scientists can never be sure that they have included all variables and modeled them accurately.

21. She would appreciate _____ (收到来信) you sometime.

22. _____ (信不信由你), his discovery has created a stir in scientific circles.

23. The trumpet player was certainly loud. But I wasn't bothered by his loudness so much _____ (而是他缺乏天分).

24. He moved away from his parents and _____ (太想念他们以至不能很好地享受) the exciting life in New York.

25. If you _____ (碰巧发现了) my lost papers while you're looking for your book, please let me know at once by telephone.

26. This hotel _____ (收费60美元) a single room with bath.

27. If I _____ (记得关窗的话) the window, the thief would not have got in.

28. Now _____ (既然我们已经完成了该课程), we shall start doing more revision work.

29. I used _____ (以前抽烟抽得很凶), but I gave it up three years ago.

30. Some women _____ (本来能够挣得一份很好的工资) in a job instead of staying home, but they decided not to work for the sake of the family.

31. _____ (无论什么困难) we may come across, we'll help one another to overcome them.

32. If you don't like to swim, you _____ (不妨待在家里).

33. Not until the game had begun _____ (他才到达) the sports ground.

34. The last half of the nineteenth century _____ (取得稳定发展) in the means of travel.

35. Investigators agreed that passengers on the airliner _____ (肯定丧生了) at the very moment of the crash.

36. The mother didn't know _____ (责备谁) for the broken glass.

37. The soldier _____ (被指控临阵脱逃) when the enemy attacked.

38. In _____ (考虑到最近的进展情况) we do not think your scheme is practical.

39. Reading _____ (字里行间的言外之意), I would say that the Government are more worried than they will admit.

40. This kind of glasses manufactured by experienced craftsmen _____ (戴起来十分舒服).

41. Over a third of the population was estimated _____ (无法获得) to the health service.　[1998.6]

42. Most doctors recognize that medicine is as much _____ (是一门科学, 也是一门艺术).　[1990.6]

43. Americans eat _____ (两倍) protein as they actually need every day.　[1998.6]

44. Please be careful when you are drinking coffee in case you _____ (弄脏了新地毯).　[1997.1]

45. There's little chance _____ (人类能幸存) a nuclear war.　[1993.6]

第二节 答案解析

1. 【答案】than stayed in New York
   【译文】事实上, 彼得宁愿去旧金山而不愿待在纽约。

   【解析】would rather... than...的用法, than 在此是一个连接词, 应该使用并列结构。前面动词用了完成式, 因此 than 之后的动词应是 have stayed 或者省略 have。

2. 【答案】calls for more attention
   【译文】这篇文章呼吁人们多关注外语教学和学习过程中的文化干扰问题。

   【解析】动词短语和名词短语搭配。call for"呼吁; 要求"。空格后的 to 表明用 attention to 表达"关注"。

3. 【答案】be sent back
   【译文】这些申请表必须在最后期限前退还。

   【解析】主语从句中的虚拟语气。主句中包括 essential, 主语从句中谓语动词形式要用"(should)+动词原形"虚拟式。

4.【答案】but that it's beyond his power
【译文】不是约翰不想帮你,而是他没有这个能力。

【解析】句子连接词。not that... but that...“不是……而是……”。

5.【答案】as was to be expected
【译文】正如预料的那样,代表们提出了很多建议。

【解析】关系代词 as 的用法,指代前文所说的现象,引导非限定定语从句。

6.【答案】monthly intervals
【译文】修高级课程的学生每隔一月要进行能力测试。

【解析】介词固定搭配。at intervals“每隔……时间/距离”。

7.【答案】being fined
【译文】每当违反了交通规则,马克常常企图逃避罚款。

【解析】动名词作动词宾语。escape doing sth.是固定用法。由于马克是动作(罚款)的逻辑宾语,因此此句中的 doing 要用被动语态。

8.【答案】before the guards discovered what had happened
【译文】昨晚有个男人越狱逃跑了,过了了很久之后警卫才发现。

【解析】句子连接词。before 在 it was a long time 或 long 之后,表示的中文意思是“……之后”。

9.【答案】other than Britain
【译文】据说除了在英国,在其他国家一天的时间内不可能体验到四个季节的气候。

【解析】固定搭配。根据句子空格前 no 的提示,用 other than,no other than 意思是“只有”。辨析类似短语:rather than“与其……倒不如,不是……而是”。

10.【答案】should be attacked
【译文】穿过山区时,所有的男人都带着枪,以免受到野兽的袭击。

【解析】状语从句中的虚拟语气。lest 引导的状语从句中,谓语动词形式要用“(should)+动词原形”虚拟式。

11.【答案】delaying making the decision/delaying making up your mind
【译文】只要不太迟,我不介意你延期做出决定。

【解析】动名词作动词宾语,mind doing sth.“介意做某事”。动宾搭配,make a decision/make up one's mind“做出决定”。空格前的 your 是动名词 delaying 的逻辑主语。

12.【答案】should adapt himself to
【译文】我建议他应该使自己适应新的环境。

【解析】宾语从句中的虚拟语气。suggest“建议”引导的宾语从句中,谓语动词形式用“(should)+动词原形”虚拟式。动词搭配 adapt oneself to sth.“使自己适应于……”。

13.【答案】to hearing your story again
【译文】我不反对再听听你的故事。

【解析】名词短语及其搭配用法。have no objection to doing sth.“不反对做某事”。

14.【答案】Neither of the two books holds
【译文】这两本书都不认为核战争的危险在日益增加。

【解析】neither of 及其用法:与它修饰的名词形成主谓关系的动词用单数第三人称。动宾搭配:hold the opinion“认为”。

15. 【答案】that you realized
    【译文】"你太自私了。你现在必须认识到你并不是这世界上最重要的人！"埃德加气愤地对他的老板说道。

    【解析】It's high/about time that 结构中的虚拟语气，从句的动词用过去式。

16. 【答案】instant it happens
    【译文】闪电一发生你马上就可以看见，而听到雷声要晚一些。

    【解析】状语从句中的连词。the instant/moment 都可引导状语从句，意思同 as soon as。

17. 【答案】to be given heavier work to do
    【译文】约翰逊先生更喜欢别人给他重活干。

    【解析】不定式作动词宾语，prefer to do sth.；Mr. Johnson 是动作(给)的逻辑宾语，因此不定式要用被动语态。

18. 【答案】he found none
    【译文】他到家时，发现家里只有老人和病人。

    【解析】固定搭配及其用法。none but"只有，除……之外都没有"，后可接表人的名词；辨析类似短语：nothing but"只有，只不过"，后可接表物的名词。

19. 【答案】to their full capacity
    【译文】不外出上班的家庭主妇们常常感到不能充分发挥自己的能力。

    【解析】固定搭配。to one's full capacity"充分施展其才华"。

20. 【答案】Even if the calculation is right
    【译文】即使计算是正确的，科学家们也永远无法确信他们已经包含了所有的变量，并且准确地建立了其模型。

    【解析】状语从句连词。even if 构成让步状语从句，表示"即使，哪怕"。

21. 【答案】hearing from
    【译文】她如能哪天收到你的来信将不胜感激。

    【解析】动名词作动词宾语，appreciate doing sth.；动词短语，hear from"收到来信"。

22. 【答案】Believe it or not
    【译文】信不信由你，他的发现在科学界引起了轰动。

    【解析】习语。believe it or not"信不信由你"。

23. 【答案】as by his lack of talent
    【译文】这个号手吹的声音确实很吵，但我烦的与其说是太吵，不如说是因为他缺乏天分。

    【解析】固定结构。not so much... as..."与其说是……不如说是……"，是连接词。

24. 【答案】missed them too much to enjoy
    【译文】他离开了父母搬到纽约，又太想念他们，以至不能很好地享受纽约那令人兴奋的生活。

    【解析】too... to...句型，"太……以至于不能……"。

25. 【答案】happen to come across
    【译文】如果你在找书的时候碰巧发现了我丢失的论文，请立刻打电话告诉我。

    【解析】动词搭配和动词短语。happen to do sth."碰巧做某事"；come across"意外发现"。

26. 【答案】charges $60 for
    【译文】带浴缸的单人房，这家旅馆收费 60 美元。

    【解析】动词搭配。charge... for..."为……而收费"，本句中的主语为名词单数形式，动词用单数第三人称。

27. 【答案】had remembered to close

【译文】要是我记得关窗的话,那贼就不会进屋了。

【解析】虚拟语气,是对过去虚拟,从句用过去完成时;remember to do sth.表示"记得去做某事",remember doing sth.表示"记得做了某事",含义不同。

28. 【答案】that we have finished the course

【译文】既然我们已经完成了该课程,我们就要开始进行更多的复习。

【解析】状语从句连接词。now that"既然"引导原因状语从句。

29. 【答案】to smoke heavily

【译文】我以前抽烟抽得很凶,但三年前戒掉了。

【解析】used to do 固定用法,表示"以前常常做某事";副词与被修饰动词的搭配用法,heavily 在此是表示程度。

30. 【答案】could have made a good salary

【译文】一些妇女本来能够挣一份很好的工资,而不是待在家里。但是为了家庭,她们决定不工作。

【解析】"could have done"表示对过去情况的假设。

31. 【答案】Whatever difficulties

【译文】无论我们遇到什么困难,都将互相帮助来克服它们。

【解析】无条件让步状语从句引导词的用法。whatever=no matter what。

32. 【答案】may as well stay at home

【译文】要是你不想去游泳,不妨待在家里。

【解析】may as well=might as well 表示"不妨"。

33. 【答案】did he arrive at

【译文】直到比赛开始,他才到达运动场。

【解析】否定词位于句首时所引起的倒装,not until 位于句首,主句主谓语要倒装。

34. 【答案】witnessed the steady improvement

【译文】19 世纪后半叶,交通工具取得稳定发展。

【解析】习惯主谓搭配,witness 前的主语经常是某个时期、某地点,但表示的含义是"(人们)目睹……"。

35. 【答案】must have died

【译文】调查人员一致认为,该班机上的乘客肯定是在坠机一刹那就丧生了。

【解析】"must+动词完成式"表示对过去情况有把握的猜测。

36. 【答案】who to blame

【译文】母亲不知道应该责备谁打破了玻璃。

【解析】who 等关系词+不定式;to blame 以主动语态表示被动意义"该(受)责备"。

37. 【答案】was accused of running away

【译文】这名士兵被指控在敌人进攻时临阵脱逃。

【解析】固定搭配。be accused of "被指控……",run away"逃跑"。be accused of 后接名词或动名词充当介词宾语。

38. 【答案】view of recent developments

【译文】考虑到最近的进展情况,我们认为你的计划不实际。

【解析】介词固定搭配。in view of "考虑到"。

39. 【答案】between the lines

    【译文】根据字里行间的言外之意,我认为政府委员们要比他们承认的更忧心忡忡。

    【解析】习语。read between the lines"体会字里行间的言外之意"。

40. 【答案】wears comfortably

    【译文】由有经验工人制造的眼镜戴起来十分舒服。

    【解析】动词和副词的搭配。主谓一致,主语 the kind of 后接单数第三人称动词形式。

41. 【答案】to have no access

    【译文】据估计,有超过三分之一的人口无法获得保健服务。

    【解析】固定搭配。have (no) access to sth."有(没有)机会/有(没有)办法做……"。

42. 【答案】an art as it is a science

    【译文】大多数医生承认,医学是一门科学,也是一门艺术。

    【解析】as much... as"同……一样"。art 以元音开头,前面的不定冠词应为 an。

43. 【答案】twice as much

    【译文】美国人每天吃的蛋白质相当于他们实际需要量的两倍。

    【解析】倍数的表达。倍数+as+形容词+as,如 three times as long as。

44. 【答案】stain the new carpet

    【译文】请你喝咖啡时小心一点,以免弄脏了新地毯。

    【解析】动宾搭配 stain sth. "弄脏某物";in case 引导的从句中动词用"(should)+动词原形"虚拟式。

45. 【答案】that mankind would survive

    【译文】如果发生核战争,人类能幸存下来的可能性极小。

    【解析】动宾搭配。survive sth.表示"从……中幸存下来"。

Part 6

第六篇

完型填空

稳拿480分完型考点突破

完型填空(Cloze)的测试形式是:在一篇题材熟悉、难度适中的短文(约200词)内留有20个空白,每个空白为一题,每题有四个选择项,要求在全面理解内容的基础上选择一个最佳答案,使短文的意思和结构恢复完整。

完型填空考查的词包括实义词和结构词,其目的是"测试学生综合运用语言的能力",即同时检测考生的篇章阅读理解能力、语法知识和词汇运用能力。要求考生在掌握语篇大意的前提下运用所学的词语搭配知识及语法结构知识解答试题。

与阅读理解类似,完型填空的文章内容主要涉及人物传记、社会文化、科普知识、日常生活等,以记叙文、说明文和议论文为主。

参照考纲,完型填空题的测试重点在于:

(1)辨别词汇(主要是名词、动词、形容词、副词等实义词)在上下文中的意义;

(2)动词的时态、语态、非谓语动词、短语搭配、连接词的选择、不定代词的用法和比较级的使用等语法知识;

(3)考生对语篇整体性、一致性、连贯性的把握;

(4)句与句、段与段之间的因果、对比、递进、让步等逻辑关系。

第一节 四级完型常用应试技巧

一、运用词汇、语法知识

1. 运用词汇知识

完型填空所涉及的词汇题主要考查实词,兼顾虚词。其测试重点有三个:①易混淆词辨析,主要是名词、动词、形容词和副词中存在的同义词、近义词及形似异义词;②一词多义类语义辨析,主要考查实词多义词在具体语境中的含义;③固定搭配,其中主要包括动词词组、介词词组、形容词词组、动词与名词的搭配等。

怎样才能做好完型填空中的词汇题呢?

(1) 运用上下文语境和构词法知识确定选项

考前复习时多记、牢记单词词义,重点记忆多义词、同义词、近义词及形似异义词,提高词语辨析能力。在保证概念清晰、记忆牢固的基础上,做题时要结合上下文语境、语义关系,借助词性、词义和构词法知识正确辨析易混淆词和多义词。

【例1】Do not talk too much to the child (during) meal times, but let him get on with his food; and do not ___76___ him to leave the table immediately after a meal or he will (soon) learn to swallow his food (so) he can hurry back to his toys.

[1997.6/T76]

A) agree   B) allow   C) force   D) persuade

【解析】根据下文"否则孩子会养成狼吞虎咽的习惯以尽快回去玩自己的玩具",空格所在句应补全为"不允许/同意他马上离开",A、B作为近义词,语义上都可以入选,但agree不能接复合宾语。[答案:B]

【例2】Neatly ___77___ and usually very frightened, they are (determined) to show that they have a good attitude and the (power) to succeed. [1998.6/T77]

  A) decorated   B) dressed   C) coated   D) worn

【解析】根据句意空白处意思应是"穿着(整洁)"。decorate"装饰",很容易被排除;wear"穿",后面需跟宾语,表示"穿着……",也可排除;coat是强干扰项,其常见词性为名词,根据构词法的词类转换知识,由该词的名词义"外套,表皮,覆盖物,层"可推测它作为动词的意思可能是"给……穿上外套;覆盖……;在……涂上涂层",这些都不符合句意,因此排除;而dress作为名词的意思是"衣服,服装",作为动词意思是"着装,穿衣",可确定为答案。[答案:B]

(2) 注意介词、副词的表意功能

  完型填空常考查介词、副词三方面的知识:基本意义、用法和相关的搭配。有关介词短语搭配的问题将在下面论述。解答此类题时,要根据介词、副词的表意功能并结合上下文语境作答。

【例3】Do not talk too much to the child ___75___ meal times, but let him get on with his food; ... [1997.6/T75]

  A) on   B) over   C) by   D) during

【解析】句子意思是说:在吃饭时不要多同孩子说话。四个介词当中,during的意思是"在……期间",是答案。而其他三个选项也可与时间名词搭配,但on只接日期;over"从……的开头直到结束";by"到……前",均与句意不合。[答案:D]

(3) 根据代词的上下文替代作用选择词语

【例4】At meal times it is a good (idea) to give a child a small portion and let him (come) back for a second helping rather than give him as ___74___ as he is likely to eat all at once. [1997.6/T74]

  A) much   B) little   C) few   D) many

【解析】根据上下文意思,可排除表示"少量的"的B、C,而空白处的词指代的应是所吃食物的量(不可数),因此为much。[答案:A]

(4) 根据词语的固定搭配选择答案

  完型填空涉及的常用短语搭配形式主要有以下几类:

  ①动词与名词、介词、副词的搭配。

【例5】The (way) you go about purchasing an article or a service can actually (save) you money, or can add ___63___ the cost. [2005.1/T63]

  A) up   B) to   C) in   D) on

【解析】固定搭配add to意为"增加,添加",可后接cost"成本";add up"加算;合计",不符合题意;其他两个介词不与add构成搭配。[答案:B]

【例6】We can change an utterance by ___72___ one word in it with ___73___: ... [2003.1]

  72. A) replacing   B) spelling   C) pronouncing   D) saying

  73. A) ours   B) theirs   C) another   D) others

【解析】72题,短语replace A with B表示"以B替代A"。[答案:A]

  73题,与前面的one呼应的应是another。[答案:C]

  ②形容词与名词的搭配。

【例7】Friendship appears to be a unique form of ___66___ bonding. [2001.6/T66]

  A) civil   B) human   C) mankind   D) individual

【解析】短语human bonding意为"人际关系"。[答案:B]

  ③名词与介词的搭配。

【例8】Unlike marriage or the ties that bind parents and children, it is not defined or regulated by ___82___. [2001.6/T82]

  A) rule   B) discipline   C) law   D) regulation

【解析】固定短语 by law 意为"按照法律"。[答案:C]
④形容词与介词的搭配。
【例9】Nevertheless, (as) the following suggestions and comments indicate, students feel ___80___ with things-as-they-are in the classroom. [2001.1/T80]

    A) satisfactory   B) unsatisfactory   C) satisfied   D) dissatisfied

【解析】固定短语 feel dissatisfied with 表示"对……不满意"。此处应有相应的上下文,否则 C 也可以。[答案:D]

2. 运用语法知识

语法不是四级完型填空的考查重点,但理解句子,特别是长难句,必须对其进行语法分析。完型填空中语法题主要是对定语从句、虚拟语气、状语从句和倒装句进行考查;其语法范畴更受上下文语境的制约。

二、运用篇章知识

完型填空要求将短文复原为意义和结构上完整的一个语篇,也就是使之成为衔接合理、符合逻辑、语义连贯的一个语言单位。连接语篇使之具备连贯性、一致性的纽带包括语法、词汇、逻辑三类。语法类纽带涉及篇章中省略、替代、照应等手段;词汇类纽带包括篇章中词汇的同现与复现;逻辑手段将在第三点中说明。

1. 利用省略、替代、照应等篇章技巧

省略、替代是为避免重复,完型填空主要考查后者。照应(reference)又叫"所指",语义上的所指关系分为人称所指、指示所指和比较所指。例如:

【例10】The (ideal) student is considered to be ___74___ who is motivated to learn for the sake of (learning) not the one interested only in getting high grades. [1993.6/T74]

    A) such   B) one   C) any   D) some

【解析】考查名词性替代。名词替代词有 one/ones, the same, the kind, the sort 等,动词替代词主要是代动词 do。另外,此题也可根据后文 not the one 的对比提示做出判断。[答案:B]

【例11】But it does affect our future ___75___ a democratic nation and as individuals. [2004.6/T75]

    A) of   B) for   C) with   D) as

【解析】考查比较照应。and 连接两个并列的 as。其他表示比较照应的词还有:as... as, than similar(ly), such, so, likewise, same, equal(ly), other, another, otherwise 等。[答案:D]

2. 利用篇章中的词汇同现、复现

词汇的同现和复现是衔接、连贯语篇的重要手段。

(1)"同现"指意义上相关的词汇出现在同一语篇中,构成以某一话题为中心的词汇链。如以下各例:

【例12】I have no doubt that (virtually) all of these people were ___74___ in school that the earth revolves around the sun; (they) may even have written it (on) a test. [2000.1/T74]

    A) advised   B) suggested   C) learned   D) taught

【解析】由于句意的限制,这里可与 school 同现的动词是 C、D,而根据语法知识,learn 作及物动词时不能以人为动作承受者。[答案:D]

【例13】Furthermore, these highways generally (connect) large urban centers which means that they become crowded with ___78___ traffic during rush hours. [1990.1/T78]

    A) large   B) fast   C) light   D) heavy

【解析】与 traffic 同现作修饰语的形容词应为 C、D,而下文 rush hours 决定这里的同现词为 D。[答案:D]

(2)词汇的复现包括原词重复、同(近)义词复现、反义词复现、概括词复现等。如:

【例14】He spoke perfect Korean—I was really amazed. He seemed like a good friend to me, (until) I saw him again in New York speaking ___85___ English instead of perfect Korean. [2002.1/T85]

    A) artificial   B) informal   C) perfect   D) practical

【解析】本题其他三个选项也可修饰语言,但上下文中重复出现 perfect 一词作修饰语,而且 instead of 前后也应为语义上并列的短语。[答案:C]

【例15】Unlike other social roles that we are·expected to (play)—as citizens, employees, members of professional soci-

eties and (other) organizations—it has its own principle, which is to promote __71__ of warmth, trust, love, and affection (between) two people. [2001.6/T71]

A) friendship   B) interests   C) feelings   D) impression

【解析】本题可利用下文中出现的近义词 affection 解题,and 为并列连词,之前名词短语的中心词应与其后的名词(或短语)对等;同时也可利用概括词复现解题,空缺词应能概括 warmth, trust, love, affection。[答案:C]

【例16】This is why the number of (signals) that an animal can make is very limited: the great tit is a case (in) point; it has about twenty different calls, (whereas) in human language the number of possible utterances is __79__. [2003.1/T79]

A) boundless   B) changeable   C) limitless   D) ceaseless

【解析】该句由 whereas 连接的两个意义上形成对比的分句组成,前一分句出现关键词 limited,因此可推断后一分句的空缺词为 limitless。[答案:C]

【例17】If you are buying a hairdryer, you might (think) that you are making the __66__ buy if choose one (whose) look you like and which is also the cheapest (in) price. [2005.1/T66]

A) proper   B) best   C) reasonable   D) most

【解析】本题如知道 a good buy "合算"这个固定搭配,就能很快选出 best。如果不熟悉固定搭配,可根据其后的 you like 和 cheapest 推断出复现概括词 best。proper 和 reasonable 体现不出最高含义;most 修饰名词是指数量,不符合题意。[答案:B]

三、利用逻辑知识

语篇是一些意义相关的句子被合乎逻辑地组织起来的语义整体。语篇衔接与连贯中的逻辑纽带能表示出作者的思路和背后的意义重心,由此非常重要。逻辑纽带主要是由表示时间与空间关系、列举与例证、比较与对比、引申与递进、让步与转折、推论与归纳、原因与结果等逻辑概念的过渡词组成的。这类词通常是一些连词和连接性副词,或者是一些介词词组、非限定分句、无动词分句等。做完型填空时,考生需正确理解并判断文章的内在逻辑关系,选用正确的过渡词。如:

【例17】Other animals, it is true, communicate with one another by (means) of cries: for example, many birds utter (warning) calls at the approach of danger; monkeys utter (different) cries, such as expressions of anger, fear and pleasure. __67__ these various means of communication differ in important ways (from) human language. [2003.1/T67]

A) But   B) Therefore   C) Afterwards   D) Furthermore

【解析】上文提到动物们以各种叫声作为交流方式,而空白处所在句指出这些方式与人类的语言有重要区别,因此可判断前后句之间为转折关系。[答案:A]

第二节 考点突破专项扫雷训练

Passage One

Now there is much more CO_2 in the atmosphere. Increasing CO_2 and other __1__ into the atmosphere are trapping more heat. The __2__ temperature will have effects on the environment and agriculture. Rising CO_2 __3__ cause increased production of some crops. Scientists have developed computer programs to show how these changes will __4__ the food supply. However, studies suggest some computer estimates __5__ be wrong.

Scientists with the Agriculture Research Service say that another gas Ozone should be __6__ in the programs. Ozone in the __7__ atmosphere has been shown to damage the plant tissue and __8__ crop production. Early studies to measure the effects of CO_2 and Ozone on crops have __9__ each gas separately. These scientists have been __10__ the two gases in tests on some crops. Their results suggest __11__ crop production in increased CO_2 __12__ may not be as high as suggested. They say the extra CO_2 may in fact __13__ crop losses caused by Ozone. But they found that rising CO_2 levels combined __14__ low Ozone levels do not always cause increased plant growth. Extra CO_2 causes some __15__ growth because the plants have more food for photosynthesis—the natural process that plants use to change __16__ into energy. The researchers observed this when the two gases were combined in __17__ tests of some crops. They also found the extra CO_2 partly closes small __18__ on leaves through which the plant exchanges gases. This reduces the __19__ of Ozone entering the water vapor released by leaves. __20__, CO_2 helps plants growing where there is too much Ozone or not enough water.

1. A) matters   B) particles   C) substances   D) gases
2. A) rising   B) falling   C) increasing   D) decreasing
3. A) number   B) amount   C) levels   D) quantity
4. A) effect   B) affect   C) infect   D) reflect
5. A) may   B) should   C) would   D) will
6. A) involved   B) contained   C) included   D) comprised
7. A) low   B) lower   C) downward   D) beneath
8. A) increase   B) raise   C) relieve   D) decrease
9. A) examined   B) inspected   C) evaluated   D) investigated
10. A) attaching   B) combining   C) connecting   D) binding
11. A) which   B) that   C) as   D) what
12. A) occasions   B) circumstances   C) surroundings   D) environments
13. A) prevent   B) allow   C) increase   D) prohibit
14. A) to   B) by   C) into   D) with
15. A) greater   B) added   C) larger   D) extra
16. A) lightning   B) sunshine   C) sunlight   D) light
17. A) field   B) scene   C) land   D) spot
18. A) blanks   B) spaces   C) cracks   D) openings
19. A) amount   B) number   C) sum   D) percentage
20. A) Therefore   B) However   C) Likewise   D) And

Passage Two

The Internet has become a commonplace for us. While __1__ the Internet, we should not __2__ the alarm bells sounding in our ears, reminding us of keeping __3__ for on-line crimes. Last year, the Melissa and Explore Zip virus caused chaos __4__ the Internet. Last week the "I love you" bug played havoc __5__ the world. What will be the next? No one knows.

Many on-line crimes are not so different to __6__ seen in the real world, the spreading of fake data, cheating and blackmail, __7__ property rights infringements and privacy violations. But computer hackers also create new forms of crime __8__ the Internet changes the world into a "global village".

With the __9__ of e-business, on-line crimes could not only cause great damage to __10__, but could also threaten the __11__ of national political, economic and cultural orders. The __12__ legal system in most countries __13__ weak when dealing with on-line crimes, __14__ to the sophisticated technology involved. For this reason, many countries are considering __15__ Internet laws to curb on-line crimes.

In China, __16__ there are millions of Internet surfers, it is more important to formulate new laws and rules on network security than to __17__ the existing ones. When drafting and __18__ new laws, China should also __19__ the relations between protecting network security __20__ the sound development of Internet.

1. A) surfing   B) operating   C) reaching   D) exploring
2. A) neglect   B) overlook   C) omit   D) ignore
3. A) guard   B) careful   C) alert   D) aware
4. A) in   B) on   C) inside   D) with
5. A) over   B) on   C) across   D) through

6. A) which	B) that	C) them	D) those
7. A) intellectual	B) intelligence	C) knowledge	D) cultural
8. A) until	B) before	C) as	D) after
9. A) blossom	B) gloom	C) blooming	D) booming
10. A) persons	B) individuals	C) country	D) society
11. A) equality	B) peace	C) security	D) safety
12. A) current	B) today's	C) nowadays	D) contemporary
13. A) proving	B) proves	C) prove	D) proven
14. A) owe	B) as	C) thanks	D) due
15. A) shaping	B) founding	C) formulating	D) setting
16. A) that	B) which	C) where	D) when
17. A) date	B) accelerate	C) upgrade	D) update
18. A) implying	B) implementing	C) importing	D) imposing
19. A) manage	B) establish	C) process	D) arrange
20. A) with	B) or	C) and	D) besides

Passage Three

A new Berlin Wall divides cultures of consumerism and poverty. Each time __1__ I am in an African village, I dream about __2__ to a city. The African countryside is not only a land of starvation. It is __3__ the worst nightmare of sleeping on a clay floor, of bedbugs and other __4__, of relentless shortages of water, but __5__ all, of darkness. In this part of the world the sun sets very early at 6 p.m. From that moment __6__ 6 a.m., one has to live in total darkness. A Chinese flashlight __7__ one dollar, but in the village in Senegal, __8__ I stayed recently, nobody had a dollar to buy one.

Societies of our planet live in two __9__ cultures: the culture of consumerism—of luxuries and abundance—and the culture of poverty, shortages, empty stomachs, and __10__ of opportunities. The border between those two cultures is marked __11__ tension and hostility. This is the most dramatic border __12__ our planet today.

If we accept the fact __13__ all people around the world, __14__ geography, history and culture, deserve lives of dignity, then we have a moral obligation to change the mentality of the people brought __15__ the culture of poverty. New ideas about how to __16__ more independence and new visions of development __17__ to be born within this culture. __18__ this the people need a new generation of intellectuals and politicians, similar __19__ those who granted them __20__ independence.

1. A) /	B) that	C) as	D) when
2. A) aiming	B) reaching	C) getting	D) arriving
3. A) even	B) also	C) still	D) nevertheless
4. A) animals	B) reptiles	C) mammals	D) parasites
5. A) above	B) for	C) in	D) after
6. A) by	B) at	C) on	D) until
7. A) spends	B) takes	C) sells	D) costs
8. A) where	B) which	C) that	D) as
9. A) contrary	B) contrasting	C) comparative	D) different
10. A) rarity	B) short	C) lack	D) none
11. A) in	B) with	C) for	D) by
12. A) dividing	B) divided	C) separating	D) separated
13. A) which	B) that	C) as	D) if
14. A) beside	B) regardless	C) except	D) despite
15. A) with	B) into	C) up	D) about
16. A) acquire	B) earn	C) secure	D) gain

17. A) has	B) is	C) have	D) are
18. A) In	B) To	C) For	D) As
19. A) to	B) with	C) like	D) as
20. A) political	B) economic	C) cultural	D) intellectual

第三节 答案解析

Passage One

1. [D]词义辨析题。matter"事情,问题;物质,物品";particle"微粒,粒子,颗粒";substance"物质;实质";gas"气体;煤气;汽油;毒气"。根据词汇同现技巧,上文出现 CO_2,这里应是其他气体,利用同现的下义词推测出上义词。

2. [A]词义辨析题。上文说到二氧化碳增加导致空气中热量增加,因此此处应为气温的升高,但强干扰项 increasing 一般不与 temperature 同现,因此选 rising。

3. [C]词义辨析题。本题四个选项都有"数量"之意,但 level 经测量所得数量、数值,更符合上下文语境,而且下文 14 题所在句出现了 CO_2 levels,根据原词复现技巧可判断答案为 C。

4. [B]形似词辨析题。effect"实现,使生效,引起";affect"影响";infect"传染,感染";reflect"反映;反射;深思,考虑"。

5. [A]语法题。此句中 suggest 表示"表明,显示",宾语从句不需用虚拟式,不选 B、C;根据句意选择情态动词 may。

6. [C]词义辨析题。四个选项均有"包含,包括"之意,但 involve 侧重指作为一个必需的部分包含起来,一般可理解成"需要"。contain 侧重指某物被容纳在比其更大的东西之内;include 侧重指作为整体的一部分或要素被包含;comprise 侧重指由某些部分或成员构成。

7. [B]词义辨析题。根据上下文,此处应为"低层大气"之意,但强干扰项 low 意为"低的,矮的",而 lower 意为"较低的,低等的;下面的,下游的",更符合文意。

8. [D]词义理解题。根据上文所说"低层大气中臭氧会破坏植物组织",因此此处意思应是"减少作物产量",排除 A、B,而 relieve 指减轻压力或负担等,因此此选 decrease。

9. [A]词义理解题。examine"检查,调查,仔细观察;考查";inspect"视察,检查";evaluate"评估,评价";investigate"调查,调查研究"。本句句意指科学家以前是分别地研究观察二氧化碳及臭氧对农作物的影响,examine 符合句意。

10. [B]词义理解题。attach"系,贴,连接;使依恋,使喜爱;认为有重要性、责任等;使附属";combine"结合,联合,化合";connect"连接,连结;联系,结合;给……接通电话";bind"捆绑,捆扎;使结合,使黏合;约束"。强干扰项 connect 表示不紧密的联系或结合,各事物保留原先特点和相对独立性。combine 强调使事物合而为一交融为一体,而下文指出两种气体是交相作用影响作物产量,因此科学家在测试中应 combine the two gases。

11. [B]语法题。该句为宾语从句且所缺词在从句中不作任何成分,选 that。

12. [D]近义词辨析。occasion"时刻,场合;重大活动;时机,机会;起因,理由";circumstance"条件,经济状况";surrounding"周围的事物,环境";environment"环境,周围状况,自然环境"。

13. [A]需根据上下文逻辑选择词汇。下文提到,"但是他们发现二氧化碳多而臭氧少的环境中作物产量不一定总是很高"。but 表明两句形成对比关系,因此该句补全后意思应是二氧化碳含量增多可能会避免臭氧所导致的庄稼歉收。

14. [D]短语搭配题。combine... with...为固定搭配。

15. [B]词义理解题。强干扰项 extra 侧重指"额外的,外加的,特别的",而上下文要求这里意义应是作物的"增长"。

16. [C]词义理解题。lightning"闪电";sunshine"日出";sunlight"日光,阳光";light"光,光线",该词表示"阳光"时用短语 the light of the sun。下文出现光合作用,根据常识,光合作用中需要阳光,所以这里同现的词应是 sunlight。

17. [A]词义理解题。根据上下文这里需表达"实地测试"之意,而只有 field 一词有"实地,野外"之意。

18. [D]词义理解题。blank"空白处";space"空地,场地;空间";crack"裂缝,缝隙";opening"洞,孔,口子"。

19. [A]词义理解加语法题。Ozone 为不可数名词,因此选 amount"数量,总额"。number 意为"数目,数量;数字";sum 意为"总和,总数";percentage 意为"百分比",均不符合文意。

20. [A]考查逻辑关系。根据文意两句间的逻辑关系为因果关系,选 A。

Passage Two

1. [A]考查动词与名词搭配。surf the Internet 表示"上网"。

2. [D]近义词辨析。neglect"忽视,忽略;疏忽,玩忽",多指有意或无意地对所做工作、应负责任未给予充分注意,常强调"忘了做"这一结果;overlook"忽视,忽略,未注意到",多指由于仓促或注意不够导致工作中出现"疏漏"这一结果,不强调态度;omit"省略,删节;遗漏,疏忽";ignore"不顾,不理,忽视",强调有意地置之不理。本句是说我们不该置已经在耳畔一再响起的警钟而不顾,强调态度。

3. [C]短语搭配。be alert for"对……保持警觉",由其他选项构成的短语是 be on guard against"警惕,提防";be careful"小心,谨慎";be aware of"意识到"。

4. [B]与 Internet 搭配的介词为 on。

5. [C]表示"在世界范围内",用介词 across。可根据介词含义选择。

6. [D]语法题。该句不是复杂句,所以不选关系代词 which;宾格代词 them 不能跟修饰语;又根据上下文,空缺词代替的是 crimes,应选指示代词的复数形式 those。

7. [A]按照习惯用法,"知识产权"的英译为 intellectual property rights。

8. [C]逻辑推理题。本句是说随着计算机将世界变为"地球村",黑客们也在发明新的网上犯罪形式,选连词 as。

9. [D]形似词辨析题。blossom"花";gloom"昏暗;忧郁";blooming"开花的";booming"激增,繁荣,迅速发展"。

10. [B]根据上下文语境及词语复现技巧解题。该句与下一分句形成对比,下文说的是网上犯罪危及"国家的政治、经济、文化秩序",因此这里是指对"个人"的危害。

11. [C]词义理解题。equality"平等,相等";peace"和平";security"安全,保障",侧重因受到保护或看护而感到安全,符合文意;safety"安全,保险",强调无危险或损害的状态。

12. [A]today's 为物主格,前面不能有介词;nowadays 为副词,不作定语;contemporary 意为"当代的,同时代的",不符文意;选 current"现时的,当前的"。

13. [B]语法题。分析句子语法结构,从句缺谓语,且根据其主语 fact 可知谓语动词应为 proves。

14. [D]短语搭配题。A 形式不正确;B 引出的是原因状语从句;强干扰项 C 所构成的短语一般跟好的原因,侧重"多亏"之意。

15. [C]词义理解题。本题可根据词汇同现技巧解题,下文很快出现短语 formulate new laws and rules。

16. [C]语法题。分析句子,空白处代替地点名词且在从句中作状语,选 where。

17. [D]词义理解题。date"给……注明日期;确定……的年代;与……约会";accelerate"加快,使增速";upgrade"提升,使升级";update"更新,使现代化"。

18. [B]形似词辨析。imply"暗示";implement"使生效,履行";import"进口,输入";impose"把……强加于;征税等"。与法律同现的词应为 B。

19. [A]词义辨析题。manage"管理,经营;设法对付";establish"建立",但放到本句中意思不通;process"加工;处理";arrange"安排,准备;整理"。

20. [C]考查介词短语搭配。between... and...是固定搭配,表示"在……和……之间"。

Passage Three

1. [A]短语搭配题。名词短语 every time 或 each time 可引出时间状语从句,不需接其他连接词或关系词。

2. [C]短语搭配题。A 不符合句意,B、D 不与介词 to 构成搭配。

3. [B]语法结构题。可根据结构同现原则解题,该句上文出现 not only 下文应该出现意义上表示递进添加的 also。强干扰项 even 只表示递进,无添加之意。

4. [D]词义理解题。可根据上、下文词复现技巧解题。上文出现下义词 bed-bugs,所缺应为与之对应的近义词 parasites"虱蚤等寄生虫"。其他选项 animal"动物",reptile"爬行动物",mammal"哺乳动物"均不妥。

5. [A]固定短语 above all"首先,尤其是";for all"尽管,虽然";in all"总共,合计";after all"毕竟,终究,究竟"。根据句意所列最后一项是尤其糟糕的事,选 A。

6. [D]短语搭配题。只有 from... until...能表达句意"从……直到……"。本题可利用介词的含义来判断选择。

7. [D]词义辨析。可利用动词本身的用法特点判断。spend 的动作发出者一般为人;take 一般需形式主语,构成句式 It takes/took sb. to do sth.;sell 意义上不符文意;cost 的主语一般为物,意义和用法上都符合要求。

8. [A]语法题。分析句子,所缺词应引出非限定性定语从句,其先行词为地点名词,在从句中作地点状语,选 A。

9. [B]词义辨析题。contrary 为名词,不能作定语;comparative 意义上不符合要求;强干扰项 different 只表示"不同的",但下文所述两种文化一富一穷,一奢华一贫瘠,contrasting"对比鲜明的,形成强烈反差的"更为恰当。

10. [C]短语搭配题。rarity 与 of 不构成搭配;short 为形容词,短语 be short of 表示"缺乏";lack of 为名词短语,表示"缺乏";none of 一般构成代词性质的短语表示"没有人或物"。根据上下文语境,能构成名词短语且意义为"缺乏"的,只有 C 符合。

11. [B]短语搭配题。固定短语 be marked with 表示"以……为明显特征"。

12. [A]词义辨析加语法题。语法结构要求此处使用现在分词;separate, divide 都有"使分开"之义,但 separate 强调把原来在一起或靠近的人或事物分开,而 divide 侧重指把整体分成若干个独立的个体。显然地球应是个整体,贫富界限使它被分割为两个个体,故选 dividing。

13. [B]语法题。根据句意可判断该处考查同位语从句,只有 B 对,强干扰项 A 引出的是定语从句。

14. [D]短语搭配题。B 不能直接与名词构成短语,需加介词 of 表示"无论";A、C 与名词所构成短语不符合文意要求;D 为介词,与文中名词构成短语,表示"无论其地理位置、历史渊源、文化状况如何",为答案。

15. [B]短语搭配题。固定搭配 bring... into...表示"将……带入某种状态"。

16. [D]词义辨析题。acquire 强调所得物量的积累,后一般接表示"才智、经验、能力、荣誉、财富等"的词;earn 表示"赚取钱财,赢得名望";secure 后一般接具体事物,含有"通过竞争、努力等好不容易才弄到手"之义;gain 指通过相当的努力或拼搏,往往是通过劳动、斗争、竞争,得到利益或有价值的东西。所缺动词后出现的宾语为 independence,D 合适。

17. [C]固定搭配 be to do sth.表将来时,有"按计划将做某事"之义,而 have to do sth.表示"不得不,必须"之义,意义上后者更符合文意。语法上,主谓一致要求选 C。

18. [C]考查介词短语搭配。上下文语境要求这里应选一表示目的的介词。

19. [A]短语搭配题。be similar to 为固定搭配,表示"与……类似"。

20. [A]本题须在理解全文的基础上结合背景知识解答。本文描述的是其经济上、文化上的贫瘠落后与不独立,不选 B、C、D。我们都知道非洲各国已实现的是政治上的独立,因此选 A。

第二章
550分完型难点突破

第一节 灵机一动猜答案

由于完型填空出现于客观题的最后一部分，在考试过程中，考生可能会因时间分配不当，导致完型填空的答题时间仓促，因此急中生智猜测答案的技巧在解答完型填空时显得尤为重要。考生可从以下几方面着重锻炼自己猜测答案的能力。

(1)根据上下文已知信息逐一排除干扰项。

【例1】At meal times it is a good (idea) to give a child a small portion and let him (come) back for a second helping rather than give him as ___74___ as he is likely to eat all at once. [1997.6]

    A) much   B) little   C) few   D) many

【解析】上文已出现"一次给小孩一点食物"之义，此处表示相反意见，因此可排除表示"少量的"B、C，而空白处指代的应是所吃食物的量。[答案:A]

(2)完型填空是一篇文章，其同一性必然非常突出，也就是说其遣词造句都是指向同一话题、说明同一主题的，而这一目的可以通过词汇的同现与复现技巧达到。因此做题时快速抓住文章主旨，抓住关键词，尽快理出与这些关键词有关的同现、复现关系，然后可以利用这些关系快速有效地猜出答案。

【例2】Unlike marriage or the ties that bind parents and children, it is not defined or regulated by ___82___. [2001.6]

    A) rule   B) discipline   C) law   D) regulation

【解析】根据上下文与背景知识，与婚姻、父母与子女关系有关的，同属一个语境的同现词应为"法律"，而不是"规则"、"纪律"或"规章、规则"。[答案:C]

> 完型填空所选文章中原词复现现象较为明显，一般来说，选项中含有上下文已出现的词汇一般就是答案。

【例3】Before you buy an expensive ___78___, or a service, do check the price and (what) is on offer. If possible, choose (from) three items or three estimates. [2005.1]

    A) component   B) element   C) item   D) particle

【解析】item有"产品"的意思，符合上下文，且后一句有该词的复现。[答案:C]

> 同根词复现在完型填空中表现得也非常明显，考生可利用同根词复现猜测答案。

【例4】Many teachers believe that the responsibilities for learning lie with the students. If a long reading assignment is given, the instructors expect students to be familiar with the (information) in the reading... When research is ___78___, the professor expects the student to take it actively and to complete it with (minimum) guidance. [1993.6]

A) collected   B) assigned   C) distributed   D) finished

[解析]本题中 If 与 When 引出的从句意义上对等。前一句中出现 reading assignment(阅读任务),相应地,后一句中研究任务也应是"被布置",所以空缺词为 assignment 的同根词 assign。[答案:B]

(3)完型填空所选文章也必然有突出的连贯性。连贯性一般由表示逻辑关系的过渡词来担当,考生有时可以不用深究某段文字暗含的意义、逻辑,而只根据自己对过渡词的了解大胆猜测出答案。

[例5]This is why the number of (signals) that an animal can make is very limited: the great tit is a case (in) point; it has about twenty different calls, (whereas) in human language the number of possible utterances is ___79___ .

[2003.1]

A) boundless   B) changeable   C) limitless   D) ceaseless

[解析]该题由 whereas 担任过渡词,连接的是两个意义上形成对比的分句,前一分句出现关键词 limited,因此可猜出后一分句的空缺词为 limitless。[答案:C]

第二节 历年典型真题突破训练

Passage One   07 年 12 月

One factor that can influence consumers is their mood state. Mood may be defined ___67___ a temporary and mild positive or negative feeling that is generalized and not tied ___68___ any particular circumstance. Moods should be ___69___ from emotions which are usually more intense, ___70___ to specific circumstances, and often conscious. ___71___ one sense, the effect of a consumer's mood can be thought of in ___72___ the same way as can our reactions to the ___73___ of our friends—when our friends are happy and "up", that tends to influence us positively, ___74___ when they are "down", that can have a ___75___ impact on us. Similarly, consumers operating under a ___76___ mood state tend to react to *stimuli* (刺激因素) in a direction ___77___ with that mood state. Thus, for example, we should expect to see ___78___ in a positive mood state evaluate products in more of a ___79___ manner than they would when not in such a state. ___80___ , mood states appear capable of ___81___ a consumer's memory.

Moods appear to be ___82___ influenced by marketing techniques. For example, the rhythm, pitch, and ___83___ of music has been shown to influence behavior such as the ___84___ of time spent in supermarkets or ___85___ to purchase products. In addition, advertising can influence consumers' moods which, in ___86___ , are capable of influencing consumers' reactions to products.

67. A) as   B) about   C) by   D) with
68. A) over   B) under   C) to   D) up
69. A) derived   B) descended   C) divided   D) distinguished
70. A) related   B) referred   C) attached   D) associated
71. A) On   B) Of   C) In   D) By
72. A) thus   B) much   C) even   D) still
73. A) signal   B) gesture   C) view   D) behavior
74. A) for   B) but   C) unless   D) provided
75. A) relative   B) decisive   C) negative   D) sensitive
76. A) given   B) granted   C) fixed   D) driven
77. A) resistant   B) persistent   C) insistent   D) consistent
78. A) consumers   B) businessmen   C) retailers   D) manufacturers
79. A) casual   B) critical   C) serious   D) favorable
80. A) However   B) Otherwise   C) Moreover   D) Nevertheless
81. A) lifting   B) enhancing   C) raising   D) cultivating
82. A) readily   B) rarely   C) cautiously   D) currently
83. A) step   B) speed   C) band   D) volume

84. A) extent   B) amount   C) scope   D) range
85. A) facilities   B) capacities   C) reflections   D) intentions
86. A) turn   B) total   C) detail   D) depth

Passage Two   07年6月

An earthquake hit Kashmir on Oct. 8, 2005. It took some 75,000 lives, __67__ 130,000 and left nearly 3.5 million without food, jobs or homes. __68__ overnight, scores of tent villages bloomed __69__ the region, tended by international aid organizations, military __70__ and aid groups working day and night to shelter the survivors before winter set __71__.

Mercifully, the season was mild. But with the __72__ of spring, the refugees will be moved again. Camps that __73__ health care, food and shelter for 150,000 survivors have begun to close as they were __74__ intended to be permanent.

For most of the refugees, the thought of going back brings __75__ emotions. The past six months have been difficult. Families of __76__ many as 10 people have had to shelter __77__ a single tent and share cookstoves and bathing __78__ with neighbors. "They are looking forward to the clean water of their rivers," officials say. "They are __79__ of free fresh fruit. They want to get back to their herds and start __80__ again." But most will be returning to __81__ but heaps of ruins. In many villages, electrical __82__ have not been repaired, nor have roads. Aid workers __83__ that it will take years to rebuild what the earthquake took __84__. And for the thousands of survivors, the __85__ will never be complete.

Yet the survivors have to start somewhere. New homes can be built __86__ the stones, bricks and beams of old ones. Spring is coming and it is a good time to start again.

67. A) damaged   B) destroyed   C) injured   D) ruined
68. A) Surely   B) Scarcely   C) Almost   D) Altogether
69. A) among   B) across   C) amid   D) above
70. A) personnel   B) equipment   C) installations   D) ranks
71. A) forth   B) out   C) on   D) in
72. A) arrival   B) falling   C) appearing   D) emergence
73. A) aided   B) provided   C) transferred   D) strengthened
74. A) yet   B) once   C) never   D) ever
75. A) mixed   B) contrasted   C) puzzled   D) doubled
76. A) like   B) too   C) so   D) as
77. A) below   B) by   C) under   D) with
78. A) implements   B) instruments   C) appliances   D) facilities
79. A) searching   B) dreaming   C) seeking   D) longing
80. A) farming   B) producing   C) cultivating   D) nourishing
81. A) anything   B) nothing   C) something   D) everything
82. A) currents   B) channels   C) lines   D) paths
83. A) estimate   B) evaluate   C) account   D) measure
84. A) out   B) up   C) aside   D) away
85. A) reservation   B) replacement   C) recovery   D) retreat
86. A) onto   B) from   C) upon   D) through

第三节 答案解析

Passage One 07年12月

67. [A]考查固定搭配的识别。该空后面的内容是mood的定义,因此应该选as,be defined as...意为"定义为……"。

68. [C]考查固定搭配的识别。动词tie与介词to属于固定搭配,表示"与……相关",故选C。如果与up搭配的话,此空后还需要介词with,构成be tied up with,也可以表示"和……有密切关系"。

69. [D]考查固定搭配的含义。句意为mood跟空后的那些emotions是不一样的,故选D,be distinguished from为固定搭配,意为"与……区分开"。derive from意为"得自,由……而来";descend from意为"从……下来";divide from指的是从群体中把个体"分出来",如:divide these patients from others表示"把这些病人同其他病人隔离开"。

70. [A]考查固定搭配的含义。根据上下文句子结构及语意,此处的词汇应该与第68题前面的tie同义,且与to搭配,be related to意为"与……相关",符合要求,故A正确。refer to意为"提及";attach to意为"附着,依附";associate与with搭配,表示"与……联系在一起"。

71. [C]考查固定搭配的识别。in a/one sense为固定搭配,表示"在某种意义上"。

72. [B]考查副词的使用。此处需要程度副词,修饰the same,much表示很大程度上,符合句意。其他各项不能直接修饰the same。

73. [D]考查语义概括。根据破折号后面的详细解释,此空的名词意义应该概括为"行为表现"(behavior),故选D。signal意为"信号";gesture意为"姿态,手势";view意为"观点"。

74. [B]考查分句之间的逻辑关系。根据此空前后的up和down的对比,应该选转折词but。

75. [C]考查语义逻辑。同样,由于转折之前用了positively,因此之后需要选反义词negative,即C。

76. [A]考查近义词及特殊词义。given有"特定的"之意,符合句意要求;granted意为"授予的";fixed意为"固定的",貌似given的近义词;driven意为"受到驱策的"。

77. [D]考查形似词辨异。be consistent with意为"与……一致",符合句意要求;resistant意为"抵抗的";persistent意为"坚持不懈的";insistent意为"坚持的,紧急的"。

78. [A]考查上下文语义逻辑。根据下文(尤其是第81题之后的原词consumer),本句的主要对象也应该是consumers,他们往往发出evaluate products这样的动作。另外,B"生意人"和C"零售商"、D"制造商"有上下义的关系,一般不作为答案。

79. [D]考查上下文语义逻辑。根据第78题之后的positive,此处应该使用褒义词,只有D"赞成的"符合要求。

80. [C]考查上下文语义逻辑。此句与前文是递进关系,而非转折关系,只有C符合。其他三个选项均为转折对比关系。

81. [B]考查近义词辨析。此空所需动词要以memory作为宾语,表示"提高,增强",应选enhancing。lift和raise都不能以memory作宾语。

82. [A]考查副词含义。readily意为"容易地",修饰be influenced,表示"容易受影响",符合句意。rarely"很少地",cautiously"谨慎地",currently"目前",均不贴切。

83. [D]考查同一范畴名词识别。此处的名词应该与前面的"节奏、音调"语义并列,修饰music,故选volume"音量"。

84. [B]考查名词间的搭配。修饰不可数名词time用amount。

85. [D]考查名词含义及搭配。此处的词应该可以与不定式搭配,表示目的,选项D"意图、目的"符合句意。facilities意为"设备";capacities意为"能力,容量";reflections意为"反射;沉思"。

86. [A]考查固定搭配的含义。in turn意为"反过来",符合句意;in total意为"整个地";in detail意为"详尽地";in depth意为"深入地"。

Passage Two 07年6月

67. [C]考查动词含义。injure"伤害,使受伤",符合句意;其余三个词都表示"毁坏,破坏"。

68. [C]考查副词含义。almost"几乎",可以修饰时间,符合句意;surely"肯定";scarcely"几乎不";altogether"总共"。

69. [B]考查介词含义。across the region表示"在整个地区",表明范围之广。本句意为"几乎一夜之间,许许多多的帐篷村落出现在整个地区。"

70. [A]考查名词含义。military personnel 意为"军事/军队人员",在句中与 international aid organizations 和 aid groups 并列,充当 tend"照顾"与 working 这两个动作的发出者,所以本题只能选有生命的人,而不能选 equipment"设备"或 installations"装置,设施,器械"或 ranks"军衔"。

71. [D]考查短语搭配的含义。set in"(季节、时令)到来,开始",符合句意;set forth"宣布;发表";set out"出发,动身";set on"前进;迎击"。

72. [A]考查名词含义。前面提到冬天开始了,接着本句的意思便是"随着春天的到来",所以答案选 arrival,而不是 falling"降落"或 emergence/appearing"出现"。

73. [B]考查动词含义。provide"提供",符合句意;aid"帮助";transfer"转移";strengthen"加强"。

74. [C]根据 close 和 permanent 的相反语义,这里需要一个表示否定意思的副词,所以答案选 C。

75. [A]考查形容词含义。根据句意"对于大多数难民来说,一想到回家他们的内心就充满了复杂的情感",复杂的情感即各种情感交织在一起,所以答案选 A。

76. [D]本题答案很直接,很容易选择,as many as 10 people"多达 10 个人"。

77. [C]考查动词与介词的搭配。shelter under sth.表示"在……下寻求庇护"。

78. [D]考查近义名词辨析。bathing facilities"洗澡设施",符合句意;implements"工具",如 farm implements"农具";instruments"仪器";appliances"电动工具,设备"。

79. [B]考查动词与介词的搭配。dream of"梦想",符合句意;search, seek, long 都是与介词 for 搭配。

80. [A]考查动词含义。前后文的 village 说明本句应为"他们想回到他们的牛群那里去,重新开始务农",所以答案选 A。其余三个词均为及物动词,且意思也与原文不符。cultivate"培养;种植";nourish"滋养,为……提供营养"。

81. [B]根据句意"但是大多数人回去的地方只不过是一片废墟而已",答案选 B。nothing but 相当于 only,anything but 真为"并不是",something 与 everything 不可与 but 构成搭配。

82. [C]考查名词含义。electrical lines"电线",符合句意;current"水流;电流;气流",不能被 repaired;channel"沟渠;海峡;频道";path"小径"。

83. [A]考查动词含义。estimate"估计",符合句意;evaluate"评估;估价";account"视作,认为";measure"测量"。

84. [D]考查短语搭配的含义。take away"带走,拿走",符合句意;take out"拿出";take up"占据;从事"。

85. [C]考查名词含义。recovery"恢复",符合句意;reservation"保留;预定";replacement"代替";retreat"撤退"。

86. [B]考查动词短语搭配。be made/built from...."由……制/建成",符合句意。build upon 是"建立在……的基础上"。

第三章
610分完型突击训练

第一节 突击训练

Passage One

Psychologically there are two dangers to be guarded against in old age. One of these is *undue* (过分的) __1__ in the past. It does not do to live in memories, in regrets for the good old days, __2__ in sadness about friends who are dead. One's thoughts must be directed to the future, and to things __3__ which there is something to be done. This is not always easy; __4__ own past is a gradually increasing weight. __5__ is easy to think to oneself that one's emotions used to be more vivid than they __6__, and one's mind keener.

The __7__ thing to be avoided is clinging to youth in the __8__ of sucking vigor from its vitality. When your children are __9__ up they want to live their own lives, and if you continue to be __10__ interested in them as you were when they were young, you are __11__ to become a burden to them, __12__ they are unusually *callous* (麻木不仁). I do not mean that one should be __13__ interest in them, but one's interest should be *contemplative* (沉思的) __14__, if possible, *philanthropic* (慈善的), but not unduly emotional.

I think that a successful old age is easiest for those who have strong __15__ interests involving __16__ activities. It is in this sphere that long experience is really __17__, and it is in this sphere __18__ the wisdom born of experience can be exercised without being oppressive. It is no __19__ telling grown-up children not to make mistakes, __20__ because they will not believe you, and because mistakes are an essential part of education.

1. A) memorial   B) absorption   C) sentiment   D) assumption
2. A) yet   B) but   C) or   D) and
3. A) about   B) in   C) on   D) of
4. A) whose   B) their   C) his   D) one's
5. A) One   B) Which   C) It   D) That
6. A) do   B) are   C) will   D) were
7. A) other   B) next   C) another   D) following
8. A) expectation   B) hope   C) desire   D) aim
9. A) brought   B) raised   C) grown   D) come
10. A) such   B) as   C) much   D) very
11. A) likely   B) possible   C) probable   D) ready
12. A) when   B) whether   C) if   D) unless
13. A) except   B) without   C) no   D) not
14. A) however   B) thus   C) and   D) instead

15. A) impossible   B) impersonal   C) impressive   D) impatient
16. A) appropriate   B) proper   C) correct   D) proportional
17. A) fertile   B) complete   C) efficient   D) fruitful
18. A) who   B) which   C) that   D) when
19. A) wonder   B) use   C) denial   D) doubt
20. A) between   B) either   C) both   D) neither

Passage Two

A subject which seems to have been insufficiently studied by doctors and psychologists is the influence of geography and climate on the psychological and physical health of mankind. There seems no doubt __1__ the general character of the landscape, the relative __2__ of day and night, and the climate must __3__ play a big part in determining what kind of people we __4__.

It is true that a few studies have been made. __5__ all the inhabitants of a particular area enjoy exceptionally good or bad health, scientists have __6__ contributory factors such as the presence or __7__ of substances like iodine, fluoride, calcium, or iron in the water supply, or perhaps types of land that provide breeding places __8__ pests like mosquitoes or rats.

__9__, we can all generalize about types of people we have met. Those __10__ in countries with long dark winters are __11__ to be less talkative and less *vivacious* (活泼的) than inhabitants of countries where the __12__ is more *equable* (稳定的). And __13__ the olive and the orange grow, the inhabitants are cheerful, talkative, and spontaneous.

But these __14__ generalizations are inadequate: the __15__ of climate and geography should be studied in __16__. Do all mountain dwellers live to a ripe old age? Does the drinking of wine, __17__ than beer, result in a sunny and open temperament? Is the strength and height of one of the Kenyan tribes due to their __18__ drinking of the blood of cows?

We are not yet sure __19__ the answers to such questions, but let us hope that something of benefit to mankind may eventually result __20__ such studies.

1. A) if   B) whether   C) which   D) that
2. A) time   B) length   C) span   D) extension
3. A) neither   B) both   C) none   D) all
4. A) are   B) belong   C) fall   D) like
5. A) When   B) That   C) Where   D) Whereas
6. A) acknowledged   B) identified   C) recognized   D) distinguished
7. A) absence   B) disappearance   C) occurrence   D) existence
8. A) by   B) to   C) for   D) with
9. A) Therefore   B) Similarly   C) Conversely   D) Moreover
10. A) live   B) living   C) stay   D) staying
11. A) due   B) apt   C) able   D) ready
12. A) weather   B) climate   C) geography   D) situation
13. A) where   B) here   C) that   D) thus
14. A) ordinary   B) average   C) commonplace   D) conventional
15. A) effectiveness B) affection   C) efficiency   D) influence
16. A) depth   B) width   C) distance   D) scope
17. A) other   B) rather   C) more   D) less
18. A) consistent   B) permanent   C) always   D) habitual
19. A) to   B) of   C) with   D) in
20. A) as   B) from   C) in   D) by

Passage Three

Most episodes of absent-mindedness—forgetting where you left something or wondering why you just entered a room—are caused by a simple lack of attention, says Schacter. "You're __1__ to remember something, but you haven't encoded it deeply."

Encoding, Schacter explains, is a special way of paying attention to a (n) __2__ that has a major impact on recalling it later. __3__ to encode properly can create annoying situations. __4__ you put your mobile phone in a pocket, for example, and don't pay attention to what you did because you're involved __5__ a conversation, you'll probably forget that the phone is in the jacket now __6__ in your wardrobe. "Your memory itself isn't failing you," says Schacter. "__7__, you didn't give your memory system the information it needed."

Lack of interest can __8__ lead to absent-mindedness. "A man who can recite sports statistics __9__ 30 years ago," says Zelinski, "may not __10__ to drop a letter in the mailbox." Women have slightly better memories than men, __11__ because they pay more attention to their environment, and memory relies on just __12__.

Visual cues can help __13__ absent-mindedness, says Schacter. "But be sure the cue is clear and __14__," he cautions. If you want to remember to __15__ a medication with lunch, put the pill bottle on the kitchen table—__16__ leave it in the medicine chest and write yourself a note that you keep in pocket.

Another common __17__ of absent-mindedness: walking into a room and wondering __18__ you're there. Most likely, you were thinking about __19__ else. "Everyone does this from time to time," says Zelinski. The best thing to do is to __20__ to where you were before entering the room, and you'll likely remember.

1. A) proposed   B) exposed   C) supposed   D) imposed
2. A) case   B) event   C) matter   D) affair
3. A) Failure   B) Success   C) Ability   D) Unable
4. A) Where   B) If   C) Once   D) As
5. A) with   B) by   C) in   D) of
6. A) hangs   B) hanging   C) hung   D) hanged
7. A) Otherwise   B) Furthermore   C) Henceforth   D) Rather
8. A) never   B) even   C) thus   D) also
9. A) from   B) for   C) in   D) within
10. A) recall   B) remind   C) remember   D) reveal
11. A) possibly   B) likely   C) luckily   D) unfortunately
12. A) it   B) which   C) that   D) one
13. A) forbid   B) prevent   C) protect   D) produce
14. A) accessible   B) acceptable   C) available   D) agreeable
15. A) eat   B) take   C) swallow   D) use
16. A) not   B) seldom   C) no   D) don't
17. A) happening   B) episode   C) chapter   D) melody
18. A) when   B) what   C) why   D) whether
19. A) things   B) nothing   C) anything   D) something
20. A) come   B) go   C) arrive   D) return

第二节 答案解析

Passage One

1. [B]词义理解题。memorial "纪念碑,纪念堂,纪念仪式"; absorption "专心致志,热衷"; sentiment "意见,观点;感情,情绪"; assumption "假定,臆断"。根据下文所述判断,此处所说第一条危险是老人过度沉湎于对过去的回忆。

2. [C]逻辑关联题。此处所说三种对过去过于沉湎的现象之间是或此或彼的关系,所以选 or。

3. [A]短语搭配题。关系代词 which 之前的介词与从句中谓语动词构成搭配 do sth. about sth.“对……采取些措施,决定”。

4. [D]语法题。此处为一独立分句,但不是定语从句,不能选 whose。该句句意是“人们的过去将随着时间的推移愈加显示其分量”。只有不定代词 one 能泛指人们。

5. [C]语法题。分析句子,此处 that 引出的从句是真正的主语,空缺词是形式主语,由 it 来担任。

6. [B]语法题。这里是让特过去和现在进行对比,前面出现 used to be,此处则出现与其对应的现在时态的助动词 are。

7. [A]语法题。利用词汇的结构同现技巧以及上下文语境推断,上一段出现 one of these (two dangers),此处必然是 the other。

8. [B]短语搭配题。固定短语 in the hope of 或 in the hope that 表示“希望”,后引出希望实现的内容。

9. [C]短语搭配题。此处提到的是“长大成人的孩子”,grow up“长大,成人”符合题意;bring up“教育,培养;提出”;raise 表“抚养,养育”时与 bring up 同义;come up“出现,发生;走上前来”。

10. [B]语法题。分析句意此处为同级比较状语从句,应由“as... as...”句型结构构成。

11. [A]词义理解加短语搭配题。短语 be likely to do sth.意为“有可能”,另外两个易混词 possible 和 probable 不用于由人作主语的系表结构中。

12. [D]逻辑关联题。此处文意是说老人在孩子成年以后就不应像以前那样关注他们,否则反而会成为孩子的负担,除非孩子对此毫不在乎。

13. [B]语法题。此处为系动词加介词短语构成系表结构,意为“我并不是说人们不应关注孩子”。由 C、D 构成的结构应是(one should) have no interest 和(one should) not have interest。

14. [C]逻辑关联题。此处 contemplative 和 philanthropic 是并列表语,由 and 连接,A、D 表示意义上对照,B 表示因果。

15. [B]形似词辨义题。impossible“不可能的,办不到的”;impersonal“客观的,非特指一个人的”;impressive“印象深刻的”;impatient“不耐烦的”。

16. [A]近义词辨析题。appropriate“适当的,恰当的”,强调某物非常适合某一特定的人、目标或事物;proper“适当的,恰当的;合乎传统的,正当的”,专指符合社会风俗、风尚、个人身份、场合要求;correct“正确的,对的”;proportional“比例的,成比例的”。

17. [D]词义理解题。fertile“肥沃的,富饶的;多产的”;complete“完成的,结束的”;efficient“效率高的,有能力的”;fruitful“有成效的,多产的”。

18. [C]语法题。此句为强调句型,所强调者不是人,所以用 that。

19. [B]短语搭配题。句式结构 It is no use doing sth.意为“做某事是徒劳无益的”。

20. [C]短语搭配题。根据句意此处应出现 both... and... 连接并列的两个原因。between... and... 指“在两者之间”,其他两项不能与 and 搭配。

Passage Two

1. [D]语法题。此处为 doubt“怀疑,疑惑”的同位语从句,用 that 引出。

2. [B]词义理解题。time“时间,时刻,时候”;length“长,长度,距离”;span“一段时间;跨距,跨度”;extension“伸出,伸展;延长部分,扩大部分”。此处意为“昼夜的相对长短”。

3. [D]词义理解题,考查代词用法。上文提到三种因素:地形特点、昼夜的相对长短和气候,因此选 all 代替它们。

4. [A]语法题。根据上下文推断,此从句为主系表结构,选 A。

5. [C]逻辑关联题。本句结构较复杂,主句是说科学家发现并确认出决定人们性格特征的一些因素,从句提到一些人们健康状况极好或极差的地区,按照逻辑,此处应填 where 表示发现地点。

6. [B]词义理解题。acknowledge“承认,承认……的权威”;identify“认出,鉴定;发现”,强调从众人或很多相似物中识别出特别的一个;recognize“认出,识别;承认,确认”,侧重指再次见面时认出某人或某物为以前曾相识的;distinguish“区分,辨别”。

7. [A]词义理解题。根据“or”判断,此处需要的是 presence 的反义词 absence。

8. [C]短语搭配题。表示“为 A 提供 B”的短语为 provide B for A。

9. [D]逻辑关联题。根据文意可以判断,空白词所在段与上一段都是科学家的发现,而后一段说,科学家对现象做了总结概括,因此逻辑上与前一段是递进关系,选 moreover。

10. [B]语法题加词义辨析题。分析句子结构,此处需要动名词与后面的内容一起作句子主语。根据句意应选 living"生活"。stay"逗留,暂住"与题意不符。

11. [B]短语搭配题。be due to sth."由于……";be apt to do sth."有做某事的倾向";be able to do sth."有能力做某事";be ready to do sth."愿意做某事"。

12. [B]词义理解题。上文提到的是有些受漫长冬季影响的地区人们的性格,而冬季漫长应是该地区的气候特征,因此此处选 climate。weather 表示短时的天气变化特征。

13. [A]语法结构题。此处需关联词引导地点状语从句,只有 where 符合。

14. [C]词义理解题。ordinary"通常的,普通的,平常的",侧重指没有特殊性或明显特征;average"通常的,普通的",侧重指正常的、缺乏新奇感的;commonplace"普通的,平庸的",强调原来期望的独特与实际情况下令人失望的平庸相差甚远;conventional"普通的,习惯的,常规的",强调符合常规。

15. [D]词义理解题。effectiveness"有效性,生效";affection"喜爱,感情";efficiency"效率";influence"影响"。

16. [A]短语搭配题。固定短语 in depth 意为"深入地"。

17. [B]短语搭配题。other than"除了";rather than"与其……倒不如……;不是……而是……";more than"多于";less than"少于"。

18. [D]词义理解题。consistent"坚持的,一致的";permanent"永久性的";always"总是,一直",为副词,不符合此处语法要求;habitual"惯常的;经常做的,习以为常的",侧重指习惯成自然的。

19. [B]固定搭配题。be sure of 为固定短语,意为"对……有把握"。

20. [B]固定搭配题。短语 result from 意为"由……而造成",后接表原因的成分,result in 为其反义短语,意为"导致",后接表结果的成分,不符合文意。

Passage Three

1. [C]形似词辨义题。propose"提议,建议";expose"暴露,显露;揭露,袒露";suppose"期望,认为应该",作此义解时,常用被动语态;impose"把……强加于"。此句意为"你本来是要记住某件事,但却未将其进行深入编码"。

2. [B]近义词辨析题。case"事例,实例;情况,事实;病例;案件";event"事件,大事;比赛项目";matter"事情,问题,情况",常用词,侧重指人们要处理的"事情",含义不太具体,但有"解决问题"之义;affair"事务;事情,事件",正式用词,可指重大或复杂的事务,多以复数形式出现,还可泛指要做或已发生的"整个事件",强调行为及其过程。

3. [A]推理题加词义理解题。空缺词在句中作主语,首先可排除形容词 Unable。根据该句的谓语成分"造成懊恼的局面",可知与 annoying 同表消极意义的词是 Failure,即答案。

4. [B]逻辑推理题。4、5、6 题所在句结构较复杂。上文提到未能正确进行编码会出现令人懊恼的情况,此句是在举例说明。主句用将来时,可以推测所举例并非发生过的事例,而是一种假设有可能发生的情况,所以此处填 if。

5. [C]短语搭配题。固定短语 be involved in 意为"参与,被卷入"。

6. [B]语法题。空缺词所在短语修饰名词 jacket,此处 hang 为不及物动词,应选择现在分词形式。此处句意是"你可能会忘记电话就放在你眼下正挂在衣柜里的夹克衫里"。注意 hung 是 hang"悬挂,吊"的过去式或过去分词;hanged 是 hang"吊死,绞死"的过去式或过去分词。

7. [D]逻辑关联题。分析上下文,此处要表达的观点是"你没有给自己的记忆系统输入它所要的信息",与上文意义上正好相反,选 rather"相反"。

8. [D]逻辑关联题。分析上下文,上文围绕心不在焉的最根本的原因"未能正确编码"展开,这一段提到"缺乏兴趣与关注",是作者所列举的第二条原因,逻辑上与前一段是添加关系。

9. [A]语法题。此处要表达的含义为"能背出 30 年前体育方面数据的人可能会忘记往邮箱里投寄一封信",根据介词含义及用法,选 from。

10. [C]词义理解题。recall"回忆起,回想起";remind"提醒";remember"记得,记住";reveal"揭露,泄露;揭示,透露"。

11. [A]词义理解题。此处是在解释原因,luckily 和 unfortunately 放在此处意义上不合适,而 likely 语法上一般作表语,不修饰原因状语从句,故选 possibly,表示可能性。

12. [C]语法题。空缺词代替的是 pay more attention to their environment,所以不选人称代词 it,而选指示代词 that。which 为关系代词,one 为不定代词,较易排除。

13. [B]词义理解题。forbid"禁止,不许";prevent"预防,防止";protect"保护";produce"使产生"。

14. [C]词义理解题。accessible"可接近的,有机会接近的";acceptable"可接受的";available"现成可使用的,在手边的";agreeable"令人愉快的,惬意的;同意的,乐意的"。

15. [B]短语搭配题。take a medication"吃药"。

16. [D]语法题。此句中主句包含两个并列分句,而第一个分句使用的是祈使语气,第二句也应是祈使语气,但意义上是否定的。

17. [B]词义理解题。happening"事情,事件",常以复数形式出现;episode"一个事件";chapter"章节";melody"旋律,曲调"。本题可根据词汇复现技巧中的原词复现来解题,文章一开始描述心不在焉的事件时所用的词就是 episode。

18. [C]逻辑关联题。此处句意为"另一个心不在焉的例子是,你走进房间,却不知道自己为什么到那儿",因此选 why。

19. [D]语法题。考查代词用法,B、C、D都能与 else 搭配,但只有 something else 符合文意。此处意为"正在想别的什么事"。

20. [D]词义理解加推理题。上文出现"走进房间却忘了来干什么",此处建议应为"回到走进房间之前的所在地"。

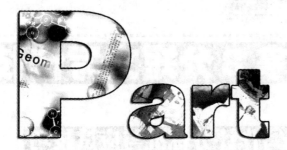

第七篇

短文写作

稳拿8分短文写作技巧

第一节 四级写作评分标准与应试技巧

英文写作自从 1987 年列入大学英语四级统考以来,一直是很多考生感到头疼的部分。大学英语四级考试大纲要求,考生在 30 分钟内按要求写出一篇 120 个单词以上的短文,形式可能是按所给的提纲写短文、描述图表或写内容提要、概述等。纵观历年四级考试,作文得分总不尽人意。毋庸置疑,四级作文要想取得好成绩,首先要了解评分标准并掌握一定的写作技巧。

一、评分标准

四级作文采用总体评分的方法,评分时考虑文章是否切题,是否充分表达思想,语言错误是否造成理解上的障碍,遣词造句是否清楚而确切地表达思想。

作文满分为 15 分,阅卷标准共分五等:2 分、5 分、8 分、11 分及 14 分。阅卷者根据阅卷标准,若认为作文与某一分数的标准相似,即定为该分数;若认为稍优或稍劣于该分数的标准,可以加 1 分或减 1 分。具体标准如下:

0 分——白卷;作文与题目不相关;只有几个孤立的词,无法表达思想。

2 分——条理不清楚,思路紊乱,语言支离破碎或大部分句子均有错误,且多数为严重错误。

5 分——基本切题,表达思想不够清楚,连贯性差,有较多严重的语言错误。

8 分——基本切题,有些地方表达思想不够清楚,文字勉强连贯,但语言错误较多,其中有少量的严重错误。

11 分——切题,表达思想清楚,文字连贯,但有少量语言错误。

14 分——切题,表达思想清楚,文字通顺,连贯性较好,基本上无语言错误。

二、应试技巧

写作能力的提高是一个长期积累的过程。但是每一个应试者都希望在短期内提高自己的写作水平,其中是否有些窍门和捷径可寻?答案是肯定的。关键是肯动脑、善总结、勤动手、多练习;特别要注意做到三个"针对":

一要针对评分标准,做到"有的放矢"。从上述评分标准来看,四级考试作文要拿高分,必须做到:内容切题,语言准确,表达清楚,文字连贯,句法多变。这就要求我们在平时练习和临场应试时,必须在文章的主题、构思、布局、结构和遣词造句等几个方面有意识地加以注意,尽量向高分的标准靠拢。

二要针对全真题型,做到"中规中矩"。认真分析历年大学四级考试作文题,可以发现很多共同特点,如题材、体裁、结构等方面,都有一定的规律可寻。另外从应试的角度来说,一方面要考虑到四级的作文是要求 30 分钟内写出一篇 120 多个单词的短文,实际上留给学生自由发挥的空间并不大,所以应注重规范性,减少盲目性;另一方面不能不注意到四级考试采用大规模集中阅卷的方式来批阅作文,所以在风格上要注意开门见山、简洁明快,绝不要拖泥带水、无病呻吟。

三要针对自身情况,做到"心中有数"。每个人在写作方面的特长和薄弱环节差别很大。有的属于词汇贫乏,有的属于思路不清,有的属于逻辑混乱,有的属于笔头太慢等等。一定要注意分析自身在写作方面存在的问题,有针对性地加强训练,才能事半功倍。

第二节 英语基本句型和扩展

句子用词准确、合乎语法规范是一篇文章最起码的要求。考生首先必须掌握英语的基本句型,并能灵活运用这些句型组词造句,才能确保拿到 8 分以上的分数。

一、英语基本句型

英语句子可谓千变万化,但基本的句子结构只有五种:

1. SV(主语+谓语)

They listened carefully.

2. SVO(主语+谓语+宾语)

A stranger visited me yesterday.

3. SVC(主语+谓语+主语补足语)

John was elected president of the company.

4. SVOiOd(主语+谓语+间接宾语+直接宾语)

在此结构中,V 是带有双宾语的及物动词。常见的带双宾语的动词有 give, ask, bring, offer, send, pay, lend, show, tell, buy, get, rob, warn 等。

He gave me a black package/a black package to me.

5. SVOC(主语+谓语+宾语+宾语补足语)

He found the door of study closed to him.

这些基本结构看似简单,但可作为检查句子是否正确的一种标准。在实际写作时并非总使用这样简单的句型,而是将其加以变化、扩展或补充各类修饰成分,来表达丰富的思想,同时增强文章的可读性。

二、英语基本句型的扩展

扩展句型指增加某些修饰或限定成分,加大句子的信息量,避免使用干巴巴的句子组织文章。适当增加某些修饰或限定成分,可以使句子结构严谨,语义连贯,表意清晰,逻辑性强。现举几例,以供参考。

1. The students work hard.

The students work very hard.

The students in our class work very hard.

In our class the students work hard from morning till night.

2. This is for us to decide.

How to use it is for us to decide.

How to use it is for us, not for the computer, to decide.

3. Do not leave the building!

Do not leave the building until instructed to do so.

4. Robinson will take a plane.

Robinson will take a plane in spite of his dislike of flying.

Robinson will take a plane, even though he dislikes flying.

句子的扩展是为了表达思想,要有目的地扩展,决不可为了扩展而扩展,而且句子的扩展应适度,无限度地增加修饰、限定、插入成分,会使句子显得冗长、啰嗦,破坏了句子的严谨性。

第三节 四步作文法

在掌握了英语的基本句型后,我们还须掌握一些写作方法。以下介绍四步作文法供大家参考,这四步分别是审题、确定主题句、三段十二句作文法、修改完善。

一、审题

审题是作文的第一步,只有审清题意,才能按照题意构思具体内容。

审题就是要把握题意和要求,确定文章的体裁。如果审题不当,就会偏题甚至跑题,以至前功尽弃。那么审题要审什么呢?

1. 明确体裁

写作之前一定要明确要写的是什么文体,这样才会按照该文体的基本要求展开内容,并体现出该文体应有的特点。就写作目的而言,文章一般分为记叙文、描写文、说明文和议论文,其中说明文和议论文是四、六级考试中最常出现的文体,而记叙文和描写文有时也可能出现在四级考试中,在这里只简单介绍一下这几种文体。

(1)记叙文

记叙文主要是叙述一件事情的经过,让读者了解事情的起因、经过和结果。在这类文章中,考生往往要回答 when, where, what, who, how 这五个问题。时间顺序往往是记叙手法的基本线索,用一些表示时间的词语(如:when, while, before, after, then, during, suddenly, at last 等)把各个细节连接起来,构成一个完整的记叙。比如"A Job Searching Experience"就是一篇记叙文。其核心内容是叙述求职的经过。一般来说,求职过程都有一个相对固定的顺序,因此要注意叙述的顺序,并做到详略得当。比如,第一段介绍获得这次求职信息的途径;第二段叙述求职经历的全过程;第三段指出自己从这次经历中得到的启发。

(2)描写文

描写文就是用文字来再现客观事物、人物、环境等的形象或画面。空间顺序往往是描写手法的基本线索。描写文分为客观描写文(只报道客观事实或描写客观环境,不加入个人评论)与主观描写文(描写人物或事实,文中带有作者的感情色彩)两种。但在实际写作中没有绝对的客观描写或主观描写,往往是交叉使用。如:My School Campus 在描写时既可以有客观描述(校园面貌),又可以有主观描述(作者对校园的看法)。

(3)说明文

说明文是四种文体中最基本的文体,常用于说明事实、情况和传达信息。写作目的重在解释、说明。在四、六级写作考题中,像 How I Overcame Difficulties in Learning English, My Ideal Job, Make Our Cities Greener, The Successful Interview 以及一些图表作文的题目等等,都可以看做是说明文文体。常用的写作方法有罗列法、例证法、因果法、比较法、对比法、定义法、时间顺序法和分类法等,通常是几种方法交叉使用。

(4)议论文

议论文用以陈述各种理由,但与说明文又有所不同。说明文着重于客观陈述,而议论文着重于发表自己的看法;说明文着重于解释,而议论文着重于"劝说"。这种"劝说"往往依靠推理和论证来阐述自己的观点,力图说服读者,使人相信某种道理或某种假设。所以,议论文要求论点明确,不要空洞或泛泛而谈;论据充分、有力;论证严密,采用的方法有归纳法、演绎法、因果法、举例法、对比法与比较法等。

从历年四、六级考题来看,这种要求考生表达个人观点的议论文命题出现频率越来越高。比如:My View on Job-hopping, Don't Hesitate to Say "No", Do Lucky Numbers Really Bring Luck?等等,都是十分明显的议论文命题,要求考生针对问题表达明确的立场、鲜明的观点和充足的理由。

2. 根据不同的体裁确定写作方法

四、六级作文往往不是单一的体裁,而是几种体裁的混合体。请看下面这道作文题:

Directions: *For this part, you are allowed 30 minutes to write a composition on the topic* **Trying to Be a Good**

University Student. You should write at least 120 words and you should base your composition on the outline (given in Chinese) below:

(1)做合格大学生的必要性

(2)做合格大学生的必要条件(可从德、智、体等方面谈)

(3)我打算这样做

很多人觉得这种类型的作文是议论文,事实上,说它是议论文是片面的。因为,第一段要求写"……必要性",这说明本段体裁是议论文;第二段要求写"……必备条件",这说明本段要求写说明文;而第三段要求写"……这样做",说明本段要求写的是描写文。考生可根据各种文体各自的特点分别进行如下的论述。

第一段为议论文。写作特点是要有论点和论据,而且往往从正反两方面来论述,所以第一段的写作思路是:做合格大学生会怎么样(这是从正面论述);不能做到合格大学生会怎么样(从反面论述),所以我们要做合格的大学生(结论)。

第二段为说明文。写作特点是从几方面来说明一个问题,可以从三方面(德、智、体)来说明做合格大学生的必备条件。

第三段为描写文。以"人"为中心描述一个"做"的过程。跟上两段相比,本段的主语多为人称代词。该段的描述要与第二段相呼应。

在大多数情况下,四、六级作文是三种体裁的混合体,遇到这样的题目时,考生更要认真审题。通过上面这个例子还可以看出,四、六级作文大多为三段式。审题的目的就在于根据不同的体裁来确定相应的写作方法和布局结构。

二、确定主题句

通过审题,考生知道了该如何确定写作的思路。接下来就是怎样写的问题。

第一步是写主题句。主题句是作者思维的起点,切题的准绳,阐述的对象,而段落主题句则统领段落中心内容。好的段落主题句,不但切题,便于围绕主题句进行扩展,而且常常给读者一种一针见血的感受。所以,确切的主题句是保证不偏题或跑题的前提,只有不偏题或跑题才有可能得及格分8分。写主题句最保险的方法就是把中文提纲的各句译成英语。例如上述作文的三段主题句分别为:

(1)It is very necessary to be a good university student. (议论文主题句)

(2)There are several respects of necessities to be a good university student. (说明文主题句)

(3)What I will do in the future is as follows. (描写文主题句)

如果给出的提纲是英语,就可以把它扩充成主题句,例如以下这篇作文:

Good Health

(1)Importance of good health

(2)Ways to keep fit

(3)My own practices

扩展后的主题句分别为:

(1)It is very important to have good health. (将名词importance变成形容词important)

(2)There are four ways for me to keep fit. (用there be句型)

(3)My own practices are as follows. (采用原词)

另外,应选用语法结构完整、内容概括、用词简洁明了的单句来作段落主题句。例如下面这篇作文:

Make the Most of School Days

(1)为什么上学

(2)在校时应与老师接触

(3)在校时只钻书本或置学习于不顾都不好

第一段,主题句当然可以用"Why do we go to school?"这种以问句开头的方式。但是为了使文章的结构更清晰,说服力更强,拟一个立意明确的主题句更好。比如:We pupils go to school to learn and to prepare ourselves for the future.就是一个很不错的段落主题句。第二段可用带建议语气的祈使句作主题句。比如:Contact your teachers as much as you can. 第三段同样可使用一个祈使句来作主题句,比如:Don't go to extremes.

三、三段十二句作文法

四级作文体裁大多是论说文,而论说文的写作方法通常采用"三段论"法,即第一段提出论题(开头段),第二段进行论证(中间段或支持段),第三段给出结论(结尾段)。下面就简单介绍一下写这三部分时的一些技巧。

1. 开头段

常言道:好的开始是成功的一半,文章的开篇出色是给评卷者留下好印象的关键。四级写作开头段根据不同的题目可采取不同的方法,常用的方法有以下几种:

(1)引用法:即以一段引言作为段落的开头,借助他人的观点来加强文章的力度。引言可以是名人格言、谚语或流行语等。如:

As the saying goes, "How time files! " How to spend one's time properly is becoming increasingly important.

(2)提问法:提出一个或一连串的问题,以激起读者的兴趣,从而引出主题。如关于"交朋友"一文的开头段:

Do you have many friends? Are they similar to you or different from you? Which kind of friends do you prefer?

(3)定义法:对题目中关键词做一些简单的(或正面或反面的)解释,限定其范围,引出主题。如:

What is decisiveness? It doesn't mean act rashly. (反面定义)

What is advertisement? It is the words or pictures used on media, TV for example, to publicize a certain product or give a warning to people. (正面定义)

(4)数字法:以针对某一问题客观报道的数字作为文章的开头,可引起读者的注意且具有说服力。这种方法尤其适用于图表作文。如:

The population of US is growing rapidly from 1800 until now. In 1800 the population was less than 1,000,000, but in 1999 the US reaches a population of 250,000,000. This rapid population growth has serious effects on the living environments of wildlife.

(5)故事法:用简单有趣的小故事引起读者的兴趣,进而提出自己的观点。如:

Most of us may have such experiences: when you go to some place far away from the city where you live and think you know nobody there, you are surprised to find that you run into one of your old classmates on the street, perhaps both of you would cry out: "What a small world! "

(6)开门见山法:在文章的开头就把自己的观点提出来,然后展开论述。如:

As a human being, one can hardly do without a friend. Society is made up of individuals, and making friends is a very important part in our life.

(7)间接开头法:以叙述别人的观点开始,引出自己的看法。如:

People often say that money can buy all things, but I don't think it is true.

Some say that love makes the world go round. Others of a less romantic and more practical turn of mind say that it isn't love. But the truth is that it is the energy that makes the world go round.

(8)概括法:先概括总结文章内容涉及的现状,然后引出主题。如:

In recent years, while our industries and businesses have developed quickly, the number of trees in many big cities has dramatically reduced. Efforts are being made to prevent people from cutting more trees, but to realize the significance of making cities greener is of great importance.

有时候具体写作时可以使用不止一种开头法,而综合上述两种或两种以上的方法。比如上述定义法中的两个例子就兼有定义法和提问法的特点。

2. 中间段(支持段)

中间段是发展、拓宽开头段中所提文章主题的段落。中间段和文章的主题紧密相关;主题限制着中间段的内容,中间段必须支持主题,即中间段的内容必须从不同的角度说明、阐述、论证文章的主题。中间段常用的表达方法主要有例证法、比较与对比法、因果法等。试看下面两篇文章的中间段:

As an English learner, I find it very difficult to form a language sense. It is because I always try to translate every word or sentence into Chinese. Whenever I want to express myself either in writing or in speaking, I often think in Chinese first, and then put it into English. As a result, I make little progress in my English study.

此中间段用因果法展开段落,说明产生问题的原因:always translate English into Chinese。

The discrimination against women is very obvious in reality. In the factory or office, it is female worker or clerk not male one who is laid off first. In the poor family, it is girl not boy who has to drop out of school.

此中间段用了例证法(In the factory or office..., in the poor family...)和对比法(it is... not...)来展开段落。段中使

用了两个平行句具体说明现实中的男女不平等现象。

3. 结尾段

结尾段是文章的总结和主题思想的升华,它应起到再次肯定和强调主题的作用。好的结尾段应简短有力、言简意赅、意味深长。总之,文章的结尾应该遵循两条原则:一是照应开头;二是总结全文,给读者一个完整的印象。和文章的开头一样,文章的结尾方法也是多种多样的,而非千篇一律。常见方法有如下几种:

(1)总结法或重述法:在结尾段概括、重述全文的中心思想,但不简单重复主题句,而在思想上保持一致,在句式和措辞上有所变化。例如在论述电视的优劣时,文章可以这样结尾:

On the whole there are more advantages than disadvantages in the use of TV. Yet different people may have different attitudes toward TV. But we must realize that television in itself is neither good nor bad. Its value to people and society depends on how we look at it.

(2)建议法:就前文提到的问题进行分析、比较之后,提出一些解决问题的方法或建议,此法尤其适用于有争议的问题或说理性的文章。如:

In fact, we should adopt both solutions because each has its advantages as mentioned above. Only in this way can we give full play to their strong points and avoid their weak ones.

It is high time for governments of developing countries to do something to encourage their people to eat the right kinds of food so as to help them improve their health conditions.

(3)评价法:在结尾处结合自己的实际,对文章中提到的观点进行评价,明确个人立场,或谈谈个人喜好、做法。比如考题要求考生写出保持健康的方法,并说明自己的健身途径,那么文章可以这样结尾:

As to my practices, I jog for half an hour in the morning every day, play basketball in the afternoon and go swimming on weekends. The regular physical exercises make me strong and healthy.

(4)引语法:用格言、谚语或习语来总结全文。所引用的名言一定要与前面的观点相符,以让读者接受论点。例如关于 books 的一文结尾:

In particular, I enjoy what Francis Bacon said—"Studies serve for delight, for ornament and for ability."

(5)预测法:依据上文提出的论点,预测该问题未来的发展,或对读者提出警告或希望。如:

The decrease of tobacco production and the non-smoking campaigns are good signs for us to predict that tobacco consumption should be going down with every passing day while people's health be getting better daily.

As far as the role of information in the future is concerned, I believe that information will play a more and more important part in our decision-making. Without information one would have to grope in the dark and find it hard to move even one step forward.

(6)展望或期望法:表达对将来的展望或倡议读者投入行动。如:

I am sure that Chinese will become one of the most important languages in the world in the next century. As China will open further to the outside world the language is sure to be spread worldwide.

If everyone has developed good manners, people will form a more harmonious relation. If everyone behaves considerately towards others people will live in a better world. With the general mood of society improved, there will be a progress of civilization.

(7)反问法:虽然形式是问句,但意义却是肯定的,具有明显的强调作用,引起读者思考。如:

Therefore, listening skills must be consciously improved. Since it is such an important means of learning and communication, why should we not develop this ability to its full extent?

So, what can we benefit from wealth if we do not have health?

以上介绍就是四级作文中常用的"三段论"法的一些写作技巧,接下来的问题是,这三段的篇幅该如何安排。四、六级考生一定希望既让作文达到字数要求又不至于写得太多,因为写得太多,一方面会更多地暴露自己语言上的弱点,另一方面又会占用过多的宝贵时间。写得太多还容易跑题。解决这些问题的一个有效办法就是采用十二句作文法。

如前所述,四、六级作文大多是三段式。依此推算,如果每段中写四句话,即主题句加两三个扩展句和一个结论句,这样全篇在十二句左右。每句十几个词,这样就是四、六级作文要求的 120–150 词。既要满足规定的字数要求,又要注意不能写得太多,言多必失。同时要注意分层次来展开主题,而不要写成流水账。例如,在论述健康的重要性时,有的同学先提出"健康非常重要",然后陈述"吃菠菜非常重要,因为菠菜含有丰富的铁,铁对人是非常重要的,因为……"。这样的作文就没有主题,像流水账。避免写成流水账的方法是不要就前一句中的一个非重点词再进行描述。

如果词数不够,可以给每一句或某些句子添加词语。例如,可以这样来加词:

主题句:

There are four ways to keep fit.→There are four or more ways to keep fit for everyone of us.

从几方面说明:

First, we should have our breakfast in the morning. (→Firstly, we should have our breakfast, with milk, eggs, bread and so on, in the morning.) Second, we should have a nap at noon. (→Secondly, we should have a short nap, even 30 minutes, at noon.) Third, sports exercises are necessary in the afternoon. (→Thirdly, sports exercises are necessary and we can do some exercises in the afternoon.) And fourth, we could have a pleasant feeling in the evening by listening to music. (→And fourthly, we could have a pleasant feeling in the evening by listening to some light music.)

这样一来,只要保持原句的主题不变,通过添加一些次要的词就能达到词数的规定标准。

四、修改完善

检查修改可分几次进行,每次集中解决一两个问题。主要分为:

1. 语篇水平上的检查

即从全局进行检查。主要检查文章的主题是否明确、观点是否可靠、内容是否切题、立论是否恰当、论证是否有力、推理是否合乎逻辑、文体风格是否合适、结论与主题是否一致等。

2. 段落水平上的检查

即局部检查。主要检查段落是否完整、段落的扩展是否充分、细节安排是否有序、段内各句衔接是否紧凑、语义是否连贯等。

3. 句子水平上的检查

即对语言进行检查。在实际考试中,由于时间的关系,不可能对文章的结构篇章做重大的修改,这也说明了审题和列提纲的重要性。所以,在应试时,主要从以下几方面做修改:

(1)大小写及单词的拼写是否正确;

(2)动词的时态、语态、人称是否正确,主谓关系是否一致;

(3)词性是否正确;

(4)名词的单复数、代词及指代关系是否一致;

(5)句子是否完整;

(6)标点符号是否正确。

也就是说,要纠正那些明显的、完全可以避免的典型错误。同时,还要遵循以下原则:

(1)尽可能把语义抽象的单词改为语义具体的单词;

(2)多用主动语态,尽量避免使用被动语态;

(3)多用短小的单词,尽量避免使用冗长的单词。

综上所述,如果我们按照以上几个步骤和方法去写作文,就可以保证稳拿8分及以上的分数。

第四节 四级写作主流题型扫雷训练

一、怎样写提纲式作文

提纲式作文是近几年来四、六级考试最常见的一种写作测试模式。所谓提纲式作文,是指出题者用中文或英文就某个标题给出提纲(有时也可能没有标题),要求考生按照提纲的思路去写,不能偏离提纲。这种作文通常包括三个段

落,也就是我们前面所说的三段式作文。写这种提纲式的作文要掌握以下要领:

1. 透析题目

对提纲进行认真、细致的推敲是写好提纲作文的关键。请看下面这道作文题:

Make Our Cities Greener

(1)城市绿化的现状

(2)绿化城市的好处(如清洁空气、美化城市、改善环境等等)

(3)怎样才能实现绿化

这一作文题列举了短文内容所包括的三个方面的提纲,要求考生根据该提纲来说明文章的主题。

从某种意义上讲,文章也就是对题目的一种阐释。所以,审题首先要审好文章的标题。在对 Make Our Cities Greener 这个题目进行分析时要注意两点:

一是 Greener 是比较级,这说明我们的城市现状一方面是 green,即取得了一定的成绩,另一方面是绿化工作还做得不够,需要进一步努力,使我们的城市 greener;二是 Our cities 是复数,前面又有 our 限定,这表明文章要求谈的不是某一个或某几个城市的现状,而是从整体上来谈我国城市绿化工作的现状。

通过审题我们发现,写作时应注意两个方面:第一,应该看到自己的成绩和进步,不能妄自菲薄;第二,要清楚地看到自己的差距和不足,奋起直追,把绿化工作做得更好。

审好标题以后,更重要的是对所给的提纲进行仔细琢磨。上述这个题目第一段要求论述绿化的现状(present state),因此"现状"是该段的中心;第二段要求列举绿化的好处(benefits);第三段则要求阐述搞好绿化所应采取的措施(ways or measures)。只有抓住提纲的精髓,写作时才不会偏题。

2. 确定主题句

提纲往往以短语形式列出,因此,考生在论述过程中,应该充分利用提纲中所提供的信息,首先写出每一段的主题句。主题句写作是段落是否紧扣主题、言之有物的关键。现在根据 Make Our Cities Greener 所列举的三条提纲来看如何写好主题句。

(1)城市绿化的现状

通过审题,可以清楚地认识到,我国城市绿化的现状是既有成绩又有不足。该段的主题句可以这样写:

The greenization of our cities has achieved much although it is still far from being satisfactory.

在这里我们把重点放在强调已取得的成绩上,一是为了便于下文的扩展,二是为了肯定积极的因素,有助于增强信心。

这个主题句如果这样写:The greenization of our cities is far from being satisfactory although it has achieved much. 强调的重点则变成了对现状的不满而显得消极,且不利于下文扩展。所以在写作中要注意词语顺序,其变换往往会使句子的语气和含义发生变化。

(2)绿化城市的好处(如清洁空气、美化城市、改善环境等等)

这一点给出了比较详细的提示,因而比较容易展开段落。这一段的核心是绿化带来的"好处"。其主题句可以这样写:

Greenery can bring people many benefits.

(3)怎样才能实现绿化

如何搞好绿化,也就是说要采取什么样的措施和办法。这一段的中心是"怎样(How)",简而言之,就是要不遗余力,想方设法把绿化搞好。具体一点就是要人人动手,多植树,多栽草,爱护花草树木,保护环境。这一段的主题句可以这样写:

Since we can get so much in the greenization, we should spare no effort to do it.

这里用了一个 since 引导的从句与上一段衔接。这样处理,上下文在意思上和语气上就比较顺畅了。主题句既是其所在段落的核心,同时也要起承上启下的作用。

3. 扩展段落

写好了段落的主题句,段落的展开就有了十分重要的依据。扩展句必须紧扣主题句展开。

第二段要谈绿化城市的好处,显然,可用列举法将提纲内括号里具体说明的几方面写清楚。参考范文如下:

Make Our Cities Greener

The greenery of our cities has achieved much although it is still far from being satisfactory. For instance, the municipal authorities have given consideration to the planting of trees and the cultivation of lawns. Citizens also have come to realize the importance of greenery in their life and most of them have grown flowers and other plants in their gardens, on their balconies. So plants have appeared quickly in many places. However, there are still some environmental problems, such as greenhouse effect, air pollution and the like.

Greenery can bring people many benefits. Plants can make the air clean and fresh by absorbing certain kinds of poisonous gases and producing oxygen at the same time. Plants can also help to make cities more beautiful. Moreover, plants are great contributors for better climate. Such pleasant and healthy surroundings are beneficial to people's mental and physical well-being.

Since we can get so much in the greenery, we should spare no effort to do it. To make cities greener, city planners should leave enough space for plants. What's more, every citizen should be aware of the importance of a green city so that they would voluntarily grow plants and protect them as well. We should try every means possible to make our cities greener.

二、怎样写图表式作文

图表作文就是命题者向考生提供图画、图表信息,然后要求考生完整、准确地表达图画、图表信息的大意。此类作文既考查写作能力,又考查观察力和想象力。它需要考生结合图表前的标题对所给图表进行分析、研究,阅读其中的文字和说明,弄清图表所包含的各种信息以及信息之间的关系;然后将这些信息进行比较、概括和归纳;最后提炼和归纳文章的中心思想。对大多数考生来说,图表作文是相当令人头疼的,看不清题意,那么整篇文章就无法下手。所以,在完成看图作文,把图表信息转换成文字信息的写作过程中应注意以下几点:

(一)要充分理解和反映图表中的信息。 既然是看图作文,首先要看懂图表,弄清图表中各个数据间的关系,分清主次,明确主题,这样才能着手写作。因此,要做到:用文字叙述时,应避免简单地将图表不分主次从头到尾复述一遍;必要时,可将图表中列举的数据或项目进行分类;观察图表时,既要掌握全局,又要善于发现其特点或规律;说明图表时,尽量无遗漏,但与图表无关的内容不要主观臆断。分析要合乎逻辑,不可牵强附会,任意发挥。

(二)注意图表的参照时间和图表所使用的单位。

(三)注意时态的选择,即采用什么时态写作。 一般来说,没有参照时间的图表或表格,通常用一般现在时;有参照时间的表格,参照时间用过去时;但如果叙述的是现在情况,则采用一般现在时。

(四)看图作文一般分三段写, 第一段说明该图表反映的总情况,第二段对数据进行仔细分析比较,归纳出增减速率,第三段写读图表后的想法或评论。

(五)对于图表类文章的开头我们可以套用下列句型:

(1)It can be seen from the (We can see from the/It has been shown from the) chart (diagram/table/graph/figures/statistics) that...

(2)The chart (graph/table/diagram/graph/bar/figure/pie) shows (indicates/presents) a/an (very) minimal (small/slight/dramatic/slow/gradual/steady/marked/large/rapid/sudden/upward/downward/sharp/uncertain) rise (increase decrease/decline/reduction/fall/drop/fluctuation/growth/trend...)

(3)According to the chart (graph/table...)

(4)As is shown in the chart

(5)Therefore/Thus/From the table (graph/diagram...) we can conclude/see/infer...

(6)From the table/graph... it can be seen/concluded/inferred/shown that...

下面以一道大学英语四级考试作文题为例,做进一步的分析:

Directions: *For this part, you are allowed 30 minutes to write a composition about **Changes in People's Diet** according to the following outline in three paragraphs. Your part of the composition should be no less than 120 words, not including the words given. Remember to write clearly. You should write this composition on the Composition Sheet.*

(1)State the changes in people's diet in the past five years.

(2)Give possible reasons for the changes.

(3)Draw your own conclusion.

Remember: You should quote as few figures as possible.

Food\Year	1986	1987	1988	1989	1990
Grain	49%	47%	46.5%	45%	45%
Milk	10%	11%	11%	12%	13%
Meat	17%	20%	22.5%	23%	21%
Fruit and Vegetables	24%	22%	20%	20%	21%
Total	100%	100%	100%	100%	100%

看过图表后,具体写作步骤如下:

(1)细读作文要求,如什么标题、要求多少段落、多少字数。从图表外提供的信息来看,我们知道该标题为 Changes in People's Diet,要求分三段,并规定字数不少于 120。

(2)将 change(变化)这一关键词牢记在心,然后仔细看图表内提供的文字信息。从表中的词汇和数字等信息我们可以得出结论,即:近年来我国人民粮食结构发生了显著的变化,这个变化就是我们要重点说明或阐释的事实和依据。

(3)组织材料,构思语言,把握整体,分析可能的理由(possible reasons)。对于这种"理由",作者可以根据自己的认识、体验来阐释,只要言之有理,思路清晰,即可得分。比如上图表中的理由可以写"物质生活十分丰富,人们有钱消费"、"现在生活水平提高了,人们对食品有较大选择余地",或"人们的饮食文化水准提高了,更加注意食物的结构,注意食品营养"等等,因而导致了食品结构发生显著的变化。

据此,我们可以组织如下的一篇文章:

Changes in People's Diet

There have been some changes in the diet of the Chinese. Grain, the main food of most people in China, is now playing a less important role. On the other hand, the consumption of high-nutrition food such as milk and meat has increased.

The changes in Chinese people's diet can be accounted for by a number of factors. First, people are much wealthier than before. With a higher income, they can afford to buy good foods which, in the past, were rarely seen on the dinner tables of ordinary families. Another factor is that people have realized the importance of a balanced diet to their health. Lack of certain amount of meat or milk, for example, will result in poor health. Finally, owing to the economic reform, meat and milk, which were scarce in the past, are produced in large quantities. For all those reasons, what was formerly called "the basket of vegetables" has become that of varied foods.

To sum up, insignificant as those changes may seem, they are the signs of the improved economic condition in China. We believe that as the effort in the modernization movement continues, there will be greater changes in people's diet in the future.

三、怎样写书信式作文

英文书信一般分为事务信件或公函(Business Letter or Official Correspondence)以及个人信件(Personal Letter)两大类。事务信件或公函主要是机构之间往来的信件,所以格式要求较为严格。一般都包括以下几部分:

(1)信头(**Heading**):包括发信人的名称、地址和日期,写在信纸右上角。写地址的习惯是从小到大,即先写门牌号和街道名,再写区、县(市)、省、国家。最后一行写日期。

(2)内文地址(**Inside Address**):包括收信人的姓名、地址和称呼。收信人地址置于左上方(日期之下一行,称呼之上)。

(3)称呼(**Salutation**):可以选择这几种:Gentlemen, Dear Sir, Dear Sir/Madam, Dear Sirs, To whom it may concern。

(4)正文(**Body of the letter**):应包括三部分:①引言部分——写信人表明身份和写信的目的;②细节部分——具体说明写信人的请求或想法等细节;③结束语部分——对信中内容进行总结并谦恭地表明希望对方做些什么事情。

（5）结束语（Complimentary Close）：一般写法有：Yours sincerely, Sincerely yours, Yours faithfully, Faithfully yours, Yours truly, Truly yours，注意结束语后要用逗号。

（6）签名（Signature）：一般低于结束语一两行，从信纸中间偏右的地方开始。

（7）附件（Enclosure，简写为：Encl.或 Enc.）：如果信中谈到附件，则在左下角注明 Encl.或 Enc.。

（8）再启或附言（Postscript，简写为：P.S.）：用于补叙遗漏的话，一般少用，郑重的函件更应避免。

其中，前六项是必备的，后两项视实际情况而定。而且，写作时要遵循"五 C 原则"，即 Correctness（正确）、Clarity（清晰）、Conciseness（简洁）、Courtesy（礼貌）和 Consideration（体谅）。

个人信件一般写给自己熟悉的人，形式很自由，只需在右上角写上日期就行了，无需信头和信内地址。直接以称呼开头，后面用逗号，比如 Dear Mary, Dear Sam，等等。

例1 事务信件

Beijing Avalon Industries

246 Baitasi Road, Xicheng District,

Beijing, 100032

P.R.C

June 21, 2003

Sales Department

Pacific Machines

212 Twin Dolphin Drive

Redwood City, Ca 94065

U.S.A

Dear Sir,

I am writing with reference to order No. AS671, which we received last week.

When we checked the machine, we noticed some damage to the case and when we turned it on, it did not work. It seems that the machine was not packed properly or tested before dispatch. Please let us know what you intend to do in this matter.

I look forward to hearing from you soon.

Yours Sincerely,

（签名）

David Wang

Production Manager

例2 私人信件

Dear John,

Congratulations on having received your doctorate in philosophy from Princeton University. I know this has meant years of study and hard work on your part, and it's an achievement you can well be proud of.

Your Aunt Emma and I have followed your progress with pleasure and interest; and we are sure, from the fine record you have made, that you will be a success in whatever you undertake.

No doubt you are tired after the strain of the past few months; and if you would like to come to Lake Talbot for a few weeks this summer, we'd be very happy to have you. We remember that you always used to like it here as a boy; and although it may be too quiet for you now, the rest and relaxation might do you a lot of good. And we'd certainly enjoy hearing about your plans, now that you have completed your college course.

Think it over, John, and let us know.

Affectionately,

Uncle Clint

第一节 漂亮句子写作技巧

句子是写作的基本单位。句子用词准确、合乎语法规范是一篇文章最起码的要求。要切实提高四级写作水平,就必须灵活掌握和运用英语的基本句型,同时在句子的完整性、一致性、简洁性和多样性上多下工夫,努力写出漂亮、精彩的句子,提高文章的可读性。

1. 完整性

句子的完整包括在语法结构上无残缺,在表达的概念上无遗漏。而句子不完整是考生常犯的错误。例如:

He was the most popular poet.

该句缺乏思想表达上的完整性。因为句中所谓的"the most popular"概念未表达完全,即在什么时间、什么范围内最受欢迎。可改为:

He was the most popular poet in his contemporaries.

再比如:College teachers are more helpful than high school.

此句原是对"大学教师"和"中学教师"进行比较,但在 high school 后错误地省略了 teachers,结果造成了"教师"和"中学"比较,显然不合逻辑。可改为:

College teachers are more helpful than high school teachers. 或 Teachers in college are more helpful than those in high school.

2. 一致性

句子的一致性包括主谓一致、代词与先行词一致以及分词、动名词、不定式的逻辑主语与句子的语法主语一致。造成句子不一致的原因有很多,主要有错用平行结构、代词指代不明、误置修饰语、转换不当以及主谓不一致等。这几种典型错误都将在第四节中详细说明。在这里就不多说了。

除了以上几点外,人称、数、时态、语态及结构上的不恰当转换也会破坏句子的一致性。请看下面的例子:

(1) He waits patiently on the platform until the train came.

这句话用了现在时和过去时,在时态上不一致。可改为:

He waited patiently on the platform until the train came.

(2) The students who want to go out for a picnic need to sign his name in the notebook.

这句话在人称的数上不一致,可改为:

The students who want to go out for a picnic need to sign their names in the notebook.

(3) He is good not only at music but also plays football well.

这句话在结构上不一致,可改为:

He is good at not only music but also football.

(4) I wrote to him, but my letter was not answered.

这句话前面是主动语态,后面是被动语态,在语态上不一致。可改为:

I wrote to him, but he did not answer my letter.

3. 简洁性

许多人常常以为句子越长、越复杂就越好。其实简洁的句子更能达到好的效果。言简意赅是我们写文章时所追求的目标之一,也是我们行文时所遵循的一个重要准则。由于大学英语四级写作考试有时间和字数上的规定,我们不可能长篇大论去写,因而尽可能用最简洁的方式表达出最多的思想信息就成为四级考生追求的目标。要达到这个目标,就必须做到以下几点:

(1)避免使用空洞、多余的短语

空洞的短语是给文章添加的累赘,通常单个词就足以表达整个空洞的短语所表达的意义。在这种情况下,要用单个的词来代替。请看下面的句子:

In my opinion, I would say that we here in China today in the last quarter of the 20th century often place a high value on the successful achievement of an education on the college level and it seems to me that the reason why we believe this is that college is the place where a young man or woman is first helped to begin to grasp and understand what the true meaning of life really is.

此句可改为:The Chinese people now value a college education highly because it helps a student to understand the meaning of life.

从上面的例子可看出,原句给人一种装腔作势的感觉,读起来使人喘不过气来,又摸不着头尾。把原句中划线部分的短语替换成更改后句子中划线部分的单词,整个句子就显得明了清楚多了。所以,在写作过程中要学会字斟句酌,使句子更清晰、简练、有力。

(2)避免过多地使用并列句

过多地使用并列关系,即盲目地把几个主要分句都用并列连词连接在一起,会使读者感到单调乏味,也无法表示分句之间的恰当关系。例如:

Eugene O'Neill was an American playwright, and he had an unhappy childhood, and he told the story of his childhood in a play entitled *A Long Day's Journey Into Night* and he said it was written in tears and blood.

改正这样的句子时,可采用主从分句、修饰性短语以及同位语等。试做改正如下:

Eugene O'Neill, an American playwright, told the story of his unhappy childhood in a play entitled *A Long Day's Journey Into Night*, which he said was written in tears and blood.

(3)避免过多地使用从句

英语中比较重要的从属概念可用从句的形式表达,其他次要的概念常用单独的词或短语来表达,因为句子比短语显得更重要。过多地使用从句会把主次概念混为一谈,削弱句子重点。例如:

He is a man who is honest, who always pays his just debts, and who observes the golden rules in his dealings with others.

可改为:He is an honest man who always pays his just debts, and who observes the golden rules in his dealings with others.

4. 多样性

多样性指的是句子形式的多样化,即句子长短、结构、类型等的多样性。句子的多样化是为作文增色的有效手段。为了使文章更具有吸引力,就要避免全文使用结构相同、长度相近的句子。全文只有一两种句式并且长度大致相等,会使文章变得单调、呆板。试比较以下句子,注意体会句中变化所带来的效果。

(1) She had been confined to bed for a long time, which had impaired the function of her ankles.

　　—Long confinement to bed had impaired the function of her ankles.

(2) If you study Mars carefully through a telescope, you will see a number of mountains and rivers.

　　—A careful study of Mars through telescope will reveal a number of mountains and rivers.

(3) People throughout the country have greatly demanded more durable goods.

—There is a great demand across the country for more durable goods.

(4) There was a rapid development in science and technology in the 19th century.

—The 19th century witnessed a rapid development in science and technology.

(5) When there is a slight improvement in their children, the parents will be really happy and proud.

—A slight improvement in the children's studies will lead to their parents' happiness and pride.

(6) Because one can not know what kind of knowledge will be useful in the future, he can't make a sound choice in taking school courses.

—The inability to predict what kind of knowledge will be useful in the future prevents a person from making a sound choice in taking school courses.

(7) More and more teenagers smoke cigarettes in recent years.

—Teenager smoking is on the rise in recent years.

(8) There are many people who complain of severe housing shortage.

—Serious housing shortage becomes the source of complaint.

句子的多样化可以通过改变句子的结构、长度、主语以及运用修辞格等方法实现。但是,不能舍本逐末,片面追求句式的丰富而忽视意义表达的连贯。

第二节 段落发展技巧

段落是若干相关的句子围绕一个中心思想或为表达一个统一的主题组合在一起的写作单位。段落由若干个句子组成,通常表达一个中心思想。因此,段落不能由一组句子随意堆砌而成,即不能把毫不相干的思想或观点放在一个段落。而是应当符合一定的模式和具有某些基本特征,并遵循一定的段落发展方法。在四级作文考试中,很多考生感到无话可说;勉强想出来补充说明提纲的句子与提纲联系不紧密,句子之间逻辑混乱,有明显的凑字数的痕迹。不知怎样展开段落,是大多数考生在四级作文考试时遇到的难题。要成功地展开段落,首先必须了解段落的基本结构。

段落构成三要素

段落由句子组成,根据段落中各句的地位及相互关系,可以将段落中的句子分成:主题句、扩展句和结尾句。而这三类句子就构成了段落的三要素。

1. 主题句(Topic Sentence)

主题句点明段落的中心内容,并限制段落展开的范围。主题句是段落的灵魂,读者可以从主题句上明了全段的中心思想。因此,考生在写作文的时候,必须围绕主题句展开段落。

主题句可以出现在文章的开头、段落中间、段落结尾处。对于四级考生来说,最好先想好主题句,并把主题句放在段落的开头,这样可以提醒考生围绕主题句展开段落,避免离题,同时也让阅卷人一目了然。

写出好的主题句是写好段落的基础,写好主题句应遵循下面三条基本原则:

第一,要有能说明段落中心思想的内容。主题句的内容应是全段内容的概括和提炼,或能限定全段内容的范围和叙述的角度。

第二,要有能体现中心思想的关键词。主题句中应该包含体现主题意义或范围的核心词或短语。这样,段落的发展才能围绕一个中心合乎逻辑地展开。

第三,主题句应该简洁明了、直截了当。当然,这决不是说句式越简单越好,而是要求在意思表达清楚的前提下尽量避免使用复杂冗长的句型和结构,以免造成理解上的障碍。

主题句的写作除了要遵循上述三条原则外,还要注意以下四个方面:

(1)立论务求严谨,合乎实情

【例1】If there were no electric power, we couldn't live and work.

这句话过于夸张,不合实际,也经不起推敲。人类历史上使用电只是近代的事情,即使在今天也还有个别地方没有电。因此,说没有电我们就无法生存和工作,显然有些绝对化,立论不够严谨。这样改可能会好一些:

If there were no electric power, many things would be in a mess.

（2）命题不要太宽，以免无从下笔

[例2]Therefore, electric power is the foundation of our society.

这句话有两个毛病：一是不合实情；二是命题太宽，无从下笔。一个段落的主题句，应该只提出本段落要说明的问题，而不是需要在整篇文章中才能讲清楚的问题。要论证电是社会的基础，这在应试作文的短短的段落中是根本无法完成的。这样改可能会好一些：

Therefore, we should sense the importance of electricity.

（3）命题不能太窄，以免无话可说

[例3]If there were no electric power, people would have to use fire to light the room in the evening.

上例命题太窄。没有电，夜晚人们便自然会用火照明，事实就是如此，一语道尽，没有余地，下文也无法继续扩展下去。这样改可能会好一些：

If there were no electric power, things would be quite different.

（4）加强语言训练，避免语言错误

[例4]Therefore, we should do our best to make the electric power in all kinds of ways.

上例中的语言毛病不少，一是动宾搭配不当，二是语义重复。这样改可能比较切题达意：

Therefore, we should do our best to generate more electricity.

2. 扩展句（Supporting Sentence）

确定了主题句之后，我们就需要用扩展句来说明、支持主题句，使读者感觉主题句更有说服力。扩展句是段落主题句的延伸和发展，起着辅助主题句、扩展段落中心的作用，对主题句的中心思想或者举例说明，或者详细解释和论证。一般来说，一个段落会有若干个扩展句。根据在段落中的地位，这些扩展句通常可以分为一级扩展句和二级扩展句。一级扩展句直接为主题句服务，二级扩展句直接为一级扩展句服务，起补充说明的作用。以此类推，三级扩展句直接支持二级扩展句。例如：

Science can do good to mankind, but it can do evil as well. When it is wisely used, it will bring benefit. For example, atomic energy can help us generate electricity. However, if it is wrongly used, its destructive power will be uncontrollable and terrible. It can claim thousands and thousands of lives in a split second.

在这个段落里，第一句是主题句，第二句和第四句是一级扩展句，第三句和第五句是二级扩展句。

扩展句是用来体现段落的主题思想的，因此必须写得清晰、翔实，不可含糊其辞或言之无物；同时，扩展句要有较强的说服力，能清楚地表达思想，绝不可只凑篇幅，凑够字数了事。另外，扩展句必须层次分明，围绕主题句展开，为主题句服务。先说什么，后说什么，应有个合理安排。也就是说，上一句要为下一句铺平道路，下一句是上一句的自然延伸，一步一步地论证或叙述主题。就四级学生写作而言，每句话的平均长度控制在10-15个词为宜。当然，随着写作水平地提高，句子的长度可相应增加。

3. 结尾句（Concluding Sentence）

所谓结尾句就是总结段落的句子，用一句话将段落内容进行归纳总结，对全段中心思想做出精练的浓缩。写好结尾句对整个段落来说是至关重要的。一个段落的结尾句写得不好，会使整个段落看上去虎头蛇尾。因为段落的内容是说明主题的，因此结尾句和段落主题句应该相互呼应，或者说是主题句的再现，并与扩展句相关联。结尾句用来总结段落，进一步强调和深化段落的主题，有时还能起到承上启下的作用，使前后两个段落自然过渡，并成为一个段落的主题句。例如：

The Influence of Advertising on Consumers

Advertisements are so pervasive nowadays that they almost guide our consuming behavior. People are more likely to buy a product that sounds and looks familiar to them. This is no doubt an advantage of ads; otherwise we'll feel a loss in a supermarket hesitating to buy even a small article. Ads save our time and lessen our anxiety in this respect. In a word, advertising plays a very important role in conducting our consuming behavior.

However, this advantage may be seen from the opposite angle as a disadvantage, like the two sides of the same coin. Ads are so persuasive that quite probably they can mislead consumers. Ads shape our consuming conception, encroaching into our private field of judging by ourselves. This has been valued as a mark of unique personal style, but now we are gradually losing it.

As a consumer, I love ads just as I hate them. Yet I don't know how to deal with my contradictory feeling, since an individual consumer is almost defenseless in front of overwhelming ads.

在这篇文章里,第一段的中心内容就是结尾句:广告在指导我们的消费行为中扮演着非常重要的角色。这句结尾句使文章向第二段自然过渡,第二段则从另一角度分析广告对我们消费理念的误导作用。考生应该注意并不是每一个段落都有结尾句。上面文章的第二段就没有总结全段内容的结尾句。

总之,主题句、扩展句和结尾句三者之间的关系是紧密相连,一环扣一环的。如果有一环脱节,文章的连贯性就会受到质疑。所以,考生在写作时,一定要处理好这三者之间的关系。

第三节 逻辑组织技巧

四级考试要求考生的作文必须结构清晰、语义连贯、逻辑性强。要做到这些,考生必须掌握一些句子和段落间的衔接技巧。

一、句子间的衔接技巧

句子与句子之间的连贯除了靠本身的意思之外,还可以通过过渡词的衔接和词汇的衔接来实现。

1. 过渡词表现出来的逻辑关系,可以大大增强文章的连贯性。如:

Smoking results in series of negative effects. To begin with, it has been proved that poisonous nicotine contained in cigarettes can reduce your fits. And what is worse, it can even cause lung cancer if you smoke constantly. That is why such warning as "smoking is harmful to our health" must be printed on the cover of the cigarette case in western countries. Furthermore, passive smoking occurs in your family members and other people as a result of your smoking at home or in public places. Consequently, their health will be unfavorably influenced. In addition, smoking adds to your financial difficulty if you happen to be short of money. Even if you are rich, you are encouraged to spend your money on valuable books, nutritious food, high-quality TV sets, etc., not on meaningless smoking. Therefore, giving up smoking is a good way to make you and your family happy.

2. 词汇衔接手段主要靠关键词的重复,同义词和近义词的关系,词的上下义关系,词的语义场关系等。如:

A good case in point is the white-tailed deer. Like most wildlife, deer reproduce, grow, and store fat in the summer and fall when there is plenty of nutritious food available. A physically mature female deer in good condition who has conceived in November and given birth to two fawns during the end of May or first part of June, must search for food for the necessary energy not only to meet her body's needs but also to produce milk for her fawns. The best milk production occurs at the same time that new plant growth is available. This is good timing, because milk production is an energy consuming process—it requires a lot of food. The cost cannot be met unless the region has ample food resources.

关键词重复:food, milk production, energy

代词:milk production—it

同义词和近义词:reproduce—give birth to; plenty of nutritious food—ample food sources; energy consuming—cost

词的上下义:wildlife—deer—white-tailed deer—a physically mature female deer; fall—November

词的语义场:grow—conceive; reproduce—produce milk

这些词通过表达出来的语义关系把相互间句子的意思连接了起来。一般来说,过渡词、词汇手段和语法结合起来使用可以大大增加文章的连贯性,从而使文章脉络清晰、逻辑性强。

二、段落间的过渡技巧

段与段的连贯过渡主要有下面几种方法:

(1)依靠上一段最后一句和下一段第一句的意思关联。请看下面选自《21世纪大学英语》第一册的三段文字:

P2.　We all know what a nerd is: someone who wears thick glasses and ugly clothes; someone who knows all answers to the chemistry or math homework but can never get a date on a Saturday night... It is a revealing fact about our language and our culture that someone dedicated to pursuit of knowledge is compared to such a freak.

P3.　Even at a prestigious educational institution like Harvard, anti-intellectualism is widespread. Many students are ashamed to admit, even to their friends, there is but a small group of undergraduates for whom pursuing knowledge is the most important thing during their years at Harvard. Nerds are looked down upon while athletes are made heroes of.

P4.　The same thing happens in U.S. elementary and high school. Children who prefer to read books rather than play football, prefer to build model airplanes rather than idle away their time at parties with their classmates, become social outcasts. Because of their intelligence and refusal to conform to society's anti-intellectual values, many are deprived of a chance to learn adequate social skills and acquire good communication tools.

第三段第一句的意思是第二段最后一句意思的继续:我们的文化竟把追求知识的人比喻成怪人,甚至连哈佛这样有名望的大学,反知识现象也相当普遍。

第四段的第一句意思又是第三段最后一句意思的继续:书呆子被人瞧不起,而运动员则被奉为英雄。这种情况在美国的中小学里也存在。

(2)依靠各段中的主题句思想的关联。还是以《21世纪大学英语》第一册的另外三段为例子:

P1.　These days, lifestyles seem to change fast. It is more than just clothing and hairstyle that are in style one year and out of date the next; it's a whole way of living. One year, people wear sunglasses on top of their heads and wear jeans and boots; they drink white wine and eat sushi at Japanese restaurants; for exercise they jog several miles a day. However, the next year they notice that everything has changed. Women wear long skirts; people drink expensive water from France and eat pasta at Italian restaurants; everyone seems to be exercising at health clubs.

P2.　Almost nothing in modern life escapes the influence of fashion; food, music, exercise, book, slang words, movies, furniture, places to visit, even names go in and out of fashion. It's almost impossible to write about specific fads because these interests that people follow can change very quickly.

P3.　In the United States, even people can be "in" or "out". Like people in any country, American enjoy following the lives of celebrities: movie stars, sports heroes, famous artists, politicians, and the like. But Americans also pay a lot of attention to people who have no special ability and have done nothing very special. In 1981, for example, an unknown elderly woman appeared in a TV commercial in which...

第一段的第一句是段落主题句。第二段的第一句也是段落主题句,它和第一段主题句的语义关系是笼统和具体的关系:现在生活方式变得很快。现代生活中几乎没有什么能逃脱潮流的影响,食品、音乐、健身、书籍、俚语、电影、家具、旅游点,甚至人名都会流行或过时。第三段的第一句又是段落主题句,它是第二段主题句意思的进一步深入:在美国,甚至人也会"流行"和"过时"。

(3)依靠全文中心思想来串联。如:

What are the basic ingredients of good manners? Certainly, a strong sense of justice is one; courtesy is often nothing more than a highly developed sense of fair play...

Another ingredient of courtesy is empathy, a quality that enables a person to see into the mind or heart of someone else, to understand the pain or unhappiness there and to do something to minimize it...

Yet another component of politeness is the capability to treat all people alike, regardless of all status or importance. Even when you have doubts about some people, act as if they are worthy of your best manners.

(《21世纪大学英语》第四册)

在这里,"What are the basic ingredients of good manners?"这一句把本段以及下面两段的思想都归纳了起来,使得三段之间非常连贯。

第四节 写作常见错误分析

通过前面的论述,我们可以看到,很多四级考生写作基本功还是比较薄弱的,从选词到造句,总是没有章法,漏洞百出。很多考生虽然做过无数的语法、词汇题目,但事实证明,会做多项选择题并不等于会在自己的写作实践中使用,一个英语学习者在语言上的漏洞在写作文时最容易暴露无遗了。

基于此,在本节我们将从遣词、造句两个方面对大学英语四级写作常见的错误进行分析,并就一些重点问题提出建议。

一、5 种用词错误分析

要想写出一篇好的文章,没有大量的词汇作为后盾是不可想象的。根据新修订的大学英语教学大纲要求,大学英语四级考生通常所掌握的词汇量应在 4200 个左右。但是,掌握了这么多的词汇并不意味着写作时能游刃有余;事实证明,很多考生在遣词造句上还是捉襟见肘、漏洞百出。问题主要表现在以下几方面:

1. 误解词义导致的用词错误

有些考生在写作时,选用自己没有完全掌握词义或用法的单词、组词造句,是造成用词错误的原因之一。如:

(1) The young man always puts on leather shoes.

(2) Both salt and sugar are easy to melt in hot water.

(3) They persuaded their son to try again, but he just turned a deaf ear to them.

(4) It is uneasy for the children to do such a thing.

英、汉两种语言中均有一词多义和一义多词的现象。对同义词、近义词的细微差别分辨不清,是导致这类用词错误发生的主要原因。现将上述 5 句错例改正如下,括号里说明了错误原因。

(1) The young man always wears leather shoes. (put on 表示穿的动作,不表示穿着的状态,而此句表达的意思是"穿着",而不是"穿上"。)

(2) Both salt and sugar are easy to dissolve in hot water. (melt 常指物体经加热后熔化或者易溶物质受热溶化,不指溶质在溶剂中溶解。)

(3) They advised their son to try again, but he just turned a deaf ear to them. (persuade sb. to do sth.是"说服某人去做某事"。如 persuade 用过去时或完成时,则意味着对方已经接受劝告而去做某事了。但此句的第二部分用了 he just turned a deaf ear to them,这在词义上造成了前后矛盾的逻辑错误。)

(4) It is difficult for the children to do such a thing. (uneasy 是由前缀 un-加词根 easy 构成,在古英语中有"不容易"的意思,但在现代英语中,uneasy 已不表示 easy 的反义"不容易"了,而是"心神不安"的意思。)

所以,在选择用词时,要从各方面对所选词的词义认真推敲,决不可"信笔漫游",想起什么词就用什么词。

2. 不符合习惯导致的用词错误

四级作文中常出现不符合英语表达习惯的用词错误。现举例说明:

(1) We all hope him to get the first prize.

(2) Mr. Smith denied my invitation to a dinner party.

(3) Who is responsible for this department?

(4) She will probably be elected woman chairman.

(5) There are jobs more dangerous than truck driving, for an instance, training lions.

在英语写作中,有些单词的使用受到诸如语法结构以及词语搭配等诸多因素的制约。写作时如果不考虑这些因素,就很可能会造成不合乎语法规范或不符合惯用法的用词错误。

现将上述 5 句错例改正如下,括号里说明了错误原因。

(1) We all expect him to get the first prize. (hope 的用法只有 hope to do sth.或 hope+that 从句结构,却不能说 hope sb. to do sth.。)

(2) Mr. Smith declined my invitation to a dinner party. (deny 可作"拒绝接受"讲,不过当表示"拒绝接受邀请"时,英语习惯一般不用 deny an invitation。)

(3) Who is in charge of this department? (be responsible for 通常指对某件事的后果负责。如果指对某一方面的工作或某一部门的工作负责,就不能用 be responsible for。)

(4) She will probably be elected chairwoman. (woman chairman,是一个词语搭配问题。一般来说,在表示职业的名词前加上 man 或 woman 可以区别男女。如 a woman doctor, a woman writer 等。但是"女主席"、"女议长"、"女诗人"等则不能用 woman 作定语。另外,英语中某些固定搭配,决不可以随便改变其结构或任意添加、省略其中的某些成分,否则就会造成不符合惯用表达的用词错误。)

(5) There are jobs more dangerous than truck driving, for instance, training lions. (for an instance 不符合英语

习惯用法。英语中"举例"的固定说法是 for example 和 for instance。虽然只举一个例子,也不能使用冠词 a/an。)

就英语单词本身而言,每一个单词都是符合英语习惯的,问题在于词与词的搭配上。在写作时,对惯用法的使用要加倍小心,平时对自己不熟悉或拿不准的习语要认真查证,才能杜绝非惯用法的用词错误。

3. 大词、小词滥用导致的错误

大学英语作文题一般限于生活、常识方面的内容,所以,在具体写作中,学生应尽量避免使用大词,尤其是生僻的词。有的学生在用词上存在误解,认为如果使用一些大词、难词会提高自己的作文档次,令阅卷老师对自己的英语水平刮目相看,从而获得较高的分数。于是花大量的时间和精力去记忆这样的难词,殊不知,这样做实在是得不偿失。一来大词难于记忆且容易拼错,如果使用错误,就难以达到预期的效果;相反,如果把同等的时间用于掌握小词,无疑会事半功倍。此外,四级写作命题范围本身就决定了写作文体只能是非正式文体。在这样的大环境下,要想用好大词,并使其与整篇作文相融合是很难的。弄不好就会弄巧成拙,事倍功半。且看下面的例子:

(1) I comprehended his statement.

(2) While we are eating breakfast, we engaged in an animated conversation.

(3) He will come in the event that it stops raining.

事实上,同样的意思完全可以用自然、简练的文字更清楚、明白地表达出来。可试改如下:

(1) I understood what he said.

(2) While eating breakfast, we have a lovely talk.

(3) He will come if it stops raining.

综观四级考生的写作水平,极少考生能保证思路清晰、表达通顺、内容完整、没有大的语法错误,为什么要舍本逐末呢?我们建议考生把有限的时间用于对核心词汇的掌握,努力做到熟练运用这些最常用的词充分表达自己的思想。

4. 误用词性导致的用词错误

英语里许多词都是一词多义,或一词多性的。在四级写作时,许多考生只注意了所选词的词义,而忽视了该词的词性,从而造成句子不合乎语法规范的严重用词错误。典型的这类错误有:错把名词当动词用,形容词、副词误用等。例如:

(1) My teacher adviced me not to go out alone at night.

(2) She doesn't aware of the importance of the study of English.

(3) Many people present at the meeting.

(4) To do this beyond my power.

(5) This road goes straightly from our school to the center of the city.

在四级考试中,有些英语基础比较薄弱的考生往往对某些常用词不像对待较生疏的词那样认真地去分析考证,而是信笔写来,常导致词性误用而"浑然不觉"。如例(1)即把名词误用为动词了。例(2)、例(3)则是把形容词误用为动词了。英语中有许多形容词具有动作含义,当它们作表语时,千万不要忘了加连系动词,常见的这类形容词有:able, absent, abundant, active, accurate, afraid, alive, asleep, awake, aware, available, backward, busy, downward, eager, faithful, feasible, fond, keen, present, late, responsible, strict, worried, concerned, interested 等。在例(4)中,误把 beyond 用作动词。英语中常见的带有动作含义的介/副词(组)还有:across, through, over, among, like, off, into, against, for, with, without, according to, along with, instead of, in accordance, on behalf of 等。另外,在使用前、后缀改变某个词的词性时,许多考生往往考虑一般规律,而忽视了例外情况,如例句(5)。

以上 5 句错例可改正如下:

(1) My teacher advised me not to go out alone at night.

(2) She isn't aware of the importance of the study of English.

(3) Many people were present at the meeting.

(4) To do this is beyond my power.

(5) This road goes straight from our school to the center of the city.

5. 用汉语思维导致的用词错误

在四级写作过程中,考生由于对英、汉两种语言、文化间的差异,以及不同文化背景所产生的不同思维方式不甚了

解,经常用汉语思维,导致用词错误。请看下面的句子:

(1) Excessive smoking will injure your body.

(2) Through inquiry, we learn that he was elected to a new leading post.

(3) We are going to visit the exhibition next week.

(4) In the basketball game, our team won the British team.

(5) We all enjoy public medicial care.

以上这些句子,在英语语言功底较差的考生作文中经常会出现。这些学生不能用英语思考,经常先在脑海里用汉语构思,然后将构思好的汉语译成英语。这种机械的对应思考方法,往往造成严重的用词错误。如例(1)、(2)、(3)就属于这种错误。另外,在表达某一概念时,两种语言的用词与搭配可能是对应的,但在表达另一概念时,其用词与搭配可能完全不同。如例(4)中,win 作"赢"解时会出现两种情况,"赢得一场比赛"是 win the game/match;"打赢某人"可以说win over sb.,但不能说 win sb.。此外,由于两种语言的用词习惯和词语搭配的不同,对于某些名词、术语、概念等,英、汉语有各自不同的说法。例句(5)的错误在于将"公费医疗"译成 public medical care。public 是指"公有的",而"公费医疗"则指"免费医疗"。

因此,在写作时,要注意英、汉两种语言的差异,要学会用英语思考,切忌把写作变成直线翻译。

现将上面 5 句错例改正如下:

(1) Excessive smoking will injure your health.

(2) On inquiry, we learn that he was elected to a new leading post.

(3) We are going to see the exhibition next week.

(4) In the basketball game, our team beat the British team.

(5) We all enjoy free medical care.

二、6 种常见句子错误分析

我们在造句的时候常会犯一些错误,这些错误主要有以下 6 种:

1. 非完整句错误

非完整句是指以完整句的形式出现的部分句子成分或非独立成分。我们知道一个意思和结构完整的句子至少有主语和谓语两部分,当然祈使句除外。若将句子中的某一部分当做一个句子,就会导致非完整句错误。考生在句子的完整性方面常常犯以下错误:

(1)非独立性从句单独成句

非独立性从句指那些由关系代词(who, whom, whose, which, what, that)、关系副词(when, where, how)或从属连词(after, before, although, as, if, because, until, unless 等)引导的句子。这些句子只能在主句中起一个句子成分的作用,因而不能脱离主句而独立存在。一旦脱离主句就会出现非完整句错误。如:

【错误】We must try hard to learn English well. Because it will be very useful in our future work.

【正确】We must try hard to learn English well, because it will be very useful in our future work.

这种错句的修改只要根据具体情况把从句归属到主句中去就可以了,当然标点和大小写需要做相应调整。对于四级考生来说,在大多数情况下,这一类错误是因为粗心或过于匆忙而用错标点造成的,同时也反映出部分考生的语感差。只要在写作时多用心一点,并在写完后有针对性地检查一下,就可以有效地减少此类错误的发生。

(2)现在分词独立成句

现在分词短语以及它的独立主格结构在句子中往往充当状语,表示原因、目的、结果、伴随状况等。学生对这类结构的掌握普遍不够扎实,应用到写作中更是错误百出。如:

【错误】They got up early that morning. Hoping to catch up the 6:30 train to Hong Kong.

【正确】They got up early that morning, hoping to catch up the 6:30 train to Hong Kong.

对于现在分词短语形式的非完整句,最好的办法就是改一下标点和大小写,视语义关系的紧密程度把它并入前面或后面一句,使其充当句子的附属成分。当然也可以加上它的逻辑主语,让它真正独立成句。

(3)细节补充独立句

句子的细节补充部分,例如举例、罗列、补充说明等一般是既不含主语也不含谓语的一组词语的罗列,如果以句子

的形式出现则肯定是错句。如：

【错误】It is hard to keep with monthly payments. Such as telephone, electric, and gas bill.

【正确】It is hard to keep with monthly payments, such as telephone, electric, and gas bill.

犯此类错误的学生往往误以为一个句子的主语和谓语可以同时对随后的一组词语起作用。所以考生要明确一点：与汉语这种讲究"意合"的语言不同，英语严格要求"形合"，即每一个句子都要有自己的主、谓语，否则就被视为错句、非完整句。

(4)无主语句

无主语句就是缺少主语的非完整句。如：

【错误】Tom dreamed of the day that he would have lots of money. And would use it to buy a nice house.

【正确】Tom dreamed of the day that he would have lots of money, and would use it to buy a nice house.

【错误】While sitting in class, she realized she had lost a ring. But happily found it on the floor after class.

【正确】While sitting in class, she realized she had lost a ring. But she happily found it on the floor after class.

这种错误的出现也是由于学生受汉语的影响，误以为既然动作是由同一主体发出，前句的主语就可以同样作用于后句，没有必要再重复了。如果是在一个并列句当中，这种做法是正确的，问题就出在又把它写成了独立的句子。这反映了部分考生对并列句的掌握不够扎实，同时和其他错句错误一样，没有培养出良好的英语语感也是一个很重要的原因。

2. 主动和被动错误

在句子写作中，要避免语态的转换，因为语态的转换会不可避免地造成主语的转换，这些转换都会破坏句子的连贯性，从而使句子显得拙劣、别扭。如：

【错误】As soon as the written examination has been finished by the student, he must take the oral examination.

【正确】As soon as the student has finished the written examination, he must take the oral examination.

【错误】We climbed to the top of the mountain and a tent was rented for the night.

【正确】We climbed to the top of the mountain and rented a tent for the night.

在英语写作中，尤其是日常写作中，并不提倡使用被动语态，这一点对以英语为母语的人来讲也是一样的。当然不提倡并不等于绝对不能使用被动语态。在某些特定情况下，被动语态的使用还是相当必要的。例如在表达诸如"据说……"、"据报道……"等没有必要指明动作发出者时，"It is said..."就比"People say that..."或"The mass media reported that..."要简洁、地道得多。

我们建议：①凡是有必要指出动作的发出者时，尽量使用主动语态；②如果没有必要指出动作的发出者时，可以恰当地运用被动语态；③在一个句子内部一定要避免语态(及主语)的转换。

3. 主谓不一致错误

主谓不一致是四级考生写作中最常见的错误之一，而这一点更多地是一个语法基本功的问题。具体来说有以下几点：

(1)存现句中的主谓一致

存现句中，如果有数个主语并列，动词的数一般与离它最近的那个一致。如：

【错误】There are a small bed, a wooden table and two old-fashioned chairs in my bed-room.

【正确】There is a small bed, a wooden table and two old-fashioned chairs in my bed-room.

但主语如果是几个并列的单数名词，谓语用复数。如：

There are a boy, a girl and a teacher in the classroom.

(2)带修饰语的主语与谓语一致

当一个主语后跟以 with, as well as, together with, like, rather than, except, but, including, accompanied by, besides 等词语开始的修饰语时，谓语动词的数只与主语本身保持一致。如：

【错误】John as well as the rest have agreed to come.

【正确】John as well as the rest has agreed to come.

主语中如果有 all of, most of, lots of, some of 等修饰限定语，谓语动词的数应与这些词之后的名词一致。如：

【错误】Most of the water in this area are polluted.

[正确]Most of the water in this area is polluted.

(3)主谓一致问题中的就近原则

由 neither... nor, either... or, not only... but also 等平行结构作主语时,谓语动词应与离它最近的那部分主语保持一致。如:

[错误]Not only the students but also the teacher have doubts.

[正确]Not only the students but also the teacher has doubts.

(4)不定代词作主语时的主谓一致

下列不定代词和复合代词作主语时,谓语一律用单数:one, no one, nobody, nothing, anyone, anything, everyone, everybody, someone, something, each, either, neither, etc. 如:

[错误]None of her friends have been to New York.

[正确]None of her friends has been to New York.

(5)定语从句的主谓一致

在定语从句中,关系代词 who, that 或 which 后的动词要与该关系代词所指代的先行词在人称和数上保持一致。如:

[错误]Computer can do many tasks which is impossible to do by hand.

[正确]Computer can do many tasks which are impossible to do by hand.

(6)集合名词作主语时的主谓一致

集合名词以单数形式出现,却常常表达复数的含义。一般来说,当这类名词用来表达整体概念时,后面的动词用单数;而当它们被用来指其组织成员时,谓语就用复数。这类集合名词主要有:audience, family, class, herd, crowd, troop, team, crew 等。由于这类搭配比较复杂,所以在这类词作主语时,考生往往在主谓一致问题上出错。如:

[错误]My family never intend to have anything to do with business.

[正确]My family never intends to have anything to do with business.

4. 修饰语问题

考生在修饰语的运用上出现的问题主要是悬垂修饰语。

所谓"修饰语悬垂",就是如果修饰语放在句首,它的修饰对象必须紧跟其后,否则,这修饰就失去了"依靠",而考生的表达意思也会被歪曲,变得模糊不清。纠正这种错误,可以有三种方法:①对句子结构做必要的改动,使状语和逻辑主语一致;②给状语加上一个适当的逻辑主语,使之成为一个独立结构;③将状语改成一个从句。如:

[错误]While talking on the telephone, the chicken soup boiled over.

这句话看上去是"鸡汤"在打电话。修饰语"while talking on the phone"脱离了被修饰语就被"悬"起来了。这种错误的出现也是受到了汉语"意合"的表达方式的影响,忘了英语对"形合"的严格要求。

[正确]While I was talking on the telephone, the chicken soup boiled over.

[错误]Looking out of the window, the grassland stretches as far as the eye can reach.

[正确]We looking out of the window, the grassland stretches as far as the eye can reach.

[错误]To swim properly, a course of instruction is necessary.

[正确]To swim properly, one needs a course of instruction. 或 If one wants to swim properly, a course of instruction is necessary.

5. 错用平行结构

平行结构要求并列的部分在结构上和意义层次上必须完全相同,如同为形容词、分词、动词、动名词等。若干个平行部分中如果有一个与其他不尽相同,就破坏了平行结构。如:

[错误]Tom enjoys playing football, swimming and to read novels.

"to read novels"破坏了句子的平行结构。

[正确]Tom enjoys playing football, swimming and reading novels.

6. 代词指代不明

　　代词按其语法功能是用来代替上文提到过的名词(短语)的,它使考生在写作中避免许多不必要的词语重复。因此,遵循英语写作简洁这一原则,充分利用代词无疑是很必要的。但在代词的使用上必须注意避免指代不明的问题。如:

【错误】He was knocked down by a bicycle, but it was not serious.

　　　　代词 It 所指的对象不明确。

【正确】He was knocked down by a bicycle, but was not seriously hurt.

【错误】He asked his brother whether he could send the girl home.

　　　　该句交代不清究竟是他要求哥哥把女孩送回家,还是他请求他哥哥同意让自己去送。句中代词 he 指代不明。

【正确】He asked his brother to send the girl back home. 或 He asked his brother to allow him to send the girl back home.

　　　　以上是大学英语四级考试中常见的 5 种用词错误和 6 种句子错误,颇具代表性。考生可根据实际情况对号入座,看看自己平常比较容易犯哪种类型的错误,然后有针对性地加强训练,减少和避免这些错误的出现。

Test 1

Directions: *For this part, you are allowed 30 minutes to write a letter of appeal calling for student participation in an aid-education project in Western areas. You should write at least 120 words following the outline given below:*

A Call for Participation in an Aid-Education Project

1. 市教委组织了一次西部支教的活动,学生会呼吁大学生积极参与
2. 活动的时间、要求及作用

写作指南:

这篇应用型习作要求考生写一篇倡议书,呼吁大学生积极参与西部支教活动。要注意语言真挚。

根据题目要求,文章结构如下:

第一段直接点题:呼吁大学生积极参与市教委组织的西部支教活动,并说明活动时间。

第二段简述此次西部支教活动的要求:

1. 具备相关教学经验;
2. 能够忍受恶劣的气候和生活环境。

第三段简述本次活动的作用,再次呼吁大学生积极参与,并提供联系方式。

范文与解析:

Sample	Analysis
July 2nd, 2006 Fellow schoolmates, 　　**[1]Under the sponsorship** of the Municipal Education Commission, an aid-education project will be held **[2]for the duration of** the summer vacation. **[3]We hereby call for** your participation to offer your kind help to students in the poverty-stricken western areas. 　　**[4]**Students **meeting** the following requirements are welcome for this project. Firstly, relevant teaching experience in	**[1]**介词词组 **under the sponsorship** 的使用,语体较为正式,意为"在……倡议下"。 **[2]for the duration of** 表示"持续时间长达……",体现了语言的正式性。 **[3]hereby call for** 意为"特此呼吁",hereby 多用于公文和布告等正式场合。 **[4]**-ing 分词作后置定语,体现了句型使用的

English, Chinese and Math is a must. **[5]**Secondly, **participants** should be confident to endure bad climate and poor living environment.

[6]This project will be a **bridge** shortening the distance between people in western areas and metropolitan cities. **[7]**Our love and devotion will benefit the teenagers there **thirsty for** knowledge. We are looking forward to your sincere support. **[8]If interested**, please contact the Student Union via email. studentunionjd@163.com.

Yours sincerely,
The Student Union

灵活性。

[5]用 **participants** 代替 students，显示用词的多样性。

[6]bridge 为比喻用法，意为"联系的纽带"。

[7]thirsty for 为比喻用法，意为"渴望"。

[8]If interested 为省略结构，当 if 从句中的主语与主句主语一致时，可以省略从句中的主语和助动词。

句型变换：

[1]
1. Under the sponsorship of the Municipal Education Commission, an aid-education project will be held for the duration of the summer vacation.
2. An aid-education project will be held during this summer vacation under the sponsorship of the Municipal Education Commission.
3. An aid-education project will be sponsored in this summer vacation by the Municipal Education Commission.
4. The Municipal Education Commission will initiate an aid-education project in this summer vacation.

[3]
1. We hereby call for your participation to offer your kind help to students...
2. We hereby call on more students to participate. In this way, we can offer our kind help to students...
3. We are looking forward to your participation and your kind help for students...
4. We earnestly invite you to participate and offer your kind help to students...

[4]
1. Students meeting the following requirements...
2. Students conforming to the following requirements...
3. Students suiting the following requirements...
4. Students satisfying the following requirements...

[5]
1. ..., participants should be confident to endure bad climate and poor living environment.
2. ..., students who are confident of their endurance of bad climate and living environment are welcome.
3. ..., participants need to make sure that they can bear the foul climate and poor living environment.
4. ..., target participants are those who can put up with foul climate and bad living environment.

[6]
1. This project will be a bridge shortening the distance between people in western areas and metropolitan cities.
2. This project will be a tie of friendship which will shorten the distance between people in western areas and metropolitan cities.
3. This project will be a link between people in western areas and metropolitan cities.
4. This project will bring people in western areas and metropolitan cities closer.

[7]
1. Our love and devotion will benefit the teenagers there thirsty for knowledge.
2. The teenagers there, thirsty for knowledge, will benefit from our love and devotion.
3. The teenagers there, in great need of knowledge, will get benefit from our love and devotion.
4. Our love and devotion will yield benefits to the teenagers there who badly need knowledge.

[8]
1. If interested, please contact the Student Union via email.
2. If you are interested, don't hesitate to contact the Student Union by email.
3. Whoever interested can contact the Student Union via email.
4. Should you interested, please feel free to contact the Student Union via email.

Test 2

Directions: *For this part, you are allowed 30 minutes to write an essay entitled **Turn off Your Mobile Phone**. You should write at least 120 words following the outline given below in Chinese:*

Turn off Your Mobile Phone

1. 移动电话给我们的生活带来了便利
2. 移动电话有时也会影响别人
3. 在某些场合请关掉手机

写作指南:

这是四级作文中典型的议论型习作,要求考生论证移动电话给我们带来的便利和造成的不良影响。结尾无须考生阐述自己的立场,而是根据题目要求呼吁人们在某些场合关掉手机。

根据题目要求,文章结构如下:

第一段:引出话题并详细论证移动电话给我们的生活带来的便利。

第二段:用例证法说明移动电话给我们带来的尴尬:

1. 在公共场所使用移动电话大声通话;

2. 在正式场合,移动电话的铃声此起彼伏。

第三段:呼吁大家在某些场合关掉手机。

范文与解析:

Sample	Analysis
【1】Thanks to the development of information technology and reduced price of communication devices, the mobile phone has become a necessity for most people. 【2】Obviously, it shortens the distance between people and makes our life more convenient. 【3】The mobile phone has made it easier for us to contact or be reached by other people anytime and anywhere. 【4】We will never miss any important meetings, great deals or admirable opportunities.	【1】第一句话开门见山,引出话题。 【2】副词 **Obviously** 起强调语气的作用。 【3】【4】对第二句做进一步的阐述,意义衔接紧密。
【5】But have you noticed sometimes the mobile phone also brings embarrassment to us? 【6】**It's not rare to** see someone shout loudly in public when using the mobile phone. 【7】And I'm sure most people have had such an experience that mobile phones ring continuously on a formal occasion. 【8】Perhaps these people have many "**life-and-death**" issues to keep the phone working at all times, 【9】but it bothers the other people.	【5】一般疑问句引出第二段,承上启下。 【6】**It is not rare to** 句型列举现象,语气缓和,表达客观。 【8】**life-and-death** 是句中的语言亮点,略为夸张的形容词使表达更生动。
【10】So if you are one of them, please shut off your mobile phone in public, especially on a quiet and serious occasion.	【10】祈使句发出呼吁,简洁有力。

句型变换：

[1]

1. ... the mobile phone has become a necessity for most people.
2. ... the mobile phone has become increasingly necessary for a vast majority of people.
3. ... the mobile phone has become part of most people's daily life.
4. ... there has been a general recognition of the mobile phone as a necessity of daily life.

[3]

1. The mobile phone has made it easier for us to contact or be reached by other people anytime and anywhere.
2. The mobile phone provides us an easier access to other people anytime and anywhere.
3. The cell phone makes it possible for us to contact or be reached by other people anytime and anywhere.
4. The cell phone enables people to keep in touch with each other anytime and anywhere.

[6]

1. It's not rare to see someone shout loudly in public when using the mobile phone.
2. People are often seen to shout loudly in public when using the mobile phone.
3. It's not uncommon to see someone shout loudly in public when using the mobile phone.
4. Shouting loudly to a mobile phone is not a rare case in public places.

[7]

1. And I'm sure most people have had such an experience that mobile phones ring continuously on a formal occasion.
2. It's a common occurrence that mobile phones ring continuously on a formal occasion.
3. I believe most people have shared such an experience that mobile phones ring continuously on a formal occasion.
4. It's an experience shared by most people that mobile phones ring continuously on a formal occasion.

[8]

1. Perhaps these people have many "life-and-death" issues to keep the phone working at all times...
2. Perhaps there are many extremely important issues to keep the phone working all the time...
3. Perhaps these people have every reason to keep the phone working all day long...
4. Perhaps these people need keep the phone working around the clock, and with good reason...

[9]

1. but it bothers the other people.
2. but the other people are greatly bothered.
3. but it's a nuisance to the other people.
4. but it brings disturbance to the other people.

Test 3

Directions: *For this part, you are allowed 30 minutes to write an essay entitled **Should College Students Own Credit Cards**. You should write at least 120 words following the outline given below in Chinese:*

Should College Students Own Credit Cards?

1. 一些银行开始向大学生开放信用卡业务
2. 人们对此看法不一
3. 你的观点

写作指南：

这是四级作文中典型的分析议论型习作,要求考生先分析人们对大学生持信用卡的不同意见及理由,然后阐述自己的观点,可选择支持、反对或中立三种立场。

根据题目要求,文章结构如下：

第一段(二句话模式):提出现象+说明争议的存在。

第二段:有的人认为信用卡对大学生有利：

1. 信用卡方便了学生的生活并能帮助他们树立健康的理财观;
2. 信用卡可以帮助学生建立良好的信用记录。

第三段:有的人认为大学生使用信用卡弊大于利:

1. 信用卡助长了大学生超负荷消费之风。
2. 信用卡可能使学生沦为"卡奴",为还债而影响学习。

第四段:持中立观点提出信用卡本身无所谓好坏,建议大学生可以使用有较低透支上限的信用卡。

范文与解析:

Sample	Analysis
[1]Some banks begin to offer credit cards to college students, which raises a general debate. [2]**People's views on the issue vary**. [3]**Some people believe** that credit card not only makes students' life more convenient, [4]but also gives students a good opportunity to develop a sound sense of financing. [5]**Furthermore**, [6]it can help them establish a good credit history. [7]**However, others think** the disadvantages weigh much more than the advantages. They argue that credit card invites students to become lavish spenders. [8]Students may spend well **beyond their means** and **end up in debt** that they can't pay off. [9]**What's more**, since interest rates are often high and penalties are severe if one fails to pay on time, [10]students may gradually become "credit card slaves" and can hardly focus on their academic life. [11]There is probably something true in both arguments, but the credit card in itself is neither good nor bad. [12]Perhaps **a happy medium** is to get a credit card that has a certain credit limit.	【1】引出现象。 【2】阐述争论的经典句型,起承上启下的作用。 【3】【7】引出对立观点的经典句型 **Some people believe... others think**。 【5】**Furthermore** 使上下文衔接得更流畅。 【7】**However** 表转折,起承上启下的作用。 【8】短语 **beyond their means** 和 **end up in debt** 是文中的亮点,使句子更生动。 【9】**What's more** 使文章更紧凑。 【11】用欲擒故纵法引出自己的观点,先承认两方的观点都有可取性,然后笔锋一转,提出自己的观点,使文章的论述更为客观。 【12】**a happy medium**(折中的办法)是语言亮点,短语的使用很贴切。

句型变换:

[1]

1. Some banks begin to offer credit cards to college students, which raises a general debate.
2. There is a general debate on the phenomenon that some banks begin to issue credit cards to college students.
3. With college students becoming eligible applicants of credit cards, there is much discussion on the issue.
4. That whether college students should own credit cards arouses controversies as some banks have allowed college students to become credit card users.

[2]

1. People's views on the issue vary.

2. People hold different views towards the issue.
3. There are many arguments for and against this practice.
4. People differ in their views on the issue.

[4]

1. but also gives students a good opportunity to develop a sound sense of financing.
2. but also helps students learn how to use money wisely.
3. but also cultivates students' financial management skills they will need to succeed in life.
4. but also prepare students for their independent life in terms of financing after graduation.

[6]

1. it can help them establish a good credit history.

2. young credit users may be able to create a good credit history.

3. it helps credit users to build up a good credit record.

4. it's helpful for young users to start a good credit record.

[7]

1. However, others think the disadvantages weigh much more than the advantages.

2. However, some other people believe there are more disadvantages than advantages.

3. However, some other people tends to view it the other way round.

4. However, some other people think there are more cons than pros in it.

[8]

1. Students may spend well beyond their means and end up in debt that they can't pay off.

2. Students are likely to spend well beyond their means and unable to pay off their debts.

3. Likely to spend more than they could afford, stu-

dents may end up in debt that they can not pay back.

4. Students may get into debt that they can't pay back when they spend more than they have.

[10]

1. students may gradually become "credit card slaves" and can hardly focus on their academic life.

2. how can a student who turns into a "credit card slave" focus on his academic life?

3. becoming a "credit card slave", a student can hardly focus on his academic life.

4. under the pressure of paying off bills, a student can hardly focus on his academic life.

[11]

1. There is probably something true in both arguments, ...

2. Perhaps both arguments are reasonable to some extent, ...

3. Perhaps both sides hold convincing points, ...

4. Perhaps the above arguments are all quite reasonable and logical, ...

Test 4

Directions: *For this part, you are allowed 30 minutes to write an essay entitled **More Private Cars or Not**. You should write at least 120 words following the outline given below in Chinese:*

More Private Cars or Not

1. 现在越来越多人买私家车,原因是什么
2. 私家车会给社会带来什么问题
3. 你认为应采取什么措施来解决私家车所造成的社会问题

写作指南:

这是典型的四级分析型习作。第一点要求考生引出现象,并作简要说明。第二点要求考生列举私家车带来的问题。最后提出建议。

根据题目要求,文章结构如下:

第一段用概括法和因果法说明为什么越来越多人购买私家车。

第二段用举例法和数字法展开主题:私家车给社会带来的问题。

最后一段提出建议并结束全文。

范文与解析：

Sample	Analysis
[1]Nowadays, thanks to the rapid **elevation** of the living standard, [2]many people have bought their own cars, or are planning to buy cars. [3]**Owning a private car can certainly help one travel more conveniently and save much precious time.**	[1]主题句引出现象,**elevation** 为亮点词汇。 [3]说明越来越多的人购买私家车的原因。
[4]But negative effects of the matter should be taken into consideration: air pollution and traffic jams and accidents. [5]As China's population is **overwhelmingly large**—1.3 billion— even a small percentage, say **10%**, of the population owning private cars, would mean an increase of **130,000,000** cars emitting waste gases to **deteriorate** the air quality and congesting the already overcrowded roads even worse.	[4]**But negative effects** 引出私家车带来的社会问题。**take into consideration** 意为"考虑" [5]**overwhelmingly large** 表示"非常多"。用3个数字说明问题,说服力强,**deteriorate** 为亮点词汇。
[6]**In my opinion**, the government should **take into account** the possible bad consequences mentioned above and hold the number of private cars under strict control until it finds solutions to the problems. The general public should try to make the most of the existing public transportation facilities rather than rush to buy a car.	[6]**In my opinion** 提出自己的建议。**take into account sth.**意为"考虑,注意"。

句型变换：

[1]

1. ... thanks to the rapid elevation of the living standard,

2. ... owing to the rapid improvement of their living standard,

3. ... because of the elevated living standard,

4. ... with the rapid elevation of the living standard,

[2]

1. many people have bought their own cars, or are planning to buy cars.

2. there are many people who are driving their own cars or going to buy cars.

3. buying cars has been on many people's mind.

4. some people have already bought cars. Others are planning to buy their own cars.

[3]

1. Owning a private car can certainly help one travel more conveniently and save much precious time.

2. Surely owing a car helps people travel more easily and save much precious time.

3. It is certain that one will travel more easily and save

much precious time if they have a car.

4. Certainly it is more convenient and time-saving if they own a car.

[5]

1. As China's population is overwhelmingly large—1.3 billion—even a small percentage, say 10%, of the population owning private cars, would mean an increase of 130,000,000 cars emitting waste gases to deteriorate the air quality and congesting the already overcrowded roads even worse.

2. As China has an extremely large population, even a small number of people owning private cars will aggravate the air pollution and congest the already overcrowded roads even worse.

3. With such a large population as about 1.3 billion, even if one in ten owns a private car in China, the emission of waste gases will cause serious air pollution and the cars will congest the already overcrowded roads even worse.

4. Because of the overwhelmingly large population of 1.3 billion in China, even 10% of people owning

private cars will amount to an increase of one hundred and twenty million cars discharging exhaust into the air and congesting the already overcrowded roads even worse.

[6]

1. In my opinion, the government should take into account the possible bad consequences mentioned above...

2. In my opinion, it is the government's duty to con-

sider the possible consequences mentioned above...

3. I reckon that the possible consequences mentioned above should be taken into consideration by the government...

4. I believe taking into account the possible consequences mentioned above should be the government's responsibility...

Test 5

Directions: *Read the following advertisement carefully, and you, by name of Wang Peng, are then asked to write a letter to apply for the job. Remember to send your letter to the company as given in the ad. You should write about 120 words.*

中国四达国际经济技术合作公司(CSCIETC)诚聘文秘一员,要求如下:

* 年龄 20-30 岁,大专以上学历

* 流利的英语听说读写能力

* 熟练的计算机操作能力

* 良好的沟通与协调能力

* 有外企工作经验者优先

应聘者请将简历和联系方式以及待遇要求寄至上海市淮海中路 0560 号揽盛大厦人力资源部

邮编:200033

写作指南:

写求职信是许多大学生就业前要经历的。求职信与一般的作文风格不同,它属于应用文范畴,有相对固定的格式和句式,考生可参考以下的格式和信中内容的遣词造句。

根据题目要求,文章结构如下:

首先,写明获得招聘信息的来源,并表明对这份工作极大的兴趣。

第二部分证明自己有能力胜任这个职位,一般叙述自己的资历、能力和能够胜任该职位所具备的条件。

最后提供一些必要的证明,并表达希望得到这个工作的恳切心情。

范文与解析:

Sample	Analysis
[1]Wang Peng No. 3120, Zhongshan Road Xu Hui District Shanghai, 200076 Jul., 28th, 2006 Department of Human Resources Lansheng Building No. 8560, Huaihai Zhong Road Shanghai, 200033	[1]寄信人地址写在右上方(日期之上),收信人地址置于左上方(日期之下一行,称呼之上)。地址按由小到大的顺序排列。

Dear Sir/Madam,

【2】I learned from *Beijing Youth Daily* on Jul. 26 that your company is offering a position for a secretary, and 【3】**it's a great pleasure for me to write to** explore the possibility of seeking the job.

【4】I graduated two years ago from Beijing University of Technology with a bachelor's degree in Business Management. During my education, I have grasped the principles of my major and skills of practice. Not only have I passed CET-6, but I can communicate with others fluently in English. And I'm skilled in computer operations.

【5】**Upon** graduation I worked in HP China as an assistant to the head of Marketing Department. 【6】My responsibilities consisted of carrying out market surveys, writing reports and organizing meetings within the department. This two-year experience has helped me a lot in many ways. 【7】In particular, I have realized the importance of **co-ordination** and **co-operation** among **co-workers**.

Enclosed please find my resume and some relevant documents as required. 【8】**If** these meet your reguirements, pleace grant me an interview. I can **be reached** at 021-66668888.

Respectfully yours,

Wang Peng

【2】【3】写信的目的及获悉这个职位空缺的途径,并表明对这份工作的兴趣。

【4】介绍自己能够胜任这个职位所具备的条件。

【5】**Upon** 结构,使句式多变。

【7】**co-ordination, co-operation, co-workers** 语言形式对称。

【8】**if** 句型,进一步丰富文章句型。**be reached** 的用法及表达十分灵活。

句型变换:

【2】

1. I learned from *Beijing Youth Daily* on Jul. 26 that your company is offering a position for a secretary...

2. I read your ad in *Beijing Youth Daily* Jul. 26 that an opening for a secretary is offered...

3. I learned from *Beijing Youth Daily* Jul. 26 that there is a vacancy for a secretary in your company...

4. In reply to your advertisement in *Beijing Youth Daily* Jul. 26, I offer myself as a candidate for the position...

【3】

1. it's a great pleasure for me to write to explore the possibility of seeking the job.

2. I'm pleased to write to apply for the job.

3. I'm writing to explore the possibility of getting the job.

4. I would like to be considered as one of the potential candidates for this opening.

【5】

1. Upon graduation I worked in HP China as an assistant to the head of Marketing Department.

2. As soon as I graduated from university, I worked with HP China as an assistant to the head of Marketing Department.

3. Immediately after graduation, I started working in HP China as an assistant to the head of Marketing Department.

4. Upon graduation I got a job in HP China and worked as an assistant to the head of Marketing Department.

【6】

1. My responsibilities consisted of carrying out market surveys, writing reports and organizing meetings within the department.

2. My work is to draft market surveys and reports as

well as organize internal meetings.

3. I was responsible to carry out market surveys, write reports and organize meetings within the department.

4. I was assigned to do the job of carrying out markets

surveys, writing reports and organizing department meetings.

Test 6

Directions: *For this part, you are allowed 30 minutes to write an essay entitled* **On Making Friends**. *You should write at least 120 words following the outline given below in Chinese:*

On Making Friends

1. 每个人都需要朋友
2. 什么是真正的朋友
3. 你的观点

写作指南：

这是典型的四级论说文题型。第一点点明文章主题：人人都需要朋友。第二点说明什么是真正的朋友。最后表明自己的观点。

根据题目要求，文章的结构如下：

开头段用概括法引出主题：人人都需要朋友。

中间段引用谚语和对比法展开段落，说明什么是真正的朋友。

结尾段用概括法总结自己的观点。

范文与解析：

Sample	Analysis
Everyone needs friends. [1]No one can sail **the ocean of life** single-handed. [2]As a matter of fact, you'll feel lonely without a friend. [3]**Moreover**, when you are in need of help, [4]whom could you turn to if you have no friends? [5]**In any case,** [6]we **find it very important to** make friends. [7]It goes without saying that everyone knows that a friend in need is a friend indeed. [8]True friendship results from understanding and trusting between each other. [9]Those who share your pain and hardship are true friends, while those who are eager to please you may be false friends. [10]In my opinion, we need to stick to the principle of making honest and reliable friends. [11]**That is to say,** a good friend should be trustworthy and dependable.	[1]No one can...使用否定词，起强调作用。 **the ocean of life** 使用暗喻的修辞手法。 [3]**Moreover** 的使用使文章条理清楚，层次分明。 [4]使用疑问句，使句式多样化。 [5]**In any case** 起强调作用。 [6]**find it very important to...**使用宾语复合结构，句式多变。 [7][8][9]并列阐述什么才是真正的朋友。 [11]**That is to say** 重申作者的观点。

句型变换：

[1]
1. No one can sail the ocean of life single-handed.
2. No one can lead a life without friends.
3. We all need friends throughout our life.
4. Friends are indispensable in our life.

[2]
1. As a matter of fact, you'll feel lonely without a friend.
2. In fact, if you don't have friends you will feel lonely.
3. The fact is that living in a world without friends can make one feel lonely.

4. A person without friends will lead a lonely life.

[3]

1. Moreover, when you are in need of help, whom could you turn to if you have no friends?
2. In addition, if you need help, whom could you turn to other than friends?
3. Furthermore, without friends you will have no one to turn to when you are in trouble.
4. Besides, you can depend on friends for help when problems crop up.

[5]

1. In any case, we find it very important to make friends.
2. At any rate, it's of great significance for us to make friends.
3. Anyway, friends are very important to us since no one lives in an isolated world.
4. Anyhow, friends are indispensable to a healthy life.

[7]

1. It goes without saying that everyone knows that a friend in need is a friend indeed.
2. As an old saying goes, "A friend in need is a friend indeed".
3. It is well known that only a friend in need is a friend indeed.
4. Everyone knows that a true friend will help you out when you are in trouble.

[8]

1. True friendship results from understanding and trusting between each other.
2. Only with mutual understanding and trusting can true friendship be developed.
3. If we don't understand or trust each other, we won't form true friendship.
4. Without mutual trusting and understanding, people can't become true friends.

[9]

1. Those who share your pain and hardship are true friends...
2. True friends are those who share your pain and hardship...
3. Only true friends will share your pain and hardships...
4. If one can't share your pain and hardship, he is not your true friend...

[10]

1. In my opinion, we need to stick to the principle of making honest and reliable friends.
2. In my view, we must have the principle of making friends with those honest and reliable.
3. As I see it, we should make friends with those who are honest and reliable.
4. From my point of view, we must follow the principle of making friends with those who are honest and trustworthy.

Test 7

Directions: *For this part, you are allowed 30 minutes to write an essay on* **How to Achieve Success.** *You should write at least 120 words following the outline given below in Chinese:*

How to Achieve Success

1. 有人说成功要靠运气
2. 有人则认为成功主要靠勤奋,与运气毫无关系
3. 你的观点如何? 并说明理由

写作指南:

这是四级作文中典型的观点分析型习作,要求考生先简述人们对成功主要因素的不同看法,然后在此基础上明确个人观点并说明理由。

根据写作要求,文章结构如下:

第一段:先简述两种不同观点,再表明自己的立场:"我"认为勤奋、投入和坚持不懈是取得成功的三个基本要素。

第二段:说明勤奋对取得成功的重要性。

第三段:说明投入对取得成功的重要性。

第四段:说明坚持不懈对取得成功的重要性。

第五段结尾段:用两句名言总结全文,重申主题。

范文与解析:

Sample	Analysis
[1]Some people say the key to success is good luck, while others claim it is hard work that really counts. [2]There is no doubt that successful people do take the advantage of opportunities. But if they do not work hard, they can only wait to see opportunities pass by. [3]So in my opinion, diligence, devotion and perseverance are three fundamental factors in success.	[1]观点分析型作文的典型开头:引述别人的观点。 [3]在主题句中明确个人观点。
[4]Diligence is **the first key to** success, which simply means to work persistently without any waste of time. Diligence makes a fool wise and a poor rich. If we work hard now we could expect a success **later on**. And If we don't, our future life will probably be **gloomy**.	[4]... **the first key to**...开门见山点出获得成功的第一个重要因素。**later on** 和 **gloomy** 为亮点词汇。
[5]Devotion, which means the concentration of our mind on doing things, is **another** key factor to success. [6]**Only** when we focus our minds on the job, **can we** do it well.	[5]用 **another** 起到承上启下的作用,进一步分析获得成功的另一个不可或缺的因素 [6]**only**+状语从句的倒装结构起强调作用。
[7]Perseverance is **also** indispensable for success. Without a strong will we can hardly overcome the difficulties.	[7]用 **also** 这个过渡词再次说明持之以恒对成功的重要性。
[8]**To conclude**, success is not something easy to achieve, and it is based on diligence, devotion and perseverance. [9]Just as the famous sayings go: "**No pains no gains.**" and "**Where there is a will, there is a way.**"	[8][9]在结尾段用 **To conclude** 和两句名言总结全文,并重申主题。

句型变换:

[1]
1. Some people say the key to success is good luck, while others claim it is...
2. Some people believe that the key to success is good luck, while other people argue that...
3. When it comes to the key to success, many people say that good luck is the most important thing, but others regard... as...
4. As far as the key to success is concerned, some people think that good luck is indispensable, whereas others hold the view that...

[2]
1. There is no doubt that...
2. There is no denying of the fact that...
3. Undoubtedly, ...
4. It is true that...

[3]
1. So in my opinion, ...
2. So from my point of view, ...
3. As I see it, ...
4. From my perspective, ...

[4]
1. Diligence is the first key to...
2. Diligence is of the utmost importance for...
3. Diligence is the foremost element of...
4. Diligence is of vital significance for...

[5]
1. ... is another key factor to success.
2. ... is also a vital factor in success.
3. ... weighs a lot to success as well.
4. ... also plays a great role in achieving success.

[8]
1. To conclude, ...

2. To sum up, ...

3. In short, ...

4. In a word, ...

.... 〔9〕

1. Just as the famous sayings go...

2. As is said in the sayings...

3. As is illustrated in the sayings...

4. Just as the famous sayings tell...

Test 8

Directions: *For this part, you are allowed 30 minutes to write an essay on **Quality Education**. You should write at least 120 words following the outline given below in Chinese:*

Quality Education

1. 中国素质教育的现状

2. 素质教育的好处

3. 怎样才能实现素质教育

写作指南：

这是四级作文中典型的分析型习作,要求考生分析中国素质教育的现状以及素质教育的优点,最后要求考生对如何实现素质教育提出个人建议。

根据写作要求,文章结构如下：

第一段:用概括法分析目前中国素质教育的现状,从而明确主题:应该在国内推行素质教育。

第二段:采用从一般到具体的方法进一步说明素质教育的多种好处；

第三段:列举一些实现素质教育的方法,并提出展望。

范文与解析：

Sample	Analysis
[1]Nowadays, educationalists advocate that **Quality Education should be promoted in the country**. [2]But the situation worries them a lot. [3]**Students are being burdened** with countless homework and various examinations, and their development of other important nonacademic qualities is hindered or totally overlooked.	[1][2]开头段引出主题 **Quality Education should be promoted in the country**,并用概括法总结目前中国教育素质的现状。 [3]说明学生的负担和目前欠缺素质教育的原因与结果。
[4]**It is obvious that** Quality Education is beneficial to students. [5]**First**, it will, to some extent, free them from homework and tests. [6]**Second**, it can broaden students' horizon and enhance their capacities. [7]**What's more**, it values ability more than memory, so students will develop their abilities in an all-round manner.	[4]采用从一般到具体的方法分析优点,先用 **It is obvious that... is beneficial to...**提纲挈领式地说明素质教育对学生是有益的。 [5]采用因果法说明素质教育的第一项主要好处。 [6][7]用递进法进一步阐述素质教育的益处。
[8]But how can Quality Education be enforced? [9]**First**, the education system should be reformed by changing the educational objectives, revising the syllabuses and so on. [10]**Second**, the workforce of teachers should be trained and new teachers with more innovative ideas and higher qualifications	[8]用问句开头,使前后两段得以自然衔接。 [9][10][11]用具体法从教育系统、教师以及先进教学方法和素材等几个方面提出了实现素质教育的方法。

should be employed. **[11]Third**, new advanced practices and teaching materials should be introduced from countries with developed education system. **[12]In this way**, a new educational prospect will be in sight in the near future.

【12】用 **In this way** 简要作结,最后提出展望。

句型变换:

[1]

1. Nowadays, educationists advocate that Quality Education should be promoted...
2. These days we often hear about educationists' favorite viewpoint of Quality Education...
3. Recently educationists put forth that Quality Education should be encouraged...
4. Currently the functions of Quality Education are attached more importance by the educationist...

[2]

1. But the situation worries them a lot.
2. Nevertheless, they are much concerned about the situation.
3. Yet the situation is not optimistic.
4. However, the current educational situation provokes their deep thoughts.

[4]

1. It is obvious that Quality Education is beneficial to...
2. It is apparent that Quality Education does good to...
3. It is with little doubt that Quality Education will benefit...
4. Undoubtedly, Quality Education has some positive impact on...

[5]

1. First, ...
2. For one thing, ...
3. In the first place, ...

4. To begin with, ...

[6]

1. Second, ...
2. For another, ...
3. Besides, ...
4. In the second place, ...

[7]

1. What's more, ...
2. Moreover, ...
3. In addition, ...
4. Furthermore, ...

[8]

1. But how can Quality Education be enforced?
2. But how can Quality Education be turned into reality?
3. But how can Quality Education be practiced effectively?
4. But how can we carry out Quality Education satisfactorily?

[12]

1. In this way, a new educational prospect will be in sight in the near future.
2. If we can follow the ideas mentioned, we would be able to expect a bright future of education.
3. All this would help a new prospect of education take shape.
4. Then there will be a positive outlook of Chinese educational reform.

Test 9

Directions: *For this part, you are allowed 30 minutes to write an essay about **Marriage of Students On-campus**. You should write at least 120 words following the outline given below in Chinese:*

Marriage of Students On-campus

如何看待在校大学生结婚的问题:
1. 国家允许在校大学生结婚

2. 人们对在校学生结婚的态度
3. 你的观点

写作指南：

这是观点型的社会热点问题习作,要求考生先阐述目前国家政策所允许的在校大学生结婚这一现象,从而引出人们对这一问题的不同看法,最后明确考生自己的观点并说明理由。

根据题目要求,文章结构如下:

第一段开头段:用问句形式自然引出颇有争议的"在校大学生结婚"这一话题。

第二段观点段落一:分析人们对此问题的负面观点。

第三段观点段落二:分析人们对此问题的正面观点。

第四段结尾段:直接点明个人见解:不应该提倡在校大学生的结婚行为。

范文与解析：

Sample	Analysis
[1]The government's **allowance that** college students may get married **triggers a controversial debate**: is it sensible to l egalize on-campus marriage? [2]**Some people welcome** this new development, **while others have expressed** their concern about it. [3]**Those who take sides against this new trend believe that** married students will inevitably have less time and energy for their academic life because they have more real-life problems to deal with than those unmarried ones. [4]One common argument, **however**, for on-campus students' marriage is **that** a number of students do have a desire for an ideal marriage. Now that they have come of age, they are entitled to such happiness. [5]I'm **in favor of** the former. [6]On-campus students are laden with academic tasks. [7]**If** they get married now, they **have to** work much harder than any other student because they **have to** solve their financial problems at the same time.	[1]这是一个很复杂的句子:主语 allowance 后接同位语从句,谓语动词生动地使用了 trigger"引发";controversial debate 和问句引出颇具争议的在校大学生结婚这一话题。 [2]Some people welcome..., while others have expressed... 引出人们截然相反的态度。 [3]用经典句型 those who... believe that 引出反对在校大学生结婚的观点。 [4]用 however 一词引出赞成在校大学生结婚的观点。另外,句中 that 引导的是表语从句。 [5]阐述个人看法:同意第一种观点。 [6][7]陈述不赞成在校大学生结婚的理由。用 if 假设从句和两个 have to 说明结婚后会遇到的各种麻烦。

句型变换：

[1]

1. The government's allowance that college students may get married triggers a controversial debate: is it sensible to legalize on-campus marriage?

2. An issue has caused wide public attention: The government has approved college students' on-campus marriage, but is it a sensible thing to legalize?

3. There is a general debate: is it wise to legalize college students' on-campus marriage?

4. These days we often hear about a controversial topic: is it sensible to legalize on-campus marriage of college students?

[2]

1. Some people welcome this new development, while others have expressed their concern about it.

2. Some people applaud this new trend while others worry about it.

3. Though there are people welcoming this new development, some firmly object to it.

4. Many favor this new idea; still others are against it.

[3]

1. Those who take sides against this new trend believe that...

2. Those who are against it believe that...

3. Those who are on the opposite side argue that...

4. Opponents assert that...

[4]

1. One common argument, however, for on-campus students' marriage is that...

2. People who are for on-campus students' marriage hold that...

3. Those sympathizing on-campus students' marriage be-

lieve that...

4. Proponents argue that...

[5]

1. I'm in favor of the former.

2. I'm on the side of the former.

3. I'm in support of the former.

4. I approve of the former.

Test 10

Directions: *For this part, you are allowed 30 minutes to write an essay entitled Styles of Living. You should write at least 120 words following the outline given below in Chinese:*

Styles of Living

1. 有些人愿意和父母住在一起
2. 有些人想自己独立居住
3. "我"的看法

写作指南:

这是四级作文中典型的比较型写作,要求考生分析目前社会上年轻人喜爱的两种截然不同的生活方式:和父母同住,或者自己独居。写作要求的第三点要求考生自由阐述个人观点,这可以是带有倾向性的选择。

根据写作要求,文章结构如下:

第一段:开门见山,分析喜欢同父母同住的原因:父母和子女可以相互照应;子女有困难时,可以得到父母及时的帮助。

第二段:分析喜欢自己独立居住的原因:喜欢独立、自由、个人空间,有机会自己面对社会。

第三段为结尾段:表明自己观点。

范文与解析:

Sample	Analysis
[1]Some people enjoy living under the same roof with their parents even after they have grown up. [2]They hold the opinion that when living with parents they can take better care of their parents and **vice versa**. [3]Meanwhile, they can turn to their parents for help if they get into trouble or have some difficulties. To them, life in a big family seems to be more enjoyable than that in a small one. [4]Others, **however**, prefer to live by themselves. [5]They cherish the idea to be [6]**independent, seek more freedom** and have **a place of their own**, in which they can do whatever they like. [7]Besides, they don't want to be overprotected by their parents but long for a chance to face the society by themselves. [8]As to me, I like an independent life style in spite of the fact that I love my parents. Living separately, each genera-	[1]Some people enjoy 引出了一部分人的观点,直接对应提纲第一点要求。 [2]固定词组 vice versa"反之亦然"的使用使语言简洁。 [3]Meanwhile 连接平行结构,引出另外一个原因。 [4]however 笔锋一转,引出了另一部分人的看法。 [6]具体说明"独立"就是追寻 more freedom 和 a place of their own,使论述丰满而不空洞。 [7]用 Besides 体现递进关系,比 secondly 更显灵活。

tion can enjoy different life styles. **[9]In addition,** by leading an independent life I can develop an ability to deal with things happening in my life and build up the confidence that I can manage my own life well.

[8][9]直接表明个人观点,愿意独居,并说明理由。

句型变换:

[1]

1. Some people enjoy living under the same roof with their parents even after they have grown up.
2. Some people like living in the same house with their parents even when they are grown-ups.
3. Some people prefer to share a residence with their parents even after they have come of age.
4. Some people choose to live together with their parents even when they are adults.

[2]

1. They hold the opinion that when living with their parents they can take better care of their parents and vice versa.
2. They are of the opinion that living under the same roof with their parents they can take better care of their parents and vice versa.
3. They favor living with their parents for they can take better care of each other.
4. They subscribe to the opinion that they can take better care of each other by living with parents.

[3]

1. Meanwhile, they can turn to their parents for help...
2. In addition, they can ask for their parents' help to them...
3. At the same time, parents can render help to them...
4. Apart from that they can get help from their parents...

[4]

1. Others, however, prefer to live by themselves.
2. Others, however, like to live by themselves.
3. Other people, conversely, would rather live independently.
4. On the contrary, others enjoy living on their own.

[5]

1. They cherish the idea to be independent, seek more freedom and have a place of their own.
2. They value the idea of not being dependent on their parents, seeking more freedom and having a place of their own.
3. It means a lot to them to be independent, enjoy more freedom and have their own place.
4. It weighs heavily on them to be independent, seek more freedom and live in their own place.

[7]

1. Besides, they don't want to be overprotected by their parents but long for a chance to face the society by themselves.
2. What's more, they like to face the society by themselves instead of being overprotected by the parents.
3. In addition, they are eager to have the opportunity to deal with their own difficulties rather than being overprotected.
4. Meanwhile, they prefer coping with all things themselves to being overprotected by parents.

[8]

1. As to me, I like an independent life style in spite of the fact that I love my parents.
2. To me, I prefer an independent life style and still I love my parents very much.
3. Personally, I would like to live an independent life, but that does not mean that I don't love my parents.
4. To tell the truth, I like living independently though I do love my parents.

[9]

1. In addition, by leading an independent life I can...
2. Furthermore, an independent life can help me to...
3. Besides, living independently I can...
4. Apart from it, an independent life style can also help me to...

第八篇

710 分考前冲刺

Model Test **1**

答题卡 **1** (Answer Sheet 1)

Part I **Writing** (30 minutes)

Directions: *For this part, you are allowed 30 minutes to write an essay entitled **School or Major?** You should write at least 120 words following the outline given below in Chinese:*

1. 选择报考的高校时,有人先考虑大学的名气,有人先考虑专业是否热门

2. 如果两者不能兼顾,你会先考虑哪个? 为什么?

School or Major?

_____

_____

_____

Part II **Reading Comprehension (Skimming and Scanning)** (15 minutes)

1. [Y] [N] [NG] 2. [Y] [N] [NG] 3. [Y] [N] [NG] 4. [Y] [N] [NG]

5. [Y] [N] [NG] 6. [Y] [N] [NG] 7. [Y] [N] [NG]

8. An alternative sentence is only suitable to be given to _____ criminals.

9. Lawbreaking companies that receive alternative sentences are required to do good to their community by contributing to relevant _____.

10. Alternative sentences, as a new kind of justice, were most resisted by _____.

答题卡 **2** (Answer Sheet 2)

Part III **Section C**

Doctors always measure the heartbeat of a patient when examining the patient's health. The heartbeat of America's stock markets is the Dow Jones Industrial Average. No other measure of stock (36) _____ is as widely known. Sometimes it is (37) _____ called the Dow. It is published by the Dow Jones Company, an (38) _____ publisher of international financial news.

The Dow Jones Company is a product of Wall Street, the area in New York City that is the financial center of the United States. Three (39) _____ , Charles Dow, Edward Jones and Charles Bergstresser, started the company in 1882. At first, they published a (40) _____ newsletter for financial workers. It was very (41) _____ . By 1889, the newsletter became the *Wall Street Journal* newspaper.

The Dow Jones Company began publishing the Dow Jones Industrial Average in 1896. The list had twelve stocks. It (42) _____ the biggest industries in the American (43) _____ at the time. Today, the Dow lists thirty stocks. They are often called "blue-chip" stocks. (44) _____. These well known companies include Coca-Cola, Eastman Kodak, McDonald's and General Electric.

When you read the Dow Jones Industrial Average, you quickly see that it is not the average price of thirty stocks. (45) _____. Ten-thousand does not seem like the average price of thirty stocks. (46) _____ _____. When the Dow goes up, it gains points, not dollars.

Part VI   Translation   (5 minutes)

87. She was complaining that the doctor was _____ (收费太高) for the treatment he was giving her.
88. They are going to have the serviceman _____ (安装电扇) in the office tomorrow.
89. Anne _____ (无法全神贯注于) what she was doing while her family were watching TV.
90. My father seemed to be _____ (没有心情) look at my school report.
91. Our company decided to _____ (废止合同) because a number of the conditions in it had not been met.

Part I Writing (30 minutes)

注意:此部分试题在**答题卡 1** 上。

Part II Reading Comprehension (Skimming and Scanning)(15 minutes)

Creative Justice

Is jail the right place for all offenders? Are there other punishments for criminal behavior that suit the interests of society? Judges in many countries seem to think so and are bringing into existence new and better ways of punishing some kinds of crime.

Does it help to put the offenders in jail?

Throwing criminals in jail is an ancient and widespread method of punishment, but is it a wise one? It does seem reasonable to keep wrongdoers in a place where they find fewer opportunities to hurt innocent people, and where they might discover that crime doesn't pay. The system has long been considered fair and sound by those who want to see the guilty punished and society protected. Yet the value of this form of justice is now being questioned by the very men who have to apply it: the judges. The reason, they say, is that prison doesn't do anyone any good.

Does it really help society, or the victim, or the victim's family, to put in jail a man who, while drunk at the wheel of his car, has injured or killed another person? It would be more helpful to make the man pay for his victim's medical bills and *compensate* (补偿) him for the bad experience, the loss of working time, and any other problems arising from the accident. If the victim is dead, in most cases his family could use some financial assistance.

Compensation

The idea of compensation is far from new: some ancient nations had laws defining very precisely what should be paid for every offence and injury. In Babylon, around 2700 B.C., a thief had to give back five times the value of the goods he had stolen; in Rome, centuries later, thieves only paid double. "Good system! " say modern judges, who know what bad effects a prison term can have on a nonviolent first offender. A young thief who spends time in jail receives a thorough education in crime from his fellow prisoners. Willingly or not, he has to associate with tough criminals who will drag him into more serious offences, more prison terms—a life of repeated wrongdoing that will leave a trail of victims and cost the community a great deal of money; for it is very expensive to put a man on trial and keep him in jail.

Alternative sentences

Such considerations have caused a number of English and American judges to try other kinds of punishment for "light" criminals, all unpleasant enough to discourage the offenders from repeating their offences, but safe for them because they are not exposed to dangerous company. They pay for their crime by helping their victims, financially or otherwise, or by doing unpaid labor for their community; they may have to work for the poor and the mentally ill, to clean the streets of their town, collect litter or plant trees, or to do some work for which they are qualified. Or perhaps they take a job and repay their victims out of their salary. This sort of punishment, called an alternative sentence, is applied only to nonviolent criminals who are not likely to be dangerous to the public, such as forgers, shoplifters, and drivers who have caused traffic accidents. Alternative sentences are considered particularly good for young offenders. The sentenced criminal has the right to refuse the new type of punishment if he prefers a prison term.

Examples

Since alternative sentences are not defined by law, it is up to the judges to find the punishment that fits the crime. They have shown remarkable imagination in applying what they call creative justice.

A dentist convicted of killing a motorcyclist while driving drunk has been condemned to fix the teeth of the poor and the elderly at his own expense one day a week for a full year. Another drunk driver (age nineteen) was ordered to work in the emergency room of a hospital once a week for three years, so that he could see for himself the results of careless driving.

A thief who had stolen some equipment from a farmer had to raise a pig and a calf for his victim. A former city treasurer, guilty of dishonest actions, was put to raising money for the Red Cross.

A group of teenagers were sentenced to fix ten times the number of windows that they had smashed "just for fun" on a wild evening. *Graffiti* (在墙壁上涂写) artists have been made to scrub walls, benches, and other "decorated" places. Other young offenders caught stealing old ladies' purses have been condemned to paint or repair old people's houses or to work in mental hospitals.

A doctor who had attacked his neighbor during a snowball fight had to give a lecture on the relation between smoking and cancer. A college professor arrested in a protest demonstration was ordered to write a long essay on civil disobedience, and the president of a film company, who had forged $42,000 worth of checks, had to make a film about the danger of drugs, to be shown in schools. The project cost him $45,000, besides the fine that he had been sentenced to pay.

The judge's creativity is not reserved for individuals only; lawbreaking companies also can receive alternative sentences. They are usually directed to make large contributions to charities or projects that will benefit their community.

Alternative sentences: good or bad?

Instead of trying new types of sentences, some judges have explored new ways of using the old ones. They have given prison term to be served on weekends only, for instance—a sentence that allows married offenders to keep their jobs and their families together. Although the public tends to find the weekend sentences much too light, the offenders do not always agree. Says one, "it's worse than serving one term full time, because it's like going to jail twenty times." But prison personnel object that it is too easy for weekenders to bring drugs and other forbidden goods to the other inmates; they have to be searched carefully and create extra problems and work for the guards.

Alternative sentencing is now practiced in seventeen states and is spreading fast. Judges meet regularly to compare sentences and share their experiences. The federal government has announced that it would provide guidelines to prevent the courts from giving widely different sentences for similar offences. The judges have not welcomed the idea; they feel that it will narrow their choice of sentences and restrain their imagination.

The supporters of the new justice point out that it presents many advantages. It reduces prison crowding, which has been responsible for much violence and crime among inmates. It saves a great deal of money, and decreases the chances of bad influence and repeated offences. It also provides some help to the victims, who have always been neglected in the past. Many judges think that alternative sentences may also be beneficial to the offenders themselves, by forcing them to see the effects of their crimes and the people who have suffered from them. The greatest resistance to the new kind of justice comes from the families of victims who have died. Keen on *revenge* (报复), many angrily refuse any sort of compensation. They want the criminal locked up in the good old-fashioned way. They believe, reasonably, that the only just punishment is the one that fits the crime. And they fail to understand the purpose of alternative sentencing. What the judges are trying to find is the kind of punishment that will not only be just, but useful to society, by helping the victims and their families, the community, and those offenders who can be reformed. "This," says a "creative" judge, "is true justice".

1. The practice of throwing the criminals into jail is now being questioned by _____.
   A) the innocent people
   B) the upright officials
   C) the judges
   D) the police

2. In ancient Rome, a thief would have to compensate _____ times the value of the goods he had stolen.
   A) two   B) three   C) four   D) five

3. Modern judges believe when a nonviolent first offender is put into jail, he will _____.
   A) learn to commit to the community
   B) be educated about the legal system
   C) be involved in more serious offences
   D) try hard to compensate his wrongdoing

4. An alternative sentence may be applied to _____.
   A) young murderers   B) life prisoners   C) careless drivers   D) rich criminals

5. Under the system of alternative sentence, a treasurer guilty of dishonesty was sentenced to help _____.
   A) the Children's Hospital
   B) the Red Cross
   C) the Animal Shelter
   D) the Home for the Elderly

6. The president of a film company had to make a film about the danger of drugs because he was guilty of _____.
   A) drug trafficking   B) illegal demonstration   C) check forgery   D) property damage

7. Prison personnel tend to think that weekend sentences _____.
   A) are too mild.   B) are more humane   C) only fit the married   D) cause more problems

8. Lawbreaking companies that receive alternative sentences are required to do good to their community by contributing to relevant _____.

9. Guidelines to prevent the courts from giving widely different sentences for similar offences will be constituted by _____.

10. Alternative sentences, as a new kind of justice, were most resisted by _____.

Part III   Listening Comprehension (35 minutes)

Section A

注意:此部分试题请在**答题卡2**上作答。

11. A) She doesn't like salad.
    C) She will do anything to help.
    B) She doesn't want any dinner.
    D) She prefers making something else.

12. A) In a businessman's office.
    C) In a professor's office.
    B) In a lawyer's office.
    D) In a doctor's office.

13. A) He has little chance to play golf.
    C) He is too old to play much golf.
    B) He's playing golf better recently.
    D) He prefers his old set of clubs.

14. A) He kept it out in case of rain on their way.
    C) The umbrella was too long to fit in his bag.
    B) He forgot to bring the umbrella along.
    D) His bag was too full for anything more.

15. A) Because the jacket does not suit him.
    B) Because he got dressed in the office.
    C) Because the jacket is too dark.
    D) Because the jacket and pants do not fit together.

16. A) Boss and secretary.
    C) Father and son.
    B) Teacher and student.
    D) Lawyer and client.

17. A) Noise in a restaurant.
    C) Service in a hospital.
    B) Facilities in a hotel.
    D) Environment at an airport.

18. A) The terrible working habit of his colleagues.
    B) The advanced equipment in the laboratory.

C) Getting off work too late in the evening.

D) Starting work too early in the morning.

Questions 19 to 22 are based on the conversation you have just heard.

19. A) To make the man feel happy.

B) To persuade the man to shop with his kids.

C) To convince the man Christmas is worth spending.

D) To prevent the man from spending too much shopping.

20. A) At a Christmas party.   B) Not long before Christmas.

C) At the New Year's Eve.   D) On some day of April.

21. A) Expectation.   B) Complaint.   C) Enjoyment.   D) Indifference.

22. A) Paying off Christmas bills.   B) Trying to earn more money.

C) Preparing for Christmas.   D) Limiting his wife's expense.

Questions 23 to 25 are based on the conversation you have just heard.

23. A) Go hill walking.   B) Go swimming.   C) Go cycling.   D) Dine out.

24. A) It has existed for a long time.

B) It enjoys very good business.

C) The owner of the restaurant is an Italian.

D) It is located on a busy street.

25. A) He cannot get the meal ready so early.

B) He didn't want to get a table himself.

C) He thinks it's too early to have lunch.

D) He has to go and see a relative before then.

Section B

注意:此部分试题请在**答题卡 2** 上作答。

Passage One

Questions 26 to 28 are based on the passage you have just heard.

26. A) Cheap clothes.   B) Expensive clothes.   C) Fashionable clothes.   D) Casual clothes.

27. A) They enjoy loud music.   B) They seldom lose their temper.

C) They want to have children.   D) They enjoy modern dances.

28. A) The speaker goes to bed very late and her sister gets up early.

B) The speaker's twin sister often brings friends home and this annoys her.

C) The speaker likes to keep things neat while her twin sister doesn't.

D) They can't agree on the color of the room and furniture.

Passage Two

Questions 29 to 32 are based on the passage you have just heard.

29. A) The great number of people engaged in cigarette producing.

B) The rapid development of cigarette-making machines.

C) The rapid development of cigarette-making factories.

D) The increasing output of tobacco.

30. A) Forty-three.   B) Thirty-one.   C) Seventy-five.   D) Forty-six.

31. A) Income, years of schooling and job type.

B) Family background and work environment.

C) Education and mood.

D) Occupation and influence of family members.

32. A) City people smoke less than people living on farms.

B) Better-educated men tend to smoke more heavily than other men.

C) Better-educated women tend to smoke more heavily than other women.

D) A well-paid man is likely to smoke more packs of cigarettes per day.

Passage Three

Questions 33 to 35 are based on the passage you have just heard.

33. A) The speed and journey of the fastest rocket soaring to the sun.

B) The brightness of the sun and its distance from the earth.

C) The size and heat of the sun compared with other stars.

D) The total heat and time a column of ice needs to melt.

34. A) 93 million degrees Centigrade.   B) 10,000 degrees Fahrenheit.

C) 10,000 degrees Centigrade.   D) Over 2,000 degrees Fahrenheit.

35. A) The sun casts its light to millions of other stars.

B) Most of the sun's heat and light are received on the earth.

C) More resources from the sun will make the earth even prosperous.

D) Appropriate amount of heat and light makes life on the earth possible.

Section C

注意：此部分试题在答题卡2上；请在答题卡2上作答。

Part IV Reading Comprehension (Reading in Depth) (25 minutes)

Section A

It is estimated that about 10 million people go into coastal waters every year to get a closer look at whales.

When the *eco-tourists* (生态旅游者) try to have a look at the ___47___ mammals rising above the water line, killer whales' lives are greatly ___48___, though they are the top of the food chain in the sea.

"We now have more whale-watch boats than there are whales," said Kelley Balcomb-Bartok of an ___49___ in Washington State that works with scientists to protect whales.

All this activity is causing people to show more ___50___ about the whales' health and survival. Some scientists say noise from all the boat traffic may ___51___ a whale's *sonar* (声纳，声波) ability as much as 95 percent. The whales need sonar to find food.

Three new studies ___52___ this month suggest the interference caused by the tourists is damaging the whales, whose population in the Puget Sound region has fallen from 98 to 80 in less than a ___53___. Scientists say all the traffic also forces the whales to move around more, wasting energy needed for ___54___ food.

"I would say that at times when there are a lot of boats and there is a lot of noise, they are ___55___," said Tom McMillen, captain of the whale-watching boat Stellar Sea, which takes out three groups a day.

Scientists say there are less food in the sea for the whales to eat, besides, the pollution in the sea is more serious; ___56___, the noise from the boats makes the life of the whales even worse.

A) threatened	B) decade	C) delicate	D) initially
E) concerns	F) cautious	G) irritated	H) hunting
I) huge	J) decrease	K) monument	L) cease
M) released	N) thus	O) organization	

Section B

Passage One

For most people, shopping is still a matter of wandering down the street for loading a cart in a shopping mall. Soon, that will change. Electronic commerce is growing fast and will soon bring people more choice. There will, however, be a cost: protecting the consumer from cheating will be harder. Many governments therefore want to extend strict regulations to the electronic world. But politicians would be wiser to see cyberspace as a basis for a new era of corporate self-regulation.

Consumers in rich countries have grown used to the idea that the government takes responsibility for everything from the stability of the banks to the safety of the drugs or their rights to refund when goods are faulty. But governments cannot enforce national laws on businesses whose only presence is on the screen. Even in a country where a clear right to compensation exists, the on-line customer in Tokyo, say, can hardly go to New York to extract a refund for a clothes purchase.

One answer is for governments to cooperate more: to recognize each other's rules. But that requires years of work and volumes of detailed rules. And plenty of countries have rules too fanciful for sober states to accept. There is, however, another choice. Let the electronic businesses do the regulation themselves. They do, after all, have a self-interest in doing so.

In electronic commerce, a reputation for honest dealing will be a valuable competitive asset. Governments, too, may compete to be trusted. For instance, customers ordering medicines on-line may prefer to buy from the United States because they trust the strict screening of the Food and Drug Administration; or they may decide that the FDA's rules are too strict, and buy from Switzerland instead.

Consumers will still need to use their judgment. But precisely because the technology is new, electronic shoppers are likely for a while to be a lot more cautious than consumers of the normal sort—and the new technology will also make it easier for them to complain when a company lets them down. In this way, at least, the arrival of cyberspace may argue for fewer consumer protection laws, not more.

57. According to the author, what will be the best policy for electronic commerce?
   A) Self-regulation by the business.　　　　B) Strict consumer protection laws.
   C) Close international cooperation.　　　　D) Government protection.

58. In case an electronic shopper bought faulty goods from a foreign country, what could he do in the present circumstance?
   A) Refuse to pay for the purchase.
   B) Go to the seller and ask for a refund.
   C) Appeal to consumer protection law.
   D) Complain about it via electronic mail.

59. In the author's view, businesses would place a high emphasis on honest dealing because in the electronic world _____.
   A) international cooperation would be much more enhanced
   B) consumers could easily seek government protection
   C) a good reputation is a great advantage in competition
   D) it would be easy for consumers to complain

60. We can infer from the passage that in licensing new drugs the FDA in the United States is _____.
   A) very quick　　　B) very cautious　　　C) very slow　　　D) rather careless

61. The "sober states" (Line 2, Para. 3) most probably refers to _____.
   A) small countries　　　　　　　　B) strict countries
   C) warm-hearted countries　　　　D) clear-headed countries

Passage Two

The quality of university life is declining under strain from the higher education, leading independent schools in

Britain complained. The warning followed survey of the impressions of campus life gained by students of school. Poor interviewing of the applicants, infrequent contact with tutors, worries over student safety, and even complaint over the food were all seen as symptoms of the pressure on universities. Head teachers said that standards could well drop if the squeeze on university budgets continued.

Although most of the 6,000 students surveyed were enjoying university life, almost a third were less than satisfied with their course. About one in 10 had serious financial problems and some gave alarming accounts of conditions around their halls of residence. Incidents mentioned included a fatal *stabbing* (用刀刺) and shooting outside a hall of residence, the petrol-bombing of cars near another residence, and two racist attacks. Nine percent of women and seven percent of men rated security as unsatisfactory in the area where they lived.

The survey confirmed head teachers' fears about contact between students and tutors slipping, with a quarter of the students seeing their tutors only every three weeks. New students, used to regular contact with their teachers, found it hard to adapt to the change. Interview techniques were a cause for concern, with the school calling for more training of university staff involved in admissions. Some headmasters complained that interviews were increasingly "odd". One greeted an applicant by throwing him an apple. Another interview lasted only three minutes. About a quarter of the students found the workload at university heavier than they had expected. There were differences between subjects, with architecture, engineering, *veterinary science* (兽医学), medicine and some science subjects demanding the most work. Veterinary science was nevertheless the most popular subject, followed by physiotherapy and history of art. General engineering, economics, computing and sociology were the least popular. The survey also confirmed previous concerns about possible racial prejudice in admissions to medical courses. Applicants with names suggesting an ethnic minority background had been rejected with qualifications as good as successful white candidates.

62. Which of the following is NOT mentioned as a sign that the quality of university life is declining?
    A) University applicants are poorly interviewed.
    B) Students can not contact their tutors often enough.
    C) Students' safety on campus is not secured.
    D) Course fees are too high for many students.

63. The author points out that the main problem existing in the interview of admission is that _____.
    A) the interviewers often greeted the applicants by throwing an apple
    B) the interviewers spent only a few minutes interviewing an applicant
    C) the interviewers were not knowledgeable to interview the applicants
    D) the interviewers lack enough training and interview techniques

64. According to the passage, minorities most probably have less chance to become _____.
    A) doctors   B) architects   C) lawyers   D) economists

65. According to the second paragraph, the students are most displeased with their _____.
    A) overall university life   B) financial situation
    C) curricular at college   D) personal security

66. We can see that the author's description of the quality of university life in Britain is _____.
    A) objective   B) subjective   C) pessimistic   D) arbitrary

Part V Cloze (15 minutes)
注意:此部分试题请在**答题卡 2** 上作答。

People living on parts of the south coast of England face a serious problem. In 1993, the owners of a large hotel and of several houses discovered, __67__ their horror, that their gardens had disappeared __68__ . The sea had eaten into the soft limestone cliffs on which they had been built. While experts were studying the problem, the hotel and several houses __69__ altogether, sliding down the cliff and into the sea.

Erosion (侵蚀) of the white cliffs __70__ the south coast of England has always been a (n) __71__ but it has become more serious __72__ recent years. Dozens of homes have had to be __73__ as the sea has crept farther and farther inland. Experts have studied the areas most affected and have __74__ up a map for local people, forecasting the year in __75__ their homes will be swallowed up by the hungry sea.

Angry owners have called on the Government to __76__ sea defenses to protect their homes. Governments surveyors have pointed out that in most __77__, this is impossible. New sea walls would __78__ hundreds of millions of pounds and would merely __79__ the problem go further along the coast, shifting the problem from one area to __80__. The danger is likely to continue, they say, __81__ the waves reach an inland area of hard rock which will not be eaten as limestone __82__. Meanwhile, if you want to buy a cheap house with a(n) __83__ future, apply to a house agent in __84__ of the threatened areas on the south coast of England. You can get a house __85__ a knockdown price but it may __86__ out to be a knockdown home.

67. A) at   B) for   C) to   D) in
68. A) overall   B) overnight   C) overhead   D) overseas
69. A) disappeared B) faded   C) lost   D) missed
70. A) on   B) near   C) in   D) along
71. A) issue   B) question   C) problem   D) matter
72. A) after   B) before   C) in   D) on
73. A) resigned   B) deserted   C) abandoned   D) erased
74. A) drawn   B) set   C) put   D) turned
75. A) that   B) which   C) it   D) what
76. A) establish   B) upright   C) erect   D) mount
77. A) examples   B) cases   C) situations   D) instances
78. A) spend   B) waste   C) swallow   D) cost
79. A) force   B) cause   C) oblige   D) make
80. A) next   B) others   C) other   D) another
81. A) until   B) when   C) as   D) after
82. A) does   B) did   C) is   D) was
83. A) uncertain   B) promising   C) indefinite   D) doubtful
84. A) that   B) some   C) many   D) one
85. A) with   B) for   C) by   D) in
86. A) stand   B) come   C) turn   D) break

Part VI   Translation (5 minutes)

注意:此部分试题在**答题卡 2** 上;请在**答题卡 2** 上作答。

Model Test 1

答案与解析

Part I Writing

写作指南：

这是典型的四级比较型习作。第一点写作要求让考生简要阐述目前学生报考高校时，面临着选择名牌大学还是热门专业的难题。然后分两段分析选择名校的优缺点以及选择一般院校热门专业的优势。最后陈述个人观点，并简述原因。

根据题目要求，文章结构如下：

第一段：引出选名校还是选热门专业的话题。

第二段：1. 名校对毕业生找工作举足轻重的意义；

2. 名校也有冷门专业，也会出现未就业先失业的可能。

第三段：1. 即使一般院校，也有热门或者独一无二的专业，可以让毕业生独具竞争力；

2. 提出个人看法：如果两者不能兼顾，选专业比选学校重要。

范文与解析：

Sample	Analysis
【1】Recent years have **witnessed** a steady increase in the popularity of such majors as international finance, finance and accountancy, etc. 【2】In the meantime, whether to choose a good university **or** a good major **has provoked a debate**. 【3】**It is true that** graduates from prestigious universities are more popular in labor markets, so many students 【4】would **spare no efforts** to be enrolled in good universities, 【5】which means **standing on the threshold of** a promising career after graduation. 【6】**But** even the **best** university has **unpopular** majors, thus graduates from these majors could encounter **much difficulty** in finding a job, 【7】let alone a good one, which means they would be out of work immediately after graduation. 【8】What about a good major then? Maybe you are studying in a common university, 【9】but your major **is of great competition**, then do you still need to worry about your future? A good major can, to some extent, ensure your future success.	【1】**witness** 用了拟人的手法开头，点出了近年来比较热门的专业。 【2】用 **provoke a debate** 引出先考虑专业是否热门还是大学是否有名气这个有争议性的话题。 【3】【6】**It is true that... But...** 结构为欲擒故纵法的核心结构，先分析优点，再重点引出劣势。 【4】**spare no efforts** 形象地刻画了考名校的竞争强度。 【5】**standing on the threshold of** 用形象的比喻手法描述了名校给人的美好期望。 【6】用 **best** 与 **unpopular** 和 **much difficulty** 形成强烈对比，说明了名校也存在冷门专业的不足之处。 【8】用问句实现自然转折，引出了专业的选择问题。

[10]If your major is exclusive to only several universities, you will surely be especially competitive in the real world. [11]Do not merely focus on the name of a university—choosing a good major suitable to you is wiser.

【9】be+of+*n.*的结构使句式多变,突出了一般院校也有热门专业,专业过硬对于找工作也是很有保障的。

【10】明确说明说明独一无二的专业能让学生颇具竞争力。

【11】承接前面的反问句总结个人观点,选择好专业胜过一味追求名校。

句型变换:

[1]

1. Recent years have witnessed a steady increase in the popularity of such majors as...

2. Recent years the majors, such as..., are becoming more and more popular.

3. The majors, such as..., are more and more welcome in recent years.

4. Such majors as... enjoy a steadily growing popularity in these years.

[2]

1. In the meantime, whether to choose a good university or a good major has provoked a debate.

2. Meanwhile, whether to choose a good university or a promising major has led to a hot discussion.

3. There is a heated debate nowadays about the problem of choosing a good university or a promising major.

4. At the same time, the issue of whether to choose a good university or a promising major has given rise to wide public concern.

[3]

1. It is true that graduates from prestigious universities are more popular in labor markets, ...

2. Needless to say, graduates from prestigious universities are more popular in labor markets, ...

3. There is probably a great deal of truth in the assertion that graduates from famous universities are more popular in labor markets, ...

4. It is of little doubt that graduates from good universities are more competitive in labor markets, ...

[4]

1. would spare no efforts to be enrolled in good universities,

2. would try very hard to be enrolled in good universities,

3. would endeavor to be accepted by good universities,

4. would make every effort to be enrolled in good universities,

[5]

1. which means standing on the threshold of a promising career after graduation.

2. which indicates standing on the threshold of a promising career after graduation.

3. which means a bright future is waiting for them right after graduation.

4. which implies that a promising future is awaiting them.

[6]

1. ... could encounter much difficulty in finding a job,

2. ... would find it difficult to get a job,

3. ... may come across a lot of troubles in job-hunting,

4. ... could be faced with many difficulties when seeking for a job,

[10]

1. If your major is exclusive to only several universities, you will surely be especially competitive in the real world.

2. Suppose your major is offered by only several universities, you will find it easy to stand out.

3. If you choose a major exclusive to certain universities only, you will undoubtedly have distinct advantage.

4. You will have unique strong points when your major is exclusive to only several universities.

Part II Reading Comprehension (Skimming and Scanning)

参考译文划线点评
有创意的制裁

所有违法者都该坐牢吗?对犯罪行为还有别的符合社会利益的惩罚措施吗?许多国家的法官看来是这么认为的,他们针对某些犯罪行为制定了一些新的、更好的惩罚措施。

把罪犯投入监狱有用吗?

把罪犯投入监狱是一种古老而广为使用的惩罚措施,但是,这种措施明智吗?把罪犯限制在一个地方,减少他们伤害无辜的机会,让他们认识到犯罪得不偿失,这看来确实是合情合理的。那些希望看到罪行得以惩处、社会得到保障的人们长久以来都认为这个体制是公平合理的。[1]然而,如今正是那些实施惩罚措施的人——法官——对这种正义形式的价值提出了质疑。 他们说,其理由就在于,监狱对任何人都没有好处。

如果一个人因为醉酒开车而致人受伤或死亡,把他投入监狱真的对社会、受害人或者受害人的家人有好处吗?让他赔偿受害人的医疗费、精神损失费、误工费,并为因该事故导致的任何其他问题进行补偿,或许将更有用。如果受害人已经死亡,在大多数情况下,其家人可以得到一些经济上的援助。

赔偿

赔偿的观点由来已久,在古代,有些国家就对每一种违法行为和伤害行为的赔偿范围制定了非常明细的方案。[2]在公元前2700年左右的巴比伦,小偷必须赔偿相当于所盗窃财物五倍的价值;在几个世纪后的罗马,小偷只需赔偿两倍的价值。"这种体制真好!"现代法官们说,因为他们明白,处以监禁会给非暴力的初次犯罪者带来什么严重的后果。罪犯坐牢的那些小偷从其他牢友那里学到更恶劣的犯罪的诀窍。[3]不管是否愿意,他都必须顺服从重刑犯从事更严重的犯罪行为,从而招致更长的刑期。在他这种重复犯罪的过程中将会有更多人受到伤害并使社会蒙受巨大的经济损失,因为对一个人进行审判并把他养在牢里是很昂贵的。

替代惩罚方案

鉴于以上考虑,许多英美法官转而尝试对一些"轻度"犯罪者采取别的惩罚措施,所有这些措施都让人很不舒服,足以令违法者不敢再犯,但同时又是安全的,因为他们不会接触到危险的伙伴。犯事的人通过帮助受害人(在经济上或其他方面)或者为社区做义工的方式来做出补偿。他们得为贫困家庭和精神病患者服务,也可以清扫城市街道、捡垃圾、植树或做别的力所能及的工作。或者,他们找一份工作,赔偿自己的一部分工资给受害人。[4]这样的处罚措施叫替代性惩罚,只适用于对公众不构成危险的非暴力犯罪,如伪造币、商店行窃和交通肇事等。替代性惩罚被认为尤其适用于年轻违法者。如果被判处这种惩罚的罪犯宁可坐牢,他有权拒绝接受这种惩罚。

事例

替代性惩罚未曾有法律明确规定,所以完全由法官决定罪犯应受的惩罚。法官们在实施他们所谓的"具有创意的制裁"时,表现出了丰富的想象力。

有位牙医酒醉开车撞死了一名摩托车司机,他被判在整整一年里自己掏钱每周抽出一天时间为穷人和老人治疗牙齿。另一个19岁的酒醉开车的年轻人被命令三年间每周到一所医院的急诊室工作一次,以让他亲眼看看大意驾驶会导致什么后果。

有个小偷偷了一个农民一些农具,他被判为受害人养猪养牛一年。[5]有位前任城市财务官员因犯有欺诈行为,被罚为红十字会筹款。

一群十几岁的孩子在狂欢之夜"仅仅为了好玩"砸烂了一些玻璃窗,他们被罚修好十倍于这个数目的玻璃窗。在墙壁上乱涂乱画的"艺术家"们被要求擦洗干净墙壁、长椅以及其他被"装饰"过的地方。还有些年轻人因为偷窃老太太的钱包被抓,他们就被责令为老人粉刷和维修房屋,或者到精神病院工作。

有位医生在打雪仗时打到了自己的邻居,他得就"吸烟和癌症的关系"作一个报告。一位参与抗议游行时被逮捕的大学教授被勒令写一篇关于"国民叛逆思想"的长篇论文,[6]一位电影公司的总裁伪造了价值4.2万美元的支票,他必须制作一部在学校放映的有关毒品危害的电影。除了被判要支付的罚金外,制作那部电影又花了他4.5万美元。

[8]法官的创造性不仅局限于个人犯罪,违法的公司也会受到替代性的处罚。这些公司通常被要求向慈善团体或者对社区有益的项目捐出大笔款项。

替代性惩罚:究竟是好还是坏?

有些法官不是尝试采用新的惩罚手段,而是探索利用现有刑罚的新途径。比如,他们判决犯人只在周末坐监服刑,这就可以使已婚罪犯保有工作,又能和家人在一起。尽管公众倾向于认为周末服刑太轻,违法者却并不同意这一点。其中一个人说:"这比一次性服完刑期更糟糕,因为这就好像坐了20次牢似的。"[7]监狱管理人员反对周末服刑,因为这样一来,罪犯很容易把毒品和其他违禁品带给其他服刑人员;周末服刑犯都得彻底搜身,这为警卫带来了额外的麻烦和工作。

现在有17个州在采用替代性惩罚,而且这种方法还在迅速扩展。法官们定期会面,比较各种惩罚措施,交流经验。[9]联邦政府宣布,将提供一些基本指导原则,以防止法庭对相似的罪行做出差别迥异的处罚。 法官们并不欢迎这样的做法,他们觉得那会限制他们对惩罚措施的选择范围,限制他们发挥想象力。

支持这种新的制裁方式的人指出,这样做有许多好处。它减少了监狱的人数,而监狱人满为患正是犯人暴力犯罪活动猖獗的原因。它节省了大笔金钱,减少了不良影响,减少了重复犯罪。它还为受害人提供一些帮助,而在以前,受害人通常是被忽视的一方。许多法官认为,替代性惩罚对罪犯也有好处,可以迫使他们看到自己所犯罪行的后果,看到人们因为他们的罪行所受到的痛苦。[10]对这种新型制裁方式抵触最大的是受害死者的家人。他们当中很多人想要报复,因而愤怒地拒绝任何形式的补偿。他们想用那种老式的好办法把罪犯关起来。他们相信,罪有应得的惩罚才是唯一公正的惩罚——这很合理。他们不能理解替代性惩罚的目的。法官们一心寻找的是一种不仅公平而且还对社会有益的惩罚手段,这种手段可以帮助受害人及其家庭,帮助社区,还能帮助那些可以改邪归正的违法者。一位"有创造性"的法官说:"这才是真正意义上的法律制裁。"

---

1. 【答案】C

   【题眼】The practice of <u>throwing the criminals into jail</u> is now being <u>questioned</u> by _____.

   【定位】第1个小标题 **Does it help to put the offenders in jail?** 部分的首段倒数第2句。

   【解析】原文该段首句表明该段内容与 throwing the criminals into jail 有关,倒数第2句中的 this form of justice 指的就是 throwing the criminals into jail,这种做法正受"judges"的质疑,因此选项C为本题答案。

---

2. 【答案】A

   【题眼】In ancient <u>Rome</u>, a thief would have to compensate _____ times the value of the goods he had stolen.

   【定位】第2个小标题 **Compensation** 部分的第2句。

   【解析】原文该句提到了古巴比伦和古罗马要求小偷赔偿的做法,古罗马要求小偷赔偿"两倍"的价值,可见本题应选选项A。

---

3. 【答案】C

   【题眼】Modern judges believe when a <u>nonviolent first offender</u> is put into jail, he will _____.

   【定位】第2个小标题 **Compensation** 部分的第5句。

   【解析】原文该句中的 drag him into...表明非暴力的初次犯罪者常进监狱后常被卷入 more serious offences,因此本题应选选项C。其他选项里的一些词虽然来自原文该段,但表达的信息没有原文依据。

---

4. 【答案】C

   【题眼】An <u>alternative sentence</u> may be applied to _____.

   【定位】第3个小标题 **Alternative sentences** 部分的倒数第3句。

   【解析】原文该句列举了那些轻微犯罪者适用于 alternative sentence,对照之下可以发现选项C为本题答案。选项A中的 murderers 不符合"nonviolent"这个条件,其他两个选项没有原文依据。

---

5. 【答案】B

   【题眼】Under the system of alternative sentence, a <u>treasurer guilty of dishonesty</u> was sentenced to help _____.

   【定位】第4个小标题 **Examples** 部分的第3段第2句。

   【解析】该句明确提到了 Red Cross 这个组织名称,其他选项并无在原文提及过,因此选项B为本题答案。

---

6. 【答案】C

   【题眼】The <u>president</u> of a <u>film company</u> had to make a film about the danger of <u>drugs</u> because he was guilty of _____.

【定位】第 4 个小标题 **Examples** 部分的第 5 段第 2 句。

【解析】原文该句中 who 引出的定语从句表明电影公司总裁所犯的罪行是伪造支票，可见选项 C 为本题答案。选项 A 和选项 D 没有原文依据，选项 B 中的 demonstration 虽有提及，但与电影公司总裁无关。

7. 【答案】D

【题眼】Prison personnel tend to think that weekend sentences _____.

【定位】第 3 个小标题 **Alternative sentences: good or bad?** 部分的首段末句。

【解析】原文该句表明监狱工作人员认为 weekend sentences 给监狱"带来额外的麻烦"，选项 D 正是这个意思，因此选项 D 为本题答案。

8. 【答案】charities or projects

【题眼】Lawbreaking companies that receive alternative sentences are required to do good to their community by contributing to relevant _____.

【定位】第 4 个小标题 **Examples** 部分的最后一段。

【解析】空白处应为名词词组。题目是对原文的两句话的概括，其中原文的 make... contributions to... 被改写为具有相同意思的 contributing to，因此，原文介词 to 的宾语就是题目的答案。

9. 【答案】the federal government

【题眼】Guidelines to prevent the courts from giving widely different sentences for similar offences will be constituted by _____.

【定位】第 5 个小标题 **Alternative sentences: good or bad?** 部分的第 2 段第 3 句。

【解析】空白处应为名词词组，为制定 guidelines 的人或组织。对比题目与原文，发现两者的用词非常相似，只是语态不同，原文为主动语态，题目为被动语态，题目要求寻找的宾语应为原文的主语，因此 the federal government 为本题答案。

10. 【答案】the families of the victims who have died

【题眼】Alternative sentences, as a new kind of justice, were most resisted by _____.

【定位】第 5 个小标题 **Alternative sentences: good or bad?** 部分最后一段第 6 句。

【解析】空白处应为名词词组。题目中的 most resisted 与原文中的 greatest resistance 意思相同，题目要求寻找谁最抵触替代性惩罚，只要在原文找到 greatest resistance 的来源即 comes from 后的名词词组就是答案。

Part III Listening Comprehension

Section A

11. M: Everybody is helping out with the dinner. Would you make the salad?
    W: Anything but that.
    Q: What does the woman mean?

[D]【解析】习惯表达题。anything but... 表示"除了……什么都行"，that 指代 make the salad，故选 D。

【点睛】①答非所问，相当于否定回答，即表示 I don't want to make the salad 含义的选项为答案，故选 D。②"听到什么不选什么"，排除 A、B、C，分别用了 salad, dinner, anything to help 作干扰。

12. W: Are these treatments really necessary? They don't seem to help very much.
    M: I'm afraid so, Mrs. Jones. Just be patient and I'm sure you'll see some results soon.
    Q: Where did the conversation most probably take place?

[D]【解析】场景题。抓住关键词 treatments"治疗"，results"效果"，可推知对话双方为医生与病人，答案为 D(在医生的办公室)。

【点睛】对话中没有出现表明商人、律师、教授身份的词汇，可排除其他选项。

13. W: Hi, Bill, have you been playing golf recently?

M: Hello, Betty. I <u>play as often as I can</u> get out of the house. And by the way, I <u>have a new set of clubs.</u>
<u>They seem to have helped my game</u>, though they are much heavier than my old set.

Q: What does Bill tell Betty?

[B]【解析】推理题。男士说新球杆帮了忙,可见比以前打得好了,所以选 B。S2 说新球杆重,有助于提高球技,并没有说更喜欢旧球杆,排除 D。

【点睛】①对于 S1 的问题,S2 尽管没有说 Yes 或 No,但 I play as often as I can 已经给出了直接回答(不能算"答非所问"),可排除 A、C。②由"听到什么不选什么"首先排除 D。A、B、C 都讨论 play golf 的问题,根据 S1,即可选出答案。

14. W: Why didn't you put the umbrella into your bag? Now we'll have to carry it on the plane with us.

M: The bag isn't too full, but I <u>kept it out.</u> <u>It looks like it might rain on our way to the airport.</u>

Q: Why isn't the umbrella in the man's bag?

[A]【解析】男士提到"看起来像是在我们去机场的路上会下雨",可见他没有把伞放在包里是因为担心在去机场的路上可能会下雨,所以选 A 项。

【点睛】中 but 题,but 后的解释内容是答题关键。而该解释部分的核心是"it might rain on our way to...",应不难听懂,选项 A 是其同义替换。B、D 与对话中的信息矛盾,C 于对话中找不到根据。

15. W: What a strange suit you are wearing. <u>Your jacket doesn't match your pants.</u>

M: I know. I got dressed in the dark, and I didn't realize my mistake until I had gotten to the office.

Q: Why does the man's suit seem unusual?

[D]【解析】女士提到"你的夹克和裤子搭配不谐调",其中 match 表示"搭配",相当于 fit,所以选 D。

【点睛】"听到什么不选什么"。S1 的 suit 是名词,选项 A 把它用作干扰;S2 说 got dressed in the dark,而 B、C 就用相关词进行干扰。注意,本题不能把 jacket, pants 看做"同音干扰",因为它们正是对话所谈到的话题,所有选项差不多都包括了这些词汇。

16. M: The <u>essays</u> you have done this <u>term</u> have been weak, and your <u>attendance</u> at the <u>lecture</u> has been poor.

W: I'm sorry, I've been busy with my <u>union</u> activities.

Q: What is the probable relationship between the two speakers?

[B]【解析】情景(人物关系)题。由标志性的单词 essays, term, attendance, lecture, union 可知应该是老师与学生的关系。

【点睛】迅速浏览便可预知是什么题型。然后听的过程中寻找标志说话人身份的关键词,做出判断。

17. M: They may be proud of their new facilities, but frankly I'm disappointed. The <u>nurses</u> are <u>not friendly</u> and <u>every-</u><u>thing seems to be running behind schedule.</u>

W: Not to mention the fact that it's <u>noisy</u>, because <u>no one observes visiting hours.</u>

Q: What are they complaining about?

[C]【解析】情景(地点)题的变体。根据标志性的单词 nurses, visiting hours,可知他们在谈论医院,因而答案为 C。

【点睛】选项 A、B 利用了 noise, facilities 作近音干扰,容易排除。D 较具干扰性,须以对话中的 nurses, no one observes visiting hours 排除。

18. W: Welcome to our laboratory. It's nice to have you with us. I'll see you at 7:30 in the morning.

M: <u>My goodness. I'm not used to getting up as early as that.</u> In London we start work at 9:00 a.m.

Q: What makes the man feel shocked?

[D]【解析】男士说他不习惯起那么早,他在伦敦时 9 点上班,而这里 7:30 上班,所以感到吃惊,故选 D。

【点睛】①最简单的答题方法是从时间副词入手,可以由 in the morning 直接而准确地判定答案为 D。②从强烈语气的角度判断,则须明白 S2 是针对 S1 中的哪一部分发出强烈语气的。选项 A、B 均是误读 S2 的语气,C 则完全从原文中找不到根据。

Now you'll hear two long conversations.

Conversation One

W: Are you all ready for Christmas?

M: No, I haven't even started. I've done zero shopping.

W: Well, [19] you'd better get going. [20] Christmas is only a week away.

M: I have to tell you that [21] I'm one of those people who really get stressed out by the Christmas rush.

W: Oh, I'm not. I love the holidays. I love the crowds, the shopping, the holidays, the music, the food, the parties, and all the presents.

M: [21] That's just the beginning. My wife always spends too much money on Christmas. That takes me till April to pay off all our Christmas bills.

W: Don't be a miser about it. Think about your kids. Didn't you use to love Christmas when you were a kid?

M: I guess so. I don't remember.

W: I know you did. You know, maybe Christmas is for kids, but you can still enjoy it through the eyes of your children.

M: [21] Well, kids enjoy it because they don't have to do all the shopping and pay all the bills.

W: Maybe that's true. [19] But you know as well as I do, that Christmas is more than shopping and trees. It's about what's in your heart and how you can make others happy.

M: You're right. You're absolutely right. [22] I'm going to try harder to be nice to people and try to keep the true spirit of Christmas in my heart.

W: I'm glad to hear it.

19. What does the woman try to do in the conversation?

[C]【解析】主旨题。整个对话内容都是围绕说话人对圣诞节的态度展开的,女士一直在劝说男士不要太在乎钱,只要开心就好。因此正确答案为 C 项。A 项不正确,女士开导男士,并非仅仅为了让他开心。选项 B、D 与原文不符。

【点睛】①读题。不定式选项,估计问"目的,打算"。四个选项的宾语均是 him,进一步确定是问女士的目的。四个不定式均有"使某人做或不做"之义。②由此,可听女士的话中是否有建议句之类表示劝说之意的句子。开始,男士说"我什么东西也没买"时,女士就说"You'd better get going."理解了本句,答案即彰显出来。

20. When does the conversation take place?

[B]【解析】细节题。女士问男士怎么还没有准备去购物,还有一个星期就是圣诞节了。因此不难判断,对话发生在圣诞节前几天。选项 B 正确。

【点睛】①情景题包括理解对话的时间、地点、人物双方关系,等。长对话开始处往往对此有所揭示。②通过读题,要预想到对话中可能出现的 Christmas, New Year, April 等字眼,并标注各自在对话中的含义。

21. What is the man's feeling about Christmas?

[B]【解析】推断题。对话一开始男士就强调圣诞节让他觉得心力交瘁(get stressed out),因此 A 项和 C 项肯定不对。接下来男士便提到他妻子会为圣诞节花很多钱,他得花很长时间才能把所有的账全部还清。显而易见,他是在抱怨,因此选项 B 正确。

【点睛】①四个选项均是表示情感、观点的名词,可以预测问题。只不过,在没有听到问题前,不能确定是问男士还是女士的态度而已。②A、B 在表示态度时,基本等价,可以同时排除;D(不在乎)一般不作答案。

22. What will the man most probably do after the conversation?

[C]【解析】推断题。到对话末尾,男士承认女士说的完全正确,并表示自己会照女士所说的去做,那么他很有可能为圣诞节积极地做准备,因此 C 项正确。A 项是他抱怨的内容,B、D 项并未提及。

【点睛】①四个动词(分词)选项表明,这是典型的长对话尾巴题,问对话中人物下一步的行动。②解题关键在最后一个话轮。③可以结合 19 题解题。本对话最后女士说:"I'm glad to hear it"(没有谁连这一句也没听懂吧?),表明女士达到了自己的目的,即说明男士准备圣诞礼物。

Conversation Two

W: It's a lovely day today! What would you like to do?

M: I really feel like doing something outdoors. Perhaps we could go hill walking?

W: Mm, I'm not really in the mood for hill walking. Why don't we just go swimming?

M: That suits me. But it will take an hour or two. Do you like to do something else first? Maybe we could go cycling?

W: I don't think I enjoy that very much. Actually I'm not a good cyclist. Maybe we could have a meal at the new Italian restaurant.

M: That's fine for me. I haven't been to that restaurant yet. [23] So that's decided then. A meal at the new Italian restaurant, then go to swim. Great! So, when should we meet?

W: [24] We'd better get to the restaurant a bit early because it might be very busy. I think we need to get there by 11:00.

M: Er, can I make it a little bit later, say, 11:20? [25] I have to visit my grandma this morning and I don't think I can make it by then.

W: No problem. I'll go straight to the restaurant at 11:00 and get you a table.

M: Great!

23. What will the two speakers do first?

[D]【解析】细节题。对话中女士说她没有心情爬山,也不擅长骑车,所以 A、C 两项肯定不对。最后他们决定先吃饭再游泳。接下来男士说"那就这样定了"。所以正确答案是 D 项。

【点睛】①由读题预测问题,并区分各选项。本题四个动词原形,应涉及某个行动:打算、建议等。②不能机械地套用"听到什么选什么"规则。当多个选项都在听力原文中出现时,须在相应选项旁做记号。本题各选项,均有男女双方的观点问题。比如 hill walking 是男士提出来的,可以标记"M√";女士否定回答,记作"W×"。③问题中的 first 涉及到先后次序,是本题难点。④划线处是总结性文字,是直接答题的关键。⑤由 24 题、25 题各选项中的词汇推断,他们的行为与吃饭、餐厅有关,可以简明地答题。

24. What can be inferred about the restaurant mentioned?

[B]【解析】推断题。女士提议去新开的那家意大利饭店,

她还建议最好早点去,因为去晚了饭店很可能(因为人多)很忙。既然是新开的饭店,那么 A 错误。饭店之所以可能非常 busy,肯定是生意好,去的人多才会很忙,因此答案为 B。意大利饭店并不一定就是意大利人开的,故 C 错误。D 对话中未提及,可以排除。

【点睛】①读题时须判断出 it 指"餐馆",则可有目的地听取信息。②作为推断题,含有一些原词干扰项出现,故也不完全适用"听到什么选什么"规则。③听到对话中的 because,须估计此处是解题关键。

25. Why can't the man meet the woman at 11:00?

[D]【解析】原因推理题。对话中,男士提出希望能 11:20 到饭店,因为他要去看望他的 grandma,11:00 之前可能赶不回来。因此选项 D 正确。

【点睛】带着问题听,才容易选对答案。由四个选项可知,本题涉及 he, so (too) early, meal, table, lunch, relative,等。有了这些准备,必不难听懂对话中男士给出的理由。

Section B

Passage One

Twin sisters are supposed to be very much alike, are they not? Well, my twin sister Jane and I do look alike, however, we are different in many ways. We like very different styles of clothing. [26] I prefer to dress informally, whereas my twin sister dresses like a model, always wearing the latest fashions. We have very similar character in most ways. [27] I do not get angry easily and enjoy being with friends, and in these respects, my twin sister feels the same. But she likes loud music and modern dances, while I find that nightclubs give me a headache. She is always with friends, is a favorite with all the teachers, and never wants to have any children, whereas I prefer to be alone at times, don't really try to impress my teachers and intend some day to have a family of my own. [28] We have tried to live in the same room several times, and even agreed on the color we like best, and the kind of furniture we want, but I like to keep things neat and orderly, while my twin sister acts as if there were a servant around to pick up all the things that get thrown on the floor. I like to go to bed early and get up early. In contrast, she doesn't seem to have any definite habits, often goes to bed very late, and then sleeps late the next day.

26. What kind of clothes does the speaker like?

[D]【解析】文中提到 I prefer to dress informally。D 中的 casual 是 informal 的同义词。

【点睛】①四个选项的中心词是 clothes,区别在前面的

定语。注意到 A 与 B 相对,C 与 D 相对。②因不知会如何提问,故短文涉及到的相关信息要简要记录。听到 different styles of clothing 后,竖尖了耳朵听,然后在 D 旁注上 I,C 旁注上 S(sister)。

27. What do the twin sisters have in common?

[B]【解析】文中提到"我轻易不会生气,喜欢和朋友待在一起。这点我们是相同的"所以选 B。

【点睛】①首先要通过读题尽量判断各选项共同的主语 they 的含义。由下一题 B 知,they 指孪生姐妹俩。②本题各选项均以 they 为主语,应当问她们的共同之处。由此,听力材料中关于两人区别的内容便可忽略。③万一"similar character"后的句子没有听到,则在其后的 but 处开始——排除 A、D、C。

28. Why isn't the speaker likely to live in the same room with her sister?

[C]【解析】最后一部分提到,她们不能住在同一个房间有很多原因,其中之一便是她是一个喜欢整齐有序的人,而她的 sister 什么东西都随手乱扔。所以选 C。

【点睛】此题难在无法从选项中预测问题,惟有判断哪个选项与听到的内容一致。四个选项内容均有提及,要在相应的主题词听到后,判断各选项的正误。其他选项中的话题都提到过,但信息不能与原文匹配。

Passage Two

Until the twentieth century cigarettes were not an important threat to public health. Since the cigarette industry began in the 1870s, however, [29] the cigarette-manufacturing machine has developed rapidly. This made it possible to produce great numbers of cigarettes very quickly, and it reduced the price.

Today cigarette smoking is a widespread habit. About forty-three percent of the men and [30] thirty-one percent of the adult women in the United States smoke cigarettes regularly. It is encouraging to note, however, that millions of people have given up the smoking habit.

[31] Income, education and occupation all play a part in determining a person's smoking habits. City people smoke more than people living on farms. Well-educated men with high income are less likely to smoke cigarettes than men with fewer years of schooling and lower incomes. On the other hand, if a well-educated man with a high income smokes at all, he is likely to smoke more packs of cigarettes per day. The situation is somewhat different for women. There are slightly more smokers among women with higher family income and higher education than among the lower income and lower education groups. [32] These more highly educated women tend to smoke more heavily.

29. What reduced the price of cigarettes?

[B]【解析】it reduced the price 中的 it 指的是前面提到 cigarette-manufacturing machine has developed rapidly。

【点睛】细节题,听到什么选什么,由读题,就要预设听到选项中的相关词汇,那么,当短文中出现 machine 时,就一定不会漏过。D 错在 tobacco;是香烟而非烟草的产量增加才使它的价格下降的。A、C 均未提及。

30. What is the percentage of American adult women who smoke regularly?

[B]【解析】可以直接听到此题答案所在:thirty-one percent of the adult women in the United States smoke cigarettes regularly。

【点睛】在不知道问题会怎么出的情况下,凡短文中出现的与选项一致的数字,一定要做好笔记。比如在 A

旁标"m(men)",B 旁标"w(women)"等。

31. What plays a part in determining a person's smoking habit?

[A]【解析】选项 A 中的三个因素是对原文 income, education and occupation 的同义表达。

【点睛】预读选项,均为名词词组。在听到的相关内容上做好标记,由此就可以加以选择、排除。

32. Which of the following is true according to the passage?

[C]【解析】最后一句话提到,受教育程度越高的女性烟瘾越大。

【点睛】A 项表达的意思与原文相反,B 项和 D 项表达不全面,只有把这两项综合起来才与原文相符。

Passage Three

Life on earth depends on the sun. Day after day we see its light and feel its warmth, but we do not often consider their origin. Yet there are many remarkable things about the sun. [33] One is its distance from the earth. This is about 93 million miles. A journey of this distance, even if it could be made, would take several hundred years even in the fastest rocket.

The sun makes us feel hot, even at a distance of 93 million miles. This is not surprising. [34] The temperature on the sun is about 10,000 degrees Fahrenheit. But we receive only a small part of the heat. The total heat of the sun could melt a column of ice two and a quarter miles thick and 93 million miles high in a second.

[33] The brightness of the sun is equally astonishing. As we said earlier, we receive only a very small part of the sun's heat. We also receive only a very small part of its light. This is sufficient for the growth of trees and plants, and for the existence of living creatures on earth. Too much heat and light would destroy the balance of life. [35] The heat and light from the sun come in just the right quantities for life on earth.

33. What remarkable things are mentioned in the passage?
[B]【解析】听到"Yet there are many remarkable things about the sun."时应该预测到后面会列举,紧接着听到"One is its distance from the earth."然后详细阐述,随后听到"The brightness of the sun is equally astonishing."及后面对该句的详细说明。因此 B 为正确选项。

【点睛】四个选项均为名词词组,要在听的时候标记听到的相关内容,然后比对。

34. What is the temperature on the sun?

[B]【解析】此题答案可以直接听到:The temperature on the sun is about 10,000 degrees Fahrenheit.

【点睛】选项为数字,听时要特别注意文中提到的数字及度量单位。短文中的数字题一般不需要计算就可以得出答案,但需要辨别易混淆的项目。

35. Which of the following is true according to the passage?
[D]【解析】"尾巴题"。D 是对最后两句的同义表达,也是本文的主题。

【点睛】A、C 未提及;B 与文中两次提及的信息"we receive only a very small part of the sun's heat"相悖。

Section C

36.【答案】value
【解析】根据预读可知此处需要一个名词,注意不要写成 valve"阀,活门"。

37.【答案】simply
【解析】此处不缺主要句子成分,而需要一个副词修饰过去分词 called;根据前后两个名字可知,此处应填表示"简单地,仅仅"的词。此词是由形容词 simple 派生而来的,由 simple 去掉 e 后加 y。

38.【答案】influential
【解析】此处需要一个形容词修饰名词。influential 是 influence 的派生词,但要注意词尾变化:ce 变成 tial,而不是 cial。

39.【答案】reporters
【解析】由空格前的 Three 可知此处需要一个复数名词;在语义上,此处需要填一个表示身份或职业的词。注意词尾是 er 而不是 or。

40.【答案】handwritten
【解析】此处需要一个修饰名词的词。形容词 handwritten 意为"手写的"。注意双写辅音字母 t。

41.【答案】successful
【解析】此处需要一个形容词作表语;根据后面的句子,此处应填表示肯定、积极含义的词。听到的是 successful,不可以只写成 success,其中的双写辅音字母一个也不能少。

42.【答案】represented
【解析】根据上下文,此处需要动词过去式作谓语。注意不要漏掉词尾 -ed。

43.【答案】economy
【解析】此处需要一个名词。注意 economy, economic,

economics 的语义和重音区别:economy n. "经济",重音在第 2 个音节;economic a. "经济的",重音在第 3 个音节;economics n. "经济学",重音在第 3 个音节。

44.【答案】These stocks represent an ownership share in companies that are considered strong
【听音关键】stocks, represent, ownership share, companies, strong
【答案重构】These stocks stand for an ownership share in strong companies
【画龙点睛】如果有怕拼写错的单词(如 represent),可以用同义词或短语代替(如 stand for)。定语从句可以简化为简单的形容词作定语。

45.【答案】For example, the Dow recently increased to more than ten-thousand for the first time in more than eighteen months
【听音关键】e.g., Dow increased to > 10,000, first time, > 18 months
【答案重构】For instance, the Dow recently went up to over 10,000 for the first time in more than 18 months
【画龙点睛】此句虽长,但是句型简单。关键是记下主谓结构和变化数据。increase to 可用 go up to 替换。

46.【答案】In fact, the Dow Jones Industrial Average does not represent a price but a mathematical average
【听音关键】not represent a price, but a mathematical average
【答案重构】In fact, the Dow represents a mathematical average instead of a price

[画龙点睛]承接前文"道琼斯工业平均指数不是指30个股票的平均价格",此处应该说明它是指什么。因为前文提到,the Dow Jones Industrial Average 有时也简称为 the Dow,所以此处可采用其简写形式。本题关键是要记录 but 后面的信息,可用 instead of 结构替换原有的 not... but...结构,强调 a mathematical average。

Part IV Reading Comprehension (Reading in Depth)

Section A

参考译文

据统计,每年有大约1000万人会不顾危险深入沿海水域近距离观看鲸鱼。

尽管逆戟鲸(也叫杀人鲸)是海底世界的霸主,处于食物链的最高一级,然而面对那些想方设法要一睹这种庞大的哺乳动物从海岸线浮出海面的壮观景象的观看者们,它们显得那么不堪一击。

华盛顿州的鲸鱼保护协会的成员凯利·鲍尔科姆·巴尔托克说:"现在观鲸船的数量已经超过了那里鲸鱼的数量。"这个组织正和科学家一起设法保护鲸鱼。

他们进行各种努力以引起人们对鲸鱼的健康和生存问题的关注。一些科学家认为来往船只的噪音会干扰破坏鲸鱼95%的声纳定位能力,而鲸鱼就是靠这种能力来寻找食物的。

本月公布的三项新研究成果表明,游客对鲸鱼带来的干扰会为鲸鱼带来灭顶之灾。菩及特海湾的鲸鱼数量在不到10年的时间内已经由最初的98头减少到如今的80头了。科学家们说,来来往往的船只还会逼得鲸鱼四处游动,这样⋯⋯⋯⋯⋯⋯⋯⋯⋯⋯⋯⋯⋯⋯⋯⋯⋯⋯⋯⋯⋯⋯⋯⋯⋯⋯

观鲸船"恒星牌"号的船长易瑞·麦克米伦说:"我坚信⋯⋯⋯⋯⋯⋯⋯⋯⋯⋯⋯⋯⋯⋯⋯⋯⋯躁不安。"麦克米伦的船每天要接待三批游客出海去观看鲸鱼。

科学家认为,如今海里鲸鱼的食物数量减少,另外海里环境污染日益严重,如此一来,船只的噪音便会严重影响鲸鱼的生存。

[词性分析]

名 词:decade 十年 concerns 关切的事;关心,担心;关系;公司,企业[复数] hunting 打猎,狩猎 decrease 减小;减少量 monument 纪念碑,纪念馆;历史遗迹 cease 停止,终止 organization 团体,机构;组织

动 词:threatened 威胁,恐吓;预示(危险)快要来临[过去式或过去分词] concerns 涉及,有关于;使关心,使担心[第三人称单数] irritated 使恼怒,使烦躁;使不适,使疼痛[过去式或过去分词] hunting 打猎,猎取;搜寻;驱逐,追捕[现在分词] decrease 减小,减少 cease 停止,终止 released 释放;解脱;放开;发布[过去式或过去分词]

形容词:delicate 脆弱的;微妙的,棘手的;纤细的;精美的 cautious 谨慎的 irritated 恼火的,急躁的;疼痛的,发炎的 huge 庞大的,巨大的

副 词:initially 最初,开始 thus 如此,这样;因此,从而

---

47. [I]此处应为形容词,修饰 mammals。本句中的 mammals 指的是 killer whales,词库中只有 huge 是描述杀人鲸体型最合适的形容词。

48. [A]此处应为动词的过去分词,与 are 构成谓语。本句 though 引出的让步状语从句表明虽然杀人鲸体型庞大,处于食物链的最高一级,但它们的生命仍然受到负面的影响,由此可以推断空白处的动词具有消极意义,词库中的 threatened 最符合本句句意。

49. [O]此处应为名词,且由前面的 an,可知是以元音开头的单数名词。本句提到的 that works with scientists to protect whales 表明说话者属于某个保护杀人鲸的组织,因此 organization 为正确答案。

50. [E] 此处应为名词,并可与 about 搭配。结合上一段提到的保护鲸鱼的组织以及本句中 about the whales' health and survival 等词,可以推断该组织正努力使人们更关注鲸鱼,因此 concerns 是本题答案。

51. [J]此处应为动词,而且是动词原形。文章至此都表明人类活动会对鲸鱼的生活造成负面的影响,因此,本句空白处的动词也应具有消极意义,表明噪音对鲸鱼的声纳定位能力会带来负面影响,由此可见,decrease 是最适合的

词。

52. [M]此处应为分词,作 studies 的后置定语。released 最符合本句句意,表明本月发表的新研究结果。

53. [B]此处应为名词。根据上下文,本句应表明在一段时间内某个区域内鲸鱼的数量急剧下降,地点已在句中提到,即 in the Puget Sound region,因此空白处应该是表示时间的名词,由此可见,decade 是本题答案。

54. [H]此处可为及物动词的动名词,food 为其宾语;也可能是形容词,修饰 food。从本句可以看出,鲸鱼 move around 的目的是为了捕食,因此本题答案应为 hunting。

55. [G]此处可为动词的分词或形容词。句末 that 引出的从句表明了船只和噪音对鲸鱼造成的干扰,因此,irritated 是最符合句意的单词。

56. [N]此处应为副词,连接前后两个分句。从两个分句的内容及句末的 even worse 可以看出,后面的分句是对全文主旨的总结,词库中只有 thus 可以起到总结或表示结果的作用,因此为本题答案。

Section B

Passage One

参考译文划线点评

对大多数人而言,购物的含义仍然是逛大型购物中心,把小推车装满。很快这种情况就会改变。电子商务正快速发展,不久就会为人们带来更多的选择。但是这也会有代价:使消费者免受欺骗将会更难。因此许多政府希望将严格的规定延伸到电子领域。不过政治家们也许更加睿智,他们将网络空间视作建立一个共同自律新纪元的基础。

富裕国家的消费者已经习惯于政府事事包办——从银行的稳定到药品的安全,或者当买到有缺陷的产品时退款的权力。但是政府无法实施全国性的法律来约束那些仅仅出现在电脑屏幕上的交易。即便在一个有明文规定索赔权的国家也很难办,[58]譬如,东京的一个网上消费者就不大可能因为买了一件衣服而跑到纽约去退款。

解决问题的办法之一是加强政府间的合作,即承认彼此的规定。但这需要经年累月的工作以及卷帙浩繁的详尽规定,[61]而且不少国家的规定过于脱离实际,使那些清醒的国家难以接受。[57]尽管如此,也还有另外一种选择:让电子商务界自行做出规定。毕竟它们这样做是符合其自身利益的。

[59]在电子商务领域,诚实交易的良好信誉将是一笔宝贵的和有竞争力的资产。各国政府也可能会争着做可信的政府。[60]例如,在网上订购药品的顾客可能会更愿意从美国购买,因为他们信任美国食物与药品管理局(FDA)的严格审查;或者他们也可能觉得 FDA 的规定过于严格,因而从瑞士购买。

消费者仍然需要运用自己的判断力。不过恰恰因为这是一项新技术,所以在一段时间内,电子商务的消费者可能会比普通购物形式的消费者要谨慎得多——而且如果哪个公司没能达到他们的期望,这种新技术还可以使他们投诉起来更容易。至少从这种意义上来说,网络空间的出现可能会导致需要更少而不是更多消费者保护法。

57. [A]推理判断题。本题考查转折处。第 3 段提出了两个可能的办法,但第 2 句指出第一种方法的不足之处,由此可见,第二种方法即电子商务界自行规定是更好的办法,最后一句以强调句式进一步说明这种方法更好,因此选项 A 正确,选项 C 错误。第 1 段第 4 句指出选项 B 很难做到,第 1 段最后两句暗示选项 D 很难做到。

58. [D]推理判断题。本题考查特殊符号处。根据结尾段中第 2 句的破折号后的部分推断答案应为选项 D。选项 A 在文中没有提及;选项 C 中的 consumer protection law 虽在文中最后一段最后一句提到,但其陈述与题目无关。

59. [C]事实细节题。本题考查对名词词组的理解。在第 4 段首句中,a valuable competitive asset 与选项 C 中的 a great advantage in competition 为同义表达。选项 A 并无原文依据,选项 B 显然与原文第 2 段表达的意思不符,选项 D 虽与原文最后一段第 2 句相似,但却答非所问。

60. [B]推理判断题。第 4 段第 3 句中的 strict screening(严格审查)和 too strict(过于严格)表明 B 为正确选项。

61. [D]词义推测题。本题解题的关键在于理解第 3 段第 3 句中的 too... to...结构。该句中的 fanciful 意为"不切实际的",too... to...结构暗示了 fanciful 和 sober 具有相反的意思,表明 sober states 不能接受这些不切实际的规定,由此可推断 sober states 是头脑清醒的国家,因此选项 D 正确。其他选项均没有上下文依据。

Passage Two

参考译文划线点评

英国主要的私立学校抱怨高等教育的压力使得英国的大学生活质量日渐下滑。关于大学生对校园生活看法的调查向人们提出了警告。[62]对报考者拙劣的面试、与导师过少的接触、对学生安全的担忧,甚至还有对食物的不满等等都被看做是高校所承受的压力的表现。校长们说,如果再继续压榨大学预算的话,大学的水准会大大下降。

[65]虽然接受调查的6000名学生中的大多数喜欢大学生活,但是有接近三分之一的学生对他们的大学生活不太满意。大约十分之一的人存在严重的经济问题,还有一些人对他们宿舍楼周围发生的事情所作的描述令人担忧。这些事件中包括一栋宿舍楼外发生的一起持械凶杀案、另一栋宿舍楼附近的汽车汽油弹爆炸案以及两宗种族主义袭击案。9%的女生及7%的男生将他们居住区域的安全等级列为不满意。

这项调查证实了校长们对学生与导师之间的接触减少的担忧,因为有四分之一的学生每三个星期才见一次导师。新生过去往往习惯和老师进行接触,他们觉得很难适应这种变化。[63]面试技巧也是引起担心的原因之一,校方呼吁对负责招生的教职员工进行更多的培训。有些中学校长抱怨说面试越来越"奇特":有人向考生扔苹果来跟他打招呼,还有的面试只进行了三分钟。大约四分之一的学生觉得大学的功课比他们所想象的更繁重。不同的学科功课量也不尽相同:建筑学、工程学、兽医学、医学以及一些理工科专业要求的功课量最大。不过,兽医学却是最受欢迎的学科,其次是物理疗法和艺术史。普通工程学、经济学、计算机和社会学最不受欢迎。[64]这项调查也证实了以前在医科招生中可能存在种族偏见的担忧。有的考生从名字可以看出其少数族裔背景,他们虽然和成功入学的白人学生资格相当,却遭到了拒绝。

---

62. [D]事实细节题。本题考查列举处。查阅文章第1段第3句,可知选项A、B、C都被提及,选项D文中未提及,故为本题答案。

63. [D]事实细节题。第3段第3句提到了Interview techniques(面试技巧)和training(培训),由此可推断,这两个就是入学面试存在的主要问题。选项A和选项B尽管文中有所提及,但并非主要问题,而只是具体个案;文中也未讨论面试考官是否有学识(knowledgeable)的问题,因此选项C也不对。

64. [A]推理判断题。从文章最后一段倒数第2句中的racial prejudice和medical courses可推断出答案。本题最具干扰性的是选项D,最后一段倒数第3句虽然提到经济学等最不受欢迎,但这并不等同于少数民族学生在这些学科内的机会更少。

65. [A]事实细节题。本题考查对course的理解及比例数字的计算。首先通过比较这些比例数字,不难发现学生最不满意的事在第2段第1句提到,第1句里的比例数字是"1/3",而其他比例数字分别是第2句的"1/10"和最后一句的"9%"、"7%"。其次要理解university course意为"大学生活",而不是"大学课程",因为course在文中是单数的。结合以上两方面的因素,就能找出正确答案为A。

66. [A]观点态度题。整篇文章作者都只是客观地转述事实、意见和调查结果,文中的所有数据都来自一项调查,全文并未出现任何诸如"In my opinion","I think","I know"等表达个人观点的字样,只有如"leading independent schools in Britain complained","Head teachers said","The survey confirmed head teachers' fears about...","New students... found it hard...","Some headmasters complained..."等类似引用别人的观点和看法的表达,因而是客观公正的,不带有任何个人感情色彩。

Part V Cloze

67. [C]短语搭配题。固定短语to one's horror意为"令人感到恐惧的是"。

68. [B]形似词辨义题。overall"总体的,全面的;总的来说";overnight"在短时间内,突然";overhead"在头顶上";overseas"在海外,在国外"。

69. [A]词义理解题。disappear"不见,消失";fade"逐渐消失,变微弱,变暗淡";lose"失去,丢失,丧失";miss"未看到,未注意到;未击中,未达到"。下文出现的副词altogether(完全,全然)决定了此处不选强干扰项fade。

70. [D]考查介词用法。根据上下文,白色的石灰质的悬崖应位于英国南部海岸的沿线,而on the south coast表示"在南部海岸地区"。

71. [C]近义词辨析题。issue指由于意见分歧而引起的"争端",需要讨论或有争议的重要"问题",还可指讨论的重点;question指说出来或写下来要求得到回答的"询问,考题";problem指客观存在的、有待解决的"困难,麻烦,难处";matter指比较重要、有义务去做的"任务,责任,事务"。

72. [C]短语搭配题。in recent years意为"最近几年来"。

73. [C]近义词辨析题。resign"辞去,放弃",有自愿放弃权利、资格等的含义;desert"离弃,抛弃,舍弃",后跟地点名词作宾语时表示使该地变得静无一人,以人为宾语时,强调在某人处于极为困难的境地时将其"遗弃、抛弃";aban-don"离弃,丢弃;放弃;抛弃",指因对某事的未来彻底失去信心或兴趣而"放弃";erase"擦掉,抹去,清除"。

74. [A]短语搭配题。draw up"起草,拟订";set up"建立";put up"建造;张贴";turn up"出现,来到"。

75. [B]语法题。定语从句所修饰的先行词是 year,此处选 which,构成 in which 引出定语从句。

76. [C]词义理解题。establish"建立,创办;确定,确立",常表示永久地建立起来,强调稳固而持久,常跟的宾语有政府、医院、学校、形象、名望等;upright"直立的;挺直着";erect"竖立,使直立";mount"登上;安放,安装"。

77. [B]短语搭配题。in most cases 意为"在大多数情况下"。

78. [D]短语搭配题。waste 意为"浪费,挥霍";swallow 意为"吞,咽",意义上不符合文意;spend 的动作发出者应为人,而此处动作发出者为 new sea walls,所以选 cost。

79. [D]语法题。四个选项中只有 D 后接不带 to 的动词不定式作宾补。

80. [D]语法题。此处要表达的含义是:"最终将问题从一地转移到另一地",应选代词 another。

81. [A]逻辑关联题。此处句意为"险情仍会持续,直到海水接触到内陆地区那些不像石灰岩那样易被海水侵蚀的坚硬的岩石",选 until。

82. [C]语法题。as 引出的定语从句中谓语部分承前省略,补全后应是 as limestone is eaten。

83. [A]词义理解题。indefinite"不明确的,含糊的";inaccurate"不精确的",一般不修饰 future;promising 显然不符合作者所说这些地区的情况,选 uncertain。

84. [D]语法题。考查代词用法。此处文意为"在英国南部沿海地区受到海水侵蚀威胁的一处地方",选不定代词 one。

85. [B]短语搭配题。短语 get sth. for a... (knockdown) price 意为"以……(超低)价买到某物"。

86. [C]短语搭配题。stand out"清晰地显出,引人注目";come out"出来";turn out (to be/do)"结果是,证明是";break out "爆发,突然出现"。

Part VI   Translation

87. 【答案】charging too much
    【译文】她正在抱怨那位给她看病的医生收费太高。

    【解析】考查 charge (sb.) some money for (doing) sth.意为"为某事(向某人)要……价"。此外,翻译时要根据句子的提示,选择正确的时态。was 提示空白处要用动词的进行时态。

88. 【答案】install an electric fan
    【译文】他们打算明天找维修人员来办公室安装电扇。

    【解析】have sb. do sth.意为"让某人做某事"。electric 以元音开头,前面的不定冠词为 an。

89. 【答案】couldn't concentrate/focus on
    【译文】当安妮的家人在看电视时,她无法全神贯注于手头的事情。

    【解析】"集中注意力于……"可用 concentrate/focus on 或 be absorbed in,但后者一般用于肯定句。

90. 【答案】in no mood to
    【译文】我父亲似乎没有心情看我的成绩单。

    【解析】固定短语 be in the/no mood to do sth.有(没有)做……的心情。

91. 【答案】cancel the contract
    【译文】由于合同中有几项条款未能兑现,我们公司决定废止合同。

    【解析】考查动宾搭配。"取消,废除"可用 cancel 一词或固定短语 call off。

Model Test 2

答题卡 1 (Answer Sheet 1)

Part I　　　　**Writing**　　　　　　　　　　　　　　　　　　**(30 minutes)**

Directions: *For this part, you are allowed 30 minutes to write an essay entitled **The Teacher-Student Relationship**. You should write at least 120 words following the outline given below in Chinese:*

1. 良好的师生关系有益于学生的发展
2. 不良的师生关系有害于学生的发展
3. 你的个人看法

The Teacher-Student Relationship

_____

_____

_____

Part II　　　　**Reading Comprehension (Skimming and Scanning)**　　　　**(15 minutes)**

1. [Y] [N] [NG]　　2. [Y] [N] [NG]　　3. [Y] [N] [NG]　　4. [Y] [N] [NG]

5. [Y] [N] [NG]　　6. [Y] [N] [NG]　　7. [Y] [N] [NG]

8. The abilities that we can make the most of life consist of _____.

9. The "learning to do" skills are also called "manual skills", which are about _____.

10. The government must examine and adapt the processes and content of education in order to gain a balance between _____.

答题卡 2 (Answer Sheet 2)

Part III　　　　**Section C**

　　Doctors estimate that about 40% of women over thirty in Britain are overweight. This figure may be (36) _____ as a large number of overweight people never (37) _____ medical advice. Many women are worried about being overweight. They feel that it shows a (38) _____ of will-power or self-control on their part. In addition, fat women do not (39) _____ to the modern ideal of beauty (40) _____ by fashion models and young film stars who are all (41) _____ thin. Apart from aesthetic reasons, there are strong medical (42) _____ for not overeating. Overweight people are (43) _____ more likely to get heart disease and are easily tired by physical activity. (44) _____ _____.

　　Some women feel guilty about being fat and their guilt is expressed by eating more. It is a vicious circle. (45) _____. Some of them end up starving themselves to death. (46) _____.

Part VI   **Translation**   **(5 minutes)**

87. Before he left for his vacation he went to the bank to _____ (取了些钱).

88. The project _____ (即将完成的) by the end of 2010 will expand the city's telephone network to cover 10,000,000 users.

89. Government reports, examination compositions, legal documents and most business letters are the main situations _____ (会用到正式语言).

90. The bed has _____ (是我们的家传之物) in the family. It was my great grandmother's originally.

91. In a time of social reform, people's state of mind _____ (趋向于跟上) with the rapid changes of society.

Part I   Writing (30 minutes)

注意:此部分试题在答题卡1上。

Part II   Reading Comprehension (Skimming and Scanning)(15 minutes)

Promote Learning and Skills for Young People and Adults

This goal places the emphasis on the learning needs of young people and adults in the context of lifelong learning. It calls for fair access to learning programs that are appropriate, and mentions life skills particularly.

Why this goal?

Education is about giving people the opportunity to develop their potential, their personality and their strengths. This does not merely mean learning new knowledge, but also developing abilities to make the most of life. These are called life skills—including the inner capacities and the practical skills we need.

Many of the inner capacities—often known as psycho-social skills—cannot be taught as subjects. They are not the same as academic or technical learning. They must rather be modeled and promoted as part of learning, and in particular by teachers. These skills have to do with the way we behave—towards other people, towards ourselves, towards the challenges and problems of life. They include skills in communicating, in making decisions and solving problems, in negotiating and expressing ourselves, in thinking critically and understanding our feelings. More practical life skills are the kinds of manual skills we need for the physical tasks we face. Some would include vocational skills under the heading of life skills—the ability to lay bricks, sew clothes, catch fish or repair a motorbike. These are skills by which people may earn their livelihood and which are often available to young people leaving school. In fact, very often young people learn psycho-social skills as they learn more practical skills. Learning vocational skills can be a strategy for acquiring both practical and psycho-social skills.

We need to increase our life skills at every stage of life, so learning them may be part of early childhood education, of primary and secondary education and of adult learning groups.

Its importance in learning

Life skills can be put into the categories that the Jacques Delors report suggested; it spoke of four pillars of education, which correspond to certain kinds of life skills:

Learning to know: Thinking abilities: such as problem-solving, critical thinking, decision-making, understanding consequences

Learning to be: Personal abilities: such as managing stress and feelings, self-awareness, self-confidence

Learning to live together: Social abilities: such as communication, negotiation, teamwork

Learning to do: Manual skills: practising know-how required for work and tasks

In today's world all these skills are necessary, in order to face rapid change in society. This means that it is important to know how to go on learning as we require new skills for life and work. In addition, we need to know how to cope with the flood of information and turn it into useful knowledge. We also need to learn how to handle change in society and in our own lives.

Its nature

Life skills are both concrete and abstract—practical skills can be learned directly, as a subject. For example, a learner can take a course in laying bricks and learn that skill. Other life skills, such as self-confidence, self-esteem, and skills for relating to others or thinking critically cannot be taught in such direct ways. They should be part of any learning process, where teachers or instructors are concerned that learners should not just learn about subjects, but learn how to cope with life and make the most of their potential.

So these life skills may be learnt when learning other things. For example:

·Learning literacy may have a big impact on self-esteem, on critical thinking or on communication skills;

·Learning practical skills such as driving, healthcare or tailoring may increase self-confidence, teach problem-solving processes or help in understanding consequences.

Whether this is true depends on the way of teaching—what kinds of thinking, relationship-building and communication the teacher or facilitator models themselves and promotes among the learners.

Progress towards this goal

It would require measuring the individual and collective progress in making the most of learning and of life, or assessing how far human potential is being realized, or estimating how well people cope with change. It is easier to measure the development of practical skills, for instance by counting the number of students who register for vocational skills courses. However, this still may not tell us how effectively these skills are being used.

The psycho-social skills cannot easily be measured by tests and scores, but become visible in changed behavior. Progress in this area has often been noted by teachers on reports which they make to the parents of their pupils. The teacher's experience of life, of teaching and of what can be expected from education in the broadest sense serve as a standard by which the growth and development of individuals can be assessed to some extent. This kind of assessment is individual and may never appear in international tables and charts.

Current challenges

The current challenges relate to these difficulties:

·We need to recognize the importance of life skills—both practical and psycho-social—as part of education which leads to the full development of human potential and to the development of society;

·The links between psycho-social skills and practical skills must be more clearly spelled out, so that educators can promote both together and find effective ways to do this;

·Since life skills are taught as part of a wide range of subjects, teachers need to have training in how to put them across and how to monitor learners' growth in these areas;

·In designing curricula and syllabuses for academic subjects, there must be a balance between content teaching and attention to the accompanying life skills;

·A more conscious and deliberate effort to promote life skills will enable learners to become more active citizens in the life of society.

Policy options—what governments should do

·Recognize and actively advocate for the transformational role of education in realizing human potential and in socio-economic development;

·Ensure that curricula and syllabuses address life skills and give learners the opportunity to make real-life applications of knowledge, skills and attitudes;

·Show how life skills of all kinds apply in the world of work, for example, negotiating and communication skills, as well practical skills;

·Through initial and in-service teacher training, increase the use of active and participatory learning/teaching approaches;

·Examine and adapt the processes and content of education so that there is a balance between academic input and life skills development;

·Make sure that education inspectors look not only for academic progress through teaching and learning, but also progress in the communication, modeling and application of life skills;

·Advocate for the links between primary and (early) secondary education because learning life skills needs eight or nine years and recognize that the prospect of effective secondary education is an incentive to children, and their parents, to complete primary education successfully.

Policy options—what funding agencies should do

·Support research, exchange and debate, nationally and regionally, on ways of strengthening life skills education;

·Support *innovative* (创新的) teacher training in order to combine life skills promotion into subjects across the curriculum and as a fundamental part of what school and education are about;

·Recognize the links between primary and secondary education in ensuring that children develop strong life skills;

·Support, therefore, the early years of secondary education as part basic education.

What UNESCO is doing

As support to governments and in cooperation with other international agencies, UNESCO:

·Works to define life skills better and clarify what it means to teach and learn them;

·Assists educational policy makers and teachers to develop and use a life skills approach to education;

·Advocates for the links between a life skills approach to education and broader society and human development.

注意:此部分试题在**答题卡1**上作答;8-10题在**答题卡1**上。

1. Many of the inner capacities which cannot be taught as subjects are often known as psycho-social skills.

2. Vocational skills are more fundamental than psycho-social skills because vocational skills determine people's livelihood.

3. One can tell how effectively a vocational skill is being used by counting how many students register for the course.

4. The progress in psycho-social skills can be measured in terms of changed behaviors.

5. One of the challenges facing the learners is to promote their life skills more consciously and deliberately.

6. The government will ensure that all curricula given to the learners will be related to life skills.

7. The function of UNESCO is to lead the governments and other international agencies to promote life skills.

Part III   Listening Comprehension (35 minutes)

Section A

注意:此部分试题请在**答题卡2**上作答。

11. A) Go to class at 1:00.　　B) Go to the cinema at 2:00.
    C) Go home immediately after his class.　　D) Go home around 3:00.

12. A) To save 150 dollars by repairing the car on their own.
    B) To sell the old car for 150 dollars and buy a new one.
    C) To spend 200 dollars buying a new car.
    D) To spend 50 dollars on the repair.

13. A) Husband and wife.　　B) Father and daughter.
    C) Doctor and patient.　　D) Teacher and student.

14. A) Tom survived the accident.　　B) Everyone but Tom was killed in the accident.
    C) Someone saved Tom's life.　　D) It did little damage to Tom's car.

15. A) Mary lost her way in learning physics.
    B) Mary is very good at physics.
    C) Physics is the least popular course in Mary's class.
    D) Mary has to pass physics exam to graduate.

16. A) He is selling cameras.　　B) He is selling electrical appliances.

C. He is selling office equipment.   D) He works in an electronics company.

17. A) He thinks that the announcer is very qualified.
    B) He doesn't believe what the announcer says.
    C) He doesn't have an opinion of the announcer.
    D) He always follows the announcer's direction.

18. A) She thinks he should call to check his score.
    B) She thinks he should take the test again.
    C) She thinks he should wait patiently.
    D) She thinks he should be more worried than he is.

Questions 19 to 22 are based on the conversation you have just heard.

19. A) Waiter and customer.   B) Good friends.
    C) Husband and wife.   D) Colleagues.

20. A) The man does her a favor.
    B) The man recommends her many good foods.
    C) The man is very patient to her question.
    D) The man decides to treat her to a meal.

21. A) There were not many Chinese restaurants before.
    B) Many people emigrated out of his country.
    C) It is famous for the different recipes.
    D) It prevents foreign languages from getting in.

22. A) He cannot understand why she always speaks nonsense.
    B) He does not think the woman knows how to enjoy herself.
    C) He believes the woman is capable of being promoted soon.
    D) He hates to choose between Chinese cuisine and French cuisine.

Questions 23 to 25 are based on the conversation you have just heard.

23. A) They are reading an article about population.
    B) They are comparing India to their own country.
    C) They are talking about homeless population.
    D) They are worrying about the homeless.

24. A) India.   B) Germany.   C) France.   D) The speakers' country.

25. A) 3 million or so.   B) 4 million or so.
    C) 2 million or so.   D) 1 million or so.

Section B

注意:此部分试题请在**答题卡2**上作答。

Passage One

Questions 26 to 28 are based on the passage you have just heard.

26. A) They want to attract attention.   B) It is fashionable to wear such clothes.
    C) They appear respectable in such clothes.   D) Riding a motorcycle makes one dirty.

27. A) It is efficient.   B) It is exciting.   C) It is convenient.   D) It is dangerous.

28. A) If he always wears protective clothing.
    B) If he can see everything around him clearly.
    C) If he is very careful.
    D) If he has a lot of defenders.

Passage Two

Questions 29 to 31 are based on the passage you have just heard.

29. A) Making noises.
    C) Combinations of different sounds.
    B) Our own system of language.
    D) A group of sentences upon our own creations.

30. A) It does good to communication between people.
    B) It encourages people to speak out their thoughts.
    C) It enlarges the vocabulary of a particular language.
    D) It hinders communication among individuals.

31. A) Words.   B) Tone of voice.   C) Sentence structures.   D) Sounds.

Passage Three

Questions 32 to 35 are based on the passage you have just heard.

32. A) By attending public schools in Bangor Maine.
    B) While serving in the U.S. Army.
    C) As a dramatist in the American theater.
    D) As a French translator while stationed in Paris.

33. A) Three years.   B) Less than four years.   C) Two years.   D) One semester.

34. A) Only one.   B) Two.   C) At least three.   D) At least four.

35. A) To make a person capable of language translators.
    B) To tap a person's best potential in language.
    C) To treat a person poorly by sending him to strange places.
    D) To assign a person a job which is not consistent with his best qualification.

Section C

注意:此部分试题在**答题卡 2** 上;请在**答题卡 2** 上作答。

Part IV Reading Comprehension (Reading in Depth) (25 minutes)

Section A

In the middle of winter, when snow is falling in many parts of the United States, scientists have sounded a warning to people who plan to spend many hours in the sun this summer. The __47__: The sun's summertime rays are more dangerous than once thought.

A team of scientists from 80 nations recently reported to the United Nations that a layer of *ozone* (臭氧) in the atmosphere, which protects humans from __48__ levels of *ultraviolet radiation* (紫外线辐射), will be thinner over the United States this summer. The thinner layer __49__ more ultraviolet rays from the sun to reach earth. The extra __50__ of ultraviolet radiation could cause an increase in the number of cases of skin cancer.

Scientists __51__ became concerned about the ozone layer in the mid-1980s when a hole was discovered in the layer above Antarctica during the winter. The hole was caused by __52__ used in refrigerators and air conditioners. When these chemicals are sent out into the atmosphere, they produce gases that destroy the ozone.

Concern about the __53__ ozone layer rose more recently when data from satellites and ground stations showed that ozone levels were __54__ over areas other than Antarctica. __55__ ozone levels were recorded in the spring and summer over the United States and over other populated areas in the world.

Although many countries have already begun stopping the use of ozone-destroying chemicals, the new findings are expected to advance the timetable for a total __56__ of the chemicals.

注意:此部分试题请在**答题卡 2** 上作答。

A) low	B) dropping	C) amount	D) harmful
E) routine	F) first	G) allows	H) ban
I) warning	J) protective	K) chemicals	L) hazard
M) superficially	N) constitutes	O) dripping	

Section B

Passage One

Before you get the idea that economics is relevant only for politics or business, we should mention that economics focuses on all the choices people make and the personal and social consequences of these choices. Some choices involve money, but many do not. Even seemingly non-economic decisions fall within the realm of economics. Most decisions involve attempts to balance costs against benefits, which may or may not be measurable with money. For example, many costs and benefits are primarily psychological.

Will you continue college? Potential benefits include higher lifetime income, the joy of learning, or good times and personal contacts; costs include expense for tuition and outlay for books, the *drudgery* (单调沉闷的工作) of sitting through dull classes, and income you could be making right now. What will be your major area of study? Will you only take classes in *lucrative* (可赚钱的) fields, or will you weigh enjoyment of the subject matter against potential monetary rewards? Where will you live and work? Should you marry? If so, when? To whom? Marriage involves both financial and psychological costs and benefits. Should you have children? If so, how many? How will you spend your limited income? Your decisions about these and other economic choices will shape your life.

Economics is important in everyday life, but you may know little about it as a field of study. You have probably heard words such as prices, costs, profit, supply and demand, inflation, unemployment, and socialism mentioned for much of your life. Right now, you may be skeptical about the models, graphs, and theories that economists use to interpret how the world works. These concepts and many more are woven into the fabric of economics. We believe that when you finish this book you will join us in the view that the economic way of thinking offers valuable insights into our everyday interaction with one another—producing, consuming, voting, and striving for the good life.

注：此部分试题请在**答题卡 2** 上作答。

57. The author's purpose is to _____.
    A) encourage people to go to college
    B) tell people how to study economics
    C) encourage people to go in business
    D) tell people how to make choices

58. According to the passage, economics _____.
    A) is concerned with choices and their consequences
    B) is especially useful for politicians and businessmen
    C) deals with costs and benefits
    D) mainly studies marriage, family and career

59. The underlined word "outlay" (Line 2, Para. 2) can be best replaced by _____.
    A) supply
    B) quality
    C) spending
    D) research

60. The author writes the second paragraph to _____.
    A) list what problems one has to face at college
    B) show both the benefits and costs when one goes to college
    C) prove how economics can influence one's life
    D) explain why economics should be chosen as one's major

61. The study of economics will lead us to _____.
    A) a better understanding of the world
    B) thorough knowledge of our daily life
    C) a wealth of information
    D) psychological confusion

Passage Two

The fact that blind people can "see" things using other parts of their bodies apart from their eyes may help us to understand our feelings about color. If they can sense color differences then perhaps we too, are affected by color unconsciously.

Manufacturers have discovered by trial and error that sugar sells badly in green wrappings, that blue foods are considered unpleasant, and the *cosmetics* (化妆品) should never be packaged in brown. These discoveries have grown into a whole discipline of color psychology that now finds application in everything from fashion to interior decoration. Some of our preferences are clearly psychological. Dark blue is the color of the night sky and therefore associated with passivity and calm, while yellow is a day color with associations of energy and excitement. For primitive man, activity during the day meant hunting and attacking, while he soon saw as red, the color of blood and rage and the heat that came with effort. And green is associated with passive defense and self-preservation. Experiments have shown that colors, partly because of their physiological associations, also have a direct psychological effect. People exposed to bright red show an increase in heartbeat, and blood pressure. Red is exciting. Similar exposure to pure blue has exactly the opposite effect. It is a calming color. Because of its exciting *connotations* (内涵), red was chosen as the signal for danger, but closer analysis shows that a vivid yellow can produce a more basic state of alertness and alarm, so fire engines and ambulances in some advanced communities are now rushing around in bright yellow colors that stop the traffic dead.

注意：此部分试题请在**答题卡 2** 上作答。

62. Manufacturers found out that color affects sales _____.

    A) by selling sugar in green wrappings

    B) by experimenting with different colors

    C) by trying out color on blind people

    D) by developing the discipline of color psychology

63. Our preferences for certain colors are _____.

    A) associated with the time of the day

    B) dependent on our character

    C) linked with our primitive ancestors

    D) partly due to psychological factors

64. If people are exposed to bright red, which of the following does NOT happen?

    A) They become alert.   B) They feel afraid.

    C) Their blood pressure rises. D) Their hearts beat faster.

65. Which of the following statements is NOT true according to the passage?

    A) Color probably has an effect on us which we are not conscious of.

    B) Yellow fire engines have caused many bad accidents in some advanced communities.

    C) People exposed to pure blue start to breathe more slowly.

    D) The psychology of color is of some practical use.

66. Which of the following could be the most suitable title?

    A) The Discipline of Color Psychology   B) Color and Its Connotations

    C) The Practical Use of Color   D) Color and Feelings

Part V Cloze (15 minutes)

注意：此部分试题请在**答题卡 2** 上作答。

Since we are social beings, the quality of our lives depends in large measure on our interpersonal relationships. One ___67___ of the human condition is our tendency to give and receive support from one another ___68___ stressful circumstances. Social support consists of the ___69___ of resources among people based on their interpersonal ties. ___70___ of us with strong support systems appear ___71___ able to cope with major life changes and daily *hassles* (困难). People ___72___ strong social ties live longer and have better health than those without ___73___ ties. Studies over a range of illnesses, from depression to heart disease, __74__ that the presence of social support helps people fend of illness, and the __75__ of such support makes poor health more likely.

Social support cushions stress in a (n) __76__ of ways. First, friends, relatives, and co-workers may let us know that they __77__ us. Our self-respect is strengthened when we feel accepted by others __78__ our faults and difficulties. Second, other people often __79__ us with informational support. They help us to __80__ and understand our problems and find solutions __81__ them. Third, we typically find social companionship supportive. __82__ in leisure-time activities with others helps us to meet our social needs __83__ at the same time distracting us from our worries and troubles. __84__, other people may give us instrumental support—financial __85__, material resources, and needed services— __86__ reduces stress by helping us resolve and cope with our problems.

67. A) good   B) superiority   C) strength   D) benefit
68. A) on   B) under   C) with   D) within
69. A) change   B) exchange   C) transaction   D) transference
70. A) Those   B) These   C) That   D) This
71. A) much   B) more   C) well   D) better
72. A) with   B) without   C) within   D) beyond
73. A) the   B) many   C) much   D) such
74. A) reveal   B) reflect   C) expose   D) discover
75. A) shortage   B) absence   C) abundance   D) existence
76. A) few   B) dozen   C) decade   D) number
77. A) evaluate   B) value   C) rely   D) stress
78. A) besides   B) spite   C) despite   D) regardless
79. A) offer   B) reinforce   C) provide   D) strengthen
80. A) define   B) relate   C) prescribe   D) account
81. A) in   B) about   C) of   D) to
82. A) Engaging   B) Involving   C) Taking   D) Being
83. A) while   B) meanwhile   C) whereas   D) however
84. A) Furthermore   B) Thus   C) Nevertheless   D) Finally
85. A) assistance   B) supply   C) resources   D) aid
86. A) what   B) that   C) who   D) as

Part VI   Translation (5 minutes)

注意:此部分试题在**答题卡 2** 上;请在**答题卡 2** 上作答。

Model Test 2

Part I Writing

写作指南：

这是四级作文中典型的分析型习作，要求考生分析师生关系对学生发展的影响。写作要求的第三点要求考生自由阐述个人观点，总结两种师生关系，明确自己的看法。

根据写作要求，文章结构如下：

第一段：开门见山提出良好的师生关系对学生发展的重要影响。

第二段：分析不良的师生关系对学生发展造成的弊端，和第一段形成鲜明对比。

第三段为结尾段：呼应主题句，通过概述利弊，提出个人观点。

范文与解析：

Sample	Analysis
[1]A **good** teacher-student relationship can **effectively further** students **to** a higher level in study. [2]Teachers with patience and understanding encourage their students **instead of** pushing or forcing them forward. [3]This sort of relationship makes learning **so** enjoyable and interesting **that** students would work hard willingly. [4]**However**, a **bad** relationship between teachers and students **seriously weakens** the achievement of teaching. [5]It **discourages** students from learning, leaving them with a **wrong and negative** attitude towards study. [6]**Thus**, teaching **also** becomes an unpleasant task, which forms a vicious circle. [7]**Now that** a good teacher-student relationship makes a teacher's job worthwhile, [8]**while** a bad one negatively affects a student's development even to the rest of his life, [9]**more importance should be attached to** the relationship between teachers and students.	[1]用 **good** 和 **effectively further... to** 简要概述良好的师生关系对学生学习的益处。 [2]**instead of** 恰到好处地突出了良好师生关系的重要性。 [3]用 **so... that...** 结果状语从句进一步申明良好的师生关系对学生的影响。 [4]**However** 笔锋一转，引出其不良影响。 [5]呼应 **discourage** 一词，用 **wrong and negative** 进一步突出不良关系的害处。 [7]**Now that** 承上启下。**while** 一词很好地概括两种师生关系的影响，重申主题。 [8]使用 **attach more importance to...**"重视"的被动形式，是语言运用上的亮点句型。

句型变换：

[1]

1. A good teacher-student relationship can effectively further students to a higher level in study.

2. Students can be inspired to go into a higher level in study with a good teacher-student relationship.

3. A good teacher-student relationship can help students

to be more effective in study.

4. A good teacher-student relationship encourages students to study more effectively.

【2】

1. Teachers with patience and understanding encourage their students instead of pushing or forcing them forward.

2. Patient and thoughtful teachers will not push or force their students but encourage them forward.

3. Patient and considerate teachers encourage their students rather than push or force them forward.

4. With patience and understanding, teachers give their students more encouragement than pressure.

【4】

1. However, a bad relationship between teachers and students seriously weakens the achievement of teaching.

2. But a bad relationship between teachers and students exerts negative impact on the achievement of teaching.

3. On the contrary, a poor relationship between teachers and students unfavorably affects the effect of teaching.

4. Unlike a good relationship between teachers and students, a bad one undermines the quality of teaching.

【6】

1. Thus, teaching also becomes an unpleasant task, which forms a vicious circle.

2. Thus, teaching also becomes boring task, giving rise to a vicious circle.

3. Therefore, teaching also becomes tedious task, which results in a vicious circle.

4. Then, teaching also becomes a dull task, which in turn leads to a vicious circle.

【7】

1. Now that a good teacher-student relationship makes a teacher's job worthwhile,

2. A teacher's job is made worthwhile by a good teacher-student relationship,

3. A good teacher-student relationship makes the teacher's job enjoyable,

4. A good teacher-student relationship makes the teacher's job meaningful,

【8】

1. while a bad one negatively affects a student's development even to the rest of his life,

2. while a bad one has negative effects on the development of a student even to the rest of his life,

3. while a student's development may be hindered by a bad one even to the rest of his life,

4. while a bad one brings ill effects on a student's development even to the rest of his life,

【9】

1. more importance should be attached to the relationship between teachers and students.

2. the relationship between teachers and students should be paid more attention to.

3. the relationship between teachers and students should be attached much importance to.

4. more emphasis should be placed on the relationship between teachers and students.

Part II Reading Comprehension (Skimming and Scanning)

参考译文划线点评
促进年轻人和成年人的学习和技能

以"终生学习"为背景,这个目标将重点放在年轻人和成年人的学习需要上。它提倡应有公平的机会去学习课程,还特别提到生活技能。

为什么定这个目标?

教育是给人们发展潜能、个性和实力提供机会。[8]这并不仅仅意味着学习新知识,还指培养能力,充分地汲取生活的养分。这些被称为生活技能,包括内在能力和我们需要的实际技能。

[1]大部分的内在能力——经常被称作"心理社会技能"——是不能作为一个学科来教授的。它与学术或技术的学习不同,但必须作为学习的一部分来塑造和促进,尤其要由教师来做。这些技能应该和我们的行为方式有关——我们如何对待他人,对待我们自己,对待生活的挑战和问题。它还包括沟通,决策和解决问题,协商和自我表达,批判性思考和理解我们的情感等方面的技能。更实际的生活技能是那些我们进行体力劳动时需要的手工技能,包括生活技能里的职业技能,例如铺砖、缝纫、捕鱼或是修理摩托车的能力。这些是人们谋生的技能,也是离开学校的年轻人经常可以学习到的技能。[2]事实上,年轻人在学习更实际的技能时,通常也就在学习心理社会技能。学习职业技能是可以同时掌握实际技能和心理社会技能的一种策略。

在生活的每个阶段,我们都要提高自身的生活技能,因此,学习这些技能也许是早期儿童教育、中小学教育和成年教育的一部分。

它在学习中的重要性

生活技能可被归入雅克·德罗斯报告所提出的分类;该报告谈到了教育的四个支柱,这和某些生活技能相呼应:

学习了解:思考能力,例如解决问题、批判性思维、决策、理解逻辑推理

学习生存:个人能力,例如应付压力和情绪、自知、自信

学习共存:社会能力,例如沟通、谈判、团队协作

[9]学习动手:手工技能,具备工作和任务所需要的技能

在当今世界,为了面对社会的迅速变化,所有这些技能都是必要的。这表明,当我们需要为生活和工作掌握新技能时,知道怎样继续学习是很重要的。另外,我们需要知道怎样应对潮水般的信息,并把它变成有用的知识。我们也需要学习如何应对社会和我们自己生活所发生的变化。

它的本质

生活技能既是具体的,又是抽象的。实际的技能可以作为一门学科直接学习,例如,学习者可以选修一门铺砖的课程来学习这项技能。其他生活技能,例如自信、自尊,其他相关的技能,或者批判性思维不可能以这样直接的方式习得。它们应该是所有学习过程的一部分。在这一过程里,教师或是讲师应该关心的是,学习者不仅在学习学科知识,而且还在学习如何应对生活,充分发挥他们的潜能。

因此,学习其他东西时,可以学习到这些生活技能。例如:

·识字可能会对自尊、批判性思维或沟通技能有很大的影响;

·学习驾驶、保健或裁缝这些实际技能可以增加自信,学习解决问题的过程,或者有助于理解逻辑推论。

这一切是否如此取决于教学方式——教师或辅导者自己的以及在学生中提倡的思维模式,人际关系类型和沟通方式。

朝这个目标发展

它要求衡量个人或集体在充分利用学习和生活上所取得的进步,或是评估人的潜能可以发挥到何种程度,或是估计人们应对变化的能力。[3]衡量实际技能的发展更容易一些,例如,通过计算注册学习职业技能课程的学生数量可知其发展。但是,这仍然不能告诉我们这些技能是否得到有效的利用。

[4]心理社会技能不能轻易地通过测试和分数来衡量,但是可以体现在发生了改变的行为方面。这方面的进步经常在教师写给学生父母的报告里提到。教师的生活经验、教学经验和最广泛意义上的教学期望值可以在一定程度上作为个人成长和发展评估的标准。这种评估是针对个人的,决不会在国际表格和图表里出现。

当今的挑战

当今的挑战与以下这些困难有关:

·我们需要承认生活技能——包括实际技能和心理社会技能——的重要性,它是教育的一部分,使人们的潜能和社会得到充分的发展;

·心理社会技能和实际技能之间的联系必须更清楚地阐明,以便教育工作者能促进这两方面的发展,并为此找到有效的方法;

·既然生活技能是作为众多学科的一部分来进行教学,那么教师就需要接受培训,学会如何传授技能,如何检测学习者在这些领域的进步。

·在设计学科的课程和教学大纲时,要平衡学科内容教学和相关生活技能的培养;

[5]·更加有意识地努力提高生活技能,使学习者能够成为社会生活中更加积极的公民。

政策选择——政府应该做的

·对教育在实现人们潜能和社会经济发展方面所起到的改造作用给予认可和积极提倡;

[6]·确保课程和教学大纲涉及生活技能的培养,并为学习者提供在现实生活中运用知识和技能以及表现学习到的种种态度的机会;

·展现各种生活技能在工作中的应用,例如,谈判、沟通技能和实际技能;

·通过教师的初始教学培训和在职培训,增加积极参与式的教学方法的运用;

[10]·检查和调整教育的过程和内容,以便平衡知识的输入和生活技能的发展;

·确保督教员不仅检查学生在教学中所取得的学习进步,还要检查在生活技能的沟通、塑造以及应用上的进步。

·由于学习生活技能需要花费八到九年的时间,应提倡把初级教育和(早期)中等教育联系起来,并意识到,良好

的中等教育能给孩子带来良好的前景,这对孩子和他们的家长来说都是一种让孩子完成初级教育阶段学习的激励因素。

政策选择——提供资金的组织应该做的?
- 支持为加强生活技能方式而进行的全国性和地区性研究、交流和辩论;
- 支持创新的教师培训,以便把提高生活技能作为学校教育的基本部分与课程科目结合起来;
- 认识到初级教育和中等教育之间的联系,以保证孩子发展良好的生活技能。
- 因此,中等教育的初期阶段也是基础教育的一部分,应当予以支持。

联合国教科文组织目前在做的事情

[7]作为对各国政府的支持者和与其他国际组织的合作者,联合国教科文组织:
- 努力给"生活技能"下更好的定义,阐明这些技能的教学意义;
- 协助教育决策者和教师发扬和使用生活技能的教育方法;
- 提倡把生活技能的教育方法和更广义上的社会和人类发展联系在一起。

---

1. **【答案】**Y
   【题眼】Many of the <u>inner capacities</u> which cannot be taught as subjects are often known as <u>psycho-social skills</u>.
   【定位】第1个小标题 **Why this goal?** 部分的第2段首句。

   【解析】题目与原文的词序虽然不同,但是用词一样,而且意思也相同,因此本题答案为Y。

2. **【答案】**NG
   【题眼】Vocational skills are more fundamental than psycho-social skills because vocational skills determine people's livelihood.
   【定位】第1个小标题 **Why this goal?** 部分的第2段最后两句。

   【解析】原文提到了 vocational skills, psycho-social skills 等,但是并没有将二者做比较,因此本题答案为NG。

3. **【答案】**N
   【题眼】One can tell how <u>effectively</u> a vocational skill is being used by counting how many <u>students register for the course</u>.
   【定位】第4个小标题 **Progress towards this goal** 部分的首段第2句和第3句。

   【解析】原文第3句中的 However 及 still may not 等词表明原文所表达的意思与题目所表达的意思正好相反,因此本题答案为N。

4. **【答案】**Y
   【题眼】The progress in psycho-social skills can be measured in terms of <u>changed behaviors</u>.
   【定位】第4个小标题 **Progress towards this goal** 部分的第2段首句。

   【解析】原文的 but become visible... 等词表明可以通过行为的改变来衡量心理社会技能的发展,也就是题目表达的意思,因此本题答案为Y。

5. **【答案】**Y
   【题眼】One of the <u>challenges</u> facing the learners is to promote their life skills more <u>consciously and deliberately</u>.
   【定位】第5个小标题 **Current challenges** 部分的最后一段。

   【解析】结合该部分的小标题,可以看出原文该段的主语指出了学习者面临的一个挑战,而题目的表语是对原文主语的同义改写,因此本题答案为Y。

6. **【答案】**NG
   【题眼】The government will ensure that all <u>curricula</u> given to the learners will be related to <u>life skills</u>.
   【定位】第6个小标题 **Policy options—what governments should do** 部分的第2段。

   【解析】原文只指出政府将确保课程中包括生活技能,但是否所有的课程都与生活技能有关并不得而知,因此本题答案为 NG。

7. 【答案】N

【题眼】The function of UNESCO is to lead the governments and other international agencies to promote life skills.

【定位】最后一个小标题 **What UNESCO is doing** 部分的首段。

【解析】原文指出 UNESCO 只起 support 的作用,而不是如题目所说的那样起领导(lead)的作用,因此本题答案为 N。

8. 【答案】the inner capacities, the practical skills we need

【题眼】The abilities that we can make the most of life consist of _____.

【定位】第 1 个小标题 **Why this goal?** 部分的首段第 2 句和第 3 句。

【解析】空白处应分别为名词词组。原文第 3 句中的 These 指代上文的 the abilities to make the most of life,题目中的 consist of 与原文 including 一词同义,因此本题答案可在 including 后找到。

9. 【答案】practising know-how required for work and tasks

【题眼】The "learning to do" skills are also known as "manual skills", which are about _____.

【定位】第 2 个小标题 **Its importance in learning** 部分的倒数第 2 段。

【解析】空白处应为名词词组。原文第 2 个冒号后的内容表明了"learning to do"具体的要求是什么,因此本题答案可在该冒号后找到。

10. 【答案】academic input and life skills development

【题眼】The government must examine and adapt the processes and content of education in order to gain a balance between _____.

【定位】第 6 个小标题 **Policy options—what governments should do** 部分的第 5 段。

【解析】空白处应为名词词组。对比题目与原文可以发现,题目中 in order to 引出的不定式与原文中的 so that 引出的目的状语从句表达的意思相同,答案可以在该从句中找到。

Part III   Listening Comprehension

Section A

11. W: Ray, are you going straight home after school today?

　　M: No. I have a class until one o'clock, and after that I'm going to spend a couple of hours at the library before going home.

　　Q: What is Ray going to do this afternoon?

[D]【解析】1 点钟下课,之后去图书馆待上两个小时,再回家。所以选 D。

【点睛】①时间计算题。听到的时间数字(one hour, a couple of hours)本身往往不能做答案,而是经过计算后的时间才会是答案。②选项 C 中的 immediately 是 S1 中的 straight 的同义替换,但 S2 开头就用 No 予以否定,可以排除。

12. W: The mechanic said it cost 50 dollars to have the car repaired.

　　M: We might as well spend 150 dollars more to buy a new one.

　　Q: What does the man intend to do?

[C]【解析】数字计算题。修旧车需要 50 美元,"might as well"表示"不如做某事",男士的提议是还不如再多花 150 美元买一辆新车。所以答案应该是 C。

【点睛】不正确的选项有一个共同点,就是再现对话中提到的数字。而对话中的数字题往往需要进行简单的运算。由此可以大胆地排除 A、B、D。

13. W: Have you found anything wrong with my stomach?

　　M: Not yet. I will let you know the result next week.

Q: What is the probable relationship between the man and the woman?

[C]【解析】标志性词语 anything wrong with my stomach, know the result next week 表明病人有胃病,医生在检查。

> 【点睛】身份关系题。只要听清标志性词语就不难解题。注意在医生、病人场景中,result 指"(化验、治疗)结果"。可参见本书 Test 1 听力第 12 题。

14. W: It's surprising that Tom came out of the accident alive.

　　M: That's true. The car crashed into the wall and was completely damaged.

　　Q: What was the consequence of the accident?

[A]【解析】A 中的 survive the accident 是原文 come out of the accident alive"在车祸中幸存下来"的同义表达。

> 【点睛】B 项和 C 项是无中生有。男士说车全毁了,D 项与原文不符,可排除。

15. M: Mary told me that she would graduate in June.

　　W: Only if she could get the physics course out of the way.

　　Q: What does the woman imply?

[D]【解析】考查对口语短语的理解。get... out of the way 意思是"使不挡住路"。女士说,只有等玛丽把物理课攻下来(即考试合格)才有可能毕业。所以 D 为正确答案。

> 【点睛】①本题就问有关 Mary 及 physics 这个话题,因此不能"听到什么不选什么"地排除含这两个词的选项。出题人唯一可以利用的同音干扰就只能在"out of the way"上做文章。由此可以先排除 A。②only if(千万要与 if only 区别开!)表示条件,四个选项中只有 D 表达了"条件与结果"关系,是正确答案。

16. W: Is your brother still selling cameras?

　　M: He has had three different jobs. Right now he is working in an electronics company. Before then he was selling office equipment.

　　Q: What job does the man's brother have now?

[D]【解析】对话中提到他现在一家电子公司(electronics company)工作,所以选 D。迷惑项 B 说他出售电器,与原文不符。A 项和 C 项时态有误。

> 【点睛】①本题的解答关键在动词。若在 sell 和 work 之间选择正确,即可得出答案。②由答非所问可以迅速排除 A。③由时态可以排除 C。单纯由时态判定难度较大。但这里"时间状语"又可以帮上大忙。

17. W: Maybe we should take Front Street this morning. The radio announcer said traffic on the freeway is really heavy.

　　M: Well, if he says to take Front Street, then we should go the other way!

　　Q: What is the man's opinion of the radio announcer?

[B]【解析】男士说:"如果他说要走 Front Street,那我们就应该走另一条路了!"由此可知,他不相信播报员所说的话,所以选 B。

> 【点睛】这种讽刺调侃题常有出现。①A、D 都是对 announcer 的正面评价,属于等价选项,可以同时排除。②C 是一个永远也不能充当答案的选项。凡多项选择题,均不会以"没有意见、观点、态度"作为正确答案。

18. M: I still haven't received my score on the computer test. Maybe I should call to check on it.

　　W: Don't worry so much. It takes at least two weeks to get your score.

　　Q: What does the woman think the man should do?

[C]【解析】女士告诉他,不用这么着急,拿到分数至少还有两周,所以选 C。

> 【点睛】①建议题。听到 Don't worry,即可推出正确答案。②从时间副词也可推知,含 patiently 的选项为答案。

Now you'll hear two long conversations.

Conversation One

M: What are you going to have?

W: I have no idea. Could you help me with the menu?

M: Yes, sure. These are starters, and these are main courses and these are desserts. See?

W: What's the alternative?

M: The alternative is to order a complete dinner. For a set price you get your choice of soup or juice, one dish with potato and vegetable, salad, bread and butter and sometimes coffee and sometimes dessert.

W: And you pay the price listed next to the main course?

M: Right. Like the roast beef dinner is $7.85—plus tax and tip, of course.

W: It all looks pretty expensive to me.

M: It's not. This is only a bit more expensive than McDonald's. [20] So enjoy yourself. We're celebrating, remember? Order anything you'd like to try; it's all on me.

W: [20] You're very kind.

M: [19] Friends are friends. I cannot get promoted often. Are you ready to order?

W: Ah, can you tell me what Hot Fudge Sundae is?

M: That's a dessert. It's an English specialty. It's a kind of ice cream with a hot sticky sauce over the top—very sweet and fattening!

W: I don't really like the sound of that. How come there is English food? I thought we agreed to eat American food.

M: [21] Our country is made up of people from all over the world, so besides collected words and phrases from every language, we've also absorbed recipes. We even have a lot of Chinese restaurants now.

W: Which is better, French or Chinese cuisine?

M: I'd say it's a toss-up. I love them both.

W: I didn't know you were so fond of foreign foods. [22] When my boss promotes me, I will take you to a French restaurant near my company. The food there is delicious.

M: [22] Oh, we will have a second dinner soon.

19. What's the relationship between the two speakers?

[B]【解析】场景推理题。题目询问两个对话者是什么关系。对话开头女士没拿定主意吃什么，希望男士提些建议，很多考生以为男士是服务员，因此选择 A。也有人因为后文出现 get promoted 和 my boss 等用语，错选 D。从全文来看，特别是男士说"friends are friends"，可知答案是 B。

【点睛】①由选项知，本题要考查对话双方的身份，在听录音时，要特别注意相关"关键词"。②本题不可贸然作答，一定要在预知问题的前提下，对相关选项一一考察排除。

20. Why does the woman think the man is kind?

[D]【解析】推理题。A 项对话中并未提及，可以排除；B 项和 C 项虽然是事实但却并非原因，故也可排除。对话中，女士觉得饭店的东西很贵，但男士让她吃什么就点什么，这才是答案所在，故选 D。

【点睛】①由选项知，本题将询及男士为女士做了什么事。各选项主语都是"the man"，而宾语都与"她"相关。②在无法知道正确的问题的情况下，看对话中涉及了什么选项。"听到什么选什么"。③若多个选项均有提及，须对各项加以区分。④本题各选项均未直接在对话中出现，而乍听起来，四个选项似乎都成立，因而难度较大。必须依据问题本身从中加以选择。

21. Which of the following statements is true about the man's country?

[A]【解析】推理题。在对话中，男士谈到他们国家有来自世界各地的人，他们带来不同的语言和烹饪方法。C 项中的 famous 与对话无关，B、D 两项与事实相悖。之后他提到现在连(even)中国饭店也有很多了，即以前没有很多，因此 A 项正确。

【点睛】①从四个选项中很难判断本题询问的要点，因而增加了难度。②本对话与"饮食"有关，B、D 属于不相干选项，故可以排除，不予考虑。③带着 A、C 的内容听录音，可以听到 recipe 和 Chinese restaurants 等字眼。不能"听到什么选什么"时，要以同义替换原则选择答案。④对话中没有出现 famous 及与其相当的词汇，而对"中国餐馆"的描述则与 A 一致。

22. What does the man think of the woman?

[C]【解析】推测题。男士虽然没直接说过 C 项中的内容，但根据他说"不久就会再次一起吃饭"的预测，可以看出他非常相信女士的工作能力，因为女士许诺升迁了也要请客，答案为 C。A、B 两项均与原文不符。题目询问的是男士对女士的看法，而 D 项描述的只是男士自己的喜恶情况，纯属答非所问，故 D 错误。

【点睛】①读题。四个选项，主语都是 He，谓语动词都表示心理情态动作，而宾语部分与"她"有关，故可推测，本题询问男士对女士的看法。②进一步判断，则可直接排除 D。③本题又属结尾部分的"尾巴题"，对话结尾处是答题要点。④若仅凭结尾男士的话，无论如何也不能得出 A、B 选项的含义；联系到本次对话的背景(因升迁而请客)，则可推出答案 C。

Conversation Two

W: What are you looking at, Tom?

M: [23] I'm reading an article about the world's homeless population.

W: What do you call "homeless population?"

M: Sociologists define homeless people as "those who have no fixed shelter on any given night." These figures show five countries with large homeless population.

W: Ha, according to the definition, I was once a "homeless person". I slept at different places every night.

M: Don't be joking. You were just on a journey.

W: Wow, that's amazing. I never realized that there were so many homeless people in Germany and France.

M: You know what? [24] Our country ranks number one among these countries.

W: Surely not! [25] India tops the list with 3 million homeless people.

M: Well, it depends on how you look at it. [25] Although we have a million fewer homeless people than India, [24] we have the highest percentage of homeless people according to the article.

23. What are the speakers doing?

[C]【解析】主旨题。整个对话围绕无家可归者的数量展开，故 C 项正确。B、D 两项以偏概全；A 项少了一个 homeless，况且由对话知，读文章的是男士，不是 they，故均不正确。

【点睛】①由四个选项的进行时态可知,本题问对方双方正在做什么事。两人的对话主题,即是答题关键。②多次重复的 homeless population/people（共计重复 9 次之多！）使本题答案非常显眼。

24. Which country tops the list of homeless population according to the man?

[D]【解析】细节题。对话中男士说，"在这些国家中，我们国家名列首位"，故选 D。

【点睛】①四个选项是国家（名称），可推知本题问哪一个国家最具有某种特点。②听到男士说"Our country ranks number one"以及女士说"India tops the list"时,要分别在 A、D 选项作标记(比如:A→W;D→M)。如此,听到问题时,便可轻松作答。

25. How much homeless population does the speakers' country have?

[C]【解析】数字计算题。根据对话，印度有 300 万无家可归者，对话者国家的无家可归者比印度少 100 万，即 200 万左右，故选 C。

【点睛】做数字题要过三关:听清数字,理解每个数字的含义;数字计算,比较各数字的关系;听清问题,做出针对性的选择。

Section B

Passage One

Nowadays motorcycling is fast becoming one of Americans' most popular sports. However, there are several things about motorcycling that [27] the average citizen dislikes. [26] Motorcyclists frequently get dirty. In fact, they are dirty. On the road there is little to protect them from mud, insects and bird droppings. For practical reasons, they are often dressed in old clothing, which looks much less respectable than the clothing of people who ride in cars. [26] For the same reason, motorcyclists usually wear dark colors. Of course, [27] the danger of motorcycling also helps account for many people's low opinion of the sport. Its defenders, however, [28] claim that careful cyclists are in less danger than it's commonly believed. He must pay careful attention to his driving. From that point of view, a man on a motorcycle is safer than a man in a car.

26. Why do motorcyclists often dress in old and dark clothing?

[D]【解析】文中提到"骑摩托车的人经常浑身脏兮兮的。因为路上没有什么东西为他们遮挡泥土，以及昆虫和鸟类的粪便。"故选 D。

【点睛】①读题,主题词包括 they, clothes, motorcycle。由此可大体推测本文的话题,从而为听的过程提供了背景。②另一种解答方式:A、B、C 均从正面角度讨论，D 从负面角度讨论，因而，只要听到有关负面词汇，便可快速选出答案。③本题符合"听到什么选什么"的原则。

27. What's the average citizen's opinion about motorcycling?

[D]【解析】①短文开头处 however 后的内容是听力重点。听到"the average citizen dislikes"可知，普通市民对骑摩托车持负面态度。A、B、C 均是正面态度，唯有 D

与此相符。②短文后面具体说到,骑摩托车危险,所以人们对其评价不高。由此也可选出 D。

【点睛】①本题选项是"it is+**adj.**"形式,可推知,它问"it"怎么样。由 26 题大体推断,这个 it 是"riding a motorcycle"。②带着这样的预期听短文,可知本文都在说驾驶摩托车的不利之处(人们不喜欢它的原因)。由此,听到问题时,就可以快速准确地作答。

28. How can a motorcyclist be safer than a car driver?

Passage Two

Speech is one of the most important ways of communicating. It consists of far more than just making noises. To talk and also to be understood by other people, we have to speak a language, that is, we have to use [29] combinations of sounds that everyone agrees stand for a particular object or idea. [30] Communication would be impossible if everyone made up their own language.

Learning a language properly is very important. The basic vocabulary of English is not very large, and only about 2,000 words are needed to speak it quite well. But the more words you know, the more ideas you can express, and the more precise you can be about their exact meaning.

Words are the main thing we use in communicating what we want to say. [31] The way we say the words is also very important. Our tone of voice can express many emotions and shows whether we are pleased or angry, for instance.

29. What are used to stand for a particular object or idea when we speak a language?

[C]【解析】根据原文中的定语 combination of sounds that stand for a particular object or idea,选 C。

【点睛】①四个选项是(动)名词词组,与语言有关。可据此听取录音信息。②符合"听到什么选什么"的原则。

30. What if everyone made up their own language?

[D]【解析】D 是对原文"如果每个人都有自己的语言,就无法进行交流。"的同义表达。

【点睛】①由选项知,本题将问"它"的作用。A、B、C 均说它好,D 说它不好,而且 A、D 属于矛盾选项。据此,可以做出大胆预定:选 D!(没有听问题就选答案!)②如果听清了问题,那不过是对选出的答案加以 confirm。③注意,在听的过程中,像"×××would be impossible if..."的句子,应该是听得很清楚的;读完选项后,×××处的 communication 也是应该听得出来的。毕竟,它

是本文的核心词汇!所以本题没有任何难度。

31. What is also important besides the main thing in communicating?

[B]【解析】the main thing in communicating 指的是 words,而问题是此外还有哪些主要的方面,答案在最后两句话中,因此不选 A 而选 B。

【点睛】①四个选项均是名词(词组),与语言有关。本题在最后,应在短文末尾处找答案。短文末尾处,要么附带说明不重要信息,要么总结全文,给出最重要信息。②听录音时,注意标记听到的词。words(选项 A):main thing。tone of voice(选项 B):important。③注意,文中的 also,besides 等引出的内容往往是考点。④正如上篇短文第 28 题所说的,"反复强调的字眼是答案"。这里,the way we say the words 即与 tone of voice 同义反复。⑤当然,本题答案的判定,最后以问题为准。

[C]【解析】原文结尾处两次提到 careful,并且说从这个角度来看,骑摩托车的人比开车的人更安全。

【点睛】①由四个条件句可知,本题将问到某个细节。②属"尾巴题",结尾处的中心词是答题要点。③反复强调的字眼一般是答案所在。④注意不可选 D。原文出现了"支持者",是介绍他们的观点。这里问的正是他们的观点的内容,而不是他们自己。

Passage Three

[32] James Anthony, who is considered to be the greatest living dramatist of the American theater was born in Bangor, Maine in 1921. He attended the public schools of Bangor and although he was the son of a poor European immigrant, he found a way to go to college. In 1939, he won a scholarship to the university of Maine, where he spent [33] almost the next four years studying. I say almost, because during his last semester he was drafted into the United States Army. He spent the next three years in the army and was honorably discharged in 1945, at the close of World War II. In the army, [34] his job was to translate French documents into English, although his best foreign language was Italian. [35] The army, in characteristic fashion, made him a French translator and for a year he was stationed in Paris.

32. According to the speaker, how did Anthony achieve his fame?

[C]【解析】文章第一句话就说明了他的成功是因为他是一个剧作家。

【点睛】①由选项知,本题问某一个人做什么事,从事什么职业。②带着这种问题听短文第一句话,必须可以听到"dramatist"(毕竟选项 C 中出现了该词,我们应该有心理准备)。③听到什么选什么。

33. How much time did Anthony spend in college?

[B]【解析】文中明确指出 where he spent almost the next four years,但不足 4 年所以选 B。

【点睛】①本题很容易预测问题。②解答关键在于区分各选项在短文中所关联的内容,并做好记录。A 中 three years is in the army。C、D 两项无原文依据。③最后,依据问题来回答。

34. Based on the passage, how many languages can we infer that Anthony knew?

[C]【解析】文中提到,他在军队中的工作是将法语文件译成英语,尽管他最擅长的外语是意大利语,所以他至少会三种语言。

【点睛】①此题看似简单,其实难度很大。解答的关键在于预期问题,做好心理准备,这样,在回想时才不致有遗漏。②若 D 正确,C 也正确,故 D 必不正确。

35. What does the speaker say is characteristic of the army?

[D]【解析】根据最后两句,他最擅长意大利语,但是部队却让他做法语翻译,而且派驻巴黎 1 年,所以部队的特点就是不能使人发挥出自己的特长来。D 选项含义最深刻,概括性最强。

【点睛】①不定式短语作选项,宾语是泛指的人,本题大概问相关目的之类。②A、B 语义正面,指发挥某人的语言特长。D 与它们含义相反。由此,大体可推测答案是 D。③C 较具体,说派人到"strange places"。文说 he 被派往 Pairs,并不是一个奇怪的地方,可以排除。

Section C

36.【答案】misleading

【解析】此处需要一个形容词或动词(的过去分词或现在分词)。misleading 表示"使人产生误解的"。按照发音规则,此词应该不难拼写。

37.【答案】seek

【解析】此处需要一个动词原形;在语义上,此处应填表示"寻求,接受"的词。seek 很简单,但不要误以为是更简单的 see,甚至 sick。

38.【答案】lack

【解析】此处需要一个单数名词,此句应意为"他们觉得这(即超重)显示了他们本身意志力与自控力的缺乏"。a lack of 为固定搭配,表示"缺乏、缺少"。不要误以为是 like。

39.【答案】conform

【解析】此处需要一个动词原形;根据句意,此处应填与 to 一起表示"符合"的词。conform to 为固定搭配。不要误以为是及物动词 confirm。

40.【答案】exemplified

【解析】根据后面的 by 可知,此处需要一个动词的过去分词,与 by 引导的介词短语一起作为定语,修饰 the modern ideal of beauty;在语义上,此处应填表示"是……的典型(或典范)"的词。不要把第二个 e 写成了 a。

41.【答案】incredibly

【解析】此处需要一个修饰 thin 的副词,incredibly 意为"令人难以置信地"。不可漏掉词尾 ly,注意拼写时不要写错元音字母 i 和 e。

42.【答案】grounds

【解析】根据前面的 are 可知,此处需要一个复数名词;根据前面的 Apart from 与 reasons 可知,此处应填表示"理由,根据"的词。

43.【答案】particularly

【解析】此处需要一个修饰 more likely 的副词,此词拼写时应注意两个 ar。

44.【答案】Losing weight would certainly make them feel healthier and increase their life expectancy

【听音关键】Losing weight, healthier, increase life expectancy

【答案重构】Weight loss would surely make them healthier and live longer.

【画龙点睛】可以利用同义替换简化原有难词,把 increase their life expectancy 变成 live longer 就更加容易拼写了。

45.【答案】On the other hand, there are women who unnecessarily lose weight in order to conform to a model of social acceptability

【听音关键】women, unnecessarily lose weight, conform, social acceptability

【答案重构】On the other hand, some women needlessly lose weight to conform to a model of social acceptability

【画龙点睛】there be 句型中的定语从句容易出错,可以简化为简单句。如果保留 there be 句型及定语从句的话,一定不可少了关系代词 who,否则就犯了语法错误。

46.【答案】So perhaps it might be better to try to remove

fat people's unhappiness than try to remove the fat

【听音关键】better to, remove, unhappiness than, fat

【答案重构】So perhaps we should try to remove fat people's unhappiness instead of their fat

【画龙点睛】注意形式主语和比较结构,记录下比较对象就很好组织句子了。

Part IV Reading Comprehension (Reading in Depth)

Section A
参考译文

在隆冬季节,当美国大部分地区还处于大雪纷飞的时候,科学家们却向准备今年夏天在阳光下度过大部分时间的人们发出了一则警告。这则警告的内容是:夏季的阳光比以前我们想象的还要危险。

最近,由80个国家组成的一个科学家小组向联合国递交了一份报告,该报告称:大气层中保护人们免受紫外线辐射伤害的臭氧层,今年夏季在美国上空会变得更稀薄。由于臭氧层变得更稀薄,阳光中也就会有更多的紫外线投射到地球上。紫外线辐射的增多将可能造成皮肤癌患者的增加。

科学家最早开始关注臭氧层是在20世纪80年代中期,那时科学家们在冬季的南极洲上空发现了臭氧层黑洞。这个黑洞是由冰箱和空调里使用的化学物质引起的。因为当这些化学物质释放到空气中时,会产生一种破坏臭氧的气体。

最近,从卫星和地面接收站得到的数据表明除了南极洲以外,全球的臭氧层水平都在下降,这使得臭氧层保护问题更加受到重视。在美国上空和世界上其他人口密集地区的上空,春夏两季时都会对低水平的臭氧层进行记录。

虽然很多国家已经开始停止使用破坏臭氧层的化学物质,但是人们仍希望不断出现新的研究成果以促使对破坏臭氧层的化学物品的总禁令早日出台。

[词性分析]

名　词:amount 量,数量;总额　routine 例行公事,惯例,惯常的程序　first 第一,冠军　ban 禁止,禁令　warning 警告,告诫,提醒;通知　chemicals 化学制品[复数]　hazard 危险,公害

动　词:dropping (使)落下;(使)下降;(使)停止[现在分词]　amount (to) 合计;(在意义、价值等方面)等同,接近　allows 允许,准许;允许……进入(或停留);同意给;承认[第三人称单数]　ban 取缔,查禁;禁止　warning 警告,告诫[现在分词]　hazard 尝试着做(或提出);冒……风险　constitutes 组成,构成,形成;设立,建立,任命[第三人称单数]　dripping 滴[现在分词]

形容词:low 低的,矮的;低等的;粗劣的;不充分的;情绪低落的　harmful 有害的　routine 例行的,常规的　first 第一的,最好的;最先的;基本的,概要的　protective 保护的,防护的

副　词:first 首先;第一次;宁可,宁愿　superficially 浅薄地;表面地

47. [I]此处应为名词。原文第1句指出科学家提出了一个警告,第2句就是该警告的具体内容,因此,空白处的名词应为 warning,冒号后面的内容是对其的解释。

48. [D]此处应为形容词。本句中的 protect... from 表明 ultraviolet radiation(紫外线辐射)很强烈,对人体有害,因此 levels 前应为 harmful 一词。

49. [G]此处应为及物动词,且为第三人称单数,在句子中作谓语。从上文提到的臭氧层和紫外线的关系可以推断,臭氧层越薄,照射到地球上的紫外线就越强,按照句意从词库中选择,只有 allows 最合适。

50. [C]此处应为名词。本句中的 The extra ____ of ultraviolet radiation 与上一句提到的 more ultraviolet rays 同义,空白处的名词应表示紫外线的"量",因此,本题答案为 amount。

51. [F]此处应为副词,作谓语 became concerned 的状语。本句中的时间状语暗示本段讲述科学家早期对臭氧层的研究,空白处的状语应表示科学家"最早"开始关注臭氧层是在80年代中期,因此 first 是最合适的副词。

52. [K]此处应为名词。本句中的 used in refrigerators and air conditioners 表明空白处的名词是一种用于冰箱或空调的物质,而根据紧接着的下一句中的 these chemicals 可知其是对此的进一步解说。关键词的再现可确定本题答案

为 chemicals。

53. [J]此处应为形容词,修饰 ozone layer。本文指出了人们越来越关注臭氧层,因为臭氧层给予地球保护,但是臭氧层不断地受到破坏,由此可见,空白处的形容词可能表明臭氧层"具有保护性",也可能表明臭氧层"受到了破坏",根据这两个语义在词库中寻找,只有 protective 适合。

54. [B]此处应为动词的分词形式或形容词,与 were 构成句子的谓语。文章不断指出臭氧层变薄,因此本题答案应为 dropping,表明臭氧层水平在下降。

55. [A]此处应为形容词。上一句提到了世界各地的臭氧层水平都在下降,因此,本句应该表明在美国等地记录到的臭氧层水平很"低",由此可推断 low 为本题答案。

56. [H]此处应为名词。根据本句句意可以推断人们希望能全面禁止使用损坏臭氧层的化学物质,因此 ban 为本题答案。

Section B

Passage One

参考译文划线点评

　　[58]在你以为经济学仅与政治和商业有关之前,我们应该提到经济学关注的是人们做出的所有选择以及这些选择所产生的个人和社会结果。虽然有些选择涉及到金钱,但是许多选择却不会。即便看起来不属于经济上的决定也仍然会落入经济学的范畴。大多数决定涉及到平衡成本和收益的努力,而这既可以用金钱来衡量也可以不用。譬如许多成本和收益主要是心理上的。

　　你会继续你的大学学业吗?可能的成本包括学费、买书的花费,学习的机会或是牺牲的可以用来赚钱的时光。[59]此处包括学费、书本费开支、修完那些规定课程的普通审以及现在你放弃工作的钱。你主要的学习领域会是什么?你是否只选容易挣钱行业的课程,或者你是否更看重学习某个学科的乐趣而不是它在经济上可能带来的回报?你会在哪里生活和工作?你会结婚吗?如果会,什么时候?和谁?婚姻涉及到经济和心理两方面的成本与收益。你会要孩子吗?如果会,要几个?你会如何支配你那有限的收入?[60]你关于这些以及其他经济上的决定将决定你的人生。

　　经济学在日常生活中至关重要,但作为一个研究领域你可能对它所知甚少。你很可能听说过这样一些在你的生活中经常听人提起的字眼:价格、成本、利润、供给与需求、通货膨胀、失业和社会主义等等。现在你可能会对经济学家用来解释世界运行的模型、图表以及理论感到怀疑。这些以及更多的概念都被编进经济学的框架之中。[57/61]我们相信你读完本书后会赞同我们的观点:经济学的思维方式为我们彼此日常的互相影响——生产、消费、选举以及为美好生活而奋斗——提供了有价值的见解。

57. [B]主旨大意题。通读全文可以发现作者写此文的目的是帮助读者正确理解经济学这门学问。第1段以及第3段都有主题句解释经济学的范畴和概念,第2段中的一系列问题及相应的选择都属于经济学的范畴,这些例证是为了帮助读者理解经济学这一看似抽象、遥远的概念,文章最后一句话更明显地表明了作者的写作目的。

58. [A]推理判断题。根据第1段开头句中关于经济学的定义就可以推断出答案。本题最具干扰性的是选项 C,因为它在第1段第4句有提及,但是该句中有 Most 这一限定词,表明选项 C 的陈述太泛。此外,选项 B 中的 politicians 和 businessmen 与文章第1句中的 politics 和 business 语义相关,但文中第1句就否定了经济学只与政治或商业有关,也并未说明经济学对政治和商业特别有用,因此选项 B 是没有根据的。

59. [C]词义推断题。从第2段第2句中的"costs include expense... and outlay..."可以推断它是一种 cost,且与 expense 的用法相同,都可接 for。由此可见,C 为正确答案。

60. [D]主旨大意题。第2段的最后一句是该段的主题句,总结了该段的中心内容是说明经济学能影响人的一生。其他选项是对该段中具体事例的总结或推断,都不能表达事例所支持的中心思想。

61. [A]推理判断题。根据文章的结尾句可以推断出答案。选项 B 中的 knowledge of our daily life 虽与最后一句中的 valuable insights into our everyday interaction 有相似之处,但 thorough 一词显得过于绝对。选项 C 和 D 无原文依据。

Passage Two

参考译文划线点评

　　盲人可以使用除眼睛以外的其他身体器官"看见"东西这一事实有助于我们理解对颜色的感觉。如果他们可以感觉到颜色的差别,那或许我们也不知不觉地受到颜色的影响。

　　[62]厂商已经通过反复试验发现,用绿色包装的糖果销路不佳,蓝色的食品无人问津,而化妆品决不能用褐色的包装。这些发现已经形成了颜色心理学的一整套规则,并在从时装到室内装饰的所有行业中发挥着作用。[63]我们的有些偏好很明显是心理作用。深蓝色是夜空的颜色,所以与消极和平静有联系,而黄色是白昼的颜色,让人联想到活力和兴奋。对原始人来说,白天的活动意味着狩猎和攻击,他不久就将鲜血的颜色、愤怒和因耗费体力而发热看成红色,而绿色是与消极防守和自我保护联系在一起的。实验显示,部分因为其心理联想,颜色也有直接的心理作用。[64]面对鲜红的颜色,人的心跳会加快,血压会升高。红色让人激动。而当面对纯蓝色的时候,人们的反应正好相反。这是一个让人平静的颜色。[64]红色因为暗含让人兴奋的性质而被选作危险的信号,但是进一步的研究表明,[65]鲜艳的黄色更能够使人进入警觉的状态,所以在某些发达的社区,成天奔忙的消防车和救护车现在都漆成黄色,以免因交通事故造成伤亡。

62. [B]推理判断题。答题的关键在于正确理解第2段第1句的短语 by trial and error(通过反复试验)。根据其后的三个从句可知试验与不同的颜色有关,从而可以推断这些发现是通过对不同颜色进行试验得出的,即选项B。选项A的用词与第2段第1句中的宾语从句"that sugar sells badly in green wrappings"相似,但这是通过试验得出的结果,而不是厂商发现颜色影响销量的方式,因此选项A不正确。选项C无原文根据。选项D将文中的因果关系颠倒,事实上正是这些发现导致形成了颜色心理学的一整套规则。

63. [D]事实细节题。答案可在第2段第3句找到。从第2段第4句开始,文章列举了各种颜色隐含的心理意义,而选项A, B, C分别只代表了一种颜色的意义,不能概括普遍情况。

64. [B]事实细节题。可用排除法明确地找出答案。第2段最后一句提到红色是危险的信号,而黄色可以产生 a more basic state of alertness and alarm,由此可知红色和黄色都可以使人进入警觉状态,所以选项A的情况属于红色所产生的心理暗示。选项C和D在第2段中倒数第5行有明确提及。只有选项B与红色无关。

65. [B]推理判断题。选项B与文章最后一句的意思相反。从文章第1段结尾句可推断出选项A,从第2段倒数第2、3句可推断出选项C,第2段第2句中的 application(应用)表明选项D是对的。

66. [D]主旨大意题。文章的标题通常会揭示文章的主题或大意,文章开头第1句中就出现了关键词 feelings about color,第2段中作者举出多种不同颜色为例,解释人们看见这些颜色时的不同感觉和反应,可以找出诸如 rage, exciting, calming 等表示情感的关键词,由此可推断本文应与颜色及情感有关,即选项D。其他选项都只是文章涉及的不同侧面细节,不能涵盖全文主题。

Part V Cloze

67. [C]近义词辨析题。good"好处,利益",作此义解时为不可数名词;superiority"优越性,优等",不可数名词;strength"强点,长处",作此义解时可数;benefit"益处,好处",为可数名词,但意义上不符合文意。

68. [B]短语搭配题。介词短语 under... circumstances 意为"在……情况下"。

69. [B]形似词辨义理解题。change"变化";exchange"交换";transaction"交易,业务";transference"转移,迁移,转让"。

70. [A]语法题。指示代词 those 可用作关系从句的先行词(those who 结构)或名词短语的中心词,如"Those (who were) present were in favor of a change."但 these 无此用法。

71. [D]语法题。此处实际是在将有较强社交关系的人与无此关系的人进行对比,所以选择比较级,而描述能力较强应用 well 的比较级 better。

72. [A]逻辑推理加语法题。根据上下文语境,这里仍在对两种人进行对比,而后半句已出现 those without ties,所以此处选 with。

73. [D]词义理解题。根据上下文,这里所说的是没有这样的社交关系的人,只有 such 可以这样复指前文,表示"上述一类的,如此的,像前面那样的"。

74. [A]近义词辨析题。reveal"展现,显示";reflect"反映;反射;深思";expose"暴露,显露";discover"发现,找到"。上文出现的主语是"研究",按照逻辑,与其同现的动词应是 reveal。

75. [B]词义理解题。本题根据词汇的反义词复现原则判断出答案。上文出现 the presence of social support,而根据文意下一分句与此分句意义上形成对照,所以此处应是 the absence of such support。

76. [D]短语搭配题。下文罗列了四个方面的内容,因此此处应该选择表示"若干,许多"之义的短语 a number of。

77. [B]词义理解题。evaluate"评估,评价";value"尊重,重视";rely"依靠;信赖",为不及物动词;stress"强调,着重"。

78. [C]短语搭配题。A 不符合文意;B、D 形式错误,应分别改为 in spite of 和 regardless of。

79. [C]词义理解加短语搭配题。provide 构成的搭配是 provide sb. with sth.。B、D 意义上不恰当,而 offer 构成的搭配是 offer sb. sth.。

80. [A]词义理解题。define"阐明;给……下定义;界定"relate"讲述,叙述";prescribe"开药;规定,指定";account (for)"说明……的原因"。根据与此空并列的词 understand 和搭配词 problems 可知本题答案为 define。

81. [D]短语搭配题。按照习惯搭配,solution 后需跟介词 to 表示"……的解决办法"。

82. [A]短语搭配题。engage in 表示"从事某活动";强干扰项 B 构成的表示"参与某项活动"的短语是 be involved in,语法上错误。

83. [A]逻辑关联题。此处文意是"同他人一起参与业余活动既有助于满足我们的社交需求,也可同时使我们摆脱焦虑烦恼的困扰",所以选 while。不可选 meanwhile,因为已出现 at the same time。

84. [D]逻辑关联题。根据文意,此段罗列出四项内容,很明显,此处所述为最后一项,选表示列举的过渡词 Finally。Furthermore 可用于列举时,但不表示"最后"之义。

85. [D]近义词辨析题。assistance"帮助,援助",强调所提供的帮助主要是协助、扶持,即接受帮助者往往强于提供帮助者,但需要后者的辅助;supply"供应;存货,必需品";resources"资源,财力";aid"帮助,援助,救助",强调所提供的帮助是受援者所急需的,受援者往往弱于援助者。

86. [B]语法题。此处考查定语从句。空格词修饰的是先行词 instrumental support,应选 that。

Part VI Translation

87. 【答案】draw some money
【译文】去度假之前,他去银行取了些钱。

【解析】draw sth. from the bank"从银行取款"。

88. 【答案】to be completed
【译文】2010 年底之前即将完成的这个项目会将该城市电话网络扩大到 1000 万个用户群。

【解析】此处需要的是定语,应该考虑非谓语动词,"即将"说明是将来的动作,要用不定式,"完成"和 project 是动宾关系,故用被动形式。

89. 【答案】where/in which formal language is used
【译文】主要是政府报告、考试作文、法律文件和大多数商务信函会用到正式语言。

【解析】根据句型分析,应该是"会用到正式语言"的 situations,需要翻译的部分作 situations 的定语,而 situations 在定语从句中作状语,故引导词可以用 where 或 in which。

90. 【答案】been handed down
【译文】这张床是我们的家传之物,它原先是我曾祖母的。

【解析】表达"家传"用 hand down;此外,句子的主语是 hand down 的逻辑宾语,此处用被动语态。含 hand 的常考动词短语还有:hand over"交出,送交";hand on"转交;传递";hand in"提出;上交"。

91. 【答案】tends to keep pace
【译文】在社会变革时期,人们的思想状态趋向于跟上社会的迅速变化。

【解析】固定短语:keep pace with 意为"跟……齐步前进;跟上……发展"。类似短语辨析:keep step with"跟……步调一致";keep in touch with"和……保持联系"。"趋向"在句中作谓语,可用短语 tend to 或 incline to。在补充句子时,要注意句子的时态及单复数。

Model Test 3

答题卡 1 (Answer Sheet 1)

Part I　　　　**Writing**　　　　　　　　　　　　　　　　　　　　**(30 minutes)**

Directions: *For this part, you are allowed 30 minutes to write an essay entitled **My View on the Income Gap**. You should write at least 120 words following the outline given below in Chinese:*

　1. 收入差距悬殊是当前社会的一种现象
　2. 人们对之褒贬不一
　3. 你的看法

My View on the Income Gap

_____

_____

_____

Part II　　　**Reading Comprehension (Skimming and Scanning)**　　**(15 minutes)**

1. [Y] [N] [NG]　　2. [Y] [N] [NG]　　3. [Y] [N] [NG]　　4. [Y] [N] [NG]

5. [Y] [N] [NG]　　6. [Y] [N] [NG]　　7. [Y] [N] [NG]

8. The cardholders could find _____ at the back of the first Diners Club credit cards.

9. Similar to what a bank's consumer loan department does, bank credit cards provide the cardholder with _____

_____.

10. When you want to get a credit card, it is crucial for you to make a careful choice due to the fact that _____

_____.

答题卡 2 (Answer Sheet 2)

Part III　　　　**Section C**

　　Jeffrey Zaslow, the advice columnist for the *Chicago Sun-Times*, grew up in (36) _____ Philadelphia. His biggest (37) _____ in life was to be a writer. "I never wanted to be anything else," he says. "I was ten or eleven when I saw *Gone with the Wind* and I wrote my own Civil War story." After (38) _____ a degree in creative writing at Carnegie Mellon University, he got a job at a newspaper in Orlando, Florida. He made his mark with his article on the rough working conditions (39) _____ by the people inside the Mickey and Minnie costumes at Walt Disney World. Later he became a (40) _____ writer for the *Wall Street Journal*.

　　In 1988, when the famous advice columnist, Ann Landers (41) _____ her job at the *Chicago Sun-Times*, the

paper launched a (42) _____ contest to find her replacement. Jeffrey Zaslow applied. Among the 12,000 contestants, women (43) _____ men nine to one, and most of them had seen a lot more of life than Zaslow, who was 28 and not married. (44) _____ "Why He'll Never Make It". But Jeffrey did make it in the finals. Today, thirteen years later, his column "All That Zazz" is read by thousands of readers in the Chicago area.

(45) _____. He is also greatly moved by the generosity, sincerity and good nature of his readers. "Wonderful people," he says, "do outnumber terrible people in this world. (46) _____."

Part VI　　　　　　　Translation　　　　　　　　　　　　　　　　(5 minutes)

87. Although many people view conflict as bad, conflict is sometimes useful in _____ (因为它迫使人们检验) the relative merits of their attitudes and behaviors.

88. The energy _____ (连锁反应所释放出的) is transformed into heat.

89. There was such a long line at the exhibition _____ (我们不得不等了大约半小时).

90. So _____ (只要他努力工作), I don't mind when he finishes the experiment.

91. The conference _____ (将持续) a full week by the time it ends.

Part I　Writing (30 minutes)

注意:此部分试题在**答题卡1**上。

Part II　Reading Comprehension (Skimming and Scanning)(15 minutes)

What Does a Credit Card Bring Us?

"Charge it! " If those two words sound familiar, it is no wonder. Over 75 million Americans use credit cards to pay for everything from tickets on American Airlines to AAA car rental. And the number of cardholders increases every month. In fact, most Americans receive at least two or three credit card applications in the mail every month.

The First Credit Card

At the beginning of the twentieth century, people had to pay cash for almost all products and services. Although the early part of the century saw an increase in individual store credit accounts, a credit card that could be used at more than one merchant was not invented until 1950. It all started when Frank X. McNamara and two of his friends went out to supper.

The Significant Dinner

During the dinner, they discussed a problem of one of McNamara's customers who had borrowed some money but was unable to pay it back. This particular customer had gotten into trouble, when he had lent a number of his charge cards (available from individual department stores and gas stations) to his poor neighbors who needed items in an emergency. For this service, the man required his neighbors to pay him back the cost of the original purchase plus some extra money. Unfortunately for the man, many of his neighbors were unable to pay him back within a short period of time and he was then forced to borrow money from the Hamilton Credit Corporation.

At the end of the meal with his two friends, McNamara reached into his pocket for his wallet so that he could pay for the meal (in cash). He was shocked to discover that he had forgotten his wallet. To his embarrassment, he then had to call his wife and have her bring him some money. McNamara vowed never to let this happen again.

Merging the two concepts from that dinner, the lending of credit cards and not having cash on hand to pay for the meal, McNamara came up with a new idea—a credit card that could be used at multiple locations. What was particularly new about this concept was that there would be a middleman between companies and their customers.

McNamara discussed the idea with his two friends and the three pooled some money and started a new company in 1950 which they called the Diners Club, and it was going to be a middleman.

The first Diners Club credit cards were given out in 1950 to 200 people (most were friends and acquaintances of McNamara) and accepted by 14 restaurants in New York. The cards were not made of plastic; instead, the first Diners Club credit cards were made of a paper stock with the accepting locations printed on the back.

The Popularity of Credit Cards

(1) Among Merchants

For a merchant, the answer is obvious. By depositing charge slips in a bank or other financial institutions, the merchant can convert credit card sales into cash. In return for processing the merchant's credit card transactions, the bank charges a fee that ranges between 1.5 and 5 percent. Typically, small, independent businesses pay more than large stores or chain stores. Let's assume that you use a Visa credit card to purchase a microwave oven for $400 from Richardson Appliance, a small retailer in Texas. At the end of the day, the retailer deposits your charge slip, along with other charge slips, checks, and currency collected during the day, at its bank. If the bank charges Richardson Appliance 5 percent to process each credit card transaction, the bank deducts a processing fee of $20 ($400×0.05= $20) for your credit card transaction and immediately deposits the remainder ($380) in Richardson Appliance's account. Actual bank fees are determined by the volume of credit card transactions, total dollar amount of credit sales, and how well the merchant can negotiate.

(2) Among Consumers

For the consumer, credit cards permit the purchase of goods and services even when the funds are low. Today most major credit cards are issued by banks or other financial institutions in cooperation with Visa International or MasterCard International. The unique feature of bank credit cards is that they extend *a line of credit* (信用贷款之最高限额) to the cardholder, much as a bank's consumer loan department does. Thus credit cards provide immediate access to short-term credit for the cardholder, who instructs the bank to pay the merchant immediately and pay back the bank later. Of course, the ability to obtain merchandise immediately and pay for it later can lead to credit card misuse. Today the average American cardholder has a credit card balance in excess of $2,000. And with typical financial charges ranging from 1 percent to 1.5 percent a month, you can end up paying large finance charges. For example, if you carry a $2,000 balance on your credit card and your credit card company charges 1.5 percent a month, your monthly finance charge will be $30 ($2,000×0.015=$30). And the monthly finance charges continue until you manage to pay off your credit card debt.

How to Get a Credit Card?

The easiest way to establish credit is to open checking and savings accounts at your local bank. Then apply for a gasoline or store credit card. These cards are fairly easy to get because retailers want you to buy their goods and services. The third step, and the most dangerous one, is obtaining a major credit card like Visa, MasterCard, or American Express.

It is important to choose a credit card carefully because terms and conditions vary widely. Annual fees range from $15 to $75 a year, but some credit card companies charge no annual fee at all. If you will be one of the growing number of people who don't pay off their credit card transactions in full each month, look for the card with the lowest interest rate. Interest rates generally range from 12 to 18 percent, though it is possible to find cards with lower rates.

Credit Card: Friend or Enemy?

A credit card can be your friend because it can get you through unexpected emergencies. And if there is a problem with the products or service you purchase with your credit card, you have an opportunity to withhold payment by asking the credit card company to "charge back" to the retailer until the dispute is settled. Monthly credit card statements can also help you keep your records in order. Finally, if you make payments on time, the card helps you to establish a good credit history.

A credit card can be your enemy because it is an invitation to purchase items you really do not need. The credit card companies' continuous offers of low minimum payments, cash advances, and even months without payments may seem like a way to skate through a money crunch. In reality, your finance charges and fees only increase, and you go deeper into debt.

How to Protect Your Credit (Card)?

If you do find yourself in trouble, do not ignore the bills. Contact your creditors to explain your problem and express your desire to pay down your card balance. If that fails, a nonprofit organization like Consumer Credit Counseling Service can assist you in getting back on your financial feet.

Protect your credit card number and your credit history. Never give your card number and expiration date to someone you did not contact first. Never write your credit card number on a personal check. Do not answer every preapproved credit card letter you receive (two or three cards are all you should need). Finally, photocopy your card, and if it is stolen, notify the credit card company immediately.

1. The credit card in the early 20th century couldn't be used at more than one merchant.

2. Diners Club was a restaurant in New York that accepted various credit cards.

3. The banks charge large stores or chain stores a higher transaction fee than they do to independent businesses.

4. Today major credit cards are issued either by banks or by Visa International or MasterCard International.

5. More and more people don't pay off their monthly credit card transactions completely.

6. The lowest interest rate for a credit card holder is twelve percent.

7. It is almost impossible to get back the payment from the retailers even if there is a problem with the products you buy with your credit card.

Part III Listening Comprehension (35 minutes)

Section A

注意:此部分试题请在**答题卡 2**上作答。

11. A) She works full-time this term.
    B) She wants to become a scholar.
    C) She needn't work part-time this term.
    D) Her grades were not good.

12. A) Policeman and driver.
    B) Salesman and customer.
    C) Teacher and student.
    D) Boss and secretary.

13. A) They are quite beautiful.
    B) They are quite comfortable.
    C) They are too expensive.
    D) They deserve more money.

14. A) He didn't work hard in school.
    B) He took a part-time job in school.
    C) He had always been serious about study.
    D) He had no interest in social work.

15. A) Share her pencils and paper with the man.
    B) Make friends with the man after class.
    C) Take notes for the man.
    D) Share her notes with the man.

16. A) To a concert.   B) To a hotel.   C) To a restaurant.   D) To a bank.

17. A) She wants to work again tomorrow.
    B) She's willing to stop working.
    C) She wants to consider half a day's work as a full day's.
    D) She's unhappy to work so long without pay.

18. A) She saw an advertisement in the newspaper.
    B) She heard about it during a TV interview.
    C) A friend informed her of it.
    D) She saw it on a list of job openings.

Questions 19 to 22 are based on the conversation you have just heard.

19. A) The difference between the US baseball team and the Chinese one.
    B) Efforts taken to promote baseball in China.
    C) The popularity and development of baseball in China.
    D) The performance of US baseball team in the game last night.

20. A) It has always been very popular.
    B) More and more people pay attention to it.
    C) It is the most important sport in China.
    D) People don't have any interest in baseball.

21. A) It will win in the 2008 Olympic Games.
    B) It is not so mature as the US baseball team.
    C) It's the best baseball team in Asia.
    D) It never wins in international games.

22. A) In the 1996 Olympics.
    B) In the 2004 Olympics.
    C) In the 2008 Olympics.
    D) In the Asian Championships.

Questions 23 to 25 are based on the conversation you have just heard.

23. A) She plans to have the man make a tour arrangement for her.
    B) She hopes that he could give her some advice on writing.

C) She wants to get some suggestions about traveling.

D) She complains to him about her boring holiday.

24. A) Bring enough cash.   B) Go with her mother.

    C) Resort to the man.   D) Reserve a room.

25. A) A busy city center convenient for shopping.   B) A peaceful seashore with beautiful views.

    C) A huge bay with a little balcony.   D) A room of standard size though noisy.

Section B

注意:此部分试题请在**答题卡 2**上作答。

Passage One

Questions 26 to 28 are based on the passage you have just heard.

26. A) Crowded houses.   B) Polluted water from factories.

    C) High crime rate.   D) Continual noise.

27. A) Traffic accidents.   B) Pollution.   C) Crimes.   D) Earthquakes.

28. A) Comparison between city life and country life.   B) Problems troubling city people.

    C) Ways to solve social problems in cities.   D) High pressure city people suffer from.

Passage Two

Questions 29 to 31 are based on the passage you have just heard.

29. A) Because he thinks dreams might be able to tell him many things.

    B) Because he likes living in dreams.

    C) Because dreams can always be realized if you study them.

    D) Because everybody dreams.

30. A) The daydreams.   B) The remembering of one's dream.

    C) The rapid eye movement.   D) The moving picture one sees in his dream.

31. A) If we wake fast sleeping people, they will feel annoyed.

    B) If we wake people during the REM, they will feel tired.

    C) Only dreaming can make us feel refreshed.

    D) If people are not constantly wakened, they will feel nothing at all.

Passage Three

Questions 32 to 35 are based on the passage you have just heard.

32. A) Fresh meat.   B) Fresh fruit.   C) Biscuit.   D) Chocolate.

33. A) To provide convenience to customers.   B) To make each product look attractive.

    C) To keep the supermarket neat and tidy.   D) To protect the products and give information.

34. A) The weight.   B) The ingredients.

    C) The production process.   D) The name of the products.

35. A) Because they usually can't see the actual product.   B) Because it is the law.

    C) Because salespeople can't be trusted.   D) Because they open the containers before they get home.

Section C

注意:此部分试题在**答题卡 2**上;请在**答题卡 2**上作答。

Part IV   Reading Comprehension (Reading in Depth) (25 minutes)

Section A

    Without proper planning, tourism can cause problems. For example, too many tourists can __47__ public places that are also enjoyed by the local people living in the country. If tourists create too much traffic, the local people become __48__ and unhappy. They begin to dislike tourists and to treat them __49__. They forget how much tourism can help the country's economy. It is important to think about the people of a __50__ country and how tourism affects them. Tourism should help a country keep the customs and beauty that attract tourists. Tourism should also advance the well-being (health and happiness) of __51__ people.

Too much __52__ can be a problem.

On the other hand, if there is not enough tourism, people can lose jobs. Businesses can also __53__ money. It costs a great deal of money to build large hotels, airports, air terminals, first-class roads, and other support facilities needed by tourist attractions. For example, a __54__ international-class tourism hotel can cost as much as 50 thousand dollars per room to build. If this room is not used most of the time, the __55__ of the hotel lose money.

Building a hotel is just a beginning. There must be many support facilities as well, including roads to get to the hotel, electricity, sewers to __56__ waste, and water. All of these support facilities cost money. If they are not used because there are not enough tourists, jobs and money are lost.

A) handle	B) destination	C) permanently	D) major
E) lose	F) invade	G) owners	H) frequent
I) curiosity	J) local	K) crowd	L) tourism
M) exerted	N) impolitely	O) annoyed	

Section B

Passage One

Dream is a story that a person "watches" or even takes part in during sleep. Dream events are imaginary, but they are related to real experiences and needs in the dreamer's life. They seem real while they are taking place. Some dreams are pleasant, others are annoying, and still others are frightening.

Everyone dreams, but some persons never recall dreaming. Others remember only a little about a dream they had just before awakening and nothing about earlier dreams. No one recalls all his dreams.

Dreams involve little logical thought. In most dreams, the dreamer cannot control what happens to him. The story may be confusing, and things happen that would not happen in real life. People see in most dreams, but they may also hear, smell, touch, and taste in their dreams. Most dreams occur in color, but persons who have been blind since birth do not see at all in dreams.

Dreams are a product of the sleeper's mind. They include events and feelings that he has experienced. Most dreams are related to events of the day before the dream and strong wishes of the dreamer. Many minor incidents of the hours before sleep appear in dreams. Few events more than two days old turn up. Deep wishes or fears—especially those held since childhood—often appear in dreams, and many dreams fulfill such wishes. Events in the sleeper's surrounding—a loud noise, for example, may become part of a dream, but they do not cause dreams.

Some dreams involve deep feelings that a person may not realize he has. *Psychiatrists* (精神病医生) often use material from a patient's dreams to help the person understand himself better.

Dreaming may help maintain good learning ability, memory, and emotional adjustment. People who get plenty of sleep—but are awakened each time they begin to dream—become anxious and restless.

57. This passage is mainly about _____.
    A) why we dream during sleep
    B) how we dream during sleep
    C) what dreams are
    D) what benefits dreams bring to people

58. What can people recall about their dreams?
    A) All people don't recall their dreams.
    B) None of the people can recall their dreams.
    C) People usually can recall the whole dream before awakening.
    D) People sometimes can recall all the dreams they have during the night.

59. Which of the following is NOT true about dream?

A) Dream is a confusing story which involves little logical thought.

B) Dream is related to the dreamer's real life.

C) Dream is an imaginary story which seems real while taking place.

D) Dream involves events that always happen in real life.

60. This passage suggests that psychiatrists can _____.

A) help the dreamer recall his earlier dreams

B) make the sleeper dream logically

C) study the benefits of dreams

D) help the sleeper fulfill his dreams

61. The least possible events that appear in dreams are _____.

A) minor incidents that happened hours before one goes to sleep

B) minor incidents that happened more than two days ago

C) the strong wishes a person has since childhood

D) the strong fears a person has since childhood

Passage Two

Cheating is nothing new. But today, educators and administrators are finding that instances of academic dishonesty on the part of students have become more frequent—and are less likely to be punished than in the past. Cheating appears to have gained acceptance among good and poor students alike.

Why is student cheating on the rise? No one really knows. Some blame the trend on a general loosening of moral values among today's youth. Others have attributed increased cheating to the fact that today's youth are far more *pragmatic* (实用主义的) than their idealistic predecessors. Whereas in the late sixties and early seventies, students were filled with visions about transforming the world, today's students feel great pressure to *conform* (顺从) and succeed. In interviews with students at high schools and colleges around the country, both young men and women said that cheating had become easy. Some suggested they did it out of *spite* (恶意) for teachers they did not respect. Others looked at it as a game. Only if they were caught, some said, would they feel guilty. "People are competitive," said a second-year college student named Anna, from Chicago. There's an underlying fear. If you don't do well, your life is going to be ruined. The pressure is not only from parents and friends but also from yourself. To achieve. To succeed. It's almost as though we have to outdo other people to achieve our own goals.

Edward Wynne, editor of a magazine blames the rise in academic dishonesty on the schools. He claims that administrators and teachers have been too hesitant to take action. Dwight Huber, chairman of the English department at Amarillo sees the matter differently, blaming the rise in cheating on the way students are evaluated. "I would cheat if I felt I was being cheated," Mr. Huber said. He feels that as long as teachers give short-answer tests rather than essay questions and rate students by the number of facts they can memorize rather than by how well they can synthesize information, students will try to beat the system. "The concept of cheating is based on the false assumption that the system is legitimate and there is something wrong with the individual who's doing it." He said. "That's too easy an answer. We've got to start looking at the system."

62. What do educators and administrators think about cheating?

A) Students who cheat are in the majority.

B) Students who cheat can be academically weak or strong.

C) Cheating is no more frequent than in the past.

D) Cheating is punished more severely than before.

63. What does the author say about students in the past?

A) They were ambitious to change the world.

B) They felt guilty when caught in cheating.

C) They did not have any desire to succeed.

D) They had to outdo others to fulfill their dream.

64. In Dwight Huber's opinion, there will be less cheating if _____.

A) the present testing methods are changed

B) teachers give more short-answer tests

C) students' memorization of facts is tested

D) teachers take action to stop it

65. The word "system" is used three times in Para. 3. It most probably refers to _____.

A) the teaching system

B) the testing system

C) the cheating system

D) the learning system

66. Which of the following will the author most probably agree with, concerned with cheating?

A) Students themselves should take the blame for the rise in cheating.

B) Students who cheat should be punished severely so as to stop it.

C) The problem of student cheating has its root in deeper problems.

D) The reason for student cheating has been clear, but nothing can stop it.

Part V Cloze (15 minutes)

注意：此部分试题请在**答题卡2**上作答。

India has about a billion people and a dozen __67__ languages of its own. One language, and only one, is understood—by an elite—across the country: __68__ of the foreigners who ruled it for less than 200 years and __69__ 52 years ago.

Today, India. Tomorrow, unofficially, the world. That is well __70__ way; at first, because the British not only built a global empire __71__ settled in America, and __72__ because the world has acquired its first truly __73__ medium, the Internet. It is __74__ that some 350 million people speak English as their first language. Maybe 250 million–350 million do __75__ can use it as a second language in ex-colonial countries or English-majority ones, __76__ 30 million recent immigrants to the United States, or Canada's 6m French-speaking Quebeckers. And __77__? The guess is 100 million to 1 billion depending on __78__ you define "can". Let us be bold: __79__ all, 20–25% of earth's 6 billion people can use English; not the English of England, let alone __80__ Dr Johnson, but English.

That number is soaring __81__ each year brings new pupils to school and carries off monolingual oldies— __82__ now as the Internet spreads. And English has __83__ dominated learned journals; German, Russian or French may be useful to their __84__ readers, but English is essential. __85__, if you want your own work published—and widely read by your peers— __86__ English is the language of choice.

67. A) minor   B) vital   C) major   D) crucial
68. A) which   B) what   C) it   D) that
69. A) left   B) came   C) conquered   D) entered
70. A) in   B) under   C) on   D) by
71. A) and   B) or   C) even   D) but
72. A) now   B) still   C) finally   D) secondly
73. A) all-round   B) widespread C) global   D) local
74. A) calculated B) predicted   C) summarized D) estimated
75. A) and   B) or   C) but   D) yet
76. A) as   B) for   C) like   D) likewise
77. A) where   B) elsewhere   C) anywhere   D) somewhere
78. A) how   B) that   C) what   D) which
79. A) for   B) at   C) in   D) after
80. A) in   B) by   C) for   D) of
81. A) while   B) as   C) with   D) after
82. A) and   B) but   C) however   D) thus
83. A) ever   B) never   C) long   D) seldom
84. A) expert   B) skilled   C) skillful   D) experienced
85. A) Nevertheless B) So   C) Although   D) Moreover
86. A) therefore   B) however   C) finally   D) then

Part VI Translation (5 minutes)

注意：此部分试题在**答题卡2**上；请在**答题卡2**上作答。

Model Test 3

答案与解析

Part I Writing

写作指南:

这是四级作文中典型的评论型习作,要求考生首先概述收入差距悬殊的现象,然后分析社会上不同人对这一现象或褒或贬的看法,最后一点要求考生表明自己的观点,并简要说明理由。

根据写作要求,文章结构如下:

第一段开头段:描写收入越来越悬殊的社会现象;

第二段分析段:分析人们对收入悬殊现象褒贬不一的看法;

第三段结尾段:陈述个人的观点和理由,简要提出解决这一问题的个人建议。

范文与解析:

Sample	Analysis
【1】Now the income gap is getting wider and wider. In some privately owned firms, joint-ventures, or foreign-funded companies, an executive's yearly income can be 【2】**ten times or even a hundred times as much as** an ordinary worker's. 　　【3】**Faced with this situation**, people will undoubtedly have different opinions. 【4】**Some believe that it benefits** the social and economic development since driving force of growth is often derived from the gap. 【5】**In other words**, the gap **inspires** people and **gives a push to advancemen**. 【6】**Others speak of its side effect.** 【7】Income gap is often **the root of** social unrest and also **contrary to** a socialist country's principle. 　　【8】From my point of view, **while** it is true that the income gap may stimulate social development to some extent, it causes trouble **as well**. 【9】An income gap that is too wide for most people to bear 【10】**can neither** contribute to the stability of a country **nor** promote its long-term economic development. 【11】Therefore, while we are pursing a rapid development of our country, we should take some actions to resolve the problem of an increasingly wide income gap.	【2】倍数+as much/many as 的比较结构更加凸显了收入差距的悬殊。 【3】Faced with 为过去分词词组作状语,语言简洁。 【4】陈述褒奖这一现象利大于弊的第一种见解。 【5】使用亮点词汇 inspires 和 gives a push to advancement 分析收入差距悬殊的积极作用。 【6】引出批评这一现象的另一种看法。 【7】用亮点词汇 the root of 和 contrary to 分析反对意见。 【8】【10】肯定收入悬殊可能带来的益处的同时,强调其带来的不良影响。 【11】重申了作者对于这一现象的处理建议和看法。

句型变换：

[1]

1. Now the income gap is getting wider and wider.
2. Now the gap between incomes is becoming wider and wider.
3. Nowadays there is a wider gap between people's earnings.
4. The income gap is now, increasingly wide.

[3]

1. Faced with this situation, people will undoubtedly have different opinions.
2. Undoubtedly, people have different opinions when faced with this situation.
3. When facing this situation, people bear various viewpoints.
4. In face of this situation, there will be pros and cons without any doubt.

[5]

1. In other words, the gap inspires people and gives a push to advancement.
2. In other words, the gap encourages people as well as gives a push to advancement.
3. Namely, people are inspired and given a push to advancement.
4. In other words, people are motivated to further progress.

[7]

1. Income gap is often the root of social unrest and also contrary to a socialist country's principle.
2. Income gap is often the basic cause of social unrest and contrary to a socialist country's principle.
3. Income gap runs contrary to a socialist country's principle and leads to social instability.
4. Contrary to a socialist country's principle, income gap gives birth to social instability.

[8]

1. From my point of view, while it is true that the income gap may stimulate social development to some extent, it causes trouble as well.
2. Personally, it is true that the income gap stimulates social development to some degree, but it also provokes some trouble.
3. As I see it, the income gap admittedly encourages social development in some ways, yet it brings trouble too.
4. In my opinion, to certain extent, income gap brings social development as well as trouble.

[9]

1. An income gap that is too wide for most people to bear
2. An income gap, so wide that most people cannot bear
3. An income gap which is so wide that most people can hardly bear
4. The wider income gap that is almost impossible for people to bear

[10]

1. can neither contribute to the stability of a country nor promote its long-term economic development.
2. cannot contribute to the stability of a country and the promotion of its economic development in a long run.
3. can neither lead to the stability of a country nor advance its economic development in the future.
4. can do no good to the stability of a country and its lasting economic growth.

Part II Reading Comprehension (Skimming and Scanning)

参考译文划线点评

信用卡给我们带来什么?

"刷卡!"如果这两个字听着耳熟,那不足为怪。超过7500万的美国人用信用卡支付一切消费,从美国航空公司的机票到3A出租车公司的租车费,而且持卡消费人数还在逐月增加。实际上,大多数美国人每个月都会收到至少两三份寄给他们填写的信用卡申请表格。

第一张信用卡

20世纪初,人们购买任何产品和服务,几乎都得支付现金。[1]虽然在该世纪早期,个别商店的赊购账户已有增加,但是直到1950年才发明了能在多个商家使用的信用卡。它始于弗兰克·X.麦克纳马拉和他的两位朋友出去吃晚饭的那个时刻。

重要的晚餐

晚餐时,他们谈到麦克纳马拉有个客户借了些钱,但不能偿还。这个特殊的客户把他的许多赊账卡(从个别的百货商店和加油站中获得的)借给急需买东西的穷邻居,结果陷入了麻烦。对于这种服务,那个人要求邻居偿还原来买东西的费用,外加一些额外的钱。不幸的是,很多邻居都不能在短时期内偿还,最后被迫向汉密尔顿信贷公司借钱。

和这两位朋友吃到最后,麦克纳马拉把手伸进口袋拿钱包,以使用现金结账。他很惊讶地发现自己忘了带钱包。令他尴尬的是,他得打电话叫妻子带钱过来给他。麦克纳马拉发誓决不让这种事情再次发生。

麦克纳马拉把那次晚餐上的两件事——出借信用卡和手头没有现金结账——联系起来,提出了一种新的想法,即可以在多个地方使用的信用卡。这个想法特别新颖之处就在于在公司和客户之间会有个中间人。

[2]麦克纳马拉与两位朋友讨论了这个想法,于是,三个人合资于1950年成立了一家新公司,把它称为"就餐者俱乐部",他们要作中间人。

第一批就餐者俱乐部的信用卡(大来卡)在1950年发放给了200人(大多数是麦克纳马拉的朋友和熟人),纽约有14家餐厅接受这种信用卡。[8]这种卡片不是用塑料做成的,而是一张纸制股票,背面印有可以接受的地点。

信用卡的盛行

(1)商家

对商家来说,答案显而易见。把收款凭单给银行或其他金融机构,商家可以把用信用卡支付的销售收入转成现金;而通过为商家办理信用卡付款交易的业务,银行赚取1.5%至5%不等的佣金。[3]通常独立经营的小商店比大商场或连锁店交纳的费用高。让我们假设你使用威士卡从德克萨斯的一家小零售店理查森电器商店以400美元购买了一台微波炉。该零售商一天下来把你的交款凭单连同当天收来的其他交款凭单、支票及现金一并存放到指定的银行。如果银行对每一笔信用卡交易向理查森电器商店收取5%的佣金,银行就从你的此笔信用卡交易额中扣除20美元($400×0.05=$20)的手续费,然后立即把余款(380美元)存到理查森电器商店的账户上。实际的银行手续费取决于有多少笔信用卡交易、用信用卡交易的销售总额以及商家(与银行)的讨价还价能力。

(2)消费者

对消费者来说,信用卡使他们甚至在资金不足的情况下仍可以购买商品和服务。[4]目前大多数信用卡都是由银行或其他金融机构与威士国际信用卡公司或万事达国际信用卡公司共同发行的。[9]银行信用卡的独特之处在于,同银行的消费信贷部一样,它们可以使持卡人获得信用贷款的最高限额。因此信用卡使持卡人可以立即获得短期贷款,由持卡人通知银行向商家即时付款,随后再把这笔款偿还给银行。当然,可以马上得到商品而不用立即付账,这会导致人们滥用信用卡。如今平均每个美国持卡人的信用卡欠款超过2000美元。由于通常融资费率为每月1%-1.5%不等,所以最后你可能得交纳一大笔融资费用。比如说,如果你的信用卡上有2000美元欠额,而信用卡公司每月收取1.5%的融资费,那么你每月须付费30美元($2000×0.15=$30)。在你付清信用卡欠款之前,每月的融资费会不断收下去。

怎样得到信用卡?

取得个人信用的最便捷的方法是在当地银行开立活期储蓄账户。然后申请一张加油卡或商店信用卡。这些卡很容易就能获得,因为零售商希望你买他们的商品和服务。第三步,也是最冒险的一步,是获得一张主要信用卡,如威士卡、万事达卡或运通卡。

[10]认真选择信用卡很重要,因为不同信用卡的条款和条件差别很大。每年的融资费从15美元到75美元不等,但也有些信用卡公司根本不收年费。[5]如果你也像越来越多的人那样不能如数偿付每月的信用卡欠款,还是使用利率最低的信用卡为好。[6]利率一般为12%-18%,有的信用卡利率可能更低。

信用卡:是友是敌?

信用卡能帮你渡过意外的难关,因而它可以成为你的朋友。[7]而当你用信用卡购买的商品或得到的服务有问题时,你可以要求信用卡公司向零售商"追回付款",这样,你就有机会在问题解决前拒付。每月的信用卡清单也可以帮助你妥善记载支出款项。此外,如果你按时付款,信用卡会帮助你建立一个良好的个人信用记录。

信用卡也可能成为你的敌人,因为它诱使你买些你根本不需要的东西。信用卡公司不断提供更低的最小偿付额、现金垫付甚至几个月的还款期限似乎会帮你渡过财政困境。而实际上,融资费与手续费只会增加,让你负债累累。

如何保护信用卡?

如果你发现自己陷入欠债的麻烦,不要置账单于不顾。向你的债权人说明你的问题并表达你想偿付卡上欠费的意愿。如果这也不成,则像消费者信贷协调机构这样的非赢利性组织可以帮助你从财力困境中恢复过来。

保护好你的信用卡号码以及你的信用记录。未经事先联系不要把你的信用卡号码和有效期告诉别人。不要把信用卡号码写在个人支票上。不要答复收到的每一封预先批准可用信用卡的(申请)信(拥有两三张信用卡就足够了)。最后,将你的信用卡影印一份,一旦失窃,立即通知信用卡公司。

1. 【答案】Y

【题眼】The credit card in the early 20th century couldn't be used at more than one merchant.

【定位】第 1 个小标题 **The First Credit Card** 部分的第 2 句。

【解析】原文指出,直到 20 世纪 50 年代才出现了能用于多家商店的信用卡,也就是说在此之前的信用卡不能用于多家商店,因此本题答案为 Y。

2. 【答案】N

【题眼】Diners Club was a restaurant in New York that accepted various credit cards.

【定位】第 2 个小标题 **The Significant Dinner** 部分的倒数第 2 段。

【解析】原文表示 Diners Club 是一家公司,是 middleman,而不是餐厅,因此本题答案为 N。

3. 【答案】N

【题眼】The banks charge large stores or chain stores a higher transaction fee than they do to independent businesses.

【定位】第 3 个小标题 **The Popularity of Credit Cards** 下的第 1 段第 4 句。

【解析】题目表明大商场或连锁店比独立经营的小商店交纳的费用高,但这与原文表明的比较关系正好相反,因此本题答案为 N。

4. 【答案】N

【题眼】Today major credit cards are issued either by banks or by Visa International or MasterCard International.

【定位】第 3 个小标题 **The Popularity of Credit Cards** 下的第 2 部分第 2 句。

【解析】原文中的 in cooperation with... 表明银行、其他金融机构、威士国际信用卡公司或万事达国际信用卡公司都不单独发行信用卡,而是共同发行,因此本题的说法不正确。

5. 【答案】Y

【题眼】More and more people don't pay off their monthly credit card transactions completely.

【定位】第 4 个小标题 **How to Get a Credit Card?** 部分的第 2 段第 3 句。

【解析】原文中的 the growing number of who... 表达的意思与题目中的 More and more 相同,因此本题答案为 Y。

6. 【答案】N

【题眼】The lowest interest rate for a credit card holder is twelve percent.

【定位】第 4 个小标题 **How to Get a Credit Card?** 部分的第 2 段最后一句。

【解析】原文 though 引出的从句说明了信用卡的利率有可能低于 12%,因此本题答案为 N。

7. 【答案】N

【题眼】It is almost impossible to get back the payment from the retailers even if there is a problem with the products you buy with your credit card.

【定位】第 5 个小标题 **Credit Card: Friend or Enemy?** 部分的首段第 2 句。

【解析】这道题与原文的真正不同之处在于 almost impossible 和 have an opportunity 的区别。前者表示"几乎不可能",倾向于否定;后者表示"有可能",倾向于肯定。两者意思相违背,因此答案为 N。

8. 【答案】the accepting locations

【题眼】The cardholders could find _____ at the back of the first Diners Club credit cards.

【定位】第 2 个小标题 **The Significant Dinner** 部分的最后一段最后一句。

【解析】空白处应为名词词组。题目中的 find... at the back 与原文 with... printed on the back 意思相同,因此,with 后的名词词组就是本题答案。

9. 【答案】a line of credit

    【题眼】Similar to what a bank's <u>consumer loan department</u> does, bank credit cards provide the cardholder with _____.

    【定位】第 3 个小标题 **The Popularity of Credit Cards** 下的第 2 部分第 3 句。

    【解析】空白处应为名词词组。题目中的 provide the cardholder with... 与原文中的 extend... to the cardholder 意思相同,因此原文 extend 后的宾语就是本题答案。

10. 【答案】terms and conditions vary widely

    【题眼】When you want to <u>get a credit card</u>, it is crucial for you to make a <u>careful choice</u> due to the fact that _____.

    【定位】第 4 个小标题 **How to Get a Credit Card?** 部分的第 2 段首句。

    【解析】空白处应为主谓成分的句子。题目中的 crucial 和 make a careful choice 分别是对原文 important 和 choose carefully 的同义替换,而且题目中的 due to the fact that 与原文的 because 功能相同,因此 because 引出的从句就是本题答案。

Part III   Listening Comprehension

Section A

11. M: Helen <u>doesn't take a part-time job</u> this semester.

    W: No. <u>Her grades</u> enabled her to earn a <u>scholarship</u>.

    Q: What is implied about Helen?

[C]【解析】女士说,Helen 的分数使她获得了奖学金,言下之意,她不用再干兼职了。

    【点睛】①对于 S1 的否定句,S2 的 No 表示"赞同"意见。由此可以得出答案 C。它与 S1 正好同义再现。②若 S2 的后半截说明只听到了片言只语,grades, scholar 纯属同音干扰,可以排除。

12. W: <u>Why are you giving me a speeding ticket?</u> I was only going 40.

    M: Can't you read? That was 10 mph over the limit.

    Q: What is the relationship between the two speakers?

[A]【解析】场景(身份、人物关系)题。标志性词汇 speeding ticket"超速罚单",limit 以及速度表达方法表明是警察和驾驶员的对话。

    【点睛】读题——辨明题型——努力听取相关解题步骤:标志词语——定位答案。

13. W: Let's stop and look at this furniture, Billy. <u>Have you ever seen more beautiful sofas?</u>

    M: <u>Quite often and for much less money</u>, too.

    Q: What does the man think of the sofa?

[C]【解析】男士说他经常看到这样的沙发,还不用这么多钱,所以他认为沙发太贵。

    【点睛】①S1 的一般疑问句,具有感叹句的含义。②S2"答非所问",表示对 S1 的话的否定。由此,否定 S1 的赞赏语气,即得出正确答案 C。干扰项均为正面的、肯定态度。

14. W: Poor Charlie. To be so close to finishing and then not to graduate!

    M: <u>If you had known how he had dealt with his schoolwork</u>, you wouldn't feel like that.

    Q: What can be inferred about Charlie?

[A]【解析】女士为 Charlie 不能毕业而感到惋惜,而男士则说,如果你知道他是怎么对待他的功课的,你就不会为他感到惋惜了。言下之意是 Charlie 不用功,不能毕业是很正常的。

    【点睛】虚拟语气题。

15. M: I forgot to bring paper and a pencil to take notes with in class.

W: That's all right. I have enough for both of us.

Q: What will the woman probably do?

[A]【解析】男士忘带纸笔做笔记,女士说她带的够两个人用,也就是表示愿意把自己的纸笔分给男士用。

【点睛】①本题不能用"听到什么不选什么"技巧,所有选项都包含了对话中的原词。②因而,本题的解答要点是弄清谈话的要点,即:S1 提出的话题是"纸笔"还是"笔记"?③S2 表示 have enough,从语义上说,只能说足够的"纸笔"而非"笔记"。

16. M: How about joining me at the hotel for lunch?

W: I'd love to, Henry, but I've got to cash a check at the bank so I can pay for our tickets to the concert.

Q: Where is the woman going now?

[D]【解析】女士说她要去银行兑现一张支票,故选 D。

【点睛】中 but 题,but 后的内容是解题关键。读完选项,听到 S2 的回答"I'd love to, but..."即可排除 S1 所说的 hotel, lunch,即选项 B、C。剩下两个选项须根据问题中的 now 加以确认。

17. M: We've worked long enough for a Saturday afternoon.

W: OK. Let's call it a day.

Q: What does the woman mean?

[B]【解析】let's call it a day 是固定搭配,表示"今天到此为止,该结束了"。

【点睛】若听不懂关键短语,可利用 S2 开头部分的简短回答解题。根据 S2 开头说的 OK,判定 S2 同意 S1 的话。与"干得够长时间了"相当的,只有"可以停止工作了"。其余选项均不合适。

18. M: How did you find your job? Was it advertised in the paper?

W: I looked and looked for months without finding anything. Then a friend told me about this job. So I applied and got it!

Q: How did the woman learn about the job opening?

[C]【解析】C 中的 inform 就是 tell 的意思,所以女士现在的工作机会是朋友告诉她的。

【点睛】①"答非所问",多表示否定,故否定 S1 中的 advertise,即否定 A。②B、C 均未提及。

Now you'll hear two long conversations.

Conversation One

W: Hello, Bill. You look very sad. What happened?

M: Don't mention it. Our baseball team was beaten by Australia last night.

W: Oh, I am sorry to hear that. I know baseball is a traditional pastime in US. But you should not expect your team to win every time.

M: Sure, I know. But it was a matter of pride for the US baseball team to win in the 1996 Olympic Games. How I wish they could win this time!

W: I also watched the live broadcast yesterday. It was a close game. They gave their best but luck was not on their side.

M: You are right. [19] How about baseball in China? Is it also very popular?

W: [20] I think it's getting more and more popular now.

M: Yeah, when I first came to China a few years ago, I couldn't find anything about the game on newspapers or in sport reports on TV.

W: I agree. I am a big baseball fan too, and I often go to the Internet to find out who has won and who has lost.

M: Right, as far as media coverage is concerned. I have seen a lot of changes in recent years in China.

W: Baseball in China is becoming an important sport now. I still remember several years ago when I went to the stadium to watch a game, there were only a few dozen spectators. But now at least thousands of fans show at every game.

M: Watching a baseball game in China now is almost like that in the US.

W: Well, even so, I believe baseball in China is not quite up to the level as other "advanced countries."

M: [21] Given some time for good training, I think Chinese baseball teams will reach world-class.

W: Did the Chinese baseball team go to play at the 2004 Athens Olympic Games?

M: [21] No, unfortunately the Chinese team lost in the Asian Championships, and therefore failed to be qualified for the Athens Games.

M: That's too bad. But I am sure with intensive training in the next few years, [21/22] the Chinese team no doubt will be qualified for the 2008 Beijing Olympics.

19. What are the two speakers mainly talking about?

[C]【解析】主旨题。对话中提到美国棒球队和中国棒球队,但并没有对二者进行比较,故 A 错误;对话中讨论了中国棒球运动的发展,但并没提到有何促进措施,故 B 也错误。整个对话由谈论美国棒球队的情况引出话题,主要是围绕着中国棒球运动的普及与发展而展开的,故 C 正确而 D 错误。

【点睛】①四个选项均是名词词组,涉及中国、美国的棒球运动,由此,大体可以推断本题为"主旨大意题"。②主旨大意题惯用规则:含 development 或 history 的选项是答案。——这条规则很好笑,但简单实用。③本对话比较特别,在提出主旨前有一段较长(占 1/3)的引子,因而可能具有迷惑性。④主旨题考查对整篇对话的把握能力。对话中出现最多的主题词才会是主旨,故可排除含 US 的选项 A、D。在 B、C 中则容易断定,efforts 语义较具体,不如 C 的概括力强。⑤主旨题的错误干扰项往往是对话中提到的词语,但却不是主题。

20. What do we know about baseball games in China?

[B]【解析】细节题。女士告诉男士棒球在中国越来越流行,并以观众人数变化为例来说明:棒球运动以前并不很流行,而现在受到人们的重视和欢迎。故答案为 B。选项 A、C、D 均与对话不符,故可排除。

【点睛】一般情况下,过于绝对的判断不会是答案,因此

可以直接排除 A、C、D。

21. What can be inferred about the Chinese baseball team?

[B]【解析】推断题。C、D 两项对话中并未提及,可排除;有望参加奥运会与在奥运会中获胜是两回事,A 项也不正确。故答案为 B。

【点睛】①虽然对话中没有明确地比较两国棒球队的水平,但是从对话中可知美国队在 1996 年奥运会中获胜,而中国棒球运动近年来才发展起来,中国队连进入 2004 年奥运会的资格都没有,由此可以判断美国队比中国队成熟。②A、C、D 属于"绝对判断"的选项,可以直接排除。

22. In which of the following games does the Chinese team still have chance to win?

[C]【解析】细节题。1996 年奥运会、亚洲锦标赛、2004 年奥运会都已经成为过去,而且是由于在亚锦赛上的失利导致无法参加 2004 年奥运会。四个选项中,只有为 2008 年奥运会拼搏还有可能,故选 C。

【点睛】①解答细节题的主要对策是在听懂的同时对关键词、强调词及时做笔记,听到问题之后根据记忆和笔记迅速锁定答案。②本题还有另一个解题思路:根据问题"在哪一场运动会上还有机会赢",那肯定是未来的运动会上,选 C 没错。

Conversation Two

W: Where did you go on May Day? [23] I called you several times.

M: Really? I have my holiday on a seaside resort.

W: Wow, that's terrific. Did you travel alone?

M: No, my wife and son also traveled with me. Where did you go then?

W: I went nowhere. I spent the whole holiday writing. I have to finish it before Mother's Day. [23] But I do plan to travel next month, that's why I'm calling you. Could you give me some advice?

M: Oh, how about the seaside? That's a really good place for a holiday.

W: Sounds good.

M: There are two hotels I can recommend while you are on your trip. [24] They are both brand new and are usually fully booked. So you'd better call them in advance.

W: I see... so what are they like?

M: Well, one is called the Hotel Bay View. It's on the coast. So, [25] it is very quiet and peaceful without noise or pollution. And the rooms are of standard size and they all have a nice little balcony, where you can overlook the ocean.

W: [25] That's great! I need to have a tranquil period to relax. How about the other?

M: The other is a city center hotel. Of course, there are no views of the sea and it tends to be a bit noisy and busy. But it is very convenient for you to go anywhere from the hotel.

W: [25] Er, it's useless for me. I don't want to go shopping or do anything like that. What about the price?

M: Well, the Central Hotel is quite a bit more expensive.

W: I know, thanks for your suggestion.

23. Why does the woman call the man?

[C]【解析】主旨题。如果能听到女士说的"但我计划下个月去旅行,那就是我打电话给你的原因。你能给我些建议吗?"就能迅速地选出正确答案 C。A、D 两项对话中并未提及;女士要征求意见,但与写作无关,B 项也错误。

【点睛】①由选项 she plans/hopes/wants/complains...知,本题问"她"的打算、目的。②对话一开头,女士说"我给你打了几次电话",由此就应紧紧抓住她自己的说明:为什么打电话。但本题由此岔开了两个话轮(一般这种插叙的话不是考查重点)小再回到主打电话问题。听的时候,要善于把握对话的发展脉络。③若能在听音时准确定位,则可由对话中的 travel, advice 迅速判断答案。

24. What should the woman do if she is to stay where the man recommends?

[D]【解析】细节题。只要抓听到 fully booked"订满"及

you'd better call them in advance "你最好提前打电话",就可以推断出女士应该要提前预订房间。D 项的 reserve 对应对话中的 book,答案为 D。

【点睛】①四个选项为动词原形;若能联系 23 题,表明本题问"建议如何做"。②带着问题听,则应该不会错过建议句型"You'd better...",从而可以迅速找准答案。

25. Which of the following environments will the woman probably choose?

[B]【解析】推断题。男士向女士推荐了两个旅馆,一个靠海、舒适、安静且便宜;一个位于市中心,方便,较贵且嘈杂。女士希望有个宁静的假期,不打算逛街购物明确表示喜欢前者。所以选 B 而排除 A。

【点睛】①四个选项均是名词词组,从其中的共现词汇中大体可以推断,本题讨论旅店房间的周围环境。②A、B 两项均可以在对话中听到,要注意标记说话人的倾向。不能完全凭"听到什么就选什么"的规则做题。

Section B

Passage One

[28] In the eyes of many people, city life is attractive with all its advantages and convenience, yet they don't see the other side of the picture. First, with the expansion of the city, housing has become a serious problem for city people. Then there is the problem of pollution. Harmful gases from vehicles and poisonous water from factories pollute our surroundings, and [26] noise continually disturbs your peace and rest and drives you mad. Thirdly, modern city life puts a high pressure upon people, you have to hurry to bump into the flood of people, bicycles, cars, buses... All day long you are under great stress. Fourthly, big cities also cause some social problems, of which high crime rate is the most serious one. [27] People are justifiably in fear of becoming victims of burglaries, robbery, murder and other crimes at any time. [28] The city should find some way or other to cope with all these problems.

26. What may drive city people mad, according to the passage?

[D]【解析】文中列举了城市生活的四大不利之处:housing, pollution, high pressure 和 social problems。其中说到 pollution 时提到 gases, water 和 noise,并且说"noise continually disturbs your peace and rest and drives you mad"。

【点睛】读完四个选项,知道本题问某种缺陷。但是,在不知道确切问题前,无法进行筛选、判断,只能在每个选项边记录相关信息:听到 A 时记录 first, serious 字

眼;听到 B 时记录"二、污染"字眼;然后听到的是 D,记录 disturbs peace, mad 字眼;最后听到 C,记录 most serious, social。听完全文,根据问题做出选择。本题考查细节记忆能力,难度较大。

27. What are city people constantly in fear of?

[C]【解析】城市的第四个缺点是社会问题,其中居高不下的犯罪率首当其冲,所以人们时刻担心成为各种犯罪的牺牲品。

【点睛】①同上题一样,从四个选项中无法确知问题的形

式。因此本题的难度在于文中提到的各选项互相干扰。②文中没提到 D,先排除。③听清问题,问"人们怕什么"。若未能记忆住原文细节,可据常识判断"合理的答案"。④问题中的 constantly 对应原文中的 at any time。

[B]【解析】全文的第一句就是主题句,指出城市生活尽管方便,但也存在着不尽如人意的地方。而最后一句又说城市应该想办法解决这些问题。因此全文重点讲的是困扰城市人的种种问题。

【点睛】首尾句往往往往是主题所在。本题比较容易。

28. What is this passage mainly about?

Passage Two

[29] <u>Man has always been fascinated by dreams.</u> He has always tried to find explanations for his dreams. Perhaps dreams tell us about the future or the past; perhaps they tell us about our deepest fears and hopes. I'll give you one or two facts about dreams. First of all, everyone dreams. You often hear people say, "I never dream" when they mean "I can never remember my dreams." When we dream, our eyes move rapidly in our sleep as if we were watching a moving picture, following it with our eyes. [30] <u>This movement is called REM, which is Rapid Eye Movement.</u> REM sleep is the sleep that matters. [31] <u>Experiments have proved that if we wake people up throughout the night during REM, they will feel exhausted the next day.</u> But they won't feel tired at all if we wake them up at times when they're not dreaming. So it is clear that it is dreaming that really refreshes us, not just the sleep.

29. Why has man been so fascinated by dreams?

[A]【解析】文章开头就说:"Man has always been fascinated by dreams."根据之后的解释可概括出 A。

【点睛】①容易推断本题问原因。②可据常识排除 B、C。③D 的内容属两大关于"梦"的事实之一,并非人们对梦感兴趣的原因。④在听到第一句后,注意听原因的陈述部分,可以据"tell us about..."选出正确答案。

30. What does REM mean?

[C]【解析】根据 This movement is called REM, which is Rapid Eye Movement.

【点睛】符合"听到什么选什么"的原则。听清了问题中的 REM,也可以从选项中找出首字母缩略词。

31. What have the experiments proved about dreams?

[B]【解析】在 REM 阶段唤醒一个人,第二天他会感到筋疲力尽,选 B,其中 tired 对应原文 exhausted。

【点睛】可以推断本题问结论、细节。实验结果的重要性不言而喻,听到就应该记录。A、D 选项无法合理推断出,C 错在 Only。

Passage Three

Are you familiar with large supermarkets? If so, then you probably know that almost everything in the market is in a container. Most food is in containers. Even fresh meat is sold in plastic packages. [32] <u>Fresh fruit and vegetables are usually the only food items that don't come in containers.</u> In fact, almost everything at the supermarket is in a bag, a box, a bottle, a jar, a carton, or a can.

This kind of packaging system is necessary at large supermarkets. Supermarkets buy large quantities of everything. Products must be protected during shipment and they must sit on shelves for long periods of time. [33] <u>Containers, therefore, protect the products. Containers have another function, too.</u> [33] <u>They give information about each product—</u> [34] <u>names, weights, materials, and ingredients, and sometimes pictures of the products.</u> This information is printed on labels or directly on the containers.

But think of this, we never see most of the things we buy at the supermarket until we get home and open the containers. When we go shopping, we look at the labels on the containers. If the container is made of glass or clear plastic, perhaps we could see a little bit of the product. [35] <u>But usually containers completely hide their products.</u>

32. Which of the following is usually not sold in containers at large supermarkets?

[B]【解析】原文提到,只有新鲜蔬菜和水果通常是不需要包装的,所以选 B。

【点睛】这道题符合"听到什么就选什么"的原则。如果听到的不只一项,则需要在旁边做笔记来帮助判断。听到文中的 only,应予以特别注意,极有可能是出题所在。

33. What are the functions of containers?

[D]【解析】D 是原文"Containers, therefore, protect the products. ... They give information about each product..."的综合。

【点睛】①不定式选项,问目的。②听到什么选什么。

34. Which of the following doesn't need to be printed on labels?

Shoppers must trust the labels.

[C]【解析】原文提到 names, weights, materials, and ingredients, and sometimes pictures,只有 C 未被提及。

【点睛】名词选项,考细节。原文中并列的词汇单独作选项出现,即为等价选项,可以一并排除。

---

35. Why must shoppers trust labels?

[A]【解析】最后一部分提到,我们在购物的时候,一般情况下,产品的包装会把产品遮得严严实实,即使是玻璃或透明的塑料包装,我们也只能看见产品的一小部分,我们没有别的办法,只能相信标签上所说的。

【点睛】①尾巴题,原因题。英文段落最后几句话往往会有出其不意的观点或信息,应该养成注意首尾句的听音习惯。②原文中的 hide 与答案 can't see 同义替换。

Section C

36.【答案】suburban

【解析】根据预读可知,此处需要一个名词或形容词来修饰后面的 philadelphia。此词由前缀 sub 加 urban "城市的"构成,意思是"郊区的"。suburb 是名词"郊区"。注意 ur 的拼写。

37.【答案】ambition

【解析】此处需要一个单数名词;根据下文的信息可知,在语义上此处应填表示"理想,抱负"的词。ambition 根据发音规则还是比较容易拼写的。

38.【答案】earning

【解析】介词后面需要动名词;根据此句可知,此处应填表示"获得,得到"的词。earn a degree 表示"获得学位"。千万别把此词错写成 urning "男性同性恋"。

39.【答案】endured

【解析】根据后面的 by 可以预测此处是过去分词作定语。注意不要把 en 拼写成 in。即使没听到-ed,也应根据语法将其补上。

40.【答案】staff

【解析】此处需要一个修饰 writer 的词,可能是名词,也可能是形容词。听到的是 staff,不要误当成 stuff。英文中有一个词语 staffman,是指"报刊的编辑、采访人员"。

41.【答案】quit

【解析】此处需要一个动词过去式;从语义上,此处应填表示"辞职,放弃"的词。quit 的过去式、过去分词都是 quit 或 quitted。根据录音应填写 quit。

42.【答案】nationwide

【解析】此处需要一个形容词或名词来修饰后面的 contest。根据发音规则,此词比较容易拼写。

43.【答案】outnumbered

【解析】此处也需要一个动词过去式,含比较意义,outnumber 表示在数量上超过。

44.【答案】When he reached the semifinals, his editors at the journal ran a headline

【听音关键】reached semifinals, editors, ran a headline

【答案重构】When he entered the semifinals, the journal's editors used a headline

【画龙点睛】注意主句的主谓宾可改写个别单词或表达。

45.【答案】His years in the advice business left him with a deep appreciation for people and their problems

【听音关键】years, advice business, deep appreciation for people, problems

【答案重构】He gained a deep appreciation for people and their problems after years of working in the advice business

【画龙点睛】可以将无生命的主语变成状语,而以人作为主语,但这样的改写需要较高的语言水平,否则还是照搬原文比较保险。

46.【答案】I have much more faith in my fellowmen than I did before. And I've read plenty of letters to back that up

【听音关键】more faith than before, fellowmen, letters, back that up

【答案重构】I trust my fellow men much more than before. And I've read many letters to back that up

【画龙点睛】注意比较句型和短语 back up 的正确使用。

Part IV Reading Comprehension (Reading in Depth)

Section A

参考译文

没有适当的规划,旅游可能引发许多问题。例如,太多游客会涌向东道国本地人也喜爱的公共场所。如果游客造成太多交通堵塞,本地人便会觉得心烦和不开心。他们开始变得不喜欢游客,对他们也不再彬彬有礼。他们不会再想到旅游能帮助一个国家的经济发展。因此,考虑旅游目的地人民的感受和旅游对他们生活的影响是很重要的。旅游应该帮助一个国家保持其赖以吸引游客的民俗风情和美丽景致,但同时旅游也应该能提高当地人的生活质量,使他们过上更为幸福安康的生活。

旅游行业的过度发展可能是个问题。

另一方面,如果旅游业不能得到充分的发展,那么许多人将会面临失业的问题,整个行业也会出现亏损。建造大型饭店、机场、航空终点站、一流的道路以及其他旅游景点所需要的配套设施都要花很多钱。例如,一家较大的国际级旅游酒店平均每个房间的造价高达5万美元。如果这个房间多数时间都闲置的话,酒店老板就要赔钱了。

建造一家酒店只是一个开始。此外还需要很多配套设施,包括前往酒店的道路、电力和处理垃圾的卫生设施、水等。所有这些配套设施都要花钱。如果它们因为没有足够的游客而被闲置的话,又会造成另一部分人失业和大量的资金损失。

【词性分析】

名　词:handle 柄,把手　destination 目的地,终点;目标　major 少校;专业,专业学生　owners 物主,所有人[复数]
　　　　curiosity 好奇(心);奇事,古玩　crowd 人群,群众;一群,一批　tourism 旅游业,观光业

动　词:handle 处理,应付,对待;操作;拿,触,摸　major 主修,专攻　lose 失去,丧失,受损失;迷路;失败,输;白费,浪费;(钟、表)走慢　invade 侵入,侵略,侵袭　crowd 群集,挤;塞满　exerted 用(力)尽(力);运用,发挥,施加[过去式或过去分词]　annoyed 使恼怒;打扰[过去式或过去分词]

形容词:major 较大的;主要的,重大的　frequent 时常发生的,频繁的,常见的　local 地方性的,当地的;局部的,狭隘的　annoyed 略感烦恼(生气)的

副　词:permanently 永久地,永恒地　impolitely 无礼地,粗鲁地

47. [K]此处应为及物动词原形,其宾语为 public places。结合上一句,可知本句的 For example 表明 too many tourists 给当地人带来了麻烦,由 too many 也可以推断游客太多,挤满了当地的公共场所,因此 crowd 为本题答案。

48. [O]此处应为形容词,与 unhappy 并列作 become 的表语。该词与 unhappy 并列,因此该词也具有消极意义,而且根据 If 条件状语从句提到的情况,可以推断 annoyed 是本题答案。

49. [N]此处应为副词,修饰动词 treat。根据前面并列的 dislike tourists,可以推断空白处的副词应具有消极意义,由此可见,impolitely 为本题答案。

50. [B]此处应为形容词或名词,修饰 country。根据本句中的 how tourism affects them 可以知道,the people of a ____ country 指的是旅游目的地的当地人,因此本题答案应为 destination。

51. [J]此处应为形容词,修饰 people。本段最后三句说的都是旅游对当地人的影响,最后一句的对象也应是当地人,因此 local 是本题答案。

52. [L]此处应为不可数名词,作句子的主语。problem 一词暗示本句是对上一段的小结,由此可见,本句主语应为 tourism。

53. [E]此处应为及物动词,其宾语为 money。从本句中的 also 一词可以推断本句应与上一句中的 people can lose jobs 结构相同,意思相似,因此 lose 是最合适的单词。

54. [D]此处应为形容词,修饰 hotel。从本句描述的酒店房间的昂贵造价来看,空白处的形容词应表明酒店是“豪华的”、“规模大的”等意思,在词库中只有 major 一词表示“较大的”,符合上下文的语义。

55. [G]此处应为名词。从本句中的 lose money 可以判断,与酒店亏损有利益关系的人应该是其所有者,因此 owners 是本题答案。

56. [A]此处应为及物动词,且为动词原形。空白处的动词表明 sewers 和 waste 的关系,通常来说,sewers 是用于处理 waste 的,因此 handle 是符合句意的词。

Section B

Passage One

参考译文划线点评

梦是一个人在睡觉时“旁观”甚至参与的一个故事。梦里的事情是想象的,却与做梦的人生活里的真实经历和需求

息息相关。这些事情在发生的时候仿佛是真的。有些梦让人欢喜,另一些让人恼火,还有一些则让人害怕。

人人都做梦,但有些人却从来想不起做过的梦。另外,有些人只能回忆起少许睡醒之前刚做的那个梦,再早一点的梦则什么也想不起来。[58]没有人能回忆起全部的梦。

梦与逻辑思维没有什么关系。在大多数梦里,做梦的人无法控制发生在自己身上的事情。梦里的故事可能乱七八糟,而且不可能发生在现实生活里的事情也会在梦里发生。在大多数梦里,一个人能看,但也可以在梦里听、闻、摸和尝。多数梦是彩色的,但是天生的盲人在梦里什么也看不见。

梦是睡着的人意识的产物,包括他经历过的事件和感情。[59]多数梦都与做梦前一天白天所发生的事件和做梦人的强烈愿望有关。许多睡前几个小时发生的小事情会出现在梦里。[61]超过两天前的事情几乎就不会出现了。强烈的愿望或恐惧——特别是那些从小就有的——经常出现在梦里,而在许多梦里这些愿望都会实现。发生在睡着的人周围的事情——譬如嘈杂的声音——可能会进入梦境,但这并不是做梦的原因。

有些梦还涉及到一些一个人自己都没有意识到的深层情感。[60]精神病医生经常利用病人梦里的材料来帮助病人更好地理解自己。

做梦可以有助于保持良好的学习能力、记忆力以及情感调节能力。睡眠充足但是每次一做梦就惊醒的人会变得焦虑不安。

57. [C]主旨大意题。本文多数段落都有明显的主题句揭示文章主题,如第1段、第3段及第4段的首句都是对dreams的定义。其他选项文中虽略有涉及,但并非主题。

58. [A]事实细节题。本题考查部分否定句的理解。选项A中的"All... don't..."是一个部分否定句,是对第2段第3句的同义替换。其他选项都与第2段的陈述相悖。

59. [D]推理判断题。选项D中的always一词太绝对,与第4段第3句中的Most dreams不符。也可用排除法逐项地找出答案,逐点在原文中找到其他选项的依据,第3段第1句支持选项A,第1段第2句支持选项B,第1段第3句支持选项C,题目问的是NOT true的选项,因此D正确。

60. [C]推理判断题。本文在倒数第2段的结尾句提到了psychiatrists的工作是帮助病人更好地理解自己,也就是意味着他们研究梦境好的方面并将其应用于治愈病人。其他选项都不是合理的必然推论。

61. [B]事实细节题。本题考查否定句的理解。第4段有多句话说明了哪些事情会在梦中出现,其中第5句是一个以Few开头的否定句,指出两天以前的事情几乎不会出现,这表明选项B正确。

Passage Two

参考译文划线点评

作弊并不新鲜。但现在,教育专家和管理人员发现学生学术作弊比以往更加频繁——却比过去更不可能受到惩罚。[62]作弊似乎得到了好生差生的一致认可。

为什么学生作弊有增无减呢?没有人确切知道。有人把这一倾向归咎于当今青年的道德价值观普遍宽松。其他人则认为这是因为当今的青年比他们那些理想主义的前辈更加讲求实际。[63]在60年代末70年代初,学生们满怀改造世界的远大理想,而现在,学生们深感顺从和取得成功的压力。在和全国各地的高中生和大学生面谈时,男生和女生都说作弊易如反掌。有些学生说他们故意这样做来报复他们不尊重的老师;另外一些学生则视之为游戏。有些说,只有被抓住后他们才会感到内疚。"人人都有竞争力,"来自芝加哥的大二学生安娜说。学生心中潜藏着恐惧。如果考不好,整个一生就会被毁掉。压力不仅来自父母和朋友,同时也来自自己。一定要进取,一定要成功。仿佛几乎是我们只有超过别人才能实现自己的目标。

杂志编辑爱德华·韦恩将学术作弊的上升归罪于学校。他认为,管理人员和教师们迟疑不决,未能即时采取行动。阿玛里洛大学英语系主任德怀特·休伯对此则有不同见解,将之归咎于评价学生的方式。休伯说:"如果我觉得自己被蒙蔽我就会作弊。"[65]他认为,只要老师们用简短问答取代问答题,只要他们依据学生能记住的事实数目来评估学生而置学生们综合信息的能力高低于不顾,学生们就会设法击败这种制度。[64/66]"作弊的概念建立在一个错误的假设之上,即制度是合法的,是作弊的人本身有问题,"他说,"这个答案过于简单。我们必须开始审视制度。"

62. [B]事实细节题。第1段最后一句中的good and poor students alike 与选项B中的academically weak or strong 同义,由此可见选项B应为正确答案。文章未提及选项A,选项C和D与第1段第2句矛盾。

63. [A]事实细节题。本题考查对复杂句的理解。第2段第5句中的Whereas引导的是一个表转折对比的复杂句,前半部分说明的就是过去学生的想法,选项 A 中的 ambitious 一词体现了他们的 visions about transforming the world。选项 B 和 D 描述的是现在的学生。文章提到现在的学生承受着成功的压力,但不能据此推断以前的学生没有成功的欲望,因此选项 C 依据不足。

64. [A]事实细节题。文章最后两句表明 Dwight Huber 认为把过错都归罪于学生是不正确的,应该重新"审视制度",把不正确的修正过来,因此,选项 A 表达了他的愿望。选项 B 和 C 恰恰是导致作弊泛滥的原因。选项 D 则是 Edward Wynne 的看法。

65. [B]词义推断题。system 所处的上下文谈的是 evaluation 和 test 的问题,也就是选项 B。其他选项都与这个中心无关。

66. [C]推理判断题。文章倒数第 2 句暗示不能简单地将作弊归咎于学生,也就是说,作弊问题有其他更深层次的原因,只有选项 C 表达了这个意思。这句话也排除了选项 A。第 1 段第 2 句虽然提到作弊的学生比以前更不可能受到惩罚,但并未就惩罚本身做出任何说明或评价,故选项 B 依据不足。第 2 段第 2 句则表明没有人真正知道作弊现象增加的原因,可排除选项 D。

Part V Cloze

67. [C]词义辨析。minor"较小的,较少的;次要的";vital"极其重要的;有生命的";major"较大的,主要的,重要的";crucial "至关重要的,决定性的"。本句需要 C 以构成"主要语言"。

68. [D]考查指示代词的用法。分析上下文替代关系,空白处词代替的是 language,而且冒号之后的内容为 of 短语,强干扰项 it 不能构成该短语。

69. [A]本题须结合上下文内容及常识来判断选择。上文出现信息 ruled it for less than 200 years,而下文出现 52 years ago,按照逻辑,这里不可能是 B、C、D 三项答案。而历史知识告诉我们印度是于 50 多年前独立的,英国殖民统治者应在那时候"离开"。

70. [B]短语搭配题。介词短语 under way 表示"正在进行之中"。

71. [D]语法结构题。依据上下文,这里表达的意思是:英国不仅曾建立了全球性的帝国,而且还曾在美洲定居。空缺词表达的应是递进之义,而上文中的 not only 决定这里需填 but (also)。本题可利用词汇的结构同现技巧解题。

72. [A]逻辑联系题。分析句意,特别是短语 at first 表示的是"最初,开始时"之义,所以本句提到的两个原因之间的逻辑关系时间上应是先后关系,意义上是对照关系,选 now。如选择 secondly 则上文出现的过渡短语或过渡词应是 first of all,first 或 firstly。

73. [C]词义辨析。all-round"全面的;全能的";widespread"分布广的,普遍的";global"全球性的";local"当地的"。此处指世界已获得其第一个真正全球性的媒介——互联网,从而体现文章主旨——英语正在变为全球性的语言,因为选 C。

74. [D]词义理解题。句型结构 It is estimated that 表示"据估计"。强干扰项(It is) predicted 表示"预计",而根据文意以及常识判断,这些数据不是预测而是事实。

75. [B]逻辑联系题。此处句意补全后应为:在前英国殖民地国家或英语占主体地位的国家可能有 2.5 亿到 3.5 亿的人口确实或能够运用英语作为其第二语言。所以选连词 or。

76. [C]根据上下文逻辑关系解题。逗号之后是对上文的举例说明,所以选 like。强干扰项 as 表示"正如"时引出的是从句,不符合此处要求。

77. [B]逻辑推理题。上文提及的数据是有关前英国殖民地国家或英语占主体地位的国家说英语的情况,按照逻辑,下文出现的数据应是有关其他地方的。

78. [A]逻辑关联题。此处句意是:据猜测,数字为 1 亿到 10 亿,具体的数字要看你怎么定义"能够说英语"。引出宾语从句的关联词应是 how。

79. [C]短语搭配题。只有短语 in all 表示所需"总共,合计"之义。其他短语:at all"根本,全然";for all"尽管,虽然";after all"毕竟,终究,究竟"。

80. [D]语法题。短语 let alone 的作用相当于连词,其后出现的成分与上文出现的成分结构上并列。上文出现的是 the English of England,这里应出现(the English) of Dr. Johnson。

81. [B]逻辑关系题。这里所空缺的含义是"随着",选 as。而下文原词已出现在 as the Internet spreads 中,也可据此判断。

82. [A]逻辑关系题。根据文意,此处前后分句之间表达的是承接关系,不是转折(B、C)或因果关系(D),选 and。

83. [C]词义理解题。此处需根据上下文和常识判断,英语长期以来一直是学术刊物所使用的语言。

84. [A]词义理解题。expert"专家的,内行的";skilled"熟练的,有技能的";skillful"灵巧的,娴熟的";experienced"有经验的"。

85. [B]逻辑关联题。根据上下文语境,此句与前一句之间为因果关系。此句意为:因为英语是学术刊物长期以来采用的语言,……所以要想使自己的文章发表并被同行所阅读,就得选择用英语来撰写论文。

86. [D]语法结构题。if... then... 为同现结构。

Part VI Translation

87. 【答案】that it forces people to test
【译文】尽管很多人认为冲突不好,但是冲突有时候也有用处,因为它迫使人们检验自己的态度和行为是否恰当。

【解析】根据此空前面的介词 in,此处的"因为"需要使用短语 in that。

88. 【答案】released by the chain reaction
【译文】连锁反应所释放出的能量被转换成热能。

【解析】考查过去分词作定语。release"释放,排放;解除,解脱;放开,松开;发布,发行"。本句中用 release 的过去分词,表示被动。易混淆动词辨析:relieve"使解脱"。

89. 【答案】that we had to wait for about half an hour
【译文】展览会前排了很长的队,因此,我们不得不等了大约半小时。

【解析】本句要求使用句型 such... that... 如此……以至于……。时态相应应为过去时。

90. 【答案】long as he works hard
【译文】只要他努力工作,我就不在意他什么时间完成实验。

【解析】如果没有开头的 so 进行限制,"只要"还可以用 as long as, if only 等短语来表达。

91. 【答案】will have lasted
【译文】会议将持续整整一周才会结束。

【解析】动词时态:by the time 后面接一般现在时的时间状语从句时,该从句是用一般现在时表达将来的动作,因此,主句用将来完成时。

Model Test 4

答题卡 1 (Answer Sheet 1)

Part I **Writing** **(30 minutes)**

Directions: *For this part, you are allowed 30 minutes to write a letter entitled **A Letter of Sympathy**. Suppose you are Frank, a friend of Li Ming. You should write at least 120 words following the key words given below in Chinese:*

1. 你从报纸上得知,朋友李明的家乡近来受到了严重的洪涝灾害。
2. 向他表示深切的慰问。
3. 表达自己愿意提供帮助,并问候他的家人。

A Letter of Sympathy

_____

_____

_____

_____

Part II **Reading Comprehension (Skimming and Scanning)** **(15 minutes)**

1. [Y] [N] [NG]   2. [Y] [N] [NG]   3. [Y] [N] [NG]   4. [Y] [N] [NG]

5. [Y] [N] [NG]   6. [Y] [N] [NG]   7. [Y] [N] [NG]

8. The Hollywood film industry gets famous throughout the world because its craftsmen are capable of _____
_____ .

9. Before the 21st century, filmmakers had to try hard to make shooting locations believable by means of _____
_____ .

10. Both film industry and car industry sell their products by _____ .

答题卡 2 (Answer Sheet 2)

Part III **Section C**

Environmental pollution is a term that (36) _____ to all the ways by which humans pollute their surroundings, for example, by damaging the soil with too many fertilizers and pesticides. We also pollute our surroundings in (37) _____ other ways. People (38) _____ natural beauty by (39) _____ junk and litter on the land and in the water. They operate machines and motor vehicles that fill the air with dangerous (40) _____ and (41) _____ noise. Nearly everyone causes pollution in some way.

Environmental pollution is one of the most (42) _____ problems that mankind faces today. Air, water, soil—all of which are harmed by pollution—are necessary to the (43) _____ of all living things. Badly polluted air can cause illness and even death. Polluted water kills fish and other marine life. (44) _____. Environmental pollution also brings ugliness to the naturally beautiful world.

(45) _____. It is complicated because so much pollution is caused by things that benefit people. (46) _____. Factories pollute the air and water, but also provide jobs for people.

Part VI　　　　Translation　　　　　　　　　　　　　　　　(5 minutes)

87. By the time you get to New York, I _____ (我将已出发前往) London.
88. He didn't come to help _____ (而是来阻碍我们的).
89. Investigators agreed that passengers on the airliner _____ (肯定是在坠机的一刹那丧生的).
90. By 1929, Mickey Mouse _____ (一样受到欢迎) children as Coca Cola.
91. If she doesn't tell him the truth now, he'll simply keep on asking her _____ (直到她说明为止).

Part I　Writing (30 minutes)

注意：此部分试题在答题卡1上。

Part II　Reading Comprehension (Skimming and Scanning)(15 minutes)

The Film Industry of the United States

"Through the movies, a Frenchman Leo Rosten remarked, the United States has effected the 'cultural colonization' of the world."

US vs. Europe

The US motion picture industry—like other entertainment businesses—works with government to make profit and culturally colonize the rest of the world. "In the mid-1960s," according to Tyler Cohen, in the April 28, 2003 Forbes.com, "American films accounted for 35% of box office revenues in Continental Europe; today the figure is between 80% and 90%."

Cohen concludes that "Hollywood films are technically advanced (e.g., special effects) and heavily advertised and publicized in the mass media. The typical European film has about 1% of the audience of the typical Hollywood film, and this difference has been growing. American movies have become increasingly popular in international markets, while European movies have become less so."

European films, slower in pace, appear to US audiences, who are very active, as unbearably heavy books filled with ideas, philosophical comments and different relationships. And, as Cohen points out, "the training of film talent in the US and Europe reflects these differences. American film schools are like business schools in many regards."

Compare the best US film schools (UCLA, NYU or USC as examples) with the cinema program at the University of Krakow in the 1950s that turned out directors like Roman Polanski and Andres Wajda. Instead of training for a job in the industry, the Polish curriculum emphasized liberal arts and humanities. Actual training for lighting, camera operation, acoustics, etc., took place in the last year of a five year program. US film schools "train" rather than "educate" from the beginning. They hold out promises that right after graduation, their trainees can become assistant editors or associate producers, defined by Fred Allen as "the only person who would associate with a producer."

From Art to Business

By the early 20th Century, business grammar captured American cinema. Entrepreneurs devised formulas to transform a new "art form" into commodities that would attract large, poorly educated audiences likely to return next week for more amazing films. Over the decades, technological perfection came to substitute for the *innovative* (创新的) dynamic of artistic creation. Indeed, the industry built its worldwide reputation on Hollywood craftsmen's ability to imitate reality. It challenged all foreign rivals and independents to match it. Hollywood enhanced the perfection of *animation* (动画) and special effects technology for examples into the principles on which mass media critics should pass their first judgment on films. Anything less than its standard of technical excellence would be the equivalent of offering a new car with a scratch on the paint job. Trace the industry from the silent, racist epic *Birth of a Nation* to the 21st Century musicals *Moulin Rouge* or *Chicago*. Technology as art wins audiences.

Besides aesthetic judgments, each Hollywood movie required, first and foremost, a business plan. To pass on a film idea, studio executives fashioned a profit-making blueprint: "give us scripts," they ordered the writers, "that will attract audiences to theaters and keep them coming back." This success formula made candy, popcorn and soft drink profits as well as Hollywood itself a special culture from which countless other industries developed. Naturally, for the first six decades of the industry, the producing studios also owned the movie theaters.

Hollywood studios helped create audience by offering what Irwin Shaw called "the American dream made visible," which included cultivating the star system. Behind the powerless but charm girls and splendid heroes of the Silent Screen, sat the multi-millionaire studio bosses who managed "the talent".

Technology

By the 21st Century, technology had rescued once challenged filmmakers from actually finding locations and figuring out how to actually render them credible through the camera and editing process. Soft ware and digital tec hnology now "render" the drama of a grand gorge or great jungle. Technology has enhanced the industry's possibilities for commercially designing and manufacturing cinema magic. It has not improved the idea quality. Indeed, few expect such "high quality" offerings.

Buying a ticket means that one leaves credibility at the box office along with the price of admission. The lights fade and impossibly beautiful people appear. They don't die in high-speed chases or falls from insufferable heights.

Truth behind Success

Behind the glitter, the film industry produces for two reasons: profit and reproduction. The motion picture industry resembles the automobile industry: big and shiny looking products on the outside. But don't look under the *hood* (车蓬) or on the cutting room floor.

Both industries rely on beauty and spectacular landscape to sell products. You've seen commercials that offer you power, sex appeal, prestige and status by owning a new SUV.

The commercial world attracts the public into the virtual setting, the theater where the available light shines on the screen, where a face (after hours in the make up room and years spent with "beauty experts") appeals to you to love it, sympathize with it, fear for it. "An emotional Detroit," actress Lillian Gish called Hollywood. The perfect look usually disguises artistic emptiness.

Hollywood's marketing success begins with the assumption that youth and undernourishment constitute universal *aesthetics* (审美观). My teenager takes these principles seriously and thus refuses to accompany us to the movies. She doesn't want to be seen in public with us.

"Why," I ask my daughter, "do gossip shows about movie stars or pop singers excite you?"

"Get real! " she responds.

I consider that since I'm no longer young enough to know everything, I should recall how teenagers went crazy about skinny Frank Sinatra in the '40s, before the skinny singer turned into a national idol—another product of the star system.

Romantic love affairs became highly profitable on the one hand and influential on the other. It can market anything. These films can indeed inspire some people to imitate the fictional characters.

Hollywood is a world-wide business whose product includes "American values", from the John Wayne so-called manlin ess or braveness notion of obeying patriotic orders to the notion that no amount of clothes is being enough, as Reese Witherspoon goes through endless costuming in her *Legally Blond* roles.

Beneath thin plot and story lines, decorated by skilled photography, special effects, set design, costuming, make up, mood music composition and the variety of photography tricks employed, one finds a world designed to delight us all—entertain at least the common.

The Hollywood sales manager instructs his team to "take this worthless waste and sell it to the world as the greatest art and entertainment ever made." God Bless America, especially the one that Hollywood invented!

1. The passage is mainly about how the American film industry achieved cultural colonization of the world.
2. American films have been dominating the film markets in Continental Europe since the 1960s.
3. American film schools usually provide a five-year training program for people who want to become a film director.
4. Candy, popcorn and soft drink businesses were three of the success formula for the Hollywood films.
5. Hollywood attracts audience by offering them a chance to realize their dream of becoming a star.
6. A film without rich plot and story lines, even produced by high technological means, cannot delight the audience.
7. Hollywood only markets films of greatest art and entertainment which are appealing to the audience.

Part III Listening Comprehension (35 minutes)

Section A

注意:此部分试题请在**答题卡 2**上作答。

11. A) Her salary will be raised.
    C) She will become a manager.
    B) She will look after all his money.
    D) She will have as much money as the man.
12. A) A manager.   B) A retiree.   C) A dentist.   D) A shop assistant.
13. A) He said that he didn't have any extra pencil.
    C) He was afraid of losing his pen.
    B) He offered her a pencil.
    D) He lent her some ink.
14. A) Whether the man really saw Paul.
    C) How Paul has been doing lately.
    B) What news Paul got in New York.
    D) How the man knows Paul.
15. A) At the airport.   B) At the library.   C) In a restaurant.   D) In an office.
16. A) They will return before Bill.
    B) The woman wants to wait for Bill.
    C) Bill will be back in just a second.
    D) Writing a message for Bill will take too much time.
17. A) Interesting.   B) Better.   C) Disappointing.   D) Exciting.
18. A) She is traveling at the moment.
    C) She is mainly a story-writer.
    B) She is a novelist.
    D) She is a travel agent.

Questions 19 to 22 are based on the conversation you have just heard.

19. A) The East Police Station.
    C) The subway station.
    B) His friend's home in the suburbs.
    D) The downtown area of New York.
20. A) He left his car about.
    C) He didn't use the crosswalk.
    B) He occupied a parking lot for a long time.
    D) He didn't comply with the traffic rules.
21. A) It's awfully tight.
    C) It eats much into his living cost.
    B) Sounds quite wise.
    D) It is sensible and acceptable.
22. A) He will refuse to pay the fine.
    C) He will cut down on spending.
    B) He won't drive any more.
    D) He will plead police for mercy.

Questions 23 to 25 are based on the conversation you have just heard.

23. A) He is going to pay the speakers a visit.
    B) He will move to Pennsylvania next month.
    C) He has been an executive for a long time.
    D) He wants to invite some of his former schoolmates to a party.
24. A) He always keeps in contact with all friends.
    B) He is one of the woman's old friends.
    C) He appreciates receiving a letter from the man.
    D) He and his eldest son will be schoolmates.
25. A) Confused.   B) Indifferent.   C) Admiring.   D) Lucky.

Section B

注意:此部分试题请在**答题卡 2**上作答。

Passage One

Questions 26 to 28 are based on the passage you have just heard.

26. A) Computer.　　　　B) French.　　　　C) English.　　　　D) Reading and Writing.
27. A) Four years old.　　B) One year old.　　C) Two years old.　　D) 18 months old.
28. A) Nicholas has a gift for language.

　　B) The teachers in the school prepared special lessons for him.

　　C) Nicholas' parents asked West London Institute for help.

　　D) Nicholas is happy in ordinary schools.

Passage Two

Questions 29 to 31 are based on the passage you have just heard.

29. A) 9 million.　　　　B) 8 million.　　　　C) 60 million.　　　　D) 10 million.
30. A) March.　　　　　B) June.　　　　　　C) August.　　　　　D) December.
31. A) They like smiling.　　　　　　　　　B) They are relaxed.

　　C) Their life is full of danger.　　　　　D) They are very hospitable.

Passage Three

Questions 32 to 35 are based on the passage you have just heard.

32. A) Eight hours.　　　B) Three shifts.　　　C) Twenty-four hours.　　D) Four hours.
33. A) Stop the other traffic on the left lane.　　B) Go into the fast lane on the right.

　　C) Go into the motorway.　　　　　　　　D) Head for the pavement.

34. A) Mark Hill is the busiest police officer in London.

　　B) Mark Hill enjoys his job because it is full of variety.

　　C) Many accidents happen because people don't follow each other.

　　D) Small motorbikes can sometimes share the motorway.

35. A) The traffic rules in Britain.

　　B) The working conditions of the traffic police officers in Britain.

　　C) Mark's work as a traffic police officer.

　　D) Why did the traffic accidents happen?

Section C

注意:此部分试题在**答题卡 2**上;请在**答题卡 2**上作答。

Part IV Reading Comprehension (Reading in Depth) (25 minutes)

Section A

　　It's an age-old dispute: Men are from Mars. Women are from Venus. Males and females show ___47___ behaviors almost from birth. Researchers say these behaviors are due to basic differences in brain ___48___ and activity. Studies show men are better at ___49___ targets and solving math problems while women are better at memorizing words and recognizing faces. Why the difference?

　　A test of the brain's electrical activity shows that women ___50___ use both sides of their brain while men rely more on one. Scientists already know that the two sides of the brain control different functions—one controlling the sense of space, for example, the other controlling language. Some researchers believe that the different ways men and women use their brains ___51___ from ancient times, when cave men hunted and women cared for the children. Men had to have good ___52___. Women had to talk to the kids.

Whatever the explanation, the battle of the sexes __53__ . And although their brains are constructed slightly differently, men and women may be __54__ capable. They may simply rely on different abilities. Take a couple __55__ over the location of their car in a parking lot. The man might use his sense of space to find it, while the woman __56__ on her recognition of landmarks. They both find the car. But chances are, they'll still argue about who's the better driver and who's better at finding the way home.

A) continues	B) arguing	C) aim	D) gradual
E) presumably	F) inferior	G) relies	H) mission
I) commonly	J) hitting	K) ventured	L) different
M) equally	N) structure	O) evolved	

Section B
Passage One

E-business requires instant decision-making and KM (knowledge management) has a tremendous role to play in achieving this as well as quality feedback. Real-time business without proper knowledge and feedback information quickly turns into real-time unsupervised and valueless chaos. Lack of adequate knowledge flow and *coherent* (连贯的) real-time views of a situation inevitably lead to disastrous consequences. The infamous Barings Bank operated a real-time futures business without real-time checks and balances, and did not ensure adequate quality of knowledge flows from the trading floor to controllers and managers. It was too-much-too-fast coupled with too-little-quality-feedback and insufficient understanding. There was too little real-time knowledge at hand and it turned out a spectacular disaster.

The missing link was KM. No serious e-business effort should be undertaken without considering planning and implementing a strong KM *infrastructure* (基础结构). Real-time knowledge must flow from those who have it to those who must be able to make the right move at the right time. And there is no time to spare. E-businesses must be equipped with interactive workflow tools and real-time business intelligence feedback in a clear and understandable format. People involved must have access to all underlying documents at all times at a snap of their fingers. Otherwise they will guess rather than make informed decisions. Or worse, in fear of making a huge mistake, people will make no decisions at all.

Take a home loan application process for example. You would most likely apply to a number of banks at the same time. They would obviously compete on pricing, but the bank that can make your credit assessment first and most effectively, process the documentation and inform you on the progress every step of the way will get your business. The rest may be stuck with less demanding, more risk-prone customers. This may affect their overall profitability, and ability to compete on price and service in the future. It could put them out of business altogether. So is there a link between e-business and KM? I surely think so.

57. By saying the first sentence, the author means that _____ .
    A) knowledge management is important for making quick decisions
    B) knowledge management is an essential element for e-business and quality feedback
    C) quality feedback cannot be achieved without knowledge management
    D) quality feedback can influence quick decision-making and knowledge management

58. One can succeed in e-business if he gets _____ .
    A) support from the government and sufficient knowledge flow
    B) sufficient knowledge flow and accurate views of the situation
    C) qualified managers and accurate views of the situation
    D) loan from the bank and support from the government

59. Which of the following is NOT the factor that makes the Barings Bank fail?
    A) Lack of knowledge flow.   B) Insufficient quality feedback.
    C) Too little understanding.   D) Incapable controllers and managers.

60. Some managers do not make decisions because _____ .
    A) they are not provided with sufficient information

B) they do not want to shoulder the responsibilities

C) they want to discuss with other colleagues first

D) they only have limited rights in their company

61. When you apply for a home loan, you tend to choose a bank which _____.

    A) offers the lowest interest

    B) gives you a first-rate credit assessment

    C) will keep you informed of the on-goings in the process

    D) is big and famous

Passage Two

    Man is endlessly inventive. But his greatest invention is noninvention, the skill of transmitting unchanged from one generation to the next the fundamental ways of doing things which he learned from the generation which came before him. Children are born and reared, houses built, fish caught, and enemies killed in much the same way by most of the members of any society; and these patterns are maintained for relatively long periods of time. From the perspective of those in each generation, and for the society as an enduring, historical *entity* (统一体), this process of cultural transmission yields enormous economy. Thanks to it, each generation need not rediscover at great cost in time and subject to great risk of failure, what those coming before have already learned. Not only is knowledge thus maintained, but the basis for community life, resting on common information and understanding is thus established. Since all those in each generation receive more or less the same cultural heritage from the preceding generation, they can more easily relate to one another and more effectively coordinate their actions.

    The grand total of all the objects, ideas, knowledge, ways of doing things, habits, values, and attitudes which each generation in a society passes on to the next is what the *anthropologist* (人类学家) often refers to as the culture of a group. The transmission of culture is man's substitute for the instincts whereby most other living creatures are equipped with the means for coping with their environment and relating to one another. Yet it is more flexible than instinct, and can grow; that is, it can store new information, infinitely more rapidly than the process of *mutation* (基因突变) and biological evolution can enrich the instinctual storehouse of any other species.

62. What does the passage mainly discuss?

    A) The relation between culture and invention.

    B) The transmission of human culture.

    C) The history of human civilization.

    D) The biological evolution of man.

63. The author points out that the process of cultural transmission _____.

    A) does not help each generation rediscover the ways of doing things

    B) brings great wealth and prosperity to each generation in the society

    C) is not as effective as inventions in promoting social development

    D) enables each generation to learn the previous skills with less time

64. The word "heritage" as used in Para. 1 is closest in meaning to _____.

    A) history   B) civilization   C) tradition   D) feature

65. It is indicated in the first paragraph that the maintenance of knowledge is possible due to _____.

    A) the great inventions

    B) the enormous economy

    C) the process of cultural transmission

    D) the common information and understanding

66. It can be inferred from the second paragraph that cultural transmission and the instincts of other living creatures are similar in _____.

    A) their functions

    B) the speed of their development

C) their ability to store information

D) the ways of passing down from one generation to another

Part V Cloze (15 minutes)

注意:此部分试题请在**答题卡 2**上作答。

These days, as leaders of all nations come together more and more to strengthen ties or resolve differences, international spokesmen rely heavily on a select band of expert linguists to   67   —often by *simultaneous translation* (同声传译)—both   68   meanings and the diplomatic *nuances* (细微差别) which can mean even more.

The   69   is terrific. One diplomatic interpreter offered a *wry* (沮丧的) description of himself   70   a man with a ruined liver and worse nerves who turns   71   in press photos between two world leaders lacking a common language. "I am the one   72   to as unidentified," he says ruefully.

Colleagues find the   73   not wholly inaccurate. Like electricity, a good interpreter is never noticed   74   something goes wrong. The *glass booth* (玻璃房)   75   which the conference interpreter usually   76   can be a private chamber of horrors that on   77   given day might feature an English delegate   78   an impenetrable Yorkshire accent; an *erudite* (博学的) Frenchman with a *penchant* (喜爱) for puns and metaphors that   79   translation; an American who will fish a piece of paper   80   his pocket, rattle off a *litany* (枯燥冗长的) of facts and figures at breakneck speed and sit down,   81   the interpreter gasping.

As   82   as being brutally demanding, diplomatic interpreting is probably the most exclusive   83   in the world. Between 50 and 100 newcomers can be absorbed each year,   84   about 20,000 rigorously screened hopefuls are at this moment enrolled in the two dozen or so recognized interpreters' schools in Europe and America.   85   these, only four—at Geneva, Heidelberg and two in Paris—are   86   by the International Association of Conference.

67. A) transfer   B) transform   C) transmit   D) transplant
68. A) wordy   B) apparent   C) superficial   D) literal
69. A) pressure   B) depression   C) press   D) recession
70. A) like   B) likewise   C) as   D) of
71. A) out   B) to   C) into   D) up
72. A) mentioned   B) referred   C) spoken   D) regarded
73. A) illustration   B) caption   C) explanation   D) image
74. A) when   B) if   C) for   D) unless
75. A) on   B) around   C) at   D) in
76. A) works   B) lives   C) inhabits   D) visits
77. A) some   B) many   C) any   D) all
78. A) by   B) with   C) in   D) on
79. A) deny   B) decline   C) resist   D) refuse
80. A) in   B) from   C) for   D) with
81. A) making   B) letting   C) leaving   D) getting
82. A) well   B) far   C) soon   D) long
83. A) business   B) expertise   C) trade   D) profession
84. A) thus   B) and   C) or   D) yet
85. A) Of   B) About   C) Among   D) In
86. A) distinguished   B) appreciated   C) identified   D) recognized

Part VI Translation (5 minutes)

注意:此部分试题在**答题卡 2**上;请在**答题卡 2**上作答。

Model Test 4

Part I　Writing

写作指南:

这是典型的四级书信型习作。要求考生先简要说明"我"是如何获悉这一不幸消息的,并描述得知这一消息时的感受。然后尽力安慰对方,并问候对方家人。

根据题目要求,文章结构如下:

第一段:明确写信的目的是表示慰问。

第二段:简要陈述自己得知这一不幸消息时的心情。

第三段:表达自己要提供帮助的强烈愿望。

第四段:简要作结,并向对方家人问好。

范文与解析:

Sample	Analysis
Dear Li Ming,　　【1】In today's newspaper, **I read about** the recent events in your hometown and 【2】**I am writing to** extend my deepest concerns.　　【3】**It hurt to see** all the pictures of destroyed homes and homeless people in the tragic flood. 【4】**I couldn't help shedding tears** when I saw a little girl crying on the roof of her house and asking for help. 【5】**I am especially worried about** you, your family, and all your friends there. 【6】I am **crossing my fingers for** you now in a hope that you are all **safe and sound**.　　【7】I can only imagine how difficult this must be for you,　and　【8】I want to extend to you my **sincere support**. 【9】Our government and many nongovernmental organizations are **initiating various campaigns to** urge people to have donate money and necessary materials to your hometown. 【10】I donated **all** my allowance that I have been saving **for years**.　　【11】**I feel extremely sorry about** this tragedy,　and	【1】简要点出了消息的来源。【2】开门见山说明的写信的目的。【3】**It hurt to see** 形象地描绘了当时的心情。【4】**couldn't help shedding tears** 意为"潸然泪下"。【5】**I am especially worried about** 再一次突出了个人的关心和担忧之情。【6】**cross one's fingers** 代替了 **pray**,让文章更加生动;**safe and sound** 为押头韵,琅琅上口。【7】【8】明确"我"个人"坚定不移的支持"。【9】政府和非政府机构的各种救援活动也会积极提供帮助。【10】**all** 和 **for years** 明确了"我"对收信人的全力支持。

[12]I am looking forward to hearing from you. [13]Please pass my concern on to your parents. Yours sincerely, Frank	[12]用 **look forward to doing sth.** 表达自己的希望，这也是书信结尾常用的表达。 [13]**pass one's concern on to sb.** 也是书信写作中结尾处常用的语句，表达了"我"对收信人家人的关心和问候。

句型变换：

[1]

1. In today's newspaper, I read about the recent events in your hometown...
2. I learned from today's newspaper the recent events in your hometown...
3. I read from today's newspaper about what has happened in your hometown recently...
4. In today's newspaper, I got to know what has happened in your hometown in these days...

[2]

1. I am writing to extend my deepest concerns...
2. I am writing to express my deepest sympathy...
3. I am writing this letter to show my sincerest concerns...
4. I am writing to pass on my concerns...

[5]

1. I am especially worried about...
2. I am deeply concerned about...
3. My concern goes to...
4. I have been concerned about...

[8]

1. I want to extend to you my sincere support.
2. I would like to extend my sincere support to you.

3. I want to let you know that I will be always by your side.
4. I would always stand by and back you up.

[9]

1. Our government and... are initiating various campaigns to...
2. Our government and... have launch a drive to...
3. Various campaigns are taken by our government and... to...
4. A variety of campaigns are sponsored by our government and... to...

[11]

1. I feel extremely sorry about this tragedy.
2. I feel heartily sorry about this tragedy.
3. I am terribly sorry about know this tragedy.
4. I am awfully sorry about this tragedy.

[13]

1. Please pass my concern on to your parents.
2. Please give my best regards to your parents.
3. Convey my deepest concern to your parents please.
4. Please bring your parents my sincerest regards.

Part II Reading Comprehension (Skimming and Scanning)

参考译文划线点评

美国的电影业

"通过电影,美国实现了对世界的'文化殖民'。"

——[法]列奥·罗斯登

美国与欧洲之争

像其他娱乐产业一样,美国电影产业与政府合作,不仅产生利润,还在文化对世界其他地方实现了殖民。[2]根据2003年4月28日泰勒·科恩在福布斯网站上的说法,"在20世纪60年代中期,美国电影占有了欧洲大陆市场35%的票房收入,而今天这个数字是介于80%至90%之间"。

科恩总结说,"好莱坞电影技术先进(比如采用了特技),而且含得花重金在大众传媒上宣传和做广告。而典型的欧洲电影,其观众只有典型的好莱坞电影的1%,而且这个差距还在扩大。美国电影在国际市场上越来越受欢迎,而欧洲电影则日受冷落"。

欧洲电影节奏较慢,对于非常活跃的美国观众来说,就像是塞满观点、哲学评论和各种不同关系的厚书一样令人无法忍受。并且,就像科恩指出的那样:"美国和欧洲对于电影人才的培训就反映了这些差异。在许多方面,美国的电影学院就像是商学院。"

将美国最好的电影学校(如加利福尼亚大学洛杉矶分校、纽约大学和南加州大学)与20世纪50年代曾培养出罗曼·波兰斯基和安德烈·瓦依达那样的导演的克拉科夫大学的电影课程加以比较。[3]波兰的课程注重文学修养和人文科学,而不是为行业职位进行培训。在五年学制中,只在最后一年才开设一些关于舞台灯光、摄像机操作和声学方面的实践课程。而美国的电影学校从一开始就是"训练"而不是"教育"。它们承诺,它们的学生一毕业就能成为助理编辑或者助理制作人——弗莱得·埃伦称之为"能与制作人合作的唯一人员"。

从艺术到商业

到20世纪初,商业法则就浸润美国电影业。企业家想出种种办法把一种新的"艺术形式"转化为商品,它能吸引广大受教育不多的观众,他们很可能为了观看更精彩的电影而在下一周再度光顾。经过几十年时间,技术的完善取代了艺术创作成为创新的动力。[8]事实上,这个行业响遍全世界的声誉就建立在好莱坞工匠们模仿现实的能力之上。它向所有外国竞争对手和独立制片人挑战,自认无人匹敌。好莱坞把诸如动画技术与特技效果是否完善提升为基本原则,成为大众传媒评论家们对电影给出第一印象时的基础。所有没达到其技术上的完美标准的电影无异于提供了一辆漆面上有刮痕的新车。追溯电影业的发展史,从无声的种族主义史诗《一个国家的诞生》到21世纪的音乐剧《红磨坊》或《芝加哥》,技术作为一种艺术赢得了观众。

除了审美标准外,每一部好莱坞电影最重要的是要有一个商业计划。要使一部电影构思得到通过,电影公司的高层会做一个赢利的蓝图,他们会要求作者:"给我们一些能吸引观众来剧院并使他们愿意再次光顾的剧本。"[4]这个成功方程式使好莱坞自身和在糖果、爆米花与软饮料业方面的赢利一起成为一种独特的文化,并从中催生出无数其他的行业。自然地,在电影业出现的前60年时间里,影片公司同样拥有自己的电影院。

[5]好莱坞的电影工作室通过提供欧文·肖所称的包括明星培养系统的"可见的美国梦"来增加观众。在无声的屏幕中那些娇弱迷人的女郎和辉煌的英雄背后,坐着操纵"才干之士"的身家数百万美元的电影公司的老板们。

技术

[9]在21世纪来临之际,技术挽救了一度受到挑战的电影制片人,使他们无需贵地寻觅拍摄场地,无需考虑怎样通过镜头与剪辑而使场景真实可信。如今,软件与数码技术"制作出"大峡谷或大丛林的场景。技术已经增强了这个行业商业化设计和制造电影魔术的可能性。然而,它并没有提高构思的质量。实际上,很少人会期望得到这种"高品质"的构思。

买了电影票就意味着人们相信票房,票价物有所值。灯光暗去,美丽非凡的人物登场了;无论是在急速的追逐中还是从不可思议的高空中坠落,他们都是不会丧生的。

成功背后的真相

在光芒的背后,电影产业为了两个原因而生产:利润和再生产。[10]电影产业和汽车工业很相像:其产品外表上看起来硕大而耀眼,但不要看车篷下面,不要看剪辑室的地板上有些什么。

[10]这两种产业都是依靠美女和引人入胜的风景来销售产品的。你应该看到过那种商业广告,说拥有一辆新的运动型多功能车就可以给你带来权力、性感、声望和地位。

商业世界吸引公众进入一个虚拟的环境——剧院里,灯光打在银幕上,那里有一张脸(在化妆间几小时的化妆和接受美容专家数年的保养之后),让你爱上它,与它共鸣,为它担心。美国默片时代的女影星莉莲·吉什称好莱坞为"情绪化的底特律"。那完美的容貌下面通常掩盖着艺术才能的空虚。

好莱坞在市场上的成功始于如下假定:年轻和营养不良是放之四海而皆准的审美标准。我那十几岁的孩子把这些原则当真,并且因此拒绝陪伴我们去看电影。她不想和我们一起出现在公众面前。

我问我的女儿:"为什么关于电影明星或者流行歌手的谈话节目使你如此兴奋?"

"它们真实!"她回答说。

既然我已经年纪太大,无法什么事情都去弄明白,我想我应该回忆一下40年代的情形,那时,十几岁的少男少女为"瘦皮猴"法兰克·辛纳屈(爵士乐演唱家)而疯狂,后来,这位精瘦的歌手就成了全国的偶像——成了这个造星体制的又一件产品。

浪漫的爱情故事一方面非常有利可图,另一方面又有很大的影响力,几乎可以凭借它推销一切。这些电影真的会激发人们去模仿那些虚构的人物角色。

好莱坞是世界范围的产业,其产品包含有"美国价值",包括约翰·韦恩所谓的服从爱国命令的刚毅或勇敢观念,也包括"衣服数量怎么都不够"的观念——就如瑞茜·威瑟斯彭在《律政俏佳人》中所扮演的角色那样服饰可以不断翻新,无穷无尽。

[6]在运用高超的摄影术、特技、布景设计、服装、化妆、配合情绪的音乐和各种不同的拍摄技巧所装饰的单薄的故事情节和故事线索中,人们找到了一个用来让我们所有人愉悦——至少给普通人带来娱乐的世界。

[7]好莱坞的销售经理教导他的团队去"接受这个没有价值的垃圾并且把它当作前所未有的最好的艺术和娱乐卖给全世界"。上帝保佑美国,特别是好莱坞所创造的那个美国吧。

1. 【答案】Y
【题眼】The passage is mainly about how the American film industry achieved cultural colonization of the world.
【定位】文章首段及各个小标题。

【解析】文章在首段首先指出了美国通过电影业实现了对世界的文化殖民,下面的四个小标题部分详细分析了美国成功实行文化殖民的方法,因此本题答案为Y。

2. 【答案】N
【题眼】American films have been dominating the film markets in Continental Europe since the 1960s.
【定位】第1个小标题 US vs. Europe 部分的首段第2句。

【解析】原文指出在20世纪60年代中期,美国电影在欧洲大陆市场占有了35%的票房收入,35%这一数字显然不足以让美国统治欧洲大陆的电影市场,因此本题答案为N。

3. 【答案】NG
【题眼】American film schools usually provide a five-year training program for people who want to become a film director.
【定位】第1个小标题 US vs. Europe 部分的最后一段。

【解析】原文只说明了波兰电影学校导演专业的学制是5年,并没有提到美国电影学校的学制如何,因此本题答案为NG。

4. 【答案】N
【题眼】Candy, popcorn and soft drink businesses were three of the success formula for the Hollywood films
【定位】第2个小标题 From Art to Business 部分的第2段第3句。

【解析】原文该句中的 This success formula 是指上一句提到的内容"使观众愿意再次光顾",而不是指本句中的 candy, popcorn 和 soft drink,因此本题答案为N。

5. 【答案】Y
【题眼】Hollywood attracts audience by offering them a chance to realize their dream of becoming a star.
【定位】第2个小标题 From Art to Business 部分的最后一段首句。

【解析】原文中的 the American dream made visible 和 cultivating the star system 都暗示观众有机会实现自己的明星梦,题目表达了这个意思,因此本题答案为Y。

6. 【答案】N
【题眼】A film without rich plot and story lines, even produced by high technological means, cannot delight the audience.
【定位】最后一个小标题 Truth behind Success 部分的倒数第2段。

【解析】原文该段提到了很多故事情节和线索以外的电影拍摄技巧,表明即使电影的故事情节和线索不够丰富,只要利用了各种高超的电影制作技巧,观众就会喜欢。题目所述与此相反,因此本题答案为N。

7. 【答案】N
【题眼】Hollywood only markets films of greatest art and entertainment which are appealing to the audience.
【定位】最后一个小标题 Truth behind Success 部分的最后一段。

【解析】原文指出美国并非只把最好的艺术和娱乐卖出去,而是把最差的电影包装成最好的艺术和娱乐,因此题目所述不正确,本题答案为N。

8. 【答案】imitating reality
【题眼】The Hollywood film industry gets famous throughout the world because its craftsmen are capable of _____.
【定位】第2个小标题 From Art to Business 部分的首段第4句。

【解析】空白处应为名词词组。题目中的 capable of... 与原文的 ability to... 意思相同,因此答案就在 ability to 后面,但是,to 后跟的是动词原形,而 of 后面应为名词,因此要把 imitate 改为 imitating 才正确。

9. 【答案】the camera and editing process

【题眼】Before the 21st century, filmmakers had to try hard to make shooting locations believable by means of _____.

【定位】第 3 个小标题 **Technology** 部分的首段首句。

【解析】空白处应为名词词组。在原文的 render them credible 中,them 是指该句前面提到的 locations,题目中的 make shooting locations believable 与 render them credible 同义,原句中引出方式的 through 在题目中同义替换成了 by means of,因此,through 后面的名词词组就是答案。

10. 【答案】beauty and spectacular landscape

【题眼】Both film industry and car industry sell their products by _____.

【定位】最后一个小标题 **Truth behind Success** 部分的首段及第 2 段首句。

【解析】空白处应同为名词词组。原文首段对比了电影产业与汽车工业,第 2 段首句中的 Both industries 就是指上一段提到的两种工业,题目是对该句的近义改写,答案可以在 rely on 后面找到,表明这两种产业销售产品的方式。

Part III Listening Comprehension

Section A

11. W: If you are promoted to manager, will you give us a raise?

M: No problem. What else would I do with all the money that will come pouring in?

Q: What will happen to the woman if the man is promoted?

[A]【解析】give sb. a raise 表示给某人加薪,男士用 no problem 给出了肯定的答复之后,又用一个反问句加强语气,所以选 A。

[点睛]B、C、D 都是利用原文中出现的个别单词进行干扰。

12. W: Are you pleased that your son wants to be a dentist?

M: Not really. I'd rather he managed my store when I retire.

Q: What does the man want his son to become?

[A]【解析】男士在否定了女士的问话后说:"我宁愿他在我退休后管理我的店。"由此可见,男士宁愿他儿子当 manager,所以选 A。

[点睛]①I'd rather 表示愿望,与问题中的 want 相当,因此其后面的内容 manage my store 是考点。②S2 否定回答 S1 的一般疑问问,可直接排除 C。③S2 说"I retire",不是指他儿子,排除 B。④D 为强干扰项。要听清 S2 说的 manage 才能排除。

13. W: Could I please borrow a pen from you? Mine is out of ink.

M: I'm afraid I don't have an extra one. Would a pencil do?

Q: How did the man respond to the woman's request?

[B]【解析】男士说,恐怕我没有多余的钢笔,铅笔行吗? 所以选 B。

[点睛]本题中,pen, ink 和 pencil 容易混淆。听清 S2 最后的一般疑问句即可得出答案。

14. M: We just saw Paul when we were in New York.

W: Really? What is new with him?

Q: What does the woman want to know?

[C]【解析】What's new with sb. 表示询问最近情况如何,所以选 C。

[点睛]①时间关系题。S1 的 just, S2 的 new 都有"刚刚"、"近来"之义,与 C 中的 lately 一致。②S2 的 really 表示强

烈语气,一般情况下,可能表示对 S1 的话持怀疑态度。但此时,really 一般不作选项的内容。根据"听到什么就不选什么"原则,排除 A。③B 是 new 与 news 的音近干扰项。④D 于原文无据。

15. M: It seems to me I've seen the dark-haired man before.

W: Sure you have. Last time when we were here, he <u>checked our luggage</u> very carefully.

Q: Where does the conversation most probably take place?

[A]【解析】关键词 check luggage 检查行李,所以对话最可能在机场发生。

【点睛】场景(地点)题。回答步骤见本书 Test 3 听力第 12 题解说。

16. W: Just a second. I want to <u>leave a message for Bill</u>.

M: <u>Don't bother</u>. We'll be back in less than an hour.

Q: What can be concluded from the conversation?

[A]【解析】男士说:Don't bother(不用麻烦了),因为我们一小时以后就会回来。言下之意,他们会在 Bill 之前回来。

【点睛】对话中未提到 wait for Bill,故 B 项错误。男士说他们会在一个时内回来,而不是说 Bill 一会就回来,C 项不对。女士有提及 leave a message,但没有说这会 take too much time,故 D 项也不对。

17. M: How did you like the movie last night?

W: Considering its interesting name, <u>we were expecting a much better film</u>.

Q: What is the woman's opinion of the film?

[C]【解析】女士说,电影的名字那么吸引人,我们原来期望会看到一部好得多的电影。言下之意,电影很差,很让人失望。

【点睛】①问及 opinion 时,若有二个选项是正面态度,一个是负面态度,或者相反,则"与众不同的选项是答案"。参见本书 Test 3 第 13 题。②S2 用 we were expecting a better film 表达一种失望之意,很值得学习、体会。

18. M: Very pleased to meet you. And what kind of things do you write?

W: Well, <u>short stories mainly</u>. Actually, at the moment I'm writing a travel book.

Q: What do we know about the woman?

[C]【解析】男士问女士写些什么,可见女士是一个作家;而女士回答"主要写短故事",可见她是个 story-writer。

【点睛】女士的回答"... short stories mainly"与选项 C 同义。B 是"(长篇)小说家",不正确。A、D 均同 travel 构成干扰项。本题也可归于"可以根据 S2 的简短回答部分解题"的类型。

Now you'll hear two long conversations.

Conversation One

M: Oh, Lucy, I've had such a terrible day.

W: You look exhausted. What on earth have you been doing?

M: Oh, I've been such a fool! You just wouldn't believe what I've done.

W: I would. Come on. [19] <u>Where have you been?</u>

M: I'm dying to tell someone. [19] <u>I planned to go down to New York to visit my friends.</u> You see, I thought I was sensible: <u>I drove down to the subway station on the outskirts of New York, and I parked my car by the station and took the train into the city center.</u>

W: Well, sounds quite wise.

M: So far, so good. I came back out of New York and went out of the subway.

W: And you forgot the car?

M: No, no. I didn't forget the car. I just got a surprise. I found a plastic envelope containing a printed form pushed under the windscreen wiper. I was fined!

W: It must be raining at that moment. The traffic warden uses the plastic envelope to protect it from being blown away [20] <u>This is a good way to discourage the drivers from occupying a parking lot. You know the car park in down-town is awfully tight.</u>

M: Yeah, maybe this is good. But how can the traffic wardens know? The meter will say that?

W: Well, actually, when the certain period of time you have paid for uses up, the meter registers "time expired". If the traffic wardens see this, he will tear one printed form from the book, write down all the details, such as your car number, the place you park the car, how much you should pay and to which police station to send the fine.

M: I must send the money to the East Police Station. [22] I have to tighten my belt this month. [21] I'd pay $200 for occupying a parking lot, which accounts for a considerable proportion of my living cost.

W: Come on, old friend. Don't be so angry. Be careful next time. I'm sure you will find this regulation sensible in the near future.

19. Where did the man plan to go?

[D]【解析】细节题。根据对话中男士的叙述,他说他打算到纽约去拜访朋友,而且后文提到 city center"市中心",即 D 项中的 downtown area,故答案为 D。他开车到纽约郊区的地铁站(朋友家并不在郊区,B 错误),然后转乘地铁去纽约市中心,C"地铁站"只是中转点而非目的地。A 是他去交罚金的地方。

【点睛】①表示地点的选项表明,本题会涉及场所。有可能是情景题,要求根据对话预测对话发生的地点;也有可能是细节题,要求明确对话中提到的场所。未听到问题前,无法明确判断,必须带着两种打算听录音。②对话中出现了 Where have you been? 男士的回答必然是听音的重点。③考虑到各选项均在对话中出现,因此要标记各项的相关信息,比如行程的先后次序等。

20. Why was the man fined by the traffic warden?

[B]【解析】细节、原因题。男士说:"I was fined!"用了强烈的语气,表示出意外、不解,女士随后给出解释,因而是听音的重点。女士说,罚款"是阻止司机占用车位的好办法",又说,市区车位很紧。因此选 B。

【点睛】四个选项均谈论"他"的违纪情况,由此可以缩小听音时的注意力范围。"parking lot"是本题答题关键。

21. How does the man find the amount of the fine?

[C]【解析】题目问男士对罚款数额的看法,原文说,这笔罚款占了他一大笔生活费。故选 C。eat into"腐蚀,花费掉"。

【点睛】①读选项,判断问题。A、C、D 主语是 It,B 是单数动词形式开头,主语也应该是 it。A、B、D 都是系表结构,对 it 加以描述;C 不是系表结构,但也表示 it 的某种性状,故可推断,本题问"it 怎么样?"。②因为不知道 it 究竟指代什么(要听到问题后才清楚),故对话中的有关描述均需标示。A 项为 car park,B 为 trip plan,C 指 fine(通过关键词 living cost 推知),D 指 regulation。③若听音时进一步注意可知,A、B、D 均是女士的话,只有 C 是男士说的。④由此,一听到问题,便可判断答案。

22. What will the man probably do?

[C]【解析】推断题。男士说他交完罚金后就要勒紧裤带过日子,由此可知两点:第一,他不会拒交罚款,故 A 错误;第二,缴完罚金后他将没多少钱,所以需要节衣缩食(cut down on spending),相当于对话中的 tighten one's belt,故 C 正确。B、D 两项对话中均未提及。

【点睛】①最后一道题,四个选项都用一般将来时将来的行动,属于是"尾巴题",需从对话最后处找答案。②听力材料一般不与文化内容相矛盾,由此可以排除 A、D。B 也太过绝对。结合 21 题和常识,可以选出答案。

Conversation Two

M: I just received a letter from Jack, one of my old buddies from college.

W: [25] That's nice! It's amazing that you're keeping in touch with each other for so many years after graduating from college.

M: Yes, we are always in contact with each other. But I haven't seen him for ages.

W: What did Jack say in his letter?

M: He said that they moved to Pennsylvania last month. Jack got a promotion recently. Now, he is a sales director.

W: He is always lucky.

M: Yes, he is, but he is always diligent in his work too. What's more, [24] his eldest son is going to the University of Pennsylvania.

W: Ah! [24] It's the university you graduated from, isn't it?

M: Absolutely right. I thought of my college life when I learned that his son would study in the University of Pennsylvania. Well, [23] in his letter he is inviting us to have a get-together with some of our old friends from college.

W: Really? That's good news. To be frank, I've been out of touch with most of my old friends. Only one or two keep me informed about what they are doing.

M: I know. It's really hard to maintain contact when they move around so much.

W: That's right. [25] But you're lucky to be in touch with your buddies for so many years.

23. Which is true about Jack according to his letter?

[D]【解析】细节题。D 中的 party 对应对话中的 get-together，而 former schoolmates 对应对话中的 old friends from college，故答案为 D。A 项未提及；Jack 上个月已经搬到 Pennsylvania 了，而不是 next month，故 B 错；C 错在 long，对话中是 recently。

【点睛】各选项均用 he 作主语，he 的身份构成听音过程的一个小难题：指参与对话的男士还是对话中的人物？这往往会干扰正常的听音过程。由对话一开始引入的 Jack，可以解决此疑点，因而准确推断出问题；在听的过程中，就可以专注于 Jack 的行为，从而方便答题。

24. What can be inferred about Jack from the conversation?

[D]【解析】推断题。Jack 的儿子即将去 the University of Pennsylvania 读书，通过说话人的一问一答，我们知道那所大学正是男士毕业的学校，而男士和 Jack 是大学同学，所以，Jack 父子也将是校友。因此 D 正确。

【点睛】①同上题可知，读选项就应明白，此题问的是对话中提到的 Jack，因而在听的时候就可以划清某些行为的归属，便于解题。②对话提到，男士(而不是 Jack)与很多朋友保持联系，并且也不是 all，而是 most，

故 A 错误；Jack 与男士是校友，但对话中并未提及 Jack 与女士的关系，故 B 也错误；C 与对话内容相悖，是男士收到 Jack 的信，而不是 Jack 收到男士的信。

25. How does the woman feel about the man's relationship with his buddies?

[C]【解析】推断题。对话初始，女士对男士毕业后那么多年还一直同朋友保持联系感到惊奇；对话尾声，女士说自己同很多老朋友都失去了联系，觉得男士能够同老朋友一直有联系，真是幸运。当听到这里时，不难推断出答案是 C，而 A"困惑的"和 B"冷漠的"显然不对。D"幸运的"是女士对男士与朋友能够保持联系的评价之一，但并不是她自己感到幸运，而是感到羡慕，因此也不对。

【点睛】①由读题可知，本题将问到某人(男士、女士或对话中提到的 he)的情感、态度。虽然在听到问题前我们不知道究竟会问到谁，但在听音的过程中就应对相关的词汇予以重视，并注意与相关的人物对应起来。本对话中，主要是女士的情感态度得到表现，因而不难作答。②对话从头至尾，女士都很羡慕男士，对话中出现的 nice, amazed, lucky 等词都是用来表现女士的羡慕之情。

Section B

Passage One

Nicholas MacMahon is a four-year-old child. [26] He is studying at college because he is too intelligent for school. Nicholas has computer lessons at the West London Institute. He spoke well before he was one year old. [27] At eighteen months he took telephone messages for his parents. At the age of two he began to learn French. The strange thing about [28] Nicholas is that he taught himself to read before he could speak. His father said, "We knew immediately that he could read. When he could speak, he corrected my spelling." When Nicholas went to school, [28] his teachers just gave him pictures to color and toys to play with and didn't have time to prepare special lessons for him. Nicholas tried two different schools, but he was bored and unhappy. Then his parents decided that [28] he couldn't stay at an ordinary school. But they had no idea what to do with him. Then [28] the West London Institute offered to help. Nicholas spends some of his time there, and also studies at home. Now he reads newspapers every day, and he can play the violin well. His father said, "Nicholas is our life. He is a clever child and we want to help him in every way."

26. What is Nicholas studying at college?

[A]【解析】原文开头提到 Nicholas 在西伦敦教学院上电脑课。因此 A 正确。

【点睛】四个选项都是学科名词，容易预知问题。听到什么选什么。

27. When did Nicholas learn to take telephone messages

for his parents?

[D]【解析】原文提到 18 个月时他帮父母接电话和做记录。因此 D 正确。

【点睛】四个选项表示年龄。多个选项在原文中都被提到，因此在听的过程中要记录不同年龄时的相应事件。为答题作准备。

28. Which of the following is true about Nicholas?

[A]【解析】文章提到,Nicholas 1 岁前就会说话,18 个月会帮父母接电话,2 岁开始学法语,还自己教自己认字,由此可见,他是一个很有语言天赋的孩子。

【点睛】①如果说四个选项有相关性的话,它们都涉及 Nicholas 的教育问题,因而有助于全篇短文的理解。②听音时,可围绕"Nicholas 的教育问题",一个个选项进行比对,随时排除与原文不符的选项。

Passage Two

[29] Last year 9 million tourists visited Thailand. From the capital city of Bangkok to the island beach resorts of Phuket, there is always lots to see and do.

Bangkok offers an amazing range of cultural experiences. Whether you are taking a taxi, visiting one of the many beautiful temples or eating out at a Thai restaurant, you will be glad that you come to Bangkok.

If you want to get away from city life, go to Phuket. Phuket offers a range of activities to suit everyone including diving, surfing and golf. If you do not want to be active, you can simply relax on one of the beautiful beaches.

The weather in Thailand is always hot and humid. [30] The best time of year to visit is during the cool season, which lasts from November to February. Whatever time of year you visit, you should take light summer clothes.

Thailand has a population of 60 million. [31] Thai people will always make you feel very much at home. No matter what you want to do, you can do it in Thailand, the Land of Smiles.

If you are looking for relaxation, culture or adventure, Thailand is the place for you.

29. How many tourists visited Thailand last year?

[A]【解析】根据开头第一句话。

【点睛】数字题。有可能几个选项所涉及的数字均有提及,要注意记录。好在短文中的数字题一般不作复杂的运算,应主要听清具体数字对应的内容。本题只有 A、C 在原文中有提及。而 C 是指泰国的人口数,非游客数量。

30. Which of the following month is the best time to visit Thailand?

[D]【解析】原文提到,参观泰国最好是凉快的时候去,从

11 月份到 2 月份。

【点睛】显然是时间题。文中"The best time..."应显得格外响亮,因为这种语义突出之处是出题的要点。

31. What is true about Thai people?

[D]【解析】D"好客的",是原文"泰国人会总是让你宾至如归"的同义表达。C 含贬义,与短文主旨大异其趣,首先排除。B 说的是读者(寻找休闲)。A 是对 Land of Smiles 的曲解。

【点睛】①由四个选项知,本题问"他们"怎么样。②最后两段开始讨论 population,应是解答本题的关键处。

Passage Three

[34] Mark Hill is a traffic police officer in Watford, near London. He works on some of the busiest motorways in Britain, the M1 and the M25.

[32] There are traffic police on duty twenty-four hours a day. There are three shifts, and each shift is eight hours. On average they have to deal with three to four accidents each shift. Here is Mark Hill talking about his job.

"We deal with anyone in the accident who is injured. That's the first thing. Then we have to clear the road and get the traffic moving again. Most accidents happen because people drive too fast—especially when the roads are wet. [34] Sometimes we get accidents that occur because drivers don't follow the rules. For example, I've seen a number of cases of drivers overtaking on the left. This is illegal in Britain. [33] If you want to overtake, you have to go into the fast lane on the right. [34] Not everyone can use a motorway in Britain. People that ride a bicycle or a small motorbike are not allowed to use it. I like my job. I have a varied working day—I never know what I'm going to do from one day to the next. And I meet all kinds of people. I don't think there's any other job that can give you that experience."

32. How long does Mark Hill have to work each day?

[A]【解析】根据原文交通警察需要 24 小时不断人,实行三班倒,每班工作 8 小时。

【点睛】数字题。需把与数字相关的信息记录下来。

33. If you want to overtake in Britain, what will you do?

[B]【解析】Mark 说如果要 overtake"超车"的话,就必须

开到右边的快车道去。

[点睛]动词原型选项,问"怎么做"。属于细节题,符合听到什么选什么原则。

34. Which of the following is true according to the passage?

[B]【解析】最后提到,Mark 很喜欢这份工作,因为每天的工作都不一样,还可以接触各种各样的人。所以选 B。

[点睛]①A、B 的主语是人名,而 C、D 则不是,因此本题可能并不具有确定的中心。这一般是细节题,须注意各选项的中心词。②其他信息点都有所提及,但是与原文信息不完全匹配。

35. What is the passage mainly about?

[C]【解析】本文主要谈的是 Mark 的工作内容,工作职责,所以选 C。

[点睛]①选项 A、B、C 均是名词词组,而 D 是个疑问句,它们均可充当主旨题的选项,因而可以判断本题的问题形式。②在此基础上,对四个选项进行排除。③主旨题要紧扣主旨,不拘泥细节。本题容易排除 A、D。属于"过分推断",也要排除。

Section C

36.【答案】refers

【解析】此处需要一个第三人称单数谓语动词;根据上下文可知,此处应填一个意为"指的是,表示的是"的词,refer to 正表示此义。refer 加 s 时,注意不要双写末尾的 r;其过去式和过去分词需要双写 r。

37.【答案】various

【解析】根据复数名词 ways 可预测此处所需的词表示"多种、多个",注意用形容词。

38.【答案】ruin

【解析】此处需要动词原形;通过此句的后半部分可知,此处应填语义上表示"破坏,毁坏"的词。

39.【答案】scattering

【解析】根据此空前面的介词 by 和之后的名词 junk,预测此处需要动名词;根据此处后面的信息预测,此处应填表示"乱扔,乱撒"之类意思的词。scattering 中的字母 c 发出的 / k / 音浊化为 / g /,既不能错写成 k,又不能错写成 g;另外,注意双写 t。

40.【答案】exhaust

【解析】根据此空后面的 and 可知,此处需要一个名词;根据此句的意思预测,机器和机动车辆应该是往空气中排出"废气"并发出噪音。exhaust 作名词时意为"(排出的)废气",h 不发音,注意不要漏写。

41.【答案】disturbing

【解析】and 连接两个并列短语,前面是形容词修饰名词的结构,因此此处需要一个形容词修饰 noise。disturbing 表示"烦扰的",注意 i 不要错写成 e,ur 不要写成 or 或 er。

42.【答案】serious

【解析】此处需要一个形容词修饰 problems;从语义上来看,环境污染应该是人类目前面临的最"严重"的问题之一。注意 serious 中的 e 和 iou 不要错写成其他元音字母或字母组合。

43.【答案】survival

【解析】the 和 of 之间必然是名词,从语义上此处应表示"生存,存活"意思的词。survival 表示"生存,幸存",动词 survive"幸免于,幸存,生还"和另外一个派生名词 survivor"幸存者"都是四级常用词汇。注意词尾变化。

44.【答案】Pollution of the soil reduces the amount of land on which we can grow food

【听音关键】pollution, soil, reduces, land, grow food

【答案重构】Soil pollution reduces the amount of land we can grow food on

[画龙点睛]此句虽不长,但是含有定语从句,为了简化句型,可以改写如上。

45.【答案】Everyone wants to reduce pollution, but the pollution problem is as complicated as it is serious

【听音关键】reduce pollution, complicated, serious

【答案重构】Everyone wants to reduce pollution, but this problem is both complicated and serious

[画龙点睛]注意转折和比较句型。其中,as... as...相当于 both... and... 之义。

46.【答案】For example, exhaust from automobiles causes a large percentage of all air pollution, but the automobile provides transportation for millions of people

【听音关键】automobile exhaust, large percentage, air pollution, automobile provides transportation

【答案重构】For example, automobile exhaust causes much air pollution, but the automobile provides millions of people with transportation

[画龙点睛]复杂的短语尽量在保持原意的基础上简化,如:将 a large percentage of 变成 much,可以大大减少书写时间和拼写错误。

Part IV   Reading Comprehension (Reading in Depth)

Section A

── **参考译文** ──

　　一个自古就存在的争论:男人来自火星,女人来自金星。男人和女人几乎从出生那一天起就有不同的行为。研究人员表示,这些行为是由大脑结构和大脑活动的基本差异所引起的。研究显示男人较善于射中标靶和解决数学问题,而女人则比较擅长记忆文字和辨识脸孔。为什么会有这种差异呢?

　　对大脑的电流活动(脑电图)的检验显示,女人通常是左右脑并用,而男人则比较倾向于使用一边的大脑。科学家已经知道左右两边的大脑分管不同的功能——例如一边掌管空间感,另一边掌管语言。一些研究人员相信,男女使用大脑方式的差异是从远古时代演化而来的,当时穴居的男人负责狩猎,女人则负责照顾小孩。所以男人必须擅长瞄准目标,女人则必须和小孩说话。

　　无论是何种解释,两性之间的战争仍在进行之中。而且虽然他们的大脑构造稍有不同,但男人和女人的能力可能是一样强的。他们只是依赖不同的能力而已。例如,一对夫妇在为他们的车子停在停车场的哪个位置而争吵时,这位男士可能会运用他的空间感来找车子,女士则可能会依靠辨认地标。两人都能找到车子,但很有可能,他们还是会争论谁的驾驶技术比较好、谁比较善于找到回家的路。

【词性分析】

名　词:aim 目标,目的,意图;瞄准　inferior 下级,下属　mission 使命,任务,天职;代表团,使团　structure 结构,构造;建筑物

动　词:continues 继续,延续,延伸[第三人称单数]　arguing 争论,争辩;主张;说服[现在分词]　aim 瞄准,对准;打算,企图;致力,旨在　relies 依靠,依赖;信赖[第三人称单数]　hitting 打,击,击中;碰撞;伤害,殃及[现在分词]　ventured 冒险,大胆行事;敢于,大胆表示[过去式或过去分词]　structure 构造,建造　evolved (使)演变,(使)进化,(使)发展[过去式或过去分词]

形容词:gradual 逐渐的,逐步的;不陡的　inferior 劣等的,次的;下级的　different 差异的,不同的;个别的,另外的;各种的

副　词:presumably 大概,可能,据推测　commonly 通常,一般地　equally 相等地,相同地;平均地;同样地

47. [L]此处应为形容词,修饰 behaviors。根据上下文说到的内容,以及 males, females, differences 等关键词,可以推断男人和女人有不同的行为,即 different 为本题答案。

48. [N]此处应为名词。本句解释为什么男人和女人有不同的行为,空白处的名词应与 activity 并列,可与 brain 构成特定搭配,在词库中只有 structure 一词合适。brain structure 意为"大脑结构"。

49. [J]此处应为及物动词的动名词形式,其宾语为 target。在词库中可与 target 搭配的动词只有 hitting,表明男人较善于射中目标。

50. [I]此处应为副词,作 use 的状语。本句要说明的是男人与女人在用脑方面的区别,而句子开头的 A test of... shows... 表明这是通过实验证明的,并不是推测的,因此 commonly 是最合适的单词,而 presumably 虽然语法上说得通,但语义不符合上下文的要求。

51. [O]此处应为动词,且为过去式。本句想要说明男女用脑方式的差异是从远古时发展而来的,因此空白处的动词应具有"发展"、"进化"之义,由此可推断 evolved 是最合适的词。

52. [C]此处应为名词。本句与上句提到的 men hunted 密切相关,因为男人负责狩猎,他们必须擅长瞄准目标,因此本题答案为 aim。

53. [A]此处应为不及物动词,且为第三人称单数。从本句的 Whatever 一词可以推断不论怎样,两性之间的战争仍然继续着,因此 continues 最合适。

54. [M]此处应为副词,修饰 capable。本句中的 although 表明主句的内容与从句相反,因此主句中的副词应与从句中的 differently 相反,再结合本句句意,equally 是最合适的单词。

55. [B]此处应为不及物动词,且为现在分词形式,可与 over 搭配。本句中的 take... 表明这是一个说明男女区别的例子,因此空白处的动词应表示"产生分歧""有不同意见"等意思,对照词库,只有 arguing 最合适。

56. [G]此处应为动词,且为第三人称单数形式,并可与 on 搭配。本句中的 while 一词表明前后两个分句意义相反但结构相似,前面的分句表明男人通常依靠空间感,而后面的分句应表明女人通常依靠辨认地标,在词库中表示"依靠"的单词只有 relies。

Section B

Passage One

参考译文划线点评

[57]电子商务要求瞬间做出决策,知识管理和优质反馈一样对实现该目标起着举足轻重的作用。没有恰当的知识和反馈信息,实时商务很快会沦为没有监管的、毫无价值的实时混乱。[58]缺乏充分的知识流、缺少对形势的连贯的实时观察不可避免地导致灾难性的后果。声名狼藉的巴林银行经营一种实时的期货交易,却没有实时的检查和结算,[59]也无法保证足够质量的知识从交易平台流向管理者和经营者们。太多太快加上太少优质反馈和了解不足,掌握的实时知识太少,结果酿成巨大的灾难。

这中间缺失的环节就是知识管理。如果没有考虑、计划并建立坚实的知识管理的基础结构,就不应当进行真正意义上的电子商务。实时知识必须从拥有者流向必须在恰当的时间采取恰当行动的人,而且这是刻不容缓的。电子商务必须以清楚、可理解的方式配备互动的工作流程工具以及实时的商务知识反馈。[60]进行电子商务的人必须随时都能够得到所有基本的文件,否则他们只能凭空臆断,不能做出有根据的决策。或者,更糟糕的是,因为害怕酿成大错,干脆不做决策。

以家庭贷款的申请过程为例。你很有可能同时向几家银行提出申请。当然,它们会展开价格竞争,[61]而只有当一家银行是第一个而且是最有效地对你的信用非凡做出评估,准备并随时通知你每一步的进展情况时,你才会和它达成交易。其他银行只能守着那些要求不高、而风险更高的客户。这可能影响它们的总体利润以及将来进行价格和服务竞争的能力。这可能使它们完全被排除出此项业务。那么,电子商务和知识管理之间有联系吗?我确信有。

57. [A]词义推断题。本题考查第 1 句的理解,解题关键是理解 this 的所指,以及 as well as 连接的两个并列成分是什么。this 应指上文的 instant decision-making。as well as 连接的成分有两种可能:它可以表示 instant decision-making 和 quality feedback 并列,也可以表示 knowledge management 和 quality feedback 并列。结合下一句,就能辨别与 quality feedback 并列的是 knowledge management,它们是影响 e-business 成功与否的要素。如能理顺句子的各部分,就可以明白只有选项 A 是正确的理解。

58. [B]推理判断题。整个第 1 段谈论的都是这个问题,从第 3 句可推断出答案应为选项 B。选项 A 中的 support from the government 原文未提到;选项 C 中的 managers 虽提到,但文章并未强调其重要性;选项 D 中的 loan from the bank 则是文章使用的一个例子。

59. [D]事实细节题。本题考查列举处。从第 1 段倒数第 2、3 句可以找出该银行倒闭的几个原因:lack of knowledge flow(选项 A);too little quality feedback(选项 B);insufficient understanding(选项 C)。选项 D 中的 controllers and managers 在文中虽有提到,但并没有对他们的能力进行评价,因此是正确选项(注意题干中的 NOT)。

60. [A]推理判断题。第 2 段强调的是信息管理的重要性,最后三句表明本题答案应为 A。本题最具干扰性的选项是 B,第 2 段最后一句表明他们害怕做出错误的决定,但并不意味着他们不愿承担责任。

61. [C]事实细节题。本题考查复合句的理解。本文最后一段第 3 句包含一个定语从句,先行词是 bank,其后的定语从句指出了你选择的银行应具有什么特点,理解了这个定语从句,就可知选项 C 正确。本题最具干扰性的是选项 B,事实上,first-rate credit assessment 意为一级信用评估,并不等同于原句中的 make your credit assessment first,原文中的 first 是"首先"的意思,与级别无关。选项 A 价格的竞争虽然也提到,但作者并不强调这一点。选项 D 文中未提及。

Passage Two

参考译文划线点评

人类的创造力是无穷的。但是人类最伟大的创造却是不创造,这是将从上一代学到的基本的行为方式完整不变地代代相传的技巧。任何社会的多数成员都以近乎相同的方式生养后代,修建房舍,下河捕鱼以及消灭敌人;而这些行为模式会持续相对较长的时间。[63]从每一代人的角度看来,而且由于社会是一个持续的历史统一体,这一文化传承过程节省了大量的人力物力。多亏这样,每一代人用不着耗费大量时间以及冒失败的巨大风险去重新发现前人已经学到的知识。[65]不仅知识是这样保存下来的,依赖于共同信息和理解的公共生活的基础也是这样建立起来的。[64]因为每一代的所有人都从上一代继承差不多一样的文化遗产,他们才能够更容易彼此联系以及更有效地协调行为。

一个社会的每一代人传给下一代的全部实物、观念、知识、行为方式、习惯、价值观以及态度的总和正是人类学家经常说的一个种群的文化。[66]多数其他生物借由一些本能来应付环境及彼此联系,人类则是用文化传承来代替这些本能的。但是它比本能更具灵活性,而且具有可发展性,即它可以贮存新信息,其速度远远高于其他任何物种在基因突变和生物演化的过程中所能扩大本能存量的速度。

62. [B]主旨大意题。关键词 cultural transmission 在文中以不同的形式或近义词出现以反复强调,如 transmitting, learned from, maintained, preceded, receive, cultural heritage, preceding generation, passes on to, transmission of culture 等,其余选项中涉及的内容只在原文中一带而过。反复出现的词及其同义词是解答主旨大意题的最佳依据。

63. [D]事实细节题。本题解题的关键在于理解第 1 段第 4 句中的 economy 和第 5 句"Thanks to it..."中 it 的所指。第 5 句可被视作是对第 4 句的进一步解释,由此可推断 economy 不是指"经济发展",而是指"节省(人力物力)",而 it 是回指第 4 句中的 this process of cultural transmission,结合这些理解,就可发现选项 D 正确。第 5 句表明选项 A 的说法不正确。如果把 economy 理解为"经济发展",就有可能错选 B。文中没有对比发明和文化传承哪个更能推动社会发展,因此选项 C 无原文依据。

64. [C]词义理解题。只要抓住该词出现的上下文,就可以推断出词义,尤其是该词前后的 receive, from the preceding generation,以及全文关键词 cultural transmission 可帮助理解。

65. [C]推理判断题。本题考查对 thus 所指的理解。有关知识的保存方式,在第 1 段倒数第 2 句有提及。解题的关键在于理解 thus(这样)是指上文提到的"通过文化传承",事实上,thus 与上句 it 的所指相同,而且本段强调的是:文化传承比发明创造重要,因此,本题正确选项应为 C。

66. [A]推理判断题。第 2 段倒数第 2 句指出人类的文化传承相当于其他动物应付环境及彼此关系的本能,由此可见,文化传承和动物本能在功能上是相似的,因此选项 A 正确。本段最后一句对比了文化传承及动物本能的不同之处,包括它们的灵活度不同、发展速度不同等,由此可判断选项 B 和 C 不是它们的相似之处。文章没有就选项 D 做对比,因此选项 D 缺乏原文依据。

Part Ⅴ Cloze

67. [C]形似词辨义题。transfer"转移,迁移;调任;转车";transform"使改观;变换";transmit"传送,传递,传染";transplant"移栽,移种;移植器官"。此处指同声传译人员传递领导人发言的字面及暗含意义。

68. [D]词义理解题。wordy"话多的,冗长的";apparent"显然的,明白的;表面上的,貌似真实的";superficial"肤浅的,浅薄的;表面的";literal"照字面的,原义的"。下文出现 diplomatic nuances(外交辞令)暗含意义上的细微差别,根据词汇的反义词复现技巧,此处选 literal。

69. [A]词义理解题。pressure"压力;压迫";depression"抑郁,沮丧";press"压,按,挤";recession"衰退,衰退期"。根据下文翻译人员描述工作带来的健康和精神问题,可知此处指的是工作的压力大。

70. [C]语法题。考查介词用法。动词 describe 构成的短语 describe... as...中使用介词 as,据此推测名词 description 之后也使用 as 表示"将……描述为……"。

71. [D]短语搭配题。此处是说"在新闻照片上翻译人员出现于两位不能用同一种语言交流的领导人之间"。turn up 意为"出现"。

72. [B]短语搭配题。refer to... as...为固定短语,意为"把……称作,把……当成"。mention 直接跟宾语,其他两词分别构成短语 speak of...和 regard... as...。

73. [D]近义词辨析题。illustration"说明,例证;图解,说明";caption"图片说明文字,字幕";picture"解释,说明,阐述";image"形象;形象的描述,比喻,象征"。

74. [D]逻辑关联题。此处意为"除非出错,否则译员永远是不被人注意的角色"。选 unless。

75. [D]短语搭配题。考查介词与名词搭配。与"玻璃房"搭配的介词应是 in。

76. [A]推理题。下文描述的是译员在会议翻译中碰到的种种难题,因此"玻璃房"应是他们工作的地方。

77. [C]词义理解题。此处意为:"随便某一天,可能就会遇到一位英国代表,满口谁也听不懂的约克郡口音;或一位法国

人,酷爱玩弄双关、暗喻,让人无法翻译;或是一位美国人,他从口袋中摸出纸片就以要命的速度迸出一连串事实和数据,等他念完坐下,译员还立在那里瞪口呆呢。"

78. [B]语法题。考查介词用法。表示"操某种口音"用介词 with。

79. [C]近义词辨析题。deny"否认,不承认";拒绝给予";decline"谢绝,拒绝",强调婉言拒绝;resist"抵抗,抵制";refuse"拒绝,不接受,不同意",表示拒绝某种请求,不接受某种提供,强调不情愿。

80. [B]短语搭配题。fish... from the pocket 意为"从口袋中摸出……"。

81. [C]语法题。leave sb. doing sth."使某人处于某种状态"。

82. [A]逻辑关联加短语搭配题。短语 as well as 表示"除……之外(也)"。此句承上启下,上一段是说口译极具挑战性,下文说它还是最难进入的职业。

83. [D]近义词辨析题。business"生意;事务";expertise"专门知识,专长";trade"贸易,商业;某种行业,手艺";profession "职业"。

84. [D]逻辑关联题。此句前后两分句意义上形成对比,前者说"每年加入译员行列的新成员只有 50 到 100 人",而后一句说"经过精挑细选有希望的侯选者则多达 20000 人"。

85. [A]语法题。此处意为"这些学校中的 4 个"。

86. [D]词义理解题。distinguish"区别,区分";appreciate"欣赏,感激";identify"认出,鉴定";recognize"承认,确认,认可"。此题也可根据原词复现技巧解题,上文已出现 recognized interpreters' schools 表示"被认可的译员学校"。

Part VI   Translation

87. 【答案】shall have left for
【译文】等你到内细时,我将已出发前往忙载了。

【解析】动词时态:by the time 后面接一般现在时的时间状语从句时,该从句是用一般现在时表达将来的动作,因此,主句用将来完成时。leave for+地点名词表示"出发前往"。

88. 【答案】but to hinder us
【译文】他不是来帮助我们的,而是来阻碍我们的。

【解析】"不是……而是……"用 not... but... 表示。

89. 【答案】must have died at the very moment of the crash
【译文】调查者一致认为机上旅客肯定是在坠机的一刹那丧生的。

【解析】情态动词+完成时的考查:对过去事实的肯定猜测,应该用 must have done。"一刹那"用 at the very moment of,very 起强调作用。

90. 【答案】was as popular with
【译文】到 1929 年时,米老鼠和可口可乐一样受到孩子们的欢迎。

【解析】考查固定搭配 be popular with sb."受到某人的欢迎、喜欢、喜爱"和 as... as 结构。

91. 【答案】until she does
【译文】如果她现在不告诉他真相,他会一直问下去,直到她说明为止。

【解析】根据上下文,此处的"说明"是指说明真相,也就是前面的 tell him the truth,翻译时为了避免重复,用 does 代替即可。

附录1 备选题型——短句问答

短句问答即简答题,为四级新题型考卷中篇章词汇理解的备选题型,主要考查学生综合应用语言的能力,考查学生是否能够在读懂原文的基础上,用笔头表达出对原文中各种信息的理解。

简答题原文材料的长度和语言难度一般都与阅读理解部分的短文相似,长度为300词左右,通常后接5个问题。问题的形式可以是问答式,也可以是填空式。

答题步骤

(1)先看问题,根据问题题干的关键词,通过略读全文定位与问题相关的原文。

(2)查读相关原文,通过总结归纳、分析推理等,用合适的单词、词组或句子表达出问题的答案。

(3)检查信息是否完整,语言是否简洁,语法是否正确。

第一节 题型分析

1. 细节题

老题型中,简答题分别在1997年1月、1999年1月、1999年6月、2002年6月、2003年6月出现过。从对真题的分析来看,考题以细节题为主。

由于简答题的宗旨在于重点考查考生的语言基本功及概括能力,所以一般来讲,简答题的细节类问题一般都能在原文中找到出处。

> 解答此类题型,首先要定位准确,即找到问题中的关键词(线索词)在文章中的大体位置,并尽可能地缩小概括范围,然后再根据要求组织答案。

[例1] **Q:** Why did Marge and her husband think it an extravagance for Marge to go back to work?

...

Perhaps the easiest choice has to do with economics. One husband said, "Marge and I decided after careful consideration that for her to go back to work at this moment was an *extravagance* (奢侈) we couldn't afford." With two preschool children, it soon became clear in their figuring that with *babysitters* (临时照看小孩的人), transportation, and increased taxes, rather than having more money, they might actually end up with less.　　[1999.6]

以题中的关键词 extravagance 为线索,查找到原文的第2段,再根据原文中的表达"... was an extravagance we couldn't afford"进一步确定答案在原文第2段最后一句。

组织答案时,要注意以下几点:

(1)答案形式要符合提问方式。

原文中提问方式为 Why,那么就应该用 Because 引导的从句回答。

(2)概括要简洁、准确,不要拖泥带水。

要回答此问题,必须对第2段最后一句的信息进行概括。如果 Marge 去工作,那么她就得为 babysitters, transportation, increased taxes 花钱,而且"rather than having more money, they might actually end up with less."这些信息可概括

为 spend more 或 more spending。

(3)注意语言表达要符合语法。

本题所问内容,是 Marge 和她丈夫的否定想法,即回答的内容可能与事实相反,故要用虚拟语气。参考答案为:

①Because they might actually end up with less money.

②Because they would spend more than their earnings.

③Because their earnings wouldn't cover the spending.

2. 推断题

> 这类题的答案在原文中是找不到的,它要求考生进行合理的推断,当然这种推断并非无源之水。文章中的某些用词、语气具有隐含意义,考生要做的只是将这种隐含意义推断出来。

【例2】**Q: The author suggests in the last paragraph that parents should be encouraged to _____.**

Parents have been particularly afraid to teach reading at home. Of course, children shouldn't be pushed to read by their parents, but educators have discovered that reading is best taught individually—and the easiest place to do this is at home. Many four-and-five-year-olds who have been shown a few letters and taught their sounds will compose single words of their own with them even before they have been taught to read. [2002.6]

本题为推断题。最后一段有两层意思,首先第一句说家长们害怕在家教孩子阅读,接着出现转折,"可教育者们发现阅读最好单独教,而最容易这样做的地方是在家里",两点结合起来进行推断可知是鼓励父母在家教孩子阅读,因此答案可概括为 teach reading at home。

3. 主旨题

> 对于此类试题,第一步是找出概括文章中心思想的主题句。对于原文中没有提供主题句的主旨题,则需要考生概括对文章的理解,自己归纳总结答案。

【例3】**Q: Which word in the first two paragraphs best explains why many women have to work?**

For many women choosing whether to work or not to work outside their home is a luxury: they must work to survive. Others face a hard decision.

Perhaps the easiest choice has to do with economics. One husband said, "Marge and I decided after careful consideration that for her to go back to work at this moment was an *extravagance* (奢侈) we couldn't afford." With two preschool children, it soon became clear in their figuring that with *babysitters* (临时照看小孩的人), transportation, and increased taxes, rather than having more money, they might actually end up with less. [1999.6]

本题是主旨题。将第1、2段概括起来可知,对许多妇女来说,不上班是一种奢侈,只有上班,她们才能生存(survive)。原文第1段提出了论点,第2段展开论证。第1段中,特殊标点符号冒号应引起我们的注意,其后内容应是本文重点内容,由此可知 survive 是答案。

4. 语义题

语义题旨在考查考生转述(paraphrase)或解释(explain)某个词或语句在特定场合下的特定含义的能力。

> 解答这类题时,可注意找出原词在文章中的同义词,如果没有,还应注意破折号、同位语从句、定语从句、插入语等具有解释、说明作用的语言成分。

【例4】**Q: The phrase "the linguistically oppressed" refers to those who were _____.**

An ongoing research project, funded by the University of Cambridge, asked a sample of teachers, educators and employers in more than 40 countries whether they regard the native/non-native speakers distinction as being at all important. "No" was the answer. As long as candidates could teach and had the required level of English, it didn't matter who they were and where they came from. Thus, a new form of discrimination—this time justified because it singled out the unqualified—liberated the linguistically *oppressed* (受压迫的). But the Cambridge project did more than just that: it confirmed that the needs of native and non-native teachers are extremely similar. [1999.1]

答案的细节部分在倒数第2句,破折号部分需重点研究,显然"linguistically oppressed"与 a new form of discrimination 及 unqualified 有关,那么进一步研究一些教师受到 discrimination 的原因是他们是 non-native speakers,再结合题

意及对原文的理解,便可顺利得到答案:①qualified but discriminated as non-native English teachers;②qualified but discriminated because of their non-native status;③qualified non-native English teachers。

第二节 短句问答题型训练

Passage One 2003年6月真题

What personal qualities are desirable in a teacher? I think the following would be generally accepted.

First, the teacher's personality should be lively and attractive. This does not rule out people who are plain-looking, or even ugly, because many such people have great personal charm. But it does rule out such types as the over-excitable, sad, cold, and frustrated.

Secondly, it is not merely desirable but essential for a teacher to have a genuine capacity for sympathy, a capacity to understand the minds and feelings of other people, especially, since most teachers are school teachers, the minds and feelings of children. Closely related with this is the capacity to be tolerant—not, indeed, of what is wrong, but of the weaknesses and immaturity of human nature which *induce* (诱导) people, and again especially children, to make mistakes.

Thirdly, I hold it essential for a teacher to be both intellectually and morally honest. This means that he will be aware of his intellectual strengths and limitations, and will have thought about and decided upon the moral principles by which his life shall be guided. There is no contradiction in my going on to say that a teacher should be a bit of an actor. That is part of the technique of teaching, which demands that every now and then a teacher should be able to put on an act—to *enliven* (使生动) a lesson, correct a fault, or award praise. Children, especially young children, live in a world that is rather larger than life.

A teacher must be capable of infinite patience. This, I may say, is largely a matter of self-discipline and self-training, for we are none of us born like that.

Finally, I think a teacher should have the kind of mind which always wants to go on learning. Teaching is a job at which one will never be perfect; there is always something more to learn about it. There are three principal objects of study: the subjects which the teacher is teaching; the methods by which the subjects can best be taught to the particular pupils in the classes he is teaching; and—by far the most important—the children, young people, or adults to whom the subjects are to be taught. The two fundamental principles of British education today are that education is education of the whole person, and that it is best acquired through full and active co-operation between two persons, the teacher and the learner.

S1. Plain-looking teachers can also be admired by their students if they have _____.

S2. The author says it is _____ that teachers be sympathetic with their students.

S3. A teacher should be tolerant because humans tend to have (1) _____ and to be (2) _____.

S4. A teacher who is _____ will be able to make his lessons more lively.

S5. How can a teacher acquire infinite patience?

S6. Since teaching is a job no one can be perfect at, it is necessary for teachers to keep improving their knowledge of the subjects they teach and their _____.

S7. Teachers' most important object of study is _____.

S8. Education cannot be best acquired without _____ between the teacher and the learner.

Passage Two

A child who has once been pleased with a tale likes, as a rule, to have it retold in identically the same words, but this should not lead parents to treat printed fairy stories as sacred texts. It is always much better to tell a story than read it out of a book, and if a parent can produce what, in the actual circumstances of the time and the individual child, is an improvement on the printed text, so much the better.

A charge made against fairy tales is that they harm the child by frightening him or arousing his *sadistic* (施虐狂的) impulses. To prove the latter, one would have to show in a controlled experiment that children who have read fairy stories were more often guilty of cruelty than those who had not. Aggressive, destructive, sadistic impulses every child has and, on the whole, their symbolic verbal discharge seems to be rather a safety valve than an *incitement* (刺激) to overt action.

As to fears, there are, I think, well-authenticated cases of children being dangerously terrified by some fairy story. Often, however, this arises from the child having heard the story once. Familiarity with the story by repetition turns the pain of fear into the pleasure of a fear faced and mastered.

There are also people who object to fairy stories on the grounds that they are not objectively true, that giants, witches, two-headed dragons, magic carpets, etc., do not exist; and that, instead of indulging his fantasies in fairy tales, the child should be taught how to adapt to reality by studying history and mechanics. I find such people, I must confess, so unsympathetic and peculiar that I do not know how to argue with them. If their case were sound, the world should be full of mad men attempting to fly from New York to Philadelphia on a broomstick or covering a telephone with kisses in the belief that it was their enchanted girlfriend.

No fairy stories ever claimed to be a description of the external world and no sane child has ever believed that it was.

1. According to the author, a fairy story is more effective when it is _____.
2. The author thinks children's symbolic verbal discharge is not an incitement to overt action, but _____.
3. If the child hears a fearful fairy story once and again, he may not feel _____.
4. Why fairy stories are objected to by some people who think the child should be taught how to adapt to reality?
5. What's the author's attitude to fairy stories?

Passage Three

What makes a good language learner? This is an eternal question to which there is no real answer. So everything I'm going to tell you is open to discussion.

Now let us look at the qualities of a good language learner. I think motivation is certainly going to be very high in our list. There are two types of motivation. One is external motivation—this is the kind of motivation which persuades a student to learn a language in order to pass an examination. The opposite of this is integrative motivation, which gets an immigrant in a country to master the language much more rapidly than someone learning in a classroom.

Personality is another major factor. You don't necessarily need to be extroverted but someone who has the confidence to make mistakes can learn much more quickly than someone who is afraid to experiment.

Intelligence isn't a factor in language learning—I would prefer to use the term learning skills. Learning skills are those abilities that allow a learner to progress faster than others; they include having a good memory, having a good ear, efficient revision and suitable organization of learning generally.

What I believe is the most important factor is independence. A learner who is independent of the teacher and who accepts responsibility for learning is always going to be not just a good language learner but the best.

1. By saying "motivation is certainly going to be very high in our list" (Lines 1–2, Para. 2), the author suggests that motivation is _____ for a language learner.
2. According to the author, if you emigrate to a foreign country, _____ makes you master the language rapidly.
3. People who are afraid of making mistakes can learn _____ than those who are confident to experiment.
4. What does the author call the abilities of having a good memory, having a good ear, efficient revision and suitable organization of learning?
5. What does the author think is the most important factor in learning a language?

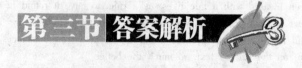

第三节 答案解析

Passage One

S1. 【答案】personal charm/great personal charm/(great) charm/(a) lively and attractive personality/attraction

【定位】根据 plain-looking 可查找到第 2 段第 2 句。

【解析】细节题。题目用 if 假设从句表达了原文 because 引导的原因状语从句内容,因此原文 have 后的宾语为答案所在。

S2. 【答案】essential/desirable/not merely desirable (but essential)/(both) desirable and essential/important and essential/important

【定位】根据 sympathetic 查找到第 3 段首句。

【解析】题目用 be sympathetic with 同义表达了原文中的 have a genuine capacity for sympathy,因此原文中的前半部分出现的表语为答案所在。原文 not merely desirable but essential 强调的是 but 后的内容,不过 desirable 也是可以接受的。

S3. 【答案】(1)weaknesses/weakness;(2)immature/induced to make mistakes

【定位】根据 tolerant 查找到第 3 段第 2 句。

【解析】推断题。原文破折号后的 but 提示了答案所在,题目中的 humans tend to 呼应原文的 human nature。注意空白处(2)前面的 be 表明该处需填入形容词或动词分词,因此需将原文中的 immaturity 和 induce 分别改写为 immature 和 induced。

S4. 【答案】good at acting/able to put on an act/a bit of an actor/like an actor/a good actor

【定位】根据 make his lessons more lively 定位于第 4 段倒数第 2 句。

【解析】细节题。原文中的 enliven a lesson 在题目中被同义替换成了 make his lessons more lively,答案较容易在破折号前面找到。

S5. 【答案】By self-discipline and self-training./(He can acquire it) through self-discipline and self-training./Discipline and train himself./Get more self-discipline and self-training./The teacher should have self-discipline and self-training./He or she should train and discipline himself or herself.

【定位】根据 infinite patience 查找到原文倒数第 2 段首句。

【解析】细节题。问题用 How 提问,因此答案需回答方式方法,可以用 by 短语或句子作答。

S6. 【答案】teaching methods

【定位】根据 keep improving their knowledge of the subjects 查找到最后一段。

【解析】细节题。no one can be perfect at teaching 在最后一段第 2 句提到,第 3 句列举了三类需要进一步了解的对象,第一类 subjects 题干已经给出,其中第二类为本题考点。

S7. 【答案】students they teach/their students

【定位】根据 object of study 查找到最后一段的第 3 句,再根据 most important 定位于该句最后一个分句。

【解析】细节题。第 3 句提出了教师的三类主要学习对象,其中由插入语 by far the most important 引出的一类最重要。注意需要把原文的 the children, young people, or adults to whom the subjects are to be taught 概括后得出答案。

S8. 【答案】full and active cooperation/good cooperation/cooperation/active cooperation

【定位】根据 best acquired 定位于最后一段最后一句。

【解析】推断题。空白处需填入名词性成分,作介词 without 的宾语。题目用 cannot... without 双重否定表达了原文的肯定意义,故原文介词 through 后的名词词组为答案所在。

Passage Two

1. 【答案】adapted by the parent/improved to be told by the parent

【定位】根据 more effective 定位于第 1 段。

【解析】细节题。作者认为,父母讲故事要比念故事好,如果能够根据实际的时间和小孩个体的情况,相应地改进书上的童话故事就更好。因此可归纳为 adapted by the parent 或者 improved to be told by the parent。

2. 【答案】a safety valve

【定位】第 2 段最后一句。

【解析】细节题。题目的 not... but 结构表明空白处需填入与 an incitement 一样的名词性结构。在第 2 段,作者反驳了对神话故事使小孩产生施虐倾向的控诉。他指出,每个小孩都有侵略性和破坏性,但他们的典型言语流露与其说是公然挑衅的行为,还不如说是安全阀(自我保护的威胁性的话)。原文的 rather... than 结构否定的是 than 后的内容,因此 rather 后的名词短语为答案所在。

3. 【答案】terrified/frightened

【定位】根据 hear a fearful fairy story once 定位于第 3 段第 2、3 句。

【解析】推断题。空白处需填入形容词,作 feel 的表语。文章第 2 段提到有人控诉神话使小孩产生恐惧感,第 3 段作者辩护这种情况通常发生在只听过一遍故事的小孩身上,熟悉故事的小孩反而会消除恐惧,感受面对和掌握恐惧所带来的乐趣。因此,应填入表"害怕的,恐惧的"之义的词。注意要用过去分词形式表示"(人)感到恐惧的"。

4. 【答案】Because they think the fairy stories are not objectively true.

【定位】根据 objected to 定位于第 4 段第 1 句。

【解析】细节题。第 4 段中,作者提到有人反对童话故事,理由是它们不真实。原文中的 on the grounds that 后的内容即答案所在。

5. 【答案】Favorable./Positive.

【定位】全文。

【解析】观点题,也是主旨题。文章类型为议论文,通过对全文的略读,特别是作者在第 3、4 段对童话故事所做的辩护,可判断作者对童话故事持肯定或赞成的态度。

Passage Three

1. 【答案】an important quality/important

【定位】第 2 段第 2 句。

【解析】推断题。第 2 段第 1 句中的 look at the qualities 表明该段将讲述好的语言学习者的特质。第 2 句中的 certainly, very high 表明对语言学习者来说,motivation 是非常重要的。

2. 【答案】integrative motivation

【定位】根据 emigrate 定位于第 2 段最后一句。

【解析】细节题。题目用 if 从句表达了原文 an immigrant in a country 的内容,因此原文定语从句中 which 的所指便是答案所在。

3. 【答案】(much) less quickly/(much) more slowly

【定位】根据 making mistakes, confident 定位于第 3 段第 2 句。

【解析】推断题。题目把原文的比较对象互换了位置,因此需要把原文的 much more quickly 改成反义比较级得出答案。

4. 【答案】Learning skills.

【定位】根据 abilities of...定位于第 4 段。

【解析】细节题。该段第 2 句解释了什么是作者认为的 learning skills,即题目所表述的内容,故答案为 Learning skills。

5. 【答案】Independence.

【定位】根据 most important 定位于最后一段第 1 句。

【解析】细节题。如果定位准确不难找到答案为该句的表语 independence。

改错是完型填空的备选题型,但历年4级真题都没有出现过,本部分以六级真题为例说明改错的应试技巧。

该部分共10个错误,分布于一篇约200词的题材熟悉、难度适中的短文或段落中。每个错误行用题号标出,每行有且只有一个错误(不含拼写或标点错误),要求考生在全面理解文章内容的基础上改正错误,使短文意思连贯、结构正确、逻辑合理。

具体答题方法

改正 将文中用错的词用斜线(/)划去,在后面横线上填入正确的词,表示替换该错词。(请注意:有些考生由于疏忽,忘记在文中划去错词,这样即便改对了也不得分。)

删除 在文中将错的词用斜线(/)划去,在后面横线上也划一条斜线(/),表示该词是多余的。

增添 在文中两词之间插入"∧",表示有遗漏,在后面横线上填入遗漏的词的正确形式。

答题步骤

解答改错题时,首先要快速浏览全文,把握文章主题和大意。然后细读要求改错的那行文字,确定错误所在及类型。如果该行或该句内找不出词汇或语法上的错误,则要联系上下文,看是否存在逻辑上的错误。做题时思路要开阔,考虑每类词汇可能出现的错误。特别注意以下考点:

1. 对于系动词、助动词,考虑单复数和时态问题。
2. 对于 *v.*-ing,考虑是否应为 *v.*-ed,反之亦然。
3. 对于介词,考虑是否能与动词、形容词、名词构成正确的搭配。
4. 对于形容词,考虑是否应为副词,或比较级、最高级等,甚至反义词;副词同理。
5. 对于连词,读一下上下文是否文意顺畅。
6. 对于代词,考虑应该是主格、宾格还是所有格,或该用单数形式还是复数形式。
7. 对于名词,考虑该用单数形式还是复数形式,单数前是否有冠词。

第一节 错误类型分析

一、词汇错误

1. 易混词的误用

英语中有很多词在拼写、语义上很相似,如动词 assure/ensure, rise/arise/raise, effect/affect,形容词 considerate/considerable, effective/efficient, economic/economical, sensible/sensitive/sentimental/sensational 等,但它们的意义及用法却可能迥然不同。这些易混词构成改错题的一个重要错误类型。

【例1】This disease mainly effects (→affects) the skin and nerves. 　　　　　　　　　　　　[2005.6/CET-6]

2. 词性的误用

此类错误通常表现在形容词、名词、副词、动词词性的误用上。解答这类改错题,首先要根据单词在句中所处的位置来确定词性是否正确。一般来说,形容词修饰名词,副词修饰动词、形容词和副词。其中最典型的是形容词、副词的误

用,因此需牢记:

> (1)系动词和感官动词后面只能跟形容词,需特别注意那些既可以作系动词又可以作实义动词的动词,如 go, become, grow, keep 等。
>
> (2)大多数副词都以-ly 结尾,但以-ly 结尾的不一定都是副词,如 likely, costly, deadly, friendly 等;有些副词和形容词同形,但意义或作用不一定相同,如 fast, early, close, direct, hard, sound, straight, fair 等;有些副词有两种不同的形式和意义,如 cheap/cheaply, close/closely, deep/deeply, flat/flatly, free/freely, high/highly 等。
>
> (3)不及物动词后面也可能跟形容词作主语补足语,如:I returned home unhappy,如果改为 unhappily,反而是错误的。
>
> (4)有些以 a-开头的形容词只能作表语,不能作前置定语,如 asleep, alive, afraid, awake, ashamed, alike 等。

3. 代词的误用

此类错误包括代词单复数、人称与非人称、主宾格或所有格、关系代词、不定代词的误用等。大部分考生都知道各类代词的语法知识,但是在篇章中,尤其要弄清代词指代的内容,不要受各种插入成分的干扰。历年的六级改错题经常考查代词的前后一致,这可以说是代词改错的核心考点。

【例2】But in the last several years, there's been a revolution in that (→what) we've learned about reading and dyslexia.

[2006.6/CET-6]

【例3】There's also convincing evidence which (→that) dyslexia is largely inherited. [2006.6/CET-6]

4. 介词的误用

介词方面的错误主要出现在动词、形容词和名词前后的介词上及固定词组中,因此,牢记固定词组能一目了然发现误用的介词。每年六级考试中都至少有一题对介词的相关知识进行考查,有时甚至多达四道题。

【例4】... she thought you could tell a well-mannered person on (→by) the way they occupied the space around them.

[2000.6/CET-6]

【例5】a very flat piece of bread that looked, to him, very much as (→like) a napkin. [2000.6/CET-6]

5. 连词的误用

连词分为并列连词和从属连词两大类。连词的误用既包括连词之间的误用,如:

【例6】However, a second person thought that this was more a question of civilized behavior as (→than) good manners.

[2000.6/CET-6]

也包括连词与介词或副词等的误用,如:

【例7】This alliance guarantees that all leprosy patients, even (→even if/even though) they are poor, have a right to the most modern treatment.

[2005.1/CET-6]

6. 冠词的误用

冠词方面的错误主要表现在错用、漏用或多用了冠词。这方面的错误虽然容易改正,可是考生往往没有意识到这么简单的内容也会出错,而忽略了冠词错误。这尤其需要细心读题,如:

【例8】In an addition (an→/) the paper instituted a content audit... [2003.6/CET-6]

二、语法错误

1. 主谓不一致

主谓不一致错误通常比较隐蔽主要出现于主语和谓语动词间隔较远处。因为长句,特别是复杂句,往往给考生造成视觉上的混淆,此时,明确主语和谓语就十分关键了。如:

【例9】... but behind it lies (→lie) two myths: ... [2002.6/CET-6]

【例10】Their improved intelligence, so vital to their old hunting life, were (→was) put to a new use. [2002.1/CET-6]

2. 时态错误

时态错误通常是由于时态与时间指示词不符,如:

【例11】Our culture's decline in reading begin (→began) well before the existence of the Patriot Act.

[2006.12/CET-6 新题型]

在没有时间指示词的情况下,则需借助文章的整体叙述基调,或通过上下文出现的谓语动词来确定时态,如:

【例 12】They became chasers, runners, jumpers, aimers, throwers and prey-killers. They cooperate (→cooperated) as skillful male-group attackers.   [2002.1/CET-6]

3. 语态的误用

最常见的语态错误是被动语态被误用为主动语态。因为在汉语的表达习惯中,有时不加"被"字也能表达被动含义,因而受母语影响,考生对被动语态往往不敏感。另外,不及物动词不能携带宾语,因而也就没有被动语态。

【例 13】Studies indicate that many girls are affecting (→affected) as well—and not getting help.   [2006.6/CET-6]

【例 14】The day the NEA report (∧was) released, the U.S. House, in a tie vote, upheld the government's right to obtain bookstore and library records under a provision of the USA Patriot Act.   [2006.12/CET-6 新题型]

4. 非谓语动词的误用

非谓语动词包括不定式、现在分词和过去分词。改错题中,可能出现非谓语动词与谓语动词混淆。

【例 15】This modern treatment will cure leprosy in 6 to 12 months, depend (→depending) on the form of the disease.   [2005.1/CET-6]

【例 16】Viewing (→Viewed) biologically, the modern footballer is revealed as a member of a disguised hunting pack.   [2002.1/CET-6]

三、逻辑关系错误

逻辑关系的混乱会使文章变得杂乱无章、难以理解。改正此类错误的做法通常是,联系上下文确定存在逻辑错误后,对每个逻辑关系点进行排查,最后发现并改正错误。六级改错题对逻辑关系的考查主要集中在连词、副词和形容词的使用上。其中副词和形容词往往是误用其反义词。如:

【例 17】But in the Information Age, no one can get by with (→without) knowing how to read well and understand increasingly complex material.   [2006.6/CET-6]

【例 18】Get someone to check for spelling and grammatical errors, because a spell-checker will (→will not) pick up every mistake.   [2006.1/CET-6]

第二节 改错题型训练

Test One

Jungle country is not friendly to man, but it is possible to survive there. You must have the right equipment and you must know a lot important things about   1. _____

woodcraft (森林知识). Then your choices of staying living   2. _____
are very good.

No one should go into the jungle without the right equipment. You need lightweight clothings, a good sheath   3. _____
knife or machete, and a compass. Fishhooks and a line, a rifle and ammunition, matches in a waterproof container, and a poncho are necessary too. Such is a mosquito net   4. _____
to protect the head.

In the jungle you can get hopeless lost within   5. _____
five minutes after leaving a knowing landmark. That is   6. _____
why you should always carry a compass. In open country, during the day, you can tell which way to go by studying the sun. At night the stars are sure of guides to direction.   7. _____

But in most places the jungle rooftop is so thick that this is impossible to see the sun or the stars. Again and again you must check the position by the compass. Keep alert. Watch the ground in front of you carefully. Stop and listen now and again. Avoid haste, and rest often. In a place where is hot and humid, the person who sets a fast pace will soon become tired. A steady, even pace is wisest on the long run.

8. _____

9. _____

10. _____

Test Two

Only a generation ago, Mauritania's capital city was many day's walk from the Sahara. Today it is in the Sahara. The sand blows through the city streets and piles up in walls and fences. The desert stretches out as far as the eye can see.

1. _____

2. _____

In some parts of the Amazon rain forest in Brazil, all the trees have cut down. The earth lies bare and dry in the hot sun. Nothing grow there anymore.

3. _____

4. _____

Over vast areas of every continent, the rainfall and vegetation necessary for life is disappearing. Already more than 40 percent of the earth's land is desert and desert-like. About 628 million people—one out of seven— live in these dry regions. In the past, they have managed to survive, but in difficulty. Now, largely through problems caused by modern life, our existence is threatened by the slow, steady spread of the earth's deserts.

5, _____

6. _____

7. _____

8. _____

Many countries first became concerned in 1970s after a terrible drought and famine destroyed Africa's Sahel, the fragile desert along the south edge of the Sahara. Thousands of people died even though there was a worldwide effort to send food and medicine to the starved people.

9. _____

10. _____

Test Three

Expressing Yourself in English is an interesting new textbook with some variations from the traditional in its approach. They would seem appropriate for self-study, especially when used in conjunction with the cassette, but is primarily intended of classroom use. Indeed, the text itself contains notes to the teachers rather than that appearing in a separate teacher's guide.

1. _____

2. _____

3. _____

Each unit contains three readings, all of which, except for those appearing in the ninth and the final unit, are illustrated. The teacher's notes indicate the teacher should refrain of answering students' questions about these readings until each student has worked through all the reading comprehension exercises without help. Among the book's distinctive features is the fact that contains a more extensive list of references than any

4. _____

5. _____

other writing for this level, in which exercises are provided and allow students to be creative with the English they learn. Again, like most comparable texts, *Expressing Yourself in English* does not formally introduce the verb until Unit 3. One hint for teachers and students likely is that students should not expect to be successful with thc examinations offered in the body of the text if they study outside of class and memorize the dialogue that introduces each unit. In order to keep the price lowly, the book is paperbound and pictures and illustrations are in black and white. The textbook was accompanied by a workbook to be published later this year.

6. _____
7. _____

8. _____
9. _____

10. _____

第三节 答案解析

Test One

1. 【答案】a lot ∧ important→of
   【解析】词组错误。a lot 作副词充当程度状语时,意为"非常,特别",相当于 very much。a lot of 则修饰名词,表示"很多"。此处 a lot 要修饰的是名词 things,因此要加 of。
2. 【答案】living→alive
   【解析】形容词误用。living 和 alive 虽同为形容词,表示"活着的",但 living 一般作定语,alive 常作表语。此处应将 living 改为 alive,与系动词 stay 构成系表结构,意为"存活下来"。
3. 【答案】clothings→clothing/clothes
   【解析】名词误用。clothing 意为"衣着",指衣服的整体而言,是衣服的总称,为不可数名词,只能用单数形式。clothes 意指全身衣服的各个部分,只可用复数形式。故 clothings 要改为 clothing 或者 clothes。
4. 【答案】Such→So
   【解析】固定结构误用。"so+be/其他助动词/情态动词+主语"倒装结构意为"同样,也",而 such 没有这样的用法,故应将 such 改为 so。
5. 【答案】hopeless→hopelessly
   【解析】词性误用。此处 get lost 为动词短语,应用副词来修饰,而 hopeless 为形容词,只能修饰名词,故应改为副词形式 hopelessly。
6. 【答案】knowing→known
   【解析】分词误用。此处 landmark 与 know 之间是被动关系,意为"知名的路标",故应将 knowing 改为 known。
7. 【答案】of→/
   【解析】be sure of sth.表示"(对获得……)有把握的",与上下文意思不符。sure 在此处意为"可靠的",为形容词,可修饰名词 guides。故应删掉介词 of。
8. 【答案】this→it
   【解析】代词误用。it is impossible/important...是常见的句型,其中 it 为形式主语,不能用其他词代替。this 通常是特指某一事件或物体,在此处不适用。
9. 【答案】where→that/which
   【解析】从句引导词误用。where 引导定语从句时,后跟完整的从句,其本身不充当主要成分。因此,此处需用可充当主语的 that/which 引导定语从句,修饰 place。
10. 【答案】on→in
    【解析】介词误用。in the long run 是固定短语,意为"从长远的观点来看,终究,最后"。

Test Two

1. 【答案】day's→days'
   【解析】名词单复数错误。此处 many 修饰 day,表示"很多天",day 是可数名词,故要用复数,因此改 day's 为 days'。

2. 【答案】in→against

　【解析】介词误用。in 是方位介词,表示"在……里面",不符合句意。against 意为"倚靠着",符合句意。

3. 【答案】have ∧ cut→been

　【解析】语态错误。此处 trees 应该是"被砍",因此应该用现在完成时的被动语态,即 have been cut down。

4. 【答案】grow→grows

　【解析】主谓不一致错误。nothing, something, anything, anybody, everyone 等不定代词作主语时谓语动词要用单数形式,故应将 grow 改成单数形式。

5. 【答案】is→are

　【解析】主谓不一致错误。此句的主语为 the rainfall and vegetation,故谓语动词应该为复数形式。

6. 【答案】and→or

　【解析】逻辑错误。根据上下文,"超过 40% 的地球陆地面积"只可能是沙漠或沙化土地,而不可能同时存在两种情况。因此要用 or。

7. 【答案】in→with

　【解析】介词误用。with difficulty 是固定搭配,表示"困难地"。

8. 【答案】our→their

　【解析】人称代词指代错误。根据上下文,从该段第 3 句开始谈的都是关于居住在干旱地区的 6.28 亿人们的环境情况,应把 our 改为 their。

9. 【答案】in ∧ 1970s→the

　【解析】漏用冠词。in the 1970s 表示"20 世纪 70 年代",定冠词 the 不可省略。

10. 【答案】starved→starving

　【解析】分词错误。此句意为"成千上万的人们还是饿死了,即使全世界都在尽力输送食品和药品给快饿死的人们"。此处应该用 starving,表示"快饿死",而不是 starved(已经饿死了)。

Test Three

1. 【答案】They→It

　【解析】代词误用。假设此处的 they 合理,则只可能指代上文的 variations,而如此一来,则会造成句意不通,且无法与下文的谓语动词 is 形成对应,故改 they 为 it,指代"课本"。

2. 【答案】of→for

　【解析】介词误用。intend for 意为"(为……而)准备",符合句意。介词 of 不可与 intend 搭配。

3. 【答案】that→those

　【解析】代词误用。此处代词回指上文的 notes,以此避免词汇的重复使用。因 notes 为复数形式,故需用 those。

4. 【答案】of→from

　【解析】介词误用。refrain 可与 from 搭配,意为"抑制,克制",不能与介词 of 搭配。

5. 【答案】that ∧ contains→it

　【解析】缺少语法成分。that 在此引导同位语从句,而此同位语从句缺少主语,因此要补上主语 it。

6. 【答案】writing→written

　【解析】分词错误。any other 指"任何其他一本书",而"书"只能是"被写",应为被动。故应将 writing 改为 written。

7. 【答案】like→unlike

　【解析】逻辑错误。根据 Again 可知,此处说的还是 *Expressing Yourself in English* 与大部分可比较的课本的不同之处,因此要将 like 改为 unlike。

8. 【答案】likely→alike

　【解析】形容词误用。likely 意为"可能的",常用于"be likely to do"结构中,不符合句意。alike 可作后置定语修饰名词,意为"相同的,同样的"。

9. 【答案】if→unless

　【解析】连词误用。unless 意为"如果不……,除非……",相当于 if... not,此处 unless 与上文的 should not 构成双重否定,表肯定,符合句意。

10. 【答案】lowly→low

　【解析】词性错误。lowly 作副词时意为"低水平,程度不高",而此处符合 keep sth./sb.+***adj.*** 的固定用法,表示"使(某物或某人)保持(某种状态)",故应将副词 lowly 改为形容词 low。

读者意见反馈卡

亲爱的读者:

　　您好! 非常感谢您对华研外语的信赖与支持。为了今后为您提供更优秀的英语图书,请您抽出宝贵的时间填写这份意见反馈卡,然后寄至:广东省广州市天河区华景北路 78 号 3103 信箱 华研外语,邮编:510630。

　　Email: huayanworkshop@163.net

《淘金高阶 4 级考试巅峰训练》

＊读者个人资料＊

姓　　名:_____　　　　　　性　　别:□男　□女

年　　级:_____　　　　　　职　　业:_____

文化程度:_____　　　　　　电　　话:_____

Email:_____

通讯地址:_____

您购买过几本华研图书:

□一本　　　　□两本　　　　□三本　　　　□四本以上

影响您购买本书的因素(可多选)

□封面、装帧设计　　　　　□封底文字

□价格　　　　　　　　　　□同学、朋友的评价

□内容提要、前言和目录　　□作者或出版社的名声

□编排逻辑　　　　　　　　□解析经典

□买过华研其他书,感觉满意

您对本书封面设计的满意度:

□很满意　　　　□满意　　　　□一般

您对本书印刷质量的满意度：

□很满意　　　　　□满意　　　　　□一般

您对本书的总体满意度：

□很满意　　　　　□满意　　　　　□一般

本书最令您满意的是：

□讲解详尽　　　□指导明确　　　□直击考点　　　□译文精彩
□一语中的　　　□定位解析　　　□有实用价值　　□有保留价值
其他 _____

您看到本书还有哪些校对错漏？

_____

_____

您希望本书在哪些方面进行改进？

_____

_____

您希望我们华研图书有哪些改进？

_____

_____

其他建议或要求：

_____

_____